Philip W. Blood

Birds of Prey
Hitler's Luftwaffe, Ordinary Soldiers, and the Holocaust in Poland

In Memory of
Professor E. Richard Holmes (1946–2011)
Soldier, scholar, gentleman.

Philip W. Blood

BIRDS OF PREY
Hitler's Luftwaffe, Ordinary Soldiers,
and the Holocaust in Poland

Bibliographic information published by the Deutsche Nationalbibliothek
Die Deutsche Nationalbibliothek lists this publication in the Deutsche Nationalbibliografie; detailed bibliographic data are available in the Internet at http://dnb.d-nb.de.

Bibliografische Information der Deutschen Nationalbibliothek
Die Deutsche Nationalbibliothek verzeichnet diese Publikation in der Deutschen Nationalbibliografie; detaillierte bibliografische Daten sind im Internet über http://dnb.d-nb.de abrufbar.

Cover image: Hermann Göring in full dress uniform circa 1940. © NARA, Hoffmann Collection. Lw. Flieger or Aircraftsman 2 Class, upon completion of basic training circa 1942 © Author's private collection.

The images marked CC-BY-SA 3.0 on pages 73, 74, 78, 90, and 295 are subject to the license terms of Creative Commons Attribution-ShareAlike 3.0 Unported (https://creativecommons.org/licenses/bysa/3.0/deed.en).

ISBN-13: 978-3-8382-1567-9
© *ibidem*-Verlag, Stuttgart 2021
All rights reserved.

No part of this publication may be reproduced, stored in or introduced into a retrieval system, or transmitted, in any form, or by any means (electronic, mechanical, photocopying, recording or otherwise) without the prior written permission of the publisher. Any person who does any unauthorized act in relation to this publication may be liable to criminal prosecution and civil claims for damages.

Alle Rechte vorbehalten. Das Werk einschließlich aller seiner Teile ist urheberrechtlich geschützt. Jede Verwertung außerhalb der engen Grenzen des Urheberrechtsgesetzes ist ohne Zustimmung des Verlages unzulässig und strafbar. Dies gilt insbesondere für Vervielfältigungen, Übersetzungen, Mikroverfilmungen und elektronische Speicherformen sowie die Einspeicherung und Verarbeitung in elektronischen Systemen.

Printed in the United States of America

Acknowledgements

> 'This is the smoking gun of all your research.'
> Professor Richard Holmes, 18 February 2001.

On 3 February 2020, I met Heinrich Schreiber for the last time. My friend and neighbour was 97 and his faculties were rapidly decining through the lethal onset of dementia. In 1943, he was called up to the German Army, severely wounded at Smolensk in Soviet Russia, and was awarded the *Allgemeines Sturmabzeichen* (general assault badge). The memory of the badge remained his foremost achievement in a lifetime of struggles faced by so many working class people born before the war. Since 1970, I was fortunate to meet many Second World War veterans but Heinrich had taught me aspects of military culture barely studied by military historians. He discussed combat reports, the importance of signals and short-hand report writing. He could read and explain the meaning of reports and would explain the limits of his experience through his platoon, company and battalion. His division(s) had long since disappeared from memory. His only observation about the reports in this book, 'so the Luftwaffe were also at it'. Perhaps a veiled reference to Nazi crimes, perhaps the universality of the military culture, or perhaps the memories of the east. From talking with Heinrich over ten years, I learned that working class German men went to war not much differently from those of other countries. The hardships of life continued after Hitler came to power, his family lost their farm tenancy when the rents were raised beyond their meagre means. Heinrich began work as a shoemaker, but his apprenticeship was interrupted by the war. After the war he became a stonemason. He passed away a month later, finally drawing to a close my contact with the war generation in Britain and Germany.

There were several key persons behind the completion of this book. The late Professor Brigadier E. Richard Holmes (1947–2011) was my doctoral supervisor. Our relationship began as professor-student, but then he turned mentor, and eventually became friends. During the research for my PhD, Richard saw the Luftwaffe records in this book and after reading my thesis summary said it was 'the smoking-gun of my Bandenbekämpfung research.' He recommended Birds of Prey should be a specific book and include the synthesis between the hunt and the military training. Richard's colleague, Professor Chris Bellamy (Greenwich) was the second supervisor and he agreed with Richard that a chapter in the thesis should form the foundation for a subsequent book. Chris encouraged more research of the underlying violence between the Soviet partisans and the Germans to explain why Bandenbekämpfung was not anti-partisan warfare. Scholarly technicalities aside, studying under Richard and Chris was a dynamic experience. A special mention should also be made for Steph Muir, Richard's assistant who was a constant pillar of support to all of us.

Beyond mentoring and friendship is another level of scholarly relationship that defies definition. During a meeting of the Anglo-German seminar group (1997-98), I met Dr. Nicholas Terry (University of Exeter). He was then a PhD candidate researching the German Army and we became immediate friends. Our friendship has spanned from the Goldhagen-Browning debates, the 'clean Wehrmacht' scandals, several conferences with publications and on into the Twenty-First Century. In 1998 we first discussed the content in the Luftwaffe files. He recommended presenting a paper at the Wiener Library event. While drafting my PhD thesis, Nick suggested signposting the role of the Luftwaffe in Bandenbekämpfung. Since 2006, Nick has been the constant advisor/mentor for this book and his was on his advice I decided upon the microhistory format.

There have also been a number of specialist advisors who have assisted me. Dr. Declan O'Reilly (London-KCL) has been a scholary conciliare and tough critic since 1998. My dear friend Dr Joe White, from the USHMM, was very supportive of my research. Following a visit to the UK, Joe recommended an article for the Holocaust and Genocide Studies Journal and introduced me to Dr. Michael Gelb (USHMM). Thanks to Michael's editing the article was published in 2010. Joe passed away in 2016 and as did Dr Geoffry Megaggee four years later. Fond recollections of those 'brown bag' lunches and lively discussions about our research. During a visit to the BA-MA archive in Freiburg in 1998, I met and discussed the life of ordinary German soldiers with Professor Jochen Böhler (Jena University). This changed my perception of ordinary German soldiers. In 2009, Dr. Tomasz Samojlik (Mammal Research Institute, Białowieźa) kindly shared his ideas on the Polish history of the forest. Tomasz very kindly supplied the forest maps that led to the digitization process central to this book. At a critical time, Professor Beatrice Heusser (University of Glasgow) offered important supervisory advice on taking the research to the final manuscript. My life partner Bettina Wunderling BSc. was important to the research by formulating the application of GIS in the cartographical research. In the latter stages of completing this manuscript, Dr. Matthew Ford (University of Sussex) gave up considerable time on modern counterinsurgency, military innovation and concepts of education, including training. He also directly edited several chapters. I would like to also thank Dr. Olaf Bachmann (King's College London) and Jake Halliday (Buckingham), for reading and commenting on the manuscript.

Since 1998 several academic institutions have been crucial to this project. Their help and support was particularly welcome since this project was self-funded. The *Bundesarchiv* (Germany), National Archives (London), Mammal Research Institute (Poland), National Archives and Records Administration (USA) provided unhindered access to records and advice. The RWTH-Bibliothek (Aachen), *Staatsbibliothek* (Aachen) and British Library (London) granted full access to holdings and inter-library loans. Germany has retained many of the traditional ideas open access learning for all and this deserves special mention in this book. The Internet Archive (Washington DC) granted unfettered access to all digitised sources, which was articularly helpful for older books outside the e-book systems. ESRI provided advice and guideance in the application of GIS software in 2010–12.

In fourteen years, many people have been involved in this book, for which I am eternally grateful: Special thanks are reserved for: Mike Buckley MA, Michael Birklein MA, Dr. Roger Cirillo

(AUSA), Dr. Halik Kochanski, Dr. Bernd Lemke (Potsdam), Professor James Corum (Salford), Professor Dennis Showalter (†), Jörg Muth (Baltic Defence College), Professor Jesse Kauffmann (Eastern Michigan), Michael Birklein (RWTH-Aachen), Tomasz Frydel (Ottowa), Michael D. Miller, and Valerie Lange and Malisa Mahler from ibidem publishing house. In 2020, I joined the Twitter community and have received very supportive advice and guidance.

Finally, to family and friends. Whereas in a second book family and friends become part of a list, unusual to this story was the extended period of serious illness launched them into a strategic role. My parents, Pamela and Peter Blood, have always supported my work and career. Also to my relatives Jan, Lauren, Colin and Dr. Alexander Ford. My dearest friend for more than forty years, Manny Phelps passed away in 2015. After major surgery and disability, he devised the means to restore my writing that led to this book. We shared an interest in the Luftwaffe and I would hope this meets with his high standards of accuracy and detail. Manny's family of Maria, Ricky, Danielle and Nicole remain precious to me. Dr. Barry Rosenthal (Baltimore) is a dear friend and supported this project with advanced computers. Harry Wise (London taxi driver) and Bradley J. Hodgson (gunsmith) spent hours explaining gunmaking, drive-hunting, and that special relationship between rifles and marksmanship. All my friends mentioned in my first book were also part of the progress to this. Thank you to German doctors and medical staff who have worked incredibly hard in my interest over the last fourteen years.

Table of Contents

Acknowledgements V
List of Tables X
List of Diagrams X
List of Maps XI
List of Illustrations XII
Abbreviations and Glossary XIV

1942 17
Excursions in Microhistory 24
An Aide-Mémoire: Reading Maps Like German soldiers 44

1. The Ogre of Rominten 59
2. The Conquest of Wilderness 89
3. *Grossdeutschland* 121
4. Bandenbekämpfung in the 'Home Forces Area' 136
5. The Białowieża Partisans 177
6. Population Engineering 201
7. *Judenjagd* 234
8. German Soldiers and Bandenbekämpfung 255
9. 1943 285
10. Göring's Hunter Killers 307
11. *Bandenjagd* 332
12. 1944: Retreat 361

Conclusion: Memories of a Never Happened History 393
Epilogue 422

Appendix 1: German Ranks 422
Appendix 2: Luftwaffe Soldiers 431
Bibliography 457
Index 477
About the Author 478

List of Tables

Table 1:	Bach-Zelewski's travel itinerary	114
Table 2:	fluctuations in manpower levels	163
Table 3:	LWSB, death by shooting, 14 August 1942	184
Table 4:	LWSB, death by hanging, 9 September 1942	188
Table 5:	LWSB, hanging 22 September 1942	189
Table 6:	LWSB, death by hanging, October 1942	190
Table 7:	Forest communities and the results of deportation	214
Table 8:	Settled out of the forest.	218
Table 9:	LWSB, death by hanging, 22 December 1942	232
Table 10:	executions through hanging, 20 November 1942	248
Table 11:	LWSB, death by hanging, February 1943	253
Table 12:	LWSB death sentences on 24 February 1943	254
Table 13:	final deployment of the LWSB on 5 March 1943	300
Table 14:	Herbst's amended body count	304
Table 15:	JSKB expenditures—fuel and ammunition	313
Table 16:	JSKB roster, 6 March 1943	320
Table 17:	JSKB muster March–October 1943	322
Table 18:	LW Signals Regiment 1 schedule	327
Table 19:	JSKB muster October 1943 to August 1944	362

List of Diagrams

Diagram 1:	*Reichsforstamt* organisation and the *Jagdamt* (1936).	64
Diagram 2:	the four categories of reported incidents	263
Diagram 3:	age range of sixth company officers and NCOs	435
Diagram 4:	age profile of sixth company	439
Diagram 5:	Original branch of Service with transfers	441
Diagram 6:	Personnel assigned from Flak regiments	442
Diagram 7:	LWSB/JSKB casualties	453
Diagram 8:	cause of fatal wounds	454

List of Maps

Map 1:	Poland divided, Nazi occupation zones in Poland, Soviet Russia and the Ukraine.	22
Map 2:	Bezirk Bialystok circa 1944.	49
Digital Map 3:	Luftwaffen Karte des Urwaldes Bialowies.	52
GIS Map 4:	Police Battalion 322 – the village deportations 25 July–15 August 1941	110
GIS Map 5:	the Kobylinski deployment	142
GIS Map 6:	LWSB strongpoints – 6 August 1942	150
GIS Map 7:	before the arrival of Fourth Company – 10 October 1942	165
GIS Map 8:	after the arrival of Fourth Company – 2 November 1942	165
GIS Map 9:	the arrival of Fifth and Sixth companies – 19 November 1942	167
GIS Map 10:	the positions of Soviet partisans killed by LWSB	196
GIS Map 11:	deportations – comparison of summer 1941 and autumn/winter 1942	225
GIS Map 12:	the total distribution of hideouts discovered by the LWSB	237
GIS Map 13:	locations of Jews killed by the LWSB	240
GIS Map 14:	The Final Deployment – 5 March 1943	298
GIS Map 15:	JSKB deployment – 6 March 1943	319
GIS Map 16:	Luftwaffe signals network and the German frontier 1943–1944	326
GIS Map 17:	JSKB hunting patrols – March to October 1943	338
GIS Map 18:	destruction of Jagdkommando Marteck	348
GIS Map 19:	the Nönning Judenjagd	352
GIS Map 20:	Unternehmen Vatertag – 3 June 1943	354
GIS Map 21:	JSKB second phase north/south final deployment	364
GIS Map 22:	Plan for Unternehmen Paul, 28–29 May 1944	370

List of Images

Image 1: left to right, Oberforstmeister Walter Frevert Rominten, Göring in his capacity as Reichsjägermeister and Oberstjägermeister Ulrich Scherping. 73

Image 2: Senior Luftwaffe and state foresters in the lounge area in Rominten. A painting of a European Bison is hung on the far wall. 74

Image 3: European Bison in Białowieźa. 74

Image 4: Reichsmarschall Göring, Lw.Generalmajor Adolf Galland, Lw.Generaloberst Bruno Loerzer and Reichminister Albert Speer, August 1943. 78

Image 5: Bernd von Brauchitsch in his cell in Nuremberg prison 1946. 80

Image 6: Preparation for a diplomatic function at Rominten. Note the Nordic runes on the picture rail under the ceiling. 90

Image 7: Sites of memory — Located beside the railway in Zabłotczyzna (2 miles from Narewka), the memorial refers to approximately 500 Jews killed on 5 August 1941. The German records show 282 Jewish men were killed at that place on 15 August 1941. 120

Image 8: A German Army Ortskommandtur: issuing daily notices and labour assignments. 125

Image 9: Captured Soviet partisans after interrogation but before execution. ...180

Image 10: Armed trusty and Nazi Collaborator. 182

Image 11: Białowieźa forest — partisan memorial in the conservation area. 200

Image 12: Civilian deportations and allocation to work or forced labour duties. ...222

Image 13: Villages destroyed and cattle taken under the Nazi food plan. 230

Image 14: Luftwaffe troops in company order. 274

Image 15: Luftwaffe troops in action in the forest. 277

Image 16: Wounded Luftwaffe troops recovering in a military hospital. 277

Image 17: Typical strongpoint construction in wood. 284

Image 18: Reichsjägermeister Göring and his prize — *Matador* — the ceremony for the dead stag — 22 September 1942. 295

Image 19: The signals was regarded as the advanced branch of the Luftwaffe. Recruits received a full training schedule equivalent to apprenticeships in industry. 328

Image 20: Sites of memory — Soviet military cemetery located within Hajnówka town. Engraving reads: Hero of the Soviet Union, Guards Junior Lieutenant Aleksii Vasilevich Florenko. Born 6 February 1922. He died in the fight to liberate Hajnówka region 25 July 1944. 392

Image 21: Sites of memory—located in the centre of Białowieża town, the memorial stands on the site where public executions were conducted during the Nazi occupation. 406

Image 22: Sites of memory—located within the Narewka town limits, the Jewish cemetery survived the Nazi occupation. 409

Image 23: Sites of memory—located nearby Białowieża town. They are memorials to the mass killings and destroyed villages in 1942. They stand in the grounds of the former German military cemetery, first constructed during the Imperial German Army occupation in 1915-18. 411

Image 24: In his position as General of Fighters, Adolf Galland approved and endorsed this anti-Semitic trope in comic form. The connections between hunting, the Luftwaffe and training had reached complete integration. 416

Image 25: Sites of memory—German dead relocated from Białowieża cemetery. The search for Siegfried Adams burial place marked by my index finger. 427

Image 26: Heimatkriegsgebiet - Luftwaffe troops in training building small unit cohesion. 436

Image 27: Dress uniforms and other duties. 437

Image 28: The Luftwaffe troops assigned to the LWSB/JSKB were generally young and often reassigned from non-combat branches. 438

Abbreviations and Glossary

AA: Arolsen Archives, located at: https://collections.arolsen-archives.org/en/search/

BArch: Bundesarchiv, including BA: Berlin (Lichterfelde); BAK: (Koblenz); BA MA: Bundesarchiv Militärarchiv, (Freiburg); BA-ZNS: Bundesarchiv-Zentralnachweisstelle (formerly in Aachen).

CMH: United States Army Center of Military History.

CP: command post.

DDSt: Deutsche Dienststelle (WASt), former Wehrmacht personnel archive.

FJK/FSK: Feldjägerkorps or Feldschützkorps, Nazi paramilitary forestry formations.

FMS: US Army Historical Branch, Foreign Military Studies (German army).

FSKAB: *Forstschutzkommando-Abteilung Bialowies*, the paramilitary forestry formations assigned to Białowieża.

HSSPF: *Höhere SS-Polizeiführer*, regional or theatre SS and Police commander.

IMT: International Military Tribunal, Nuremberg.

IWM: Imperial War Museum, (London).

Jagen: a 1 kilometre square sector, a measurment to micro-manage trees and game reserves.

JSKB: *Luftwaffe Jäger Sonderbataillon Bialowies* zbV. (March 1943–August 1944).

Ln. : *Luftwaffenachrichten*, Luftwaffe signals.

Luftwaffe: German Air Force.

Lw.: Luftwaffe abbreviated for ranks and units.

LWSB: *Luftwaffe Sonderbataillon Bialowies* zbV. (July 1942–March 1943).

MGFA: *Militärgeschichtliches Forschungsamt*, Bundeswehr's military history department since changed to ZMSBw, see below.

NARA: National Archive, College Park annex, Colombia Park Maryland, USA.

NCOs: German *Unteroffiziere* and non-commissioned officer ranks.

OP: observation post.

ORs: other ranks, non-commissioned military personnel.

PB: police battalion.

PoW: Prisoner(s) of War.

RFA: *Reichsforstamt* — Nazi ministry of state forestry.

Soltys: Lithuanian, refers to the local head person of a village.

SSPF: *SS-Polizeiführer*, district SS and Police commander.

TNA: The National Archives, formerly the Public Records Office (PRO), London

TsAMO Bestand 500 Findbuch 12452: Deutsch-Russisches Pojekt Zur Digitalisierung Deutscher Dokumente in Archiven Der Russischen Föderation (digitised captured

German records). Located online at: https://wwii.germandocsinrussia.org/de/nodes/2410-findbuch-12452-oberkommando-der-luftwaffe-okl

USHMM: United States Holocaust Memorial and Museum, Washington DC, USA.

Waffen-SS: militarised *Schutzstaffeln*, the military expansion from Hitler's bodyguard detachment.

YVA: Yad Vashem, The World Holocaust Remembrance Centre, located at: https://documents.yadvashem.org

zbV: zur besonderen Verwendung, special duties or special deployment.

ZMSBw: *Zentrum fur Militärgeschicte und Sozialwissenschaften der Bundeswehr*.

1942

In January 1942 a popular German hunt magazine published a remarkable story about Luftwaffe Colonel Adolf Galland. During the German army's attack on Moscow, in the winter of 1941, the famous fighter ace took time out to go hunting. He was an expert hunter, like so many Luftwaffe officers, and wanted to extend his record to the forests of the east. Galland together with his adjutant set off without an armed escort into a gloomy forest just north of Dünaberg (today Daugavpils in Latvia). The forest was renowned for its game but was badly scarred by war. The Soviet Red Army had put up a spirited defence, however the Germans forced them to retreat. The Russians had abandoned their trenches leaving behind the detritus of war; discarded equipment, clothing and weapons littered the forest floor. As the two hunters strolled deeper into the forest, they disturbed a herd of Roe deer. They decided to separate, and Galland took up a position in a bush by a clearing and a stream. Very soon he observed and shot a roebuck. The single shot wounded the buck and it sprinted away. Galland set off in pursuit but stumbled into a ditch breaking through ice immersing himself and coat in sticky mud. He sloshed around in the freezing muddy water trying to break free from its suction. By luck, his hunting rifle hadn't got wet and continued the search as he followed a blood trail. Covered in sticky wet mud, Galland trudged deeper into the gloomy forest and eventually located the buck, it was dead. An impressive trophy, 'I am overcome with joy! I did not expect such strong antlers.' Galland put down his rifle, took up his hunter's blade, and began preparing the carcass.

Suddenly, and without warning, Galland faced three armed Russians. 'We were all surprised' he exclaimed. Galland shouted 'sstaj', presumably meaning stop or halt, but a Russian fired at him. He took up his rifle and fired back, 'one of the Russians clasped his chest and collapsed.' Galland tried to shoot again but his rifle wasn't loaded. He struggled to pull a bullet from his coat pocket, but it was snagged in sticky mud. Unable to gauge the Russians' intentions, Galland opted to back off. He was temporarily forced to abandon his trophy later recalling, 'only a hunter will understand how I felt!' After a short time, he returned for his trophy: 'I don't think I will ever value a set of antlers more than those for which I had to fight with considerable luck.' Galland penned his hunting tale, 'in my shelter while being heavily bombarded by Russian artillery during the great offensive against Moscow that promises final victory'. He pondered the shortcomings of hunting in the 'paradise of farmers and workers' (contemptuous Nazi brogue for the Soviet Union), and that most wildlife had fled the forests as the front lines approached. The animals that remained had been exterminated rendering minimal hunting opportunities. To conclude his tale, Galland warned his fellow hunters and foresters to seek permission before hunting in the forests of the east: 'A number of dangerous bandits are still roaming the large forest areas between the River Memel and Lake Peipus and will do for a long time to come.' Galland's parting shot was to assume his 'report' offered sound advice to those who recognise the value and the importance of German protective security in the east.[1] Within a year, the random confrontations with partisans had turned into a major Soviet insurgency campaign.

On 1 December 1942, Adolf Hitler faced a military calamity. A week before, the Soviet Red Army had encircled Stalingrad, isolating the Sixth Army from adequate supplies or relief. Since the beginning of 1942, a raging Soviet insurgency had undermined all efforts to pacify the German occupied territories.[2] The increased Soviet partisan penetrations had become a priority discussion for that evening's military conference. Hitler introduced the *Draft of Official Regulations for the struggle against banditry* and explained:

---

1 Adolf Galland, 'Oberst Galland', *Wild und Hund*, No. 47, 1941–42, pp. 357–358.
2 See Chris Bellamy, *Absolute War: Soviet Russia in the Second World War*, (London, 2007) and Evan Mawdsley, *Thunder in the East: The Nazi-Soviet War 1941–1945*, (London, 2016).

1942

> The goal must be to destroy the bandits and restore peace and order. Otherwise, we will end up in the same situation that we had once in our domestic affairs, with the so-called self-defence clause. This clause led to the situation that no policeman or soldier actually dared to use his gun in Germany.[3]

The progress of Hitler's policy, from proposal to directive to doctrine to dogma, had followed a predictable path. In late 1941, Hitler invited Heinrich Himmler, chief of the SS and German police, to find a solution. In June 1942, Himmler initiated a planning process with particular instructions to his senior SS-Police officers. He demanded their proposals must include the vilification of the 'partisan' as an illegal 'bandit'. Then from the proposals Hitler issued: Führer Directive No. 46, *Richtlinien für die verstärkte Bekämpfung des Bandenunwesens im Osten* (Instructions for Intensified Action against Banditry in the East) in August 1942.[4] The policy was tried and tested under SS auspices, and in parallel, the chief of staff of the Army issued general instructions to form *Jagdkommando* (hunting-squads) to combat the 'bandit bands'. All rear area forces were directed to exterminate the 'bandits' with the utmost ferocity. Also, cruel sanctions were imposed on civilians for assisting the bands, including execution or slave labour, their homes burned, and crops destroyed. The *Bandenbekämpfung* doctrine was officially introduced on 27 November but the doctrine's architecture and language were already institutionalised by the summer of 1942.[5]

The Luftwaffe's participation in Bandenbekämpfung was critical to security operations on the Eastern Front. In April 1942, the Luftwaffe committed ground forces and support units. At that stage, German security and counterinsurgency still conformed to the army's regulations and tactical doctrines. From August, the SS

---

3   Helmut Heiber, David M. Glantz (ed), *Hitler and his Generals: Military Conferences 1942–1945*, (New York, 2002) pp. 14–17.
4   NARA, T175/140/2668141-355, Weisung Nr. 46: Richtlinien für die verstärkte Bekämpfung des Bandenunwesens im Osten, Der Führer, OKW/WFSt/Op. Nr. 002821/42g.K., Führerhauptquartier, 18 August 1942.
5   Philip W. Blood, *Hitler's Bandit Hunters: The SS and the Nazi Occupation of Europe*, (Virginia, 2006), pp. 3–28.

became the guardians of Bandenbekämpfung dogma within all the Third Reich's civil-military authorities, while the Wehrmacht gradually filtered the terminology into reports. On 31 December, the *Luftwaffen Kommando Ost* issued a report on the entire period since April. The report opened:

> The increasing activities of the bandits since 1941/42 in the rear of Army Group Centre, presents a serious danger to the supply and the conduct of the war by the army and air force, or exploit or colonize local economies. Although large-scale operations and smaller actions to combat the bandits were conducted successfully by the security units, the bandit activity increased, especially in the frontline or area of the frontlines. This was aggravated by Red Army Frontlaufer, or stragglers, often supplied by the Red Air Force, and the bands' press-ganged local people and trained them.[6]

The Soviets had organised raiding parties or bands of 200–400 men with specialists—scouts, messengers and saboteurs. These bands had constant and reliable communications with the Soviet Union, through signals, messengers and aircraft, which enabled re-supplies and reinforcements. These Red Army bands were properly organised and well armed, and ranged deep into occupied territory.[7] The local populations were either directly assisting them or supplying food. The Germans were also disturbed that the band's weapons were good quality and included mortars, anti-tank guns, and field artillery, and warned against underestimating the 'bandits'.[8]

In response to the partisan threat the Luftwaffe had been forced to take 'special measures' to protect the airfields. *Luftwaffen Kommando Ost* recognised that the few security troops could not stem the advance of the bands. In response, on 24 April, Göring granted permission for the formation of *Lw.Infantry Regiment Moskau* from surplus manpower from tactical formations, building

---

6   TsAMO 500-12454-623, Bericht über die Bandenbekämpfung durch Einheiten der Luftwaffe im Bereich des Lw.Kdo.Ost von 10.4. bis 31.12.42, 8 Jan. 1943.

7   S.A. Kovpak, *Our Partisan Course*, (London, 1947). Stalin's directive, 1 May 1942, instructed the bands to cause sabotage and destruction behind German lines.

8   TsAMO 500-12454-623, Bericht über die Bandenbekämpfung.

and construction units, as well as signallers and staff cadres. Training was shortened and the regiment was deployed in June. For a period, the regiment was the only available infantry in the entire area of *Luftwaffen Kommando Ost* and were committed to security tasks in sectors with high concentrations of partisan infiltrations. They were also briefly engaged in the frontline when circumstances demanded their commitment to conventional warfare. The 'bandits', according to the Luftwaffe's colourful use of the emerging *Lingua Franca*, were committed to widespread *Bandenanschlägen* (acts of terror), with attacks on railways roads, stores, bridges, dairies, landed estates, warehouses, and kidnapping mayors (collaborators). The insurgency increased into Autumn 1942, which led the Germans to take more radical measures. The bands posed a serious threat to the occupation, the supply of the front and military communications. The Luftwaffe had facilitated a general replenishment of all its units, with increased training and reinforcements. The only limitations to the increases were inadequate shelters for the troops with the onset of winter. The army and Luftwaffe imposed similar mission targets of *Befriedungsräume* (entirely pacified area) — achieved through pacification, cleansing, and destruction. The *Luftwaffen Kommando Ost* report included a Butcher's Bill: body counts with destroyed villages and lists of captured booty. The list of destruction included: 19 'bandit-camps', 88 enemy villages, 140 bunkers destroyed, 1,284 partisans shot after capture, and lists of equipment. Subsequent research by James Corum uncovered the *Lw. Infantry Regiment Moskau* was responsible for the destruction of 5,000 houses and killed seventy-six hostages.[9]

---

9 James Corum, "Die Luftwaffe und Kriegsverbrechen im Zweiten Weltkrieg." in Gerd Überschär, Wolfram Wette (Hrs), *Kriegsverbrechen im 20. Jahrhundert*, (Festschrift für Manfred Messerschmidt), (Potsdam, 2001), p. 298.

Map 1: Poland divided, Nazi occupation zones in Poland, Soviet Russia and the Ukraine.
© J. Noakes & G.Pridham, *Nazism 1919–1945 Volume 3, Foreign Policy, War and Racial Extermination*, A Documentary Reader, University of Exeter Press, Exeter 1995, p. 1222, courtesy Liverpool University Press.

The report closed with a series of post-operational observations, which indicate that Göring's lieutenants were not only experts in the application of security warfare, but were well versed in the politics of *Bandenbekämpfung*. The first observation concerned the local population vis-à-vis the *Bandenlage* (bandit situation): if the locals were peaceful, they were usually 'happy' to be protected by German troops; in *bandenbeherrschten Gebieten* (bandit-controlled areas) the locals work for the 'bandits'; however, in the *bandenverseuchten Gebieten* ('bandit' diseased areas) the locals expected to be targeted by both sides. One comment concluded that local co-operation was necessary for the successful pacification and exploitation of an area, and it was therefore, critical to impose German rule. A second observation concerned the compromise of Nazi propaganda by security operations. It was recognised that burning villages for revenge or retribution might backfire, especially if the locals were both harmless and helpless. However, if an area was collaborating with the 'bandits' it was necessary to 'cleanse with a firm hand.' The third observation noted how the morale of the troops suffered when expected to combat the 'bandits' with inferior weapons. The bands were well supplied with superior and heavy weapons, and several times Luftwaffe flak artillery engaged in direct firing against heavily armed 'bandits'. Another point mentioned the high level of mobility adopted by the 'bandits', which meant the Luftwaffe depended on the army's security units to effect a mobile counter-strategy. A further observation criticised the absence of a unified command, and there had been reports of chaotic incidents. This had led to a centralisation of all Luftwaffe forces and the reorganisation of command structures. There had also been an introduction of strongpoints at important hubs along the railway lines, with Luftwaffe troops assigned to guarding junctions. A final point noted how the 'bandits' adopted 'sneaky' tactics, which required strong forces to counter and eradicate them. There was a palpable reluctance in a recommendation to conduct night-time actions and the troops to be trained to work in 'night and fog' — the distasteful notion of resorting to 'bandit' tactics to counter the 'bandits'. Operational training was acknowledged as the key to success and especially in learning to exploit the same methods as the 'bandits' — the use of cunning, and ruthlessness.[10]

---

10 TsAMO 500-623, Bericht über die Bandenbekämpfung.

Excursions in Microhistory

Writing history has history. The Luftwaffe's participation in the Holocaust had always been on the fringe of history. Although Hitler's air force was known to have held an instrumental part in the war, it was not associated with killing Jews, civilians, and partisans. The senior officers of the Luftwaffe tried to destroy the evidence in 1945 and very nearly succeeded. A small section of files survived that served as a catalyst for in-depth research of the Luftwaffe. The central thread of the narrative of this book is about ordinary Luftwaffe soldiers, the *Landser* and the Holocaust. The *Landser* is a slang word for the common soldier akin to the British *Tommy*. There was only partial evidence of the *Landser's* footprint in the military documents. Consequently, painstaking research was adopted to piece together and collect scraps of evidence to construct a microhistory. From its origins in my PhD research, *Birds of Prey* was destined to be a microhistory. The research for this book, however, took a scientific path and applied historical GIS methods as forensic means to map the movements and the spatiality of the *Landser*. The outcome is this microhistory of Luftwaffe security troops in occupied Poland during the period 1942–44.

The general hypothesis underpinning this book re-confirmed my original research conclusions. Hitler's Bandenbekämpfung was not conventional anti-partisan warfare or counterinsurgency. Bandenbekämpfung was not a bureaucratic reclassification of anti-partisan warfare without consequences, and the Wehrmacht was no longer able to conduct security operations within the parameters of its traditional guidelines. The application of Bandenbekämpfung was relatively easy and ideologically inexpensive. In practice, it vilified opponents, placed civilians under suspicion, and rendered them defenceless to exemplary punishment. Within its historiography, the school of military history has perpetuated the myth of Partisanenbekämpfung or anti-partisan warfare rather than recognise Bandenbekämpfung and its genocidal implications. This approach downplayed the place of Nazi ideology, as it sought to make sense of anti-partisan warfare. Given the evidence, this is no longer a sustainable argument. *Bandenbekämpfung* evolved from the forester's battles with poachers and bandits. Christopher Hale makes a compelling argument that Bandenbekämpfung originated in the Thirty Years' War. The word existed long before it was institutionalised as a doctrine of militarised security in the Nineteenth Century. *Bandenbekämpfung* was radicalised as an operational doctrine within Imperial Germany's colonizing security warfare, and was extended into the German way of war from 1908. *Bandenbekämpfung* was Germany's approach to security warfare from 1942 onwards.[1]

The setting for the book's research was Białowieża forest in eastern Poland. This primaeval forest lies in the historical region of Podlasie and is famous as a habitat for the European bison. Białowieża established a reputation for hunting and since the 1500s was a hunting reserve for the Polish kings. The forest and surrounding areas became populated with Poles, Lithuanians, Belorussians and Jews. There were few municipal conurbations, other than Białystok, but many small towns, villages, and shtetls. The forest had a long history of authoritarian and violent occupation. After 1795, following the third partition of Poland, Białowieża was subject to consecutive annexations: Prussia, Russia, Imperial Germany and then Nazi Germany in 1941. After 1918 this region once again returned to Poland, but war with Soviet Russia turned the region into one of the shattered lands of the east. After the experience of German Army occupation, during Great War, the Nazis increasingly craved the forest as a trophy. Hermann Göring pursued Hitler's ambitions for *Grossdeutschland* (Greater German Reich) on the eastern frontier by locking Białowieża forest into a defensive plan. This defensive plan envisaged a primaeval wilderness as a natural barrier to the threat of the 'Bolshevik' horde. In theory, this geopolitical strategy was scientifically sophisticated, but proved wholly naive as a defence line. This was Germany's Maginot Line on the eastern frontier.

---

1 Christopher Hale, *Hitler's Foreign Executioners: Europe's Dirty Secret* (Stroud, 2011).

The research set out to explore how other ranks (ORs), or the rank and file, adapted to Bandenbekämpfung in Hitler's race war. From 1942, the common soldiery perpetrated genocide in most theatres of the war: without overt ideological indoctrination; without being ordered by junior officers to commit crimes; and with everyday killing normalised to within military procedures or routines. There was no evidence the troops resisted this work. Indeed, trained into aggressive military concepts such as Auftragstaktik (mission-tactics) the soldiers were roused to heightened levels of violence.[2] The research synthesized Göring's geopolitical ambitions with the study of the Landser as perpetrators of genocide. In many ways this contradicted the general opinion that Göring disappeared into the shadows after Stalingrad. However, the findings set him apart from Hitler and Himmler. Whereas Hitler wanted to be excluded from the killing process, Himmler was a keen visitor to the extermination sites. Göring, in contrast, participated in the planning and willed its execution, but never visited the killing sites, or Białowieża after the Nazi-occupation in June 1941.

My research focused upon Göring's manipulation of two key institutions within his mandate as a Nazi leader. The German hunting fraternity and the Luftwaffe. Both institutions contained influential social elites and controlled a large proportion of the population. The hunt created the Nazified honour code for his 'court etiquette', and the Luftwaffe was the foundation of a 'revolutionary' military order. Together they merged the nstitutional symbolism of 'The Blue' (Luftwaffe) and 'The Green' (state forester-hunters). This was the culmination of Göring's corporatism. By exploiting this institutional dynamic, Göring set about his plans for a permanent national frontier in the east. Stalin was determined to frustrate these plans and waged an intense insurgency campaign within Białowieża. Göring escalated the conflict by sending Luftwaffe security troops to destroy the Soviet partisans. Jews fleeing to the

---

2 Jeff Rutherford & Adrian E. Wettstein, *The German Army on the Eastern Front*, (Barnsley, 2018), p. 41. They refer to Auftragstaktik as 'Mission Command', a commander ordered a mission, arranged forces and set the goal but then left it to a junior officer or NCO to complete the mission as they saw fit.

forests to escape the Holocaust were caught in the middle and became victims of Göring's hunter killers — the *Landser*. This microhistory was demarcated by three groups: Göring and the Nazi leaders plotting from the hunting lodges in East Prussia, the Luftwaffe soldiers on the ground hunting partisans and Jews, and the German hunt officials serving as the authoritarian lynchpin in the middle. Together, they all worked towards winning Hitler's race war, but Göring had his own views how this should be achieved. This is a challenging book, but as close as possible it is a real-time reconstruction of Nazi-occupation of Białowieża, German soldiers and the Holocaust. Michel Trouillot's words are evocative: 'This is a story within a story — so slippery at the edges that one wonders when and where it started and whether it will ever end.'[3]

The acquisition of sources

The research was hindered by the absence of a central repository of records and archives to anchor the book. The grouping of documents was like different corners of a jigsaw puzzle without an original picture to bring them together. There were mismatches between known actions, where histories had percolated into myths and no bridges to span any connection between maps and documents. My doctoral research into *Bandenbekämpfung* doctrine was helpful, as was defining *Sicherheitskrieg* (security warfare) as a traditional German response to armed resistance in occupied and colonial territories; but it was not yet clear how all of this applied to the Białowieża case.[4] There was a vague outline for a case study article, but too thin to stand alone as a book. Richard Holmes recommended I pursue my post-doctoral research along multiple lines of investigation. The primary sources from six key topics included: Hitler's Luftwaffe, the hunt and environmental history, military geography, Colonialism and Nazi *Lebensraum*, the Holocaust, and the war in the east. Gradually, the evidence was acquired from a

---

3   Michel Rolph Trouillot, *Silencing the Past: The Power and Production of History*, (Boston, 1997), p. 1.
4   Blood, *Hitler's Bandit Hunters*, passim.

variety of sources, but with a common cut-off date of 1945. This evidence was then categorized into victims, perpetrators, and bystanders. Some postwar evidence that directly contributed to the narrative was included to explain how the perpetrators escaped justice and manufactured 'new' lives. This methodological approach of synthesising multi-disciplinary research satisfied some but generated criticism from others.

There was also a story about the Luftwaffe records. On 3 August 1945, US Army intelligence officers interrogated Karl Mittman, formerly deputy commander of the Historical Section of the *Luftwaffe* (*8. Abteilung*). Mittman, born in Frankfurt in 1896, had served in the Great War and afterwards had established a career as an industrial merchant. In 1935 he was called up and joined the *Luftwaffe*. His work had initially involved publishing a history of the war in the air 1914–1918. The onset of the Second World War suspended all previous work, as the section began collecting material for the present conflict. The section also expanded, employing well-educated officers with experience in writing historical narrative. Lw. Brigadier General Herhudt von Rohden (1899–1951) was placed in overall command. Section eight had six subsections: *Auswertung* (evaluation), *Kriegsgeschichte* (war history), *Wehrwissenschaftliche Gruppe* (military science), *Bildgruppe* (photographic section), *Technische Gruppe* (technical) and *Archiv* (archives). Mittman claimed the purpose of military history was to establish the basis for a world history, a medium for the education of service personnel, and to present 'a responsible account to one's own war.' He identified three categories of military history: a political history of the war, a history of the military strategy of the war, and a 'history for the education of the people.' During the war, the section had completed a review of the period 1939–43; fifteen annuals of air war accounts including Poland, France et al; had compiled special instructional guides for officers; and had published pamphlets on aspects of the air war. All this work and output, according to Mittman, had been carried out without political controls or interference. Then, as the war drew to a close, the section made several moves from Berlin to Thuringia, Bavaria, and Czechoslovakia. Driving from Karlsbad to

Bavaria, as allied thrusts quickened, Mittman decided to destroy the material. Fifty cases reached Vorderriss near Bad Toelz, mostly maps and material regarded as 'little importance', were stored in a forester's office. Mittman helpfully offered tips to the allies how the archive could be reconstructed.[5]

More than fifty years later, I was in the *Bundesarchiv-Militärarchiv* in Freiburg-Im-Breisgau, the last day of a long research trip. Frau Noske, the resident but kindly official, presented a print-out of files that had just arrived in the reading room. They were a small collection of diaries of a *Luftwaffe* security battalion and a *Luftwaffe* 'special commando'. They were assigned to security actions against Soviet partisans in 'Bialowies', the German spelling of Białowieża, during 1942-44. The battalion was the *Sicherungsbataillon der Luftwaffe Bialowies zbV*. The battalion was raised on 18 July 1942, disbanded on 18 March 1943. The other formation was *Jäger-Sonderkommando Bialowies der Luftwaffe zbV*. This smaller unit was activated on 6 March 1943, but was increased to battalion size from October 1943, and remained in Białowieża until the great German retreat in July 1944. It was immediately apparent they were an important source. Panic: hasty photocopy requests in bulk, hatched and dispatched, in the age before digitalisation. Subsequent deflation: under scrutiny, it was apparent that the primary content was locked in obscure map references. Richard Holmes recognized this was the 'smoking gun' of the research, but only so long as all the evidence was collected and deciphered.[6] In lieu of managing the maps, a search process was started to locate the personnel records of the men. The *Deutsche Dienststelle* (WASt), in Berlin, held the Wehrmacht's card index records. The *Wehrmachtsauskunftstelle für Kriegsverluste und Kriegsgefangene* (WASt) maintained a complete record of combatants, casualties, and POWs for all the Wehrmacht. Alongside the names extracted from the diaries with the casualty

---

5   NARA, RG165 721A, Seventh Army Interrogation Center APO 758, Final Interrogation Report, Historical Section of the OKL, Ref. No. SAIC/FIR/51, 3 October 1945.

6   Philip W. Blood, 'Bandenbekämpfung, Nazi occupation security in Eastern Europe and Soviet Russia, 1942-45,' PhD diss. (unpublished), Cranfield University, 2001.

records, a prospective list was sent to the *Bundesarchiv-Zentralnachweisstelle* (BA-ZNS), previously in Korneliemünster, near Aachen, to locate records. That archive held several personnel files of some officers and ordinary ranks (ORs), including postwar claims for service pensions.

In their memoirs, *Luftwaffe* aviators have acknowledged the tactical implications of *Bandenbekämpfung* for the *Luftwaffe's* ground forces. In particular, the change from the defence of installations to aggressive local search and destroy actions. Hans-Ulrich Rudel recalled his airfield being exposed to Red Army probes and no longer any '... battle-worthy ground forces screening our front ...'. As 'Ivan' probed, the commander of the airfield staff company, 'gets together a fighting company drawn from our ground personnel and those of the nearest units and holds the airfield.' Rudel observed:

> Our gallant mechanics spend their nights, turn and turn about manning trenches with rifles and hand grenades in their hands, and during the day return to their maintenance duties. ... Our Luftwaffe soldiers at the beginning of the war certainly never saw themselves being used in this way.[7]

The question of the airfields in the 'bloodlands' had not entirely gone unnoticed. In July 1952, US Counter-Intelligence officials began an investigation of the Vinnytsia massacre, where Soviet secret police had murdered 9–11,000 Ukrainian civilians. The grave pits were discovered in 1943 and, the Germans used the evidence as a propaganda coup against the Soviet Union. The Nazi Ministry of Eastern Affairs assigned pathologists from nations across occupied Europe. Several former Luftwaffe personnel, present when the site was uncovered, were later interrogated by the Americans. Alfred Holstein (born December 1891), from Rothenburg, remembered visiting the excavations several times and recalled how the Ukrainian mayor (a Nazi collaborator) had called them victims of their religion. He was persuaded to give a detailed testimony, which revealed he was the commander of the Luftwaffe labour battalion working at the nearby airfield. Following a period of heavy rain and rapid drainage, the ground had formed strange shapes. In May

---

7   Hans-Ulrich Rudel, *Stuka Pilot*, (Exeter, 1952), p. 36.

1943 they began digging and discovered the massacre site. Georg Müller (born 1894), had served with the *Luftwaffe*, was transferred to the airbase in Vinnytsia and testified:

> At one time, I was going from Winia (sic) to the airport when I saw many people coming down the street accompanied by SS Guards. The people were Jews (men, old women and children). They were taken to the prison. A few days later, they were taken by truck to the place of execution (approximately one kilometre from the airport). They had to undress and walk into the pits which were already dug. There they were shot. There also partisans were disposed of in the same manner.

He also recalled engaging with a group of 60 Jews — slave labour working on the airfield. He discovered they were to be shot. A truck arrived that evening (6.00 pm) and took 10 to the place of execution — 8 managed to escape. He was later transferred to a Luftwaffe facility in Lemberg, in Poland, and Müller learned of an execution site in the locality. The CIC report concluded: 'no further investigation of subject massacre is intended by this detachment unless otherwise directed ...'.[8]

> In the 1950s, former German Army and *Luftwaffe* generals recast themselves as honourable professional soldiers, irrespective of being among Hitler's cohorts.[9] They were praised in military histories of the Luftwaffe, which persisted in focusing upon strategy, operations and technology; affirming a reputation for elitism, rather than scrutinising the allegiance to Hitler and its darker implications.[10] Marrying murderous acts on the ground to knightly aerial warfare is not difficult to establish. The behaviour of the airborne forces in Crete (1941–42) continued a trail of crimes that began in the Spanish Civil War and included bombing civilian settlements in Soviet Russia and Yugoslavia on the spurious grounds of 'suspected' partisan hideouts. The *Luftwaffe*, as demonstrated in this book, was quite capable of breaching its legal codes to commit murder, even without the vilification of racial enemies.

---

8   NARA, RG319, Winiza (sic) massacres, September–October 1952, 66 Counter-Intelligence Corps Detachment, 17 October 1952.
9   Autorenkollektiv, *Bilanz des Zweiten Weltkrieges – Erkenntnisse und Verpflichtungen für die Zukunft*, (Oldenburg, 1953).
10 H. Boog, *Die deutsche Luftwaffenführung 1935–1945*, (Stuttgart, 1982); W. Murray (1996), *The Luftwaffe 1933–45: Strategy for Defeat*, (Washington DC, 1996); J.S. Corum, *The Luftwaffe: Creating the Operational Air War, 1918–1940*, (Kansas, 1997).

Engaging with microhistory

This book was conceived at a particularly lively period of historical discourse and debate. The contemporary interpretation of Hitler's war had begun to take shape in the 1980s. For example, Omer Bartov had noted, 'The collaboration of the army with the Nazis and its role as the instrument which enabled Hitler to implement his policies, were most evident during the war against Russia.'[11] Since German rearmament in the 1950s, the story of the Wehrmacht's complicity in Nazi crimes had been resisted. Bartov's book was an uncomfortable reminder of the reality of the war, just as the Cold War was about to end. By the 1990s the literature was directly questioning the mass mobilisation of manpower as directed towards the Holocaust. Christopher Browning had observed, '... the German attack on the Jews of Poland was not a gradual or incremental program stretched over a long period of time, but a veritable blitzkrieg, a massive offensive requiring the mobilization of large numbers of shock troops.'[12] In Germany, the *Wehrmachtausstellung* opened in Hamburg, an exhibition that explained the Wehrmacht's participation in Nazi crimes. A controversy over the content forced the exhibition to close and one of its organisers forced to step aside.[13] Hannes Heer, having stepped down from the exhibition, published his interpretation of the crimes of the *Wehrmacht* on the eastern front and included his essay on combating partisans.[14] In 2000, I was able to discuss my ideas with Heer and soon recognised we shared similar conclusions about *Bandenbekämpfung*, as a means to bringing ordinary soldiers to Holocaust killing without an overbearing ideological hierarchy.

---

11 Omer Bartov, *The Eastern Front, 1941–45, German Troops and the Barbarisation of Warfare*, (New York, 1986), p. 3.
12 Christopher Browning, *Ordinary Men: Reserve Police Battalion 101 and the Final Solution in Poland*, (New York, 1998).
13 Hamburger Institut für Sozialforschung (Hg.), *Vernichtungskrieg. Verbrechen der Wehrmacht 1941 bis 1944*, (Hamburg, 1995). Hamburger Institut für Sozialforschung (Hg.), *Verbrechen Der Wehrmacht: Dimensionen Des Vernichtungskrieges 1941–1944*, (Hamburg, 2002).
14 Hannes Heer, *Tote Zonen: Die Deutsche Wehrmacht An Der Ostfront*, (Hamburg, 1999).

The Holocaust was also embroiled in lively debates in the 1990s. For a long time, Raul Hilberg's three-volume study framed Holocaust scholarship.[15] Then Daniel Goldhagen exploded the accusation that Germans had been willing executioners, '... this book endeavours to place the perpetrators at the centre of the study of the Holocaust and to explain their actions.' He argued the '... institutions of killing detailed the perpetrators' actions, chronicled their deeds, and highlighted their general voluntarism, enthusiasm, and cruelty in performing their assigned self-appointed tasks.'[16] Since 1940, deportations had collected Jews from across occupied Europe concentrated them in Polish ghettos. In June 1941, the *SS-Einsatzgruppen* ranged across the rear areas in the wake of the German Army's advance into Soviet Russia.[17] In the *Holocaust by Bullets*, the SS killed or murdered upwards of two million Jews.[18] From mid-June 1942 the destruction of the ghettos set off another wave of deportations to killing centres, but this also sparked outbursts of Jewish resistance.[19] By December 1942, Hitler's war against the Jews had escalated into a three-part process involving deportations, killing centres, and mass deaths. The evidence collected for *Birds of Prey* confirmed that Luftwaffe troops were assigned to this process.

There were other challenges to collecting evidence. During the period 1941–44, Białowieża forest came within *Bezirk Bialystok*, a Nazi occupation zone administered from East Prussia. Göring's ambition was to bind East Prussia and Ukraine in a common frontier with *Bezirk Bialystok*—a land bridge between the two. This represented a racialized colonial frontier of fewer than 3 million Germans under Erich Koch, ruling over 35 million people (Ukrainians, Belarussians, Poles, and others). This particular region was under-

---

15   Raul Hilberg, *The Destruction of the European Jews*, (New York, 1985 revised).
16   Daniel Jonah Goldhagen, *Hitler's Willing Executioners: Ordinary Germans and the Holocaust*, (New York, 1996).
17   Yitzak Arad, Shmuel Krakowski, Shmuel Spector, *The Einsatzgruppen Report*, (New York, 1989).
18   Father Patrick Desbois and Paul A. Shapiro, *The Holocaust by Bullets: A Priest's Journey to Uncover the Truth Behind the Murder of 1.5 million Jews*, (New York, 2009).
19   Shmuel Krakowski, *The War of the Doomed: Jewish Armed Resistance in Poland, 1942–1944*, (London, 1984).

researched, but for Christian Gerlach's published doctoral thesis, which is cited in the narrative of this book.[20] In *Hitler's Empire* (2008), Mark Mazower referred only to Ukraine and noted that the SS had difficulties working with Koch, who became virtually untouchable after turning East Prussia into a pro-Nazi state.[21] Koch could rely on both Hitler and Göring to back him during internal squabbles. The greater challenge to my research, however, was the glaring absence of evidence about *Bezirk Bialystok* in the archives.

Before applying Historical GIS (explained in chapter 1) to the research, several attempts were made to construct a more traditional historical structure for the manuscript. The classic study of a German town, under Nazi rule, was also considered a viable option because it was compact.[22] There were parallels of cultures, anthropology and localism. Allen claimed his 'microcosm studies' were unrepresentative of the Nazi regime but encouraged detailed analysis, which initially made it an important option. The closely relevant study was Christopher Browning's *Ordinary Men* (1992), the study of a police battalion in the Holocaust.[23] The book examined records from Federal German investigations, compiled from perpetrator interrogations and testimonials conducted more than twenty-five years after the war. Browning concluded the Nazis had unleashed a 'blitzkrieg' against the Jews, and ordinary men had carried out the killings. There were parallels of scale between police and Luftwaffe battalions, but whereas Browning could construct a case based on postwar testimonies, this was not available for a study of the *Luftwaffe*. Memory-based evidence has limitations, even with Federal investigations, but the greater problem was the lingering myth of the 'clean Wehrmacht', which included the Luftwaffe. Overcoming the myth was challenging.

---

20 Christian Gerlach, *Kalkulierte Morde: Die deutsche Wirtschafts- und Vernichtungspolitik in Weissrussland 1941 bis 1944*, (Hamburg, 1999).
21 Mark Mazower, *Hitler's Empire: Nazi Rule in Occupied Europe*, (London, 2008), pp. 153–4.
22 William Sheridan Allen, *The Nazi Seizure of Power: The Experience of a Single German Town 1922–1945*, (London, 1984).
23 Browning, *Ordinary Men*, passim.

The impact of the Historical GIS research is explained in detail in 'Reading Maps Like German Soldiers' (chapter 1), but it should be recognised that it was central to redirecting the research. The final microhistory version adapted for the book as a consequence of working with the GIS maps. Several scholars were identified as endorsing the benefits of microhistory long before its actual appearance as a specific methodology. Eric Hobsbawm defined 'grassroots history, history from below or history of the common people'. This is referred to as *Alltagsgeschichte* by German historians or everyday history.[24] Hosbawm's Marxian interpretation of 'history of the common people' was a dialectic that might be applied to the history of the common soldier. In comparison to Hosbawm's observations about the traditions of oral history to the working class, similar characteristics exist for the common soldier. The lowly soldier's social structure was confined to a traditional militarised hierarchy, with orders from above forcing 'confrontation or co-existence' with officers and NCOs. To construct an interpretation of how the soldiery responded to Nazi dogma required a deeper understanding of the Wehrmacht beyond the battles and operations. This also involved an understanding of the cultural transformation from conventional combat to occupation, and vice versa, with some comprehension of how the soldiery survived the war beyond the usual glib interpretations of luck. Hosbawm's ideas greatly suited the social history of the soldiery.

A wholly unexpected outcome from my research was the prominence of the German hunt in shaping events (on this see chapter 2). This coincided with a new study that advised: 'military history, ... is a promising candidate for ... microhistory', and later added 'military history gives ample scope for the microhistorian.'[25] This was a significant theoretical development, but there were no examples to support the claim. The application of microhistory in Holocaust history also illuminated how the intimate scrutiny of Nazi perpetrators could transcend everyday life and everyday

---

24 Eric Hobsbawm, *On History*, (London, 1997), p. 201.
25 Sigurdur Gylfi Magnusson and István M. Szijártó, *What is Microhistory? Theory and Practice*, (London, 2013), p. 164 and p. 166.

killing.[26] These microhistories seemed to fit the environmental and forestry conditions of Białowieża. The conditions had formed a peculiar impression of Białowieża on the Germans, which they dubbed *Urwald Bialowies*. The Mammal Institute (Białowieża) had published several important publications, which have discussed life during the occupation.[27] Historically, forestry and hunting have been dominant themes in German literature for centuries, while foreign observers have been rather whimsical about the national fixation with 'gloomy forests'.[28] The weight of forestry literature threatened to overwhelm the research for this book, but it should be recognised that the power of Białowieża dominated the collective mindset of the Germans.[29] Throughout the Luftwaffe war diaries, there were constant references to *Urwald Bialowies*, in almost an arena like context. *Birds of Prey* has attempted to reproduce that notion of an arena of killing, where the Germans imagined themselves as warriors of antiquity.

The hunting culture was politicised by Göring to serve as a code of honour, which enforced the operational dogma in Białowieża. Senior hunt officials perpetrated genocide from their first orders for extermination, which continued for the duration of the occupation. The hunter's mission was set by Göring, but their actions at the local level were defined by individual responsibility. Beatrice Heuser recommended pursuing a deeper examination of hunting and war through Barbara Ehrenreich's *Blood Rites*.[30] This ground-breaking interpretation of war and hunting led to further reading. In particular, Simon Harrison touched on much darker

---

[26] Claire Zalc and Tal Buttmann (ed), *Microhistories of the Holocaust*, (New York, 2017).

[27] Tomasz Samojlik, *Conservation and Hunting: Białowieża Forest in the Time of Kings*, (Białowieża, 2005), Bogumila Jedrzejewska and Jan M. Wójcik, *Essays on Mammals of Białowieża Forest*, (Białowieża, 2004); see also Jan Walencik, The Last Primeval Forest in Lowland Europe, (Białowieża, 2010).

[28] Simon Winder, *Germania: A Personal History of Germans Ancient and Modern*, (London, 2010), p. 17.

[29] Simon Schama, *Landscape and Memory*, (New York, 1995), pp. 75–120.

[30] Barbara Ehrenreich, *Blood Rites: Origins and History of the Passions of War*, (London, 2011).

kinds of hunting and human behaviour in war.[31] Under the Nazis, the German hunt turned into an elitist social class. One observation with hindsight, these findings could have been contextualized within Michel Foucault's theories of power and discipline. An etiquette of power shaped the mannerisms of the hunters, especially in their relations to non-hunters. The hunt's social elitism, in the absence of monarchy and aristocracy, was directed towards the ritualisation of professionalism. Foucault's doctors and patients could be almost role-reversed into the hunters and non-hunters. These threads formed an image of the naked display of power and professionalism, as depicted in the symbolism of the 'hunter-warrior' of Luftwaffe propaganda, labouring with genocide, in the wilderness arena of Białowieża.[32]

The necessity to conduct field research in Białowieża came from reading *Riding The Retreat*. In the preface, Holmes discussed his 'growing reservations with what we might term 'arrows on maps' military history' and being drawn to the 'microterrain, that tiny detail of ground and vegetation that means so much to men in battle.'[33] Holmes had previously engaged with the history of memory through the anecdotes of soldiers. Both *Firing Line* (1985) and *Dusty Warriors* (2006) were influenced by memory, the 'other soldier' in the case of the former, and himself in the latter as an observer on the ground. Holmes listened to veterans after the Falklands War in 1983, but in 2005 gave an impression of being on the ground in Iraqi. This transformation in Holmes' writing, from listener to witness, was a lesson in historical change, that went largely unnoticed in reviews. A further contemporary impression of the dichotomies of military culture came from *The Junior Officers' Reading Club* (2010). The author warned the readers that incidents in war are not recalled in exact detail. Hennessey reflected upon a war from yet another standpoint of soldiers' responses during a hostile

---

31 Simon Harrison, *Dark Trophies: Hunting and the Enemy Body in Modern War*, (New York, 2014).
32 See Michel Foucault, *The Birth of the Clinic: An Archaeology of Medical Perception*, trans. A.M.Sheridan Smith, (New York, 1994).
33 Richard Holmes, *Riding The Retreat: Mons to the Marne – 1914 Revisited*, (London, 2007), p. ix.

occupation. There are always doubts over the accuracy of reports and this was more prominent in wartime where accounts were often accepted at face value.[34] There was one important study that could not be incorporated into the research findings. Thomas Kühne has written extensively and profoundly about soldiers within the context of identity and comradeship.[35] Repeated attempts to incorporate his ideas failed due to fundamental gaps in the evidence. This was primarily due to the lack of personal evidence of the Luftwaffe soldiers, their shortened periods of service together, and the absence of any identifiable primary groups. In the final version, it was a collective of Hosbawm, Holmes, and Hennessey that pointed the way. The consistent reference to documentary evidence, but the caution of the unreliability of the bureaucracy underpinning that evidence was a constant finding in my research.

At the heart of this book is the German soldier — *the Landser* — the common soldier. The motivation behind this book was to understand who they were and how they were — in effect, a socio-cultural military history. Scholars and writers have reflected on who they were, why they fought for Hitler, and remained faithful to the bitter end; but the soldiers themselves have remained aloof, distant, and impenetrable. During the war, British military intelligence examined German fighting traits through PoW interrogations.[36] US Army intelligence carried the subject into a wider analysis of

---

34 Peter Hennessey, *The Junior Officers' Reading Club: Killing Time and Fighting Wars*, (London, 2010).
35 Thomas Kühne, *Kameradschaft: Die Soldaten des nationalsozialistischen Krieges und das 20. Jahrhundert*, (Göttingen, 2006). See also Kühne, *Belonging and Genocide. Hitler's Community 1918–1945*, (New Haven, 2010) and 'Kameradschaft – "das Beste im Leben des Mannes", Die deutschen Soldaten des Zweiten Weltkrieges in erfahrungs- und geschlechtergeschichtlicher Perspektive,' *Geschichte und Gesellschaft* 22 (1996) S.504–529, and Kühne, *The Rise and Fall of Comradeship: Hitler's Soldiers, Mass Bonding and Mass Violence in the Twentieth Century*, (Cambridge, 2017).
36 TNA, WO 208/3608 CSDIC SIR 1329, Establishment of a Jgdko by Secret order of the Befehlshaber Südost, interrogation of UFF'S Kotschy and Boscmeinen, 13 December 1944. WO 208/3979, A Study of German Military Training, Combined Services, May 1946.

military methods and innovation.[37] After the war, civil-military relations scholars applied the interrogation reports to a 'cohesion and disintegration' thesis (1947). The authors identified a 'primary group' concept, which claimed to hold the fighting or combat troops together. The article also cited an interrogation report of a captured German NCO about the political opinions of his men — the reply was instructive:

> When you ask such a question, I realise well that you have no idea of what makes a soldier fight. The soldiers lie in their holes and are happy if they live through the next day. If we think at all, it's about the end of the war and then home.[38]

The timeless words of veterans' attitudes from all armies. The article was widely read but with a limited appeal. A general perception of the German soldier remained of the well trained and highly disciplined soldier. Nazism had socialised the soldiery, which tightly bound the myths of the Landser during the war. In the postwar age, Germans grappled with the uncomfortable realities of the war. In the 1950s, foreign observations, like that of *The Scourge of the Swastika*, were directed at German society struggling to come to terms with the war and Nazism.[39] From the 1980s, scholarship began to follow an empirical/analytical path, while popular genres embellished uncontested German veterans' anecdotes which has continued to this day.[40] In 1983, a study compared the respective performances of the German Army and US Army during the war.[41] Omer

---

37 TNA, WO 208/3000, 'The German Squad In Combat, Military', Intelligence Service, US War Department, Washington DC, 25 January 1943. WO 208/3230, US Army Pamphlet 20-231, 'Combat in Russian Forests and Swamps', Department of the Army, July 1951. Military Intelligence Service, No.15, *The German Rifle Company*, (Washington DC, 1942), 1942, partial translation of Ludwig Queckbörner, *Die Schützen-Kompanie: Ein handbuch für den Dienstunterricht*, (Berlin, 1939).
38 Edward A. Shils and Morris Janowitz, 'Cohesion and Disintegration in the Wehrmacht in World War II,' *The Public Opinion Quarterly*, Vol. 12, No. 2 (Summer, 1948), pp. 280-315.
39 Lord Russell, of Liverpool, *The Scourge of the Swastika*, (London, 1954); Russell was a judge advocate officer and had worked on numerous war crimes trials.
40 For example, Max Hastings, *Overlord*, (London, 1986).
41 Martin van Creveld, *Fighting Power: German and U.S. Army Performance 1939-1945*, (London, 1983).

Bartov published his research of Hitler's soldiers, which adapted the 'primary group' thesis to German fighting formations.[42] I was fortunate to be placed in London at a time when several leading scholars discussed their ideas about common soldiers and war. Following a London University German history seminar in May 1997, there was a discussion with Bartov. He believed there was a shortfall of records, in particular the German NCOs, thereby reducing the prospect for serious research.[43] In a subsequent conversation with Joanna Bourke, following a lecture at the Wiener Library, she argued men killing in war, stripped of military identity and political ideology, could be the basis for a comparative study.[44] Bourke's impressions closely matched the acts of men in Białowieża. However, the resort to public killings by the Germans represented extreme exemplary violence, which placed them in a separate category of Second World War belligerents.[45] This basic idea for comparative analysis, however, never entirely disappeared.

The *Landser*, as portrayed in this book, emerged from scholarly engagements with German colleagues. Following discussions with the late Professor Wilhem Diest and Professor Stig Förster at conferences, a different path of research was set emphasizing the interactions of social class.[46] An impression drawn from conversations with German veterans about their impressions of 'combat', 'firefights', and their sense of gratification from memories of being soldiers.[47] In lengthy discussions with Professor Jochen Böhler, about German soldiers and their private letters, a richer impression of the *Landser* emerged. The culmination of the research identified the Luftwaffe soldiers as either reservists (mostly officers with civilian professions) or conscripts (mostly ORs from the lower classes). The

---

42 Bartov, *Barbarisation*, passim.
43 Institute of Historical Research: School of Advanced Study, University of London, German History seminar, Professor Omer Bartov, 21 May 1997.
44 The Wiener Holocaust Library, lecture 'Intimate Killing', 26 February 1999 presentation of Joanna Bourke, *The Intimate History of Killing*, (London, 1999).
45 Michel Foucault, *Discipline and Punish*, (London, 1991).
46 Arbeitskreis Militärgeschichte e.V., Essen conference, August 1999.
47 In particular: Henry Metelmann (panzer—Guildford), Heinrich Schreiber (infantry-Aachen), Paul S** (Luftwaffe-Magdeburg), Frederick Baumann (infantry-Berlin) and Boso L**(Waffen-SS).

only professional soldiers were the senior NCOs (no more than six), and none of their papers has survived. If these men were judged by their careers, they cut a cross-section of Third Reich society: farmhands, industrial workers, clerks, low-skilled technicians, tradesmen, trainees, beat police, and junior civil servants. They were a rag-tag collection of men mustered into small units. They did not represent the cream of the crop, and even Göring held little sway over manpower selection at the point of recruitment. They were poorly organized and were turned into cannon-fodder — even the non de plume 'the poor bloody infantry' did not describe their circumstances. They were not particularly well-armed; their first weapons were captured enemy booty from the Great War. Neither unit colours and class identity, nor duty and discipline, explained their motivations. They performed occupation security as dedicated perpetrators, but then gave a reasonable account of themselves as German soldiers in retreat. The fog of war.

Terminology

Some issues remained unresolved. There was evidence of Polish collaboration with the Germans, especially in hunting and as forest guides. Identifying those persons was impossible as Germans reports did not include names. The problem of confused languages was an added complication. German soldiers, usually clerks in headquarters, compiled combat reports that struggled with Polish and Russian names. In Białowieża, the occupation bureaucracy cast transliterations of Polish and Russian. Today, the only impact of this chaos is to cause confusion to researchers. An example: the Polish town of Hajnówka was translated by the Germans as Gainovka during the Great War, and Hainowka under the Nazis. The Germans translated Białowieża as Bialowies in both world wars. Pruzhany in Belarus was Pruzhany when it came under Poland before 1939, and Pruzana under German occupation. The GIS maps adopted the German and narrative took the present-day Belarus form. The other prominent towns including Narewka, Topiło, Czolo, and Popielewo, Suchopol, Bialy Lasek, and Kamieniec-

Litewski have remained unchanged. The Germans referred to Narewka Mala in their reports and that name is used throughtout the manuscript in accordance with the German records. Many villages disappeared and their names later replicated far beyond the original site. Others cannot be identified on any maps and the reader has to accept that some villages are now lost from record and memory.

Since the war, there have been several changes in the political boundaries of the region adding further confusion to place names. To identify such places, the original name is adopted, but in brackets the present name and nation: for example, Nassawen, East Prussia (Lessistoje: Kaliningrad Oblast). Any faults in translations are of course mine. Time was also a critical factor in this book, because a certain level of real-time has been restored to events. The 24 hours clock regulated military life, with the Luftwaffe reports adopting that time system, but which time zone were they working towards—Berlin or Moscow? The Białowieża occupation was a confusion of time. The Germans imposed curfews between dusk and dawn, which the partisans and Jews ignored. Luftwaffe patrols rarely began before dawn or continued after dusk; the partisans attacked when there were no patrols. The atmospherics of darkness and lightness is better reflected by am/pm, which is adopted throughout the book.

In principle, the citations for the archival sources follow the original text. However, certain sources the shortand, the notes and the unclear dates led me to anglicize dates and document pages to ensure clarity. For example, this German citation include document number in the diary and the anglicized date: "BArch, RL 31/2, document 3, Wehrmacht-kommandantur Bialowies Tgb.Nr 686/42, An des Lw.Sicherung-Batl. z.b.V. Bialowies, 29 July 1942." Words can have legal implications for academic research in Germany. In 1992, Christopher Browning accepted the restrictions of Federal German laws for data protection on the use of names of individuals. Those laws are still in force at the time of writing, and I also agreed to abide by the strict code of privacy. In an article about Białowieża from 2010, I adopted pseudonyms.[48] Since then, several German books have placed the names of many individuals that were assigned to serve in Białowieża in the public domain. My research database is more extensive than those books, and so I adopted a mix of anonymity and openness. For those persons not yet published in the public domain and in the interests of anonymity, I have adopted the first name with the first letter of the surname followed by two ** — for example, Rudolf F**. The names of men already published remain in full — for example, Walter Frevert. The ranks of those from criminal organisations, such as the Nazi Party and the SS, have been kept to the original.

---

48 Philip W. Blood, 'Securing Hitler's Lebensraum: the Luftwaffe and the forest of Białowieża 1942-4', *Holocaust and Genocide Studies*, (Oxford, 2010).

An Aide-Mémoire:
Reading Maps Like German soldiers

A.J.P. Taylor once wrote: 'Every German frontier is artificial, therefore impermanent; that is the permanence of German geography.'[1] The Luftwaffe's mission in Białowieża was part of a policy of erecting a permanent frontier on the eastern borderlands. Beyond this 'new' frontier lay Belorussia, Soviet Russia, and Ukraine, in effect Hitler's Lebensraum empire. A permanent eastern frontier represented a geopolitical goal for the Nazis. Göring's three-part plan to bring this about included racial population engineering in Białowieża. The first and fundamental goal was to bring about the eradication of Eastern European Jewry. The second goal involved the reduction and deportation of Slavs, dubbed Untermensch (sub-humans), from the large group of forest settlements. In the third stage, Göring's plan called for the settlement of ethnic Germans, mostly repatriated from the east. Hitler's invasion of Soviet Russia complicated this plan, slicing through the former Pale of Settlement from Tsarist times, a vast territory that was still homeland to several millions of Jews.

The problem I had to overcome concerned the relationship between the *Landser* and the environment. How did 650 German soldiers effectively secure 256,000 hectares of Nazi-occupied Białowieża? The command and control of space or terrain have always been a strategic concern of nations, colonisers, army commanders, and security forces. During the Iraq insurgency (2003–11), the American army was forced to adopt a 'population-centric' strategy.[2] For this research, the first step was to recognise that the expansion of the Białowieża Forest, by the Nazis, was the creation of a frontier security zone. I called this frontier security zone the Białowieża arena, to reflect the full extent of Göring's territorial ambitions in this region. This arena was secured on the basis of a ratio of one soldier per

---

1   A.J.P. Taylor, *The Course of German History: A Survey of the Development of German History Since 1815*, (London, 1961), p. 2.
2   Dan G. Cox and Thomas Bruscino (ed), *Population-Centric Counterinsurgency: A False Idol? SAMS Monograph Series, CSIP, US Army CAC*, (Kansas, 2011).

1.52 square miles. How did the Germans fill the command and control of space, and was it effective? These questions challenged my research because they fundamentally alter our understanding of how Nazi occupation and colonisation was practised. In 2010, the research began the application of Historical GIS to solve these challenges and look afresh at how the Germans organised security. Consequently, this chapter is an aide-mémoire to the GIS maps that were generated and are included in full within the narrative.

I. The Nazis and military geography

Nazi aspirations were particularly focused on the frontier of East Prussia. Following an ultimatum to Lithuania, in March 1939, Memelland (today — Klaijpéda in Lithuania) was annexed, an area covering 3,000 square kilometres.[3] After Memelland, there were more acquisitions of former Polish territory in the south-east, named Regierungsbezirk Zichenau. This added another 12,000 square kilometres. Further annexations increased the state's landmass to 52,731 square kilometres (5,270,000 hectares), with a total population of 3,336,771. In July 1941, three forests became the anchors for further expansions. The Elchwald (Elk forest) designated Forstamt Tawellningken (due west of Tilsit and running north/south along the Kupisches Haff) was expanded to 100,000 hectares with localized annexations. The Kaiser's former hunting estate at Rominten was increased to 200,000 hectares with Polish acquisitions. The third was Białowieża forest, a trophy from the Nazi invasion of Soviet Russia in June 1941. Between 1915 and 1939, the approximate forest area was 160,000 hectares. Göring's plan required an increase of 90,000 hectares, increasing the gross area of the forest to 256,000 hectares. One hectare is equivalent to Trafalgar Square (London) or the area of an American football stadium. Shenandoah National Park boasts 200,000 acres, which converts to 81,000 hectares. This brought the eastern forest plan to a gigantic total of 560,000

---

3 AŠarūnas Liekis, *1939: The Year That Changed Everything in Lithuania's History*, (Amsterdam, 2010), pp. 82–83; see also Norman Davies, *Europe: A History*, (London, 1996), p. 904.

hectares. In forest mass alone, East Prussia's 1933 borders had increased by twenty-five per cent.⁴ This occupation area, including Białowieża, was designated Bezirk Bialystok and administered from Königsberg as domestic territory.

Where this expansionism was leading is not altogether clear, since Nazi dogma, strategic ambitions, and geopolitical annexations were all at odds. Erich Koch, as ruling Nazi Gauleiter of East Prussia, not only presided over all these expansions but was also gifted with the Reichskommissariat Ukraine. Koch was turned into an overlord of a racialized colonial frontier. In effect, East Prussia and Bezirk Bialystok symbolised the fulfilment of the eastern frontier of the Greater German Reich—virtually replicating the brief existence of New East Prussia (1795–1806). The annexation of Ukraine, however, represented a fulfilment of Hitler's Lebensraum ambitions. Thus, Bezirk Bialystok was also a geopolitical land bridge between Nazi Lebensraum and an Imperial style Greater German Reich. The creation of a colossal forest wilderness, dubbed an Urwald (primitive forest), also had strategic and cultural implications. There was a belief in the defensive military qualities of forest wilderness, which will be discussed later. Culturally, the creation of a massive forest pointed to the recreation of the ancient forests of Germania. In parallel, there were biological-zoological ambitions to recreate long-extinct animals, like the Aurochs that once roamed the ancient forests. In effect, Zoologists had institutionalised the notion of the racialized game. These mindsets lay behind the German occupation' transformation of Białowieża into a wilderness arena, however, even this story was loaded with contradictions.

In the military context, the expansion of the eastern frontier produced significant security administration requirements of a colonising scale, rather than for a political annexation. The challenge for the military-security services was to meet the Nazi goal. To excel in military geography was the German officers' mantra. Field Marshall Schlieffen's staff rides, his battlefield tours, were lessons in

---

4   Walter Frevert, 'Zehn Jahre Jagdherr in Rominten', *Wild und Hund*, (1943), pp. 148–153.

reading maps to better understand the nature of battle.[5] Göring's fitness for command could be partly gauged by his map skills and understanding of the terrain. In the first instance, he had acquired knowledge as a user of military geography. As an officer cadet, he was schooled in terrain and geography; as an airman-observer, he was an expert of map interpretation; and as a squadron leader conducted his command through maps — but was he suited to command-control Białowieża from the comfort of Rominten? In the Second World War, German military cartographers not only plotted the movements of armies and the positions of enemies, but also the distribution of populations and strategic raw materials. The search and acquisition of local information were paramount to military and civilian occupations. Consequently, the daily production of maps was essential to both warfare and racial engineering. By 1942–43, it is estimated were that the armies in the east were printing and distributing upwards of 25,000 maps per day.[6]

German military geography was not well documented to assist this research,[7] but an indication of the German cartographical system can be located in other sources. In July 1945, British Army intelligence interrogated a senior NCO from the Wehrmacht's military geography branch. His interrogators isolated the German administration of military geography as the focus of their questions. They learned that Lieutenant General Gerlach-Hans Hemmerich (1879–1969) was reactivated in October 1936 as Chief of Abteilung für Kriegskarten- und Vermessungswesen, the Mapping and Surveying department within the Chief of Staff of the Army (OKH). He remained chief of army mapping until April 1945. The department was designated MIL-GEO, with its head office in Berlin and with smaller satellite departments dispersed throughout the army. Maps remained its primary mission throughout the war.[8] Following the

---

5 Robert T. Foley, *Alfred von Schlieffen's Military Writings*, (London, 2003).
6 Discussions with archivists of the Bundesarchiv Militärarchiv. At the time of writing, there is uncertainty over the numbers of maps produced by the Wehrmacht.
7 Edward P.F Rose, Dierk Willig, 'German Military Geologists and Geographers in World War II', in *Studies in Military Geography and Geology*, 2004, pp. 199–214.
8 TNA, WO 208/3619, Interrogation Reports, CSDIC (UK), SIR 1706–1718, interrogation number 1709, German Army Warrant Officer Dr. Bartz 19 July 1945.

outbreak of war, MIL-GEO's offices and personnel expanded through the conscription of elderly professors and civilians with geographical expertise. The Berlin university system was particularly important in providing staff. Professors also recommended good students for staff posts, and the army designated them Heeresbeamter, a military-civil service rank. This process of conscription was later extended to geography schoolteachers and local government surveyors. Following Germany's early conquests, the MIL-GEO established outposts in most occupied cities. The scope of their work extended to gathering information recorded on a card index system. The breadth of data collected included physical geography, economics, water sources, traffic routes, roads, and anything deemed essential to military operations. Once compiled into maps and reports, they were packaged in comprehensive volumes and distributed to the higher commands as topographical intelligence. In effect, each high command of the army received a collection of detailed maps and cartographical information to conduct operations.

The British interrogators also raised questions about (Lw) Lieutenant Otto Schulz-Kampfhenkel (1910–1989), chief of the Forschungstaffel zbV des OKW. They learned that Schultz-Kampfhenkel was a geographer and was Göring's special advisor on political-military geography. Before the war, he founded Forschungsgruppe-Schultz-Kampfhenkel, a consultancy with a reputation for applying a 'total approach' to explorations and surveys. He led an anthropological-cartographical expedition to Amazonia (1935–37) in a joint venture organised by the Kaiser-Wilhelm-Institut für Biologie and Brazil's National Museum.[9] The expedition's mission was to examine Urwald and understand its special qualities. During the war, his Forschungstaffel was turned into a small office, attached to the OKW, and called Sonderkommando Dora.[10]

He was described as a university geography lecturer, who returned to Germany after working in the USA and was conscripted into the army.

9   Sören Flachowsky und Holger Stoecker (Hg), *Vom Amazona an die Ostfront. Der Expeditionsreisende und Geograph Otto Schulz-Kampfhenkel (1910–1989)*, (Köln, 2011).

10 Hermann Häusler, 'Forschungsstaffel z.b.V. Eine Sondereinheit zur militärgeografischen Beurteilung des Geländes im 2. Weltkrieg.' Schriftenreihe, *MILGEO Institut für Militärisches Geowesen*, Heft 21/2007.

Schulz-Kampfhenkel was also tasked with exploring and surveying parts of North Africa. As the chief exponent of Urwald, Schultz-Kampfhenkel advocated the incorporation of forests into the German national defence system. While there was a sacred relationship between the German hunt and Urwald, Schulz-Kampfhenkel's ideas for a forested border in the east gained a powerful grip on Nazi homeland security. Schulz-Kampfhenkel's 'hidden-hand' was behind Göring's plans for Białowieża. In effect, the forest was set to become part of Germany's national boundaries, and with a central strategic purpose of defence.

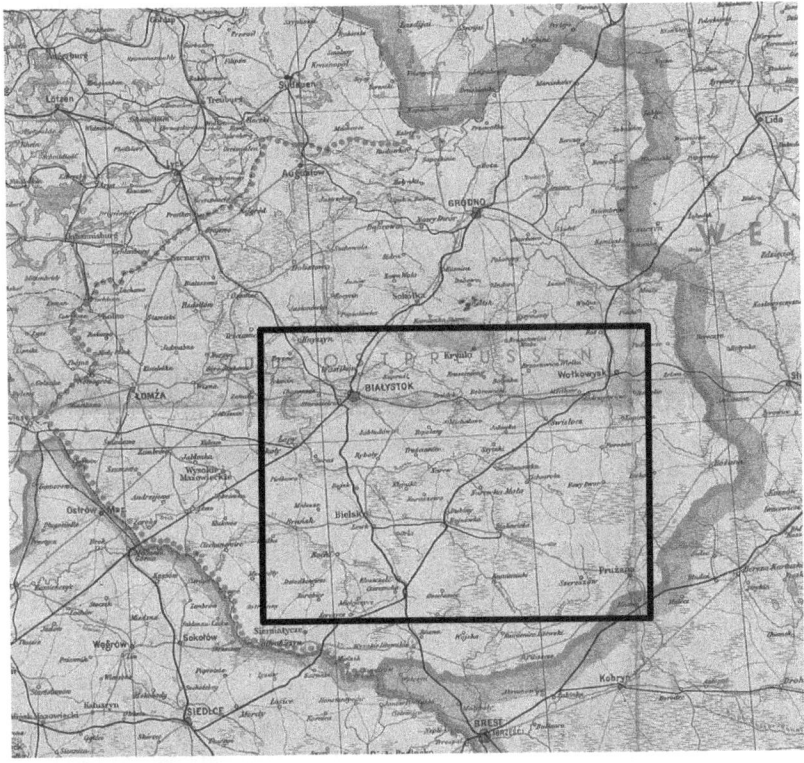

Map 2: Bezirk Bialystok circa 1944.
The area within the black box approximates to the Białowieża security arena discussed in this book.
Source: Wikicommons | Public Domain

The Luftwaffe's Białowieża operation's map the Karte des Urwaldes Bialowies is held by the Bundesarchiv-Militärarchiv. The map has a 1:100,000 scale and was produced in digital format of six sections. When put together they filled a small lecture room. The map had a legend that included the positions of troops, strongpoints, command posts, and wireless posts. During the war, the map was arranged as a single item on a large map-table in the Tsar's former hunting palace, that served as the battalion's headquarters. Trying to reconstruct the battalion's cartographical activity was impossible: trying to locate the position of companies and squads beyond the major towns was a 'hit and miss' exercise. A conundrum materialized that came from not being able to integrate the map with the documents. The operational administration and orderly filing of the Luftwaffe combat reports contrasted with the content of the reports, that implied random, haphazard, and chaotic killing. Actions were too far at odds with reporting. The actions in the combat reports did not reflect the known understanding of the German way of war or small-unit actions. The maps were the primary form of command and control for German operations, and were pertinent to the Białowieża story. Reports without the maps were largely incoherent beyond killing, fighting, or deporting. If the behaviour of the Germans was deliberate, it could only be proven by unlocking the map codes. A neutral, and important, issue within the documents, was the geographical references buried within the combat reports. These references could not be disputed. Attempting to reconstruct cartographical movements with this map approved impractical with marginal results. This confirmed Hobsbawm's dictum that grassroots history has its challenges: it 'doesn't produce quick results, but requires elaborate, time-consuming and expensive processing.'[11]

II. The science of maps

The aphorism 'a map is worth a thousand words' was never more pertinent than in the research behind this book. The conversion to historical GIS (Geographical Information System) was a drawn-out

---

11   Eric Hobsbawm, *On History,* (London, 1997), p. 201.

process. Today, GIS is routinely applied to a full range of historical fields, including the Holocaust.[12] Before that time, we relied on discussions with the geographers at the Bundesarchiv to try to understand how the maps were used. There was some confusion because there was no working reference to how the Germans had used the maps. In discussions with Bettina Wunderling, a qualified GIS technician, we examined the theory of applying alternative methods to unlock the maps and connect them to the war diary. We agreed upon an experiment that should use the digitized map of Karte des Urwaldes Bialowies as the platform for conducting GIS-based forensic analyses.[13] Transferring the research to a scientific basis was not an entirely alien prospect. During my MBA at Aston Business School, assignments involved quantitative analysis of large data sets, computer programming, systems engineering, and design, and had devised a research method for managing large quantities of diverse information. There were hidden benefits that Richard Holmes recognised, that elements of my MBA, which included management systems, organisational theory, and social psychology, would help to broaden the historical research.

In the second decade of the Twenty-First Century, it might appear strange to discuss working with Historical GIS in a large area of Europe, without geo-referencing. The challenge was to combine old map skills with the new science of mapping. The first stage involved learning by doing. Initially, little could be done because the 'Bialowies' map lacked spatial coordinates and the projection was unknown. These are common problems when working with historical maps. As a consequence, it was not possible to use the map in a GIS system or make visualizations and analyses. We visited the Mammal Institute, in the UNESCO World Heritage park of

---

12   Anne Kelly Knowles, Tim Cole, Alberto Giordano (ed), *Geographies of the Holocaust*, (Bloomington, 2014). See also the essential secondary source was Ian N. Gregory and Paul S. Ell, *Historical GIS: Technologies, Methodologies and Scholarship*, (Cambridge, 2007); also, Anne Kelly Knowles (ed), *Past Time, Past Place: GIS for History*, (California, 2002).

13   Bettina Wunderling BSc. Geology (Göttingen), a certification in GIS (Kiel), and has studied at Aachen-RWTH. The GIS modelling was carried out with ARC GIS version 10.0 by ESRI Software.

Białowieża in eastern Poland, and Dr. Tomasz Samojlik. He showed us the institute's collection of historical maps and five highly detailed maps drafted in the 1920s by Polish geographers. After some preliminary examination, we realised the Germans had based their military map on the Polish maps. Tomasz provided the projections and coordinates to digitize these maps. In the search for comparative national/local maps from 1941, we found a consistent absence of borders between Białowieża and East Prussia to the north, which indicated political annexation. A military map of the Pinsk-Pruzhany area to the south, drafted in July 1943, confirmed a national boundary towards the east. This confirmed the territorial expansion of East Prussia, as the national frontier with a wilderness bastion to the Greater German Reich in the east.[14]

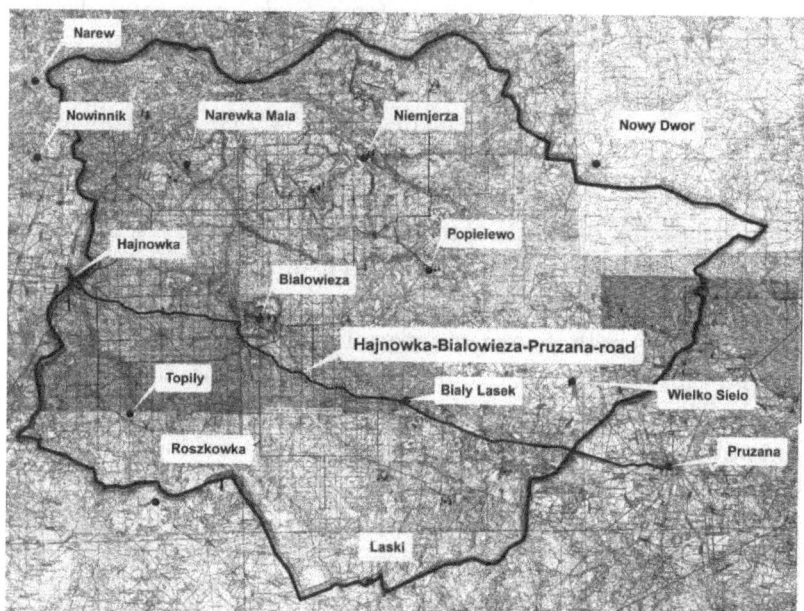

Digital Map 3: Luftwaffen Karte des Urwaldes Bialowies.
© Bettina Wunderling.[15]

---

14 Hein Klemann & Sergei Kudryashov, *Occupied Economies: An Economic History of Nazi-Occupied Europe,* 1939–1945, (London, 2012), plate 1.
15 This digital map represented the longest period of research and analysis prior to the full application of historical GIS.

In 2009, it was virtually impossible to identify the lost villages and the scenes of many incidents in the forest. The preparations for being able to conduct forensic modelling came from comparing the documentary records to the application of historical GIS to research and using textbooks as guidebooks. There were few textbooks about GIS in historical research or how to apply GIS to forensic analysis. One of the few was published by ESRI Press, the in-house publishing arm of the leading GIS software company.[16] The chapters were instructive. One chapter examined the importance of maps in GIS.[17] The authors explained the values of reliability and accuracy in GIS modelling. They highlighted the visual impact of terrain. A second chapter focused on battlefields and detailed the essential processes from fieldwork to desktop mapping.[18] Another important book confirmed the peculiarities of working with both historical data and maps.[19] A visit to Białowieża was necessary to log important data into the database: the positions of old photographs, specific map references, and geo-reference points. The processing of the Luftwaffe map sections was a laborious and time-consuming task that involved adjusting different maps to a single useable map. Bettina began an advanced GIS course, and the department allowed the process of digitisation and the GIS mapping to be tested under university conditions. A high degree of expertise emerged that the university endorsed with a letter of commendation.[20] Bettina began to incorporate more advanced methods of historical GIS.[21] To better understand the full breadth of Historical GIS and the basic operating principles, there were online seminars available to beginners. In May 2013, I joined an historical GIS course hosted by the Institute of Historical Research, London University.

---

16   Anne Kelly Knowles (ed), *Past Time, Past Place: GIS for History*, (Redland, 2002).
17   David Rumsey and Meredith Williams, 'Historical Maps in GIS', in Knowles (ed), ibid., pp. 1–18.
18   David W. Lowe, 'Telling Civil War Battlefield Stories with GIS', in Knowles (ed), ibid., pp. 51–63.
19   Ian N. Gregory and Paul S.Ell, *Historical GIS: Technologies Methodologies and Scholarship*, (Cambridge, 2007).
20   Geographisches Institut, Christian-Albrechts-Universität zu Kiel, May 2009–March 2010.
21   Jonathan Raper, *Multidimensional Geographic Information Science*, (London, 2000).

This involved working through an ArcGIS project in the classroom. This course reinforced the importance of managing several issues, including, digi-maps, geo-referencing, vector data and coordinates, symbolising data, pixelization, spatiality, data parcels, cartograms, and copyright.[22] By the completion of the first stage and the preparatory work, we had produced a map (Map 3 below) in a digital, georeferenced form that would make possible a variety of analyses.

The second stage involved identifying data from the documents or qualitative content to form into specific layers. In a sense, this was akin to unpicking the spaghetti of data and trying to isolate common data sets. The significance of GIS is the integration of seemingly unrelated data and its reordering into meaningful information. Layers were identified from different sources. Infrastructure like roads, swamps, railways, roads, bridges, farms, and estates were digitized from the original Polish maps. The Luftwaffe had drawn information on their maps, such as the position of strongpoints, companies, and *Jagdkommando*. This data was integrated with the Polish maps and digitized. The next task involved data mining from the surviving diaries of the Luftwaffe. There were two defined periods with different commanders, tactics, and dogma. This was a very time-consuming process because of the form of handwriting. Sütterlin is not taught in German schools today, but was widely utilised during the war. Once the barrier of the handwriting was overcome, page by page, line by line, (about 120 pages) we were able to present the results for review by a German veteran, who explained more nuances about that writing form under combat conditions. The overall outcome was a wealth of details and data. This led to multiple complex layering and we began to compare colour pixelization against the black-white map format. We opted for the latter. There were so many map options we decided to compile a series of test maps. Copies of these maps were sent to the late Dr. Joe White and his team, at the US Holocaust Memorial and Museum in Washington DC in 2013 for an evaluation. We also began to examine the nature of time and its impact on the

---

22   Institute of Historical Research, Historical Mapping and GIS, (research training), May 2013.

events. A partial experiment, involving multiple modelling was used to test the visualisation of progressive troop movement and patrols through segments of the forest. The outcome came down to tracking platoon, squad, and Jagdkommando movements, by minutes, hours, or days, depending upon the detail of supporting data.

Stage three involved formulating forensic analyses based upon the findings from the GIS layering tests. The key forensic mappings was classified under: the orders of battle or deployment of companies; the Bandenbekämpfung actions; population engineering; *Judenjagd* or Jew hunts; and larger operations. A 3-D model was drawn from the isolines of the maps. The outcomes of the analyses confirmed the working value of Historical GIS in a forensic dimension. How we presented and organized this evidence became crucial because the format selected would profile the narrative. The choices were: a military history format, the judgemental form of a war crime investigation, or a socio-cultural study of violence. In discussions about Bandenbekämpfung with retired US Army General Richard Trefry, comparisons emerged from Vietnam and Iraq.[23] He recommended the US Army's official report on My Lai as a structural model. The report incorporated a full schedule of maps and movement diagrams, which enabled comparisons with the logic behind the GIS mapping.[24] Comparing post-war atrocities, such as My Lai, with Bandenbekämpfung was not the intention, but following the structure of the report of integrating maps in the narrative did seem appropriate. In 2013, a test of the mapping and narrative was made of the area where Siegfried Adams was killed in combat in June 1943 (see epilogue). The geo-data, geo-references, and qualitative content proved complete for Adams. The results were spectacularly successful.

A final test was to compare the findings to the content from Geographies of the Holocaust. This book had set the benchmark for

---

23 Association of the US Army, Annual Conference, October 2006.
24 US Army Colonel Roger Cirillo, PhD retired supplied a copy: 'Report of the Department of the Army Review of the Preliminary Investigations into the My Lai Incident', Volume 1: Report of the Investigation, 14 March 1970.

applying historical GIS to the Holocaust. The book revealed the potential for a multidisciplinary approach to the Holocaust, but also the limitations when applied to military matters, and both are due to issues of spatiality. In a chapter about hunting Jews, the application of GIS was focused on time and space. The base data required a large body of data statistics including names, homes, mass deportations, and camps. In another chapter devoted to the killing grounds, the authors attempted to reconstruct the specialities of hunting Jews in Belarus. The chapter highlighted the formulation of 'locational models of killing', with GIS applied to map the movement patterns of killing units. There was graphical presentation of killings, a diagrammatic schedule of killings by time, and functional images of soldiery duties, which culminated in the summary — testimony, technology, and terrain. In both chapters there was an absence of integration and limited forensic outcomes. If the same methods had been applied to Białowieża, they would have produced only minimal results.[25] This did not reflect against the authors, but rather explained how different documentary evidence requires different historical GIS methods. We concluded that Historical GIS had unlocked the Luftwaffe's mission and methods in Białowieża. Historical GIS served three purposes: firstly, it had highlighted the prominent geographical features of the forest. Secondly, it recreated all military movements by timelines, operations, and outcomes, such as individual crimes. A deeper forensic analysis was achieved from mapping and visualising the effects of discipline, the routine, and orderliness of the killings. Thirdly, GIS exposed how a national political frontier divided responsibilities, but also explained the internal rivalries. In conclusion, GIS had exposed a grandiose Nazi scheme, Göring's ambitions, and the soldiers' behaviour — probably for the first time since 1945.

---

[25] Alberto Giodano and Anna Holian, 'Retracing the "Hunt for Jews": A Spatio-Temporal Analysis of Arrests during the Holocaust in Italy', and Waitman Wade Beorn and Knowles, 'Killing on the Ground and in the Mind' in Knowles et al, *Geographies of the Holocaust*, (Bloomington, 2014).

III. The GIS maps

This book contains more than twenty maps, the majority are from the Historical GIS analyses. The map below (uncaptioned) is an example of our first results. This is a composite map and although highly detailed it's also a picture of information overload caused by the density of layering and grayscale. The 'buffers', or roundels, represent patrol distances within company areas and also radio signals ranges for small wireless devices. Arrow lines give general directions of patrols and deportations. The Germans incorporated the *Jagen* system, which represented a square kilometre ground — reflected in the grid pattern. This was an old Tsarist form of measurment used in Białowieża for forestry management. The squares were mapped into the German maps and renamed *Jagen*. All of these factors have remained constant. However, in an effort to reduce the sense of clutter, we experimented with single layer maps and then with specific theme maps.

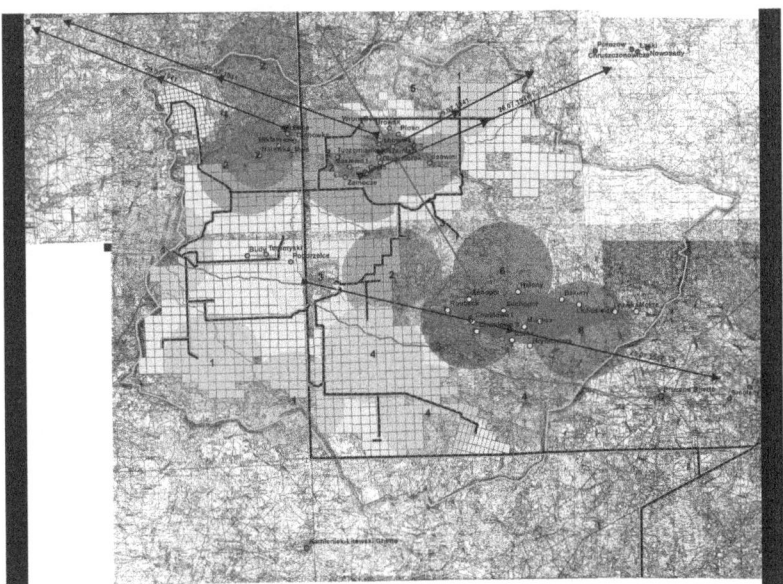

The solution we finally decided to accept were specific to the general findings from the research and forensic in design. The maps were finalised after series of experiments with colour, black and white, multiple layering, and single layer analysis. The GIS maps are in a specific set of representations: the orders of battle or deployment of companies (maps: 3, 4, 12, 13, 14, 20); the Bandenbekämpfung actions (6, 10, 16, 17); population engineering (5); *Judenjagd* (7,8,9, 11, 18); and larger operations (19, 21).

Alongside the GIS maps, the number of photographs were selected to contrast contemporary images of war with postwar memory. The aim was to visualize the concept of 'victims, bystanders and perpetrators' so prominent in Holocaust literature.

The conjunction of memory and mapping represents how communities co-exist within a landscape scarred by war and the Holocaust. Memories cast in the stone memorials stand in all Eastern European and Russian communities; this is an aspect of the Holocaust that is unique to the landscape. Maps and memories are germane to any microhistory of the region.[26]

---

26 For an example of this, see the travelogue in Omer Bartov, *Erased*.

1. The Ogre of Rominten

Knuff was a crafty and cuddly stag as his name implied, but he was elderly, and his days numbered. Although this mighty stag had large antlers he was reduced to the status of a commoner. There were too many weak points in his vital statistics that denied him a place in the regal stock book. Regardless of *Knuff's* less than noble pedigree, Hermann Göring had honoured the beast by selecting him for his hunting record. In his last hours, *Knuff* led Göring on a merry dance across der Romintener Heide. Göring stalked the stag for a week but the 'old gentleman' simply refused to surrender. For only the briefest moments *Knuff* tantalisingly presented his flanks but never long enough to be shot. After five hours of fruitless stalking in the morning, Göring was resigned to failure and trundled off to breakfast. Just about to tuck into a hearty platter, the mighty hunter received a telephone call from a forester that *Knuff* had been sighted. Leaving his continental breakfast behind, he dashed off eager for the kill. Göring mounted a shooting stand, took aim, and with a masterful shot he killed *Knuff*. This was the supreme moment—the sublime one-shot kill, a '… staggering phenomena that successful fighter pilots are good shots', wrote Göring's biographer.[1] While anecdote has shaped the myths about Göring, the tale of *Knuff* represents a narrative about the hunt and the Luftwaffe lost from history.

Hermann Göring is a complicated character, with a façade that is not always reflected in the literature. In the past, his biographers have been compelled to condemn rather than delve beyond the superficial. In this literature, Göring is painted as the Nazi archetype of failure. This notion is also reflected in the balance of books on the man: mostly about Göring and the Luftwaffe; a few books about Göring and the Nazi economy; and a handful of books about Göring and forestry. Consequently, we know more than we need to know about his failings with the Luftwaffe but know less than is

---

1   Erich Gritzbach, *Hermann Göring, Werk und Mensch*, (München, 1938), pp. 114–116.

necessary to fully comprehend his part in the Holocaust. These depictions do not give us a rounded view of Göring. For example, in 1945 when examined by allied psychiatrists, he was regarded as the most intelligent and unscrupulous of the Nazi war criminals held in the Nuremberg cells. In the courtroom, he rallied from apathy to become the last champion of Nazism and the guardian of his legacy. To start at the end, therefore, would inevitably lead to the conclusion that he was a deviant, unscrupulous, clever, dogged by physical issues, had an addiction to morphine, but ultimately cheated the hangman with suicide.[2]

Deep within Göring's psychology, was a story of violence that began with hunting and continued through soldiering. As a child, he was taught to hunt by his Jewish godfather on palatial estates. Then he was removed from this opulent lifestyle at an impressionable age and sent to a military academy with its strict discipline. Göring became an army officer and was posted to a Bavarian regiment garrisoned in Mulhouse in the Alsace, an area annexed after the Franco-Prussian war 1870/1. Göring experienced occupation first hand. He served in the disputed frontier area and was present in the region during the political unrest that led to the Zabern Affair (1913).[3] In 1914 he served in the trenches and later transferred to become a pilot. Göring was a fighter ace, served in and then commanded the famous *Richthofen Circus* and was awarded the *Pour Le Mérite*. Although Göring politicised his war record, it was not until he came to power that it became the central core of a radical political-military idea. In November 1918, Göring gave the farewell address as commanding officer of the *Richthofen Circus*, he recalled their combat victories and casualties. Fourteen years later, as President of the Reichstag, Göring recalled saying Germany would once again be allowed to fly, and 'I would be the Scharnhorst of the German air force.' Gerhard von Scharnhorst (1755–1813) was the driving force behind the reforms of the Prussian Army. An interesting

---

2   Robert Gellately (ed), *Leon Goldensohn, The Nuremberg Interviews: An American Psychiatrists Conversations with the Defendants and Witnesses*, (London, 2006), p. 128.

3   Richard W. Mackay, *The Zabern Affair 1913–1914*, (Lanhan, 1991).

role model since Scharnhorst was known to be, 'silent and withdrawn, a man who looked more like a schoolteacher than an officer of the king.' His 'calm tenacity in adversity' was in stark contrast with Göring's temperament.[4] When the Great War ended, Göring was at the peak of his physicality, a war hero with attitude, but unemployment forced him to search for direction—he met Hitler in 1922.

Göring's Nazi biographer called him the 'Führer's paladin' and pitched the narrative to his master's achievements in rebuilding the nation. He had come a long way from his squalid street battles in Munich after the war. 'From hero to zero', in modern parlance informs a trajectory of violence that culminated in a bullet wound during Hitler's Munich putsch (1923). The wound changed his physical being and the rest of his life. Göring saw himself as broken like Germany. His mission to create a Greater German Reich was as much a reflection of his condition as it was his endorsement of Hitler's ambitions. Göring's Nazism was different to that of Himmler, Rosenberg and Goebbels because it had been born in pre-war nationalism and fuelled by the events of 1918–1923. His belief in a Nazi military revolution was wholly different to both the SS and the army. His ideas were grounded in his self-constructed Germanic-romanticized-renaissance, bound by honour codes, Nazi etiquette, privilege and patronage. Richard Overy has argued that as the leading Nazi defendant at the Nuremburg war crimes, he bullied, chided and coaxed his fellow inmates. His inflated self-importance, egomania and ebullience left little room for contrition. In 1939 the allied politicians had believed Göring to be a moderate but at Nuremburg he proved to be as extreme as the rest of Hitler's circle. Overy believed Göring was an old-fashioned nationalist with a radical personality.[5] In 1933, as Prime Minister of Prussia, Göring enforced police regulations to smash Germany's left-wing

---

4   Wolfgang Paul, *Hermann Göring: Hitler Paladin or Puppet?* trans. Helmut Bögler, (London, 1998) p. 39. See also Stefan Martens, *Hermann Göring: "erster Paladin des Führers" und "Zweiter Mann im Reich"*, (Paderborn, 1985). Gordon Craig, *The Politics of the Prussian Army, 1640–1945*, (Oxford, 1978), p. 40.
5   Richard Overy, *Interrogations: Inside the Minds of the Nazi Elite*, (London, 2001), pp. 141–152.

movement. From 1933, under his guidance, the forestry and hunting fraternities examined future legislation and regulations, which led to the National Hunting Law (1934) and the National Nature Law (1935). These ecological laws were subtle devices that conformed to the Nazi *Volksgemeinschaft* and the evolving police state. In March 1935, Hitler agreed to the formation of an independent Luftwaffe, within the Wehrmacht following rearmament, and Göring was made its supreme commander. The forestry service would incubate the birth of the Luftwaffe.

Göring's Nazism was motivated towards restoring German national honour, but his institutional ambitions reached deeper into Third Reich society. Peter Uiberall was Göring's official interpreter during the Nuremburg trial, and claimed the prosecutors were unable to reach deep inside Göring. Uiberall argued that confronting Göring with crimes committed in the name of Nazi Germany was pointless. He labelled Göring a 'Condottieri type of personality' who didn't recognize right or wrong or know the difference between good and bad. As far as Göring was concerned the nation was an organism, a 'body politic' that had to be secured and protected by any means.[6] Göring the Condottiero is an enduring image of corruption, Machiavellianism, and capriciousness. He was an enigma of countless variations. The political ambition, to make Germany great again—a political tract with remarkable durability—fused his ideas across the breadth of Nazi orthodoxy. Shaping a modern military institution out of forestry, hunting and aviation, which combined the elements that were most Germanic in spirit to raise a frontier police with the capability to strike at enemies from long distance. This was a breath-taking strategic concept even by Nazi standards. Frontier security reinforced with a hard punch was fundamentally defensive, but also colonialist and nation-building. The killing of *Knuff*, therefore, can be seen as symbolic of Göring's representations of Germany—past, present and future.

---

6   Peter Uiberall on Göring, in Adam Curtis, 'The Living Dead', BBC, 1995.

I. The Green

The social engineering underpinning Göring's organisational ambition was both racial and hierarchical. The green uniform of the state foresters and game wardens drew on the symbol of centuries-old traditions from German culture. There was a bizarre compromise between Hitler's anti-blood sport rhetoric and Göring's bloodthirsty passions. Their compromise settled on the institutionalisation of *völkisch* culture throughout the Germanic forest and Germanic game. On 3 July 1934, Göring introduced the *Gesetz zur Überleitung des Forst- und Jagdwesens auf das Reich* (the bill for the National Laws for the Centralisation of the forests and hunting).[7] On 1 April 1935, the *Reichsjagdgesetz* (National Hunting Law) was enacted and the *Jagdamt* (hunting department) was established as a department within the RFA.[8] Diagram 1 is an organisational chart of the *Reichsforstamt*, highlighting the *Reichsjagdamt Abteilung IV*. The diagram was drawn from the military plans for the forestry industry and the hunting fraternity for mobilisation into the Luftwaffe in the event of war. The national hunt law centralised management, regulated hunt discipline, incorporated the preference for *Urwald* or primaeval habitats and introduced a scheme for the advancement of the Germanic game. The politics of the hunt involved corralling the power and influence of the predominantly middle-class fraternity and propagating Nazi racism through the hunt's classifying culture of social Darwinism.

---

7   Andreas Gautschi, *Der Reichsjägermeiste: Fakten und Legenden um Hermann Göring*, (Suderburg, 1999), p. 53.

8   See on this: Stefan Dirscherl, *Tier- und Naturschutz im Nationalsozialismus: Gesetzgebung, Ideologie und Praxis*, (Göttingen, 2012), and Tier- und Naturschutz im Nationalsozialismus: Gesetzgebung.

Diagram 1: *Reichsforstamt* organisation and the *Jagdamt* (1936).
Compiled from multiple sources filed under NARA, RG242, T77/100/145/301, (OKW WiRu Amt) Reichsforstmeister.

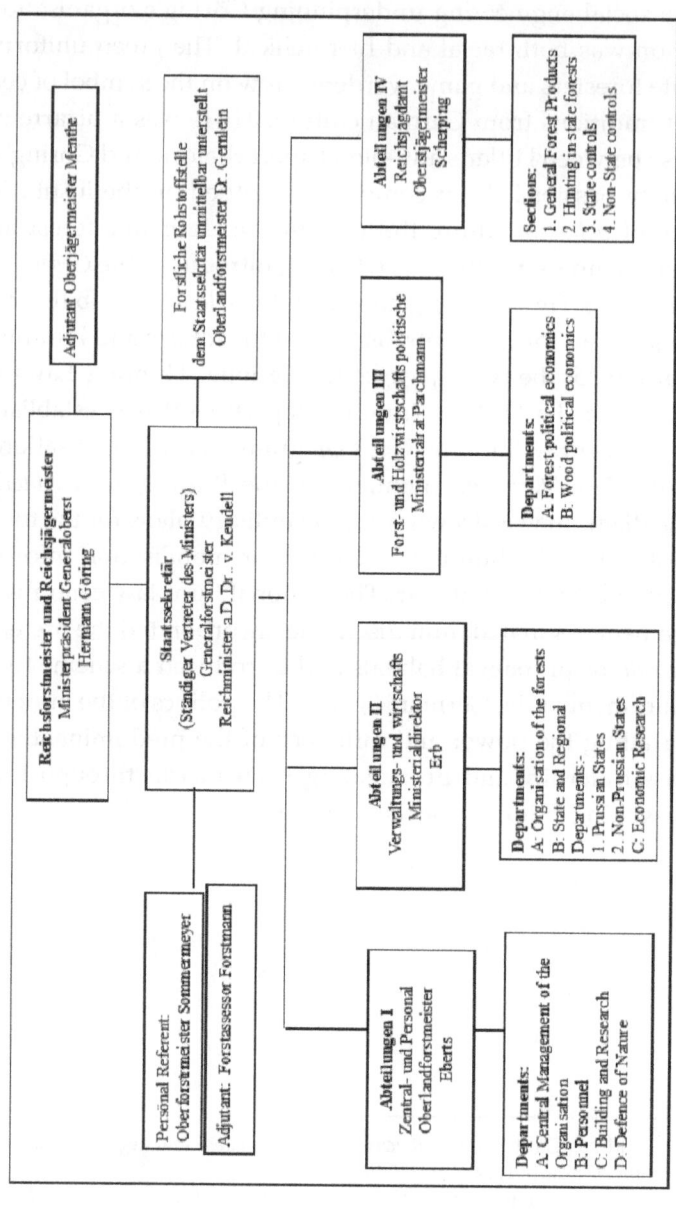

The German hunt was liberalised through laws made in 1848. The laws stimulated middle-class hunting, a social-cultural phenomenon in Germany. This process of culturalization was accelerated by industrial innovation in advanced gun design and manufacturing, mass-produced accoutrements and the mass distribution of cheap popular hunt literature.[9] During the Great War, hunting became a symbol of the inherent warrior masculinity of German soldiers. The collapse of monarchy caused an ideological void within the hierarchy of the hunt regardless of the increasing influence of the middle-class. The middle-class hunt was bereft of ideology because of the preponderance of a *modus operandi* steeped in professionalism. There was a great outpouring of hunt literature after 1848, but there had been no single volume codifying a general hunt etiquette until 1914.[10] Raesfeld's hunting manual was written from a professional standpoint and became the standard reference because he avoided dogma and didn't offend anyone. Fritz Röhrig, a senior forester on the staff of Greifswald University, later published a cultural history of German hunting with an undisguised national-conservative bias.[11] Like most from his profession, the first edition condemned *völkisch* myths of the *Germanen* tribes, *Germania* and the growing desire for ritual from within the hunt. A later edition incorporated a nuanced Nazi narrative. He argued the period immediately after 1848 had led to the endangerment of game, especially the extensive killing of elk, deer and beaver. This was coded language for maligning the middle-class as 'trophy vultures'. Röhrig however, was hostile towards both dominant social groups of the hunt. He criticised the 'privileged classes' (aristocracy) for their irresponsibility in opening the estates to "guest-hunters". He railed against the middle-class for transforming the hunt into a shooting exercise. The local shooting clubs and rifle associations were also a target of his ire. Röhrig claimed the hunt declined after 1919 partly caused by

---

9 https://www.academia.edu/43096984/Weidmanns_Heil_a_history_of_Social_Hunting_and_the_German_Middle_Class_1848_1914_ 27 April 2020.
10 Ferdinand von Raesfeld, *Das Deutsche Weidwerk: Ein Lehr- und Handbuch der Jagd*, (Berlin, 1914).
11 Fritz Röhrig, *Wald und Weidwerk: In Geschichte und Gegenwart*, (Potsdam, 1933, 1938 and 2003).

the alienation of the *Jagdjunker* (hunting aristocrats) and the vilification of foresters as royalist lackeys. Thus, between Raesfeld and Röhrig, there had been an observable politicisation of the hunt.

Röhrig's ideological resentment was vented against the Communists with the accusation that they had machine-gunned game as symbols of capitalism. He attacked the societal craze for money where profiteering proliferated and endangered the lives of foresters with a sharp increase in murders. There had been an increase in poaching, and he blamed the complicity of 'unsavoury characters' like the *Salonjäger* (saloon hunters), *Schiesser* (shooters) or *Fleischmacher* (meat-makers). Röhrig criticised the 'red' press, satirical newspapers and *Artfremde* (aliens) for lampooning the hunt with cheap and vile satire. He generalised that all postwar periods, throughout history, were disastrous for hunting because unemployed former soldiers turned to poaching and banditry. Poachers had never been tolerated by the hunt. If arrested, the punishments were severe with the loss of an eye or hand, or public execution. His chapters took a racial dimension when he described how Hessen had regulated against Jewish traders by making them swear an oath to report any illegal trade in furs. In Prussia, Jewish traders were forced to purchase certificates to trade furs.[12] Röhrig accused Weimar politicians of hypocrisy, patronising the hunt's feudalism and participating in private hunts, but ridiculing the hunt in parliament. The rising values of wood, forced Weimar governments to improve the lot of state foresters. This brought about improved training and schooling, but the social emphasis had shifted away from the hunt. The decline in the domestic game forced hunters to seek alternatives overseas, in safaris and hunting dangerous game in primaeval habitats.[13] Writing after the Nazis were in power, Röhrig congratulated Hitler. He was grateful for the eradication of the "red" menace. The Nazis were the saviours of Germany and Göring had protected both the forest and game. Röhrig called Göring's 1935 hunting law a "monument in his own lifetime" widening the national

---

12 Ibid., p. 176–178.
13 Ibid., p. 205–209.

and classless appeal of the hunt and realising the goal of harmony with the *Volksgemeinschaft*.[14]

Göring as chief of forestry and master of the hunt was responsible for an institution of diverse talents. The first *Generalforstmeister* of the *Reichsforstamt* (RFA) was Dr. Walter von Keudell (1884–1973), a long serving Prussian civil servant. He was removed from office in 1937 because he refused to implement Göring's policy for cutting quotas. He was replaced by Friedrich Alpers (1901–1944), who had studied law at Heidelberg University and became a committed Nazi in 1929. Alpers took an honorary SS officer rank and in 1941 worked on the infamous hunger plan that led to the starvation of millions of people in the east. The *Jagdamt* (the hunt bureau) was organised as a department within the RFA. The chief of the *Jagdamt* was *Oberjägermeister* Ulrich Scherping (1889–1958) who was accountable to Keudell and later Alpers, but in practice reported directly to Göring. Scherping was the architect behind the hunting law and was deeply committed to the process of Nazification. He was born in Pomerania and began a career in the army as a cavalry officer, and like Göring was an early devotee of hunting. During the Great War, his bravery was rewarded and was promoted to the general staff of an infantry division. In August 1915, Scherping arrived in Białowieża and was left awestruck at the magnitude of the forest. After the war, he joined *Freikorps Rossbach* at the same time as Rudolf Hess, Hitler's first deputy.[15] Scherping took up a career as a professional hunter and a staff writer for *Der Heger* (a hunt journal). In 1927, he became general manager of the *Deutsche Jagdkammer* (German Chamber of Hunting) an organization founded in 1920 and a year later the *Reichsjagdbund* (National Hunting Union). He gained a reputation as the hunt's leading political activist and the exponent of right-wing dogma. In 1934 he acquired the title *Oberstjägermeister* (Colonel of the Hunt) and became Ministerial director of the *Jagdamt*. The adoption of *Oberstjägermeister* with its royalist resonance, a rank placed seventh in importance among the two

---

14 Ibid., p. 213–215.
15 Nigel H. Jones, *Hitler's Heralds: The Story of the Freikorps 1918–1923*, (London, 1987), pp. 124–125.

thousand positions in the Kaiser's royal household, made him a target for lampooning from Nazi rivals of which there were many.[16] Scherping clung to Göring in all matters of policy, politics and rivalries, but was astute enough to cosy up to Himmler and serve on his SS personal staff.[17]

Aldo Leopold, the American naturalist, visited Germany in 1935. He made observations of Göring's reforms at work and visited Silesia to meet Günther-Hubertus Freiherr von Reibnitz, the *Gaujägermeister* or Regional Director, with his assistants the *Kreisjägermeisters*. The meeting was held in a local police station where Reibnitz's offices were located, which reflected the future of German forestry and the Nazi police state, but Leopold did not report on anti-Semitism.[18] Scherping was responsible for the Aryanisation of the hunt. In 1935 the hunt acquired self-policing powers that allowed the implementation of an Aryanised membership base. In 1937 he announced, 'the hunt had become a closed shop to outsiders and had restored its noble reputation', and then added that 'the law had removed anti-social elements that gave hunters a bad name' — he meant the Jews.[19] Rules were drafted to define those persons excluded from the hunt as 'foreigners without German nationality', which also meant Jews.[20] In *The Nazi Seizure of Power*, Allen discovered that all the local shooting associations were quick to discriminate against Jews, cancelling their memberships once the Nazis came to power.[21] Then Nazi hatred for the Jews exploded into violence on 9–10 November 1938, during *Reichskristallnacht* (Night of Broken Glass), which led to the arrest of more than 30,000 Jews and more than ninety killed. A few days after the violence subsided Göring hosted a conference of state officials at the Reich Air Ministry. He joked the 'Jews could

---

16 Michael Vale, *The Princely Court: Medieval Courts and Culture in North-West Europe, 1270–1380*, (Oxford, 2002), p. 184.
17 Gautschi, *Der Reichsjägermeister*, p. 44.
18 http://digital.library.wise.edu/1711.dl/AldoLeopold/Writings Miscellaneous Manuscripts; Lectures; Yale Reports; German notes pp. 938–944. 27 April 2021
19 Ibid.
20 Kurt Mantel, *Reichsjagdgesetz*, (München, 1934), pp. 23–25.
21 Allen, *The Nazi Seizure of Power*, p. 221.

be restricted to forest areas inhabited by elk, which, like Jews, were marked by their large, crooked noses.'[22] The tragic culmination of Nazi race policies was the assistance given by the RFA in East Prussia to supply timber for the construction of the Stutthof concentration camp in 1941.[23]

Long before the Nazis came to power, the hunt had departed from the natural science classifications of the renaissance to the rigid social Darwinism of the Nineteenth Century.[24] In post-colonial Weimar Germany, the hunt spun fantastical and exotic accounts of the ancient and extinct game. Under the Nazis, the recreation of the Germanic game became part of a racialised zoology, game and habitat research. The science of hunting began to follow many research trajectories. In 1936 Göring founded an institute of hunting science in Hannover, which later transferred to the University of Göttingen. The Heck brothers, Lutz (1892–1983), and Heinz (1894–1982) had also been experimenting with their breeding back programme to restore the long-extinct Aurochs. Their work involved the mass observation of European cattle breeds to isolate what they believed was the special characteristics of the Aurochs. The first breeding experiments led to a breakthrough in 1934 when they sired a bull later called 'Heck cattle'. Lutz declared the research funded by Göring was the greatest value to science and a 'the symbol of German power and courage.' From 1938 Rominten's game population was re-engineered. Wild boar and five *Heck Cattle* were released under Göring's orders. Eventually, five lynxes were released, the precise number recommended for game management purposes.[25] Leopold described the prevailing conditions of the hunt in Germany, 'Every acre of forestland in Germany, whether state or

---

22   Alan E. Steinweis, *Kristallnacht 1938*, (Cambridge Mass., 2009), pp. 104–105. See also Susanne Heim & Götz Aly, 'Staatliche Ordnung und 'organische Lösung'. Die Rede Hermann Görings 'über die Judenfrage' vom 6 Dezember 1938', *Jahrbuch für Antisemitismusforschung 2*, 1993, pp. 378–404.
23   BArch, R3701/2033, Reichforstamt, Forstamt Steegen, SS-Lagers Stutthof 15 August 1941.
24   Michel Foucault, *The Order of Things*, (London, 1989), pp. 137–179.
25   Lutz Heck, *Auf Tiersuche in Weiter Welt*, (Berlin, 1943), pp. 232–296.

privately owned, is cropped for game.'²⁶ He blamed this on the German obsession for hunting deer, which outweighed the damage herds caused the habitat. He believed there would be long-term consequences, especially among game birds. He was deeply critical of foresters who 'sprinkled' hardwood trees among pine forests to achieve mixed forests but were unable to create a balance in-game management.²⁷ Leopold and other foreign either overlooked or ignored the prevailing Nazi racialism—both the game stock and the people were being Aryanised.

The long-term implications of decisions to the national ecology were a constant theme of discussion. Leopold learned of the German appreciation for predators in preventing the degeneration of game, and the status of the wolf as the noble animal of the wilderness. Decades later he claimed this idea for himself.²⁸ However, not all predators and aggressive game were appreciated. A postwar rumour circulated that Göring had a morbid fear of snakes. His senior hunter disclosed this secret to explain Göring's absence from hunting in wild forests and his preference for high stands. During a visit to Darss, a nature protection park, Göring was shocked and petrified to learn it was the habitat for poisonous Adders. An unnamed forester informed Göring that hedgehogs killed snakes. He immediately called Lutz Heck and ordered 300 hedgehogs brought to Darss. He was persuaded there was no veracity in the story that hedgehogs killed snakes. Göring immediately departed from Darss never to return.²⁹ If Göring had a morbid fear of snakes, it represents an important insight about his fears, but also points to his enthusiasm for eradicating all Jews as vermin.

---

26 http://digital.library.wisc.edu/1711.dl/AldoLeopold, Clifford F. Butcher, 'Every Farm in Wisconsin to Be a Game Preserve', The Milwaukee Journal, Sunday, January 5, 1936, p. 2 and p. II, 27 April 2021.
27 Aldo Leopold, 'Deer and Dauerwald in Germany. I. History', Journal of Forestry 34, No.4 and 5 (1936), p. 366–7.
28 Aldo Leopold, *A Sand County Almamanac: And Sketches Here and There*, (New York, 1949).
29 Walter Frevert, *Rominten*, (München, 1957), p. 216.

In 1938 Lutz Heck was promoted chief of nature protection and natural monuments within the RFA.[30] He set about a building programme of national parks and game reservations. Heck wanted the people to observe native animals and the habitat to comprehend how the Nazi culture social Darwinism functioned to the greater benefit of German society. Mass public education through micro-models of game habitats was conceived as a means to concentrate the people's 'organic gaze' on the biological values of everyday existence. These early forms of bio-zone were predicted to elevate social Darwinism as the normal natural order of life. Heck believed he was fulfilling the national will because Hitler's genius was his understanding of nature and its centrality to nation-building. The national parks were put to service in the Nazis' policies for national recovery.[31] The ambition to restore the Germanic game was the mirror of the Aryan being. The Aryan man and Germanic game co-existed in the timeless myth of antiquity. Heck's ambitions were not limited to Göring, he accepted honorary membership to the SS (June 1933) unusually before joining the Nazi Party (May 1937). He served Himmler's *SS-Ahnenerbe* (society for Ancestral heritage) founded in 1935. This SS institute advanced research into racial theories and championed Aryan primacy. Among this group of Nazis, the plans for Białowieża were conceived.

The ideological lynchpin necessary to complete Göring's corporatism and institutionalisation was some form of honour code. In 1936 Scherping, under Göring's orders, instructed Walter Frevert (1897–1962) a state forester and hunter, to write a book about Nazi-German hunting customs. The *Jagdliches Brauchtum* (1936) drowned the reader in *völkisch* claptrap but proved to be an instant political and public success. Scherping's foreword to the book was opaque, 'The German people are grateful to the Führer for restoring and awakening old and beautiful customs.' The success of the book led to Frevert's elevation to Göring's inner circle and later as a *Leibjäger*, a personal hunter and confidante, an important position in the hunt

---

30 Frank Uekoetter, *The Green and the Brown: A History of Conservation in Nazi Germany*, (Cambridge, 2006), p. 72
31 Heck, Auf Tiersuche in Weiter Welt, pp. 215.

hierarchy. Frevert was born in Hamm (Westphalia), his father was a dentist; but, after a distinguished war record as a young volunteer, and a period in the Freikorps, he chose to become a state forester specialising in the hunt. His first forestry rank was *Forstassessor* and was promoted in 1928 to *Forstmeister* while serving in Battenberg. Frevert had joined veterans' associations but in May 1933 became a member of the Nazi Party, and in the summer joined the SA. Frevert's Nazi membership initially looked like career opportunism, but his subsequent behaviour singled him out as a racist zealot.[32]

The *Jagdliches Brauchtum* was an orchestrated departure from the traditions set down by Ferdinand von Raesfeld in 1914. Frevert dispensed with historical accuracy, ignored quips about pompous hunters, and revelled in any applicable German sources. He adapted a poem by Ernest de Bunsen (1819–1903) to express his sentimentality of the hunt: 'The origin of the hunter is in the long past close to paradise. There were no trade people, no soldiers, no doctors, no priests, no lawyers but there were already hunters.'[33] However, a serious shortfall in sources about German hunt customs and even fewer German methods led him to invent material for his book. The final version of *Jagdliches Brauchtum* was a Nazi fantasy composed of made-up stories, plagiarised ideas and foreign rituals. He confessed his reasons were for a good cause, but nobody cared because the book met the approval of all things völkisch prevailing at the time.[34]

The climax of the inventions was the *Bruchzeichen*, a centrepiece of ritual and a ceremony of 'breaking' the dead game. Once the animal was killed and retrieved, the *Bruch* was started. The ceremony opened with a tune from a hunting horn to the dead animal. The hunter then placed a sprig in the animal's mouth representing its *Letzter Bissen* (the last meal). The sprigs were taken from oak, spruce, fir, alder or pine trees. The hunter then placed a sprig over

---

32 Andreas Gautschi, *Walter Frevert, Eines Waidmanns Wechsel und Wege*, (Melsungen, 2005), see also BArch, Lw. Personalakte, Walter Frevert.
33 Ibid., p. 12
34 Gautschi, *Der Reichsjägermeister*, pp. 89–92.

the beast's heart and another covering its nether regions. The hunter's companion then dipped a sprig of leaves into the animal's blood, drew his dagger with his left hand, placed the sprig on the blade, and presented it to the hunter. The hunter then took the sprig with his left hand, uttered the words *Weidmann's Dank* (the hunter's thanks), and fixed the blood-soaked sprig to the left side of his hat. If a bloodhound had participated in the kill, it also received a twig placed in its collar. Once the first part of the ceremony was completed the hunter opened up the carcass and removed the entrails.

Image 1: left to right, Oberforstmeister Walter Frevert Rominten, Göring in his capacity as Reichsjägermeister and Oberstjägermeister Ulrich Scherping.
Source: Bundesarchiv, Bild 146-1979-145-13A / CC-BY-SA 3.0

Image 2: Senior Luftwaffe and state foresters in the lounge area in Rominten. A painting of a European Bison is hung on the far wall.
Source: Bundesarchiv, Bild 146-1979-144-15A / CC-BY-SA 3.0

Image 3: European Bison in Białowieża.
Source: Author, 2009.

Once completed, the hunter began the *Totenwacht* (guard the dead), an hour-long vigil over the carcass. During this hour the hunter was expected to reflect on the sublime kill and recall past hunts with all their joys and miseries. The carcass was then included in the total tally for the final rituals. The dead carcasses were arranged in order of nobility, size, and by rank, like soldiers on a parade ground. If it was a large tally, braziers and flaming torches were added to the ambience of the moment. The results of the day's hunt were then read aloud. The horns sounded several more tunes, announcing the end of the hunt at which point the hunters and their guests would raise their right arms in the *Hitler Gruss* (Nazi salute). Then followed the final horn sounding the *Halali* (tally-ho). After the ceremonies were over the hunters retired to the dining room to partake in the *Tot-trinken* (toast to the kill). The antlers were placed on tables, with candles and more sprigs added for decoration. Dinner was then served by silver service.[35]

Deconstructing Frevert's invention is not difficult. David Dalby has explained the *Bruchzeichen* was a French ceremony. He claimed when German nobles were offered the ritual in the Middle Ages, they expressed no interest.[36] The *Letzter Bissen* originated in James Frazer's *The Golden Bough* (1922), which was conveniently published in German in translation in 1928.[37] Frevert's justification, was the *Totenwacht* had increasingly appealed to hunters in the two decades since circa 1916. This had associations with the widespread death cults and ceremonies that emerged during the Great War. Frevert confessed two music scores were composed for the book by Professor Cleving (Berlin). They were the *Muffel tot* and the *Halali*.[38] Gritzbach, Göring's Nazi biographer, claimed the *Jagdliches Brauchtum* restored the 'heroic realism' and traditions of the past. He enthused over the combination of faith in *Urwald* (primaeval

---

35 Walter Frevert, *Jagdliches Brauchtum*, (Berlin, 1936), pp. 51–69.
36 David Dalby, *Lexicon of The Mediaeval German Hunt: A Lexicon of Middle High German Terms (1050–1500) associated with the Chase, Hunting with Bows, Falconry, Trapping and Fowling*, (Berlin, 1965), pp. i–v.
37 Sir James Frazer, *The Golden Bough: A Study in Magic and Religion*, (London, 1993), p. 521.
38 Frevert, *Jagdliches Brauchtun*, 1936, p. 68.

wilderness) and its relationship to Germanic hunting customs. He believed Frevert's efforts would form the common etiquette for all German hunters.[39] The institutionalisation of the *Jagdliches Brauchtum* brought uniformity, while the reinvention of customs and traditions helped assimilate Nazi ritualism within the hunt. Ceremonies were devised that honoured the dead and invoked pagan pre-Christian style rituals that had never been associated with German hunt lore.[40] The death ceremony was an invention and few in history have been quite so blatant. This bizarre story of the invention, however, found its way into Nazi ceremonies and rituals that preceded the Holocaust. To paraphrase Hobsbawm, 'nothing appears more ancient, and linked with an immemorial past than the customs' of the German hunt. In 1970 the German hunt handbook still referred to the ideas of *Oberforstmeister* Frevert and Scherping.[41] Hosbawm opined that customs are not a brake on innovation and precedent can be changed when appearing to bring about 'social continuity and natural law'.[42] Like Faust, Frevert had made a pact with the devil.

II. The Blue

The Luftwaffe uniform colour was blue-grey. The colour selection was to distinguish the Luftwaffe uniform from the grey-green of the army and Kriegsmarine. 'The Blue', unlike state forestry was a 'new' Nazi elite. From the outset it was as an institution burdened with internal tensions and riddled with mediocre leadership. A postwar narrative of Luftwaffe history was manufactured by Adolf Galland's based upon his memories and fantasies. In *The First and the Last* (1950) Galland effectively neutralised his political involvement in the Nazi state. He acknowledged Göring as the founder of the Luftwaffe, but was reluctant to discuss the deeper Nazi

---

39 Gritzbach, *Hermann Göring*, p. 118.
40 Ibid., p. 33 and 134.
41 Richard Blasé, *Die Jägerprüfung*, (Melsungen, 1970), p. 17 referred to Frevert and p. 268 Scherping.
42 Eric Hobsbawm/Terence Ranger, *The Invention of Tradition*, (Cambridge, 1983), pp. 1–4, 6, 104.

pedigree. He also recognised that Göring had allocated forty per cent of total rearmament costs to the Luftwaffe, while he was responsible for the Third Reich's economy.[43] His most serious criticism was also toward Göring, as 'supreme commander', for surrounding himself with his Great War cronies. Galland claimed they shared a common failing of not understanding modern aviation.[44] Where Galland was less forthcoming was how the Luftwaffe had been incubated through the RFA's paramilitary structure. The Luftwaffe's organisation, air bases, depots, manpower, structure and ideology were acquired from RFA resources. Galland dropped a hint of this relationship in reference to the *Elchwald* estate that served as the headquarters for his command. Göring turned over his palatial lodges into Luftwaffe headquarters for the duration of the war. The RFA facilitated the rapid mobilisation of the Luftwaffe across the estates and bases in East Prussia.

The reasons for Galland's myth-making are not difficult to deconstruct. Stephan Bungay argued the Luftwaffe was as much political as it was a military organisation.[45] He pointed to the Göring and Ernst Udet (1896–1941) relationship, as the champions of the warrior-hero ethos. They introduced the notion of 'romantic amateurism' as the ideological glue of the officer corps. Bungay believed this stunted the Luftwaffe's military development. The Luftwaffe had been raised from a broad cross-section of the population, unlike the army it was recruited nationally rather by state like the army.[46] Bungay focusing aircrew noted that by 1939 the officer corps had reached 15,000 comprising of pilots, army officers, and the technical services. In basic training, the Luftwaffe instilled an attitude of common experience and service. During the Spanish Civil War, according to Bungay, the German aces became poisoned by 'romantic amateurism'. Galland was a typical example of this clique. He was known to have recommended the removal of radios

---

43   Adolf Galland, *The First and the Last: The German Fighter Force in the World War II*, (London, 1970), p. 100.
44   Ibid., pp. 13–17, p. 55.
45   Stephan Bungay, *The Most Dangerous Enemy: A History of the Battle of Britain*, (London, 2010), p. 80 and p. 188.
46   Ibid. p. 92.

as unnecessary in the cockpit of fighting aeroplanes, in a dubious challenge to modernity.[47] Bungay was deeply critical of Göring, Udet, Galland and others but blamed this on traits of the 'Herrenvolk' and the temporary loyalty of the pack that followed whoever was leader.[48] There was a persuasive argument but not entirely accurate and misunderstood the nature of Nazism. The deteriorating fortunes of war encouraged a rise in the cliques but their loyalty to Hitler never waivered.

Image 4: Reichsmarschall Göring, Lw.Generalmajor Adolf Galland, Lw.Generaloberst Bruno Loerzer and Reichminister Albert Speer, August 1943.
Source: Bundesarchiv, Bild 183-J15189 / Lange, Eitel / CC-BY-SA 3.0

Göring's military ambitions for the Luftwaffe was more sophisticated and corporate than Bungay could imagine. There are signposting clues in the literature and archives. In the foreword to the 1933 edition of Richthofen's biography Göring wrote, 'I was honoured by the confidence shown in me when I was appointed the last commander of the *Jagdgeschwader Richthofen*. This appointment

---

47 Ibid., p. 88.
48 Ibid., p. 82.

has bound me forever and I will carry this responsibility in the spirit of Richthofen.'⁴⁹ During a meeting in 1944, Lw.General of Paratroops Hermann-Bernhard Ramcke confronted Göring over the command of the airborne formations. The reply was unexpected. Göring explained why they must remain under his command: 'I'm glad that I have them under my own wing in the Luftwaffe so that they are steeped in the spirit of the Luftwaffe ... it's the spirit that counts. In the same way ... the French revolutionary army ... in Paris simply swept away all the old French guards who'd had years of training.'⁵⁰ In allied captivity, in 1945, Galland testified to British interrogators that Göring told him in early 1941, 'In a few months we shall attack Russia ... the whole affair was meant to last ten weeks at the most. After that the army was to be reduced to sixty 'Divisonen[sic]'. But they were to be elite troops to hold the west, and the remainder of the 'Divisionen'[sic] so released would be used ᶠᵒʳ building an Air Force. Everything was to be put in the Air Force. That was the Führer's plan.'⁵¹ These three anecdotes reveal something about Göring's concepts of leadership, organisation and fantasies.

The subject of leadership has always raised questions about Göring's ability. His senior Luftwaffe adjutants were known colloquially as the 'small general staff'. The most significant member of this clique was Lw.Colonel Bernd von Brauchitsch, nephew of Colonel-General von Brauchitsch, chief of the army until 1941.⁵² There was no official job description for his post, but under cross-examination before the Nuremburg tribunal, in March 1946, Brauchitsch explained:

> I was the first military adjutant of the Commander-in-Chief of the Luftwaffe. I held the rank of chief adjutant. I had the job of making the daily arrangements as ordered by the Commander-in-Chief and working out the

---

49 Manfred Freiherr von Richthofen, *Der Rote Kampfflieger*, (Berlin, 1933), foreword: 'Manfred von Richthofen zum Gedächtnis – Hermann Göring.'
50 Sönke Neitzel (ed), *Tapping Hitler's Generals: Transcripts of Secret Conversations, 1942–45*, trans. Geoffrey Brooks, (Barnsley, 2007), pp. 113–117.
51 TNA, WO208/4170 C.S.D.I.C. (UK), S.R.G.G. 1230(C), Generalleutnant Galland (JV44), Captured Tegernsee 5 May 1945, interrogation on the 17 May 1945.
52 BArch, RL31/3, Kriegstagebuch LWSB, 6 August 1942.

adjutants' duty roster. The military position had to be reported daily; military reports and messages only to the extent that they were not communicated by the offices themselves. I had no command function.[53]

Brauchitsch's importance to Białowieża was his role as an intermediary forwarding Göring's orders to the battalion(s) and in return collating their regular reports. Galland offered his allied interrogators an abrasive opinion of Brauchitsch. On 16 May 1945 he said:

> Brauchitsch has been with him [Göring] for four or five years and he had a very bad influence, in that he always concerned himself with politics and didn't hold himself aloof; as a chief 'Adjutant' he should have — the varying information should be condensed, but not selected.[54]

Image 5: Bernd von Brauchitsch in his cell in Nuremberg prison 1946.
Source: NARA, Hoffmann Collection.

Setting aside Galland's dislike of Brauchitsch, the evaluation that he was inclined to side with decisions and sift reports was not unusual in Göring's world. Galland of course was an integral member

---

53 The Avalon Project, at http://avalon.law.yale.edu/imt/03-12-46.asp Cross-examination by Dr. Stahmer, 12 March 1946.
54 TNA WO208/4170 C.S.D.I.C. (UK), S.R.G.G. 1228(C), Generalleutnant Galland (JV44), Captured Tegernsee 5 May 1944, interrogation on the 16 May 1945.

of the same command structure and his reputation was never really tested over his influence on shaping the fighter command. However, what can be drawn from the observations by the senior echelons of the Luftwaffe was the absence of 'band of brothers' style fraternity.

The RFA/Luftwaffe mobilisation documentation highlights an intensive period of planning around 1935–7 and subsequent annual updates. Evidence of this mobilisation planning can be found in other scholarship.[55] From 1935 apprentice foresters and gamekeepers were required to serve for one year in the army (later the Luftwaffe) before becoming foresters. Older candidates were expected to participate in a three-month military refresher course alongside other Nazi officials.[56] Michael Imort has argued this, 'was all it took to remilitarise the forest service.' The Luftwaffe's organisation and peacetime expansion was based upon a general mobilisation calendar drawn up by the RFA in the mid-1930s and continually updated to 1940.[57] Göring was determined to set in motion plans for the mobilisation of the *Reichsforstbeamte* (RFA's public servants) including all members of the hunt offices to the Luftwaffe. This process behind a mobilisation calendar issued precise instructions for the transfer of all forestry officials to the Luftwaffe command structure. In 1936 forestry manpower numbered 870,000, and even by 1945 although greatly depleted forestry could still supply conscripts under the general Wehrmacht reserve assessment.[58] The RFA's mobilisation in the event of war was bound to the *Wehrwirtschaftstab* (economic warfare staff) of the Luftwaffe with wood and timber both regarded as strategic raw materials. During the war, forestry manpower was mobilised through the Luftwaffe

---

55 James Corum, *The Luftwaffe: Creating the Operational Air War, 1918–1940*, (Kansas, 1997).
56 Michael Imort, '"Forestopia": the use of the forest landscape in naturalizing National Socialist policies of Volk, race and Lebensraum 1918–1945', PhD Thesis, Queen's University, 2000, pp. 485–486.
57 BArch RW 19/936.Wehrwirtsschaftstab, Mobilisation Kalender (Berlin, 26 April 1939). File indicated in the event of war the Reichsforstamt would be mobilised under the Luftwaffe.
58 NARA, RG242, T77/780/5506284-5506484 Wehrmacht Ersatzplan 1945, section 62, Reichsforstamt.

although foresters served in specialist forestry units of the army, navy and Waffen-SS.[59] Further evidence of organisational synchronisation can be found in the blue-grey uniforms with green insignia that recognised foresters serving in the Luftwaffe.[60] From very early on the Luftwaffe was imbued with National Socialist spirit and by August 1944 it numbered between 2.8 and 5 million men, women and youths depending upon on which authority. The largest number of troops were in the ground forces and, in terms of manpower alone, the *Luftwaffe* constitutes a significant historical entity.[61]

In meeting Hitler's expectations, the Luftwaffe departed from the traditional military formation, incorporating the dogma behind ideological warriors. The roots of this politicisation began in 1929 when Göring informed the Reichstag of the inevitability of a future German air force.[62] Once in power, Göring's first priority was to consolidate political power. As Minister-President of Prussia, Göring ordered the raising of reserve police and volunteer paramilitary units. They combined his military expertise, with paramilitary policing methods, in security actions to crush left-wing political parties and communists. The police flying squad (*Polizeiabteilung z.b.v. Wecke*), named after its commander was mustered on 23 February 1933, with a force of 14 officers and 400 men. This formation was garrisoned in the Friesenkaserne, in Berlin, and became 'godfather' to the first SS detachments sealing that special relationship between the SS, police, and the Luftwaffe.[63] *Wecke's* first police actions were on 2 March 1933, rounding up communists and Marxists in Berlin. In 1936 this unit was turned into Prussian police regiment

---

59 NARA, RG242, OKW Wehrwirtschafts- und Rüstungsamt (OKW Wi Ru Amt): T77/100/824182 on RFA manpower and T77/145/880000-50, RFA mobilisation to Economic Warfare Staff.
60 Roger James Bender, *The Luftwaffe: Air, Organisation of the Third Reich*, (Atglen, 1997).
61 NARA, RG242, T77/780/5506284-568, OKW-WEA, Wehrmacht-Ersatzplan 1945, recorded an all-branches manpower level of 1,966,862 on 1 October 1944, while the Air Ministry (1948), *The Rise and Fall of the German Air Force (1933 to 1945)*, London: Pamphlet 248, p. 395, recorded an estimate of 2,304,500 on 15 December 1944, for all branches.
62 Air Ministry, p.4. Air Ministry (A.C.A.S.[I]), *The Rise and Fall of the German Air Force (1933 to 1945)*, (London 1948). Thanks to Manny Phelps for the loan of this book.
63 Rudolf Lehmann, *The Leibstandarte*, trans. Nick Olcott, (Winnipeg, 1987), p.1.

General Göring and was then transferred to the Luftwaffe to form a bodyguard. By 1944, this bodyguard had transformed from a regiment to the panzer division Hermann Göring, and by the war's end was designated an airborne-panzer-corps.[64]

The social appeal of Luftwaffe recruitment was the proximity to advanced technology, aviation and the sense of speed. Compared to the SS, the Luftwaffe represented a larger and more interesting option for the nobility deeply bound by its class, its racism and elitism. Under Göring's leadership flying, hunting and highbrow socialising offered an extension of the prestige, privilege and stimulus they were socially accustomed to. The list of nobles that joined the Luftwaffe included: Philipp Landgrave of Hesse (Nazi party member 1930), Nikolaus von Below (Hitler's Luftwaffe adjutant), Günther Freiher von Maltzhahn (fighter ace and senior officer), Wolfram Freiher von Richthofen (cousin of Manfred, senior field commander), Heinrich Prinz zu Sayn-Wittgenstein and Egmont Prinz zur Lippe-Weissenfeld (both night fighter aces) and Hans Graf von Sponeck (airborne forces commander). However, like the German hunt, the majority of would-be flyers hailed from the middle-class with strong social values that were based upon professionalism, technocracy and innovation. Even working-class boys saw advantages of technical training and apprenticeship that offered greater opportunities for career advancement.

The proximity to the hunt did not appeal to all flyers. There was a significant group of flyers who rejected the hunt from their entrenched National Socialist ideology. The leading exponent of this group was Hans-Ulrich Rudel. He was a highly decorated flyer who rejected the hunt as a true disciple of Hitler, but was also a guardian of his social class. Göring's different treatment of Rudel and Galland was influenced by social backgrounds. Both men went to great pains to explain their social backgrounds in their memoirs. Rudel was individualistic, the son of a Lutheran pastor, drank milk, didn't smoke and spent most of his free time enjoying sports

---

64   This division was eventually designated the Fallschirm-Panzer-Division 1 Hermann Göring. For simplification purposes this formation is referred to the Hermann Göring Division throughout the rest of the book.

(athletics and skiing).⁶⁵ Galland's father was the bailiff of Graf von Westerholt's estate; a position held by generations and a Huguenot family that left France in 1742. From the age of seven, Galland's father taught him to shoot and hunt. He was encouraged to fly gliders and enter for the Lufthansa entrance examination.⁶⁶ Rudel had to wait until he joined the Luftwaffe before he learned to fly. Rudel's meetings with 'the chief' (Göring) were uncomfortable and brief in comparison with his meetings with Hitler. Rudel was the Führer's favourite and similar characters. Galland recalled hunting a stag in Rominten—a gift bestowed by Göring, 'it was really a royal beast, the stag of a lifetime.'⁶⁷ Recently discovered films show Galland at ease in meetings and during meals in the relaxed atmosphere of Göring's headquarters.⁶⁸ During a visit to one of Göring's castles, Rudel came face-to-face with the Reichsmarschall 'rigged out in German hunting costume and shooting with a bow and arrow.'⁶⁹ This was a counter-narrative about the 'other' *Luftwaffe* as a Nazi organisation that embraced polycratic persuasions.⁷⁰ Rudel's ideas came close to the blood and soil rhetoric of the SS and their 1936, claim to be an anti-Bolshevik combat organisation.⁷¹ In this regard, the SS and the *Luftwaffe* were both sides of the same coin. SS zealotry was drawn from pagan myths of blood and soil, while the Luftwaffe drew on the mystery of the forest and the skies. Both Rudel and Galland remained blindly obedient to Hitler.

III. Raising a social-military order

The *Jagdliches Brauchtum* symbolised more than a Nazification of the hunt. It was an attempt by Göring to anchor invented traditions to the German past, but looking forward to a new ill-defined

---

65 Rudel, *Stuka Pilot*, pp. 1–9.
66 Galland, *First and the Last*, pp. 1–9.
67 Ibid., p. 88.
68 https://collections.ushmm.org/search/catalog/irn1002569 27 April 2021.
69 Rudel, *Stuka Pilot*, p. 118.
70 Ibid., p. 354.
71 Bernd Wegner, *Waffen-SS: Organization, Ideology and Function*, trans. Ronald Webster, (Oxford, 1990).

military order. Frevert had formulated an honour code. This was a synthesis of cultures both German and Nazi, hunting and military. It was system for social induction and regulation. The most important feature was the honour system. The Waidgerechtigkeit (hunt justice) raised localised courts of honour. This code was grounded in the strict discipline of the laws and regulations of the hunt. The simplicity of the system made it transferable to wider society and shared similar procedures to the later Nazi people's courts. This was regulation through a moralistic almost Kantian code, for example: unlicenced shooting and feeding game were serious crimes, while shooting game struggling in a metre of snow was regarded as ungentlemanly conduct. Wounded game had to be located and killed before any further hunting. The hunter was cautioned not to shoot from too great a distance in case he missed. The hunter was warned not to dishonour the dead by sitting or standing on the carcass. The game was not to be fed during a crisis like severe winter conditions or drought. The application of this morality code found its way into Luftwaffe etiquette and manuals of discipline. In 1940 Göring formed an honour court over a disagreement that developed during the Norway Campaign, between Stuka pilots and paratroopers. There is no known outcome.

Frevert recommended no alcohol while hunting because it weakened responsibility and raised the bloodlust. This was a reaction to the popularity of the small *Jägermeister* pocket bottles, dubbed *Göring's Schnapps*, which was distilled by Mast-Jägermeister SE (Wolfenbüttel) and distributed from 1935. He also encouraged the *Schüsseltreiben* (social gatherings) when all hunters dined communally. The single course of *Eintopf* (stew) with Sauerkraut and pork, was hailed as the noble family dish for the *Volksgemeinschaft*. Frevert only allowed drinking in the lodge after the days' hunting. The alcoholic toasts for these gatherings included the communal *Horrido*. He described the *Horrido* as being of equal importance to the Nazi party's *Sieg Heil* or the army's *Hoorah*. During the toasts, a jug of beer was passed around for each member to raise a toast, drink and shout the *Horrido*. All drinking parties had rules and for the evening a kangaroo court judged party delinquents who were placed before three 'noble' judges. The punishments ranged from communal ridicule to fines for serious breaches of etiquette. All monies were given to orphans or to winter aid. Frevert also insisted all hunters, without exception, venerated 3 November as the sacred *Hubertustag* (St. Hubertus day — patron of hunting).[72]

The *Jagdliches Brauchtum* was the ideological glue that sealed the officer corps of both the Blue and the Green within Göring's court. Frevert advocated a code of conduct for 'the noble or aristocratic pleasure ... the highest form of masculine yearning ... culture bearers of the nation.'[73] All hunters were to be militarised, regimented and armed; in this context, the *Jagdliche Brauchtum* contributed to building Göring's military doctrine.[74] A significant part of the book was the adoption of invented culture and traditions that had no precedent in the German hunt. The sole purpose was to instil an *esprit du corps* through the introduction of ceremonies, the correct use of hunting horns, the application of field signals to raise communications, and the introduction of self-regulated courts of honour. Frevert complained about the social barriers of rural society that had become entrenched in the division between the hunt and agriculture. To reconcile this problem, he plumbed the depths of *völkisch* idealism in a polemic about capitalism's destruction of the German way of life and promised the old ways would be restored. He dismissed the existence of any underlying social and cultural differences between the peasant farmer and the elitist hunter hailing both as *völkischer Kulturträger* (culture bearers of the nation). They would be militarised, regimented and armed; in this context, the *Jagdliche Brauchtum* was not just an almanack of invented traditions but served as the basic honour code for Göring's court and organisations.[75] This dogma underpinned the ideas for Białowieża.

This system failed and calamitous consequences. Göring and Udet had been comrades in war and peace. Frevert had recollections of Udet as a regular guest at Rominten who was known for

---

72 Ibid., pp. 112–121.
73 Ibid., p. 33 and 134.
74 Ibid., p. 6, and 104.
75 Ibid., p. 6, and 104.

fun and frivolity. Everyone noticed that Göring and Udet used the informal and friendly 'du' when greeting and when together. Frevert recalled Udet sketched Göring on a beer mat stalking on his stomach. He drew a large posterior and on each rear cheek was stamped with the German cross and German Hunting Association shield, so as no one in his company could be offended. Göring enjoyed such jokes and thought the sketch was funny. According to Frevert, Udet was known as a great fighter ace but he was a lousy rifleman having missed several stags. Göring would often jibe Udet for his failings. One day a stag was caught in wire and Göring jokingly told him they had 'wired the stag for Udet to shoot'. Uncertain over whether he should shoot or not Udet hesitated, but just as he pulled the trigger the stag broke free and he missed. Göring was convulsed with laughter. Udet eventually killed the stag with a second shot but the jokes were on him.[76] Frevert recalled Udet's suicide in 1941 was a hard blow for Göring. Before killing himself, Udet had scrawled in red on the headboard of his bed: '*Reichsmarschall*, why have you deserted me?' Frevert concluded, they had been comrades and hunted together, but Göring convened a court of enquiry with a view to a posthumous court-martial.[77]

Göring deserted Udet because there were other men, more pliable and willing to do his bidding; men like Walter Frevert and Adolf Galland. In the early years, they worked towards the successful synthesis of The Blue and The Green. They were behind a civil-military institution that synthesised the politics of ecology, the politics of advanced warfare and the politics of racial extermination. Göring's ideological ambitions were colossal, perhaps limitless, but the merger of 'The Green' and 'The Blue' served his corporatism. Eventually, this turned into an uncomfortable and wieldy marriage further unsettled by Göring's notorious lifestyle. With the outbreak of war, the Green estates became operational headquarters for the Blue command system. This placed the hunt within close proximity to headquarters staff, making it more than just a rest and recuperation reward for combat weary troops. The Carinhall hunting estate,

---

76   Frevert, *Rominten* (1957), p. 223.
77   Cajus Bekker, *The Luftwaffe War Diaries*, (London, 1972), p. 401 and p. 295.

forty miles northeast of Berlin, was erected in the Schorfheide, a nationalised nature reserve. This grandiose complex was described by Frank Uekoetter as the most 'pompous' and costliest of all Göring's residences. However, he overlooked how the intermingling of functions, between military headquarters and hunt lodges, skewed the social order of the Luftwaffe command system. Under Göring's supreme control, patronage was politicised that inturn ramped up the prestige. Diplomacy and politics continued from Carinhall,[78] Rominten became the favoured retreat, but Göring's headquarters train, *Robinson* became the centre of decision-making in regards to the Białowieża mission. By April 1945, Göring had destroyed both Carinhall and Rominten.[79]

---

78 Volker Knopf, Stefan Martens, *Görings Reich. Selbstinszenierungen in Carinhall*, (Berlin, 1999).
79 Frank Uekoetter, *The Green and the Brown: A History of Conservation in Nazi Germany*, (Cambridge, 2006), pp. 101–7.

2. The Conquest of Wilderness

Combining diplomacy and hunting proved to be lucrative politics for Göring. From 1934 he led the negotiations with Poland over Danzig and later took control of German-Polish relations. There are accounts that Göring was repeatedly invited by the Polish ambassador to hunt in Białowieża from 1934[1], but the only official and detailed account came from February 1937. The hunt was set to a time when the snakes were in hibernation. The Polish hunting officials agreed a lynx would be a suitable trophy. The gamekeepers cornered a Lynx, but it managed to escape the night before Germans arrived. Göring was well received but on the day of the hunt, his tally was small with three wolves and two wild boars. Scherping, however, not only bagged more game but also killed a young lynx. Before the Nazi delegation departed, Göring announced that he better appreciated the difficulties of hunting in a "Polish primaeval forest".[2] In November 1937, Germany hosted the International Hunting Exhibition in Berlin. The RFA promoted this as an international event comparable to the Olympic Games (1936). The Polish contingent included representatives from Białowieża national park. Adolf Hitler's appeared, on 6 November, and was hailed by the RFA as the high point of the exhibition.[3] The exhibition was a triumph for Göring. During the exhibition, Göring told the Polish ambassador the Jews and Bolshevism were dragging the world into war.[4] In 1938 Göring secured Poland's agreement to German demands during the Sudeten crisis promising it was Germany's 'last territorial claim.' Göring's confidence was riding high after the Luftwaffe's success in the Spanish Civil War. The Nazi author commissioned to write the operational history incorporated Göring's ambition of the Greater German Reich as the purpose of his diplomacy and war-making.[5]

---

1 Schama, *Landscape and Memory*, p. 67. Detlev Peukert, *Inside Nazi Germany: Conformity, Opposition, and Racism in Everyday Life*, (London, 1987).
2 Simona Kossak, *The Białowieża Saga*, (Warsaw, 2001), pp. 445–448.
3 Gautschi, *Der Reichsjägermeister*, p. 84.
4 Richard Overy, *Goering*, (London, 1984), p. 81, 89, 100.
5 Werner Beumelburg, *Kampf um Spanien: Die Geschichte Der Legion Condor*, (Berlin, 1939).

Image 6: Preparation for a diplomatic function at Rominten. Note the Nordic runes on the picture rail under the ceiling.
Source: Bundesarchiv, Bild 146-1979-138-33 / CC-BY-SA 3.0

Diplomacy, hunting and rituals reached its apotheosis during the Polish crisis (1938–39). An important account of these events came from Sir Neville Henderson, British ambassador to Berlin. There were doubts over his selection as ambassador. He joined the diplomatic service in 1905. Henderson had a reputation for 'jujitsu methods in diplomacy', a tendency to 'go native', and was prone to hero-worship. Anthony Eden's secretary thought he might be 'another Ribbentrop to Berlin.' Peter Neville found sources that noted Henderson could shoot adding to his suitability.[6] Henderson's memoirs recalled his visits with Göring at Carinhall in 1938 and being taken around the European Bison breeding pens. Göring subsequently invited him to hunt in Rominten Heide. His observations about the leading officers of 'The Green', in their political heartland, was insightful. Henderson noted the lodge was a 'simple shooting-box with a thatched roof'. The serving staff included maids and a

---

6   Peter Neville, "The Appointment of Sir Nevile Henderson, 1937 – Design or Blunder?", *Journal of Contemporary History*, London: Sage Publications, Vol 33(4), 1988, 609–619. Peter Neville, *Appeasing Hitler: The Diplomacy of Sir Nevile Henderson, 1937–39*, (London, 2000).

servant, working in a comfortable but relaxed atmosphere.⁷ Henderson was introduced to the leading RFA and *Jagdamt* officials and went hunting with them. The party included: "One of his [Göring's] Swedish brothers-in-law, Count Rosen, was the only other guest, and the rest of the party consisted of Oberstjägermeister Scherping, Oberstjägermeister Menthe, and a young air officer A.D.C., von Brauschitz [sic Brauchitsch], a son [nephew] of the present German commander-in-chief." Absent from the recollection, but known to be present, was *Oberforstmeiser* Walter Frevert. The ambience of the wilderness and the solemn rituals captivated Henderson and he described the Bruchzeichen and *Totenwacht* ceremonies. He heard 'the *hallali* [sic] ... sounded on the horns of the *jägers* [sic] ...'⁸

Henderson explained the differences between "stag-shooting" in Europe to deer stalking in Britain. The stags cannot be found so easily in the dense European forests, so were tracked by their roar during the rutting season. A *Hochstände* (high stand) was usually placed where the stags grazed or rutted. According to Henderson, all the huntsmen had to do was climb the stand and shoot the stag. Henderson's first hunt included Scherping and Menthe as companions. He lay on his stomach and crawled to a good shooting position and killed a stag. When Göring was told, he allegedly roared with laughter having previously bemoaned that British hunters were very capable with shotguns, but not so with rifles. He was amused by the image of Henderson on his belly and announced to his courtiers it was the perfect place for diplomats. The 'jujitsu diplomat' melted under Göring's generosity and liked him. Henderson recalled how Göring confessed his youthful support for the Boer guerillas but admired the British pirates like Sir Francis Drake. He regretted the British had been 'debrutalised'.⁹ In 1940 Henderson blamed Göring for his lack of moral integrity that led to the outbreak of war.

---

7   Sir Nevile Henderson, *Failure of A Mission: Berlin 1937–9.* (London, 1940), p. 89.
8   Ibid., p. 90–1.
9   Ibid., p. 80.

I. War

The Second World War in Eastern Europe began at 4.45 am on 1 September 1939 when the old German battleship *Schleswig-Holstein* opened fire on Polish fortifications in Danzig (Gdansk: Poland).[10] The Bialystok-Białowieża area came within the Soviet zone, under the protocols of the Nazi-Soviet Pact. The German Army advanced into Białowieża ten days before the Red Army. The 413th Infantry Regiment, 206th Infantry Division, arrived in Hajnówka on 12 September.[11] Rumours claimed the *Luftwaffe* bombed the Tsarist styled Orthodox Church and a Soviet military hospital by accident. The 'Berlin Bear' symbol made an appearance as the 3rd Panzer Division's vehicle insignias as it drove through towards Brest-Litovsk.[12] Locals claimed Göring declared the forest a *heiliger Hain* (sacred grove) and under his protection. During the brief occupation the innkeeper of the Żubr tavern, Michał Zdankiewicz, was killed for venting criticism against the Germans. Before shooting Zdankiewicz, it's rumoured the soldiers set their dogs on him.[13] The Germans withdrew once the Red Army arrived on 21 September 1939.[14.] The Soviet occupation was marked by terror during a sustained period of violence, disorder, deportations and mass killings.[15] Contemporary Polish allegations blamed the Ukrainians, Byelorussians and Jews within the communities of welcoming the Red Army as liberators. Jan Gross has argued that the Soviets encouraged violence against Poles as 'thousands were killed, often with primitive and premeditated brutality.' Peasant vigilantes were raised to administer 'justice', which led to atrocities.[16] The Polish state bureaucracy and archives were ransacked and taken by the

---

10 Halik Kochanski, *The Eagle Unbowed: Poland and the Poles in the Second World War*, (Cambridge, 2012), p. 59
11 BArch, Lw. Personalakte, Erich Weinreis.
12 Kossak, *Białowieża Forest Saga*, p. 462.
13 Waldemar Monkiewicz, *Białowieża w cieniu swastyki*, (Bialystok, 1984), p. 36.
14 Czesław Madajczyk, *Die Okkupationspolitik Nazideutschlands in Polen 1939–1945*, (Berlin, 1988), p. 143.
15 Jan Tomasz Gross, *Revolution from Abroad: The Soviet Conquest of Poland's Western Ukraine and Western Belorussia*, (Princeton, 2002). p. 4.
16 Ibid., p. 35–38. See also Kossak, *Białowieża Forest Saga*, p. 463.

Soviet secret police (NKVD) to Moscow.[17] There were mass arrests (130,000) and deportations (370,000) of Poles by the summer of 1941.[18] The Soviets introduced the oblast (division), a regional system of government. The Bialystok oblast included Bielsk and incorporated Białowieża as a sub-district.[19]

A local account has described the Soviet occupation of Białowieża. Since 1937, trained NKVD agents were being infiltrated into Poland, their mission was to destabilise the borderlands. Paid collaborators organised communist cells and initiated strikes. Once the Soviets took control of the bureaucracy they instituted a system that isolated all inhabitants' since the end of the Polish-Soviet War in 1921. Stalin ordered widespread arrests. On 19 December 1939 the Soviet commissar of Belarus released lists of persons for deportation. From February 1940, there were arrests and deportations of forestry officials and forest dwellers. An NKVD captain from Bialystok led the action, assisted by a lieutenant from Bielsk, who arrived with a list of 1,463 persons. This list included local farmers, public officials, and national park staff (92 clerk's families and 46 families from the palace, museum and gamekeepers). The NKVD organized about 113 snatch squads each of three men to round up all those listed for deportation. The deportation trains were stabled in Białowieża, Hajnówka, Narewka, and Bielsk Podlaski. The snatch squads, with dogs, started rounding up victims in the early hours. They forced people to pack and prepare their children and belongings within two hours. They bundled the people onto horse-drawn sledges and took them to the freight trains; the action was completed in one day.[20] Almost two years later the Germans returned.

---

17 Ibid., pp. 50–68.
18 Ibid., pp. 126–179. Gross had originally presented figures of one million deported and 400,000 arrested.
19 Daniel Boćkowski, *Białostocczyna w radzieckiej polityce okupacyjnej 1939–1944*, (Lublin, 2005).
20 Kossak, *Białowieża Forest Saga*, pp. 463–466. Kossak provides no record of how many people returned, although her account does include subsequent testimonies by victims.

II. The Battle for Białowieża (22–30 June 1941)

In the early hours of 22 June 1941, Hitler unleashed *Operation Barbarossa*, the invasion of Soviet Russia. Army Group Centre was designated the task of conquering the area that included Białowieża. The army group formed on the west bank of the River Bug. The operational plans called for a pincer movement forcing destructive encirclements on the Red Army. Białowieża came within the scope of the Fourth Army's southern pincer. The troops in the first wave were tasked with capturing Bialystok and Minsk. They were to advance at all costs, ignoring their flanks, leaving pockets of strong Soviet resistance. The second and third waves were tasked with mopping up isolated pockets of Red Army forces to sustain the momentum of the advance. Fourth Army commander, Field Marshal Günther Hans von Kluge, assigned the task of breaking through the forest to IX Army Corps, commanded by General of Infantry Hermann Geyer.[21] The IX Corps' fighting formations were three infantry divisions (137th, 253rd, and 292nd).[22] Facing them were the Red Army's 13th Mechanised Corps, and elements of the Tenth Army under Major-General Golubev.

In the early hours on 22 June, IX Corps struck out and within a matter of days, the 13th Mechanised Corps had disintegrated with stragglers dispersing throughout the forest.[23] IX Corps' official war diary has few details about the first week's fighting. In 1942 Hermann Geyer was sacked during Hitler's purge of the generals. He subsequently wrote an account of the campaign, recalling the first ten days as the 'most beautiful in the long and heavy battle which started on the 22 June.' There were many opportunities for independent decisions and actions; the troops 'were fresh, full of hope and successful.' The Germans crossed the River Bug and quickly

---

21 The search for archival evidence included a visit to NARA's microfilm collection of records of German field commands and corps compiled under finding guide 55 for IX Armeekoprs. Microfilm series T314/404-8 were examined but with no results to explain the Corps' drive through the forest.
22 Horst Boog et al, trans. Ewald Osers, *Germany and the Second World War: Volume IV The Attack on the Soviet Union*, (Oxford, 1998), p. 528.
23 Catherine Merridale, *Ivan's War: The Red Army 1939–1945*, (London, 2010), pp. 144–147.

developed the breakthrough 'with a pursuit full of verve.' The opening barrage began at 3.15 am and Geyer recalled it was an 'impressive sight!' Pioneers from the 78th Infantry Division (XIII Corps) finished the first pontoon bridge shortly after 9.00 am. With no concerted counterattacks by the Soviets, the Germans pushed across the river unimpeded. Although more pontoon bridges were constructed bottlenecks soon developed as the distance lengthened between the advancing forces and those moving up behind. Upon reaching the east bank of the river German troops struggled with the terrain. The 263rd Infantry Division was slowed by deep sand clogging the movement of horses and men. Fortunately for the Germans, there was no Red Army presence and the advance completed twenty kilometres on the first day.

Th next day there were sporadic outbursts of Soviet resistance. In Brjansk, Geyer became embroiled in a firefight as Russian tanks attempted a desperate breakout. His account again mentioned the sandy ground and forest terrain as serious obstacles in moving forward. The 263rd and the 137th Infantry Divisions struck out towards Bielsk on 23–24 June. The 137th, tasked with reaching Bielsk, was ordered to turn eastwards, while the 292nd faced a difficult situation. Its line of advance was fifty-five kilometres and followed a zigzag pattern plotted to avoid Soviet strong points. Its progress was hampered by the breakdown of its signals' communications. At the same time, resistance from scattered Red Army units kept interrupting the division's progress as it pushed on towards Kleszele on the River Nurzec. There were some ferocious skirmishes and on 23 June Colonel Christiani, commander of its 508th Infantry Regiment, was killed in action. The 508th was so heavily engaged that only with the timely arrival of assault guns was the line held against concerted Russian pressure. On 24 June Geyer attended a progress conference and his army group commander, Field Marshal Fedor von Bock warned: 'I expect my army group to act as it did in Poland and the West.' Geyer understood Bock's meaning and issued a general order of the day for his divisions to press on regardless, ignoring their flanks. He recalled that it was not his job to close up with German units approaching from the north but only to gain ground. The 292nd led the drive toward Hajnówka, then on to Białowieża, and finally Porozow. It was a painful march, sixty kilometres over sandy soil, undulating terrain, and along narrow waterlogged roads.

By 25 June the 292nd had made deep inroads into the forest but its rear echelons were under constant enemy fire from all sides. Geyer recalled it was not very pleasant, it sapped the energy of the troops and wasted time. It was difficult to establish command and control or conduct supply. The following day, the 292nd was still fighting its way through the forest to reach the advance units of the Ninth Army and close the pincers around Bialystok. The signals problems continued to hinder the 292nd as it struggled through the forest. Three days later on 28 June Geyer decided to visit the division to clarify the situation because of the ongoing signals problems. Its losses were mounting, during the period 22–24 June 250 men had been killed while in the period 25–28 June 300 men were killed (there was no reference to Soviet casualties). By the sixth day of the campaign, the Corps had advanced 150 kilometres east of the River Bug. An Order of the Day (2 July 1941) referred to the advance through Białowieża:

> We had to deal with eight complete divisions (two tank divisions) and parts from ten other divisions. Up to the evening of 1 July, we captured 27,000 men. The bloody losses of the Russians were very high. ... Huge stores of fuel, rations and equipment of all kind were captured in Bocki, Bielsk, Hajnówka, Wolkowysk and Cholstowo.[24]

The Fourth Army finally joined the encirclement of Bialystok, and IX Corps continued to advance to close up with other German forces.

In 1962 the old comrades' association of the 137th Infantry Division compiled a unit history that included anecdotes from the Barbarossa campaign. Wilhelm Meyer-Detring, by then a corps commander in the post-war Bundeswehr, had been a staff officer

---

24 Herrmann Geyer, *Das IX Korps im Ostfeldzug*, (Vowinckel, 1969), pp. 10–92. Wilhelm Meyer-Detring had an original draft after Geyer committed suicide in 1946 and wrote the book's foreword. The Red Army units were the equivalent in size to a German division.

with the division in 1941. He recalled Geyer was from the old school officer class, but constantly pressed his men to achieve their objectives. Their regiments were forced to skirt through the western edge of the forest. The troops were anxious in the face of a swamp, sand, Urwald, poor roads and Russian snipers. Meyer-Detring complained that the Germans, unlike the Soviets, had not been trained to fight in such forests. On 25 June the 449th Infantry Regiment met stiff resistance on the western edge of the forest. Both the advance guard and mounted reconnaissance troops were reluctant to engage the Russians in a nocturnal fight inside the forest admitting, 'they were more cautious than cavalry should be'. They waited until dawn and pressed forward only to find the Russians had already withdrawn. They pressed on and reached the main Bialystok road the evening of 26 June but were in a difficult situation. The divisional signals kept in contact with the regiment through its 100watt receivers handling over a hundred coded messages to maintain contact and press the advance. A corporal of ammunition supplies recalled an incident when a horse and cart became stuck in swamp mud. The horse's hind legs sunk into the deep thick mud just as the divisional commanding general arrived. A senior NCO was beating the horse so hard that deep red marks were cut into its hindquarters. The corporal pushed the NCO into the mud just in time for General Bergmann to witness the scene. Bergmann ordered the muddied NCO to stop beating the horse and told the corporal off for pushing the NCO. He then ordered the cart unloaded of its cases of hand grenades each weighing fifty kilos and the troops to carry the boxes two hundred meters to dry ground. The corporal recalled the general carrying a case of grenades, and that image remained with him long after the war.[25]

To the south of the forest and IX Corps, Colonel General Heinz Guderian's *Panzergruppe 2* crossed the River Bug unmolested and began striking out through Red Army territory. However, upon

---

25   Wilhelm Meyer-Detring, *Die 137. Infanterie-Division im Mittelabschnitt der Ostfront*, (Eggolsheim, 2006), pp. 24–25. The original was published by the old comrade's association that was called Divisionskameradschaft General Bergmann (137. I.D.). Bergmann was killed in action on 21 December 1942.

reaching Pruzhany on the first day his 18th Panzer Division suddenly became locked in a tank battle. To the south, the Red Army also put up a bitterr resistance in Brest Litovsk's fortress that denied Guderian the use of road and rail communications. He also experienced stiff Red Army resistance first hand on 25 June when he was forced to seek shelter as two Russian tanks broke cover and turned on a German supply road. Guderian received orders to assist in preventing the Soviets from breaking out of Bialystok and was assigned to the Fourth Army. He was not keen on the decision but pressed his senior commanders with the same energy as Geyer. The XXIV Corps commanded by General of Panzer Geyr von Schweppenburg was moving forward supporting Guderian's attack on Bobruisk. Guderian recalled that Schweppenburg's corps headquarters was set up in a castle once owned by the Radziwiłł family, one of the grand old families of Eastern Europe. The soldiers found a photograph of a hunting party with Wilhelm II.[26] One of Schweppenburg's formations was the 1st Cavalry Division, under General of Cavalry Kurt Feldt, advancing towards the Kobryn-Beresa-Kartuska road. By 28 June it was located in the Drohiczyn area. The cavalry was given the order to clear the area of the Pripet marshes of Red Army forces.[27] Among the cavalry's advance, in the Pripet marshes on the southern flank, was Artillery Captain (reserve) Walter Frevert leading his mounted batteries forward.

The lead formations of IX Corps had moved out of the forest by 27 June. David Glantz noted that Army Group Centre 'had accomplished this classical pattern of destructive manoeuvre brilliantly during the battles of Belostok and Minsk, by doing so, liquidating the western front's first echelon armies and savaging the Stavka's first strategic echelons whose mission was to defend the border region.'[28] The histories of *Barbarossa*, however, do not take proper account of the heavy fighting that continued in the rear

---

26 Heinz Guderian, *Panzer Leader*, trans. Constantine Fitzgibbon, (Aylesbury, 1974), pp. 152–160.
27 Boog et al, *The Attack on the Soviet Union*, p. 526.
28 David M. Glantz, *Barbarossa Derailed: The Battle for Smolensk, the Encirclement Battle, and the First and Second Soviet Counteroffensives, 10 July–10 September 1941*, (Solihull, 2010), p. 39.

areas after the frontlines had shifted eastwards. Deep inside the German rear area, there were still large numbers of Red Army forces putting up stiff resistance. The task of mopping up Białowieża was given to General of Infantry Hans-Gustav Felber's XIII Corps.[29] The XIII Corps had three infantry divisions: 17th, 78th and 87th.[30] The job of clearing the forest was assigned to General of Artillery Curt Gallenkamp commander of the 78th Infantry Division,[31] which 'distinguished itself in the battles of Białowieża ...'[32] The stiff Red Army resistance forced the Corps to push more troops vicious fighting left a deep scar on German memories.[33]

The Corps published an account of its *Barbarossa* experience in 1942, including deeds of valour in Białowieża. The operations covered the period 29–30 June 1941 and the account opened with a description of the situation:

> [T]he forest of Bialowies is wonderful. Huge beech trees, ancient oaks, a lot of thickets, making the forest a paradise for hunters. A few poor settlements exist along its border areas. A single road leads through it. This road is surrounded by the green twilight of the primaeval forest, with huge trees, which are hundreds of years old. *Reichsmarschall* Göring went hunting together with Marshall Pilsudski here. There is still large numbers of noble game and the last remaining bison. They live in the swamp area, in the alder tree thicket, which appears to be impenetrable.[34]

The hunting clichés turned into typical heroic pathos: 'Now another hunt started in the Bialowies Urwald.' Strong Red Army forces

---

29 Felber was born in July 1889 in Wiesbaden, had been a soldier since 1908. In 1940, he was promoted to General of Infantry after the French campaign. Felber took command of the corps in October 1940. He served throughout the war and died in 1962.
30 W. Borcher, 'Der Todeswald von Bialowieza', *Der Landser*, (1961). In August 2009, I received a copy of this pulp pamphlet before a visit to Białowieża. The content traced the events and places in close detail.
31 Ludwig Merker, *Die 78. Infanterie- und Sturm-Division 1938–1945*, (Berlin, 1981). Gallenkamp (1890–1958) received the Knight's Cross of the Iron Cross. After the war, he was found guilty of war crimes against British and American servicemen. He was released from prison in 1952.
32 Samuel W. Mitcham, *Hitler's Legions*, (London, 1985), p. 96.
33 Fritz Vetter, *Die 78. Infanterie und Sturm-Division 1938–1945: Eine Dokumentation in Bildern*, (Bad Nauheim, 1981), p. 37.
34 Generalkommando des XIII. *Armeekorps, An Der Mittleren Ostfront: Ein Deutsches Korps im Kampf gegen die Sowjets*, (Nürnberg, 1942), pp. 25–8.

concentrated deep inside the forest and settled into a stubborn pattern of resistance. German intelligence identified the Red Army's 4th Tank Division, fully intact, as the main opposition.[35] The fighting turned into a confusion of conventional warfare of open-ended encirclements, and 'shoot n' skoot' tactics. The Russians dispersed during the day and concentrated at night. Snipers picked off German messengers or signallers attempting to lay telephone cables. The Russians replaced their supply through scavenging or turning around discarded weapons including artillery pieces, machine guns, flak artillery, and tanks to sustain the fight. They formed a formidable array of ad hoc fighting units. The Germans vilified the Red Army soldiers as 'communistic fanatics, who bullied their men to fight on regardless of their losses and their shortages and supply difficulties.' The corps was ordered to 'smoke out this nest' from an area roughly estimated at eighty-five kilometres long and thirty-five kilometres wide.

The Germans could not identify the precise positions of the Russians but suspected they were somewhere to the north. Gallenkamp ordered his troops to march through the forest towards Rudnia, and occupy security positions of the forest's northern border. He planned an encircling drive to push the Russians out and press them against German fixed positions. The divisional plan included placing a tactical command post in the town of Popielewo. Two infantry regiments the 195th (on the left facing north) and 215th (on the right flank facing north) were assigned to secure the town. The second and third battalions of the 215th Infantry Regiment were to lead the main attack forming a left hook coming around and behind the Russians. The 195th was to drive northwards expecting to close the encirclement of the Russians in an area north of Popielewo.[36]

From the beginning the Germans found themselves at a disadvantage *Vorkommando* (advanced guard) of the divisional staff came under artillery fire while advancing into Popielewo. The Russians opened fire on the Germans from houses. Then a German

---

35   Ibid.
36   Vetter, *Die 78. Infanterie*, p. 37.

reconnaissance report identified strong enemy forces concentrated to the east and south of Popielewo.[37] The Germans assumed this to be difficult if not impassable terrain within extensive marshland. Supported by artillery, machine guns, and tanks, however, the Russians mounted a surprise attack launched from the marshland terrain. They battled their way into Popielewo and came face-to-face with advanced units of the 215th Infantry Regiment. Irrespective of local Russian superiority the Germans held their ground in a tenacious defence with artillery, infantry and anti-tank troops deployed to enfilade the Russian attacks.

The situation became precarious as the Germans accused the 'Bolsheviks' of underhand methods: 'the vicious and sneaky tactic, of cunningly occupying a field. Many Red Army riflemen set themselves up in the treetops and trained their rifles with telescopes.' Some Russian snipers were accused of wearing civilian clothing and shooting concentrated rifle fire into the masses of German lines. The German plan was aimed at forcing a meeting engagement to identify the Russian positions. The strength of the Russian attack turned the fighting into a 'struggle for survival' against 'a near invisible enemy that clung to their piece of soil.'[38] The Germans were at a disadvantage because the forest thicket made it impossible to bring down artillery or Luftwaffe close support. The desperate fighting turned into a hand-to-hand struggle or *Nahkampf* (close combat) with bayonets. Another German infantry battalion was ordered into the fight to sweep the Russians from the forests north of Popielewo. While another battalion, trying to turn the Russian flank, was entangled in fighting before it could jump off.

The battalion command assumed 'both companies were advancing quite well', but the Russians watched and waited. The sixth infantry company, from that battalion, crawled alongside the edge of a wood through tracks in the thickets and beside a stream. The fifth, from the same battalion, seemed to move through the wood on the right flank. At the moment the Germans assumed the Russians had fled, 'suddenly it was hell on earth':

---

37 Ibid.
38 Ibid., Armeekorps, p. 26.

> A hail of murderous fire was unleashed. The snipers, hidden in the treetops, again opened fire into the rear of both companies. At the same time, both companies came under fire from machine guns, artillery and flak guns shooting straight at them from well-camouflaged positions.[39]

All contact between the battalion and the companies abruptly ceased. Isolated groups of German soldiers clung to the ground under a withering hail of bullets and shells. The officer commanding the sixth company took the critical decision — he ordered his men to charge. The was a quick dash, some vicious close combat, but they captured a Russian artillery position. At 4.00 pm the remaining companies were released in an all-out assault. The counterattack broke the Russians and they scattered, disappearing into the woods. The Germans searched the area systematically: 'Eventually some Bolshevists came out of the thicket with their hands up. The rest retreated and many more had been killed in combat.' The fifth company was rescued and contact with the sixth company restored. The account summarised the mopping-up process:

> We walked by comrades killed in action. The Bolshevists had killed even those of our men only slightly wounded. They were inhuman and a beastly enemy that thought they could stay in the forest of Bialowies. The prisoners of war were mainly Mongols who hardly speak any Russian. They are simply instruments in the hands of their commander. The German soldier shows no mercy towards these people. This was proven by the battle for Popielewo, a small and shabby village in the large forest of Bialowies. The battle for Popielewo will remain an honourable memory in the history of this division.[40]

III. The Green in the ascendancy

From his mobile headquarters, Göring ordered his train to be stabled in a forest siding in Johannisburger Heide and convened a conference. On or around 1 July 1941 the hunt leadership of Göring as Jagdherr (master of the hunt), his hunt deputy Oberjägermeister Ulrich Scherping, Landjägermeister Friedrich Ostermann (senior hunt official of East Prussia) and Oberforstmeister Walter Frevert the

---

39 Ibid., Armeekorps, p. 27.
40 Ibid., p. 28.

chief game warden of Rominten Heide (and recently artillery captain) discussed the future of Białowieża under Nazi rule. The priority was to incorporate an extended eastern frontier into Göring's nation-building mission of the Greater German Reich. The second point was how the forest and associated economies, communities and wild game could be brought under a forestry and hunting administration. What was said and decided in the meeting is unknown, but in December 1941 Scherping published an article about Urwald Bialowies. The contents of the article are the only detailed account of the forest under the German administration during the first stage of occupation.[41]

Some months before *Barbarossa*, it is believed Göring requested the files on Białowieża, but there is no explanation of why.[42] This could have been related to the economic planning behind *Barbarossa* or the proceedings of *Wirtschaftsstab Ost* (economic staff east). *Generalforstmeister* Friedrich Alpers ((1901–1944), chief of the RFA, was Göring's representative in the preparations behind the infamous hunger plan, as reported on 23 May 1941: 'The population of this area [the forest regions] especially the urban population, will inevitably face a great famine … Many tens of millions of people will be superfluous in this area and will die or have to emigrate to Siberia.'[43] On behalf of Göring's conference, Frevert was recalled from duty with the 1st Cavalry Division and returned via Białowieża. He reported that Białowieża had suffered damage, but the former Tsarist's palace, the bison compound, and the forest industries were still functional. Göring decided Scherping with the others should travel to Białowieża and conduct a survey of the forest. The Scherping party set off in a military staff car, on 5 July, armed

---

41 Scherping, 'Bialowies wieder in Deutscher Verwaltung', pp. 317–325. See also Gautschi, *Frevert*, p. 78.
42 Thaddeus Sunseri, 'Exploiting the Urwald: German Post-Colonial Forestry in Poland and Central Africa, 1900–1960,' *Past & Present*, Vol.214, Issue 1, February 2012, pp. 305–342, and in particular p. 336.
43 Christopher Browning, 'A reply to Martin Broszat Regarding the Origins of the Final Solution, in Michael Marrus (ed), *The Nazi Holocaust: Historical Articles on the Destruction of the European Jews*, vol.3, (Meckler, 1989), pp. 168–87; see also the original "Zur Genesis der Endlösung.' Eine Antwort an Martin Broszat." *Vierteljahrshefte für Zeitgeschichte*, 25(4), 1984, pp. 739–775.

with machine pistols and their hunting rifles. The party included a driver and 'R', or Richter an ethnic German gamekeeper, according to Heinrich Rubner.[44] Scherping and Richter had known each other from hunting in Białowieża before 1939. He had escaped Soviet captivity in Bialystok and taken employment as an overseer of a mill in the Warthegau (western Poland). Richter had intimate knowledge of Białowieża, the inhabitants, and was fluent in Russian (Belorussian dialect) and Polish which made him indispensable. The journey took them on a route, Lomza, Bielsk, Hajnówka and Białowieża. The party travelled roads littered with the detritus of war; crosses of German dead lined the roadside, with destroyed vehicles, and abandoned Russian artillery. The party arrived in Hajnówka at dusk and were greeted by German troops. They continued to the town of Białowieża. The 78th Infantry Division headquarters staff were stationed in the former palace and welcomed Scherping's party.[45]

Scherping's article then described his horror at the racial degeneration destroying Białowieża. He accused every village or settlement of scaping away at the forest through their subsistence lifestyles. The settlement had caused damage before the war and he noted, 'The forest people were already fully occupied with their usual work and the clean-up of war damage.' The party counted more than a hundred villages and settlements. Many settlements were on the land of poor soil which forced villagers, 'to plunder the forest for their livelihood. They didn't care whether it was right or wrong to steal wood from a state reservation.' Scherping described how villager's, when they required space, cleared an area of forest and when they need food, set traps and shot game. A major concern was how domestic animals were allowed to roam the forest, they caused extensive damage to nursery trees, and destroyed natural rejuvenation. Scherping judged the 'forest people' brought no added value, and 'the inhabitants breed like rabbits'.[46]

---

44 Heinrich Rubner, *Deutsche Forstgeschichte 1933–1945. Forstwirtschaft, Jagd und Umwelt im NS-Staat*, (St.Katharinen, 1997), p. 193.
45 Scherping, 'Bialowies wieder in Deutscher Verwaltung', pp. 317–325.
46 Ibid., pp. 317–325.

Scherping's racial profiling was scathing about the Poles and Russians, calling them all thieves. The small settlements were known to be disrespectful toward the property of the state. Scherping believed the inhabitants were notorious criminals, all murderers, bandit leaders and poachers. Ironically, he contrasted: 'the living area of the criminal had become too small beside the living area of the game'. This was Nazi rhetoric for isolating anti-social elements. The evidence came from routine searches of the settlements where the 'criminals', mostly professional poachers resided. During the searches, the party received oral evidence from unnamed locals, who expressed deep loathing for the Jews and Soviet commissars. Scherping levelled his venom against the Jews and Bolsheviks. 'The Jews, if not employed in workgroups doing something useful, gather in crowds in the towns.' Białowieża, Narewka Mala and Narew were identified as centres of 'the worst and lowest kinds of Jews.' Scherping vilified them as vermin: 'Their looks and filth can only be compared with rats.' This racist polemic was intended to stir up tension among the *Wild und Hund* readership:

> The Bolshevist in his childish naivety about matters of human existence is the most devious and most vulgar criminal. It was simply unimaginable what the Bolshevist system, the devil's own invention, has done to the Russian people over a quarter of a century. Jews and commissars, usually one of the same, have initiated *Zersetzung* (subversion) and have resisted any sense of order in Białowieża.[47]

This narrative reinforced why it was critical to remove the Jews and Communists: 'so long as they lived in the villages and settlements, they were the cause of passive resistance, strikes, acts of sabotage, and other problems.' Once the 'subversive elements' were removed, Scherping promised normality would return to the forest. He claimed the Germans received 'sufficient assistance' from 'orderly locals' to combat subversives and removing Jews. He discussed the severity of fighting and the Red Army had not buried their dead and they 'littered the forest'. The stench of death, especially in the heat and humidity of summer, was overwhelming. The

---

47   Ibid.

Jews were forced to work on the clean-up, 'it took us weeks, together with the Semitic inhabitants of the forest, to restore order and fresh air again.' Scherping led his readers into the vilification of the Jews but did not inform them of the killings.

Accounts of the mass killings, during July–August 1941, come from multiple sources. After the 78th Infantry Division moved out, responsibility for the area passed to the 221st Security Division stationed in Bialystok. On 6 July the division initiated security operations in the Bialystok and Białowieża area. The mission was 'to secure two major highways and to pacify the area of Bialystok and Białowieża forest so that Reich Marshal Göring could convert the forest into a game park'.[48] On 8 July, the diary of the 221st Security Division noted that mopping operations in Białowieża were increasingly hazardous because the local Jews supported the partisan bands.[49] On the same day Major Karl Haupt, the division's operations officer, ordered: 'The immediate and complete evacuation of all male Jews from the villages north of Białowieża has therefore been ordered.'[50] There is evidence that locals denounced Red Army stragglers and Soviet functionaries in hiding. Another report noted how the Division made Jews 'toil in the mid-summer heat improving roads.'[51] In his diary for the 14 July, SS-Gruppenführer Erich von dem Bach-Zelewski recorded discussions with General Max von Schenckendorff and confirmed receipt of 'Generalforstmeisters' Göring's' order to clear the forest. The contents of Göring's order remain unknown. Bach-Zelewski lampooned Göring as a mere forestry general, but he might have confused him with Alpers. Then on 30 July, Bach-Zelewski received a *Fieseler Storch* reconnaissance aeroplane from Göring's Luftwaffe. This kind of benefit was granted to few army commanders and reflected the

---

48 Ben Shepherd, *War In The Wild East: The German Army and Soviet Partisans*, (Cambridge Mass., 2004), p. 61.
49 Hannes Heer & Klaus Naumann, *War of Extermination: The German Military in World War II 1941–1945*, (Oxford, 1995), p. 65.
50 Ibid., pp. 65–66.
51 Ibid., p. 65.

importance Göring and the Nazi leadership placed in Bach-Zelewski's mission.[52]

Bach-Zelewski's diary also noted his primary responsibility was securing *Rollbahn I*. The *Rollbahnen* were improvised strategic roads that the German Army depended upon for their logistics.[53] *Rollbahn I* was the major supply and lines of communication highway for Army Group Centre. The route of *Rollbahn I* eastwards followed in an arc through Brest-Kobrin-Bereza-Baranowicze-Minsk-Orsa-Smolensk. Feeder roads, running along a north/south axis, which connected to the east-west central highway. A typical feeder was the Bialystok-Hajnówka-Białowieźa-Prużany road that connected with Rollbahn 1 at Bereza. The road opened between Pruzhany and Białowieźa in 1903[54] and continued north to Bialystok and Königsberg. This became the main highway for the Nazi administration connecting East Prussia with Ukraine.[55] Bach-Zelewski began resettlement actions against the forest communities in the vicinity of the transport system. He followed military occupation regulations: villages close to railways were routinely placed under martial law or even cleared. A second road, south-east from Bialystok, skirted the northern and eastern edge of the forest in parallel with the railway line to Baranowicze. The Imperial Russian railways constructed the Brest-Moscow line in 1861 as part of the main Moscow-Warsaw railway line. Both railway depots, in Hajnówka and Narewka Mala, became essential to the strategic railway network installations in the

---

52 BArch, R 20/45b Kriegstagebuch von dem Bach, 14 July 1941, p 4. Bach-Zelewski changed his name many times during his lifetime, mostly to fit the governing political situation. During Barbarossa, he was known as Erich von dem Bach having dropped the 'Zelewski' part to suit SS sensitivities over his Slavic heritage.
53 Anthony Clayton, *Warfare in Woods and Forests*, (Bloomington, 2012), pp. 102-3.
54 Małgorzata Krasińska & Zbignew A. Krasińska, *European Bison: The Nature Monograph*, (Białowieźa, 2004), p. 68.
55 Andrej Angrick, Martina Voigt, Silke Ammerschubert, Peter Klein, 'Da hätte man schon ein Tagebuch führen müssen: Das Polizeibataillon 322 und die Judenmorde im Bereich der Heeresgruppe Mitte während des Sommers und Herbstes 1941', in Helge Grabitz, Klaus Bästlein, Johannes Tuchel, *Die Normalität des Verbrechens: Bilanz und Perspektiven der Forschung zu den nationalsozialistischen Gewaltverbrechen*, (Berlin, 1994), pp. 332-333.

Białowieża area. These networks were the core of the Wehrmacht's strategic transportation system, and Białowieża was a central hub for the military operations. The geopolitical-environmental duality of Białowieża, under Nazi occupation, later caused turf wars and rivalries.

The SS-Police documentation detailed the next stage in the occupation. Several police battalions had piggybacked on the 221st Security Division as it arrived in Bialystok. Their job was to initiate SS-Police actions, in the wake of the Wehrmacht, and as a precursor to turning over the area to the civil administration.[56] Police Battalion (PB) 309 raised in Cologne in September 1940 was assigned to follow the 221st Security Division into Bialystok.[57] The city was barely under German occupation on 27 June when PB 309 became embroiled in an alcohol induced killing spree. Upwards of 3,000 Jews (men, women and children) were slaughtered in extreme acts of savagery, culminating with hundreds of Jews being locked in the Great Synagogue and burned alive.[58] On 3 July, PB 309 were ordered to collect, and stockpile captured Russian weapons in the Stoczek and Białowieża areas. The following day it led 150 Jews on a work detail to clean up the Pruzhany road and was also involved in a cleansing action in the Chwojnik area. According to Peter Longerich, on 8 July Himmler ordered his SS-Police troops to treat every Jew as a partisan. Then on 11 July, the senior police formation in the sector (*Polizeiregiments Mitte*) issued a general order to its three PBs (307th, 316th and 322nd) to shoot all Jewish males aged 17–45 under arrest for looting.[59] The arrival of Police Bicycle Battalion 322 initiated a change of *modus operandi*. This battalion was mustered in Vienna in April 1941, served in Warsaw, and was ordered east cycling ninety-four kilometres on

---

56   Philippe Burrin, *Hitler and the Jews: The Genesis of the Holocaust*, (London, 1994). Browning, *Ordinary Men*, pp. 437–8. This police regiment was assigned to Bach-Zelewski as part of the pre-Barbarossa preparations.
57   AA, 1.2.7.6. 9038100 Incarceration Documents, Notices and reports o Pol. Batl.322 Operation against Jews in Białowieża, Bialystok, Narewka Mala.
58   Peter Longerich, *Holocaust: The Nazi Persecution and Murder of the Jews*, (Oxford, 2010), p. 203, Emil Ditlev Ingeman Kjerte, 'A Comparative Study of the My Lai and Bialystok Massacres: The Social Mechanismsof Perpetration and their Casual Determinants', MA Thesis, Uppsala Universitet, 2015.
59   Ibid., p. 198.

paved roads. Over the period 10–14 July, the war diary recorded killing seventy-one Jews and two Red Army PoW's. This battalion briefly served as guard of Dulag 185 (prison camp) and shot five Jews 'while trying to escape'. Then it participated in searches of Bialystok's Jewish quarter. From 19–21 July, the PB 322 transferred to Bereza on *Rollbahn I* for transport security duties.

On 23 July 1941, *Polizeiregiments Mitte* issued further instructions about the forest's inhabitants. The order explained that all locals (excluding Jews) were friendly and should be treated correctly. The locals had been 'patient' during searches and had remained 'nice' even when contraband was removed from their homes. Many locals accepted paid work for the Germans. The instructions were followed by an order from OKW, recorded in PB 322's war diary, regarding the burial of the Russian dead.[60] The burial process did not allow priests or any religious service and denied any salutes or decorations. This was justified on the grounds of Soviet war crimes, the order alleged they had used illegal 'dum-dum' bullets. The police diary referred to difficult internal issues, including signals problems and insufficient sanitary facilities for the ninth company. They were not allocated showers until they arrived in Baranowicze (Baranovichi: Belarus). GIS Map 4 illustrates the area of deportations in the northwest corner of the forest. This area contained the highest concentration of Jews in the forest and in particular the town of Narewka Mala.

---

60 Kriegstagebuch Pol.Btl.322, Stichwortartiger Bericht über Einsatz des Batl. In Bialowieza, pp. 1–2. There are multiple copies of the war diary of Police Battalion 322 in circulation that have been collected by several national archives and then variously cited by scholars. For example, Ernst Klee, Willi Dressen and Volke Riess (ed), *'The Good Old Days': The Holocaust Through the Eyes of the Perpetrators and Bystanders*, (London, 1991) referred to the BArch Ludwigsburg reference: CSSR 1, Ordner 147, whereas Christian Gerlach, in *Kalkulierte Morde*, referred to BA F56753 (a former Bundesarchiv reference); and Yad Vashem (Jerusalem) the reference is: 0.53 – Ludwigsburg, USSR Collection, file number 86 or 127. All sources have been scrutinised in this research but for simplification and to avoid confusion the shortened German document title is adopted in this section of the book.

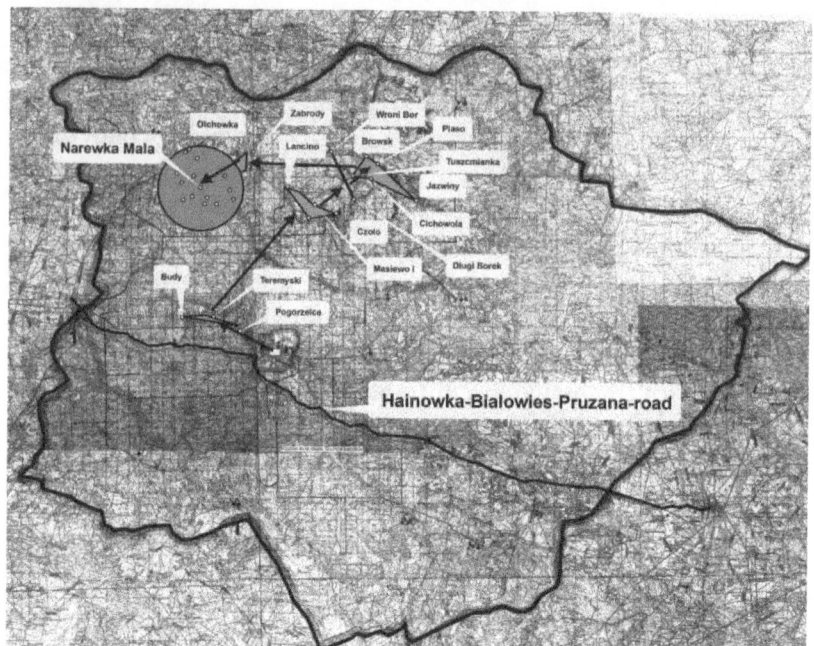

GIS Map 4: Police Battalion 322 — the village deportations 25 July–15 August 1941
The map was generated from the diary in PB 322's war diary. The layers were drawn from specific locations in the diary, as well as Scherping's article and Bech-Zelewski's diary. The concentrations reflected the area covered by Scherping's party.

Deportations from Białowieża started on 25 July 1941 (GIS Map 4). Bach-Zelewski issued a proclamation, posted in each town centre for persons bound for deportation. Every inhabitant brought their property on carts; they had two hours to pack; there was a warning if the people returned, they would face capital punishment; they had to leave behind all tools, and cattle.[61] PB 322 began deporting people from villages from ten kilometres northwest of Białowieża town (see map 4). The police used twenty-four trucks to deport 921 persons (103 families) and transported them to villages eleven kilometres beyond the forest border. Nothing is known about how these people were received, housed or integrated into these villages. The next day 200 families (1,210 people) were deported from

---

61   Kossak, *Białowieża Forest Saga*, p. 462.

villages fifteen kilometres northeast of Białowieża. They were transported forty-five kilometres northeast to Laski (a common village name in that region). During the process, they shot a communist and a 'Jew for plunder'. On 27 July the police burned down the empty villages. The following day they deported 160 families (945 persons) from villages twenty kilometres northeast of Białowieża. On 29 July they deported a hundred families (570 persons) from villages also twenty kilometres northeast of Białowieża. They transported the people to the Porosow area. The next day they deported 1,135 persons (320 families) from villages eighteen kilometres north of Białowieża to Sabludow about fifty kilometres to the northwest.[62]

A report from the third company's diary (PB 322) described how the deportations were conducted, and official photographers were on hand to record the process (note the illustrations). The company removed people from Zabrody, using twenty-eight horse-drawn carts to convey fifteen families, a total of a hundred people. They also carried people from Lesna, with sixty-six horse-drawn carts conveying thirty families, a total of 180 persons. The diary recorded four families of twenty-eight persons had departed the day before, indicating the police were not restricting all movements to set schedules. The police report explained their lorries were being maintained and could not be used. The carts were loaded with pregnant and old women, old men and children. They took along seventy-two cattle but handed over twenty-three cows, forty-four calves and forty-four horses to the Germans. The people were warned if they returned, they would face a death sentence. The carts were formed into a column and led away with the last gone by 10.30 am. The company commander reported the shooting of two communists. The company remained in Lesna overnight before moving on. They deported 1,619 persons from twelve villages in the Narewka Mala area on 31 July. The deportees were taken fifty kilometres beyond forest borders. The total deportations for the

---

62   War diary Pol.Btl.322, Einsatz der Pol.-Batl.322 in Białowieża Forst.

period 24–31 July was 6,446 persons and thirty-four villages destroyed.[63]

In Berlin in the early evening of 31 July 1941, Reinhard Heydrich (Himmler's deputy) presented Göring with a letter for official signature. The appointment in Göring's diary was marked with "Heydrich" 18.15–19.15hrs, and the letter stated:

> To supplement the task that was assigned to you on 24 January 1939, which dealt with the solution of the Jewish problem by emigration and evacuation in the most suitable way. I hereby charge you with making all necessary preparations with regard to organisational, technical and material matters for bringing about a complete solution of the Jewish question within the German sphere of influence in Europe. Wherever other governmental agencies are involved, these are to cooperate with you. I request you further to send me, in the near future, an overall plan covering the organisational, technical and material measures necessary for the accomplishment of the final solution of the Jewish question which we desire.[64]

The letter was Göring's direct culpability to the Holocaust. Many Holocaust scholars regard this as the key document that led to the 'final solution' of the extermination of European Jewry. In his masterwork, Raul Hilberg explained that the letter granted Heydrich a 'mandate' for the extermination process.[65] Adolf Eichmann's prison confession included a reference to the paragraphs he drafted that Göring signed.[66] Peter Longerich in *The Unwritten Order* (2002) reduced the letter's importance and linked it to a more important draft from March 1941. In that version, Göring requested an amendment to include the territories planned to fall under Alfred Rosenberg's civilian administration of Soviet Russia and Ukraine. In a subsequent study, Longerich explained that Göring's amendment included Rosenberg's territory indicating the 'final solution' was

---

[63] War diary Pol.Btl.322, Stichwortartiger Bericht über Einsatz des Batl. In Białowieża, pp. 1–2.
[64] J. Noakes & G. Pridham, (ed), *Nazism 1919–1945, A Documentary Reader: 3. Foreign Policy, War and Racial Extermination*, (Exeter, 1995), p. 1104, document 825. See also the Notizen: 'Die Aufzeichnungen Herman Göring's Im Institut Zeitgeschichte', *Vierteljahreshefte für Zeitgeschichte, Jahrgang 31*, (1983) Heft 2.
[65] Raul Hilberg, *The Destruction of the European Jews*, (New York, 1985), p. 163.
[66] Raul Hilberg, *Sources of Holocaust Research: An Analysis*, (Chicago, 2001), p. 153.

planned for the east.[67] In Saul Friedländer's opinion, the letter sealed Himmler and Heydrich's authority over the Jewish question.[68] Mark Roseman connected the letter to an earlier order by Göring to Heydrich to form the Reich Central Office for Jewish Emigration in 1939. The 1941 letter was an extension of the mandate leading to the infamous Wannsee Conference.[69] Christopher Browning initially agreed with Longerich over the March 1941 draft which Göring agreed in principle, but then required the amendment.[70] Browning later argued that the final document was the go-ahead to prepare a 'feasibility study' for mass extermination. He added that Heydrich required the document because 'he now faced a new and awesome task that would dwarf even the systematic murder program emerging on Soviet territory.'[71] Another explanation was how the letter granted official approval, even in the illogical polycracy of the Third Reich. On 10 February 1941, Göring became vice-chancellor of Germany, or deputy Führer, and in that capacity, his signature represented the state approval for Himmler and Heydrich to proceed.

Probably coincidental to the Göring-Heydrich letter, but the next day (1 August) Scherping met with Bach-Zelewski in Białowieża—a critical meeting of perpetrators. The only record of the meeting is a PB 322 war diary entry. The detail confirmed the meeting, in Białowieża, and the agreement to shoot seventy-two locals. We can assume with certainty that this killing action signified the Scherping's party pivotal role in the police killing actions, because they knew the locations of the Jews and Communists. From Bach-Zelewski's perspective, his war diary is highly reliable on his military activities, but woefully unreliable regarding the Holocaust.

---

67   Longerich, *Holocaust*, pp. 175–6.
68   Saul Friedländer, *The Years of Extermination: Nazi Germany and the Jews, 1939–1945*, (London, 2007), pp. 237–8.
69   Mark Roseman, *The Villa, The Lake, The Meeting: Wannsee and the Final Solution*, (London, 2002), p. 15.
70   Christopher Browning, *Nazi Policy, Jewish Workers, German Killers*, (Cambridge, 2002), pp. 20–21
71   Christopher Browning, *The Origins of the Final Solution: The Evolution of Nazi Jewish Policy 1939–1942*, (London, 2004), p. 353.

His diary has no reference to the meeting on 1 August, but there are indications of his presence in a busy travel schedule (see table 1). The *Fiesler Storch* enabled Bach-Zelewski to keep constant track of the killing process. It also meant he could coordinate the assault against the Jews across the entire rear area of Army Group C. Apart from Minsk and Mogilev, his two visits of Białowieża were significant markers in the killing period. The schedule highlights his centrality to the killing process and the importance Białowieża.

Table 1:   Bach-Zelewski's travel itinerary

July		Aug		Sept		Oct		Nov	
1	Bialystok	1	Białowieża						
8	Warsaw	2	Pripet	3	Minsk	4	Vitebsk	5	Mogilev
10	Bialystok	10	Baranowicze	5	Turov	5	Toropets	9	Mogilev
12	Grodno	14	Minsk	6	Minsk	6	Mogilev	12	Smolensk
18	Pripyet	17	Breslau	8	Mosyr	13	Sick-Mogilev	13	Berlin
30	Receives Storch	19	Baranowicze	13	Choiniki	14	Sick	14	Breslau
31	HSSPF staff	20	Turov	16	Mogilev	16	Toropets	18	Berlin
	still in Breslau	22	Starye Dorogi	17	Smolensk	17	Cholm	27	Warsaw
		23	Pinsk	24-26	Training	18	Vitebsk	28	Mogilev
		24	Baranowice	29	Pripet	27	Mogilev	30	Smolensk
		25	Białowieża			30	Riga		
		26	Mogilev						
		27	Starobin						
		30	Minsk						

PB 322's war diary and supplementary correspondence recorded a period of sustained killings. On 2 August, seventy-two people (including five Jews and six women) were rounded up and shot. They also included nineteen persons having been arrested for participating in an illegal labour action in a factory in Hajnówka.[72] Among the diary's papers, there is a 'daily report' that itemised third company from the assembly at 3.00 am in Białowieża to the 'blitz' hunt for communists forty minutes later. They searched houses, arrested

---

72   War diary Pol.Btl.322, Stichwortartiger Bericht über Einsatz des Batl. In Bialowieza, p. 2.

people, and took prisoners to a collection camp under the command of Order Police Lieutenant Giebner, who was part of the local garrison. The company arrested four Poles, eleven Byelorussian men, three Byelorussian females, six male Jews and a Jewish woman. They were searched and the Jews were accused of holding occupation money vouchers, which the Germans confiscated. The second company, from the PB 322, rounded up more prisoners. The Germans shot all of them and the final report confirmed no one had tried to escape.[73] Writing later, Kossak claimed Scherping had handed a letter to the SS identifying the persons he wanted to be arrested and shot, but this may be based on rumour.[74] Interestingly, on 3 August the commander of PB 322, recorded receipt of correspondence from Scherping which was passed on to *Polizei-Regiment Mitte* that confirming actions taken but there is no known copy of the letter.[75]

The remaining companies PB 322 departed from *Bezirk Bialystok,* on 4 August, but the third rifle company remained behind in Białowieża. The company wholly relied on Scherping and Frevert to complete the mission. On 4 August, the third company executed those persons arrested on 2 August. The company then literally worked through the Bodbiala area killing fifty-one men and three women. On 8 August they shot another nineteen people. All male Jews, aged 16–45, were rounded up on 9 August, and the next day seventy-seven persons were killed in Białowieża prison camp (location unknown). Some photographic evidence indicates the police adopted the 'sardine packing' killing method. The victims were made to lay face down in a long ditch as the police fired a single shot to the back of their necks. The next group of victims were made to lie on the dead bodies and were then shot. This continued until all were dead. There were several shootings on 11 August, including a Jewish man and two 'Belorussian plunderers'. Third company and army troops were ordered to participate in a fruitless action to hunt for 'bandits' on 14 August. The order came from *Kreiskomman-*

---

73 War diary, Pol.Btl.322, Tagesmeldung an Pol. Btl.322, 2 August 1941.
74 Kossak, *Białowieża Forest Saga,* p. 466.
75 War diary, Pol.Btl.322, Einsatz der Pol.-Batl.322 in Bialowieza Forst.

dantur Pruzhany (district level garrison) and took place east of Białowieża near Suchopol. A daily report excused their failure for starting too late, and then the police regiment commander ordered it halted.[76] On 14 August 1941, Göring was overheard saying there would be a great loss of life through a lack of nutrition in the east and added, 'the Jews in the territories dominated by Germany had nothing more to seek.'[77]

Goring's timing preceded events in Białowieża by just twenty hours. The third company conducted a *Judenaktion* (Jew action) in Narewka Mala, on 15 August. They corralled 282 Jewish males (aged 16 to 65) and a Pole. Their families (259 women and 162 children) were immediately taken to a holding facility in Kobryn (Belarus) about 90 kilometres away. The men were forced to walk 2 kilometres through the high street, a public display of degradation, and led to a remote place beside a railway line. They crossed the line and made to dig ditches in the axis of a second branch line were shot. There are no precise details of the killings, but the task was completed by the end of the day. Christopher Browning described the scenes of a police company conducting a mass shooting. The process included the identification of a remote site, digging mass grave pits in advance, bringing the Jews to the place of execution, and forcing them to disrobe. Browning noted there was the consumption of alcohol by the troops, with as many as twenty per cent trying to avoid the shooting by doing 'other' duties. The NCOs walked around selecting firing squads of eight to ten men. Small groups of Jews were then made to run through a police cordon of about thirty metres to the pits where they were lined up and shot. The rotation between firing squads was kept to five or six shots per man. Based upon Browning's findings the shootings were normally completed in three hours.[78] After the killings, the police held a convivial campfire party with beer and beef on the roast.[79] On 18

---

76 War diary, Pol.Btl.322, Tagesmeldung an Pol.Btl.322, 14 August 1941.
77 On this see, Browning, 'A reply to Martin Broszat Regarding the Origins of the Final Solution'.
78 Browning, *Ordinary Men*, pp. 78–87.
79 War diary, Pol.Btl.322, Tagesmeldung an Pol.Btl.322, 14 August 1941. p. 4.

August, the third company conducted a 'communist hunt' and accounted for twenty-six shot dead.[80] The last daily report by the third company was issued on 19 August when they departed from their strongpoints in Olschewka, Skubewo, Masiewo I and Chichowola handing over duties to the second company of PB 323.[81] Today the site of the Narewka Mala killings is remote but there is a monument above the mass grave, incorrectly dated 5 August 1941, and the area has been largely planted over with pine trees. The destruction of the Jewish community marked the end of a two-hundred-year Białowieża history.

IV. A cultural synopsis of genocide

The journey from Rominten's calm diplomacy to the genocide in Białowieża was three short years. After the outbreak of war, Henderson reflected: 'There is no rabid nationalism in sport [hunting], or at any rate that kind of sport, nor Socialism either, in the midst of unspoilt Nature, where all men are equal. From my host downwards everyone was simple, unaffected, and extremely friendly.' Henderson had regaled his participation in a Nazi pseudo-pagan death ceremony. He had hoodwinked himself into treating Göring and his court as 'gentlemen'. He could fairly argue that genocide was not explicit in 1938, but there was evidence of the mounting terror against the Jews. The ritualisation of death should have been a warning even to Henderson in 1938–39. Silence in Nazi Germany was not golden. Scherping's December 1941 article publicly announced Nazi ambitions to the German hunt and the role of the Green in genocide. Leading officials tried to maintain tight security regarding leaks. From late August 1941 British intelligence intercepts of German police signals began to decipher messages about atrocities.[82] In July police signals from Bialystok requested films to

---

80 War diary, Pol.Btl.322, Stichwortartiger Bericht über Einsatz des Batl. In Bialowies, pp. 8–9, Gerlach, Kalkulierte Morde, p. 562.
81 War diary, Pol.Btl.322, Tagesmeldung an Pöl. Bl. 322, 19 August 1941.
82 Richard Breitman, *Official Secrets: What the Nazis Planned, What the British and American Knew*, (New York, 1998).

'assist' in their conduct of atrocities.[83] Another decrypt had identified and confirmed: 'Pol.batl.309, based on Stozcek near Białowieża, has had similar work in the woods around the latter.' In the same decrypt, the British noted: 'Pol.batl.322 is to see an evacuation of the population from Białowieża.'[84] On 17 August PB 323 arrived in Białowieża from Tilsit in East Prussia. This concluded PB 322's assignment in the forest. The transfer was identified in another British decrypt although incomplete it stated: '… both Białowieża and Bialystok are being reinforced: Pol.Batl. 323 arrives at the former on 18 August 1941.'[85] On 25 August Bach-Zelewski returned to Białowieża 'to meet with SS-Untersturmführer von Härtel (sic) to see for himself how the clearances were progressing.' He also wanted all the horses taken from the locals to be led on a march to an SS domain in Minsk.[86] In September 1941, a British Intelligence report summarised:

> The execution of 'Jews' is so recurrent a feature of these reports that the figures have been omitted from the situation reports and brought under one heading … Whether all those executed as 'Jews' are indeed such is of course doubtful; but the figures are no less conclusive as evidence of a policy of savage intimidation if not of ultimate extermination.[87]

The events in Białowieża in 1941, bisected theories of Imperial German colonialism and Nazi Lebensraum. In 1936, the amalgamation of the SS and the Police had brought about the Nazi police state. Under Kurt Daluege, the chief of the Ordnungspolizei, the beat police were radicalised through a crash course of militarisation.[88] On 21 January 1941, Daluege spoke to the day of the Police inspectors conference. He discussed the Kolonialfrage (colonial

---

83   TNA, HW 16/6, part one, MSGP 27, 21 August 1941, p. 2.
84   Ibid.
85   TNA, HW 16/6, part one, MSGP 28, 12 September 1941, p. 6.
86   BArch, R 20/45b Kriegstagebuch von dem Bach, 25 August 1941, p. 10. Bach-Zelewski misspelt von Hertel's name. Hertel was the commander of the third company.
87   TNA, HW 16/6, part one, British decrypts of German police signals covering period 15–31 August 1941 General situation assessment.
88   Philip W. Blood, 'Kurt Daluege and the Militarisation of the Ordnungspolizei', in Gerard Oram, *Conflict and Legality: Policing Mid-Twentieth Century Europe*, (London, 2003), pp. 95–120.

question) still lodged in German thinking about empire. His speech referred to two SS-Police schools, Berlin-Oranienburg and Vienna (Austria). They both ran training programmes on behalf of the Colonial Police Department, within the Hauptamt (central offices) of the Ordnungspolizei. Daluege claimed he had stumbled across the Berlin Colonial School, which was a surprise since they trained annually: 600 policemen and 1,500 Beamten (officials).[89] The training of the police, according to Daluege, was to transform them into the 'best quality' manpower; and to the shame of the older colonial powers like England'. The functions of these two colonial police schools, in April 1941, also pointed to the strategic thinking of the SS-Police about security and policing Hitler's empire.[90] The colonial police academies adapted to the guidelines for colonial military tactics that were placed on general distribution to police departments. In methodology, the preferred skills were simplistic—adopt silence, march with care, and attack the enemy with skill. There was a racial tone injected into colonial lectures: 'racialism is strongly represented in Judaism'. Colonial warfare was reframed to fit Nazi war-making: 'The aim of the fighting in this war, in the west the destruction of their [allies] abilities to continue fighting, but the war against Bolshevism is their destruction per se.'[91] This chapter has shown how 'the Green' revelled in its invented rituals and exploited them to bamboozle foreign diplomats. The rituals emboldened the RFA to navigate genocide. 'The Green' killed Jews like vermin and was akin to the gamekeeper's modus operandi. This was the end of the first stage of radicalisation, there could be no going back, and events will show how it worsened.

---

89 NARA, T580/216/0473. Ansprache des Chefs der Ordnungspolizei anläßlich der Tagung der Inspekteure der Ordunungspolizei am 21. Januar 1941, 24.
90 NARA, T175/13/2515813-2515890, Die Völker der Erde.
91 NARA, T175/13/2515813-2515890, Richtlinien für die kolonialtaktische Ausbildung an den Kolonialpolizei-Schulen (n.d.).

Image 7: Sites of memory—Located beside the railway in Zabłotczyzna (2 miles from Narewka), the memorial refers to approximately 500 Jews killed on 5 August 1941. The German records show 282 Jewish men were killed at that place on 15 August 1941.

Visitors to the site have included relatives of victims:
https://kehilalinks.jewishgen.org/Narewka/HolocaustMemorials.html
Source: Author, 2013

3. Grossdeutschland

By July 1942, Białowieża could no longer be regarded as a Green colony. In the summer of 1941, Ulrich Scherping saw the realisation of his *Urwald Bialowies*, through deportation and genocide; one year later that political initiative was squandered to his rivals. Göring's ambitions, regardless of his hunting-forestry interests, remained fixated on the geopolitical priorities. Under Göring's nationalist umbrella, the full administrative bureaucracy had descended on *Bezirk Bialystok*. The entire retinue of strategic, political, and cultural offices took over Białowieża, Bialystok and East Prussia. There were also those historical echoes of former borders, which Erich Koch was determined to exploit. The Third Partition of Poland in 1795, led to Prussia's territorial acquisition of the area around Bialystok which was briefly known as New East Prussia (1795–1806).[1] During the Great War, Imperial Germany had expectations of reconstituting New East Prussia out of the occupation in which Koch had served as a soldier.[2] Koch had no interest in restoring the old monarchy, but his greed was fuelled by the recent rapid growth of East Prussia. There had been a twenty-five per cent increase in East Prussia's territorial expansion from the war including *Bezirk Bialystok*.[3] This was largely due to his special relationship, even friendship, with Göring.

On 16 July 1941, a Hitler conference was convened to discuss the administration of the conquered territories in the east. Martin Bormann kept the minutes and wrote, 'The Reich Marshal [Göring] thinks it was right to incorporate into East Prussia several parts of the Baltic country, e.g., the Forest of Bialystok.'[4] Hitler agreed to

---

1. Ingeburg Charlotte Bussenius, *Die preussische Verwaltung im Süd- und Neuostpruessen*, (Hamburg, 1960).
2. Ralf Meindl, *Ostpreussens Gauleiter: Erich Koch – eine politische Biographie*, (Osnabrück, 2007), p. 300.
3. Frevert, 'Zehn Jahre Jagdherr in Rominten', pp. 148–153.
4. 'Document L-221: Memorandum For the Record, 8/17/1941 [translation]', in Nazi Conspiracy and Aggression, Volume VII, US Government Printing Office, District of Columbia, 1947, pp. 1086–1093.

assign *Bezirk Bialystok* (district of Bialystok), including Białowieża to East Prussia. It is probable Koch, Göring and Hitler had come to a pre-conference arrangement. After the conference, Göring returned to his field headquarters in Johannisburger Heide. Lw.General Ramcke and Lw.General Student was present when Göring was greeted by Koch brandishing a map of the Bialystok region, claiming it had once belonged to East Prussia. Koch pointed to Białowieża and Göring said, "of course East Prussia gets that too."[5] Hitler later confirmed Koch's acquisitions in the 'Führer decree on the Provisional Administration of Bialystok district', which included the Ukraine.[6] According to a British intelligence report, *Bezirk Bialystok* was placed under Koch by decree on 1 August 1941.[7] Alexander Dallin thought, 'The Bialystok district of Belorussia, Polish until 1939, was attached to East Prussia as of 15 August 1941, thus linking the latter with Ukraine.'[8] *Bezirk Bialystok*, including *Urwald Bialowies* (part of the incorporation renaming of Białowieża into German officialdom), had joined Koch's fiefdom, stretching his geopolitical landmass from the Baltic to the Black Sea.[9]

German soldiers had fought and died in the East Prussia-Bialystok-Białowieża, and this led to the assignment of military cemeteries as honoured ground. The *Wehrmacht* war graves commission, designated the occupied east the *Wehrmacht-Gräbenoffiziere im Osten* (WGO) and graves in *Bezirk Bialystok* became listed as WGO-36. Captain Plaumann, the local WGO officer, routinely referred to the Greater German Reich on cemetery location maps, and in all official correspondence.[10] This both symbolized and confirmed the

---

5   TNA, WO 208/4168, SRGG 1065, General Ramcke, September 1944.
6   Cologne District Court Judgement 30-11/67, The People vs Kurt Wiese and Henry Errelis, Federal Republic of Germany, 27 June 1968; for Ukraine see Wendy Lower, *Nazi Empire-Building and the Holocaust in Ukraine*, (Chapel Hill, 2007).
7   TNA, WO 208/3009 Nazi-Occupied Europe, 1944, pp. 14-5.
8   Alexander Dallin, *German rule in Russia 1941–1945: A study of occupation policies*, (London, 1981), p. 90. See also Czesław Madajczyk, *Die Okkupationspolitik Nazideutschlands in Polen 1939–1945*, (Warsaw, 1988), pp. 143–6, 518–39.
9   Dallin, *German Rule*, p. 301.
10 NARA, RG 242, T78/880, Kriegsgräberfürsorge, II band 1943–1944, various WGO papers.

centrality of Göring's nation-building. The defeated region had been administered by the Poles and Soviets within less than three years. There were traces of both still in the system. The prevailing jurisdiction in the Bialystok region, after the Nazi occupation, was skewed by confusion. East Prussia was the German state or Nazi Gau, but each national institution claimed self-regulation. *Bezirk Bialystok* came within German national laws and codes, but there were multiple interpretations of jurisdiction. There were layers of civilian administration competing with military, political and ideological organisations. Within in each organization, there were layers of bureaus, management departments or field offices. Officials were paid home salaries and received foreign service subsidies. Soldiers in the field faced dual reporting structures divided between occupation and homeland authorities.

I. Prussian administration

East Prussian officialdom swamped *Bezirk Bialystok* with all manner of administrators. The politics of bureaucracy expanded in line with Parkinson's Law with the corresponding rate of incompetence as defined by the Peter Principle.[11] From 25 August, the civil administration in Könibgerg sent out officials to fill the political landscape. Christian Gerlach observed that Koch and Scherping met with representatives from the Interior Ministry and Heydrich's RSHA to discuss boundary and population changes in autumn 1941.[12] *Bezirk Bialystok* was divided into different civilian administrative districts. The *Oberpräsident der Zivilverwaltung des Bezirkes Bialystok* (President of the Civilian Administration for *Bezirk Bialystok*) established an *Amtskommissar* (local district Commissioner) in Białowieźa, Schereszow and Suchopol. At the lowest levels, German mayors adopted a policy of 'divide and conquer', exploiting the antagonisms between Poles and Byelorussians.[13] Koch's first

---

11   Gerlach, *Kalkulierte Morde*, p. 179.
12   Laurence J. Peter and Raymond Hull, *The Peter Principle* (London, 1970), C. Northcote Parkinson, *Parkinson's Law or The Pursuit of Progress*, (London, 1958).
13   Meindl, *Ostpreussens Gauleiter*, p. 306.

president of the civil administration was Waldemar Magunia (1902–1974). He took up his post on 15 August 1941 but transferred to Ukraine on 31 January 1942. He was replaced by Dr Friedrich Brix (1898–1969) as president on 1 February 1942 and remained in position until 27 July 1944. Like most officials, he was transferred from the *Landrat* (district commissioner) of Tilsit, in East Prussia. Brix gained a reputation acting independently because of Koch's long periods of absence. He encouraged a large influx of Germans and *Volksdeutsche* (ethnic Germans). On 4 March 1942, *Bezirk Bialystok* was declared a *Regierungsbezirk* in line with districts in Germany.[14] By November 1942 around 20,000 Germans (administrators, professional, agriculturalists, merchants and foremen) were recorded living and working in *Bezirk Bialystok*.[15]

By tradition, custom and practice, the German Army was the dominant national institution in East Prussia. The army was divided between the Field army (fighting component) and the *Heimatkriegsgebiet* (Home Forces Area), which handled the administration. The army's *Wehrkreis* (military district) system was responsible for recruitment and mobilization, as well as handling the administration of armies in the field. *Wehrkreis 1* was the home forces military district for East Prussia, with a headquarters in Königsberg. This military district was affiliated to nearly forty front line divisions and an unrecorded number of ancillary formations and bureaus. The army raised *Divisionskommando.z.b.V "Bialystok"* (abbreviated to *Kdr.d.Div.z.b.V Bialystok* in SS reports). According to Georg Tessin, the division replaced the 221st Security Division. The commanding officer was General Hans-Erich Nolte and was garrisoned in Bialystok and Oesterode on 1 August 1941.[16] The *Division z.b.V., Bialystok* (adopted in Luftwaffe reports) came under the

---

14 TNA, WO 208/3009, Nazi-Occupied Europe, 1944, pp. 14–5.
15 TNA, WO 208/3009, Nazi Occupied Europe, 1944, pp. 14–5. The report maintained the entire Bezirk area was 32,000 sq.km., in 1942, and numbered 1,650,000 inhabitants.
16 Georg Tessin, *Verbände und Truppen der deutschen Wehrmacht und Waffen-SS im Zweiten Weltkrieg 1939–1945, Sechzehnter Band*, (Osnabrück, 1996), p. 54; see also, Wolf Keilig, *Das Deutsche Heer 1939–1945, Gliederung, Einsatz, Stellenbesetzung*, (Bad Nauheim 1956), Band 3, 173/17–18.

Kommandeur der Ersatztruppen (headquarters of the replacement army) in Allenstein (1939). This division was the reserve army representative for *Bezirk Bialystok,* responsible for training and supplying infantry replacements for *Wehrkreis 1* affiliated front line divisions. The division combined operational training and security duties. The division's major task was to secure the supply traffic that was assigned to Army Group Centre. Although a Home Forces formation, *Division z.b.V., Bialystok* adopted an occupation configuration. Evidence points to the division's *Landesschützenbataillon 238* (Local Defence Battalion), under Major Wittke, which deployed its full complement of six companies and carried out guard duties around strategic installations.[17]

Image 8: A German Army Ortskommandtur: issuing daily notices and labour assignments.
Source: NARA, Hoffmann Collection.

The staff installed an *Ortskommmandantur Bialystok* (a commandant garrison) typical for military security of an urban area. This bureau opened a number of satellite offices including *Wehrmacht-*

---

17 Ibid., Tessin, *Verbände und Truppen,* , p. 54 listed the Lds.Schtz.Btl's: 208, 229, 617, 664, 854 but not 238.

kommandantur Białowieża commanded by Manfred von Kobylinski. This office reported to the *Wehrkreis I* and to *Division z.b.V., Bialystok*. The *Wehrmachtkommandantur Białowieża* (later renamed *Wehrmacht-Kommandantur Abwicklungstelle-Bialowies*) was based in Hajnówka and reported directly to *Ortskommandantur Bialystok*. The names indicate it was the army's resettlement or demobilizing centre, but no details exist. Kobylinski's presence in the forest has proven almost impossible to clarify. He was not the commander of PB 322 as has been claimed or an Order Police officer.[18] The forest remained unpacified even after the 1941 actions and the division had assigned patrols to counter the partisans.[19]

The SS-Police established a hybrid bureau, a compromise because of an old Nazi squabble. During a conference in the 1930s, Erich von dem Bach-Zelewski arrogantly led his SS band out in a public protest. Erich Koch was the host and harboured deep animosity towards the SS. This forced Himmler into creative designs for the administration.[20] Bialystok became the supply hub for all SS-Police/*Waffen-SS* operations in the Army Group Centre theatre, and under Bach-Zelewski who was *HSSPF-Russia-Centre*. This explains his importance to the Białowieża deportations and killings in 1941. However, Koch refused to countenance Bach-Zelewski's permanent presence and Himmler was forced to instigate a compromise. Hans-Adolf Prützmann (HSSPF-Russia-South) was named substitute commander of *Bezirk Bialystok* but the physical administration was handled through Bach-Zelewski's offices of HSSPF-Russia-Centre. Prützmann had formed a working relationship with Koch in Ukraine, and in this regard, it was a workable solution. The Order Police senior command structure and PB's reflected an extension of the East Prussian police region. The designated *SS-Polizeiführer* (SS and Police Leader—SSPF) based in Bialystok and responsible for Białowieża was Werner Fromm (1905–1981) until

---

18   Schama, *Landscape and Memory*, p. 71. Kobylinski published a book *Bunte Strecke* (1935), which was about East Prussian hunting community and the Great War.
19   Kurt Hilmar Eitzen, *Deutsch-Englisches Militär-Wörterbuch*, Berlin: "*Offene Worte*", (Berlin, 1936), p. 114.
20   Blood, *Hitler's Bandit Hunters*, p. 80.

January 1943. He was supposed to report to both Prützmann and Bach-Zelewski, although the latter was officially his senior, but Himmler received all reports directly and interfered directly in the decision process.[21] The senior ranking Order Police officer was *Generalmajor der Polizei* Rudolf Müller (1 March 1942 to 5 August 1944) based in Königsberg. He was determined to incorporate *Bezirk Bialystok* into the Order police district system and with full operational integrity. The designated battalions assigned to *Bezirk Bialystok* were PB 13 (Königsberg) and PB 323 (Tilsit), both mustered with local men.[22] There were other police formations including the gendarmerie, rural police and frontier detachments, but too small to itemise.

There were two German national institutions with a significant presence in the forest. The *Deutsche Reichsbahn* (German State Railways) absorbed the existing central maintenance facility in Wolkowysk and two sub-workshops in Hajnówka within its operational structure. Within the forest the *Reichsbahnstation Bialowies* (Hajnówka) and *Reichsbahnstation Narewka Mala* were mainline railway sub-offices, coordinating connections with the Białowieża narrow gauge network, which was operated RFA. The DR assigned *Eisenbahntruppen* (railway troops) for defence duties, securing lines and installations.[23] The *Reichspost* (German state postal service) opened four centres in the forest area, *Postamt Bialowies, Postamt Narewka Mala, Postamt Schereszow,* and *Postamt Suchopol.* The SS protected these offices with the armed postal police force.

German and Polish scholars have tried to explain the inner workings of *Bezirk Bialystok,* but their efforts have been hindered because few records survived the war. Christian Gerlach concluded the Nazis behaved differently in *Bezirk Bialystok* and treated it, unlike any other occupied territory. He judged the Nazis were trying to administer the region under a system based upon the German

---

21 Mark C. Yerger, *Allgemeine-SS: The Commands, Units and Leaders of the General SS*, (Atglen, 1997), p. 27, 70.
22 Wolfgang Curilla, *Die deutsche Ordnungspolizei und der Holocaust im Baltikum und in Weissrussland 1941–1944*, (Paderborn, 2006), p. 587 and p. 696.
23 Eugen Kreidler, *Die Eisenbahnen im Zweiten Weltkrieg*, (Hamburg, 2001).

civil code that emphasised the *Landfriedensbruch* (breach of the public peace) procedures, rather than the usual martial law and extreme measures. Compared with other eastern occupations there was not the same scale of random shootings, reprisal killings, and other war crimes. There were civil courts and drumhead court-martials, albeit dispensing summary justice. Białowieża was the most eastern part of the Greater German Reich and subject to domestic law.[24] Ralf Meindl concurred with many of Gerlach's findings in his biographical study of Erich Koch. He argued that *Bezirk Bialystok* was administered like German occupation authorities in the west Alsace, Lorraine and Luxembourg. The national currency, the *Reichsmark*, rather than occupation bills, was the common currency. There was less exposure to the full extent of economic exploitation or the hunger plan. Meindl found the summary courts-martial system was introduced in April 1942, but it was only used for serious crimes. The evidence is contradictory. From 30 September 1942, *Bezirk Bialystok* introduced the full German legal code, although it did not provide for non-Germans or Slav locals. In matters of security, the occupation legislation was dictated by collective responsibility.[25] The process of Germanisation was planned to transform the *Bezirk Bialystok* within ten years and this means it's difficult to gauge how far the civil structure would change. This is rendered more difficult because Koch's working methods and attitude towards *Bezirk Bialystok* are largely unknown. Gerald Reitlinger accepted an older interpretation of Koch, the tyrant that preferred to remain lodged in his East Prussian fiefdom except to go hunting.[26]

II. The Białowieża arena

Göring confirmed the annexation of *Bezirk Bialystok* to East Prussia on 25 August, in a document outlining the RFA's administrative responsibilities in Białowieża.[27] The orders were first issued when

---

24 Gerlach, *Kalkulierte Morde*, p. 933–934.
25 Meindl, *Ostpreussens Gauleiter*, p. 300.
26 Reitlinger, *The House Built on Sand*, pp. 175–184.
27 BArch, R 37001/2231, RFA, Organisation der neuen Ostgebiet Bialystok, nach vom 20 August 1941.

the forest was occupied and again reissued once Bialystok was attached to East Prussia. The RFA introduced the *Oberforstamt Bialowies* (Higher Forest Department) with a full complement of forestry staff and also the *Staatsjagdrevier* (state hunting district), which adopted a range of titles including *Jagd Bialowies*.[28] The order also instructed all sawmills, turpentine stills, agricultural areas, and power stations to be placed under the *Oberforstamt*'s administration. Scherping became chief of the forest, and Fritz Nüsslein his second-in-command of *Jagd Bialowies* (the Białowieża hunt).[29] *Oberforstmeister* (senior forest-superintendent) Wagner became *Chef des Oberforstamtes Bialowies* with orders to establish a *Reichsjagdgebiet* (National Hunting Reserve). Frevert was designated Göring's plenipotentiary or senior official of the hunt and the forest.[30] This assignment was from 1 July 1941 to 1 April 1942, which differed from his army records that had granted a special release for 1–20 July 1941. His official duties from July 1941 to April 1942 were not recorded in his army papers, which indicates he was assigned a range of tasks including genocide.[31]

The *Oberforstamt Bialowies* administered several *Forstämter* (forest departments) each under a *Forstmeister*. The central office was based in Białowieża and administered the entire forestry operations including tree stands for cutting, the narrow-gauge railway, timber distribution centres, wood and paper mills, and derivative factories such as the turpentine stills. There is no known organisational chart for the Oberforstamt. Seven *Forstämter* were raised that followed the German army's *System Bialowies* model (1915–18) they were: *Forstamt Hajnówka, Forstamt Czerlanka, Forstamt Podolany, Forstamt Bialowies, Forstamt Narewka Mala, Forstamt Eichowola-Süd*, and

---

28 BArch, R 37001/2231, Der Reichsjägermeister – Leitung des Staatsjagdreviere an die Abteilung III des Reichsforstamts, 25 August 1941.
29 Rubner, *Deutsche Forstgeschichte*, pp. 190–195. Fritz Nüsslein (1899–1984), a Bavarian forester, became part of Scherping's staff within the Jagdamt.
30 BArch, Lw. Personalakte: Walter Frevert. Promotion to 'Sonderauftrag für des Reichsmarschall zwecks Befriedung und Evakuierung des Urwaldes Bialowies'.
31 BArch, Lw. Personalakte: Walter Frevert, Vorschlag zur Beförderung eines Offizieres (d.B.) zum nächsthöheren Dienstgrad, 3 May 1943.

Eichowola-Nord. *System Bialowies* had concentrated its activities to within an area north and west of a rough line running from Nowy Dwor to Bialy Lasek and then to Roszkowka on the maps. *Urwald Bialowies* was a replication of *System Bialowies* from the Great War. There was a search for trained manpower and army Lieutenant Erich Weinreis was reassigned. A professional forester, he was a regimental sergeant major during the short occupation of Białowieża in 1939. In December 1939 he was promoted and assigned to Göring's court staff. In 1941 he transferred to the army command in Bialystok, but then became the district forester of Podlany under the *Oberforstamt Bialowies*.[32] The details behind similar transfers, matching experience with the position, indicated the extent of searches for candidates.

In 1941, the combination of the army, RFA, SS-Police and local collaboration imposed a powerful security presence in Białowieża. Referring again to Scherping's article he had outlined, 'it was necessary to cleanse the forest of arms and unsuitable races.' The 'clean up' was initiated by the 78th Infantry Division. Scherping singled out the *Feldgendarmerie* (military police) battalion for special praise because of their enthusiasm in the actions. Once the 78th departed, the SS-police troops and a company of FSK (*Forstschutzkorps* — forest defence troops) were responsible for policing and security. The RFA raised an *FSK Hundertschaft* to guard the forest's mills and estates; and, they tackled the forest clean up, the protection of valuable assets, restarting forest industries, and transporting valuable wood supplies. Scherping continually referred to the assistance of 'locals' or collaborators, but there is no evidence of who they were or where they came from. However, despite the intensified security measures the Soviet insurgency was increasing in intensity. There was an unsubstantiated story from December 1941 that the Luftwaffe bombed a concentration of five hundred partisans in the northeast area of the forest. By March 1942 the security situation had deteriorated for the Germans and Frevert was even forced to abandon catching a lynx for Rominten because the partisans posed

---

32   BArch, Lw. Personalakte: Erich Weinreis.

a serious threat.³³ He was admitted to hospital on 23 March and only returned to light duties in Rominten on 2 April 1942. He remained plenipotentiary of Białowieża, but his health prevented his involvement in countering the partisan incursions.³⁴ Partly because of his absence, the Germans made a concerted effort to rationalise their security effort.

There was a detachment of FSK in the forest from July 1941 to March 1942.³⁵ Although there are no specific records of their performance, other organisations noted they were disbanded because of the intensity of the insurgency. The FSK was first raised in the General-Government of Poland. Hans Frank made a general appeal for extra police due to the increase of poaching and banditry in the forests.³⁶ Heinrich Rubner has written about the FSK and explained that Dr Kurt Eisfeld took charge of *Hauptabteilung Forsten* in the General-Government of Poland. Eisfeld was a professional forester, an SS man, and part of Friedrich Alpers' clique within the RFA. On 29 October 1939, Eisfeld reported to Alpers that the forest administration in Poland urgently required an increase in forces. The fear of a breakdown in rural authority was a regular complaint among many authorities. In March 1940 the *Gaujägermeister* in the *Reichsgau Wartheland* (western Poland) wrote to the RFA in Berlin complaining that Polish children were hunting illegally.³⁷ In April 1940 SS-Oberstgruppenführer Kurt Daluege, chief of the Order Police, wrote to Scherping about the illegal discharge of weapons in the forests, and the need for a *Jagdschutz-Kommando* (Hunting Defence Force).³⁸ On 5 September 1940, the British decoded a corrupted

---

33 Waleri Ripperger, & Wjatscheslaw Semakow, *Der Traum vom Urwald: Streifzüge durch die Bialowieser Heide*, (Tessin, 2008), p. 321.
34 While under convalescence Frevert remained accountable for Bialowizca and during this period transferred to the Luftwaffe.
35 Ripperger et al, *Der Traum Vom Urwald*, pp. 302-309.
36 Wilhelm P.B.R. Saris and Mathieu de Wolf (2008), 'Das Forstschutzkommando des Reichsforstmeisters', in *Internationales Militaria-Magazin*, Mai-Juni, pp. 27-33.
37 NARA, T580/222, Bekämpfung des Wildererunwesens im Warthegau, 8 March 1940.
38 NARA, T580/222, letter from Chief of Order Police Kurt Daluege to Scherping, 8 April 1940.

intercept indicating the police had been conducting actions against Polish bandits in forests around Cholm.[39]

Landforstmeister Ernst Boden became the FSK's senior officer. According to Rubner, the FSK mustered young forest workers as *Forstschützen* (ORs) and *Zugführer* (platoon or section leaders) from the *Revierforststand* (the class of district foresters). The Luftwaffe supplied the equipment, uniforms and weapons usually from captured stocks. By April 1940 there were nine companies of 2,000 men with the task of securing the supply of timber from Poland. The FSK had three primary functions: first—forest security, securing the forest administration, monitoring, and guarding polish labourers, and forest/game protection; Second—managing emergencies such as storms, beetle infestations, and fire; and third—instructional or training Polish labourers, maintaining equipment, meeting work quotas, and ensuring general efficiency. Once an FSK unit was operational in occupied territory its priority was to recruit local foresters preferably with some military training, but also craftsmen, fitters and drivers. Rubner has argued the FSK had an educational role in improving Polish work methods but this reads too much like German stereotypes. He also claimed Polish 'trusties' were given sawmills taken off the Jews, but that Eisfeld was going to gift the mills to German men after the war.[40] FSK detachments were first raised in the Polish towns of Radom, Lublin, Tarnow and Lemberg—all with large Jewish ghettoes. In 1940 the forestry school's yearbook carried an article about the old *Feldjägerkorps*, the military foresters of Prussia, and the nobility of armed foresters.[41] From spring 1943 the increase in partisan activity forced Eisfeld to lower the race barriers for Poles to serve. There are no accurate figures but of those Poles that joined the FSK many deserted to the partisans taking their weapons with them.[42] The FSK was introduced into Białowieża but failed.

---

39 TNA, HW 16/6, MSGP 13, 11 September 1940.
40 Rubner, *Deutsche Forstgeschichte*, p. 196
41 Fr. Jentsch, 'Das Preussische Reitende Feldjägerkorps', *Tharandter Forstliches Jahrbuch*, Band 90, Heft ¾, 1940.
42 Rubner, *Deutsche Geschichte*, p. 201. During five years of its existence, 9,500 men served in the FSK. It's believed that 130 were killed in accidents or by partisans,

Since August 1941, PB 323 was in Białowieża until it departed for the eastern front in January 1942. The FSK and the army units mentioned proved inadequate on their own. On 9 March 1942, the first company of Reserve PB 13 transferred into Białowieża, with the mission to combat partisans and restore law and order. During its assignment, the company ventured into the marshlands in pursuit of partisans and carried out searches of several villages. There were random incidents including firefights, searches for bunkers or hideaways, and shooting fugitive Red Army PoWs. The police killed two men for wielding axes, killed partisans in firefights, and arrested four Jews. In one incident they arrested five Poles because they had been in contact with the partisans. The Poles were then shot on the justification of running away. On 12 May the company formed an execution commando (an officer and forty ORs) and killed sixteen persons without trial. On 2–3 June, the company with a gendarmerie unit was in a short firefight with partisans in Kapitaszyzna. Three partisans were captured, interrogated and killed. The next day, in a revenge action, the village was destroyed, and the inhabitants deported. On 8 June, the first company, the second company arrived with the SD they conducted actions that burned down several villages (listed as Skryplewo, Postelewo and Sowiny Grunt). They searched Lipiny, a village nearby to Hajnówka. On 16–17 July the first company instigated reprisal actions in Lichacze and Krasice. A week later, 25 July, the company commander led another execution commando of twenty-four troopers in Pruzhany. They shot and killed ninety-six people including fourteen women. By the end of the assignment, the police had suffered three fatalities in combat. Later PB 13 joined 2nd SS-Police Regiment and the first company departed for Bialystok on 10 August 1942, signifying the withdrawal of the police from Białowieża.[43]

---

and 400 were killed in the last year of the war, and captivity. According to Rubner, Eisfeld shot himself beside his parents because of his SS membership and he was listed as a war criminal by the Polish government for killing hostages. Rubner also claimed many foresters escaped to the west and the FSK became part of the 40th Infantry Division for all those born in the year 1927.

43 Curilla, *Die deutsche Ordnungspolizei*, pp. 595–8, see also YVA 0.53/15, War Diary of the 1.Kompanie of Reserve-Polizeibataillon 13, during 1941–42.

III. The hunt

Seemingly oblivious to the rising insurgency the senior RFA/Jagdamt officials went hunting. On 19 January 1942, a hunting party set out with Scherping, *Oberjägermeister* Nüsslein, Lutz Heck, Heinz Heck (director of Munich zoo), *Elchjägermeister* Hans Kramer (master of the Elk hunt at *Forstamt* Tawellningken), and *Oberforstamt Bialowies* superintendent Hans Krause. They were photographed hunting wolves and boar.[44] In 1942 a pureblood bison released into a Białowieża reservation and Heck claimed this was the first attempt at reintroduction in modern history. Heck praised Göring for the 'truly magnificent promotion of bison in the *Urwald Bialowies*'. He explained that the forest was large enough to sustain several herds of bison and the Heck Cattle.[45] There are snippets of evidence about Heck's work in *Urwald Bialowies*. It is known that twenty-two Heck Cattle were reared in Rominten, and in 1942 sixteen were transported to Białowieża, and released into the forest. It's also believed that in 1945–46 the entire stock of twenty-three Heck cattle was slaughtered by the Soviets because they were deemed 'fascist beasts'.[46] Heck assisted Georg Moesges, the inspector of Berlin zoo, who had been rounding up panje horses and wild horses in Poland and was assisted by the Reiter-SS (SS cavalry). In August 1941 Bach-Zelewski noted in his diary the rounding up of Białowieża's horse stocks and taking them to the SS cavalry stables in Minsk.[47] The removal of all horses had a devastating socio-economic impact on the forest communities.

Wartime allowed Heck to dabble with the lure of predators and he began to experiment with the brown bear. The first bears were released in Białowieża in June 1943. A trial release of two young bears born in a Russian zoo was founded on the assumption that their character suited Białowieża's habitat. When they were released from their boxes, they ravished a horse carcass prepared in

---

44 Ripperger et al, *Der Traum Vom Urwald*, p. 320.
45 Lutz Heck, 'Hermann Göring, der Schützer des deutschen Urwildes', *Wild und Hund*, 1943, No. 39–40, pp. 154–157.
46 Ibid., pp. 324–330.
47 Heck, *Auf Tiersuche*, second edition, 1943, p. 285.

advance. They were disturbed by the keepers and ran into the forest exciting several young dogs. The bears then fought playfully with each other and finally disappeared. According to reports, they had left the forest and were resident seventy kilometres to the north. An older female brown bear was later released. The bear calmly left its box and dragged a horse leg into the impenetrable area of the marshland and then disappeared. This bear became unpopular with the locals because it killed cattle and attacked humans; locals later slaughtered it. An article about the bears claimed the Germans introduced five bears. In 1942 a bear killed two people and poachers later set out to kill it.[48] Heck knew the dangers but the temptation of unlimited research free of liability removed all caution with his experiments.[49]

Two documents place Heck at the heart of Nazi racial engineering theories. In May 1942 he completed an agreement between two Nazi agencies over settlements in the east. He claimed the east had to be conquered and transformed into a Germanic landscape.[50] One of the agencies was the *Lebensborn* (the well of life) project, Himmler's plan for 'creating a twentieth-century race of janissaries by kidnapping "Nordic" children from non-German areas …' The Nazis rounded up thousands of children even during their retreat through Russia and Poland at the end of the war.[51] The second came from the minutes of a board meeting held at Berlin's *Zoologische-Garten* on 15 May 1942. Heck announced that during a business trip to the Polish-Belarusian border he had collected six young White Russian workers from *Urwald Bialowies*.[52] Although these documents are not conclusive, they highlight Heck's role in transforming Białowieźa into an Aryanized reservation.

---

48 Samojlik, 'The brown bear', p. 68.
49 Heck, 'Hermann Göring', pp. 154–157.
50 Uekoetter, *The Green and the Brown*, p. 160.
51 Robert Lewis Koehl, *RKFDV: German Resettlement and Population Policy 1933–1945*, (Cambridge Mass., 1957), p. 219
52 Monika Schmidt, '"Heute haben Sie wieder eine Carla im Zoo" Der Berliner Zoologische Garten und seine jüdischen Aktionäre,' in Hans Frädrich und Heinz-Georg Klös, Bongo, *Beitrage zur Tiergärtnerei und Jahresberichte aus dem Zoo Berlin*, Jahrgang 158, Band 32, 2002, p. 87.

4. *Bandenbekämpfung* in the 'Home Forces Area'

On 18 August, Hitler signed *Führer Directive 46: Richtlinien für die verstärkte Bekämpfung des Bandenunwesens im Osten* (Instructions for Intensified Action against banditry in the East).[1] Under the clause — 'auxiliary and other forces' — the Directive was quite specific:

> The arming of the *Reichsarbeitsdienst* [Reich Labour Service], *Eisenbahntruppen* [railwaymen security troops], *Reichsforstamt* [RFA], agricultural overseers, etc., will, where required, be improved. They should be able to defend themselves with the most effective weapons available ...

The directive placed a particular onus on Göring to redeploy units in the east:

> The Luftwaffe, the mobilisation of the *Reichsforstamt* and the Luftwaffe field forces. Commander-in-Chief Luftwaffe will arrange for the transfer of Luftwaffe establishments to the areas threatened by bandits, in order to reinforce the garrisons in the Eastern territories.[2]

The *Heimatkriegsgebiet* or Home Forces Area represented the Wehrmacht's national military territorial structure from 1 August 1942. Bezirk Bialystok had been annexed into the Greater German Reich. Göring's position as Hitler's deputy made him responsible for nation-building and securing the frontiers. Although not written specifically, it could be assumed Göring was responsible for the prosecution of Bandenbekämpfung in *Urwald Bialowies*. In this context, at 11.00 am, 2 July 1942, Himmler arrived in Rominten for meetings with Göring.[3] In the days that followed, Scherping met Koch on 5 July to raise money for the *Reichsjagdgebiet*,[4] but also to inform him

---

1 Blood, *Hitler's Bandit Hunters*, p. 70–80. NARA, RG242, T175/140/2668141-355, Weisung Nr. 46: Richtlinien für die verstärkte Bekämpfung des Bandenunwesens im Osten, Der Führer, OKW/WFSt/Op. Nr. 002821/42g.K., Führerhauptquartier, 18 August 1942.
2 Blood, 'Bandenbekämpfung', PhD, p. 288.
3 Peter Witte et al (Hrg), *Der Dienstkalender Heinrich Himmlers 1941/42*. (Hamburg, 1999), p. 476.
4 Rubner, *Deutsche Forstgeschichte*, pp. 190–195.

about the forthcoming security arrangements in Białowieża. A week after the Göring-Himmler meetings, the Luftwaffe mustered and dispatched a security battalion to *Urwald Bialowies*. This encouraged the partisans to greater incursions believing the Germans were overstretched. Himmler began preparations for *Unternehmen Wisent* (Operation Bison) from 1 September to 15 October 1942, to counter the intensified insurgency in *Bezirk Bialystok*.[5] On 7 August, Himmler issued instructions for *Unternehmen Wisent* to be coordinated from Fromm's offices at SSPF-Bialystok.[6] The operation was synchronised with *Unternehmen Sumpfieber*, a larger operation that was set to start on 15 August in the Belarus area. Himmler placed a dual command in the field, with *Order Police-Generalmajor* Müller, and HSSPF-Ukraine Hans-Adolf Prützmann. *Wisent* was a blockade action running along the eastern borders of *Bezirk Bialystok*, Belarus and Ukraine. All local Wehrmacht and the SS-Police forces were assigned military or security tasks. The forces committed to *Operation Sumpffieber* were expected to drive the partisans, forcing them into fighting or flight. This was a common tactic and was based upon the *Treibjagd* (partridge drive), where the partisans were forced from *Sumpffieber* to run headlong into the prepared positions of *Wisent*. The heightened security level led to a near absence of documents. The barest of details remain with no final report. Christian Gerlach estimated 350 people were killed during this operation.[7] *Unternehmen Wisent* officially ended on 15 October 1942.[8]

From reading the original evidence, it quickly became apparent that the Wehrmacht was unable to conduct security operations

---

5 Nuremberg document, NO-1667, Der Reichsführer-SS, Kommando Abt Ia Tgb Nr. Ia 490/42 g.Kdos, Unterdrückund der Bandentätigkeit in Regierungsbezirk Bialystok, 7. 8. 1942. 'Wisent' – Prützmann, SS-Brigadeführer und Generalmajor der Polizei Müller. I would like to thank Dr. Nicholas Terry for a copy of this order.
6 Gerlach, *Kalkulierte Morde*, p. 933.
7 Ibid., p. 935.
8 IMT, NO-1667, Der Reichsführer-SS, Kommando Abt Ia Tgb Nr. Ia 490/42 g.Kdos, Unterdrückund der Bandentätigkeit in Regierungsbezirk Bialystok, 7.8. 1942. 'Wisent' – Prützmann, SS-Brigadeführer und Generalmajor der Polizei Müller.

within the parameters of its guidelines on occupation. However, *Bandenbekämpfung* was not a bureaucratic reclassification of anti-partisan warfare without consequences. On the contrary, in practice, it vilified opponents, placed civilians under suspicion, and rendered them defenceless to or from exemplary punishment. The application of *Bandenbekämpfung* was relatively easy and ideologically inexpensive. As a result, all parts of the German armed forces could apply it. This has not stopped military historians perpetuating the myth of *Partisanenbekämpfung* or anti-partisan warfare. The last vestiges of German Army *Partisanenbekämpfung* as the standard dogma ended in May 1942.[9] Instead, military historians have inadvertently perpetuated the idea of the 'clean Wehrmacht'. As a consequence, military historians have licensed an interpretation of counterinsurgency that focuses on the conventional forces against insurgency rather than recognise *Bandenbekämpfung's* deeper genocidal implications. Thus, Cold War interpretations of counterinsurgency have downplayed coercion and focused on protecting the population from the insurgent. This unwillingness to engage with the brutal reality of *Bandenbekämpfung* has undermined their arguments and led more critical scholars to expose the linkages between counterinsurgency, colonialism and the politics of terror. Given the evidence, any temptation to dismiss the evidence *Bandenbekämpfung* as simply another form of anti-partisan warfare is no longer credible. In Germany, *Bandenbekämpfung's* evolution came from the forester's battles with poaching and banditry, was radicalised within Imperial Germany's colonies, and was extended into the German way of war from 1870. By 1942, however, *Bandenbekämpfung* had been radicalised by the Nazis and became their sole method of security warfare. This chapter will examine how the Luftwaffe responded in the first few months of Hitler's directive.[10]

---

9   Boog et al, Jürgen Förster, 'Securing 'Living Space',' *Germany and the Second World War*, volume 4, (Oxford, 1998), pp. 1224–1225.
10   Blood, *Hitler's Bandit Hunters*, passim.

I. Rude arrival

Luftgau I (air district) was the Luftwaffe's home command for East Prussia and *Bezirk Bialystok* in 1942. This office was established in Königsberg to administer all *Luftwaffe* interests in parallel to the army's *Wehrkreis* on 1 August 1938. From 21 January 1941 to August 1943 the *Luftgau* was commanded by Lw.Lieutenant General Richard Putzier. The prevailing regulations (1938) made *Luftgau I* responsible for all flying and ground organisations, local fighter forces, all flak installations and command, all reporting and bureaucracy, air defence, and supply and administration (including flying schools and rear area detachments). The catchment area of *Luftgau I* was extended to include Bialystok and Białowieża in July 1941. Five days after the Göring-Himmler meeting, *Luftgau 1* issued command order No.506/42, on 7 July 1942, mustering *Sicherungsbataillon der Luftwaffe Bialowies* (hereafter referred to as LWSB). The opening entry of the LWSB's *Kriegstagebuch* (war diary) confirmed the order although no copies have survived. The battalion was assigned the *Feldpost* number L49006 in Königsberg and was administered as a home garrison unit.[11] The war diary has a subsequent entry (18 July) that recorded the arrival of the first cadre and the stockpiling supplies at depots in the Rominten, nearby Göring's hunting lodge.[12]

On 19 July, the diary recorded the inclusion of a command staff and two companies quartered in Gerdauen (today: Schelesnodoroschny in Oblast Kaliningrad, Russian Federation). The battalion continued equipping for a further three days. The troops received the basic items, but there were shortages especially rank and file clothing and equipment. The motor vehicles were in poor mechanical condition. The assigned drivers lacked experience with heavy vehicles. The battalion's efforts to make good ran out of time. On 22 July, the LWSB was declared operational. On paper, the

---

11 The documents in the DDSt record the battalion was activated on 27 July 1942.
12 Tessin, *Verbände und Truppen*, ibid., p. 56. According to Tessin there was virtually no Luftwaffe presence in Bezirk Bialystok before 1944.

battalion had five officers, twenty-seven NCOs and 209 ORs. The transfer to Białowieźa was arranged for 9.18 am on 22 July. This was abandoned when the railway trains failed to arrive. By that stage of the war, troop convoys no longer received priority transport, especially in home district transfers. An *ad hoc* motor truck convoy was assembled and at 10.25 am the battalion set off for its destination. Truck travel in the 1940s was slow and exceedingly uncomfortable. Depending upon the seating arrangements, soldiers either sat side-by-side or back-to-back on wooden benches and their cumbersome personal equipment piled at their feet. Bucket latrines, light rations and slow progress are the usual recollections of veterans. Officers were only slightly better off travelling in their uncomfortable and squat command cars. The convoy had to take long breaks, mostly because the vehicles required continual maintenance. The convoy arrived in Prostki (written as Prostkeu) at 5.20 pm and set off again at 8.00 pm. They arrived in Bialystok at 2.00 am on 23 July and rested until 6.30 pm. They arrived in Czernanka (unknown) at 9.00 pm and rested.[13] The convoy set off for Hajnówka at 12.25 pm on 24 July and arrived at 10.15 am. Following the same route now takes about four to six hours, driving at an average speed over metalled roads. The war diary poignantly declared, 'We have no information about the task of the battalion.'

    The LWSB arrived in Hajnówka, the battalion was 'greeted' by Major Manfred von Kobylinski. He informed them they had been re-assigned to his command and Wehrmachtkommandantur Bialowies. They learned, to their surprise, that the mission was to combat partisans in Białowieźa forest. This may have been a case of miscommunication. It is probable Kobylinski had been receiving recruits for operational field training. Being a Home Forces Area, Kobylinski was receiving troops from Wehrkreis 1 for conversion training to the infantry. The army was also bound by Hitler's directive, this incident reveals how far training and security had been institutionalized. Kobylinski divided the battalion into two parts:

---

13 Probably Czerwonka and another indication the troops were not familiar with the area or the directions.

the first company was ordered to remain in Hajnówka and Lw.Lieutenant Zanke, in temporary command, was sent to Białowieża town with the second company and headquarters troops. The convoy finally arrived in Białowieża at 9.00 pm. Zanke was informed by RFA officials that the battalion was under the command of Ortskommandanten Bialowies in direct contradiction to Kobylinski. The battalion headquarters were housed in Schloss Bialowies while the second company was assigned quarters in an abandoned school. The quarters had been 'prepared by an army bicycle squadron' that was being transferred out. The reaction to the mission was shock. The war diary contained a short entry: the 'fighting contingent' believed they were neither sufficiently trained nor properly equipped for the mission. A battalion clerk observed, 'What rifles the battalion has received? Belgium Luftgewehre, Modell 89. These weapons are unsuitable for combat in a forest because they are too long with their fixed bayonets.' The battalion had not received spare barrels for its MG 08/15 machine guns, there were no signal flare pistols, no compasses, and no field glasses. They had been issued with only limited ammunition, the recommended amount for march/convoy security. The only comment about Kobylinski was a short entry, 'the first company, in Hajnówka, is no longer under the battalion but under the command of Wehrmachtskommandantur Bialowies.' A request was issued to exchange the Belgian rifles for the standard-issue Mauser K98 carbine and replace the vehicles for the Kübelwagen (jeep type vehicle). The war diary reiterated the inadequate preparation and training for their mission. The deployment of the battalion by Kobylinski, in relation to all the other security forces was mapped, see GIS map 5.

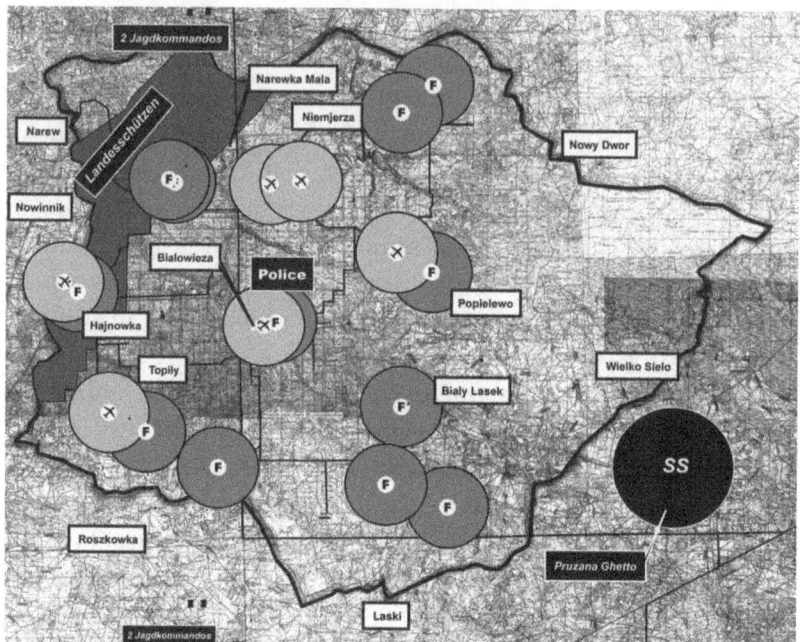

GIS Map 5: the Kobylinski deployment
Major Manfred von Kobylinski briefly took command of the LWSB when it first arrived and Białowieża was crowded with security forces.
Legend: symbols in the centre of the circles, or roundels, represent the formations — 'an aircraft' in the lighter grey circles are the LWSB; 'F' in the darker shades of the grey circle is the FSK platoons. The army's reservists (Landesschützen), the SS and the police gendarmerie are also included.

The LWSB's first deployment in the forest was the evening 25–26 July. The diary recorded a day of 'firsts': the first 'employment of the first platoon with two squads from the second platoon' in their first patrols. The squads and patrols were not organised along the usual military lines with a squad leader, light machine gun, and rifles. They were *ad hoc* police styled rifle squads. This was a feature of the small-unit tactics until the final days of the deployment. The troops took up positions in two *Partisanenwechsel*, a known partisan crossing point in an area of open ground within the forest. The term originated from hunting, a *Wildwechsel* (game crossing), a place that was the known for passing game that hunter's exploit. From 7.00 pm until the next morning troops mounted patrols following three sets of paths known to be used by partisans but there were no incidents. The first engagement was on the evening 27–28 July 1942. Earlier that day Kobylinski issued an *Einsatzbefehl* (operational order) to the second company to deploy *Feldwachen* (pickets). Nine picket positions were assigned to three road bridges; the railway bridge over the Narewka River near Kosy-Most; three road junctions; and two crossing points in the forest. A position at *Jagen* 170/120, where two *Jagen* crossed designated as a *Banditenwechsel* (conforming to Himmler's mantra).[14] The troops travelled from Stoczek by special train on the forest railway, prepared in advance by the *Reichsjagdverwaltung* (hunting bureau) at 4.00 pm.[15] Three Polish foresters joined the train at Konczik to guide the troops to their positions. The troops brought two translators to coordinate communication between the picket commander and the Polish guides. The operation was expected to terminate at 8.00 am on 28 July. The train and its crew remained in position, under guard, and were to return with the troops the next morning. The exercise turned into a calamity:

> Mission: following the operational order of the *Wehrmachtkommandantur Bialowies*. A section fired at three partisans who did not answer the fire. A second group exchanged fire with partisans. Aircraftsman K** received a straight shot through the right side of his arse. The private walked into the friendly fire of a machine gunner and was shot. The machine gunner was not responsible.[16]

Kobylinski issued fresh orders on 28 July. A second company platoon was set to depart from Stoczek at 2.00 pm bound for Czolo. They were greeted by *Oberförster* Kaiser from Zamosze, about two kilometres west of Czolo, and arranged quarters. The platoon was expected to remain in the Zamosze area until 1 August. A train was arranged with the crew ordered to remain with the platoon, and

---

14 The *Banditenwechsel* later became the site of a gallows for exemplary executions and public warnings.
15 The LWSB war diary and Herbst's reports didn't distinguish between *Oberforstamt Bialowies*, *Reichsjagdgebiet* or *Reichsforstgebiet*.
16 BArch, RL 31/2, document 2. Wehrmacht-kommandantur Bialowies Tgb.Nr 676/42, An 2. Kompanie Sicherungsbataillon d. Lw Bialowies, 27 July 1942.

four squads assigned to guard duty.[17] *Oberförster* Kaiser was determined to conduct patrols day and night and brought in local foresters to act as guides.[18] Kobylinski also ordered an NCO to lead a squad to guard an *Oberforstamt's* estate in Popielewo.[19] He issued more orders for the evening 29–30 July, assigning the second platoon (second company) to the Czolo area. They dispersed into three picket positions. The first contact with partisans occurred at 11.00 pm and skirmishes lasted until 5.40 am. Another post became engaged in a fifteen-minute firefight at 3.15am. The third post was involved in a gun battle from 3.45-to-4.15am. Elsewhere seven partisans attacked and looted a gamekeeper's house in *Jagen* 25. The gamekeeper's wife and daughter were forced to flee into the forest. In Lipiny nine partisans broke into the gamekeeper's house at 11.00 pm. They threatened the gamekeeper for food. They wore a mix of Soviet uniforms and civilian clothing. There were several other incidents and sightings of roving partisan bands.

The Luftwaffe's overall cohesion was restored when Lw.Major of Reserve Emil Herbst arrived in Białowieża. His first report from 6 August confirmed, 'I arrived in Bialowies on 29 July 1942, after discussing the order of battle of the battalion with the quartermaster-general of *Luftgaukommando I Königsberg.*'[20] Herbst's appointment came directly from Göring and there are indications he visited Carinhall to receive his orders personally. Herbst's success was dependent upon his relationship to Lw.Colonel Bernd von Brauchitsch, Göring's adjutant.[21] Herbst was determined to restore control over the first company. The second company, quartered in a Białowieża school, was re-assigned to permanently securing the

---

17   The train remained with the troops possibly because, without radios, in the event of a large attack it was the only means of escape and to warn headquarters.

18   There is no list of names of collaborators employed by the Germans, they only referred to national status.

19   BArch, RL 31/2, document 3, Wehrmacht-kommandantur Bialowies Tgb.Nr 686/42, An des Lw.Sicherung-Batl. z.b.V. Bialowies, 29 July 1942.

20   According to Ripperger et al., *Der Traum Vom Urwald*, p. 292, Herbst alleged after the war that he received his orders from Göring at Carinhall but his own situation reports seem to contradict him.

21   BArch, RL 31/3, Kriegstagebuch LWSB, 6 August 1942.

Czolo-Zamosche and Popielewo areas. The battalion staff company (two officers, three NCOs and fifty-one ORs) was stationed in Białowieża. Herbst assessed the staffs as largely unfit for operational duty due to 'physical shortcomings and insufficient intellectual dexterity'. He was aware the battalion had been allocated a third company, with more armaments, better equipment and set to arrive in due course. Herbst attributed the friendly fire incidents to the troops' lack of training and inadequate equipment. *Luftgau I* accepted Herbst's demands for replacements and equipment, especially ammunition. On 30 July, the battalion staff completed a transfer into the Tsar's hunting palace, while the RFA's *Oberforstamt* moved into the adjacent administrative buildings. An NCO and five ORs were sent to an outpost in Topiło, a similar-sized group was assigned to escort duties for the district forester of Hajnówka. A picket, with a two-day overlapping shift, was assigned to both companies to guard the forest railway at Sorje, and the neighbouring turpentine distillation complex. These pickets were caught in a firefight that lasted ten minutes without casualties.[22]

The next day (31 July) there were more skirmishes. At 4.45 am two firefights erupted both lasting thirty minutes. The strength of the partisans was estimated at twenty men per band. The troops identified two machine guns among the partisan's firepower. A subsequent search of the area at 5.30 am found no traces of the band. The battalion scribes noted that the partisans were using German carbines and pointedly remarked that 'a G-2 bullet had hit the casing of a machine gun, which was extracted and identified.' There was a sour comparison, 'our troops still have to fight with their Belgium rifles.' At 11.00 am up to thirty partisans crossed the railway track at *Jagen* 471/472 moving towards the south. The partisans were thought to be heading for the gamekeeper's house in Podzerkow seeking shelter from the heavy rain. The LWSB deployed to box them in, and elements from the second company were sent to lush them out but were unsuccessful. Troops from the first platoon

---

22   BArch, RL 31/3, document 2, report 1, period to 6.8.42, Major Herbst, 6 August 1942.

drove a truck beside the hunter's shooting stands and advanced north via Podzerkow following the forest railway between *Jagen* 523 and 524. At 3.00 pm inhabitants of Budy observed three armed partisans on the move. A squad was immediately sent out to intercept them but failed. At 6.30 pm second platoon (second company) reoccupied its earlier positions near Sorje railway station. They had contact with partisans at 10.00pm, and an intensive firefight opened at 10.30 pm and lasted until 6.10am when the partisans withdrew. Herbst reassessed the situation and reported his findings to Brauchitsch. In his first report, he explained that the LWSB's arrival had triggered intense partisan activity. He explained the fighting on 27-31 July in the northern area, around the Czolo-Zamosze outpost, was under constant attack. A particularly aggressive attack during the evening of 31 July led to several partisans being severely wounded, but they made good their escape. A dead partisan, left behind by the band, was found lying in front of the German firing positions.[23]

II. Turf war

Torrid tales of rivalry fills the narrative of histories about the Nazis. The sub-plots that underpinned everyday life in the regime could spark serious rivalries. Białowieźa was no exception. The problem, however, is how to explain the squabbles that emerged in August-September 1942. Hitler's Bandenbekämpfung directive contained both specific and vague instructions. The German Army was responsible for the front line/operational areas. The SS-Police was given overall control in the Reich Commissars in the east (*Ostland*, Ukraine etc); the army and SS were expected to work in close cooperation. The army was to transfer two replacement divisions in the General-Government of Poland when it became a Home Forces Area and all ancillary formations were to transfer from the General-Government to Ukraine. Five army replacement divisions were to be transferred to the Ukraine and *Ostland* (Baltic territories). The *Heimatkriegsgebiet* or Home Forces Area was not mentioned in the

---

23   Ibid.

directive, in effect, *Bezirk Bialystok* remained under German jurisdiction of the army, party, SS, Luftwaffe, RFA etc. Göring was instructed to transfer all formations to reinforce garrisons in the 'eastern territories'.[24]

Since the summer of 1941, the army had lodged claims on Białowieża. The army had been combating partisans in the forest for over a year. It is possible the army was making claims through its security operations because there was no other rival force. When the LWSB first arrived in Białowieża it's probable the army assumed they were recruits for conversion, but it's equally possible Kobylinski was initiating a stand on behalf of the army. Herbst from the outset took the stance he was in a turf war, but it's likely he was primed. Before arriving in the forest he had met Göring, in private, and was granted the personal authority to act in the name of the *Reichsmarschall*. Little is known about Herbst. He was born in Cuxhaven, and in the 1930s was a Bremen-based business director. Before his assignment to Białowieża, he was serving in the German occupation of Bosnia.[25] Perhaps his selection was orchestrated by Göring because Herbst adopted a pseudo-managerial stance, typical of boardroom battles rather than local garrison politics. He set forth on two priorities: to resolve the 'difficulties' with rivals by neutralising them; and counter the partisans with the utmost ferocity, while terrorising the civilian communities into passivity. His opening letter was brusque, to Göring's headquarters about the serious lack of cooperation from other security forces noting 'there is little support for the LWSB or the tasks it was to undertake.'[26]

---

24 Blood, *Hitler's Bandit Hunters*, p. 70–80.
25 Gautschi, *Reichsjägermeister*, p. 218; Ripperger et al, *Der Traum vom Urwald*, p. 292. They claim Herbst was commander of Fliegerabteilung der Kampfgruppe Westbosnien, which was combatting Tito's partisans. See Ben Shepherd, *Terror in the Balkans: German Armies and Partisan Warfare*, (Cambridge, 2012), pp. 161–235. Shepherd has comprehensively explained how the Bosnian occupation was dominated by German atrocities against civilians and especially Jews.
26 BArch, RL 31/3, document 2, report 1, period to 6.8.42, Major Herbst, 6 August 1942.

Herbst then set about using the LWSB's poor performance to expose leadership Kobylinski's failings. This was ruthless politics, leveraging the calamitous performance of the period 27/28/29 July to expose his opponent. Herbst quite literally used the death of soldiers to hammer his rival. He opened with the case of Corporal W** mistakenly named Aircraftsman K** in the war diary. Corporal W** had wandered from his position, against repeatedly being ordered to stay put. At 5.00 am a machine gunner noticed movement in the bushes to his front and shouted for the parole or password. There was no reply. A rifle appeared to rise from behind a bush, the machine-gunner opened fire and Corporal W** was dead. Under normal conditions, this might have reflected badly against the Luftwaffe promotions board, for promoting an inept corporal. There was a second incident, not in the diary, but mentioned in Herbst's report and referred to as Private R**. On the evening of 28/29 July 1942, Private R** was on outpost guard duty. He was warned that a nearby house quartered forest employees. He was instructed under no circumstances were the guards or anyone else allowed to shoot in the general direction of the house. At 1.00 am a skirmish erupted. The district forester, accompanied by another forester, ran from the house towards the outposts while shouting the password. Private R**, scared witless, missed the password and began firing towards the house. He shot and severely wounded the district forester in the upper thigh. An investigation recommended Private R**'s immediate transfer on grounds of mental incapacity. Private R** was previously relieved from a medical unit owing to his unsuitability for service. Herbst followed textbook methods and introduced a training schedule for all troops, which was another albeit indirect swipe at Kobylinski for failing to appreciate the weaknesses of the troops. He astutely claimed over hasty mustering would be resolved through strong leadership.[27] Herbst had combined managerial posturing with textbook military culture in a devastating takedown of a political rival.

---

27 Ibid.

Kobylinski, considerably weakened, was forced to defend himself against the accusation of poor leadership, failing to comprehend the condition of the troops, and reckless endangerment of the troops. Meanwhile, Herbst reorganized the battalion, as illustrated in GIS map 6, with the main axis in the upper half of the Białowieża, where the main RFA assets were concentrated. Herbst also reported on his relationship with other security services within the Białowieża arena. He sent a telegram, either to Brauchitsch or *Luftgau I*, with the request to be granted authorisation to establish a uniform chain of command throughout the forest. He made overtures to *Generalmajor* Nolte and *SS-Standartenführer Fromm*, SSPF-Bialystok.[28] Fromm responded unfavourably, claiming that he alone was responsible for the civil jurisdiction of the forest. However, he acceded to Herbst's authority from Göring, and offered 'collegial cooperation and cooperative solutions to all questions'.[29] Herbst had presented himself as Göring's man while suggesting he was a team player. Herbst the team player didn't last long. On 15 August 1942, he reported a *Landesschützen* patrol in *Jagen* 275 had killed a bear without authority. Herbst also accused another army *Jagdkommando* of shooting forest predators, 'we have a report in which a *Jagdkommando* patrol confirmed that they had not shot at partisans, but at a wolf. Afterwards, the troops received eggs, dripping, and honey as evidence for the success of their enterprise.'[30] In blaming the army for interfering in a natural experiment, Herbst was able to expose their actions as vandalising Nazi culture.

---

28 Tessin, *Verbände und Truppen*, Zehnter Band, p. 223. The division was based in Bialystok and included three reserve infantry regiments (each with three battalions) based in Modlin, Bialystok and Allenstein (East Prussia).
29 BArch, RL 31/3, document 2, report 1, period 27.7–6.8.42, Major Herbst, 6 August 1942.
30 BArch, RL 31/3, document 2, report 2, period 6.8–17.8.42, Major Herbst, 17 August 1942.

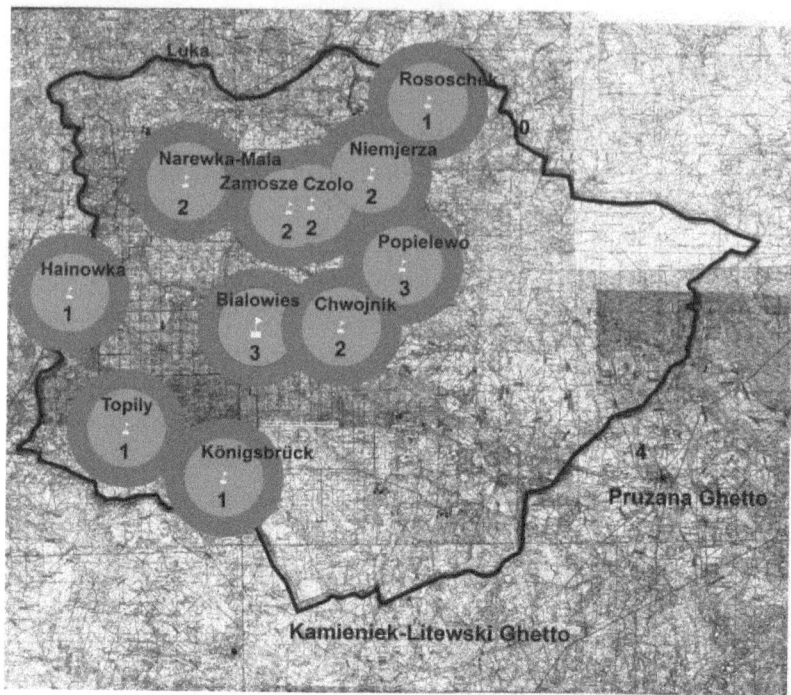

GIS Map 6: LWSB strongpoints – 6 August 1942[31]

This map depicts the LWSB's first temporary phase of operations (July–October 1942); changes to the size and deployment were already in preparation when these positions were being arranged. The circles represent the layers of patrols. The radius was staggered at 500 metres, 4 kilometres and 12 kilometres. This deployment would change as more companies arrived. The crucial point is the hunter's maxim that a good position determines the success of the hunt.

On 17 August, Herbst issued a report and once again raised the command issue: 'Successful combat against the partisans in the forest area could only be guaranteed if a unified command was granted authority over all the forces in Białowieźa.'[32] This time Herbst named and shamed General Hans-Erich Nolte (commander Army Division z.b.V., Bialystok) as well as Kobylinski and Fromm

---

[31] The strong points at this stage indicate how concentrated the battalion was to the western side of the forest and little association to the ghettoes administered by the SS-Police.

[32] BArch, RL 31/3, document 4, report 2, period 6.8–17.8.42, Major Herbst, 17 August 1942.

for their complete lack of cooperation. According to Herbst, Fromm and Nolte believed they commanded all forest security forces. Fromm was adamant the forest area was under the command of the civil administration and challenged Herbst's authority regardless of Göring's backing. Nolte argued Göring had no authority in Białowieża and claimed the army high command was the governing authority. Herbst advised that neither the SS-Police nor the army had assigned the forces necessary to impose law and order. He recommended a state of emergency (martial law) be declared, to reinforce the LWSB with more troops, and dispense with all cooperation with the army and police, 'which is any way without any practical value.' Herbst then wrote to Fromm with intelligence for his 'SS colleague' about the black-market activities in Bezirk Bialystok. This was another calculated move, using full letter headed paper to reinforce his status as 'Battalion commander and Plenipotentiary for the Reichsmarschall in Urwald Bialowies'. Göring's authority was advertised in the paper trail and distribution lists. The letter was bureaucratic style divide and rule, all 'stick and carrot'. He sharply criticised the army and civil servants in Bialystok for profiteering from black markets but offered the carrot of cooperation to the SS.[33] The allegations not only exposed the lax discipline of the army but there was also a mild rebuke of SS-Police suggesting they clean up their backyard before venturing into 'his' forest.

The turf war was interrupted when Herbst was informed, he was to participate in *Aktion Reinhard,* the Nazi plan for the destruction of Polish Jewry. On 19 July 1942, Himmler issued an order to Krüger *HSSPF-GG-Poland* to accelerate the extermination process, with a completion date set for 31 December 1942.[34] All armed forces in the connected regions were included in the distribution of this general order. In Herbst's third report, he discussed a face-to-face meeting with *Generalmajor* Müller in Bialystok where he was informed of Himmler's confidential order to conduct a *Sonderaktion*

---

33 BArch, RL 31/3, document 8, letter Major Herbst to SS-Standartenführer Fromm, 17 August 1942.
34 Christian Gerlach, *Krieg, Ernährung, Völkermord: Forschungen zur deutschen Vernichtungspolitik im Zweiten Weltkrieg,* (Hamburg, 1998), pp. 205–206.

(special actions) in the *Ostgebiet* (Ukraine, Byelorussia and Bialystok) against the partisans. This was an extension of *Unternehmen Wisent*, extended into *Aktion Reinhard*. He was informed that all actions and operations were being coordinated between the *HSSPF-Ostland* under *SS-Obergruppenführer* Jeckeln; and *HSSPF-Nordost and Ukraine* under *SS-Obergruppenführer* Heinz Prützmann, the chief of SS operations in the Ukraine and *Bezirk Bialystok*. This was planned to begin on 1 September, and the LWSB was assigned to the blocking role on the eastern perimeter of the forest. Specifically, to close all roads, and prevent and Jews from escaping the cordons.[35]

During Herbst's meeting with *Generalmajor* Müller, on 20 August 1942, they discussed the progress of *Aktion Reinhard*. An indication of this can be found in a copy of the letter from the Chief of Staff of *Luftgau I*, which confirmed that Herbst had met with Müller on that day. The wording of the letter was unusual since the content referred to clause 11 of an order that stated: 'The OKW instructs all Wehrmacht commanders to take over blockades and security tasks to such an extent, as the military security tasks allow it. The chain of command is with the HSSPF.' In *Bandenbekämpfung* doctrine, institutional authority for the rear areas was automatically placed under the SS. The inclusion of this clause points to a different purpose. The letter indicates Herbst had requested official confirmation that the LWSB was assigned to assist SS operations. Besides, there was confirmation that Bialystok had been placed under the overall command of *SS-Obergruppenführer* Heinz Prützmann, which was verbally conveyed to Herbst by Müller. These exchanges included a reference that Müller had met the commander of *Army Division z.b.V., Bialystok,* on 25 August, to discuss 'agreements and cooperation.' The army had assumed the division came under Byelorussia, Ukraine, or even under General-Government of Poland. In every way, the army was reluctant to serve under SS command in *Bezirk Bialystok*.[36]

---

35 BArch, RL 31/3, document 12–13, report 3, period 18–31.8.1942, Major Herbst, 17 August 1942.
36 BArch, RL 31/3, document 21, Abschrift von Abschrift, Chef d. Stabes Luftgau I, 27 August 1942.

Without any prior warnings, on 22 August, the army announced their absolute claim over Białowieża. The was no explanation other than Major Wittke, the commander of *Landesschützenbataillon 238*, wrote to inform Kobylinski of his operational sectors and tactical boundaries, included in his operational orders.[37] Wittke's units patrolled the area either side of the forest railway and covered at least 26 *Jagen* (roughly 28 square kilometres) as well as the towns of Narewka Mala, Niklaszewo, and Olchowka, Borowiki, and Siemienniakowszczyzna in the east, and the *Jagen* on both sides of the River Narew.[38] Kobylinski forwarded copies to Herbst, to the commander of SS-Police Regiment 2, to the RFA, and to the FSK. He claimed the area north and south was not patrolled because of 'the demands placed on the battalion.'[39] In effect, the army had prioritised the RFA authority to within its full operational scope and expected the LWSB and SS-Police to fill the gaps. Two days later, *Oberfoster* Krause wrote to Scherping in Berlin about the growing tensions and lack of unified command:

> For some weeks a security battalion of the Luftwaffe has been placed in Urwald Bialowies under the leadership of Herr Major Herbst. He is under the direct command and has extensive authority from the Herr *Reichsmarschall*, to provide overall protection in the forest. He should attempt to bring the military and the civilian services into working together.
> However, in reality, there is an undercurrent of confusion because, alongside the Luftwaffe, there are police, Landesschützen, Reichsbahn security troops, individual army Jagdkommando, and a bicycle squadron etc. The employment of these units is in principle positive; the Jagdkommandos and the bicycle squadron did particularly well. It is, however, regrettable that there is no unified chain of command for these units. There are daily incidents.
> The Police, for example, enter the middle of the forest without the Luftwaffe being informed. This is a completely unacceptable condition. The RFA does not know anything about the commitment of this police battalion, and I only

---

37 Tessin, *Verbände und Truppen*, Achter Band, p. 170. The Landesschützenbataillon 238 had been a border guard unit until September 1939, in Gumbinnen and later in 1941 a guard unit for PoWs. It was eventually destroyed in fighting the Red Army near Warsaw in January 1945.

38 BArch, RL 31/3, document 17, Landesschützen Bataillon 238, Tgb.No.1o37/42, Major Wittke, 22 August 1942.

39 BArch, RL 31/3, document 16, Wehrmachtkommandantur Bialowies, Tab.No.772/42, Major von Kobylinski, 24 August 1942.

got to know by accident that police pickets are set up in the middle of the forest. There are no thoughts of effectively combating the bandits in this chaos. Apart from the fact that it's only a miracle that different units, when partly camouflaged, are prevented from fighting each other.

As a consequence, I ask the responsible administration to clarify the chain of command in *Urwald Bialowies*. It is absolutely necessary that the bandit fight in the primaeval forest is directed by a single administration. The military and police authority not only in the primaeval forest but also in the border areas must be assigned to this administration because these areas are included in the overall fight against the bandit.[40]

Although there is no known reply, the content stirred a reaction from Göring. What happened is reconstructed from subsequent reports.[41] Herbst was requested to attend *Luftgau I* in Königsberg on or around 26–27 August 1942. He received the copy of a telegram (Br. B.Nr. 932/42 Secret 26 August 1942) sent by Brauchitsch to Fromm, Nolte and Kobylinski with a list of questions they had to address. The responses:

> First question: 'what was the mission of the Landesschützen and the police battalion; and was their mission confined exclusively to the Białowieża area?'
>
> Answer: 'In and around Urwald Bialowies the Landesschützen are employed in securing the Hajnówka-Wolkowysk railway line. In an agreement with Major Herbst they are also to secure an area north-west and five kilometres south-east that are part of the forest.'
>
> The second question: 'what is their present mission and deployment?'
>
> Answer: 'the army is combating bandits inside and beyond the forest borders. Inside the forest in cooperation with Major Herbst.' Four police battalions operating in the Bialystok and forest area, are committed to pacification duties, and 'The commander of the East Prussia Order Police employs these battalions depending on the situation.'
>
> Third question: 'what are the consequences for the LWSB of implementing a state of emergency in the forest?'
>
> Answer: 'The state of emergency is practically permanent. The native population is not allowed to leave their houses at night. They are arrested or shot if they try to flee.'

---

40 BArch, RL 31/3, document 15, Krause zu Reichsjägermeister, Leitung des Staatsreviers Berlin, Bekämpfung der Banden im Oberforstamt, 24 August 1942.

41 BArch, RL 31/3, document 13, report 3, period 18–31.8.42, Major Herbst, 31 August 1942. BArch, RL31/3, document 14, Luftgaukommando I, Königsberg/Pr./, den 27. Aug.42, Chief of the staff, Führungsgruppe Ia Nr./42 secret, Betr: Auftrag Major Herbst – Fragen des Chef-Adjutanten, Stabsamt of the Reichsmarschall No. 932/42, Chef des Stabes Luftgau I, 27 August 1942.

Summary: the public declaration of a state of emergency would have little impact. If a state of emergency was initiated the LWSB, the RFA and Nazi officials would all fall under army control. The SSPF would be assigned to general security and public order throughout Bezirk Bialystok, but the local SS-Police forces were inadequate for large-scale missions and would require army assistance.[42]

Herbst was requested to respond to the replies as contained in a telegram (Az, 40Br.B.Nr. 78/42 – no known copy). He wrote to *Luftgau I* on 28 August: 'The reality of the situation differs from the picture as they presented'. According to Herbst's reply, the army had a dual command structure. There were units assigned by the *Stellvertretendes Generalkommando I*, in effect quartermaster units such as *Wehrmacht-Kommandantur Bialowies* and *Landesschützen Bataillon 238*. While General Nolte's *Army Division z.b.V., Bialystok* was releasing independent *Jagdkommandos* and other units to patrol the forest. Herbst had earlier met with Kobylinski and officials to clarify the army command but concluded the army's replies about cooperation were only partly correct. Herbst noted the Police Battalion was also conducting independent patrols assigned by the SS-Police command system.[43]

With the army's bluff called, Herbst began his second bureaucratic campaign to finish the job. Three days after the Q&A telegram, Herbst wrote to the commander of *Division z.b.V., Bialystok*: 'Even though the *Stellvertretendes Generalkommando I* recently confirmed to Luftgau I that units employed in the forest and perimeter areas should be willing to work in harmony with this battalion, we are sorry to say that this mutual agreement still does not exist.' He was concerned with the potential for 'collisions', those friendly-fire incidents where formations accidentally fired on each other, only 'tight cooperation between the units, which operate in the same area is necessary for preventing collisions.' Herbst also raised the case of three partisans captured during an operation against Krzywiec. The security police with a company of *Landesschützen*

---

42 Ibid.
43 BArch, RL 31/3, document 18, Anfragen des Reichsmarschalls, Az.40 Br.B.No.77/42, Major Herbst, 28 August 1942.

from Narewka Mala had carried out an action and captured the partisans. The *Wehrmacht-Bereichsstandortältesten Bielsk* had ordered the transfer of the prisoners to Białowieźa prison for interrogation.[44] Despite this order, Major Wittke had transferred the captives to a PoW camp (*Kriegsgefangenenlager*) in Bialystok.[45] Herbst complained that it was 'not the usual custom to keep bandits in a PoW camp'. He continued: 'There is now, unfortunately, the real danger that these dangerous bandits will be released', and added, 'as a consequence the commander of the *Landesschützen* was admonished and asked not to hinder the LWSB in the future.'[46]

On the last day of August 1942, the rivals withdrew. Herbst reported the army and police had withdrawn nearly all their units from the forest. Each had left behind one company, employed for the protection of the forest railway between Hajnówka and Narewka Mala. Herbst pressed the issue of two companies acting independently within his area when he wrote to Brauchitsch:

> The independence of the different units employed in Bandenbekämpfung has repeatedly been in danger of fighting each other. This danger is increased because they often operate in disguise and not in their regular uniforms. It is fortunate that to date no accidents have occurred. It is irresponsible to continue working in this way.[47]

Herbst was like a broken record but continued to press his demands for a unified command. The turf war had turned into a slugging match and only his bureaucratic stamina would succeed. He raised the stakes by calling for aggressive action against 'clearly identified, complex organisations of the bandits in the villages, towns, and border region of *Urwald Bialowies*. The pursuit of tracks, leading

---

44 Główna Komisja Badanaia Zbrodni Hitlerowskich w Polsce Rada Ochrony Pomników Walki I Męchzenstwa, Obozy hitlerowskie na ziemiach polskich 1939–1945: Informator encykloedyczny, (Warszawa, 1979), p. 99. There was a prison established in 1941 that continued in service until 1944. It seems to have served as a holding jail prior to court martials, executions or deportation.

45 Tessin, *Verbände und Truppen*, Sechzehnter Band, 'Bezirk Bialystok', p. 55. The only known camps in the Bialystok area were Stalag 57 and Stalag 316.

46 BArch, RL 31/3, document 22, An die Army Division z.b.V. Bialystok, Az.40 Br.B.No.89/42, Major Herbst, 31 August 1942.

47 BArch, RL 31/3, document 13, report 3, period 18–31.8.42, Major Herbst, 31 August 1942.

into the forest's border areas, must be continued.' He also confirmed that twenty prisoners were being held in a local prison and six were ready for sentencing by the courts-martial. He claimed there were more persons identified for arrest but could not be enforced due to the shortage of prison holding capacity, and his limited manpower.[48] In effect, Herbst was calling and recalling the army's bluff.

Success came less than a week later. On 4 September, Herbst received a letter from Kobylinski confirming he had written to the *Wehrmacht-Bereichsstandortältesten Bielsk* the day before. The *Landesschützen* were no longer permitted to conduct independent actions within the forest. They were to continue safeguarding the railway lines, carry out counteractions against the partisans, and support LWSB as and when required.[49] Further restrictions were placed on the *Landesschützen* detachments attached to the *Army Division z.b.V., Bialystok*. Regarding Wolkowysk-Hajnówka-Siemiatycze mainline railway section: they were restricted to patrols to within a 3–5 kilometres strip running either side of the railway line and defending the corridor against partisan incursions. An order stated: 'Active *Bandenbekämpfung* in the area of the *Reichsjagdgebiet* is normally only conducted in accordance with Major Herbst in Bialowies. There are no restrictions on the employment of the battalion in *Bandenbekämpfung* related actions outside the *Reichsjagdgebiet*.'[50] This was Herbst's first political success, establishing limits on the movements of the *Landesschützenbataillon 238*. In his fourth report (11 September 1942) Herbst referred to further local changes in command structures that were to his benefit. The operations officer of *Army Division z.b.V., Bialystok* later reported that the *Wehrmachtkommandantur Bialowies* was being closed. Henceforth, Kobylinski would serve as the division liaison officer working alongside the

---

48 Ibid.
49 BArch, RL 31/3, document 28, Wehrmacht-Kommandantur Abwicklungsstelle Bialowies, Tgb.U 815/42, An den Wehrmacht-Bereichsstandortältesten Bielsk, 4 September 1942.
50 BArch, RL 31/3, document 29, Divisionskommando z.b.V (Bialystok) Der Militärbeauftragte Abt. Ia Nr. 402/42 geh. Bezug: Div. Kdo. z.b.V. Abt. Ia Nr. 282/42 geh. V.7.7.42., Bialystok, 4 September 1942.

Oberforstamt Bialowies. On 5 September, Kobylinski suffered a serious loss of face, went on leave and never to return.[51]

Problems with the army lingered until 22 September, when Herbst was relentless when he wrote to Nolte about lack of cooperation. He complained that following the withdrawal, the army units had left only a liaison officer and a handful of troops for the protection of the railway line around Narewka Mala.[52] The petty bickering also continued. For five weeks Herbst had repeatedly requested the Army Division z.b.V., Bialystok, the offices of 'the Kommandanten von Bialowies', the Wehrmacht-Bereichsstandortältesten Bielsk, and the divisional liaison officer requesting the release of a small family house to quarter his troops. Herbst alleged the Landesschützen commander had finally declined to vacate the house stating: 'He would not leave his quarters for a lieutenant.' Herbst complained, 'I did not bother to report to you that this gentleman behaved like a peasant towards me because I have no time for such trivial personal quarrels.' On 21 September, an army Major told Herbst, 'Hajnówka did not fall under the area of the RFA'. Herbst complained to Nolte about how he was being treated: 'Although I am not prepared to contribute in this utter bureaucratic nonsense. For example, a private asked me yesterday over the telephone, in the name of the commander of the garrison to visit next morning at 8.00 am and provide him with exact information about the strength of my company in Hajnówka.' He added, 'I obediently ask you to set demarcation lines of the garrison of Hajnówka in such a way that the factories of the Oberforstamt and company quarters of my battalion, which is employed there, are no longer included in the garrison area [Standortgebiet] of Hajnówka.' Herbst concluded 'I would like to apologise for bothering you with these matters, which the duty posts in question could have solved on their own and with goodwill. I would like to thank you

---

51 BArch, RL 31/3, document 23, report 4, period 1.9–10.9.42, Major Herbst, 11 September 1942. BA MA, RL 31/3, document 27, Divisionskommando z.b.V (Bialystok) Der Militärbeauftragte, Abt. Ia Nr. 895/42, Bialystok, 4 September 1942.
52 BArch, RL 31/3, document 33, Major Herbst to Generalmajor Nolte, 22 September 1942.

for your benevolence and hospitality, which I experienced when I reported personally to you.'[53] The final act in the army saga came in October 1942, Nolte was promoted Lieutenant General and transferred to Stabsamt von Unruh (an economic warfare office). Army Division z.b.V. Bialystok was renamed Ersatz Divisionen Stab 461 (461st Reserve Infantry Division).[54] Herbst noted at the time, 'There was a formation change of the Army Division in Bialystok', he gloated adding incorrectly, 'It is now called "Ersatz-Divisionen 251". Nolte has moved on and his replacement is General Wenk.' Herbst added that Nolte visited Białowieża for a final meeting. The army chief of the general staff had arrived on the same day in Luftgau I for a meeting together with his operations staff officer in Białowieża.[55]

The final act in the turf war came in December 1942. Herbst was a judge in a scandal of SS internal affairs. The case of Sophie Kuryla and Fritz Krause involved crimes against the *Reichspost* (German state postal service). An arrest report detailed Sophie's interrogation and confession. She was a Belarusian, arrested following an investigation into theft from the field post office. This story began when she joined the Narewka post office as a cook in August 1942. She was engaged in a sexual relationship with Fritz Krause, her boss at the post office. Sophie explained she joined the post office with several other women including Jadwiga and Janina Kulbatzki from Miklaschewo, and Olga from Luka. Later, other girls joined the post office including Maria Marusa (previously employed by the priest of Popen) and Nadzia from Trosnaka. The girls spent the night in the post office, implying there were sexual liaisons with all the German men. After a few months, three men of the *SS-Postschutz* arrived. They spent every second night in the office

---

53 Ibid.
54 Tessin, *Verbände und Truppen*, 'Bezirk Bialystok', p. 54. In some correspondence in the files it was designated as Ersatz Division 461. Section 173, Mitcham, *Hitler's Legions*, p. 277, Keilig refers to 461 Division. Nolte was replaced by army Lieutenant-General Richard zu und von Wenk. Nolte retired from March 1943 and died in Detmold in 1964.
55 BArch, RL 31/3, document 47, report 8, period 11–21.10.1942, Major Herbst, 23 October 1942.

and the women spent the night in the men's rooms.[56] Sophie told Herbst that Karl Rodinger, a postal official, was on friendly terms with Olga. She handled a 'busy' exchange of stolen goods and sent Rodinger's ill-gotten gains back to Germany. At the end of October, Karl gave Sophie a parcel that belonged to a man called Schenka who came from Luka. The parcel contained a pullover, a dress, a blouse, a blanket and a white skirt. She handed items to Schenka's sister. Sophie admitted she had stolen two more parcels. Karl knew of this but had not interfered. She then itemized the items in the parcel including three dresses, two blouses, three skirts, a pullover, a pair of shoes and two shirts. These parcels had also been posted in Narewka and were addressed to Poles working in Germany. Maria Sobeska was also involved in the crimes but had not kept any items for herself. Sophie also accused Marusa of also stealing parcels. She claimed Rodinger had given Marusa a parcel that was addressed to a man in Luka. She was to take the parcel personally and deliver it. Under interrogation, Olga said she had lost the parcel and after a month an unnamed man had demanded two kilos of yeast in compensation for the loss. Rodinger told Sophie not to say anything and she seems to have lied to the police before finally admitting her guilt to Herbst.[57]

Herbst wrote to Fromm of his decision to arrest, postal employee Karl Rodinger, Sophie, and Alexander Luschinski (Sophie's stepbrother). He explained that investigations had shown their continual theft of parcels from the Narewka Mala post office was aggravated by the 'intolerable behaviour' — the sexual relations of SS men and Slav women. Herbst's apparent prudishness was probably an outpouring of Nazi race laws and sexual ethics bombast. It was also deeply political and directed at his rival. All postal employees in Narewka Mala were found guilty of tolerating these crimes and neglecting their duties. Rodinger confessed under interrogation that all the men of the *SS-Postschutz*, notably

---

56 BArch, RL 31/3, document 70, report 11, period 21.11–14.12.42, Major Herbst, 14 December 1942.
57 BArch, RL 31/3, document 77, letter to SS-PF Bialystok, Major Herbst, 9 December 1942.

Otto Schäfer, Rudi Müller and Bernhard Müller, were running a booming black-market business of Saccharin for booty from local villages. Rodinger confessed to sending 830.00 Reichsmarks home in just a few weeks. Herbst collected transfer receipts totalling a similar amount from among Rodinger's papers. He also found letters from the former chief, Fritz Krause, among Rodinger's papers that indicated Krause and Sophie were lovers. The letters contained harsh criticism of the German Army and civilian administration. This was regarded as more serious than petty theft. Herbst instructed the security police in Wolkowysk to arrest Fritz Krause.[58] Sophie Kuryla's tale closed without concluding events. The investigation of the *SS-Postschutz* had wider implications. Herbst had struck a final devastating political blow against his SS rival. Fromm's failings were exposed, and he was transferred from Bialystok to *Polizeigebietsführer-Sarajewo* under the command of *HSSPF-Kroatien* on 30 January 1943. This was a demotion, being removed from one of the prime posts in the east to a smaller city command in Croatia.[59]

III. Manpower fluctuations

In Białowieża the forest's size was a major factor in determining the placement of companies and troops, and that, in turn, had a direct bearing on the battalion's performance. When the first companies of the LWSB arrived in the forest at the end of July they came under Major Kobylinski and were deployed for priorities set by the army. There was no indication Kobylinski was aware of Göring's orders or the mission. On 22 July 1942, the LWSB's recorded strength on paper was 5 officers and 236 NCOs/OR's, formed into a command staff and two rifle companies.[60] Once Herbst took over there were reshuffles. In the second report of 17 August, Herbst referred to the arrival of more companies: 'The formation of the fourth company

---

58　Ibid.
59　Yerger, *Allgemeine-SS*, p. 79.
60　BArch, RL 31/3, document 12, report 3, period 18.8–31.8.42, Major Herbst, 31 August 1942.

of the battalion in Neukuhren will be completed in some days, according to the latest report.'[61] This comment indicates the expansion was already planned by Göring, and the LWSB's arrival was treated as an advanced settling the phase before the arrival of new formations and equipment. By 31 August the LWSB had increased to three companies and the staff re-designated as the headquarters company. Each company was assigned three officers but had different counts for NCOs (first company: 18, second: 19, third: 26), and OR's (from 113 to 123 troopers). After the third company arrived, Herbst formed a battalion reserve and raised several Jagdkommando on the company level for long-range patrols.[62] Before September 1942, the LWSB was not in a condition or position to intercept Jews escaping into the forest.

The fluctuations in the LWSB's manpower levels continued until November 1942 when the battalion was increased to six companies. A tabulation of this expansion can be found in table 9. Once the expansion was complete Herbst announced that his battalion secured the entire forest. The placement of companies confirmed the LWSB's mission priorities: First, Second and Third remained within the Oberforstamt Bialowies area; the Fifth was positioned north but due south of Bialystok, and was a safety-net force blocking Jews and partisans from entering the forest and reaching the remote swamp areas; while the Fourth and Sixth deployed in the south where Jews escaping from two nearby ghettoes would seek sanctuary. With the destruction of the ghettoes, the companies closed down their outlying positions.

---

61 BArch, RL 31/3, document 4, report 2, period 6.8–17.8.42, Major Herbst, 17 August 1942.
62 BArch, RL 31/3, document 30, report 5, period 11–20.9.1942, Major Herbst, 22 September 1942.

Table 2: Fluctuations in manpower levels[63]

Date	Accuracy	Officers	NCOs	Men	Notes
Staff		2	6	51	Remained constant throughout period
22.7.42	Documented	5	27	209	
1. 8. 42	Documented	11	69	406	Arrival of Third Company
31. 8. 42	Documented	9	63	355	Fluctuations due to combing out
22. 9. 42	Documented	10	55	325	Fluctuations due to combing out
30. 9. 42	Documented	9	58	328	
10.10.42	Documented	10	56	338	
Estimates					
16. 10. 42	Estimates	11	81	478	1 officer, 25 NCOs and 140 OR's
16. 11.42	Estimates	12	107	618	Arrival of fifth/sixth companies
5. 3. 43	Documented	13	139	496	Figures based on JSKB opening muster and final LWSB operational report

Internally, the expansion process triggered several changes in deployment. Upon arrival, each new company raised a command post (CP) situated within its central strong point. Then outlying picket posts were placed to extend the company's sphere of control. In design, the strong points ranged from a fortified hamlet to the forts commonly associated with the US cavalry on the American plains. An examination of the map terrain surrounding these strongpoints and outposts utilising GIS found that an all-around clear 'line of sight' dictated their position. They were placed to enforce control within their locality. Their construction incorporated good observation to regulate local movement, and concentrated firepower to fend off partisans. Several strong points in the south were positioned on high ground with well-planned fields of fire; their spheres of control extended beyond local communities; and, effectively divided a locality into sectors of security zones. There were different patterns of patrols between those in the locality and the *Jagdkommando*. A typical *Jagdkommando* patrol could range for days, hopping between outposts, or terminating at a different company

---

63 BArch, RL 31/4, from all reports of the LWSB Kriegstagebuch 22 July 1942 to 3 March 1943.

strongpoint. This implied the companies buddied-up in operation procedures: the first, third, and fifth worked jointly on civilian deportations; while in the south, the fourth, and the sixth patrolled in the vicinity of two Jewish ghettoes at Prużany[64] and Kamieniec Litewski.[65]

Major Herbst's positioning and deployment of companies were planned. To understand the spatiality in his methods several GIS maps were generated to illustrate the impact this had on the forest. By examining the position of companies at different stages shows the gradual build-up forces in step with SS operations to liquidate the ghettoes. In each GIS map, a company is represented by a roundel(s) with its tactical number, highlighting the patrol areas from strongpoints and outposts. The companies often used several strong points. The GIS maps were generated to show the distribution of a company from its primary positional reports in the war diaries. The roundels identified the three regular patrol distances. Local patrols were conducted within a radius of 500 metres from the strongpoint; an area constantly patrolled throughout daylight. They were too small to ring in the GIS maps but are represented by the small flag in the centre of each roundel. The next level, identified by the lighter grey inner area of the roundel, represented patrols conducted within a radius of 4 kilometres from a strongpoint. The patrols concentrated on local duties such as guarding convoys, food production or securing communities. The last band in the roundel represented the 6 kilometres patrol area, the maximum strongpoint patrol distance based upon the records. It is important to note the regular patrols were entirely different from the *Jagdkommando* patrols—with troops assigned to one or the other and possibly rotated by company schedules.

---

64 Katrin Reichelt, Laura Craigo, and Martin Dean, 'Pruzana', United States Holocaust Memorial Museum Encyclopedia of Camps and Ghettos, ed. Geoffrey P. Megargee, Vol. 2, *Ghettos in German-occupied Eastern Europe,* ed. Martin Dean, (Indianapolis, 2012), pp. 939–942.

65 Laura Craigo and Alexander Kruglov, 'Kamieniec Litewski', United States Holocaust Memorial Museum Encyclopedia of Camps and Ghettos, ed. Geoffrey P. Megargee, Vol. 2, *Ghettos in German-occupied Eastern Europe,* ed. Martin Dean (Indianapolis, 2012), pp. 904–906.

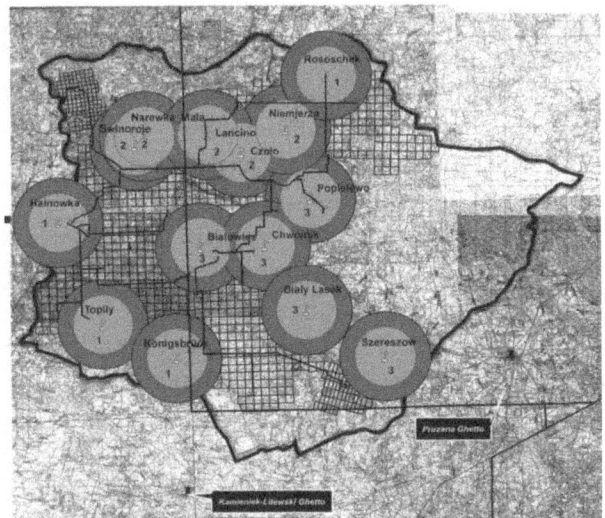

GIS Map 7: before the arrival of Fourth Company – 10 October 1942

This map visualises the period just before the arrival of the fourth company. In preparation, the third company raised an advanced outpost in Szereszow. The LWSB used the central Hajnówka-Pruzhany road as a line of advance.

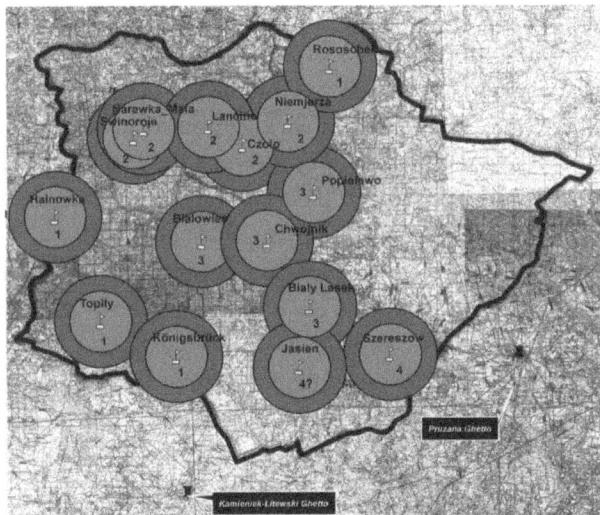

GIS Map 8: after the arrival of Fourth Company – 2 November 1942

This map marks the arrival of the fourth company and its establishment in the south as the third company withdrew back into the centre of the forest as the LWSB's reserve. This was ten days before the destruction of the Kamieniec-Litewski ghetto.

GIS Maps 7 and 8 were generated to explain the spatiality in the deployment of the companies. They map the arrival of the fourth company into a build-up area in the southeast. We know very little about the fourth other than it was critical to Herbst's plans in the period November 1942 to February 1943. The fourth hunted Jews, conducted Bandenbekämpfung operations, and policed deportations. There is no record that the company underwent special ideological conditioning before its arrival or after. The fourth was raised at the Luftwaffe training airbase in Neukuhren in East Prussia (Pionerski: Russian Federation) in October 1942. The fourth was originally planned to arrive between 22 September and 1 October but was held up by a delay in receiving weapons. In preparation for its arrival, the third extended its positions southwards and acted as an advance guard. The fourth finally arrived on 16 October. It was assigned to the southeast sector of Urwald Bialowies, initially based in Strongpoint Czeresow (written as Schereschow in the original) but later around Strongpoint Wiskula. It was finally deployed in the immediate vicinity of Kamieniec-Litewski ghetto. In a corresponding movement, once the fourth arrived the third returned to the Białowieża area as battalion reserve. The positioning of the fourth company was completed ten days prior to the destruction of the Kamieniec-Litewski ghetto.

The arrival of the fifth and sixth companies followed a similar pattern to that of the fourth. Herbst wrote, 'the formation of the fifth and sixth companies of the battalion will be conducted in Neukuhren and shall be completed by 21 October 1942 (a reference to Lw. order: Lg.Kdo.I Ib (Fl) Nr. 1744/42 from 28 September 1942, there is no known copy).'[66] In his ninth report, Herbst noted that the fifth and sixth companies were expected on 21 October but were in Neukuhren awaiting the assignment of officers. Luftgau I confirmed to Herbst on 1 November that officers had been assigned.[67] Eventually the fifth (1 officer, 25 NCOs, 140 ORs) and sixth companies

---

66 BArch, RL 31/3, document 34, report 6, period 21–30.9.1942, Major Herbst, 1 October 1942. Herbst referred to Lw order: Lg.Kdo.I Ib (Fl) Nr. 1744/42 geh. from 28 September 1942 – no known copy.

67 BArch, RL 31/3, document 50, report 9, period 22–31 October 1942, Major Herbst, 2 November 1942.

arrived on 16 November. The only known muster roll for the sixth lists 2 officers, 21 NCOs and 109 ORs. The sixth company's *Vorkommando* (advance party) arrived on 6 November with two NCOs and eight ORs.[68] It was located initially in the area of the fourth and was assigned to Strongpoint Chwalowo II and Haleny. Later it occupied the strong points: Murawa, Haleny and Wielko-Siolo. The company's *Jagdkommando* were designated 'buzzard', 'heron' and 'shrike' respectively. Once the sixth was positioned, Herbst confirmed, 'the entire Reichsforstgebiet was divided into six company sections after the arrival of the fifth and sixth companies.'[69] GIS Map 9 was generated to highlight how the fourth company increased the number of outposts, as the sixth began to erect its strong points.

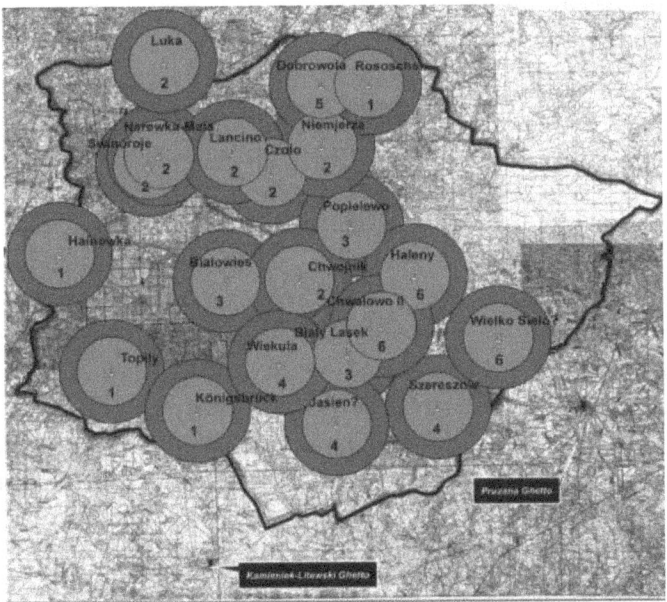

GIS Map 9: the arrival of Fifth and Sixth companies—19 November 1942
The expansion of the fourth company had continued just as the sixth company began building its strongpoints. Seven days after the destruction of the ghetto and still, the LWSB was building forces in the south.

---

68 BArch, RL 31/3, unnumbered document, daily report extracts 1–20 November 1942, 21 November 1942.
69 BArch, RL 31/3, document 70, report 11, period 21.11–14.12.42, Major Herbst 14 December 1942.

The fourth, fifth, and sixth companies were raised to support the SS plans to liquidate the ghettoes. The companies were deployed in a timely fashion, to be in position ready to intercept the first escapees from the deportations. The planning and coordination behind these moves were not explained within the war diary and the coordination with the SS conducted verbally and without a formal record. Remove the timing of the SS ghetto actions and these company-level deployments look like normal military movements. There were no tasks, missions, or patrol schedules for the companies to follow, but the after-action reports show their tactical purpose was to hunt Jews.

There was no documentary evidence of local civilian collaborating in the hunt or killing of Jews. This was an important point because the reports were written by Germans for Germans, which was an important viewpoint of Polish-German relations. Herbst did present Brauchitsch with a proposal to form an Ortswehren (civil guards), a self-defence militia mustered from locals. The issue came down to the supply of weapons to Slavs, despised as Untermenschen (sub-humans) in Nazi ideology. Herbst's expectation that 2,000 foreign rifles could be issued to loyal locals had not materialised.[70] In the report, Herbst referred to a request (A.Qu. Nr. 201/42 secret—no known copy) sent to Brauchitsch to press Göring into issuing the order to deliver captured 'western European rifles.' They could guarantee the security of the settlements either independently or in cooperation with the Wehrmacht. Herbst wrote that service in the civil guard was Ehrendienst (unpaid service) for all male citizens aged eighteen to fifty with a spotless record and a reliable reputation. The volunteers had to inform their local Soltys, who would announce them to the designated Amtskommissar. The Amtskommissar would then pass lists of names to Herbst for final approval. A leader and a deputy had to be appointed for every militia unit and Herbst would confirm them after a thorough examination. The main task of the militia was

---

70   BArch, RL 31/3, document 47, report 8, period 11–21.10.1942, Major Herbst, 23 October 1942. The rifles in question were known to have come from the captured stocks from the 1940 campaign in the west.

village protection at night. They each had had to be strong enough to provide sufficient guard posts and patrols during the evening, with a rota to enable men to rest and continue their daily work.[71] Herbst thought he faced a wall of silence, but the delay was the RFA's plodding bureaucracy.

IV. The bureaucracy of Bandenbekämpfung

Hitler's Bandenbekämpfung directive included a mission statement. This bound Göring, Alpers, Scherping, Wagner, Frevert and Herbst to adhere to four mission principles:

> 1. The confidence of the local population in German authority must be gained by handling them strictly but justly.
> 2. A necessary condition for the destruction of bandit gangs is the assurance to the local population of the minimum requirements of life. Should this fail, or – what is particularly important – should available supplies not be fairly distributed, the result will be that more recruits will join the bandits.
> 3. In this struggle against the bandits the cooperation of the local population is indispensable. Deserving persons should not be parsimoniously treated; rewards should be really attractive. On the other hand, reprisals for action in support of the bandits must be all the more severe.
> 4. Misplaced confidence in the native population, particularly in those working for the German authorities, must be strictly guarded against. Even though the majority of the population is opposed to the bandits, there are always spies to be reckoned with, whose task is to inform the bandits of all action contemplated against them.[72]

These principles were quite specific to the RFA and Luftwaffe and particularly pertinent to the conditions in Białowieża. There were also instructions to recruit and arm loyal or reliable 'native units'. Troops in the training areas were also assigned to Bandenbekämpfung duties and all troops in the rear areas were directed to combat the partisans with the utmost ferocity. Hitler's mission statement bound Herbst to certain bureaucratic forms.

---

71 BArch, RL 31/3, document 78, Major Herbst, Bevollmächtigter des Reichsmarschall des Großdeutschen Reiches, O.U., 29.11.1942, Call to the population of the Reichsforstgebiet.
72 Blood, 'Bandenbekämpfung', PhD, p. 134.

Combat reports are critical to military and security operations. Herbst utilised two report formats—the record of tactical everyday actions and the periodic official summaries for the higher authorities. Documents and diaries were the responsibility of the battalion scribes, the headquarters clerks who reported directly to the battalion adjutant. The clerks were in the unusual position of drafting reports destined for Göring or his Luftwaffe aide Brauchitsch. The basic battalion record was the war diary, with the first entry on 7 July 1942. Every Wehrmacht formation from battalion upwards maintained a war diary. The diaries remained in the battalion's possession until disbanded and handed over to the offices of military records. The diary entries were either handwritten or typed. The handwriting form was usually *Sütterlinschrift*, a style commonly taught during the first half of the twentieth century. *Sütterlinschrift* is notoriously difficult for people to read today. From November 1942, Herbst changed the diary format. The handwritten diary was suspended and replaced by typed situation reports. These reports went to Brauchitsch and it can be assumed Göring was made aware of the contents. Scholars have taken it for granted that war diaries were accurate and not altered or corrected after events. This is an error because diaries were constantly being updated with after-combat details or even censored of details regarded as inappropriate for the final record.

The typewritten documents had several formats: the regular situation reports; the extracts of the daily report; and the general reports. The 'daily report extracts' indicated the existence of company level diaries or logbooks that no longer exist. The text format indicates the clerk's used standard keys on normal typewriters, without the extra Nazi keys such as runic lightning-SS symbols or Swastikas. The quality of typing was generally accurate with few grammatical errors. The contents were succinct, usually a list of events with minimum details. Sometimes a short sentence for an entire day—'no operations today due to snowfall'. The reports did not always follow numerical or chronological or date order, there were random reports that were outside of the routine sequence, but without explanation. The 'daily report extracts' were not collated or summarised in a single report. Herbst was very selective in his reporting to Göring, and some information was not forwarded unless by telephone, of which there is no record.

The reports provide an impression of the clerks' duties. Their greatest challenge was overcoming the spelling of Polish and Russian words. Names were either in the original form, Germanised, or spelt phonetically. There are no general killing orders in the diaries or supplementary reports. Although Herbst did not issue a general killing order, killings were germane to the reporting culture. After-action reports often referred to various acts of killing and remained largely uncensored on the record. Herbst did issue specific orders for reprisals or the execution of captives, and this was referenced in his reports. When reprisal orders were issued, Herbst never mentioned names, there was always anonymity. The reports do not mention burial parties or any arrangements for the dead. They were probably left as public examples, or warnings, of what would happen if caught assisting the partisans or Jews. German casualties were always named with a short explanation of their injury or death. The locals were only mentioned in the context of collaboration, usually favourably or vilified as criminals. The partisans were vilified as 'bandits', with details of their crimes, the circumstances of their capture, interrogation, and killing. Partisan leaders, if known, were named.

Herbst deployed the battalion in a fixed defensive system—strongpoints for area control with local routine patrols and *Jagdkommandos* patrols of deep penetration into the forest. The strongpoints were positioned on higher ground, with good fields of fire, and within reach of the battalion signals coverage. The downside was the isolation, being at least an hour from the nearest local reinforcements. The companies assigned to the strong points carried out the rotation with the battalion reserve. During daylight hours the strong points served as platforms for patrols, but also controlling the flow of traffic through the forest. At night-time partisans often took potshots at strongpoints with little effect other to rattle the Germans' nerves. In local support of the *Oberforstamt*, troops were tasked with protective duties while the harvest was being gathered.

The food priorities meant security duties were extended to farms, collection centres, and storage facilities. Herbst's responsibilities included timber-related industries, the forest railway, large farm estates and the game reserves. Herbst's lowest priority, based on the comments in his reports, was the protection of villagers and communities. There was a sense of ambiguity levelled against the locals. He recorded all the attacks against villages, but troops were not always sent to investigate afterwards. The very few cases when troops were assigned to village protection were not explained.[73]

The details in Herbst's reports highlight his priorities, and an example can be drawn from various incidents on 3 August 1942. Just after midnight, a large band destroyed the tar oven (priority) in *Jagen* 910. The partisans shot the site boss (not a priority), set the turpentine stores (priority) aflame and blew up the tar-oven (priority). At 6.30 am the forest railway station at Poerzerkow (priority) called for help via the telephone. A platoon (second company) was sent but arrived to be told fifty partisans had appeared in the grounds of a nearby estate at 9.50 pm. They had plundered an RFA managed farmhouse (priority) taking official documents including forestry defence regulations. They threatened to kill the farmer and family if he reported to the Germans. They then moved out at 3.00 am taking a pig. The delay in raising the alarm was assumed to be a lack of telephones in a remote area of the forest. Some days later on 11 August, a supply train (priority) on the forest railway was carrying LWSB and FSK troops on a mission to ambush the partisans. As the train reached a bend in *Jagen* 28 it came under heavy fire from three enfilading machine guns. The troops 'answered fire with fire', but the unnamed officer-in-charge decided not to stop the train and rode through the bullets. He later claimed the intense firepower showed he was outgunned. A district forester and an FSK trooper were killed, a Luftwaffe corporal, two FSK men and a district forester were wounded. The report mentioned two partisans killed, but it isn't known if this was confirmed. The file was closed without follow up or further action.

---

73   BArch, RL 31/3, document 23, report 4, period 1.9–10.9.42, Major Herbst, 11 September 1942.

Transport and communications were the strategic priorities and a constant in many reports. On 9 August, four partisans attacked the railway section in Laski, in *Jagen* 808, and plundered a railwayman's house. A squad from the third company was dispatched. The squad leader, a sergeant, took action: he sacked the head of the railway section, stripped him of all his possessions, and evicted him from his apartment. The sergeant claimed the man had been derelict in his duties and was suspected of contacting the partisans. Herbst upheld the decision. During a two-weeks (15–30 August) partisans pinned notes to a forest railway vehicle that warned 'anybody who uses the forest railway after 7.00 pm will be shot.' There was no attempt by Herbst to intercept the messengers. On 6 September, four partisans tried unsuccessfully to burn down the railway bridge near Kosy-Most. The damage was contained, and the bridge quickly repaired. On 8 September partisans attacked a military supply transport nearby Masiewo II at 2.40 pm. The escorting troops opened fire and the partisans returned fire as they fled. Two hours later a couple of construction-maintenance trains on the forest railway were set on fire by a small band. In the evening Herbst despatched pickets to guard a series of tactically important sites including Jasien, Chidry Male, the Laski bridge, the western forest bridge, the north forest bridge, the south-east road junction, the central forest bridge, the forester's house in Wiskula, a bridge near Solomenka, and finally the road junction in *Jagen* 752.[74] It is possible the partisans had interpreted Herbst's actions and responses and had coordinated incidents to overstretch LWSB's assets.

On 3 October partisans carried out concerted attacks against the railway. At noon, in *Jagen* 833 four partisans entered the junction box at Debowe and stole a telephone. At about the same time five partisans entered the forest railway facilities at Wroni-Bor and questioned the railway staff about the strength of the Czolo, Masiewo and Hajnówka strongpoints. They removed petroleum jelly from a locomotive to lubricate their weapons. At 3.30–4.00 pm

---

74 BArch, RL 31/3, documents 24–25, daily report extracts 1–10.9.1942, 11 September 1942.

seven partisans carried out a 'stop and search', they were searching for Germans on a train near Wroni-Bor. Many more partisans had taken up ambush positions hoping to cut down any Germans fleeing the train. The plot failed and in frustration the partisans beat up a Polish railway worker instead. On the same day at 5.00 pm, a partisan armed with a rifle and pistol appeared on a new length of railway track near Popielewo and held up a train. He threatened the driver with a grenade in the firebox unless he took the train to Skipowo. Arriving at Kontschyk he forced the driver to stop the train and took him to the junction telephone switchboard operator. The partisan threatened to shoot the operator if she reported the incident to the Germans. At 3.00am two partisans brandishing carbines and hand grenades were seen loitering beside the Białowieża-Hajnówka road. The presence of partisans at that point was surprising since the road was under constant patrols as the army's central highway through the forest. When a motor vehicle approached, they fled across the road and into the forest. At dusk, two partisans with rifles appeared before a group of female field hands, southeast of Rudnia. They questioned the women about the strength of Strongpoint Niemerca. Only then did Herbst allow a search, but this led to nothing.

    On 4 November, three partisans entered the railway station in Lipiny, just north of Hajnówka. They took tobacco from the stationmaster and threatened to shoot him if he reported the incident. They returned several hours later with a companion. They forced the stationmaster to send a message repeatedly through the telephone network (details unknown). The telephone was then ripped from the table and a partisan beat the stationmaster with it until he collapsed unconscious. They then stripped him, sat him by the front door, and set fire to the station building. Once the fire took hold the partisans dragged the stationmaster to a nearby group of forest labourers. A fourth partisan, possibly the leader, checked their names against a list he was carrying. He warned them of the same treatment if they told the Germans what they had witnessed. Herbst believed the partisan leader had waved a document in front of the labourers as evidence of his authority from Moscow.[75] Once again the partisans had struck against multiple targets and Herbst had not responded.

From November 1942 until March 1943, Herbst's operational remit was extended beyond *Urwald Bialowies*. This was partly in response to the draining of military assets from *Bezirk Bialystok* due to the growing crisis in Stalingrad, and partly due to the increasing scale of partisan incursions. The increases enabled Herbst to deploy across the forest and covering the borders. The first indication of the growing problems came in the form of a memo on 9 October 1942, from the operations officer of *Oberfeldkommandantur 392* (Minsk). This was widely distributed to all Wehrmacht and SS-police forces in the Bialystok-Białowieża area. The memo warned of increased partisan activity. Collaborators in Belarus had informed the Germans that partisan staff officers were striking out towards Białowieża. They planned to lodge themselves in Bialystok and concentrate the bands under a unified command.[76] The following day Lieutenant Bernhard, an operations officer of the Wehrmacht garrison in Bielsk, wrote a short memo to his counterpart at 461st Reserve Division regarding partisan activities, adding to a climate of heightened security awareness.[77] The German fears proved groundless, but the heightened security status was not lifted.

In November 1942 Herbst changed the format of his reports', to reflect both sectors of operations: (a) inside the *Reichsforstgebiet*,

---

75 BArch, RL 31/3, document 63, daily report extracts 1-20.11.42, Major Herbst, 21 November 1942.
76 BArch, RL 31/3, document 57, Abschrift: Kdtr. des Sich, Gebietes Weissruthenien (Oberfeldkommandantur 392) Abt. Ia, Minsk, 9 October 1942.
77 BArch, RL 31/3, document 69, Abschrift: Wehrmacht-Bereichsstandortältester Bielsk, Department Ia, Tgb.Nr. 3268/42 – An die Ersatz Division 461, Abt.Iat, Bialystok, 10 October 1942. Betr.: Bandenumtriebe. Troops from Landesschützenbataillon 238 had received information from a forest official of partisan activity. At 3.45 PM on 31 October a patrol stumbled on evidence of a band of about 30-50 partisans in the Bielsk area. The partisans had taken food from locals and a village guard had been hit over the head with an axe handle. A German railway officer in Czerenzca ordered a patrol (two NCOs and seventeen OR's) to travel by train (a locomotive and a carriage) to a siding in Wietowo (12 kilometres south-west of Hajnówka) because the partisans the reported in the village.

and (b) outside the *Reichsforstgebiet*. There are no instructions on file indicating why, although Herbst wrote: 'The reports of the gendarmerie show clearly that there are still many partisans' activities surrounding the area of *Urwald Bialowies*.' The LWSB had located bunkers in the forest, and it was believed, 'the majority of the partisans hide in the villages surrounding the area.' Herbst described a new mission: 'We intend to search thoroughly the villages in the border area of the forest during the wintertime in cooperation with the police, which has only weak forces.'[78] His twelfth report summarised the shift in partisan activity. There were twenty-eight attacks on farms and villages outside of the forest, but only two attacks on villages and five on local workers inside *Urwald Bialowies*. Partisans had appeared in the northeast and southeast but had been 'very cunning' using 'shoot-and-scoot' methods. He explained that nineteen partisans had been killed in firefights and another 185 captured partisans and their supporters had been shot with another eighty-five hanged (mostly after the Ciré reprisal mentioned later). A further fifty persons were in a police prison awaiting execution. In comparison, the battalion had suffered ten dead and five wounded. Herbst observed that as a consequence of these actions and reprisals, 'the locals once again favoured the Germans rather than the Bolsheviks and the partisans.'[79] In reality, the locals swung to whichever side was brandishing a gun.

---

[78] BArch, RL 31/3, document 63, daily extract 1–21.11.1942, Major Herbst, 21 November 1942.
[79] BArch, RL 31/3, document 81, report 12, period 15.12. 42–1.1943, Major Herbst, 5 January 1943.

5. The Białowieża Partisans

Who were the partisans, and how did they sustain their campaign? There has been a wealth of literature about the Soviet partisans originating from before the war ended. Allied propaganda represented both Stalin and Tito's partisans as heroic symbols of resistance and hope for liberation. This representation changed during the Cold War where partisans were recast as the insurgent arm of Soviet ideological warfare and politics of violence. During the war, the Soviet partisans worked to destabilise the Nazi occupation from within. This caused societies to become dysfunctional and contributed to turning regions into a dystopia. The cause was the partisan culture, where bands behaved like rampaging gangs rather than bearers of hope and liberation. The odd snippets of information about the Białowieża partisans were far from flattering. The Germans identified a myriad of profiles that were recorded in Herbst's reports. The reports painted the partisans from two perspectives: the accurate intelligence-based assessments and the Nazi propagandised stereotypes.

Herbst's reports always labelled the partisans 'bandits', without exception, and sometimes qualified this with 'Russian bandit', 'Soviet bandit' or 'Bolshevik bandit'. There were a few references to Polish or Jewish bands or 'armed Jews' or Jews fighting alongside 'bandits'. On 6 August 1942 Herbst formed a rough assessment of the partisan situation, 'the bandits are Russians who either escaped from PoW camps or labour camps', and mostly wore Russian uniforms. Herbst urged *SS-Standartenführer* Fromm to initiate countermeasures within all PoW and labour camps to prevent escapes. Stalin had publicly denounced Soviet PoW's as traitors, but Herbst assumed there was an informal clemency being practised that encouraged escaped Red Army PoWs to join a senior Soviet partisan officer calling himself the 'commander of the primaeval forest'. There was a kernel of 'Bolshevik' soldiers, believed to be 'hard-liners' sent by Moscow on missions to establish 'bandit gangs' or partisan bands, and also to coordinate smaller isolated bands of partisans.

Several reports referred to former Soviet mayors or officials having been arrested or had surrendered to the Germans. A major reason why fugitive Soviet PoWs were prepared to take their chances with the partisans was the ill-treatment by the Germans. During a meeting with Count Ciano (Italian Ambassador in Berlin) Göring joked, 'In the camps for Russian prisoners they have begun to eat each other.'[1]

A study of the German Army's treatment of Red Army PoWs revealed a deliberate policy of starvation, killings, and men forced as guinea pigs in gas experiments in Auschwitz.[2] Herbst's attitude reflected the Nazis' racial contempt for Russian people as sub-human. In October 1942, Herbst received a telegram from the court-martial of *Luftgau I*. The court requested a detailed report of all sentences delivered by his courts martial.[3] Herbst responded: 'I am not under the control of any courts-martial because of the special authority granted by the *Reichsmarcshall*. I dispense judgments after a short trial.'[4] He enclosed an extract from a report already sent to Göring on 11 October in which he stated: 'six Russian PoWs escaped from the Popielewo *Oberforstamt* camp on 3 October. They were employed on farms outside the camp. Four of the remaining PoWs received death sentences from the courts-martial for assisting in the escape. They were shot after sentencing.'[5] On 6 December, a 'Soviet-Russian PoW' was shot while running away. Another Soviet PoW, called Satuwje, was shot while running away in

---

1   Alan Bullock, *Hitler: A Study in Tyranny*, (London, 1952), p. 606
2   Christian Streit, *Keine Kameraden: Die Wehrmacht und die sowjetischen Kriegsgefangenen 1941–1945*, (Stuttgart, 1978); see also Christian Streit, 'Soviet Prisoners of War in the Hands of the Wehrmacht', in Heer and Nauman, War of Extermination, pp. 80–9.
3   BArch, RL 31/3, document 54, telegram, ref. No. 0373, A LKLG, 16.19 hrs, 24 October 1942.
4   BArch, RL 31/3, document 55, letter to Luftgau I Br.B.Nr. 208/42, Major Herbst, 26 October 1942.
5   BArch, RL 31/3, document 41, report 7, period 1–10.10.1942, Major Herbst, 11 October 1942. On 4 October 1942, the LWSB court sentenced the men to death by shooting for aiding and abetting the escape of their six comrades. In other words, the remaining PoWs were all shot for not running away. That evening the six escapees were observed in Murawa begging for food but were never apprehended.

Jasienowka. At the time he was already under suspicion of being a partisan.[6]

In August, Herbst predicted an increase in the number of partisan bands.[7] However, two months later his reporting was more specific:

> [Our] *Jagdkommandos* had repeatedly come into contact with small groups of bandits. A number of strongpoints had taken fire from small groups of bandits. ... The gangs are divided, a few stronger gangs but much smaller gangs with only a few members. The reason for this is probably due to supply difficulties. For this reason, the activity of the gangs was concentrated along the perimeter of Urwald Bialowies.[8]

He was aware that during the winter months the partisans went into a form of hibernation until the weather improved. They stockpiled supplies in the autumn and then went to ground in well-camouflaged bunker complexes built deep inside the remote areas of the forest. In this regard, the Luftwaffe were working against the clock to locate and eradicate the partisan bunkers. By February 1943, the tone of his penultimate report was less assured: 'Several *Jagdkommandos* were deployed along the border areas to assist the weak *Gendarmerie* duty posts that are powerless at this time because of the increased activity of bandits having been forced out of the forest area.' The large bands had departed the forest, but a few individuals or small groups still took shelter after raids or used the forest to evade the Germans. Herbst explained that an operation had been mounted in the western edges of the forest against 'stragglers, bandits hiding in the villages and bandit supporters, and many prisoners had been taken.'[9] Herein lay the *Catch-22* of Herbst's methods: if the partisans were forced into areas policed only by lightly armed Gendarmerie there was a sudden surge in

---

6   BArch, RL 31/3, document 71-73, daily report extracts 21.11-14.12.1942, Major Herbst, 14 December 1942.
7   BArch, RL 31/3, document 2, report 1, July-August 1942, Major Herbst, 6 August 1942.
8   BArch, RL 31/3, document 35, report 6, period 21-30.9.1942, Major Herbst, 1 October 1942.
9   BArch, RL 31/3, document 93, report 15, period 2-12.2.1943, Major Herbst 12 February 1943.

violence that overwhelmed local police detachments. This was the conundrum of policing vast area with limited assets and uncoordinated missions.

Image 9: Captured Soviet partisans after interrogation but before execution.
Source: NARA, Captured German photographic collection.

I. Surveillance, counterintelligence and luck

Following the defeat of his rivals in the turf war, Herbst became the Nazi judge and executioner of *Urwald Bialowies*. In his first report (6 August 1942), he alluded to more deportations and resettlement plan devised by the *Oberforstamt*. From a jurisdiction perspective, he faced a confusion of civil, corporate and 'martial law' due to the ongoing transition from occupation to colonisation/annexation and from the strictures imposed by the Hitler directive. His powers were being defined shaped by a 'new' security vocabulary. The crime of suspicion was extended to all *Bandenhelfer* (bandit-helpers), while the presence of *Bolshevik-Banditen* (Soviet agents and partisans) initiated counterintelligence investigations, and both came within the Bandenbekämpfung directive. The *lingua franca* of security policing was also utilised: *Überwachung* (surveillance), *Verdacht* (suspicion), *misstrauisch* (suspicious), and *verdächtig* (suspect), to elevate missions beyond local areas. These criminal classifications were already racialised to extend to selection and population controls, social engineering, and public executions. The consequence was a reassessment of petty crime and an escalation of accusations/denunciations of saboteurs, spies and bandits. From August 1942, *Urwald Bialowies* experienced a strange form of Nazi genocide that in some ways was akin to a sinister socio-biological community experiment. Whether this was due to the RFA's involvement was difficult to judge, but Herbst's methods exposed a deviant personality of the petty bureaucrat and feral killer.

Herbst was merciless in the prosecution of suspicion, as was evident from the first report: 'Between the 30 July and 5 August 1942, the battalion arrested thirty-five persons; thirty-two were shot, and three jailed for further interrogation.' On 5 August he received word that a 'trusty', had identified a partisan arms supplier in Bielsk, a person called *Schorsa* and ordered *Schorsa's* arrest. The trusty was a reliable collaborator, called *V-Männer* or *V-Leute*, and employed to infiltrate the bands. At the same time Herbst placed a formal request with *Luftgau I* send a trained signals officer to monitor intercepts of partisan signals traffic. He also requested infiltrators (trusty cadre).[10] On

---

10 BArch, RL 31/3, document 2, report 1, period to 6.8.42, Major Herbst, 6 August 1942.

7 August, the diary noted that the Topiło district forester had advised the battalion that a 'bandit' had entered his yard, his hands up, and offering intelligence for clemency. Herbst dispatched a *Sonderkommando* (special commando) of two officers, two NCOs and twenty-six men and motor vehicles from the headquarters staff, to collect the 'bandit deserter'. The 'bandit' was Nicolai Laptiev (details later in this chapter) and the information he offered led to the arrest of twelve suspects accused of supplying food, information and weapons to the partisans.[11] Herbst delivered summary justice: seven were shot, three hanged, and two remained in prison under interrogation. The interrogations led to further information about a complex partisan supply chain working the Brest-Litovsk/Bialystok area. Herbst, the *Sonderkommando* and Nicolai travelled to Brest-Litovsk, on 12 August: 'After being in touch with the SSPF and together with the security police I arrested twenty-two Bolshevists. The majority were women.'[12]

Image 10: Armed trusty and Nazi Collaborator.
Source: NARA, Captured German Photographic Collection.

---

11   BArch, RL 31/1, Kriegstagebuch des Sicherungsbataillon entry 3 August 1942.
12   BArch, RL 31/3, document 8, letter Major Herbst to SS-Standartenführer Fromm, 17 August 1942. This case of the black market was mentioned earlier.

A few days later in Topiło (11 August), the district forester reported that thirty partisans were seen nearby the bridge spanning the Lesna River. A platoon officer led two sections on a reconnaissance patrol along either side of the river. One section guarded the hunting lodge when Nicolai surrendered, and the other the bridge. A partisan armed with a machine gun crossed the bridge at 6.15 pm, but the troops judged the distance too far to open fire. At 8.00 pm the bridge section heard gunfire from the direction of the hunting lodge and then received incoming fire from across bridge. The firing ended abruptly. At 1.00 pm a patrol was sent out and encountered thirteen partisans. A skirmish developed, but the partisans withdrew firing random shots as they made good their escape. At 7.50 pm the section stationed at the hunting lodge came under sustained fire from positions believed to be thirty metres away. The firefight lasted fifteen minutes and there were casualties: squad leader Walter B** (killed — shot in the head) Corporal Ernst S** was wounded in the shoulder, and Private Wilhelm H** took a bullet to the hip. The wounded men were treated in the reserve military hospital in Bialystok.[13]

The incidents at the Lesna River and elsewhere raised Herbst's suspicions. He claimed enemy agents had infiltrated the inner workings of the *Oberforstverwaltung*. He instigated an internal investigation because his plans were being 'betrayed'. During the encirclement actions, the partisans had unaccountably changed positions, several times, and strayed into neighbouring areas just before his *Schwerpunkt*. 'Traitors' were identified among the employees and arrested. Several persons were summarily executed including Nicolai Protasewitsch, a 'White-Russian hunter' from Dlugi-Brod, and a Polish couple named Barmuda, a railway worker and his wife, both hanged in public. Herbst claimed they were guilty of passing information to the partisans in advance of operations. He also had three forest railway employees and three women arrested

---

13 DDst, Sicherungsbataillon d. Lw. z.b.V. Feldpostnummer L49 006 Luftgaupostamt Königsberg/ PRNamentliche Verlustmeldung Nr. 1, 1–31 August 1942 (27.7–29.8.42).

(possibly their partners).[14] On 14 August, Herbst held a conference with Fromm on the handling of civilian prisoners. Following this, he confirmed an order to execute 'twenty-one Bolsheviks from Białowieźa [among them two women] executed as revenge for the raid against the forest railway.' The list of those killed can be found in table 3.

Table 3: LWSB, death by shooting, 14 August 1942[15]

No.	Name	First name	Home	Grounds for shooting
1	Fenke	Piotr	Saulek Nr. 2	Bolshevik.
2	Newerowitsch	Sergiej	Browsker Weg	Bolshevik.
3	Diatel	Alexander	Browsker Weg	Bolshevik.
4	Podlaschtschik	Leon	Podolany	Bolshevik.
5	Schpakowitsch	Roman	Brows A 6	Bolshevik. (Agent of the N.K.V.D.)
6	Schpakowitsch	Sergeij	Stoczek 228	Director (Agent of the N.K.V.D.)
7	Schpakowitsch	Maxim	Stoczek 234	Saboteur
8	Stankiewitsch	Juljan	Baracke	Bolshevik acting as an agent provocateur
9	Radkiewitsch	Wladimar	Zastawa 81	Active N.K.V.D. agent
10	Buszko	Michael	Zaulek	Active Bolshevik
11	Lickiwicz	Justyn	Podolany 28	Bolshevik Propaganda worker
12	Buczel	Alexander	Zastawa 154	Bolshevik agitator
13	Grabowski	Micheal	Tropinka 80	Bolshevik agitator
14	Zorin	Wlodimir	Stoczek 197	Bolshevik agitator
15	Wolkowycki	Alexander	Zastawa 144	Bolshevik agitator
16	Dron	Ignatz	Tropinka	Bolshevik agitator
17	Kuwszynow	Dimitry	Krzyze 20	Bolshevik Under cover
18	Szpac	Helene	Waldkolonie 31	Wife of a German Communist, spy and saboteur
19	Rudzki	Kasmir	Grudki	G.P.U. Agent
20	Kozlowski	Stanislaw	Forsttr. 83	Nationalistic Pole – political agitator
21	Kozlowski	Marianna	Forsttr. 83	Nationalistic Pole – political agitator

Unusually, Herbst went to some lengths to explain his reasons: 'The arrest of all Bolsheviks and their families, who still live in the forest

---

14 BArch, RL 31/3, document 4, report 2, period 6.8–17.8.42, Major Herbst, 17 August 1942.
15 BArch, RL 31/3, document 7, Verzeichnis der an 14 August 1942 erschossenen Personen. The war diary stated that at 2.00 pm fourteen men and two women were executed as revenge for the assaults. The dead soldiers were buried in the

area of Białowieża. They are exclusive elements that moved into the Białowieża area from Soviet Russia after the war started. They are dangerous.' There is an indication that the continuation of forestry administration imposed by the RFA had incorporated a Polish, a Russian and a German staff. Herbst's methods had led to the arrest of twenty-two persons on 12–13 August, but this had not been possible without the initial information from Nicolai Laptiev. The majority arrested were wives of Russian officers, local public servants, and intermediaries for the partisans. They had supplied passes, weapons, ammunition, and quarters.

Once Herbst got hold of the partisan network's documents identifying agents and suspects accelerated. The first was Nicolai Karso, a public official in the *Stadtkommissariat,* in Brest-Litovsk, his job involved issuing movement orders and work passes. His underground contact was codenamed 'Nina', a Soviet agent, who fled the city with one of the passes before her arrest. The 'pass-forger' as Herbst called 'Korsa' possibly a file typo, was arrested and under interrogation had confessed to forging ten passes for 'Nina'. The last batch was delivered to 'Nina' for 50 Reichsmarks per item. All the passes were accurate, correct in every detail. A Soviet *Ortsgruppen* (district group) with agents named 'Natja', 'Olga', 'Kostja' and 'Tosja' were identified as working from a house at 16 Bialystoker-Strasse. The intermediaries for the group were Gregori Rewa and his wife. The partisans had approached him and he introduced them to 'Lida Marjatowa' and 'Sola Podutschiena', suppliers of weapons, ammunition and passes. Rewa and his wife fled to the partisans. Another person, 'Alex Marasow' was denounced by 'Sergeij Stepanow' another 'bandit deserter' and arrested. Lieutenant 'Marasow' was believed to be a political commissar and a PoW fugitive. He was arrested walking the streets. At the time of his arrest, he was in possession of a forged pass in the name of 'Schdanow'.[16] On 17 August

---

early evening in Bielsk military cemetery. The Soviet GPU (state political directorate) was accountable for state security. The NKVD was the People's Commissariat for Internal Affairs presiding over the regular and secret police.
16   BArch, RL 31/3, document 11, file note, 14 August 1942.

Herbst wrote to *SS-Oberführer* Günter, the *SSPF-Brest-Litovsk*, about the twenty-one persons arrested on 12–13 August:

> I would like to ask you again not to release any of the arrested persons. I believe it is necessary to remove these people in the interest of the mission even if it might not be possible to prove the active participation of one or other Bolshevist woman. The reason is that we have to prevent released persons from passing information to other members of this organisation about the manner of my investigations or the discovery of the facts.[17]

The investigations continued into October and Herbst reported the arrest of two more partisans. They were carrying forged passes issued by a man called 'Woid' from southeast of Lomscha, beyond the area of his remit. Herbst's investigations also exposed the Soltys (headman) of Miodusy, he sold two sets of passes for 100 Reichsmarks to two Soviet operatives. Members of the Polish population in the area south-east of Lomscha had assisted in the crime and were handed over to the SS. From turf war to cooperation, relations between the SS and Luftwaffe seemed to improve.[18] According to Herbst, Nicolai's intelligence was truthful and had enabled the LWSB to arrest 'bandit-helpers' living on the forest border. He had closed down the underground forgers in Brest-Litovsk and arrested or destroyed a major part of the organisation. The SD in Brest-Litovsk reported fifty people had been arrested. According to Herbst, 'Laptiev had offered us valuable service in the pursuit of the partisans and their connections in the rear area. He will stay with the battalion for further special tasks.'[19] Nicolai's information was undoubtedly useful, and the evidence suggests he was the most important partisan turncoat during Herbst's time in the forest.

September was critical for both Germans and partisans preparing for winter. The partisans established camps and stockpiled food supplies for their winter-long hibernation. The locals were busy gathering in the harvest for the winter and meeting the ration quotas for

---

17 BArch, RL 31/3, document 10, letter to SS-Oberführer Günther, Brest-Litovsk, Major Herbst 17.8.42.
18 BArch, RL 31/3, Report 9, period 22–31 October 1942, Major Herbst, 2 November 1942.
19 BArch, RL 31/3, document 46, Abschrift, Aktenvermerk über den Nikolai Laptiew, undated.

the Nazi administration. Civilians hiding food and partisans seeking shelter placed them in confrontation, which was even more jumbled by Herbst's order for house-to-house searches. The locals faced both German and partisans largely unarmed. On 1 September, two platoons (from first and third companies) were dispatched to the southeast sector to assist the police in searches. The mission involved individual house searches having first encircled, and then sealed off the settlements of Przedielsk, Wielko-Siolo, Lezaika, and Zadzieny. The mission was a calamity since the Soltys had not only correctly listed all the inhabitants of the villages but had included all new arrivals. The new arrivals were mostly women and children, pre-processed and assigned to villages by the Nazi *Amtskommissar*. There was no illegal stockpiling and no trace of partisans. However, Herbst monitored the action from above flying his Fieseler Fi 156 *Storch* reconnaissance aeroplane, over the area, watching for partisan escapes. Meanwhile, a 100 strong partisan band, acting mob-handed, descended on Pazuki to the south encircled and infested the hamlet. They took food and winter clothing without any German interference.

On 4 September, a trusty reported the presence of nine Russian families in an unnamed village falling within the area designated as 'police section II'. The families had supplied the partisans with food, while the menfolk had joined the bands. An immediate search of the village was unsuccessful partly because the trusty who denounced the village mysteriously disappeared mid-way through the action, suggesting it was a partisan ploy. Early next morning, Krizyva was surrounded and searched by the LWSB, and five persons were arrested on suspicion. On 8 September, *Jagdkommando Eule* reported they had shot and killed a partisan leader. He was carrying information about persons providing aid to the partisans. Herbst arrested seventeen suspects including five women. The next day after a brief consultation with Fromm, Herbst confirmed their execution. At 3.00 pm, on 9 September, they were hanged on public gallows along Białowieża high street nearby the Orthodox Church, (table 4 includes their names).[20] This was Herbst's public warning to the community.

---

20 BArch, RL 31/3, document 24-25, Auszug aus den Tagesmeldungen (hereafter referred to as daily report extracts) vom 1–10.9.1942, Major Herbst, 11

Table 4: LWSB, death by hanging, 9 September 1942[21]

No.	German SurName	Spelling First Name	Polish SurName	Spelling First Name	Home
1	Klimus	Anrej	Klimus	Andrezj	Boroditsche
2	Schimtschak	Anton	Szymczak	Antoni	Boroditsche
3	Hantschuk	Antonia	Hanczuk	Antonina	Kamieniuki
4	Hantschuk	Olga	Hanczuk	Olga	Kamieniuki
5	Hantschuk	Wera	Hanczuk	Wiera	Kamieniuki
6	Hantschuk	Marie	Hanczuk	Maria	Kamieniuki
7	Hantschuk	Ignac	Hanczuk	Ignacy	Kamieniuki
8	Nasarewitsch	Wlodmir	Nazarewicz	Wlodzimierz	Kamieniuki
9	Nikitiuk	Dimitrik	Nikitiuk	Dymitr	Kamieniuki
10	Nasarewitsch	Stefan	Nazarewicz	Stefan	Kamieniuki
11	Lis	Alexander	Lis	Aleksander	Kamieniuki
12	Prokoptschuk	Nicolai	Prokopczuk	Nikolaj	Kamieniuki
13	Nasarewitsch	Andrej	Nazarewicz	Andrzej	Kamieniuki
14	Dobunewitsch	Ignaz	Dubaniewicz	Ignacy	Boroditsche
15	Kalischuk	Michael	Kaliszuk	Michal	Boroditsche
16	Lobanowski	Alexi	Lobanowski	Aleksy	Waldbahnhaus Jagen 828
17	Sonnenschein	Vera			Seemiatytsche

There were more public executions on 22 September after another series of surveillance actions. The report confirmed ten persons received death sentences handed down by Herbst's drumhead courtmartial. The Celey couple, in table 4, were man and wife.

September 1942. The Germans went to some trouble to Germanise their victim's names. Two families suffered badly: five from the Hanczuk family and three from the Nazarewicz family.

21 BArch, RL 31/3, document 26, Verzeichnis der am 9 September 1942 erhängten Personen.

Table 5: LWSB, hanging 22 September 1942[22]

No	Name	First Name	Home	Birth
1	Kolunbiego	Iwan	?	27 May 1916
2	Kendis	Iwan	Piaski	4 February 1922
3	Chanowski	Josef	Koniuchowa	1 February 1915
4	Sabolotni	Elonidas	Bielsk	15 April 1916
5	Stanko	Peter	Kschywez	15 May 1908
6	Celey	Boleslaw	Cherlonka	3 September 1895
7	Celey	Maria	Cherlonka	January 1901
8	Gorotschik	Anton	Cherlonka	22 July 1901
9	Gabiecz	Jan	Czwirki	1922
10	?	Iwan	Lumno	?

During October, seven persons accused of being *Bandenhelfer* (bandit-helpers) were hanged. They are listed in table 5. The SS carried out the executions in Bialystok. There is a file note from the 6 October report about a meeting held in Bialystok, hosted by SS-Police *Generalmajor* Müller. Those in attendance included an unnamed battalion commander from Waffen-SS Regiment 8, *Oberst* Hirschfeld the Order Police commander of Bialystok, state official Dr Altenloh, the commander of the security police in Bialystok, and District Propaganda Director Wagner. The Bialystok security police had located the central partisan organization originally identified by Herbst in August. An unknown number of members of this organization were reported killed. Herbst in earlier reports had recommended the best conditions for combating partisans effectively involved the destruction of 'Bolshevist' functionaries, and their followers, in the rear areas, and especially those groups established in the cities. Herbst correctly assumed the police leadership shared his opinion. Müller announced that he would strive, under all circumstances, to clear the rear area and the cities of these elements. Müller placed all senior officers responsible for large-scale actions on notice. Order Police Oberst Hirschfeld argued that positive propaganda might lead some partisans to abandon the movement and

---

22 BArch, RL 31/3, Verzeichnis der aus 22.9.1942 vom Standgericht des SS und Polizeiführers Bialystok, zum Tode durch Erhängen verurteilten Personen.

return to their former peaceful professions. He cited an example where the police had succeeded in Pruzhany encouraging a partisan leader to return to his farm. Herbst objected to a major propaganda campaign, as it would not serve their purpose and might prove counterproductive. Experience had shown him that, with the onset of winter, the vast majority of partisans tried to disguise themselves as harmless farmers. He wanted to prevent them from doing this before they returned to their partisan activities in spring. Müller agreed, determined to prevent the partisans from hiding among the civilians during winter.[23]

Table 6: LWSB, death by hanging, October 1942[24]

No	Name	Vorname	Home	Born
1	Warinow	Boris	Not known	-
2	Zukur	Dimitri	Not known	-
3	Perkowski	Waclaw	Wdigkon	21 August 1913
4	Potoptzow	Theodor	Gut Karoleen	27 February 1922
5	Matkow	Georg	Wojnowka	20 May 1919
6	Pawlik	Grigory	Ohne (sic)	11 July 1914
7	Wereniul	Iwan	Dubiny	10 October 1910

II. The Trusty

There is one complete report from a trusty. It concerned the case of the Soviet partisan deserter Nicolai Laptiev (Germanized as Lapitew). He was the 'partisan-deserter' who denounced twenty-two persons he had formerly worked alongside. He was born on 21 December 1921 in Tschurdurew near Kharkov in Ukraine. His father Sergej was a middle school teacher; shot by the Soviets in 1939. His mother Lilli was from Kharkiv and still alive when he was conscripted into the Red Army in March 1940. He trained with the 137th battalion and then the 29th Tank Division. He was then

---

[23] BArch, RL 31/3, document 45, Abschrift: Aktenvermerk, Major Herbst 6 October 1942.
[24] BArch, RL 31/3, executions by SSPF Bialystok, of inhabitants from the district 22 October 1942. The LWSB courts martial handed out a death sentence for seven people found guilty of being Bandenhelfer. They were all hanged.

transferred to the 178th Independent Tank Battalion, attached to the 10th Army based in Slonim. Before *Barbarossa*, his unit moved to tank training grounds near Bialystok. Once hostilities opened his unit began retreating towards Grodno, but this turned into a rout. He was wounded in the right upper thigh by a bomb splinter on 22 July 1941. His entire unit was captured near Minsk. The majority of the Soviet PoWs were led to a camp in Minsk where Nicolai was taken to a field hospital inside the camp. His injury was not severe but after a few days, he was transferred to a field hospital in Brest-Litovsk. He eventually left the field hospital just before winter. He was then forced to work in the Poligon factory in Brest-Litovsk. According to him, there were several 'Bolshevist' women employed there and they persuaded the Soviet prisoners into escaping.

Nicolai escaped during daylight hours in May 1942. He made contact with a woman called Lydia who lived in Topolower Street, Brest-Litovsk. Lydia allowed him to live in the house for a couple of weeks until he received a set of papers and passes. Nicolai paid Nina, a 'Bolshevist agent' and an employee of the pass administration, 50.00 Reichsmarks and two bottles of corn liquor for forged papers. While living with Lydia, Nicolai discovered the underground cell had a large network. It was then that he decided to denounce the cell because the 'Bolshevists' had killed his father. He dropped the plan when he discovered this female cell was only a sub-organisation of a larger 'partisan' organisation. His next ploy was to collect as much intelligence as possible to offer the Germans, so he agreed to join one of the bands. He was collected by two liaison partisans (bearing false names Heinrich Sauer and Klava) from the forest in Brest-Litovsk together with Gregor, another escaped PoW, sometime around 20–25 May 1942. They received weapons and munitions in an old school. The group then marched for four or five days into the forest. They were expected to join a Zwischenkommando (intermediate commando) based in Piaski. This commando had a hideout in a small forest in Ploschdscha near Sipurka. They were seven men led by a Red Army lieutenant; the band remained in the area for two weeks. They received information from gamekeeper Krupitsch that the Germans were searching the area. The Germans later shot Krupitsch and burned his house down on the strength of Nicolai's information.

Nicolai and his band retreated into the forest. He recalled a group of thirty-two escaped Soviet PoWs passed by on the opposite bank of the River Bug. Their leader, Lieutenant Vassilev, demanded their machine guns but Nicolai's band of twenty-four partisans was able to resist his demands. On another day a seventy strong band of former PoWs passed by led by Captain Vladimir, having also come from the River Bug area. This band had contact with Vassili Trofimowitsch Consendeilo's band of predators mentioned earlier. At this time the female agent Klava joined Vladimir's band. Nicolai explained how well organised they were: the leadership was made up of a lieutenant in command of three-second lieutenants, three political leaders, and two local youths (Wassil and Stefan) who served as forest scouts. Twelve men remained in the camp when the others went out on a raid.

Nicolai was assigned to a splinter group and told how they returned to Ploschdscha because their women lived in the locality. He explained that although small it was administered on military grounds with strict discipline, and with the threat of capital punishment for any sexual contact with women from the villages. Their tasks were fundamentally different from other bands. At first, they had been armed with only three rifles and one machine gun but they gradually acquired more weapons. Villagers gave them supplies without the partisans having to threaten them. They were also ordered to prepare bunkers to store food and quarters for wintertime. They were unable to meet the task only managing to build a small cellar for food storage. They moved every day but used a camp in Jagen 576 as their focal point. Their daily patrol range was as far as twenty-five kilometres away from their camp. Nicolai's band had never been attacked or pursued by the Germans. It only made contact with small bands usually composed of Byelorussians and Poles. There were no firefights between them, but Nicolai's band usually confiscated their weapons. The smaller bands were warned and threatened with death if they attacked and robbed villagers in the forest. These 'local partisans' were then released. Nicolai explained that his band did not want to create any animosity with the local villagers or interrupt their source of supply.

III. A view from within

Rudolf Ludwig was a German Army driver, who escaped from the partisans and was debriefed by the LWSB on 28 November 1942. After the partisans captured Ludwig, they led him into the forest where he learned they were a twenty strong band camped in a secluded enclave of the forest. A former Red Army soldier questioned Ludwig in fluent German, asking him about the general situation, and the size of the military/police forces. Ludwig claimed he hadn't given up information but recalled the interrogation lasted thirty minutes. Then he was given a cooked meal of meatballs and bread and was told, 'that I would soon become fat. The Germans should see how much food the bandits had.' He claimed their conversation often included criticism of the Nazi party, the police, and Hitler, but no one passed criticism of ordinary working-class German soldiers. During the first days in camp, the partisans pitched tents and lit large fires to reduce the effects of the winter cold but were forced to seek shelter from locals when the temperature dropped. A female partisan, the wife of the commander served as the medical orderly. On 18 November 1942, thirty more men joined the band including fifteen Jews. He said, 'the Jews were not particularly popular. They were covered in lice and caused the other men to literally tear off their clothing. The partisans told the Jews they should not be allowed to stay here after the war but sent to Palestine.'

Ludwig learned the partisans received regular military supplies through the Red Air Force; but added, 'I did not observe connections with aviation although the bandits had tracer ammunition and signal cartridges.' They were in constant contact with Moscow through a signals relay station and received news about the rest of the war. He claimed, 'It was obviously a great joy to them to hear about the losses of the Germans and Italians in Africa, and of the defeat of Japan.' He discovered the band's plan to attack Zelwa and the Zelwa-Zlonim railway line. Ludwig was impressed by the partisan's soldierly bearing: 'The bandits gave a good impression and were well armed and every one of them had a rifle; some had automatic rifles or machine pistols.' The partisans were excellent weapons handlers, 'It was obvious that the bandits looked after their weapons well. They spent every free minute attending to them.' He had seen a heavy machine gun and estimated that there were twenty light machine-guns, and a lot of ammunition. The camp had a large store with two barrels of pork; meat from four cows; a cart loaded with bread and, several hundredweight of corn. Ludwig explained, 'The bandits said they would not worry about future supplies because the farmers in the area were very bandit friendly.'

Ludwig made good his escape on 24 November. The partisans were bathing at a farmhouse when he made his getaway. A police border patrol picked him up and he was taken to Mosky where he was handed over to the military railway duty station of *Landesschützen Kompanie 208*. He was then collected by the *Hauptwachmeister* of *Heimfahrkolonne I/8* (Ludwig's unit) and taken to the LWSB for a debriefing by the adjutant. The adjutant concluded the debrief:

> I should mention that Ludwig's statement included a reference to bandits in the forest area—600 men allegedly north of Derczyn and 2,000 men in the area of Baranowicze-Slonim. They are mainly composed of Russians *Volksstämme* (different tribes). Also, some natives are among them. They are 18–35 years of age. They are convinced Soviets and proud of their task to destroy the transport system in our rear area. They feel secure in their hideaways and absolute masters. They are not scared of the police. The inhabitants of the district cooperate with them and support them in many ways.[25]

The LWSB employed Russian trusties to infiltrate the bands or for counterintelligence and propaganda.[26] They had to identify Soviet agents in villages then locate, infiltrate and destroy the bands from within. They were primarily Russians, Belarusians and Ukrainians, and brought an added dimension of 'mistrust' adding to the prevailing mindset among all sides in Białowieża. In November 1942, the adjutant completed a report on the circumstances of three Russian

---

25 BArch, RL 31/3, document 80, Auszugsweise Abschrift aus der Vernehmung vom 28. 11. 1942 des Fahrers Rudolf Ludwig (Heer) der bei den Banditen in Gefangenschaft war.
26 Bogdan Musial, *Sowjetische Partisanen 1941–1944: Mythos und Wirklichkeit*, (Paderborn, 2009), pp. 63–65. The partisan commander of the Lenin Brigade in a report from 1 December 1943 explained that Soviet 'trusties' had provided the intelligence to flush out Polish spies from the forests. The Lenin Brigade was reported in the Bialystok area on 22 December 1943 by German military intelligence but there were no serious incidents recorded between November and January.

trusties serving with the battalion. They set out on 20 October with the mission to scout north of Białowieża in search of partisan camps. They were expected back on 24 October but were missing, and a search was initiated three days later. Two were found dead, hidden away in a deserted partisan camp in *Jagen* 223. The next day the search party found the third man dead, buried in another deserted camp in *Jagen* 224. The report assumed they had been uncovered by members of an *Unterbande* (sub-band) led by a partisan called *Kryslof*, one of several dubbed the 'commander of the forest'. Kryslof had issued a warning on 13 October against all trusties. The same report noted three other trusties had scouted to the northeast and had infiltrated a small band but had returned without success. Their efforts had been undermined by 'inappropriate behaviour of the police in a sub-station', which was not clarified in the final report.[27] In December 1942 a short report was filed about *Sonderjagdokommando Lüttge*. Lieutenant Theodore Lüttge was the oldest of Herbst's officers and commanded a column of nine former Red Army officers and locals serving as trustiess.[28] None of Lüttge's reports have survived.

IV. Countering the bands

From the outset, putting *Bandenbekämpfung* into practice was a complicated mission for Herbst. GIS map 10 illustrates the distribution of partisans killed in Herbst's reports. Not all the bands were working towards the same mission from Moscow. On 31 August he compiled a report that encapsulated all his problems.[29] On the afternoon of 28 August, the first platoon (second company) had captured a partisan west of Narewka Mala. Under interrogation, he claimed his band was attacked by the German army the previous evening and had been scattered. It was later discovered, however, that it was

---

27 BArch, RL 31/3, document 58, Concerning: Lieutenants Iwan Nitschukow, Grigorij Tepljakow, and Second Lieutenant Iwan Kuljeschow, for the army records division Bialystok, Major Herbst, Br. B. Nr./42, O.U, 1 November 1942. Ist possible they were ill-treated by the police.
28 BArch, RL 31/3, document 70, report 11, period 21.11–14.12.42, Major Herbst, 14 December 1942.
29 BArch, RL 31/3, document 12, report 3, period 18–31.8.42, Major Herbst, 31 August 1942.

neither the German army nor police, but a rogue band led by Captain Wassily Trimowitsch [sic]. This band preyed on other partisan bands and attacked small German units. It was partly equipped with German uniforms and weapons. The first platoon later clashed with the Trimowitsch band in *Jagen* 15, estimated to be 30 strong. During the clash, the LWSB suffered a self-inflicted casualty when Aircraftsman Johann K** was *Schuss durch das Gesäss* (shot through the arse) by friendly fire, according to the medical report.[30] The platoon captured the band's entire baggage train including tools, ammunition and diaries/papers. To summarise Herbst's problem: the partisans didn't play by the rules of conventional warfare, the LWSB was not trained in security tactics, many of the troops were not fit for combat, and they were poorly armed. The task facing Herbst however was not just to forge the LWSB into an effective 'anti-bandit' force, he was also expected to fulfil an ideological mission.

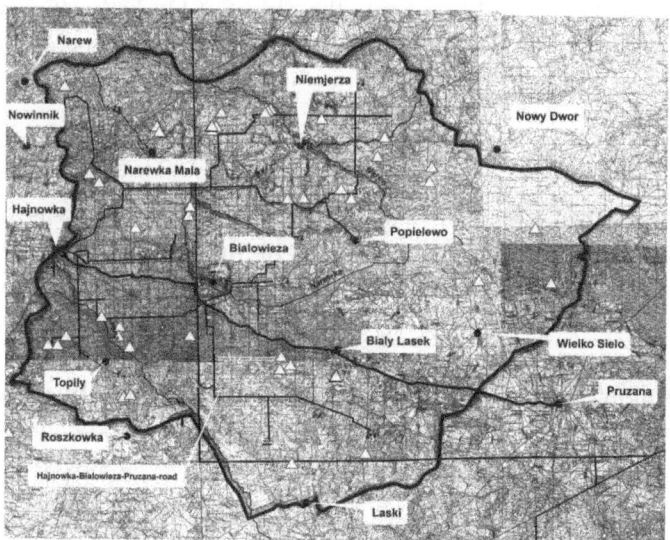

GIS Map 10: the positions of Soviet partisans killed by LWSB
This is a visualises of partisan fatalities across the forest, during the duration of the LWSB's deployment. There is an absence of concentrated areas of killing, which reveals how widespread partisan activity was throughout the forest.

---

30   DDst, Sicherungsbataillon d. Lw. z.b.V. Feldpostnummer L49 006, Luftgaupostamt Königsberg/ PR Namentliche Verlustmeldung – Nr. 1, 1–31 August 1942 (27.7–29.8.42).

On 8 September *Jagdkommando Eule* shot a partisan leader in combat. He was carrying information about *Bandenhelfer* (bandit-helpers) as well as persons targeted for execution by the Soviets. As a consequence of getting the information, seventeen people accused of being *Bandenhelfer* were arrested.[31] A platoon from the third company patrolling *Jagen 218* on 2 October intercepted an *Unterbande* (small sub-band). This band formed an advance scouting party and was led by 'Russian' Captain Vassili Trofmiovitz Conzendeilo[sic] who was shot and killed in a subsequent firefight.[32] In Herbst's fourteenth report (February 1943) partisan leader Wassili Petrowitsch, aka Wassili T. Conzendeilo also known as a 'Russian captain', was identified in a house in Zbucz, a hamlet ten kilometres west of Hajnówka. He was shot when he tried to make an escape through a window. Herbst did not correct the reports or acknowledge the troops' success.[33] There was a pattern of endorsing smooth efficiency rather than high performance, focusing on a few successes rather than achieving a major clear up.

On 26 October (2.00 am), three partisans armed with rifles appeared in Wolka. They took a horse and a cart from a farmer and drove in the direction of Kuraszewo. Five hours later, three *Jagdkommando* (fourth) and a troop from Strongpoint Bialy-Lasek retraced the tracks and found a deserted camp in *Jagen* 753 and the remains of a pig carcass. As the group moved in a south-westerly direction, they stumbled upon another camp with twenty partisans. Although surprised they immediately opened fire, but the partisans escaped, with two believed wounded. They secured the camp and booty of fifteen coats, two pairs of boots, two bags of bread, a salted pig, a radio, some clothing and other items. One section followed the tracks in a northerly direction, and after 550 metres came upon a dead partisan.[34]

---

31 BArch, RL 31/3, documents 24–25, daily report extracts 1–10.9.1942, 11 September 1942.
32 BArch, RL 31/3, document 48, daily report extracts 11–21.10.1942, Major Herbst, 11 October 1942.
33 BArch, RL 31/3, document 48, report 14, period 8.1–1.2.1943, Major Herbst, 1 February 1943.
34 BArch, RL 31/3, document 52, daily report extracts 22–31.10.42, Major Herbst, 11 October 1942.

The report ended without further details. On 28 October, *Jagdkommando Wisent* stumbled into a large partisan camp while on patrol in *Jagen* 254. The camp lay at the heart of a forest clearing and only recently deserted. It was well constructed with spring wells, sleeping bunks, solid wooden shelters and beyond the camp a secret weapons locker (*Schützenlöcher*). The troops pulled a male corpse out of the well and found two more male corpses on the outskirts of the camp. A Russian rifle, maps and other pieces of equipment were secured.

On 11 November, Wladimir Schakewitsch (sic) surrendered himself to the second company. He was a former Soltys confessed that he had gone into hiding for two months because he was frightened of the police.[35] There is an impression that he took a chance in surrendering instead of being captured and killed by a *Jagdkommando*. On 25 November, two dead partisans were found southwest of Luka. They had been beaten and shot in the face to avoid identification. A Russian military pass and Russian rifle ammunition were found on one of them. Two days later ten partisans appeared in Waski and a *Jagdkommando* from the fourth company was sent to intercept them. As the *Jagdkommando* approached Waski the partisans opened fire with machine guns. The onset of darkness curtailed a search of the village. Herbst believed the quick reaction *Jagdkommando* had prevented the partisans from taking away five fully loaded horse carts of food and clothes. On the same day, Serjey Charkewitsch (sic) the former mayor of Lewkowe-Stare surrendered to the second company. He had fled to the forest in 1941 when the Germans arrived and led a five-man band existing in a hideout in *Jagen* 70. He was under the impression there was an amnesty.

The Germans also attempted to offer amnesty to those partisans who surrendered, but it represented such an ideological contradiction that it didn't find favour in all circles. *SS-Standartenführer* Fromm posted a declaration offering amnesty to any partisans in the forest. Fromm's amnesty announced: 'the consequences of the war had particularly affected this area, forcing part of the population to leave their homes. Some people fled into the forest because

---

35 BArch, RL 31/3, document 63, daily report extracts 1–20.11.42, Major Herbst 21 November 1942.

their homes were destroyed during the fighting. They went into hiding because they feared the Germans. The area had been peaceful for more than a year and the Bolshevists did not and will not return.' Fromm claimed this was achieved by German soldiers fighting thousands of kilometres away on the Volga River (meaning Stalingrad) or in the Caucasus. He called upon the forest folk to recognise the Germans had brought security and peace, enabling them to work undisturbed. The final paragraph of the amnesty contained a remarkable gesture given that it came from an SS officer:

> Many of you who fled from us have wanted to return home. More so because of the onset of wintertime with all its hardships. We want to make this move easier for you. We assure everybody, who now lives in the forests or hides somewhere as a bandit or for a political or other reason, they will not be punished if they return in the space of three weeks, announce themselves at the Soltys, and hand over their weapons. In this case, we will make sure that accommodation is given to them in their hometown or in another place of their choice and will be given a job there. So please take this opportunity which is only offered to you once.[36]

This amnesty was issued just three months after the introduction of the *Bandenbekämpfung* doctrine. The timing was strange since both the SS and *Luftwaffe* had claimed the upper hand over the partisans. It was announced publicly the day after *Unternehmen Wisent* ended. Herbst was not convinced by Fromm's amnesty and wrote to Göring: 'Amnesty was against my advice to the *SSPF-Bialystok*, and it only led to the surrender of three partisans, who had hidden in the forests', although several other men had also surrendered themselves to police posts along the forest's borders. In a subsequent report, Herbst again raised his concerns over the amnesty. He referred to the case of a former resident from *Amtsbezirk Czereszow* who re-appeared before the town's strongpoint. He had been kidnapped along with eight other men by a band of ninety partisans several months before and had negotiated his release from the band. Upon his return, he was asked to go back to the band to request their surrender and their weapons. Herbst noted that 'in

---

36   BArch, RL 31/3, document 66, Amnesty, posted by SS-Standartenführer Fromm, 16 October 1942.

compensation, the partisans would only be sent to a PoW or work camp—hardly a fair bargain.'[37] Herbst thought Fromm's offer was too miserly and without substance:

> I didn't intervene because the time period, mentioned in the amnesty, had already expired but I pointed out that it does not serve any purpose to pardon the bandits, who are escaping into the forest. They would only spend the wintertime in glorious conditions and then return to the bandits in the spring.[38]

There was a postscript to Fromm's amnesty. On 18 February 1943, twenty partisans participated in the assassination of a man accused of being a German stool pigeon. That evening partisans also killed three men; deserters that accepted Fromm's amnesty.[39] Herbst's complaints about the amnesty were couched to imply the SS was 'soft on terror'.

Image 11: Białowieża forest—partisan memorial in the conservation area.
Source: Author.

---

37 BArch, RL 31/3, document 48, daily report extracts 11–21.10.1942, Major Herbst, 21 October 1942.
38 BArch, RL 31/3, document 62, report 10, period 1–20.11.42, Major Herbst, 22 November 1942.
39 BArch, RL 31/3, document 100, Auszug aus den Tagesmeldungen vom 13.2–4.3.1943.

6. Population Engineering

How was *Bezirk Bialystok* and in particular Białowieża to be administered? Whether through Imperial German style colonisation or Nazi *Lebensraum*, the administration was bound to race, populations and social engineering policies. The usual interpretation of Hitler's *Lebensraum* is the cobbled-together agenda of social Darwinism drawn from a range of genres like anthropology meshed with Nazi eugenics and *völkisch* fantasies.[1] There was a utility to this kind of dogma which granted ease of application from theory to practice. In areas further to the east than Bezirk *Bialystok*, mindsets attuned to achieving *Lebensraum* quickly — through extreme racial engineering and genocide — were prone to wild behaviour and poorly administered killing actions. In territories closely connected to the homeland, there appears to have been a greater sense of control over racial engineering and genocide. This can be seen in German occupation methods in *Bezirk Bialystok*, where administrative structures were overlayed onto existing establishments. As was found in the previous chapter, the Nazis erected overlapping layers of administration with similar terms of reference which sporadically sparked rivalries. This administrative surplus was not a permanent fixture, but before the setbacks after Stalingrad, it made it possible for the Nazi leadership to follow war and racial policies in parallel. Nazi leaders like Heinrich Himmler understood this and Erich Koch fully exploited it in *Bezirk Bialystok*. In the period 1941–42, the mass deportations of Jews and Poles, caused the system neither to lurched nor jolt, but adjusted to the task. In Nazi governance, this level of integrated response served both ideological and functional tasks. Even the security warfare organisations — the SS-Police, the army, and the Luftwaffe — were forced to consider a broad range of rationales than simply applying brute force. Sometimes civilian authorities and the security services were out of kilter, but on the whole, there was synchronisation towards

---

1 Gretchen E. Schafft, *From Racism to Genocide: Anthropology in the Third Reich*, (Illinois, 2004) and George L. Mosse, *The Crisis of German Ideology: Intellectual Origins of the Third Reich*, (New York, 1998).

expediting tasks swiftly and efficiently. Where differential behaviour did appear, it was always about interpretation, never about the outcome. *Bezirk Bialystok* was different but not 'normal'. It was a powerful securitised state, working to a peculiar set of rules, where genocide and the Holocaust were incorporated in a highly regulated and controlled administration.

Białowieża's story, however, is punctuated with inconsistencies and ambiguities partly because the evidence is incomplete or one-sided, and partly due to its exceptional standing within *Bezirk Bialystok* as a place of environmental biodiversity and ecological culture. The *Urwald* (forest wilderness) was an old German and Nazi fantasy, but Białowieża was no longer an *Urwald* in the true sense of the meaning. This contradiction materialized in many ways and forms and confounds any final estimation of what the Nazis were trying to do in Białowieża. Plans were known to have been drawn up by the *Oberforstamt Bialowies*, under the guidance of the RFA's central offices in Berlin. There is no copy, but the diary of the *Sicherungsbataillon der Luftwaffe Bialowies* repeatedly referred to a plan. It is impossible to confirm whether this plan was drawn before the invasion in 1941 or after. Scherping's published report from December 1941, alluded to a plan to return the forest to its natural wilderness. He claimed many settlements were destroyed and the locals deported because they vandalised the forest. However, an assumption that all the communities were wiped out in wholesale exchange for wilderness is incorrect. The deportations were followed by 'colonies' of ethnic Germans, also cited by the Luftwaffe diary as per the plan. The expansion of the Białowieża arena, into the so-called *Urwald Bialowies*, widened the catchment of civilian communities. These 'additional' communities were not related to Białowieża's pre-1939 communities. The main forest road from Białowieża to Pruzhany, sixty-three kilometres long, imposed limitations on the peasant communities and their panjewagens. The middle class, an important thriving social group in the Hajnówka area were more likely to relate to Bialystok than Pruzhany. A photographic collection reveals Białowieża was no longer a rural backwater in the 1930s.² Scherping's memories of 1915 were no longer comparable to 1941. There was also wealth to be plundered from the raw materials of the timber industry and the derivatives of tar or wood pulp. If the value of the forest's timber was combined with the wealth of the wild game stocks, it could be fairly assumed that Białowieża was the jewel in the crown of *Bezirk Bialystok*. This established Białowieża as a target for another group, the carpetbaggers, individuals that existed below the institutional radar with no other purpose than acquiring wealth. They were epitomized by Oskar Schindler, who went to occupied Poland in search of a fortune.³

I. Accounting for wilderness

The general rule governing modern organisations and institutions, military or civilian, would normally be an 'incomes and expenditures' method of public accounting. The financial statements of *Oberforstamt Bialowies* for the period 1942–44 were submitted to the Reich Ministry of Finance (RMF) and they followed the 'incomes and expenditures' format. This collection of budget statements referred to the RFA's activities in *Urwald Bialowies* and are the only original documents from the occupation that have survived. There is correspondence confirming this was a closing budget statement for the financial year ending April 1944, but the supplementary documents are from the previous period. The statement presented gross financial totals for 1943, including revenues of 8,060,687.40 Reichsmarks and expenditures of 5,746,849.29 Reichsmarks, with a nominal surplus of 2,314,238.11 Reichsmarks. By taking the closing figures for the 1942 budget and the opening balance for the 1943 period, it is possible to recreate an impression of the business activities through to April 1944.

The covering letter from the RFA identified two extraordinary items: 200,000 Reichsmarks for the *Ortswehren*, the civil guard (see also chapter six), described by the RFA as *Selbstschutzkampf*, and 726,250.00 Reichsmarks set aside for the *Forstschutzkorps* (FSK).

---

2 Alla Gryc (ed), *Hajnówka W Starej Fotografii*, (Hajnówka, 2007).
3 Thomas Keneally, *Schindler's Ark*, (London, 1982).

Both items were described as directly attributable to the fight against Soviet partisans. The *Ortswehren* was a local defence militia recognized by Major Herbst in October 1942. He requested permission to arm the locals to combat the partisans and Brauchitsch passed on his request to the RFA in Berlin assuming it was a civilian matter. The RFA, in turn, requested an extraordinary budgetary amount from the RMF on 20 October 1943 to meet the costs. The RMF accepted the request and release funds, with an additional provision for extra funding. Herbst had assumed the process was unnecessarily ponderous, whereas the budget statement indicates the officials followed normal budgetary procedures. The *Ortswehren* does identify a two-speed process, between the Luftwaffe and Berlin, which might have been attributable to *Bezirk Bialystok's* standing as home territory.

There is a confusion of evidence about local civilians collaborating with the Germans. Herbst sent Brauchitsch a proposal to raise an *Ortswehren* (civil guards), a self-defence militia mustered from locals. In the report, Herbst referred to a request (A.Qu. Nr. 201/42 secret—no known copy) sent to Brauchitsch to press Göring into issuing the order to deliver captured 'western European rifles.' The issue of weapons did not come down to the supply of weapons to Slavs but rather receiving budgetary approval from Berlin. This represented a conundrum between Nazi ideology and the racial concept of *Untermenschen* (sub-humans) and arming Slav collaborators on grounds of security necessity. Herbst's recommended 2,000 foreign rifles to loyal locals but this had not materialised.[4] Herbst thought he faced a wall of silence, but it was the RFA's plodding bureaucracy. Berlin had approved the weapons, but the decision was delayed within the budgetary process. Herbst wrote that service in the civil guard was *Ehrendienst* (unpaid service) for all male citizens aged eighteen to fifty with a spotless record and a reliable reputation. They could guarantee the security of the settlements either independently or in cooperation with the

---

4   BArch, RL 31/3, document 47, report 8, period 11–21.10.1942, Major Herbst, 23 October 1942. The rifles in question were known to have come from the captured stocks from the 1940 campaign in the west.

Wehrmacht. The volunteers had to inform their local Soltys, who would announce them to the designated *Amtskommissar*. The *Amtskommissar* would then pass lists of names to Herbst for final approval. A leader and a deputy had to be appointed for every militia unit and Herbst would confirm them after a thorough examination. The main task of the militia was village protection at night. They each had to be strong enough to provide sufficient guard posts and patrols during the evening, with a rota to enable men to rest and continue their daily work.[5]

In 1942, the RFA rented accommodation for thirty employees, seven staff were granted access to dining facilities in *Schloss Bialowies* (Tsar's palace) at a total cost of 5,000 Reichsmarks. This was presumably the headquarters staff of *Oberforstamt Bialowies*, quartered within the grounds of the former Tsarist offices. These figures did not change in 1943. A cook was employed among seven extra staff, at a daily rate of 1.50 Reichsmarks raising the total expenditure from dining of 5,000 Reichsmarks in 1943. Receipts from agricultural sales included a contribution back to the *Schloss* of 2,750 Reichsmarks for vegetables and 4,000 Reichsmarks for meat. The hunt was administered from the *Schloss* for 12,000 Reichsmarks for 1942 and 1943. The 'red light' in the figures being the extra allowances. As *Beamte* (officials) the members of the RFA received a generous allowance in addition to basic salaries. They covered food, clothing, travel and quarters, and subsidies to German families with spouses on 'overseas service'. Another contradiction of *Bezirk Bialystok* administered as a home territory with civil servants receiving allowances for foreign service.

Beyond the headquarters, the estate managers were responsible for overseeing forestry and agricultural business. An estate manager received an annual salary of 450 Reichsmarks, which was noted as an extraordinary item within total salaries of 5,400 Reichsmarks. The war diaries point to almost all these managers being German, but necessarily RFA employees. A large surplus was

---

5   BArch, RL 31/3, document 78, Major Herbst, Bevollmächtigter des Reichsmarschall des Großdeutschen Reiches, O.U., 29.11.1942, Call to the population of the Reichsforstgebiet.

generated from agriculture: 15,000 Reichsmarks in 1942, this increased to 50,000 Reichsmarks in 1943. By comparison, there was a smaller level of cattle trade at less than 5,000 Reichsmarks. This might reflect Scherping's order to remove the cattle in 1941. Forestry and wood were the main sources of revenue. Timber sold to the *Deutsche Reichsbahn*, to the sawmills, and to the forest railway raised a total of 2,090,000 Reichsmarks. This income came from the sale and distribution of cut timber and bark. The RFA rented factories to private persons or companies, but the rental levels were not disclosed. There was extensive timber cutting throughout the occupation, proving once again the inconsistency with the wilderness fantasy. The statement listed the sawmills in Hajnówka, Grodek, Podolany and Rorschek, all fully operational. Labour assigned to the timber and sawmills in 1942 cost 24,000 Reichsmarks in wages, but this plummeted to just 2,000 Reichsmarks in 1943. This was due to several factors including the employment of cheap and slave labour. The 'foreign workers' employed were identified as 'Polish' with total wages of 90–140,000 Reichsmarks. The numbers of workers and the daily wage rate are unknown. The budget showed the RFA was the main supplier of electricity to the forest, but there were no revenues. The forest railway received a fixed budget. A large part of the income came from carrying timber to the main distribution points of the *Deutsche Reichsbahn* or the sawmills. In 1942 this had generated 390,000 Reichsmarks, which increased to 506,000 Reichsmarks by the close of 1943. Interestingly, the use of oil and fuel reduced from 120,000 Reichsmarks to 65,000 Reichsmarks possibly due to more effective maintenance and wood-burning. The revenues generated from railway operations included transporting labourers from their quarters or camps to workplaces. The salaries of the railway workers increased from 80,000 in 1942 to 155,000 Reichsmarks in 1943. Track maintenance, workshops and loading bays increased in cost to 330,000 and 440,000 Reichsmarks respectively over the period.[6]

---

6   BArch, R 2/4699, RFA, Forstwesen, Urwaldgebiet Bialowies, Reichsfinanzministerium, abt.1, May 1944; Ausserordentlicher (Kriegs) Haushalt XVIIa Teil

The RFA's budgets are a small window into the workings of Białowieża. The statement presented the *Oberforstamt Bialowies* as an efficient governmental organisation, and without significant operational issues. In this context, they disguise more than they reveal. The partisans were treated as an extraordinary item, a temporary problem confined to the duration of the war. Scherping's ambitions were not reflected in the budget. His long-term ecological plan was at odds with the day-to-day management of the RFA. The Białowieża project was progressing but not within the bounds of a wilderness fantasy. Any public bookkeeper, filing this budget in Berlin, would no doubt conclude *Urwald Bialowies* was a quiet backwater with a minor social violence problem. Whether this Nazi project was succeeding or failing remains unknown.

II. The curious case of Roczkowka

The case of Roczkowka was curious because the Germans did not kill anyone. The evidence behind this incident began with a letter from *SD-Befehlsstab-Bialystok* to the LWSB on 24 September 1942.[7] An *SS-Sonderkommando*, possibly raised from the Kamienicec-Litewski ghetto guard, had reported serious partisan activity within its vicinity *SD-Befehlsstab-Bialystok*. An SS wrote to Herbst with evidence of a 'suspicious' village:

> The village Roczkowka, which is south of Kaminiki, has been declared under partisan-bondage *(bandenhörig)* by several authorities. Liaison agent 0228 was assigned to find out about the reliability of the village people. He is officially a technician. We now have the result of his latest observations. According to agent 0228, the village Roczkowka serves as a sort of bandit settlement *(Bandenniederlassung)*. There is permanent coming and going from the village to the forest by bandits.[8]

XXI Unterteil I; Haushalt für das Oberforstamt Urwald Bialowies, Staatsjagdrevier in Bialowies für das Rechnungsjahr 1943.

7   BArch, RL 31/3, document 38, Auszugsweise Abschrift des Schreibens des Inspekteurs der Sicherheitspolizei und des SD Befehlstab Bialystok vom 24 September 1942. There is no evidence of Agent 0228's identity its possible he was Polish or Belarus but was proven to be unreliable.

8   Sometimes written as Roszkowka and Kaminiki meaning Kamienicec, illustrate the range of spellings.

Agent 0228 alleged Anton Protaszewicz, the Roczkowka *Untersoltys*, of being overheard making derogatory remarks about the Germans:

> The situation will not always be as it is at the moment. We all know that the bandits are good men, but the damned Germans are worse than the bandits. We are all sticking together, and we do not deliver each other to the Germans. The time will come when we all will become bandits. The German tanks cannot drive into the forest and they are not going to search for us in the forest.[9]

The SS concluded the *Untersoltys'* comments were typical of the prevailing attitude among the community.

The SD letter to Herbst explained, on 15 September Afanasi Panasiuk, a villager had returned from the forest in the evening from an area to the northwest of the village. He was joined by two or more men from the village. They were carrying an illegal alcohol still that had been hidden a short distance away in the undergrowth. The SD assumed that the illegal distillers had supplied the forest's partisans with Samogong, wood alcohol like Vodka. The SD classified the village as *Bandenhörigkeit* (under partisan-bondage) and hostile to the Germans. The complaint added the Soltys had failed to report the appearance of partisans, as bound under the occupation regulations. This was judged the typical behaviour of a village under *Bandenhörigkeit*. The SD advised they could not accept a permanent partisan presence in any village. Agent 0228 also claimed to have observed Alexander Kuczynski, a villa farmer, acting suspiciously. He had driven a pig, a sow and five piglets to pasture but returned in the evening with only the sow and piglets. When Agent 0228 asked him about the pig, he said he did not know where it was. The SD argued:

> We are convinced that he received an order to deliver the pig to the bandits in the forest. The overall impression from the liaison agent is that the bandits are permanently supplied with food from the villages of the forest. We can also assume that the bandits pass information from the Soviets to the population of these villages. Parts of Roczkowko's pastures lie deep inside the forest area. The pastures are close to a favourite Jagen used by the bandits for temporary camps. This permanent connection with the bandits is now blatantly obvious.[10]

---

9 Ibid.
10 Ibid.

Alexander Protaszewies was accused of complaining that the partisans had taken (stolen) iron rods from the school's roof structure and that Roczkowka had been made to provide vehicles to transport building materials. According to the SD, Protaszewies had said, 'its damned work. We drove the building material for the Germans to Dimitrowicze. We loaded it up with our hands but soon the Germans will be harnessed to the cart and they will have to load up the material with their teeth and drag it back here.' The SD also accused the village of being lax over security matters. The local Nazi *Amtskommissar* (department commissioner) had ordered each village to raise a night guard. The Roczkowka guard was often found asleep. The SD concluded: 'They are obviously not afraid of the partisans because they support them. The same is said for the village of Chwojanowka, which lies southwest of Roczkowka.' The letter concluded that Agent 0228 would return to the village in a few days to continue his surveillance.

Six days after receipt of the SD letter, Emil Herbst added a note in the diary: a decision was taken to make an example of Roczkowka. An action was planned for 28 September 1942. The plan incorporated a 'commando' (three officers, 120 ORs) from SS-Police Regiment 2 and three LWSB *Jagdkommandos*. The village was to be encircled and occupied. The inhabitants were to be informed that they were subject to a special action because the village was accused of *Bandenhörigkeit*. All the adult inhabitants were to be shot. The children aged twelve or younger were to be adopted by families of surrounding villages. Girls (aged 12–22) and boys (aged 12–17) were to be sent to Germany as slave labourers. There was a rather contradictory comment as to what would happen to the village. In one statement Herbst indicated the village would be burned to the ground. In another, the village was to be assigned to selected inhabitants from the villages of Eljazucki, Nichnowka and Cherlonka, which were to be evacuated later under the resettlement program. As the senior civilian police authority in the region, *SSPF-Bialystok* sanctioned all these measures.

On the morning of 28 September, the inhabitants were given two hours to load their belongings onto trucks. At the same time, the seventy-three teenagers listed for labour in Germany were prepared to be taken to Białowieża. The *Hilfsdienst* (collaborators) and inhabitants from other villages were ordered to round up the larger farm animals and lead them away. The small farm animals were loaded onto panje-wagons and taken to the designated livestock collection area. The list of farm animals included: 113 horses, 258 beef cattle, 458 sheep, 115 pigs, and 363 chickens. These numbers indicated a relatively prosperous village. After dealing with the farm animals the Germans began herding the people. Women from other villages collected all the children below twelve (156) in panje-wagons, and the seventy-three teenagers were led away to the Nazis' forced labour centre. The village manifest listed twenty-four absent inhabitants. They were accounted for as employed in other villages under Nazi labour regulations. There were seven persons excluded from the condemned because they were 'certainly not sympathizers of the Bolshevists.' They included an anti-communist Cossack of the old *Denikin* army (a reference to the White Russian army), the mother of a child serving in the *Hilfdienst,* and the wife of a serving German soldier. The Germans selected eight persons 'each with a bright and vivid expression' to be taken to Białowieża and 'interrogated intensely'. The remaining 264 adults of a total community of 532 persons were to be killed. The grave pits were dug by the intended victims and the execution squad lined up.

The '264' were led before the grave pits. Herbst questioned several of them one final time. He spoke to the Soltys a second time. He learned in the spring of 1942, the village had suffered from an outbreak of typhus and the partisans avoided all contact. There were two incidents when the partisans did try to enter the village, but the local gendarmerie post had been informed. During one incident, the villagers chased off the partisans with sticks and stones. Herbst, later noted in his report, when the Soltys was told they were to be shot, 'he left a strong impression as an upright man'. He was reassured by the Soltys' who was not *hündisch* (dog-like), even before the grave pits. The Soltys had refused to pass on any false names of bandit-helpers, even when such accusations would have saved him considerable misery. Herbst accepted the villagers were not 'bandit-helpers'. He re-questioned Alexander Kuczynski, accused of taking his pigs to the partisans. His children had chased the pigs and piglets into the woods, but they were still part of the farm stock. However, the children had been arrested by the gendarmerie. Herbst's concerns doubts shifted to the reliability of Agent 0228, but there was no evidence of what happened later.

Herbst, no longer convinced the village was *Bandenhörigkeit*, rescinded the execution orders. However, innocent or not, the '264' remained standing before the grave pits as he harangued them about the punishment for assisting the partisans. The children and animals were returned. In his report, Herbst concluded: 'We have to believe that the village will beat-up any partisan who even comes near to the village.' All senior officers from the different Nazi offices agreed that sparing the inhabitants this time served the occupation. Those persons taken to Białowieża for interrogation only confirmed Herbst's decision to grant 'mercy', and the last returned to the village on 30 September 1942.[11] In his sixth report, Herbst referred to the Roczkowka action:

> The operation on 28 September, against the village of Roczkowka was stopped at the last moment. It was planned to execute all 270 adult inhabitants of the village. The mass grave was already dug and the people stood in front of it. The reason for it being halted was that the accusations by the SD and other agencies could not be proven.[12]

Generalmajor Müller hailed the outcome as a valuable propaganda coup and believed its consequences should be analysed and assessed. The case was discussed among Nazi official circles in Bialystok. They agreed to hold meetings of regional and local commissioners from the area to examine the ramifications. There was a general recognition that officialdom should better plan resettlement actions in the *Reichsforstgebiet* and the borders.[13] One author has noted that the grave pit remained open when Herbst led a visit

---

11 BArch, RL 31/3, document 39, Aktenvermerk, 29 September 1942.
12 BArch, RL 31/3, document 34, report 6, period 21.9.-30.9.1942, Major Herbst, 1 October 1942.
13 BArch, RL 31/3, document 34-35, report 6, period 21-30.9.1942, Major Herbst, 1 October 1942.

of dignitaries from Bialystok on 22 November. The lessons of Roczkowka were still being taught.¹⁴ It is believed that in 1967, while under criminal investigation, Herbst claimed that Roczkowka was an act of his 'mercy'. Subsequently, German writers have largely accepted Herbst's defence to explain his behaviour.¹⁵ The West German war crimes investigators did not pursue the case against Herbst. The evidence contradicts Herbst's defence. He gloated over the result as yet another snub to his rivals and basked in his spiteful manipulation of psychological terror.

III. Making wilderness

The levels of German administration that had descended on Bialystok-Białowieża made a mockery of Scherping's claims of turning the forest into a wilderness. However, it is incorrect to assume the deportations were a cloak for Nazi racial resettlement. A report by Herbst referred to the plan to bring about wilderness through mass deportations. He paraphrased Scherping about the locals' behaviour: 'The absurd clearances in earlier years into the forest area has weakened the local land economy and led to vast clearing of trees.' He confirmed the existence of a plan to deport civilians from the entire *Urwald Bialowies* area as well as a contingency for policing the remaining communities:

> We work on a radical evacuation plan in cooperation with the *Oberforstverwaltung* and the representative of the civil administration, *Amtskommissar* Schargenorth. I made the suggestion to leave only the part of the civil population in the area of the primaeval forest, which is necessary for the forest economy and to concentrate the population to certain *Stützpunkte*, which need to be determined by the *Oberforstverwaltung*.

It is probable that Göring had agreed with Herbst's 'evacuation plan' after taking soundings from *Oberforstmeister* Wagner (see table 7 for the list of remaining indigenous communities).¹⁶

On 24 September Herbst met with *Generalmajor* Müller and other local civilian administrators in Bialystok. They discussed the

---

14 Ripperger et al, *Der Traum Vom Urwald*, p. 295.
15 Ibid., pp. 320–1 and see also Gautschi, *Der Reichsjägermeister*, pp. 218–9.
16 BArch, RL 31/3, document 2, report 1, Major Herbst, 6 August 1942.

evacuations and the possibility of arming the remaining locals as civil guards. A first stage plan was coordinated to remove 4,000 inhabitants from: Rybaki, Slobodka, Luka, Eljaszuki, Michnowka, Lewkowo-Stare, Narewka, Niemionowka and Czerlonka.[17] On 30 October, Herbst announced the proposals to those locals destined for deportation:

> We intend to resettle a part of the population into Bialystok and to make them available for work in local industries. The purpose of the resettlement is the creation of clear forest and agricultural economical conditions as part of the restructuring process of the *Reichsforstgebiet*. The *Reichsmarschall* has given the order to conduct these resettlement actions avoiding all unnecessary hardships as repeatedly occurred during previous evacuations. Therefore, everything will be prepared for the resettled people at their new location and every family will receive a new home. Income and food will be guaranteed by their immediate employment in the local industry. The resettlements will only proceed after we have received confirmation about the completion of these preparations. Enough time will then be given to the population to prepare their resettlement.

Herbst's language was not hostile or aggressive. His words promised a decent life, but for those being forcibly deported the prospect was not paradise. He went on to explain the personal belongings and allowances the locals could take with them:

> In principle, they will be able to move all their transferable processions. Every family shall only take up to two pounds of potatoes, their flour store and small quantities of eggs, butter, fat and so forth. They are also allowed to take four chickens. Food will be made available at the new localities. The remaining cattle and chickens will be sold at fixed prices to the responsible *Amtskomissar*. They are allowed to sell possessions, which cannot be transported on the free market and the Amtskomissar will buy the stuff for estimated prices. The transports will be conducted with horse carts in close convoy and with military escort.

The caring approach was extended to the deportations and he expected those being deported to cooperate with the move:

> In principle two carts shall be provided for each family. It is possible to provide one cart more for families with more than six children. Only carts, which are provided by the *Amtskommissar*, shall be used for the transport. You will not be allowed to take your own carts or horses into Bialystok. These

---

17 BArch, RL 31/3, daily reports extracts 21.9–30.10.1942, 1 October 1942. BArch, RL31/3, document 41, report 7, period 1–10.10.1942, Major Herbst, 11 October 1942.

preparations will help avoid unnecessary hardship and all families will receive an improvement in their living conditions at their new homes. Consequently, we expect the population to follow orders and the appointed actions and not interrupt the conduct of this large-scale resettlement work ...

The caring approach could not last an entire document and Herbst warned at the end, 'Whoever disobeys or causes unnecessary difficulties has to expect severe punishment.'[18]

Table 7: Forest communities and the results of deportation.[19]

No.	Community	Original Population	Still Resident	Total Households	Total Farms
1	Annopol	290	117	407	58
2	Bakuny	517	303	820	85
3	Chwalowo 1	345	135	480	68
4	Chwalowo II	554	58	612	96
5	Haleny	266	240	506	73
6	Hryniewicze	214	54	268	50
7	Izbice	149	50	199	36
8	Leschajka	362	261	623	78
9	Lichosielce	597	495	1092	120
10	Mokre	293	323	616	59
11	Murawa	926	372	1298	192
12	Nowosiolki	641	147	788	131
13	Roubeck	1237	346	1583	224
14	Suchopol	714	430	1144	136
Total		7105	3331	10436	1406

Herbst reported that his negotiations with the president of the regional government in Bialystok, and other police and civil administrators were proceeding along positive lines. The city authorities in Bialystok offered 35,000 lodgings, to resettlement locals from the forest, which would be increased to 49,000 as required. He expected

---

18 BArch, RL 31/3, document 59, Bevollmächtigter des Reichsmarschalls des Grossdeutschen Reiches Br.B.Nr. 821/42. Aufruf an die Bevölkerung im Reichsforstgebiet, Major Herbst, 30 October 1942.
19 BArch, RL 31/3, the list of original population figures and the remaining numbers following the first resettlement actions in 1941.

to begin the resettlement actions within ten days around 2 November, writing: 'We have the possibility to enforce such a settlement policy in the *Reichsforstgebiet* and the bordering communities that will finally serve the desired outcome.' He proposed discussions with the *Oberforstamt* about other priorities of economic importance and to then finalise matters with Göring. A list was passed to Brauchitsch with an explanation of how badly prepared the deportations of Suchopol had been in 1941 and why the community had not recovered. There had been 7,105 people in the town in 1941 but only 3,331 persons remained. Table 7 listed the effect on the town, after the deportations, and a large number of empty properties. There is little doubt the remaining locals lived in a constant state of concern over their future. Herbst confirmed, 'We have already taken the decision to create a *Reichsdomäne* (state-run estates) in the area around Suchopol, which is very suitable for farming', and populated with ethnic Germans.[20] The deportations of Suchopol were set to begin on 5 November, after the harvest.[21]

Lw.Lieutenant Schultrich was designated the LWSB's *Umsiedlungsoffizier* (resettlement officer). He agreed on an outline plan with Dr. Brix in Bialystok, and with the Bielsk land commissioner and the *Amtskommissars* of *Suchopol*, *Czerezow* and *Bialowies*. The mechanics of deportation were set in two phases. The first phase began with selections indicating these deportations were not about entire communities. The target group of the deportation list were those persons without a steady income, or 'healthy existence', or identified as without the right to exist (*Existenzberechtigung*) in any form in the forest. The resettlement was conducted in convoys each of 500 persons and under military escort. The military escorts were arranged: *Amtskommissariat Bialowies* with troops from the first company; the *Amtskommissariat Suchopol* with troops from the third company; and the *Amtskommissariat Czerszow* with troops from the fourth company. The Bialystok's *Oberbürgermeister* agreed to accept the convoys during a 48-hour window when care and quarters

---

20 BArch, RL 31/3, document 47, report 8, period 11–21.10.1942, Major Herbst, 23 October 1942.
21 BArch, RL 31/3, document 50, report 9, period 22–31.10.1942, Major Herbst, 2 November 1942.

would be prepared. The convoys were to depart from: *Amtskommissariat Bialowies, Suchopol* and *Czereszow* on a strict rotation basis. The *Amtskommissars* were to provide each resettled family with a stamped and signed resettlement document including all their personal details. The escort commander received a list of those being deported signed and stamped by the *Amtskommissariat* containing the names of all persons in the convoy. Copies of these transit lists were distributed to the *Oberbürgermeister*, the LWSB and a third copy retained with the *Amtskommissar*.[22]

Schultrich explained how the convoy system was to work. Two carts would be provided for each family from other communities. The carts would be taken from those families not being resettled. Each cart received a plate on its left side with its number in the convoy and the number of the family members (the given example was 1/5, meaning the first cart with five persons). The commanders were ordered to regulate the loads on the vehicles. The carts travelled in a convoy and the sequence was given the example 1, 2, 3 etc. The military escort included the convoy commander, a company sergeant major, a translator, and nine troopers each supplied with a bicycle. The convoy commanders were allocated four days from start to finish. The convoy route was divided into sections: the first section Czerszow-Suchopol-Białowieża; the second section Białowieża-Halody; the third section Halody-Ryboly; and the fourth section Ryboly-Bialystok. The route had an approximate distance of 90 kilometres, mostly along secondary lanes or rough tracks. The troops and all-male deportees were to guard the carts at night. The women and children were allowed to spend the night in houses of villages along the route; the Soltys were to provide quarters in their villages. The horses were to be watered regularly. In the event of any problems, convoy commanders were given the authority to requisition fresh mounts or carts from villages. Schultrich insisted at the end of the day the horse-drawn carts were to form a

---

22   Ibid.

Wagenburg (protective circle) for security. Once again confirming German fascination with American frontier culture.[23]

After arriving in Bialystok, the convoy commanders were to deliver each transport in the sequence of the transit lists. The escort and translators were to return by the first available train to Białowieża, having received their travel warrants before departure. Bicycles had to be carried on the train and handed back in Białowieża. In the event of any incidents, the NCOs were to report to the LWSB's headquarters in Białowieża. Locals were appointed to lead the horses and empty carts back to Białowieża unguarded. There is no indication of how they were to defend themselves against partisans or receive fodder and rations. The *Amtskommissars* issued passes enabling the drivers to travel through checkpoints between Bialystok and Suchopol with free passage by the police. The instructions for the drivers and the deportees were first read aloud in both Russian and Polish to local headsmen or Soltys on 30 October. This same procedure was followed two or three days before departure with the instructions being again read aloud to the deportees by translators. Any questions raised at the readings had to be answered by the *Amtskommissar* or resettlement officer. Once the details about the process were completed, those being deported were given another reading, in Polish and Russian, about the positive benefits of resettlement.

The question of property and plunder were the constants of German plans irrespective of how caring the instructions might first appear. Schultrich explained that the Amtskommissar were to purchase any property that could not be transported on an estimated value basis. Purchased cattle were to be taken to the slaughterhouses but the remaining animals not purchased by the *Amtskommissar* were sold to the inhabitants of neighbouring villages. Estimates over the quantities of corn left behind were made and sold to the inhabitants of other villages. The *Amtskommissar* was expected to estimate in financial terms the number of uncollected crops that was also sold to other villagers. The buyers were

---

23 Susanne Zantop, *Colonial Fantasies: Conquest, Family, and Nation in Precolonial Germany 1770–1870*, (Durham, 1997).

forced to hand over two-thirds of the crop but were 'generously' permitted to keep one-third. They were ordered to take the crops, straw and other produce to their storage facilities because the abandoned villages would be demolished afterwards. Crops were to be threshed by machines supplied by the Nazi farm association and agreed quantities delivered depending on the weather. One resettlement schedule is outlined in table 8.[24]

Table 8: Settled out of the forest.[25]

I. Amtskommissariat Bialowies	Total	1,114 persons
Transported in:		
a. 6.11.1942	446 persons	
b. 10.11.1942	295 persons	
c. 16.11.1942	373 persons	
II. Amtskommissariat Suchopol		1,212 persons
Transported in:		
a. 5.11.1942	464 persons	
b. 11.11.1942	399 persons	
c. 17.11.1942	349 persons	
III. Amtskommissariat Schereschow		
Transported in:		
a. 7.11.1942	422 persons	
b. 13.11.1942	425 persons	
c. 19.11.1942	466 persons	
		1,313 persons
Up to 20.11.1942	Resettled:	3,639 Persons

During the deportations, there were several incidents with partisans. The most serious occurred at noon on 4 November when five partisans attacked a convoy from Königsbrück and Borodyce as they progressed towards Białowieża. The partisans were armed

---

24 BArch, RL 31/3, document 60, Richtlinien zur Durchführung der Umsiedling in den Amtskommissariaten Bialowies, Suchopol and Czerszow, Oberleutenant u. Umsiedlungsoffizier Schultrich.
25 BArch, RL 31/3, document 67, Umsiedlung aus dem Reichsforstgebiet.

with two machine pistols, revolvers and 'undisclosed rapid-firing weapons.' The German escort returned fire and the partisans withdrew.[26] In response to the random partisan attacks, Herbst felt compelled to reassure the locals. On 29 November he addressed the locals and began by blaming the partisans for continuing to infiltrate the forest on the false pretext of patriotic or 'Bolshevist' duty. They call themselves 'Russian partisans' and believe in the pointlessness of fighting behind the German army's frontline and added:

> The inhabitants of the *Reichsforstgebiet* and surrounding settlements have had more than once an opportunity to witness how the partisans rarely attacked the German army. These lazy villains, without conscience, have terrorized and plundered the population. As a consequence, the partisans have shown they are the enemies of the peaceful and orderly people despite their opposite claims.[27]

Herbst addressed the resettlement plan and its aims. He explained that over several weeks, families had been resettled but the remaining families would be concentrated into closed forest settlements. Action would be taken to secure the inhabitants, to protect their lives and property against both partisans and anti-social elements. However, he cautioned those who remained in the forest that they only received 'the full protection of the Reich' if they were ready to take on extra duties. 'The only inhabitants who can be tolerated in the forest,' he cautioned, 'must prepare themselves completely with this order and who are willing to cooperate in the protection and construction of the area.'[28] Herbst threatened them with joining the militia or deportation, or worse being left to the mercy of partisans. His words and actions implied those remaining in the forest had been reduced to slaves.

---

26 BArch, RL 31/3, document 63, daily reports extracts 1–20.11.42, Major Herbst, 21 November 1942.
27 BArch, RL 31/3, document 78, Bevollmächtigter des Reichsmarschall des Großdeutschen Reiches, 29.11.1942, (call to the population of the Reichsforstgebiet), Major Herbst.
28 BArch, RL 31/3, document 78, Major Herbst, Bevollmächtigter des Reichsmarschall des Großdeutschen Reiches, O.U., 29.11.1942, Call to the population of the Reichsforstgebiet.

By autumn 1942, the demographic balance in the forest altered as *Urwald Bialowies* began to take shape. The deportations of locals had been replaced with an influx of German migrants under Lebensraum initiatives. The large presence of the SS-Police, army, German post office and the Nazi civil administrations, including the RFA, raises questions as to whether *Urwald Bialowies* could still be classified as a true wilderness. On 8 December, Herbst turned his attention to the German women and children residing in the forest. The civil administration of Bialystok had issued orders that placed the city under tight security. In response to this heightened state of security, Herbst distributed a circular to all German institutions in the forest called *Urwald Bialowies*. He warned, 'Staying inside or approaching the primaeval forest is every person's responsibility and dangerous. The Reich and its duty posts cannot accept any liability whatsoever.' All forest officials were warned that the decision to allow German women in the forest was their responsibility. He acknowledged that several German women and children had temporary permission to stay in the villages of Białowieża, Stoczek and Zastawa. There were German female employees in the RFA, and civil administration offices located in Suchopol and Czereszow. They were granted the permission to remain. He forbade women and children from leaving their settlements or wandering into the forest without armed escorts. Herbst pointed out that 'ignoring these instructions will lead to the immediate cancellation of all residential permits.' He also strictly forbade German women from travelling beyond the settlements of Białowieża, Stoczek, Zastawa, Suchopol and Czereszow. All other women and children, in settlements or in strongpoints within the *Oberforstamt*, were ordered to leave immediately and granted until 15 December 1942 as a deadline.[29] There were constant alarms that a large partisan presence was about to descend on the forest, but these fears never materialised.

---

29   BArch, RL 31/3, document 76, An die deutschen Dienststellen im Gebiete des Oberforstamtes 'Urwald Bialowies', Az.11 Br.B.Nr. 1770/42, Major Herbst, 8 December 1942.

Herbst wrote to Scherping about the security situation. He had already informed Luftgau I and Dr. Brix in Bialystok that the *Reichsforstgebiet* should be treated as an occupied territory rather than administered as part of the German homeland. He explained to Scherping that Wehrkreis I and *Luftgau I* shared his opinion that *Bezirk Bialystok* region should be treated as occupied territory under the German military code (Nr. 46 Ziffer 2736 from 9 November 1942). This meant all women and children related to military officers, public officials and party members should not be allowed to remain in the area. Herbst faced the dilemma of imposing military security in territory mandated as homeland. His mission instructions forced him to reconcile the wishes of the civil administration with the authority granted to him by Göring. He freely criticised Wagner for pressing the permission to employ German women and accept the presence of family members of RFA officials in the forest. Herbst explained he was in no position to grant permission and admitted that he had tolerated their presence until finally, Göring had ordered their departure. Wagner had applied for several exceptions including the German women employed in *Revierförsterei Bialy-Lasek*; the wife and sister-in-law of the *Revierförsterei Swineroje*; and a residential permit for the wife of *Revierförster* Erich Weinreis and his two small children in *Revierförsterei Podolany*. Herbst requested Scherping intervene against these requests for exemptions.[30] There is no known reply from Scherping. This letter adds further weight to the probability that Scherping was the architect behind *Urwald Bialowies*.

---

30   BArch, RL 31/3, document 75, letter Major Herbst to Oberstjägermeister Scherping, 12 December 1942. Herbst cringingly signed off his letter 'your devoted Herbst'.

Image 12: Civilian deportations and allocation to work or forced labour duties.
Source: NARA, Hoffmann Collection.

On 14 December, Herbst confirmed in correspondence that the resettlement process due to end the next day had been completed except for 1,000 persons assigned to Bielsk still in progress. To date, 8,000 persons had been resettled into Bialystok. A survey of those resettled showed they were sufficiently quartered and provisioned apart from some deficiencies caused by the delays in the Jewish 'evacuations'. This note indicated how far the deportations were harmonised to the transportation of Jews to extermination camps. The resettlement process involved removing the Jews from the ghetto and giving their homes and jobs to the deported from *Urwald Bialowies*. Herbst relayed to Brauchitsch how 'happy' the people were working in Bialystok's industries and that the employers had judged them, satisfactory workers. It seems the deported locals were arriving in Bialystok just as the Jews were being forcibly removed. In these circumstances, it's hardly surprising that the forest folk didn't give their new masters any opportunity for criticism. The resettlement programme was planned to continue into mid-January. Herbst also confirmed discussions held in Białowieża with thirteen Russian-orthodox priests from the forest on 14 December. He noted, 'We have reason to assume that the priests will have a positive influence on the population, and this will certainly lead to good cooperation.' It's difficult to gauge how far this represented priestly collaboration with the Nazis or the priest's part in calming the people before their deportation.[31]

In January 1943 Herbst observed: 'It would be easy for somebody, who is not familiar with the mentality of the white-Russian population, to use these modest and incredibly patient people for the development of this area.' He cautioned the troops, under all circumstances, that they must avoid '… running wild in such a way that even the most good-natured and harmless farmers are driven into the arms of the Bolshevists.' Herbst claimed the locals took for granted that Göring sanctioned the actions of German soldiers.

---

31   BArch, RL 31/3, document 70, report 11 period 21.11–14.12.42, Major Herbst 14 December 1942. There are no references to the Catholic priesthood in any LWSB documents.

Herbst had told the people that Göring had given a special order to prevent any unnecessary hardships befalling the population. The Russian-orthodox clerics had communicated this policy of care to the population. He added, 'there is a great sense of gratitude and confidence among the people.' As a consequence, there had been well-meaning messages and presents from forest locals for Göring on his fiftieth birthday.[32] The statements indicate a number of Russian or Belarusian communities remained in the forest and were collaborating with the Germans.

Meanwhile, the evacuations in Białowieźa drew the attention of other Nazi agencies in Berlin. A letter by Nazi minister Albert Speer from 1 February 1943 stated:

> I have been informed that a major resettlement operation is underway in the district of Bialystok. Roughly 40,000 Jews are to be evacuated from the Bialystok ghetto. In order to eliminate the last partisan strongholds remaining in the forests around Bialowitze [sic], the White Ruthenians living there — also about 40,000 people, predominantly peasants — are to be evacuated and transferred to the dwellings in Bialystok that used to house Jews. Because these are insufficient for the rural population, the additional housing shortage is to be alleviated by a wooden housing scheme, or barracks, with a capacity of 20,000 people ...[33]

The full extent of deportations across the period 1941–42 are illustrated in GIS map 11. The map illustrates the concentration points that were the direct consequence of expanding Białowieźa into the *Urwald Bialowies* scheme. This note explains the extent of the deportations and how far the preparations involved other agencies. It's not altogether clear whether the Nazis intended to build a wooden community to house some of the deported or erect labour camps.

---

32 BArch, RL 31/3, document 81, report 12, period 15.12 to 5.1.1943, Major Herbst, 5 January 1943.
33 Götz Aly, *Final Solution: Nazi Population Policy and the Murder of the European Jews*, (Oxford, 1999), pp. 269–70.

POPULATION ENGINEERING

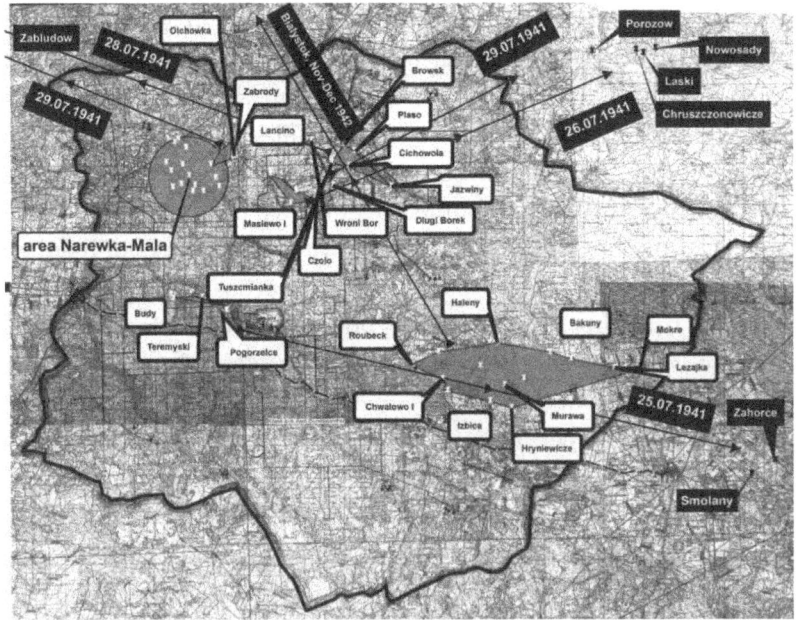

GIS Map 11: deportations — comparison of summer 1941 and autumn/winter 1942
This comparison of the two phases of deportations highlights the concentration of German effort and the determination to create a wilderness. Depopulated areas experienced a subsequent increase in patrols by the LWSB. Major Herbst argued for arming the remaining communities to establish self-protection zones in collaboration with the Germans. However, evidence also suggests the Germans were prepared to tolerate locals as 'bait' to lure the partisans. There was also a move to settle ethnic Germans in the forest but there are no known names of towns.

IV. Reprisals and revenge

In December 1942, Herbst announced that his allocation of troops allowed him to cover the entire area. *Urwald Bialowies* was divided into six sectors, and each sector had been allocated a company. This due to the arrival of the fifth and sixth companies. More strongpoints were constructed and *Jagdkommando* patrols stepped up. Large snowfall had helped the *Jagdkommando* conduct patrols more effectively and as a consequence had located several occupied bunkers. He noted this had led to a further decrease of partisan activities inside the forest. Small numbers of splinter groups continued to enter the forest from time to time but caused relatively little harm. Beyond the forest, the partisan activities had increased to such an extent that 461st Reserve Division and the gendarmerie were reporting regular attacks against villages on a daily basis.[34] Thus, Herbst's efforts in effect pushed the partisans away for someone else to solve. Herbst counted twenty-two days of reported incidents during December. The breakdown was: ten days of the theft of food; seven days of serious attacks by partisans on locals; three days of firefights between strongpoints and partisans and, nine days of *Jagdkommando* interceptions. There were other sporadic incidents throughout the month.

On 1 December, *Jagdkommando Fuchs* (second) was alerted by tracks in the snow. They observed two partisans running along the railway tracks, but they disappeared through fallen trees and thickets. After close inspection of the ground, it was thought the partisans had changed direction during their flight. Then it was thought the partisans had altered their tracks by placing a false heel on the tips of their boots to confuse their trackers. On 4 December, three partisans appeared in an unnamed community and handed an eight-month-old child into the care of a woman. They took nothing and threatened nobody. An unarmed partisan was shot dead in Ohotynowo as he tried to escape arrest. During the early hours of 7 December, eight partisans armed with rifles attacked the turpentine installation in Radatz. They were seeking information about the garrisons in the neighbouring strongpoints but also stole food and clothing. *Jagdkommando Geier* (fourth) was on patrol in the afternoon and found an empty but well-camouflaged bunker with a store of potatoes. The *Jagdkommando* followed fresh tracks of up to fifteen partisans leading from the bunker to another camouflaged bunker in a neighbouring *Jagen*. The Germans found fifteen pounds of potatoes, two pounds of meat in barrels, three cowhides, and other foodstuffs. The *Jagdkommando* destroyed the bunker but could not pursue the

---

34 BArch, RL 31/3, document 70, report 11 period 21.11–14.12.42, Major Herbst, 14 December 1942.

tracks because dawn was about to break. On 9 December a *Jagdkommando* (second) led by its company commander observed a thin trail of smoke in *Jagen* 119. As the *Jagdkommando* approached several partisans began to fire. The troops returned fire and a partisan was severely wounded. He was later finished off with a bullet to the back of the neck. A second partisan, believed to be Jewish, was wounded in the leg and taken captive and a third partisan escaped.[35]

The Jewish captive was interrogated on 11 December, and afterwards, the village of Nowinnick was placed under suspicion. A battalion *Sonderkommando* was raised and carried out an action against the village. The population was deported. The Soltys and two militiamen executed before the villagers, and then the village was destroyed Carthaginian style.[36] Herbst wrote to SSPF-Bialystok:

> I want to pass on information about the activities of the inhabitants of Nowinnick, seven kilometres south of Narew. Following the interrogation of a Jew, who was wounded and captured during a firefight on 9 December. It became clear that three bandits had robbed large quantities of meat, bread and other food from Nowinnick on or about the evening of 7 December.

Herbst later explained, 'the captured Jewish boy intimated the other two bandits were directed towards houses by the village guards during their raids. Neither the Soltys, his deputy nor the village guard or any of the other inhabitants offered the slightest resistance or raised the alarm or reported the incident.' According to Herbst, 'the two guards, Lasdwiewilnt and Bankowska confessed to these allegations under interrogation.' The Soltys and his deputy had only confessed that the partisans had been in the village and had not received anything. Herbst believed the partisans entered the Soltys' house and were given food. He noted: 'the three men, mentioned above, will be shot today by order of the courts-martial. This is because investigations have clearly proven that

---

35 BArch, RL 31/3, document 71–73, daily report extracts 21.11–14.12.1942, Major Herbst, 14 December 1942.
36 BArch, RL 31/3, document 70, report 11 period 21.11–14.12.42), Major Herbst, 14 December 1942 and BArch, RL 31/3, document 71–73, daily report extracts 21.11–14.12.1942, Major Herbst, 14 December 1942.

most inhabitants of the village supported the partisans. They will be resettled after a short period.'

An *Amtskommissar* from Narew, along with local auxiliaries and troops from the LWSB, were assigned to conduct a round-up. The inhabitants were allowed to take all moveable belongings. Fourteen horse-drawn carts (twelve from the village) with additional carts from the villages of Kotlowka and Losinka, helped take the deported to Narew at 2.00 pm. The column moved out on 12 November for Bielsk where they were resettled. Herbst noted: 'the Narew *Amtskommissar* will sell the non-moveable possessions and the villager's cattle and the profit will be paid into a resettlement fund which I set up.' The buildings of Nowinnick were dismantled and sold to their neighbours in Kotlowka and Losinka. The sale of the building materials was dependent upon the buyer removing them within ten days. The horses and carts taken to Bielsk were also sold with the profits paid into the resettlement fund. Herbst concluded: 'I will encourage the responsible farming association as we already discussed to exploit this action against the people of Nowinnick for propaganda purposes. This will be a warning to the population of the district not to support the partisans with an indication of more severe actions in the event of further incidents.'[37] Herbst wrote to all *Amtskommissars* confirming that he had opened a bank account in the name of the 'resettlement fund *Bialowies*' with the district *Sparkasse* (savings bank). This was also agreed with Erich Koch. The money was to be used to support the poorest among the resettled to find homes and work in the Bielsk district. Herbst also requested the transfer of all revenues from selling the property and this confiscated cattle that were slaughtered for profit.[38]

---

[37] BArch, RL 31/3, document 74, Major Herbst to SSPF Bialystok, 11 December 1942.

[38] BArch, RL 31/3, unnumbered document copy of a letter from Major Herbst to Amtskommissars Bialowies, Czereszow, Suchopol, no. 1845/42, 12 December 1942.

On 15 December, the LWSB received word that twelve well turned-out partisans had appeared. The information referred to their cleanliness; smart uniforms with Sam Brown belts and were assumed to be Red Army officers. They were armed with machine pistols, carbines and revolvers. A patrol was sent with urgency to intercept them but without success. Elsewhere a patrol stumbled on a partisan in a house who refused to surrender and tried to hide in a loft. He was killed in a brief shootout. At 1.00 pm four partisans brazenly appeared on the railway line in *Jagen* 207. They took food and tobacco from railway labourers and then interrogated them about the strength of the local strongpoint. *Jagdkommando Panther* located a bunker during a patrol in the marsh area of *Jagen* 30. The bunker was empty and was blown up to prevent it from being re-used. Another bunker was detected during a *Drückjagd* (pressing hunt) in *Jagen* 120. The partisans escaped by sneaking through the gaps between the 'beaters'.[39] On 18 December, the commander of Strongpoint Czolo reported that a man begging for bread ran to the woods when a German sergeant approached him. The sergeant shouted 'halt' but a rifleman shot him from fifty metres. They searched the body and found scars from recent injuries.[40] On 19 December, there was a further intensification of partisan activity. Thirty partisans, armed with machine pistols and rifles, attacked a patrol in the forest nearby Bransk at about 11.00 am. The patrol was assisted by a gendarmerie detachment and together they counter-attacked. Heavy fire and concentrated shots came from an isolated house. The partisans were gradually pushed back, and the house encircled. There was a sudden series of explosions in the house and barn as the buildings erupted in flames and the partisans burned to death. At 11.00 am a band twenty strong, armed with machine guns, machine pistols and rifles struck Czabachy. An hour later the same band struck Chitowszcyzna stealing clothing and food.[41]

---

39 BArch, RL 31/3, documents 82–84, daily report extracts 15.12–5.1.1943, Major Herbst 5 January 1943. A Drückjagd was similar to 'partridge drive' beaters force game towards shooting stands.
40 Ibid.
41 Ibid.

Image 13: Villages destroyed and cattle taken under the Nazi food plan.
Source: NARA, Hoffmann Collection.

Those six days of intensive activity culminated in a more serious incident. On 21 December 1942, Lm. Senior Lieutenant Walter Ciré was the fourth company's second-in-command was on the move.[42] He was accompanied by corporals Huckle (clerk/bookkeeper), Kleinert, and Göke their driver. It was company payday and routine inspections. They were travelling in the company's staff car, a Steyr-Kübel military staff car along the fourth company's designated road from Jasien toward Bienwald. At 11.30 am *Strongpoint Bienwald* reported the sound of machine-gun and rifle fire (counting approximately 300 shots) from the direction of Jasien. A patrol was dispatched and found the field car along the Jasien-Bienwald road in *Jagen* 24. The vehicle was riddled with bullets and its occupant's dead. The dead Germans had been stripped of all their weapons including a machine pistol, three .08 pistols, and a Hungarian 7.65 model pistol. In addition to the weapons, the partisans scavenged ammunition, boots, coats and Ciré's pay book.[43] There is no evidence the dead were stripped or mutilated postmortem. The immediate shock to the battalion was that Lw.Lieutenant Walther Ciré had distinguished himself by becoming the first officer to be killed-in-action. The response was reprisal and revenge.

The investigation of the ground, around the incident, indicating a chain of events. The partisans had taken up an ambush position on the south side of Jasien-Bienwald road about forty meters from the clearing of *Jagen* 24. They had positioned and camouflaged a machine gun in a ditch by the roadside. They were prepared in advance for LWSB traffic but it's unknown if Ciré was targeted. As Ciré's vehicle approached from the west, a hand grenade was thrown landing in front of the car before it reached the clearing. It was well placed because at that point in the road the driver had to drop gears to traverse the sandy incline. The grenade exploded about fifteen metres in front of the car on the north side of the road. It was thought Ciré and his comrades then tried to fight back from within the car, which was riddled from left to right with machine

---

[42] BArch, RL 31/4, Namentliche Liste der Offiziere und Beamten (officer roll, 18 March 1943), Walter Ciré, arrived on 16 October 1942 with fourth company. He was called up on 1 May 1942.

[43] BArch, RL 31/3, document 85, report on the attack of 21.12.1942, Major Herbst, 29 December 1942.

gun bullets. The investigation estimated the Germans had fired twenty shots before being overwhelmed. They were unable to vacate the vehicle and were killed by multiple bullet wounds to the head, chest and stomach. Empty cartridge cases, bullet strikes against trees and tracks indicated they faced about twelve well-armed partisans. It was assumed to be the same band that had conducted similar attacks but with less success a few days earlier. Herbst thought the band was camped out to the south beyond the forest.

The response was a reprisal-revenge action. That evening all companies of the LWSB received orders to arrest known communists, suspicious elements and 'Bolshevist' in border villages in an area covering ten kilometres beyond the forest. They were told to employ all available forces, trucks and horse carts, and to move rapidly to designated jumping-off points (unknown). This action was carried out on 22–23 December. Herbst's courts-martial sentenced nine persons to death on 22 December (table 9) accused of *Banditenbegünstigung* (aiding and abetting bandits). The courts-martial sentenced another 148 hostages (former 'bolshevik' functionaries, bolshevist followers and suspicious elements) to face death by shooting (there is no surviving record of their names). The four Germans, killed-in-action was buried with full military honours in Bielsk military cemetery at 11.00 am, on 24 December 1942.

Table 9: LWSB, death by hanging, 22 December 1942[44]

No	Name	First Name	Home	Born
1	Kosatschuk	Andrej	Wolkostawicz	1902
2	Jaroschuk	Piotr	Omelaniec	17 June 1912
3	Wlodatschik	Iwan	Kamieniki	1905
4	Ssajewitsch	Andreas	Wiluki	1899
5	Tankowski	Josef	Siemienowka	1912
6	Semienaka	Alexander	Siemienowka	1921
7	Sadowski	Wassil	Siemienowka	1907
8	Lesota	Josef	Siemienowka	1910
9	Hanczuk	Alexi	Kaniniec	1905

---

44 BArch, RL 31/3, document 84, court martial sentences to hang, 22 December 1942. A note on the referred to victim number nine who hanged himself in his cell.

The reprisals had no deterrent effect. The year closed with yet more incidents. On 22 December, forest workers found two kilos of explosives on the railway tracks three kilometres west of Narewka Mala at 9.45 am. Two detonators and a safety fuse were recovered. At 11.00 am, a farmer travelling south of Siemieonowka was shot at by partisans firing machine pistols and machine guns. The shots killed his horse and a bullet passed through his jacket. He fled but later failed to identify who fired at him. A railway worker found a detonator and a half-kilo of Russian explosives under the railway track a kilometre east of the railway station at Narewka Mala at 3.15 pm. It took an hour to disarm. On 24 December, fifteen partisans attacked Siemionowka. They were armed with carbines and pistols and took clothing and food. The next day, twenty partisans, armed with machine guns, machine pistols and rifles attacked Molosiaty. They remained in the hamlet for two hours and seriously injured a farmer shooting him in the upper thigh. They departed with clothing and food. On 29 December a Polish band, one of the few recorded in the files, was observed entering the forest, they were dressed in civilian garb.[45] There were no further references to them in the files.

---

45   Ibid.

7. *Judenjagd*

The story of Herbst and the *Sicherungsbataillon der Luftwaffe Bialowies* reached the inevitable point of barbarisation with the *Judenjagd* (Jew-hunt). 'The Jew is the Partisan, and the Partisan is the Jew', was the potent ideological message that came out of the *Barbarossa* campaign (1941).[1] Himmler's SS-Police regulatory and planning bureaus had been set to the task of rationalising the 'Jewish question', the 'Jewish-Bolshevik' and the 'Jewish-Bandit' to Hitler's war. The Wannsee Conference in January 1942 was followed in March by *SD-Einsatzgruppen* reports that heightened security fears of Jews (the rising occupancy within ghettoes and camps across Poland). The tone of the reports ominously represented the Jews in the past tense. One report noted that Polish and Soviet resistance movements had increasingly found a common cause against the Germans and that since the end of 1941 Jews had been joining the partisans. The report exaggerated the vague details of a *Judenaktion* (an action by Jews), when a sizeable German force was routed and destroyed in an 'unequal fight' by Jewish partisans.[2]

By mid 1942, the Jews in Poland were in a perilous situation as the SS-Police began deportations to extermination centres. The dismantling of ghettoes and clearing concentration camps, were co-ordinated with security operations that included resettlement. The clearance of Bialystok ghetto saw the former homes and jobs filled by Poles deported from Białowieża. This 'out-in' processing of people was also carried out to ensure the minimum interruption to work. The consequence for the security forces in the Home Forces Area was the reassignment of the Order Police to ghettoes/camp

---

[1] Hannes Heer, 'Killing Fields: The Wehrmacht and the Holocaust in Belorussia, 1941–1942', *Holocaust and Genocide Studies*, V11, N1, Spring 1997, pp. 79–101.
[2] Yitzhak Arad, Shmuel Krakowski, Shmuel Spector, *The Einsatzgruppen Reports*, (New York, 1989), pp. 352–4.

guards and convoy duties on the deportation trains. This led to a shortfall in the security presence, which meant battalions like the LWSB stationed in the Home Forces Area received a wider operational brief. In Białowieża, the evidence for this came from the Luftwaffe records meticulously maintained by Lw.Major Emil Herbst. This unique record of hunting Jews, by ordinary German soldiers, opened another window on the Holocaust. The record isolated military personnel, under operational training, being assigned to hunt and kill Jews. However, the implications of this policy and its implementation goes further than another story of soldiers killing civilians. The rigorous methods behind German operational training point to both the absence of the usual inducements offered to perpetrators and a heightened level military discipline. This story leads us out of military history and into the politics of violence with the initiation of young men into killing — or being bloodied before conventional combat. Herbst maintained individual anonymity, we only know the primary perpetrators were the Sixth Company (see appendix 2). The patrols followed military procedures, the *Jagdkommandos* applied *Auftragstaktik* and the military system heightened efficiency by encouraging the killing of 'soft' targets. The records indicate the soldiers were given a choice to kill or arrest Jews intercepted in the forest. Regardless of their choice, the arrested Jews all faced public execution. These reports were not suppressed or censored but Herbst's descriptions did not glorify or embellish the killings.

There is no comparison in the literature to the Luftwaffe in *Urwald Bialowies*. There was a 1984 study of Parczew and Wlodawa forests in the Nazi-occupied region designated the GG of Poland. That forest area covered 3,500 square kilometres, compared with the Białowieża arena (the full security zone) of 2,560 square kilometres. Forest in Parczew and Wlodawa covered 35 per cent of the area, in Białowieża forest and swamp covered approximately 75 per cent of the area. In addition, the Białowieża arena had 5,000 square kilometres frontier, with constant Soviet partisan incursions. The deep winter, from mid-November, forced partisans and Jews to search for bunker space to survive (see GIS Map 12). This placed the Jews in a direct confrontation with the partisans over bunkers, as well as trying to avoid the German patrols. In the General Government, Shmuel Krakowski observed that: 'The partisan movement was not a realm of armed struggle for Jews alone, the vast forests served as natural bases of activity for non-Jewish partisans as well.'[3] The Jews of Parczew/Wlodawa were congregated in fourteen towns and rural settlements. The destruction of this community began on 23 May 1942, almost a year after the cleansing actions in *Urwald Bialowies*. The cleansing actions forced Jews to escape. From June until the end of the year, there were many escapes with more turning fugitive through 1943. They were joined by other people on the run including slave labourers, outlawed Poles, and Red Army PoWs. From November 1942, Krakowski described how large-scale hunts were set against the partisans and the refugees in the Parczew forests. The Order Police conducting scouting and intelligence missions, but then the Germans committed military formations of company and battalion size. He believed the Germans, 'estimated that hundreds of Jews were in hiding lost their lives.'[4]

---

3 Shmuel Krakowski, *The War of the Doomed: Jewish Armed Resistance in Poland, 1942–1944*, (New York, 1984).
4 Krakowski, ibid., p. 30.

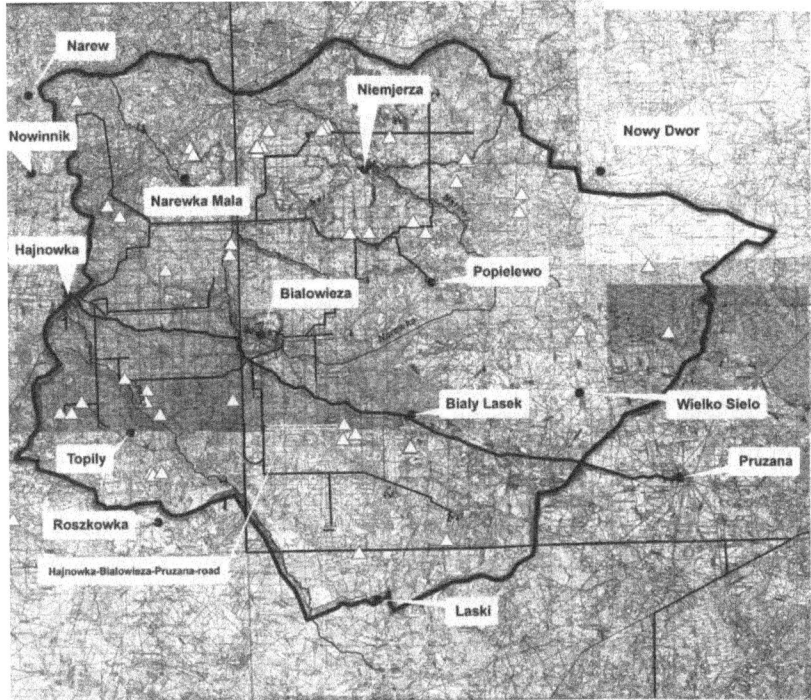

GIS Map 12: the total distribution of hideouts discovered by the LWSB[5]
The white triangles are the positions of bunkers identified by the Germans as holding Jews or partisans. The bunkers in the vicinity of Popielowo were nearby swamplands and saw a concentration of partisans. The cluster of bunkers around Topiło included partisans and Jews. The bunkers in the Bialy Lasek area were nearly all holding Jews when discovered.

Christopher Browning addressed *Judenjagd* and that it '… was an important and statistically significant phase of the Final Solution.' He was interested in how the 'hunt' impacted upon the psychology of the perpetrators. Browning observed that the Judenjagd was 'tenacious, remorseless and an ongoing campaign'.[6] Recent scholarship has also focused upon the *Judenjagd* in the GG. The word has

---

5   Report 14, Herbst wrote: 'The number of bunkers that were so far destroyed is an indication that a large proportion of the bandits expected to spend the winter in the area of the Reichsforstgebiet. It can be said that only a few bandits stayed here. The majority of the bandits hide in the villages in the surrounding area.'
6   Browning, *Ordinary Men*, p. 132.

been examined but without specific connection to the German hunt. Jan Grabowski has argued that, 'the expression of the *Judenjagd* ... was used by German police and gendarmes to describe the search for Jewish refugees who ran away. There is no question that this kind of hunt became one of the most important tasks of the German police during the fall and winter of 1942/43 it was, no doubt, their most important task.'[7] Grabowski focused upon Polish collaboration and isolated the area of Dąbrowa Tarnowska with the Dulcza forest. A Polish forest ranger informed the Germans where a group of about fifty Jews were in hiding, which led to the killing of thirty people. A survivor has left a testimony of this incident.[8] There was an earlier interpretation by a Polish writer that ran counter to Grabowski's account. This has been questioned, which is part of the regular to and fro of contemporary studies about Polish collaboration.[9] Tomasz Frydel has raised this subject with a hard-hitting research and discussion about *Judenjagd*. He writes, 'ethnic Poles had a larger say in the fate of 200,000 fugitive Jews who did not survive' and this added a 'load-bearing question of Polish responsibility ...' Frydel argues that Polish 'peasant society participated in the capture and killing of Jews, but mostly within locally situated dynamics of communal fear and survival ...' Frydel does not attribute this to nationalistic extremists or race, but noted this came '... after the structures of village authority were reconfigured for the purpose by the occupation authorities.' Frydel believes his approach reveals the deeper complexities of the *Judenjagd* that went beyond Jews and included Red Army PoWs, informers, and the dual personality of collaborating perpetrators. Frydel argues that Nazi genocide from above can now be distinguished from the Poles killing Jews from below.[10]

---

7   Jan Grabowski, *Hunt for the Jews: Betrayal and Murder in German-Occupied Poland*, (Indiana, 2013), p. 1.
8   Ibid., Grabowski, p. 88.
9   Adam Kazimierz Musiał, *Krwawe Upiory*, (Poznan, 1993).
10 Tomasz Frydel, 'Judenjagd: Reassessing the role of Ordinary Poles as Perpetrators in the Holocaust', in Timothy Williams and Susanne Buckley-Zistel, *Perpetrators and Perpetration of Mass Violence*, (London, 2018), pp. 187–203.

The works of Grabowski, Frydel and Krakowski contrast with the events in the Białowieża arena. There was a far greater concentration of Jews in the GG. By the end of 1941, all the Białowieża Jews had been removed from the forest/arena. The security warfare campaign waged in the GG, incorporated old style colonial policing, with Bandenbekämpfung rigorously applied by SS-Police, and the extermination camps. *Judenjagd* in the GG was also used as means to train soldiers through Bandenbekämpfung, extending the practice of blooding younger troops. However, *Judenjagd* was interpreted differently by many institutions and regions. In Bezirk Bialystok the troops came under Home Forces Area jurisdiction. Killing, without trial, was a breach of the East Prussia criminal codes. This also went against the 'ten commandments', fixed in the soldiers paybooks, in Article 7 declared, 'civilians are untouchable.' Herbst adopted a strict military solution, the more difficult question to answer is where that idea originated? The likely candidates were: Göring, Scherping, Frevert or Herbst.

From the war diary, we can identify both the key components of the plan for the forest and how that plan was implemented. Activities were broken down into three-parts: to continue the deportations of non-Jewish locals, to combat the partisans, and to eradicate all Jews from the forest. The first two were initiated upon the arrival of the LWSB into the forest, and the final part began in earnest in November. The Jew hunts were delayed due to the delayed arrival of the Fourth, Fifth and Sixth companies. There is no evidence that the delay was caused by the troops being ideologically pre-conditioned before arrival.

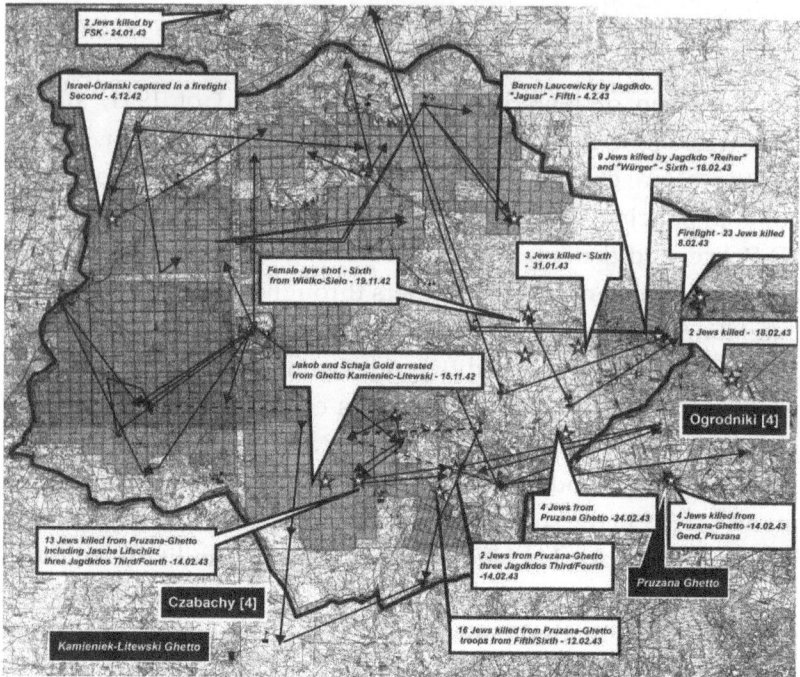

GIS Map 13: locations of Jews killed by the LWSB
This map identifies where Jews were either killed or arrested by the LWSB's patrols. The stars identify each incident, and the captions add details from the LWSB war diary. The files pointed to random or chance contact, but the application of GIS revealed the patrols were set in the highest expectation of intercepting Jews fleeing from either of the two ghettoes to the south.

The GIS based findings from maps 12 and 13, explained the relationship between the German search for bunkers and the pattern of killings of Jews. The killings, whether in the field or after arrest were not chaotic or disorderly. The clusters of located bunkers (GIS Map 12) explains why the Germans placed cordons to the south to deter Jews from escaping to the north and gaining shelter and food. The clusters in GIS Map 13, represent the positions where Jews were recorded killed or arrested in the forest. The GIS mapping visualised three main points of action — from the strongpoint, the local patrol, and the killings usually by the *Jagdkommandos*. GIS mapping of the fourth and sixth companies identified them as the main culprits, but the fifth company also participated. Although there were procedures put in place to dragnet the area, there was still an element of chance to the interceptions of Jews. The papers taken from the Jews killed, or captured, identified them as fugitives from either Pruzhany or Kamieniec-Litewski ghettos. Once the ghettoes were destroyed, all the companies called in their pickets and pulled back north into forest area positions. This identified their positioning was set to a dragnet-killing plan.

I. In step with the Jagdkommando

General Franz Halder, chief of the German army general staff, was a self-declared passionate hunter. In consolidating Hitler's Bandenbekämpfung directive, Halder proposed and introduced the *Jagdkommando* order, in which he specifically called for the adaptation of hunting techniques to counter the partisans.[11] The *Jagdkommando*, or hunting-detachment, had the dual task of preventing the partisan bands from gaining a firm foothold in an area, while at the same time maintaining *bandenfreies Vorfeld* (partisan-free areas). A typical *Jagdkommando* might include a senior NCO and ten OR's with a civilian scout(s) skilled in tracking. They were armed with a machine pistol, two light machine guns, 2,000 rounds of ammunition and 25 grenades. In combat against partisans or saboteurs, the *Jagdkommando* was ordered to take no prisoners. In the 'combat' zone, they were expected to imitate the *Kampfweise* (fighting style — tactic or doctrine) of the partisans — roaming free, setting ambushes, exploiting ruses, and using cunning.[12] In effect, Halder's recommendations for combating partisans were comparable to gamekeepers battling poachers. The conduct of *Bandenbekämpfung* was dangerous and not always the straightforward killing exercise some historians have tried to claim. Few German soldiers enjoyed

---

11 Military Intelligence Service, *German Military Abbreviations*, Washington: War Department, 12 April 1943, p. 91. *Jagdkommando* means hunting kommando but US Army translated them as 'raiding detachment' and the British Army as 'raiding parties'.

12 BArch, RH 27-1/98 1st Panzer Division, general orders 18 August–10 September 1942. Zusammenstellung von Jgdkos zur Bandenbekämpfung, (31 August 1942), also Blood, *Hitler's Bandit Hunters*, pp. 123–5.

this kind of fighting, but nearly all those posted to the east after August 1942 experienced it in some form.

The Białowieża arena, in the winter of 1942–43, was a hostile place of rugged terrain and with social society increasingly turning to a dystopia. Under the Tsarist Empire, the region was part 'pale of settlement' where Jews were allowed to settle. Many of those settlements, like Narewka Mala, had a heritage dating back to the early 1800s and were still in place in June 1941. There had been cases of terror, like the pogroms, and the Soviet occupation had turned the synagogue into a grain store, which later burned. The Jewish cemetery has remained to this day, marking the once cultural heritage that was exterminated in August 1941.[13] During September 1942, the deployment of conventional military forces from *Bezirk Bialystok* to SS command for *Aktion Reinhard* was in serious progress. The LWSB was made responsible for preventing fugitive Jews from escaping into the forest, but the specific period was ill-defined to somewhere between September 1942 and February 1943. This was not a small task, and an estimate can be drawn of the mission. To the north was the Bialystok ghetto, with about 160,000 Jews; to the south, Pruzhany another 10,000 and, to the southwest Kamieniec-Litewski a ghetto of 2,000. In September the LWSB was a battalion of 300 men expected to cover 256,000ha of *Urwald Bialowies*, but in November the numbers increased to 650. In September Herbst claimed the troops were of doubtful ability and lacked the necessary skills. While it is debatable whether the skill levels improved, the LWSB was compensated by increased numerical strength.

The first impression of Herbst's reports, for this period, pointed to an overall increase in aggressiveness. This was assumed to be LWSB's longer deployment in the forest and the 'new' companies enabled an arena wide security screen. On close inspection, however, the overall results and performance, given the expansion in companies were marginal. This marginality was anchored in the performance of the *Jagdkommandos*. The onset of winter led Herbst

---

13 Tomasz Wisniewski, *Jewish Bialystok and Surroundings in Eastern Poland*, (Ipswich, 1998), pp. 93–95.

to shift tactics to 'search and destroy' forest bunkers. The local population used storage bunkers during the winter for food supplies and wood. They were also hiding places for Jews fleeing the ghettoes and partisans sheltering for winter. The *Jagdkommandos* had the task of locating the local bunkers, identifying partisan constructed bunkers and destroying those used by partisans and Jews. All the companies were deployed in the dragnet to intercept the fleeing Jews. Herbst allowed a dual system of 'choice' over whether to kill or arrest Jews caught in the forest. The arrested Jews were brought to Herbst's headquarters to receive an official sentence for trespassing in the forest and public execution.

In report 14, Herbst wrote: 'The number of bunkers that were so far destroyed is an indication that a large proportion of the bandits expected to spend the winter in the area of *Urwald Bialowies*. It can be said that only a few bandits stayed here. The majority of the bandits hide in the villages in the surrounding area.' The partisans could construct elaborate bunker complexes as described in two *Jagdkommando* reports. The second and fourth companies achieved moderate successes on their own and in joint actions. On 8 January *Jagdkommando Keiler* (second) located and destroyed a bunker in *Jagen* 7. They later found a complete bunker complex used as sleeping quarters although deserted. The construction measured 5 metres by 6 metres by 0.75 metres and was built into the forest floor. The bunker's doors had glass windows and inside there was an oven, and a back door was sealed with nails. The front door was booby-trapped with an improvised explosive device, made from a pressure plate with detonators attached to a 10.5cm mortar grenade. The troops disarmed the booby traps and found ammunition and clothing. On 8 February *Jagdkommando Keiler* also located a bunker about five metres by six metres in diameter. They were astonished to find a complete Soviet 10.5cm mortar, perhaps related to the grenade mentioned above.[14] During the evening 16–17 February partisans stole a horse cart from the forester's house in *Jagen* 28, which they used for transporting their casualties. *Jagdkommando Geier* (fourth) began

---

14 BArch, RL 31/3, document 94–95, daily reports extract 2.2–12.2.1943 Major Herbst, 2 February 1943.

a pursuit following their trail. They surrounded what they thought was a command bunker. *Jagdkommando Falke* (fourth) was drawn up as reinforcement. The command bunker turned out to be a supply bunker. They continued the search and stumbled on partisans and immediately opened fire, but the band made good their escape. A barracks bunker was detected about a hundred metres from the supply bunker, large enough for fifty partisans! The Germans secured a machine gun, potatoes and clothing. A twenty strong band crossed through the railway control sector of Tarnopol and Siminowka, moving along the railway embankment at 8.00 pm. A *Jagdkommando* (second) joined a pursuit at 8.45 pm. They lost the trail in the deep marshland. Partisans brazenly bearing their arms entered Ciesowka wearing vertical red linen stripes on their hats. The band entered the village and asked locals for material to wrap around their feet.[15] At 5.00 pm on 8 February partisans opened fire on a fourth company automobile three kilometres north of Brody. The troops answered, 'fire with fire', but there were no losses and the partisans fled. The car had bullet hits to the left front wing and windscreen.

The most successful *Jagdkommandos* during the period from New Year to the end of February 1943 came from the fifth company. The company record began ominously on 1 January, when a staff sergeant led his *Jagdkommando* in pursuit of partisans. He crossed a clearing at *Jagen* 29/30 and stepped on a mine that blew off his right foot and caused minor injuries to his lower left arm. Upon detonation, the Germans came under concentrated fire from surrounding thickets. They returned fire forcing the partisans to withdraw. The troops were unable to follow them or their tracks due to the lack of visibility. On 9 January *Jagdkommando Luchs* (fifth) stumbled on two bunkers near Kolonna used to store potatoes. The floor was covered with straw, indicating use as a quarters. On 8 February a picket from Strongpoint Niemerca secured a sledge and horse at midnight. Two sentries from Rudnia village guard secured two horses roaming free. An unnamed *Jagdkommando* was dispatched, and they

---

15 BArch, RL 31/3, document 100, daily reports extract 13.2–4.3.1943.

found three more sledges and four horses without drivers. The sledges and horses were from nearby villages on the northern border of the forest previously infiltrated by partisans. On the same day, *Jagdkommando Luchs* discovered a bunker filled with potatoes. Three days later the gendarmerie in Nowy Dwor (east of the forest) reported that a hundred partisans had attacked them at dawn. A local policeman was killed in the firefight. The fifth company sent a *Jagdkommando* in support but failed to locate any partisans.[16] Luck favoured *Jagdkommando Jaguar* during a patrol on 22 February when it 'bumped' into a partisan patrol in *Jagen* 181. A partisan was shot, his automatic rifle and explosives were secured. Later that day *Jagdkommando Luchs* discovered a small one-man bunker in *Jagen* 91, which they destroyed.

The least prominent companies in the reports were the first and third. *Jagdkommando Elch* (first) discovered an empty camp in *Jagen* 822 and located another section nearby in *Jagen* 822B. The first section of the camp was empty but in the second section, five partisans were sat around a campfire. A partisan was shot in a short firefight, but the others escaped into the thicket. The Germans pursued but gave up after two fruitless hours. The dead partisan was armed with a rifle and ammunition. Also, clothing and pieces of equipment were secured from searching the campsite. On 11 January a *Jagdkommando* (third) stumbled on two bunkers in *Jagen* 127. The bunkers were empty as were two bunkers discovered in *Jagen* 153, all were blown up. On 13 January *Jagdkommando Wisent* (third) found a small camp in *Jagen* 611 with two men who fled and evaded pursuit. This was the sum of their activities from all reports.

On 14 February 1943, four partisans armed with automatic rifles and machine pistols took clothing from a road official who lived and worked on the *Rollbahn* (military highway) Pruzhany-Widomla. They shot him in the leg. The next day twelve partisans with three horse carts entered Dohle. They held the civil guard at gunpoint and took ten horses. The partisans moved on to

---

16 BArch, RL 31/3, document 103, Abschrift: Telefonische Meldung des Gend. Kreises Grodno vom 10.2.1943, 18.30 Uhr, Leutnant u. Adjutant Weinreis.

Suchowszcyzna where they tied up the local Soltys and plundered the hamlet. A *Jagdkommando* (fourth) set off in hot pursuit but faced a hail of machine-gun and rifle fire. As the band escaped the troops observed eight men mounted on horseback and another five mounts without riders. At lunchtime on 27 February, five soldiers from Strongpoint Jasien (fourth) drove with six Panjewagens to Debowe to fetch wood. On the return, partisans fired at them and a brief exchange followed with the lead horses of the first and second carts being killed.[17] The *Jagdkommando* engagements against the partisans in the New Year period, although small in number were significant enough to force Herbst to adopt an aggressive advance. This set the mindset of the *Jagdkommandos*.

II. Hunting Jews

The first evidence that the LWSB was conducting more than just targeting partisans emerged from the blocking operations for the SS. Herbst informed the *Gestapo* in Berlin that:

> During an exercise in co-operation with the SD in this territory, there were several arrests of people operating in our rear area with a partisan organisation including the '*Juden* Scherschinowski' from the Bielsk ghetto. He had on his person a photograph of *Kreisleiter* [Nazi district leader] Möller-Crivitz in Party-Leader-uniform, which had the following dedication on the back: 'Best wishes Herr Schersch with fraternal greetings, Heil Hitler Möller-Crivitz.'
> An interrogation of the Jew Sch.[sic] testified that he and Möller-Crivitz were friends and held meetings together. He has met Möller-Crevitz on more than one occasion, visited his home and carried out the dedication for his publishing factory. The friendship of a political leader, a National-Socialist, with a Polish Jew is moderately strange. Perhaps you would like to deal with this problem, I have enclosed the photograph.[18]

In October 1942 the RSHA issued an order to liquidate the Bialystok ghetto and deport the Jews to extermination camps. The deportations began in mid-October 1942 and continued through to mid-

---

17 BArch, RL 31/3, document 100/2, daily reports extract 13.2–4.3.1943.
18 BArch, RL 31/3, letter Herbst to Gestapo, Prinz-Albrecht-Straße 10, Berlin SW, Az. 7 Br.B.Nr. 285/42, 1 September 1942, document 41. To conclude his investigation, Herbst told the Gestapo that he found that the 'Jew Sch.' had lodged with Frau Wrede, at 11 Ansbacherstrasse in Berlin.

February 1943. In March 1942 the Nazi administration of *Bezirk Bialystok* issued a census report of Jews still in residence. By the end of the period, about 36,000 Jews remained in the Bialystok ghetto. A census report recognised the *Reichsjagdgebiet Bialowies* and referred to the security methods administered by *Reichsjagdverwaltung Bialowies* since July 1941, with the mass deportations under Göring's protocols.[19] Decades later, Dr. Szymon Datner, wrote that the difficult period began on 2 November when 'the destruction of the ghettoes in the region of Bialystok began ...', and continuing, 'in the months of January through March 1943, about 130,000 Jews from the Bialystok region perished in gas chambers and in the ovens of Treblinka.' Some managed to flee: 'They escaped to the forest where most of them died, of starvation and of frost or from the bullets of the German gendarmes, or at the hands of their local persecutors or those hired by the Germans ...'[20] The LWSB's documents confirm Datner's statement there is no evidence that the local or village militias collaborated in the killings. During the entire period of its stay, the LWSB never received any denunciations of Jews by the locals.

From 1 November 1942, the LWSB's summarised daily reports referred to the public execution of Jews, by firing squad or hanging. The reference to arrests in the after-action reports indicates the troops had a 'choice' of kill or capture. Jakob and Schaja Gold were arrested at 12.30 pm on 15 November in *Jagen* 852 near Kamyanyets. When they were questioned, they admitted to being fugitives from the Kamieniec-Litewski ghetto. Their original home was in Mokrany near Brest in Belorussia. The distance they had covered from the ghetto, before their capture, was in excess of 20 kilometres and in the most extreme conditions of the forest in winter. They were placed before Herbst's drumhead courts-martial and found guilty of being in the forest without permission. An offence that carried the death penalty and, in Table 10, Jakob and Schaja Gold

---

19 Zivilverwaltung Bialystok, *Der Bezirk Bialystok*, (Bialystok, March 1942), p. 30.
20 Szymon Datner, 'Eksterminacja ludności żydowskiej w Okręgu Białostockim', *Bulletin of the Jewish Historical Institute*, Warsaw, October–December 1966, no.6: pp. 3–29.

are included in a list of all persons executed on 20 November; the others found guilty for being communists and 'bandits'. Their classification as 'Jews' in the list is at odds with the court-martial sentences of trespass.

Table 10:   executions through hanging, 20 November 1942[21]

No	Name	First Name	Home	Born	Crime
1	Koroway	Peter	Politscha	1 October. 1903	Bandit
2	Ochryniul	Matdy	Starzyna	1900	Bandit
3	Gerasimiuk	Gregor	Politschna	November 1905	Bandit
4	Michalowski	Alexander	Wojnowka	23 March 1896	Bandit
5	Majeski	Makar	Wolkostawze	1903	Bandit
6	Ryback	Iwan	Tafilowsze	August 1915	Communist
7	Stanischewski	Wlodimir	Pokoniewo	March 1907	Communist
8	Krupta	Alexander	Chlewischtsche	25 August 1905	Communist
9	Ryschtschuk	Wladimir	Rogatsche	1915	Communist
10	Gaponiuk	Stefan	Molotschki	27 December 1906	Communist
11	Gold	Jakob	Mokrany	25 December 1907	Jew
12	Gold	Schaja	Mokrany	12 October 1925	Jew

Another summarised daily report from 18–19 November noted that a patrol from the sixth company set out from Strongpoint Wielko-Siolo to investigate partisan tracks. They lost the tracks in lowland swamps north of Radek. On their return, they stumbled across 'a half-famished Jewish female' (perhaps a fugitive from Pruzhany ghetto). They excused shooting her on the dubious grounds that having been given a choice she refused to go with them.[22] This was the first incident by a sixth company patrol and happened three days after their arrival.

---

21 BArch, RL 31/3, document 68, court-martial sentenced to hang, 20 November 1942. The file note added: 'persons no.1 1–12 are Jews'. They were hanged together with the others, following a decision of the security police because they had escaped from a ghetto and were in the primaeval forest without passes or approval.'

22 BArch, RL 31/3, document 65, daily report extracts 1–20.11.42, Major Herbst, 21 November 1942.

On 22 November, Herbst's tenth report explained a temporary halt in the resettlement process that also shows how it was also coordinated with *Aktion Reinhard*:

> The resettlement started on 5 November as scheduled. It was conducted according to the plan in spite of significant difficulties, 3639 people have so far resettled to Bialystok from the Reichsforstgebiet. We intend to resettle altogether about 40,000 people: 15,000 people from the three Amtskommissariaten and another 25,000 from the villages of the border areas. There will probably be an interruption between mid-December until mid-January as the deportation of the Jews from Bialystok is suspended because the Deutsche Reichsbahn is committed to other tasks.[23]

The shortage of rail traffic was more than likely due to the pressure on Wehrmacht's operations and the crisis in Stalingrad.[24] In addition traffic within *Bezirk Bialystok* was organised from *Reichsbahndirection Königsberg*, which meant organising trains on a north-south axis, rather than an east-west, meant diverting traffic across two fully operational army group rear area supply corridors on maximum effort.[25] This revealed the complications of mission: the coordination of deportations, resettlements, and the hunting of Jews. The mission also required the coordination of national, city and local agencies, as well as the SS, Army, and civilian authorities across the region.

Brief notifications about the killing of Jews continued into February 1943, but with fewer and fewer details. For example, on 2 December troopers shot 'four escaped (*flüchtige*) Jews' near the village of Sykki. Two days later eighteen Jews were discovered in 'holes in the ground' (*Erdlöcher*) and were shot and their 'holes destroyed'. In the early afternoon of 7 December, a patrol ventured beyond the limits of the forest and shot fourteen Jews northwest of Kol Sady. On 9 December Herbst's daily reports noted that 'a Jew is shot in

---

23 BArch, RL 31/3, document 62, report 10, period 1–20.11.42, Major Herbst, 22 November 1942.
24 Raul Hilberg, *Sonderzüge nach Auschwitz*, (Mainz, 1987), pp. 50–61.
25 AA, 1.2.7.7. Incarceration Documents, I. Train Car numbers from the German railroad, railroad administration Königsberg, 29.22.1942–18.8.1943. The manifest and route plans indicate the trains were treated as low-level priority freight, assigned to mostly secondary lines, and with older rolling stock.

the forest of Bransk-Rukra at 1530 hrs.' During another skirmish with partisans, men of the second company captured Israel-Orlansk and he was hanged in public the next day.[26] Two weeks later a midday patrol of four troopers was shot at from a farmhouse lying between Wolka-Zaleska and Seichy. Barricaded inside the farmhouse were three partisans and two Jewish women. They continued to fire at the Germans. A hand grenade was thrown into the house, but two partisans managed to escape. The two women and the third partisan were shot, and the house burned down on top of them.[27] On 6 January 1943, two *Jagdkommando* from the sixth were involved in a firefight, they shot three partisans and wounded three others.

On 28 January 1943, the SS began the action to demolish the Pruzhany ghetto. Their plan involved the transportation of 10,000 Jews to Auschwitz, and many were expected to escape. The SS action was completed on 31 January, the same day the sixth shot three Jews claimed to be 'while running away'. A report from 8 February confirmed one of its patrols had shot a Jew 'trying to escape'. A *Jagdkommando* (sixth) killed three 'bandits' in the forest and captured several Soviet weapons on the same day. At 6.00 pm on 6 February, the next day twenty-three Jews were killed during a firefight with the LWSB nine kilometres northwest of Truchonowicze. There were no details of the weapons the Jews were using. On 11 February a partisan camp was reported in the area of Ur-Krywiersz. The LWSB's fifth and sixth companies were deployed that evening. The camp turned out to be a tented settlement with sixteen Jews. They had fled from the Pruzhany ghetto and all sixteen were shot as they 'attempted to flee'.[28] On 18 February, *Jagdkommando Buzzard* (sixth) discovered a bunker nearby Samosze occupied by Jews, seven attempted to defend themselves with egg-shaped hand grenades but all were killed. One section of the *Jagdkommando* remained behind

---

26 BArch, RL 31/3, document 71–73, daily report 21.11–14.12.1942, Major Herbst, 14 December 1942.
27 BArch, RL 31/3, documents 82–84, the daily report from 15.12–5.1.1943, Major Herbst 5 January 1943.
28 BArch, RL 31/3, document 94–95, daily report extracts 2.2–12.2.1943, Major Herbst, 2 February 1943.

in the bunker while the rest set out in pursuit of the four Jews who escaped. They caught up with them and shot two, but two others escaped. The Germans found six egg-shaped grenades, ammunition, a slaughtered calf, clothing and valuables inside the bunker. On 24 February an unnamed Lw.NCO and a bystander observed four suspicious persons a short distance from the settlement Przedielsk. When the NCO shouted a warning, they tried to flee but while 'resisting arrest' they were shot dead. Their papers identified them as Jews escaped from Pruzhany ghetto.[29]

Once the LWSB extended its Bandenkekämpfung beyond the forest, Herbst began to compile a record of other agencies' killing Jews. On 20 January two Jews were shot by the gendarmerie in Czereczowo and officials from a customs office in Zarwercze shot another. By February 1943 the killings appeared to increase in step with the ghetto clearances as more Jews escaped. On 5 February a gendarmerie patrol shot seven Jews in Drohczym. A patrol from the gendarmerie post in Ciechanowiec 'shot a Jew while running away'. The next day a gendarmerie patrol from Topczewo 'shot a Jew trying to run away'. On 13 February the gendarmerie from Kaladycze shot 'four Jews who were running away' and another four next day. On 18 February two Jews were shot 'while running away' in Koladyce. In Polanowa, three kilometres north of Pruzhany, the alarm was raised when 'twelve armed Jewish bandits stole a team of horses with a sledge, food, clothing, and slaughtered a calf on the spot.' In Smanklice on 27 February, six Jews were killed by the Drohiczyn gendarmerie.[30] Herbst made a point of recording an incident in which 'a Jew seriously injured a Pole in Dobuczun, eight kilometres northeast of Pruzhany ghetto'.[31] As a reward for the troops' performance in hunting Jews and partisans, Herbst petitioned his bosses to negotiate leave and the release of Christmas

---

29 BArch, RL 31/3, document 100, daily report extracts 13.2–4.3.1943, Major Herbst 5 March 1943.
30 Ibid.
31 BArch, RL 31/3, document 94–95, daily report extracts, 2.2–12.2.1943, Major Herbst, 2 February 1943.

parcels.[32] Simon Schama had called the 1941 killings 'open season against Jews', however the evidence shows this was the killing actions of the LWSB.[33]

The LWSB's contact with armed Jewish bands was minimal and a few Jews were identified serving within partisan bands. In a report from February, Herbst described the ongoing mission beyond the forest as 'actions against stragglers, partisans hiding in the villages and the supporters of the partisans.'[34] The LWSB interrogated two captured partisans and from their confessions, thirty persons from villages northwest of Hajnówka were arrested. They had delivered food, weapons, ammunition and items to the partisans. Several *Hilfskräfte* working for German agencies: an auxiliary policeman, a male secretary of an *Amtskommissar*, a Soltys, and several others were arrested in the district of Dmitrowicze to the south. They were accused of terrorising the local population and encouraging the formation of bands. The courts-martial convened on 1 February, in Białowieża, and condemned twenty-two prisoners to death (see table 10). Four others recovered concentration camp sentences, and two released. An investigation found that the bands were systematically targeting *Ostmänner* (Eastern European collaborators). Table 11 included two Jews listed among those executed who were denied any legal process and found guilty of entering the forest without permits.

---

32   BArch, RL 31/3, document 70, report 11, period 21.11–14.12.42, Major Herbst 14 December 1942. Herbst wrote: 'I asked you to confirm that the battalion is employed in the eastern campaign or on a 'special mission' so that we can receive tickets for holiday trains, the distribution of parcels and other matters. The confirmation of the general staff Gen. Qu. 2 Abt. Nr. 11 818/42 secret (III e) from 28.11.1942 is not sufficient for this because it only confirms that the battalion belongs to the field army. I ask again, therefore, for a sufficient confirmation.'
33   Schama, *Landscape and Memory*, p. 70.
34   BArch, RL 31/3, document 93, report 15, period 2–12.2.1943, Major Herbst, 12 February 1943.

Table 11: LWSB, death by hanging, February 1943[35]

No.	Name	First name	Home	Born
1	Radetzki	Alexander	Wielka-Kollonna	27 August 1907
2	Radetzki	Jan	Wielka-Kollonna	4 May 1922
3	Bielinski	Stanislaus	Bialowies	21 November 1873
4	Wegera	Lucian	Gulewicze	12 December 1902
5	Skepke	Philipp	Hajnówka	1902
6	Jankowski	Gregor	Kamien	1913
7	Segien	Nikifor	Kamien	12 November 1907
8	Niczuboruk	Nikolai	Krywice	14 October 1910
9	Ignasiuk	Alexander	Kamien	28 September 1910
10	Golonko	Nikolai	Kowela	17 February 1923
11	Golonko	Stefan	Kowela	12 August 1905
12	Golonko	Anna	Kowela	1912
13	Dubke	Theodor	Chrobustowka	10 October 1912
14	Stapaniuk	Omelam	Kuraschewo	1878
15	Pasieka	Anton	Starczyna	5 January 1901
16	Grigoruk	Piotr	Kojly	1910
17	Solomienko	Iwan	Usmarczyna	1882
18	Moroz	Josef	Usmarczyna	1887
19	Wisniewski	Alexander	Wulki	12 December 1922
20	Miczeke	Antoni	Weschanko	1920
21	Miczeke	Iwan	Weschanko	23 May 1924
22.	Gulkowicz	Sylvester	Nesterki	21 December 1897
Jews				
1	Goldberg	Wela		
2	Kabinowitsch	Lew		

A hunter called Bräuer (unknown origin) raised the alarm on 13 February. He had overheard voices and noises in *Jagen* 791 south of Bialy-Lasek. Three *Jagdkommando* (from third and fourth companies) were immediately sent out with a local forest guide, the hunter, and FSK riflemen led by Lw. Captain Rüttcher. They observed a group of eight men near a bunker. Rüttcher decided to surround them but before they could get into position a German

---

35 BArch, RL 31/3, 1 February 1943 in Białowieża. The court-martial, on 1 February 1943, pronounced 22 death sentences by public hanging. Four others were condemned to a concentration camp and two prisoners were released.

opened fire without permission. The troops were forced to attack the partisan camp, which was discarded as only partly completed with half-finished bunkers. They accounted for ten partisans in the firefight and a number of wounded. Three Soviet rifles, a machine gun, several carbines and other materials were later secured but some partisans escaped. A pursuit force followed their trail south, but after five kilometres the *Jagdkommando* stumbled on another band fourteen strong. The troops opened fire and killed thirteen including two women, and they captured a female partisan. They belonged to 'a Jewish band under the command of a Jewish gardener called Sascha Lifschütz.' They had all escaped from Pruzhany ghetto in February. Two other members of the band were shot nearby Suchowszyna. The Germans abandoned their pursuit of the partisan band to kill the Jews.[36] This 'Jewish band' was almost certainly unarmed because the troops did not itemise any captured weapons and there was no mention of a firefight. On 24 February the Białowieźa courts-martial declared six persons guilty of *Banditenbegünstigung* (bandit-supporters); they were all sentenced to death by hanging (see Table 12 below).[37]

Table 12: LWSB death sentences on 24 February 1943

No.	Name	First Name	Home	Born
1	Zylluk	Illarien	a Hajnówka	21 April 1904
2	Zylluk	Tatjana	Hajnówka	1910
3	Michalczuk	Jan	Dubini	10 September 1921
4	Radczenko	Alexander	Nowosady	20 March 1916
5	Labinski	Wladislaus	Dubini	11 November 1920
6	Sawczuk	Wladimir	Saki	1910

36 BArch, RL 31/3, document 100/1, daily reports extract 13.2–4.3.1943.
37 BArch, RL 31/3, document 104/105, Verzeichnis der am 24.2.1943 vom Standgericht Bialowies zum Tode durch Erhängen, Leutnant und Adjutant Weinreis, 25 February 1943. The list of persons sentenced to death by hanging by the court martial in Białowieźa. They had been found guilty of being 'bandit-supporters'. There was a stay of execution and they were transported to the SD headquarters in Bialystok.

8. German Soldiers and Bandenbekämpfung

On the first impression, a microhistory of a Luftwaffe battalion conducting Bandenbekämpfung in the Home Forces Area does not appear unusual in the world of Nazi military violence. The 'lower quartile' of battalion killings and deportations will not alter opinions over the mass murders and the deportations. However, presenting this story with only original documents from pre-1945 removes any postwar contamination by anecdotes and or false testimony. What this shows is that the German Army's replacement army was conducting operational training through security tasks. Soldiers trained in units conducting security operations and rotated out to frontline commands having learnt their trade. This raises wider questions about the entire Wehrmacht training and replacement system following the Bandenbekämpfung directive and implies that prevailing interpretations about small unit cohesion are incomplete. We must confront the discreditable practice that has become deeply ingrained within the field of military history of advocating German doctrines as a superior form of warfare.

The *Wehrkreis I* was affiliated to nearly forty combat divisions and ancillary forces. If the Army's ambition was to reduce training time by 'blooding' men against weak opponents, then this presents an entirely different interpretation of the determination of German soldier to continue the fight to the bitter end. The army trained recruits and replacements in the effective use of weapons, terrain and tactics against non-threatening human targets, as per Kobylinksi's training regime. When framed this way the value of the LWSB story is heightened. This is especially the case given the absence of relevant historical literature or theoretical framework which might help with interpreting the LWSB's microhistory. A 1983 study of German fighting power was not particularly relevant to post-1942 training/replacement methods, or the Germans overwhelming concentration of effort on the eastern front.[1]

---

1   Martin van Creveld, *Fighting Power: German and US Army Performance 1939–1945*, (London, 1983).

An ambition of this book was to attempt to walk in step with ordinary German soldiers. This reveals that walking in step with soldiers also involves walking in step with killers. This is not based on postwar testimony or anecdote,[2] since the reports were written and filed by the battalion within the Nazi military system while it was still functioning. For decades, leading military historians have warned of the absence of research into training and the operational preparation of soldiers for war. In 1947 a study of men in combat discussed how the soldier, 'has been schooled to maneuver with his weapons in such a way that his employment of the ground will give his weapons maximum effectiveness and himself a degree of protection.' The soldier had been trained to make an 'automatic response', to learn about the limitation of weapons in combat, and to achieve 'high initiative in the infantry soldier'.[3] Richard Holmes claimed training had 'two clearly identifiable functions — weapons handling and minor tactics.' He believed in the Second World War the German recruits received 'solid basic training' — 16 weeks for infantry 'sound training'. In 2006, after observing war at first hand, Holmes was even more convinced over the importance of training.[4] Despite the concerns about lack of understanding, writers of the German Army in the Second World War have barely researched how the troops were trained or how the replacements were prepared for war.[5]

In *Fighting Power*, Creveld noted, 'Replacement Army units were moved into the occupied countries, assumed the burden of security operations, were occasionally called on to lend a hand in times of crisis and were consequently unable to properly carry out their training functions.'[6] The evidence from the previous chapters

---

2   Browning, *Ordinary Men*, passim.
3   S.L.A. Marshall, *Men Against Fire*, (Alexandria, 1947), pp. 38–41, 135.
4   Richard Holmes, *Firing Line,* (London, 1985), pp. 36–55; and *Dusty Warriors*, (London, 2006), p. 76.
5   Gerhard P. Gross, *The Myth and Reality of German Warfare*, (Lexington, 2016) compared with Robert M. Citino, *The German Way of War: From Thirty Years' War to the Third Reich*, (Kansas, 2005), Ben H. Shepherd, *Hitler's Soldiers: The German Army in the Third Reich*, (London, 2016).
6   Creveld, *Fighting Power*, p. 72.

of this book not only refute Creveld's assumption but raise much more critical issues. Victor Madej adopted an economic phrase to describe the Replacement Army as the 'invisible hand' of the German Army. He argued that warfare was a test of military efficiency, where only the case study approach can expose the nuances of the system. Madej understood the importance of affiliation between field formations and their training units, in building 'solidarity' among the troops, where it was important to establish strong teamwork for battle. The *Wehrkreis* system was critical to replenishing this process and sustaining Hitler's war.[7]

If training is highly valued for achieving maximum efficiency, performance and military success, then alternatives to ideology, social group and dogma as motivators must be assessed. This book's research from 'below' involved evaluating younger soldiers in training, carrying out security tasks. The absence of primary groups meant looking at alternatives such as functional jobs in soldiering. Functionality in the killing was machine-like in manner and served the system as much as it perpetrated Nazi crimes. Reaching optimal performance in weapons handling, as a prerequisite for the infantry, meant more than simple re-education for troops previously trained in a different service. This meant machine-like-training for machine-like-performance within a period of rotation of less than three months. These findings come from the Luftwaffe records and reflect Madej's opinions. He was dismissive of the primary group hypothesis in military studies. In his opinion, the Germans placed greater value on maintaining unit integrity and this, in turn, raised military efficiency. This 'efficiency' permitted 'a few close knit men to replace many.' To achieve high levels of efficiency, he argued that 'efficient application of combat power will determine success. Success can be described as being proportional to skill multiplied by efficiency, multiplied by motivation.' Madej argued: 'Warfare aims at the "production" of enemy losses through destructive power and involves similar motivation. ... Battles are lost because men are killed and wounded.' Small units collapse through

---

[7] W. Victor Madej, *German Army Order of Battle: The Replacement Army, 1939–45*, (Allentown, 1984).

casualties and the advent of long-range weapons have made casualties unpredictable. This suggests Herbst's methods of sustaining the integrity of the battalion and his command, was the appropriated tactical methodology. Madej thought, 'the expertise grew and hardened in the crucible of continued conflict, manifesting an underlying military professionalism.' Given the evidence he was perhaps more accurate than he realised when he wrote, 'the cold reality of German technology bred combat success.' Success in this context meaning the correct and effective use of weapons. In this regard, Madej believed the system was not coercive, which had parallels to Herbst's reports and he concluded: 'the nature of German leadership and teamwork at the small unit level was patently significant.'[8]

Traditionally in civil-military relations, German military formations were assigned to political, ideological and policing-security missions. To conduct this kind of security warfare, the German leadership trusted the training of the soldiers. As Creveld noted, from 1906 German military regulations, '… combat demands thinking, independent leaders and troops capable of independent action.'[9] There is an important question: did organised murder or killing, conducted as work, undermine German military efficiency or enhance it? In specifically referring to the actions/motivations of the troops within *Sicherungsbataillon der Luftwaffe Bialowies zbV.*, under Herbst, we can draw specific conclusions. Nazi dogma or personal rewards played no part in inducing the troops to kill. We also know line officers and senior NCOs were not present on patrols forcing ORs to kill. Herbst did not issue written orders to junior NCOs leading patrols to arrest or kill. The ORs routinely killed defenceless people without facing arrest or courts-martial, making the reasonable assumption that authority was conveyed verbally. We also know, through deduction, that Herbst relied on military discipline, the command hierarchy and 'trust' of his men for them to fulfil his intentions during patrols. Those intentions varied between arrest or killing, which further confirms there was a central mission with differential outcomes

---

8   W. Victor Madej, *Hitler's Dying Ground: Description and Destruction of the German Army*, (Allentown, 1985), pp. 3–38.
9   Creveld, *Fighting Power*, p. 35.

depending upon circumstances. For example, whether the killing was immediate or an exemplary public execution to act as a warning. We can safely assume therefore, Herbst expected his men to function within the bounds of routine and was not disappointed by their performance. We know he identified proficient men to transfer with him. Based upon these findings it must be concluded that *Auftragstaktik* was the overarching operational culture, underpinning the actions and motivations of the LWSB.

If the military is a microcosm of the culture they fight for, then *Auftragstaktik* has to be treated in the wider context of Nazi ideology. From this perspective, Herbst in his civilian career as a commercial lawyer would have been professionally proficient in the Nazi legal codes of *Arisierung* (the exclusion of Jews from business), the *Führerprinzip* (leader principle), the *Volksgemeinschaft* (people's community) and the national mission of *Lebensraum*. In other words, Herbst was responsible for leading his troops in enforcing racial purity and colonisation for the German people. Blending *Arisierung, Führerprinzip, Lebensraum* and *Auftragstaktik* offered no room for civilised behaviour. Herbst was ordered to wage genocide because it was Göring's intent, he was bound ideologically by *Führerprinzip* and by *Auftragstaktik* militarily. Whether Herbst approved, or not, there was no avenue for an appeal to reason or speak truth to power even if he had wanted to object.

The real culprit was the prevailing combat dogma instilled into all German soldiers from basic training — *Auftragstaktik*; a word that fuses together *Auftrag* — 'order, task, mission' and *Taktik* — 'tactics, tactical art'.[10] The word *Auftragstaktik* connotes a raft of meanings and interpretations that has been written into many military histories. Anglo-American scholars have adopted 'mission command', as the optimal translation, with the usual explanation:

> Auftragstaktik is based on the principle that a commander should tell his subordinates what to do and when to do it, but not necessarily tell them how to do it. In accomplishing their missions, subordinate commanders are given a wide degree of latitude and are expected to exercise great initiative.[11]

---

10 Kurt Hilmar Eitzen, *Militär-Wörterbuch,* (Berlin, 1936), Auftrag, p. 25, Taktik, p. 192.
11 Bruce Condell and David T. Zabecki, *On the German Art of War: Truppenführung: German Army Manual for Unit Command in World War II,* (Mechanicsburg, 2009), pp. 3–4.

German historians have expressed less interest in *Auftragstaktik* to perhaps avoid the seriousness of its implications.[12] A direct comparison of German and American interpretations can be seen in their respective treatment of the German way of war. While Gerhard Gross makes no references to the word, even in translation, Robert Citino makes several specific references.[13] The puzzle is why the word had not been confronted in military history or in its application by modern armies.[14] Social and Holocaust histories have similarly shied away from incorporating *Auftragstaktik* or similar military terminology to explain the perpetration of crimes.[15]

Ben Shepherd has been an advocate of using the word to explain the Wehrmacht's way of war. Throughout his book, from introduction to conclusion, Shepherd effectively referenced *Auftragstaktik*, untranslated, but defined the term for his readers as 'mission tactics'. There is a thread of *Auftragstaktik* running through his narrative with a powerful collection of military-cultural words to embellish its impact: doctrine, training, improvisation, tactical mastery, coordination, impetuous, flexibility, incentive, motivation, daring, and aggression.[16] Regarding war crimes, however, Shepherd does not comment on whether *Auftragstaktik* stimulated actions or behaviour. In an earlier book about crimes, Shepherd entirely avoided using the word.[17] We can only assume, given the

---

12 Stephan Leistenschneider, *Auftragstaktik im preussisch-deutschen Heer, 1871 bis 1914*, (Hamburg, 2002), and Marco Sigg, *Der Unterführer als Feldherr im Taschenformat. Theorie und Praxis der Auftragstaktik im deutschen Heer 1869 bis 1945*, (Paderborn, 2014).
13 Gross, *The Myth and Reality of German Warfare* compared with Citino, *The German Way of War*, refers to Auftragstaktik in multiple references.
14 Bartov, *Barbarisation*, passim, Jeff Rutherford, *Combat and Genocide on the Eastern Front: The German Infantry's War 1941–1944*, (Cambridge, 2014), and Waitman Wade Beorn, *Marching Into Darkness: The Wehrmacht and the Holocaust in Belarus*, (Harvard, 2014).
15 For example: Richard Bessel, *Nazism and War*, (London, 2004) or Christopher Browning, Ordinary Men, passim.
16 Ben H. Shepherd, *Hitler's Soldiers: The German Army in the Third Reich*, (London, 2016).
17 Ben Shepherd, *Terror in the Balkans: German Armies and Partisan Warfare*, (Harvard, 2012).

evidence as presented that Shepherd refers to *Auftragstaktik* in the purely conventional military context. In contrast, this book argues that the lethality of violence was heightened by Auftragstaktik and that under Nazism genocide and the military was a comfortable partnership.

I. Herbst and Bandenbekämpfung

The LWSB's Bandenbekämpfung campaign was concentrated into two phases: July–October 1942, and November 1942 to February 1943. The first phase was largely defensive and concentrated on defending the north-western third of *Urwald Bialowies*, an area that equates to the present-day Polish forest. The second phase involved the expansion of the LWSB into the larger area of *Urwald Bialowies*, which falls into Belarus today. Herbst adopted the tactics of static defence based upon a system of strongpoints, observation posts (OP), and pickets, erecting a screen across the entire area. In both phases, 'search and destroy' techniques were part of the tactical operation of extensive local and *Jagdkommando* patrols. There were several undercurrents within Herbst's reports including the level of partisan firepower in relation to the Germans and, the partisan's brazen attacks on LWSB's positions. There was also the division in time, the twenty-hour clock, where the Germans ruled in daylight and the partisans ruled at night. This chapter is not a blow-by-blow reconstruction of events. However, analysis of Herbst's *modus operandi*, his leadership, and his interpretation of the mission, reveals the inner workings of a security battalion in Bandenbekämpfung.

Forming a breakdown of incidents for the entire period from July 1942 to February 1943 presents many inconsistencies. The reports of incidents changed in content with the seasons, different terrain conditions, and with the expansion of the LWSB. Terrain played a major part on German casualties and this identified some of the tactics adopted by both sides. The Germans suffered less than a handful of casualties from mine explosions, the vast majority were caused by shots to the head and body (see appendix 2).

The partisans preferred the ambush or 'shoot-and-scoot' (shooting and running away) tactics. The undulating ground deep in the forest led many German soldiers to be shot in the head, neck and upper torso as their patrols crested the small plateau, which is a feature of the forest. The plateau constantly changed and are caused by deep soil erosion due to the concentration of heavy rainwater, the overflow of streams, and small rivers swelled by rain or melting snow. In some parts of the forest marshland, swamps, and lakes added further restrictions on movement, which also forced the Germans to expose themselves to partisan gunfire.

There were 169 *Jagdkommandos* incidents, all during patrols. In his fifth report (11–20 September 1942) Herbst disclosed the intention of adopting *Jagdkommando* patrols in his tactical planning. In his thirteenth report (6–7 January 1943) he explained that each company deployed a *Jagdkommando* in response to the intensification of partisan activity. The *Jagdkommando* were tasked with 'search and destroy' missions. They were also used as pursuit troops, held in reserve as a rapid-response force, or deployed as reconnaissance or scouts. The *Jagdkommandos* were named after animals. The first company *Jagdkommando Elch* or elk comprised of an officer, two NCOs and fifteen OR's, whereas *Jagdkommando Falke* (hawk) of the third company had two NCOs and thirteen ORs. The second company raised two Jagdkommando designated *Keiler* (male wild boar) and *Fuchs* (fox); while the fourth company raised four designated *Kranich* (crane), *Falke* (falcon), *Sperber* (sparrow hawk) and *Geier* (vulture). The fifth company raised four *Jagdkommandos* designated *Wildkatze* (wild cat), *Jaguar*, *Luchs* (lynx), and *Panther*; and Sixth company three *Jagdkommandos* designated *Buzzard*, *Reiher* (heron) and *Würger* (shrike). *Jagdkommando Kranich* had the smallest compliment with two NCOs and ten OR's.

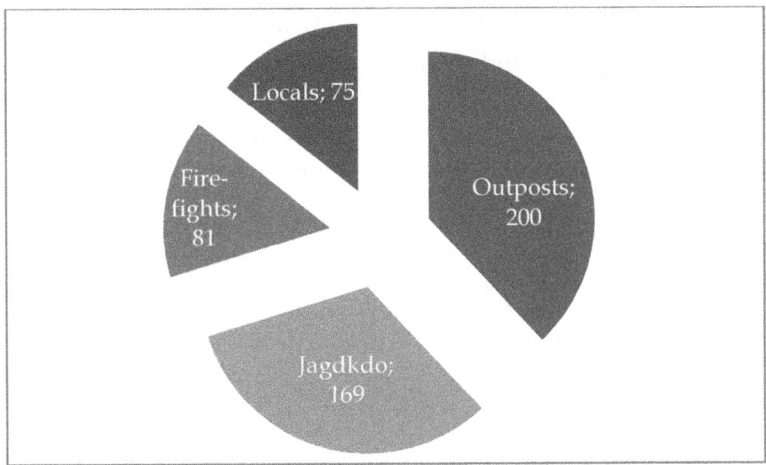

Diagram 2: the four categories of reported incidents

There were more than 200 incidents involving *Vorposten* or OPs and strongpoints mentioned in the documents. The troops assigned to outposts ranged from a platoon, a *Jagdkommando*, or just a section depending upon the mission. OPs served several functions including *Schildwache* (sentry posts), *Feldwachen* (picket detail) or *Feldposten* (picket posts) and were placed in positions of good visibility.[18] The routines of OP duty depended upon the corresponding threat levels, in some areas they were the advance reconnaissance of known infiltration points or partisan concentration; and, in other cases were platforms for deep ranging patrols. Strongpoints were wooden forts, following a similar pattern to those erected by ancient Romans or the wooden forts of the US cavalry in the American west.[19] Andrew Charlesworth has written 'Himmler's line of SS settlements penetrating deep into Russia can be seen as the eastern

---

18 Ludwig Queckbörner, *Die Schützenkompanie: Ein Handbuch für den Dienstunterricht*, (Berlin, 1939), p. 265. The prescribed model for forming a security screen began the centre oft he formation based in village or strongpoints. Then three Feldwache were formed on the entry-exit roads; then Feldposten set up further out at important points like a wood, hill or bridge; and then scouts (Spähtruppe) led patrols beyond the security zone gathering information on the movements of the enemy.

19 Ripperger el al, *Der Traum vom Urwald*, p. 306. The authors caption a picture of the Woitowy Most strongpoint illustrating a wooden fort more akin to a US cavalry fort during the Plains War or an earlier Roman fort.

equivalent of the US Cavalry forts from which SS troops would test their military prowess and chivalrous ideal by sallying forth against hostiles, in their case Slavic partisans.'[20] Herbst's strongpoints seemed to confirm Charlesworth's observations. After the war a German general described the construction of a typical strongpoint:

> Wooden walls to cover buildings in a stockade form. The wooden walls were 3 metres from the main building walls. Trunks, 30–40cm thick fallow were planted at the corners, gaps were left for flanking machine-gun fire. Fire steps were added to allow troops to fire over the wall. There was only one entrance usually on the railway side. The wooden shutters were 5cm thick to guard windows against grenades. An observation position was placed on the roof. Water towers were similarly protected with wood and all the buildings were linked by trenches. The area was surrounded by barbed wire obstacles and chevaux-de-frise to block the road.[21]

There were eighty-one *Feuergefechte* (firefights) in the records. The firefights came in several forms. On 8 August a firefight in the Czolo area lasted from midnight to 6.00 am. There were no other details, which was typical of so many reports. The evening of 8–9 October was quite lively because at 6.15 pm thirty partisans occupied Gruski, loading up everything that could be carried. They then set fire to the village. Every house except the foresters was destroyed. Later at 7.30 pm, an alarm was raised in Rudnia when fifteen partisans entered the village. A detachment from Strongpoint Niemerca was dispatched. At 9.30 pm the partisans shooting from within the confines of the village initiated a firefight. They increased the intensity of shooting to make good their escape. At midnight partisans attacked Strongpoint Niemerca, the Germans returned fire, but the partisans withdrew. Several hours later a sniper killed a sentry with one shot, this sparked a double-flank firefight. A *Jagdkommando* (third company) was sent to reinforce Niemerca but failed to intercept the band. In the afternoon a patrol from Strongpoint Niemerca came across two partisans; they ran away, but the Germans began random shooting without effect. At 7.00 pm

---

20 Andrew Charlesworth, 'The Topography of Genocide', Dan Stone (ed), *The Historiography of the Holocaust*, (Londond, 2004), p. 248.
21 NARA, RG242, FMS, D-257, Heinz Krampf, 'Anti-Partisan protection of the railways'.

Strongpoint Niemerca received incoming fire. The Germans assumed it was because the partisans had observed the *Jagdkommandos* depart and thought it was safe to attack.[22]

The accounts of serious attacks on local civilians, by the partisans, were barely investigated. Herbst recorded these cases but did not express any sympathy or go out of his way to offer assistance. On 1 August, twenty-five partisans entered Oezem wearing civilian garb and carrying a few weapons. They forced the people into a courtyard and announced the hamlet was to be torched to prevent the Germans from turning it into a strongpoint. They beat a man accused of passing information to the Germans. They then raped an unspecified number of women. A twenty-year-old female attempted to flee across the river, but a partisan gave chase and shot her in the back. At 8.00 pm the partisans set fire to the village. Five minutes later smoke was observed by troops at Strongpoint Popielewo. The villagers managed to save their cattle and a few possessions. Eventually, the partisans departed in a northerly direction taking eighty pounds of honey, seventeen loaves, and twenty pounds of butter. The survivors claimed the partisans were all escaped Soviet PoWs.[23] No troops were sent to investigate or pursue the partisans.

In a two-week period (15–30 August 1942) there were several serious attacks on locals. A band a hundred strong occupied Woguzka, in the furthest south-west border of the forest at 2.00 am. The civic guard attempted to fight back and was overwhelmed. A villager was killed and another injured. The partisans stole food, clothes and a pig. They carried the swag in four horse-drawn carts, but they were returned later. A partisan took a pot shot at a patrol from Königsbrück. He evaded capture but left behind his rifle. The LWSB responded by encircling and searching Krieziec. Empty Russian ammunition boxes for machine guns were found in a house, and the homeowner was placed under arrest. Meanwhile, three partisans entered a house several kilometres north of Hajnówka

---

22 BArch, RL 31/3, document 43, daily report extracts 1–10.10.1942, Major Herbst, 11 October 1942.
23 BArch, RL 31/1, LWSB Kriegstagebuch, 2 August 1942.

and stole a cooking pan. On 30 September twenty-five partisans, one wearing a German police uniform, three in civilian clothing and the rest in Red Army uniforms, occupied Izbica a hamlet nearby Suchopol. They were well armed with rifles or machine pistols and hand grenades. They overwhelmed the civil militia and disabled the alarm tripwire to the LWSB. They took food and clothes and 120 Reichsmarks of *Gemeindegeld* (communal funds). Before they departed, they interrogated the locals about the strength of the gendarmerie in Suchopol and the *Hilfsdienst* (auxiliary service). Fifty partisans appeared in Zarzeze near Czereczow, they were well armed with two light machine guns, bolt-action rifles, pistols and hand grenades. They encircled the village cutting it off and isolating it before taking food and clothes.[24]

Many reports reflected uncertainties over partisan intentions. On Saturday 19 September, at the end of the workday, two railway maintenance waggons were parked in a siding in *Jagen* 378. The waggons were loaded with spare rails. Two days later at 6.00 am, the workers found the waggons in *Jagen* 640 and the rails tipped into a ditch. Herbst couldn't decide if it was an act of vandalism or a case of failed sabotage.[25] The forest's terrain added to the general unpredictability in reporting incidents. The forest restricted German movement, but camouflaged partisan activity. One report from 1 October noted that an unknown number of partisans carried out a 'hit and run' attack against *Jagdkommando Fuchs* (second company) in the area of *Jagen* 277. The Germans clung to the claim that the impenetrability of the forest made pursuits impossible. The lack of daylight and the problems associated with coping in darkness were also regular excuses for abandoning the chase. On 4 October, a *Jagdkommando* patrolling in the same *Jagen* 277 stumbled across four partisans. They slipped away during a short firefight. The Germans gave chase, but the pursuit ended with the onset of darkness. Once darkness set in the Germans usually ceased all activities surrendering the night and the locals to the mercy of the partisans

---

24 BArch, RL 31/3, document 36–37, daily report extracts 21.9.–30.10.1942, Major Herbst 1 October 1942.
25 Ibid.

The random acts of partisans led the Germans to conclude it was intended to terrorise the locals. The evidence points to that conclusion. At lunchtime on 26 October, partisans intercepted wedding guests driving in three horse-drawn carts from Nowasady to Narewka Mala. As they travelled through *Jagen* 94, the last cart carrying seven people was stopped by four partisans wielding rifles. The partisans demanded tobacco and cigarettes but received nothing. They eventually allowed them to continue their journey.[26] On 28 October eighteen partisans occupied Schwalowo, they took boots, clothes and fur coats. A woman tried to fight back but was given a serious beating.[27] At lunchtime on 1 November, a band held up three local men on the road to Jasien-Obrudniki. They scrutinised their travel documents and confiscated the papers of a miller from Taszuki. Several partisans walked behind trees with his pass while the others stood guard. They returned twenty minutes later and accused the miller of being a spy. They led him away and nothing was heard of him again, but the others were released. At dusk on 5 November, the gamekeeper of Nieznany-Bor came faced eight partisans in his house while another thirty surrounded the building. They demanded butter, fat and other produce, but the gamekeeper refused. The partisans beat up his wife and the others in the house. They threatened to rape his daughter and eventually he surrendered all the supplies they could carry. On the evening of 21 November, a twenty strong band attacked Michnowka. A farmer had all his money and a pass taken. The partisans threatened to kill him if he reported the incident. A gamekeeper called Schutkowski was held up on the way from Brody to Jasein by six partisans wielding machine pistols. They pushed him into a thicket, questioned him about the Germans, and then robbed him. He was forced to promise to get ammunition and deposit it under a bridge in the forest. The Germans did not use him in a ploy to ambush the partisans. At 2.00 pm on 23 November, twenty partisans intercepted eight

---

26 BArch, RL 31/3, document 52, daily report extracts 22–31.10.42, Major Herbst, 11 October 1942.
27 BArch, RL 31/3, documents 51, 52, daily report extracts 22–31.10.1942, Major Herbst, 31 October 1942.

horse-drawn carts on the Luka-Michnowka road. The carts were plundered, and money taken from the drivers. The partisans wore complete Soviet army uniforms with fur coats and armed with machine pistols.[28]

Among the LWSB's documents are several operational reports that were exceptions. They reported the LWSB's cooperation with rival agencies during joint operations. The paperwork was treated with care and attention, with full letter headings and the correct forms of address. Typical of these reports was *Unternehmen Czolo* (Operation Czolo), the first joint mission with the SS. It was planned to take place ten kilometres northeast of Białowieża town and expected to last 1–2 August. The first company, with two additional platoons from the second company, joined elements of an SS-Police gendarmerie company. Their mission was to crush the partisans with coordinated actions against Czolo and Zamosche with cordons by the LWSB's pickets. The plan involved setting an ambush, utilising the partridge drive method. The troops were to form several *Absperrposten* (cordon of sentries) covering roads and across forest firebreaks. Herbst explained:

> We have learned from previous experience, after night-time attacks the bandit's retreat in easterly and westerly directions, seeking shelter in their forest hideaways. We shall under no circumstances *nachdrücken* [push the enemy] from Czolo to Zamosze because we do not want to risk endangering our forces in the east. We have to point out to the squads that unnecessary, wild shooting is forbidden and that only identified objectives shall be placed under fire.[29]

On 2 August, Herbst released further orders concerning *Unternehmen Czolo*. Both second company platoons were to advance in a northerly direction conducting a 'search and destroy' action. A company of PB 13 was to be transported in trucks from Popielewo to Jagen 112. From there they were to advance, on foot, in a westerly

---

28   BArch, RL 31/3, document 71–73, daily report extracts 21.11–14.12.1942, Major Herbst, 14 December 1942.
29   BArch, RL 31/2, document 4, Einsatzbefehle Br. B. Nr. 15/42 secret, Einsatzbefehl für 1. Kompanie, Major Herbst, 1 August 1942. Without explanation, Lieutenant Mailowsky (third company) was assigned command of the returning troops to Hajnówka.

direction toward the partisans, and forming an encirclement of Czolo. The LWSB's troops were to press on along the known tracks of partisans' movements over the previous ten days. A local hunter led the police to prepared positions along a forest firebreak near Dlugi-Borek. At dawn, the company was to destroy the partisans believed to be moving in an easterly direction.[30] There was no follow-up report because the partisans departed the area several days before the mission. Herbst was frustrated about the waste of time and effort. He also believed his plans were betrayed, hence the decision to conduct internal investigations.

Concerning Himmler's *Unternehmen Wisent*, there were no direct references to the LWSB's participation. However, on 1–2 September 1942, Herbst conducted aerial reconnaissance in his Fieseler Fi156 *Storch* in support of a *Polizeiaktion* (police action) over sectors designated as *Urwald Bialowies* (Przedielsk, Wielko-Siolo, Lezaika, Zadzieny). He was observing the movements of a partisan band seven kilometres northwest of Truchonowicze. He landed in Pruzhany to confer with *Generalmajor* Müller and *Oberst* Hirschfeld. They agreed upon a joint mission arranged to begin on 4 September. The plan required the LWSB's pickets to remain in their positions while Herbst flew search missions to assist the police in locating a partisan encampment. On 24 September, Herbst met with Müller in Bialystok and received a promise of more support from an unnamed Waffen-SS regiment to aggressively combat the partisans up until 7 October. The regiment was to search through villages. Then alongside elements of the second battalion, SS-Police Regiment 2 and detachments from the Waffen-SS (8th and 10th Infantry Regiments) were to take up positions along the southern border of *Urwald Bialowies*. The SS commander and his regimental staff transferred to Białowieża for the duration of these operations.[31] There was no after-action report regarding the outcome.

---

30 BArch, RL 31/2, document 5, Einsatzbesprechung, Br. B. Nr. 16/42 geheim, Einsatz für Unternehmen Czolo 1–2 August, Major Herbst, 2 August 1942.

31 BArch, RL 31/3, document 35, report 6, period 21–30.9. 1942, Major Herbst, 1 October 1942. See also Gerlach, *Kalkulierte Morde*, p. 935.

There is one report that covered a joint operation between the LWSB, SS and trusties. On 13 September, Herbst visited Witowo to meet with a trusty. The man identified three partisan camps in *Jagen* 628, 629, and 597. The camps were located and searched; they were described as shabby having been deserted for a long time and it was believed the partisans had not been in the Witowo area since 28 August. Trusties and reconnaissance patrols had observed a group of partisans settled in nearby Sipurka. They were identified as a *Leit- und Verteidigungsstelle* (scout-guide group holding a defensive position) for all the bands in the forest. The trusties discovered that these partisan scouts were leading smaller bands from the River Bug into the forest. The partisans had barred local inhabitants from entering 'their' part of the forest and threatened to kill anyone who dared try to enter. Herbst believed the LWSB was not capable of tackling these partisans alone. He approached Hirschfeld to conduct a joint action, but he refused. Hirschfeld was reluctant because the previous large-scale operations had failed. Herbst approached Müller who agreed and immediately ordered the encirclement of the band by a Waffen-SS battalion, elements of the LWSB, and the 2nd SS-Police battalion. On 28 September the Waffen-SS took command, the LWSB provided trusties, and Herbst once again took to the air to reconnoitre the area. During the operation thirteen partisans were killed, twelve arrested including two women but an unknown number escaped. The troops located a large, well-constructed and fortified bunker camp capable of quartering forty-five persons. The troops secured one machine gun, food, and clothes.[32] This was one of Herbst's most notable successes.

The reports leave a confused impression. They reveal a lot but explain little. They reveal how active the partisans were, but do not explain why the Germans were reticent. Hitler's directive expected aggression and initiative, but Herbst seemed determined to maintain the integrity of his command. The absence of radio wireless equipment and signals capability was a major disadvantage for the *Jagdkomandos*. The inability to maintain regular contact or call for assistance

---

32 BArch, RL 31/3, document 39, Aktenvermark über das Unternehmen Wald Sipurka am 28 September 1942, Major Herbst, 30 September 1942.

was an important reason for the German reluctance to press the partisans deep into the forest. The relative youth, poor training, and general condition of the troops were also important reasons for Herbst's reluctance. Even after the battalion expanded, Herbst was still reluctant to press the troops to take greater initiative. Herbst was not prepared to allow his forces to go toe-to-toe against the partisans, this absence of faith in the troops is a fascinating issue about German command attitudes. The troops were not up to the task and this is the central theme of Herbst's reporting. However, in other tasks, the troops excelled, and this will be examined in subsequent chapters.

II. NCOs: command spine in the field

In the absence of senior NCO records, it has been difficult to construct a complete description of the junior officer system. As a result, it has become necessary to address a number of questions from alternative perspectives. There is an assumption in military history that cold-blooded killing undermines military discipline. How then did Wehrmacht units maintain discipline during the Holocaust? The prevalence of initiative biased military dogma, such as *Auftragstaktik*, cannot entirely explain how discipline was maintained. The company, the squad and the *Jagdkommando*, the primary fighting units in Białowieża, were all micro-military detachments usually led by NCO's. They were intimate communities of young men where the vulgar, the base and puerile vernacular were the everyday *lingua franca*. Delving into the 'real life' within small units is notoriously difficult, even in modern wars with troops carrying smartphones and recording their combat experiences. Although the troops did similar work and duties, each small unit had its own identity and was shaped by the squad leader. The US Military Intelligence Service published *The German Squad in Combat,* a small booklet. It was a translation of an original German training booklet for squad leaders. The English translation carried a foreword that added, 'These tactics differ somewhat from those of the US squad, mainly in that the enemy unit is built for tactical purposes around the employment of the squad's light machine gun.' The structure of the original included such themes as the organisation of squad formations; followed by 'combat methods'; and then a right or wrong section of 'correct' or 'false' examples of how to conduct squad combat tactics. The section on combat methods observed: 'The efficiency of a squad depends essentially on the personality of its leader, his conduct in emergencies and in danger, his example, his power to make decisions, and his coolness.'[33] According to the booklet, 'A good leader, one with a good personality means a good unit, and a poor leader means a poor unit.' To aspire to good leadership the squad leader had to take training seriously but also:

> He must learn the way to the hearts of his subordinates and win their confidence by understanding their feelings and their way of thinking, and by justice and solicitude for their welfare. The subordinate wants to feel that his superior has a heart for him, looks after him and intercedes on his behalf. It is only in this way that in the field the squad leader can be at the same time a stern father and a kind mother.[34]

The 'stern father and a kind mother' points to the family concept at the heart of the German squad culture. The NCO was the most prominent figure of authority. The functions of the NCOs were to serve as a nervous system of the battalion. In combat, the NCO's held the fighting troops together, but their more substantial role was to build the feedback loops providing information to the commanding officers on the condition of formations and the well-being of the troops. The NCO shaped morale and was the long arm of the commanding officer in the field. In basic training, the NCO is rarely depicted as a kindly instructor. Rather they were the harsh bullying taskmaster, screaming at bewildered recruits.

There is a basic training film, of the *Horstkompanie (E) 11/xIII* at a *Fliegerhorst* (airbase) near Przemysl in Poland, during the winter of 1942. Scenes illustrated the character of NCO how they enforced discipline. The airbase comprised of barrack buildings set up around a large square with trees and a lawn. Parades and drill were conducted on a wide road lined by pavements. Around the parade grounds,

---

33   TNA, WO 208/3000, 'The German Squad In Combat, Military', Intelligence Service, US War Department, Washington DC, 25 January 1943.
34   Ibid.

Polish civilian onlookers watch the troops while tending the gardens. Six NCOs were filmed training a detachment of twenty-eight recruits. The senior NCOs looked middle-aged and portly, the junior NCOs lean and youthful. In this atmosphere of harsh discipline, both the instructors and the recruits carry out their exercises with smiles.

Was fun an essential part of everyday life in the Luftwaffe? The film shows the senior NCOs standing around joking with each other and smoking. Alcohol was absent, reinforcing the impression of traditional German military discipline. This compared with the lax behaviour prominent among non-conventional Nazi paramilitaries like the SS. The discomfort of the recruits is obvious. The young NCOs bark orders as the men march, making them hold their carbines correctly and standing properly to attention on parade. One NCO marched beside a recruit to ensure the recruits raised their legs to the correct level in the 'goose step'. The recruits dressed in a mix of shabby uniforms or drill overalls and without insignia, in contrast to NCOs in crisp full-dress uniform. The training NCOs stood rigid as they barked their orders with such force their bodies visibly jerk. The recruits were in a mixed age range, and each issued with a 98k carbine and leather webbing. They constantly run at the double and their exercises included the correct form of the Hitler salute. For a brief clip in the film, the recruits wore their full-dress uniforms during a parade. Later the film passed to the training fields and a nearby forest where the recruits were taught to 'run and drop' with their carbines in preparation for combat. An officer joined the exercise, he lay in a firing position, and then leapt up running forward. This instructed the men to move quickly with their weapons in the correct position. Later, there was a brief clip of an inspection by a *Luftgau* general with his large staff and the salute being taken. The film ended on the firing range with a large number of NCOs attending to their weapons for a shooting competition. A *Luftwaffe* clerk kept the scores in a shooting book in what appeared to be a very convivial affair.[35] If the LWSB was still training it might have still been going through those same activities of discipline, shooting and manoeuvre.

---

35 Polar Films, 'Alltag im Fliegerhorst', Gescher, 2004.

Image 14: Luftwaffe troops in company order.
Source: Author

Omer Bartov's *Hitler's Army* examined the primary group hypothesis, men who served together in a unit from its inception, and their destruction through increasing combat casualties. He formulated an 'anatomy' of war experience, motivation, social organisation, and perceptions of reality.[36] The evidence from the *Luftwaffe* personnel files indicated his views about the primary group were

---

36 Bartov, *Hitler's Army*, pp. 3–11.

incorrect. The *Luftwaffe's* troopers experienced multiple transfers, before and after service in Białowieża, and many with multiple postings across Europe in the front line or rear area duties. If the primary group ethos was crucial to the German way of war, why did the military bureaucracy constantly break them up? The question has never been satisfactorily solved. However, Bartov's ideas on how the German Army absorbed genocidal doctrines, and his examination of the 'perversion of discipline' remains fundamental to any research. Harsh discipline was a strong cultural thread across all the armed forces and remained constant throughout the rise of modern warfare. This harshness enabled the German Army to establish a reputation for 'battlefield steadfastness' and 'brutalization'. However, Bartov's general theory was mostly concerned with the application of discipline 'from above', from senior commanders and the officer corps. It helped explain the harsh treatment of civilians, Red Army PoW's, Jews, and Soviet commissars. Bartov focused on the orders and rulings set by generals but there was no counter-balancing study of the military environment and the individual soldier — in other words, no examination 'from below'.

Sönke Neitzel and Harald Welzer study of German PoWs in British captivity took a different approach. Their approach pushed a social-psychological-institutional emphasis on the primary group hypothesis, but also included ideology, military values, and violence. They presented the concept of 'war as work', as the extension of work-related traits and characteristics into wartime. Their opinions were shaped by sources from combat troops and largely avoided the occupied zones. The German armed forces, unlike the other belligerents, had for decades institutionalised a rear area and occupation organisation within its order of battle. An entire establishment of German soldiers were specialists or trained in making an occupied area serve the army and the frontlines. A broad comparison of *Soldaten* and the findings from this book identified the prominent absence of ideological prerequisites. Białowieża was a garrison rear area and service were shaped by personal security, strongpoints, and extreme violence. this military community encouraged a bureaucratic regime not far short of a modern 9-to-5-

working day existence.[37] The 'war as work' culture paints Białowieża as an extremely violent community, ruled by Herbst, and policed by aggressive young men and licensed to shoot-to-kill. Patrols set out in the morning and were back before darkness. The troops had access to soldiers' bars and alcohol when off duty; relaxation enabled them to bond, and as comrades in a common cause could dissolve the psychological stress of killing unarmed Jews and civilians. It is also known from the 1943 budget (see chapter 6) that hunting and general entertaining continued throughout the occupation.

The German Squad in Combat provided insight into small unit doctrine but should be read in conjunction with *The German Rifle Company* on the questions of orders.[38] That book contains a reference to the company's 'combat orders', drawn from the rules set down in the army's *Truppenführung* (field service regulations). Under these regulations, all higher command orders had to be written or typed, whereas the same regulations stipulated that 'lower commanders use the oral order.' We should take care not to attribute too much to textbooks as official guidance and control. Hitler's Bandenbekämpfung directive broke with German military traditions in training and establishing a professional code. The final evidence is the findings from the GIS maps, which remove any doubt over the troops killing Jews. The NCOs' commanded the patrols. The sixth company was assigned five senior non-commissioned officers but none of their personnel papers has survived. The most senior NCO was Company Sergeant Major Heinrich P** born in Wagenau on 27 December 1912. Below him were four younger sergeants. The eldest was Paul G** born on 17 June 1909 in Danzig, and the youngest Rudolf P** born in Freudenthal in February 1920.[39] They, in turn, were assisted by a further twenty junior NCOs. We do know these men led the patrols rather than the company officers. In effect, the NCOs were the lynchpin between Göring, Herbst and the junior officers, and the ordinary men.

---

37 Sönke Neitzel, Harald Welzer, *Soldaten, On Fighting, Killing and Dying*, (London, 2012) pp. 334–343.
38 MIS No.15, *The German Rifle Company*.
39 No senior company, or battalion NCO personnel files were located.

Image 15: Luftwaffe troops in action in the forest.
Source: Author

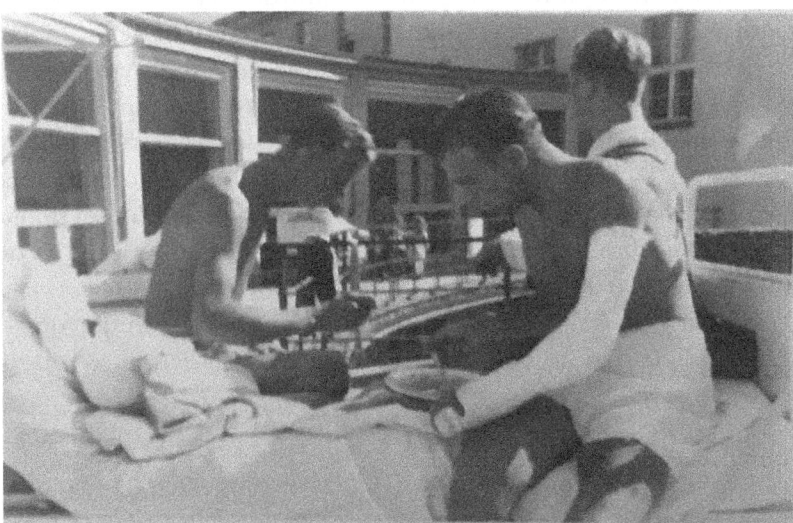

Image 16: Wounded Luftwaffe troops recovering in a military hospital.
Source: Author

III. Military dogma, military order or military efficiency?

Theories about military dogma cannot explain why young German troops in training killed Jews. The German instruction book *Die Schützenkompanie* (The Rifle Company) contained no reference to morale, but one section referred to *Kameradschaft und Manneszucht* (comradeship and discipline). Comradeship, the text advised, bound the troops together especially in the life and death struggle of war. Regarding discipline, the maxim was 'obedience and comradeship' but not 'blind obedience'. The book instructed that blind obedience was the 'escape route for cowards shirking their duty.' Discipline and obedience, in this context, represented the psychological and educational preparedness to endure the hardship and heroism of combat.[40] Thomas Kühne has written extensively of the Landser's complicity in war crimes. He investigated comradeship as both a virtue in morale but also as a moral deficiency through the conspiracy of murder. The importance of male bonding is now regarded as a common trait of masculinity, and Kühne recognized its importance to the military system.[41] Kühne's work is compelling and probably had some applicability to the men of the LWSB, but there was no documentary means to confirm it. The companies rarely remained fixed for more than six months, with a regular turnover of the rank and file through transfers. There was no evidence of pre-existing primary groups or their formation during assignment to companies or *Jagdkommando*. We know the *Jagdkommando* tracked Jewish fugitives in the forest. Killing them had no noticeable bearing on their continued effectiveness as soldiers.

---

40   MIS No.15, The German Rifle Company, Washington DC, US Government Printing Office, 1942. The book was a partial translation and rough reprint of Ludwig Queckbörner, *Die Schützenkompanie: Ein Handbuch für den Dienstunterricht*, (Berlin, 1939), p. 5.

41   Thomas Kühne, *Kameradschaft: Die Soldaten des nationalsozialistischen Krieges und das 20. Jahrhundert*, (Göttingen, 2006) and Kühne, *The Rise and Fall of Comradeship: Hitler's Soldiers, Mass Bonding and Mass Violence in the Twentieth Century*, (Cambridge, 2017).

Joanna Bourke has observed, 'the characteristic act of men at war is not dying, it is killing.'[42] Is that true, or is the characteristic of men in war their determination to survive? Constant fear of death rendered the common soldier pliable to their army's dogma and military orthodoxy. As a 'sophisticated military conflict' a military historian thought the soldiers at every level in the Second World War were expected to perform with both 'technical expertise' and 'individual initiative'. He opined, 'small unit tactics laid quite a new emphasis upon dispersal, mutual support and a flexible responsiveness to the demands of the local situation.'[43] The skills level and soldierly imagination of the modern infantryman turned them into highly effective fighting men after only three months of basic training. The 'infantryman' was the embodiment of survival in modern warfare. The 'poor bloody infantry' of the Second World War shouldered their weapons and equipment, carried them across all kinds of terrain and weather, dug a hole for their personal protection, and awaited the battle. In *Urwald Bialowies* geography and terrain imposed an unusual existence. Patrolling the forest was a major physical challenge for the troops. Long-range patrols could last several days covering distances of well over twenty to thirty kilometres. The forest's floor undulates with small hills, ravines, and large holes from fallen trees, with large trunks, and mixed tree stands. A multitude of streams forms a watershed with springs, streams and rivers; water collects in ponds, lakes, marshes and deep swampland. Pools formed in tree holes causing landslips creating small plateaus. In winter poor light, extreme cold, and waist-deep pools of frozen water exacerbate these conditions. In the area expanded into *Urwald Bialowies*, the terrain included swamplands, and water meadows, and several isolated communities.

The LWSB's structure does not explain why the troops were killers. A battalion was the smallest formation with a war diary that was also capable of operating independently. The battalion

---

42 Bourke, *An Intimate History of Killing*, p. 1.
43 John Ellis, *The Sharp End of War: The Fighting Man in World War II*, (London, 1980), p. 10.

headquarters had a number of functions and was the nerve centre of information and signals. The LWSB's headquarters were quartered in the Tsar's former hunting palace. The headquarters function was crucial to their performance. It was the control centre for the commander; it received orders from higher commands and distributed orders to the platoons/strongpoints. The headquarters, the CP for the duration of the occupation, had a large map room for planning patrols, killing actions and resettlements. The headquarters also handled the administration. The battalion clerks typed the reports that included the extent of the killings. The battalion staff handled all transportation requirements, especially for the resettlement plans. Headquarters, like all head offices, were the rumour mill for all gossip. The British Army captured a document that explained the workings of a German army battalion staff. The senior-level or *Führerstaffel* — the command group — comprised of three officers: the battalion commander, the adjutant, and the *Ordonnanz* or Ordnance officer (also known as the deputy adjutant). The document instructed about the role of the battalion commander 'alone commands and bears the responsibility' and 'he alone gives orders and settles all important matters'. The commander issued all orders, 'settles all important matters, initiates reconnaissance, situation reports' to higher authorities and liaison with neighbouring or 'flanking units'.[44]

The battalion second senior officer also served as the adjutant but was the 'assistant to the commanding officer' and relieved the commander of all correspondence, general duties and 'takes minor detail off his shoulders.' The function of the adjutant was to manage the everyday administration of the headquarters; the preparation and distribution of orders; maintained contact with neighbouring formations; compiling the war diary; map reproduction and was expected to organise command group motor transport. Adjutants administered battalion discipline, political instruction, transfers and reinforcements, officers and NCO appointments, and training.

---

44 TNA, WO 208/3777, Vorschlag zur Gliederung und Aufgaben-Verteilung des Bataillons-Stabes im Gefecht und im inneren Dienst. Acquired February 1945.

Little is known of the LWSB's adjutant, second lieutenant Heinrich W**.⁴⁵ The third headquarters officer was the *Ordonanz*. The *Ordonanz* served as the deputy adjutant and arranged all headquarters security. His duties included 'control over the use of ammunition, supply of ammunition, equipment and rations, bringing up transport echelons.' There were several clerical positions in the headquarters hierarchy with the first, second and third battle clerks (*Gefechtsschreiber*). The First Battle Clerk handled orders and messages distributed to the commander and adjutant. The first battle clerk maintained rough logbooks of messages and summarised oral orders, and handled despatch riders. They kept an account of arms and equipment, weapons training, supplies including petrol, intelligence, welfare, complaints and punishments, and horse transport. They were joined by the reporting section made up of runners, dispatch riders and horse handlers, usually under the command of an NCO. The battalion NCO handled the smooth running of the headquarters and command staff. His responsibilities included 'protection, camouflage, digging in'; they assigned sentries at guard posts; headquarters runners, the placement of road signs, and the battalion flag. The senior NCOs identified and assigned roads, conducting traffic control and closing roads. There was a horse section, a battalion aid post (battalion medical officer, medical NCO and driver), and an ammunition section.⁴⁶

Richard Holmes had written, 'At the very heart of war, wrapped in layers of boredom and anticipation, veiled by confusion, and eerily lit by terror, anguish, and savagery, lies the experience of combat. Yet war and battle are not synonymous.'⁴⁷ The examination of the *Landser* of the LWSB focused upon gauging who the men were and building a social profile. Knut Pipping's

---

45 All that is known is that he arrived from Flieger-Horst Kommandantur (E) 44/XI on 20 July 1942 and departed for Wachbataillone der Luftwaffe Robinson Ost 2 on 15 March 1943.
46 TNA, WO 208/3777, Distribution of duties in the HQ of an Infantry Battalion, 1 March 1945.
47 Richard Holmes, 'Battle: The Experience of Modern Combat', in Charles Townshend ed, *The Oxford History of Modern War*, (Oxford, 2000), pp. 224–244.

study of a company was one framework adopted to examine the rank and file of the LWSB. In 1943, Pipping served as an NCO of a machine-gun company in the Finnish army and was a veteran of the invasion of Soviet Russia. As a qualified sociologist, he decided to research his comrades in a primary group study of men in combat. Pipping examined: the history of his company; its composition; the company's 'lines of action'; the social groups; 'compliance with formal and informal norms' and, 'attitudes to outsiders'. He argued that the social structure of his company was complex and diverse. The men belonged to several distinct groups including the rank group, military group, age group, home district group, and their mess group. His observations enabled him to conclude: the men found a sense of cohesion and loyalty within these groups. The individual soldier developed a particular social role within each specific group.[48] Not all Pipping's methods and ideas could be adapted to the LWSB, but his general frame of reference assisted in streamlining the documentary evidence from the sixth company.

In conclusion, why did the men of the sixth company kill Jews and civilians? The Occam's razor solution must be that the German soldiers killed Jews and civilians because it raised their efficiency in weapons handling and skills in minor tactics. The evidence presented young soldiers working toward fulfilling their role within the infantry section—rifleman, machine gunner or squad leader—and the defenceless people were used as targets in an extreme form of blooding before combat. A social-historical interpretation might point to ingrained Nazi ideology, for more than ten years, or the military discipline and allegiance to the Luftwaffe organisation. A military cultural interpretation might rather rest on Sönke Neitzel and Harald Welzer's interpretation of 'war as work' and less on Joanne Bourke's 'characteristic' of killing. My sense from the research tends to side with the unique dynamics of

---

48   Knut Pipping, 'Infantry company as a society', PhD diss. published, Helsinki: National Defence University, 2008.

the company as described by Knut Pipping and following conversations with Richard Holmes. The uniqueness of the LWSB's records, as a military formation, intrigued Holmes. The LWSB represented a unique example, where other European powers would not commit troops to any form of active service before in-depth preparations. From the company perspective, I would combine the poor-quality weapons, the ill-fitting uniforms, the general lifestyle, the weaknesses of the manpower, and the immaturity that comes with youthfulness. Then I would underpin them to the *Jagdkommandos* where patrol performance was more important than bonding, primary groups, masculinity or any other number of variables. Pipping discussed how men were trained to know their role and place in the company mechanism. The men of the LWSB were not long enough together to form permanent bonds or primary groups. The formations of pickets, sections, *Sonderkommando* and platoons revealed similar low-level preparations, ad hoc selection and random allocations. The *Jagdkommandos* were raised locally within the company, they went out on 'soft' patrols and killed Jews. They were not drenched in alcohol or greatly intimidated. They were men being re-trained into infantry methods against enemies not regarded as particularly dangerous or threatening. Bandenbekämpfung in the shadows of the shattered lands of the east was mainstream policy, but with a low military profile. The men were socialized into *Auftragstaktik* until it was an automatic, response prior to being prior to being shipped off to fighting units. The dogma of Mission Command has been understood in terms of military efficiency but it also enabled the *Judenjagd*.

Image 17: Typical strongpoint construction in wood.
Source: NARA, Captured German photographic collection.

9. 1943

The story of Nazism and the German hunt reached its zenith on 22 September 1942, when Göring shot *Matador*. *Matador* was a magnificent pedigree stag, the finest ever recorded in Rominten. Six years on from the killing of *Knuff*, the politics of the hunt had traversed genocide in Narewka Mala, but the killing of *Matador* represented the ultimate form of Nazi race dogma, the Hitler's Holocaust against the Jews. *Knuff* represented the sacrifice of a common stag to an honour code and professionalism of the hunt. The newsreel of the *Matador* rituals was choreographed to the *Totenwacht* in the *Jagdliches Brauchtum*. The ceremony took place on a hillock overlooking a river in a solemn setting. The carcasses of *Matador* and two other grand stags were arranged sprinkled with leaves and twigs. Two large braziers, with burning logs, were placed to the right and left of the line stags, while Göring posed before *Matador's* dismembered and decorated carcass. He was dressed in his leather hunters' jerkin, a broad-bladed dagger at his side, and his hunting jacket draped over his shoulders. Hatless, Göring gave the final sermon for *Matador* while Scherping, Frevert, Brauchitsch and others looked on in silence. This was Nazi blood theatrics, conducted by the high priest of the hunt, but behind the scenes, the entire machinery and manpower of extermination were being released.

The *Matador* ritual was part of a critical period — 22–29 September 1942 — in the progress of the war and the Holocaust. Professor Erwin Gohrbrandt (1890–1965) shot *Theodorisch*, another grand pedigree stag. Gohrbrandt was a world-renowned surgeon from the central Berlin hospital and serving as senior medical inspector of the Luftwaffe. He had attended SS Dr. Simon Rascher's infamous conference on 10 September 1942, when the results from the freezing medical experiments requested by the *Luftwaffe* and carried out on inmates from Dachau concentration camp were released.[1] Gohrbrandt's reward for flouting his medical ethics and

---

1   Wette et al, *Himmlers Dienstagbuch*, 1941–42, p. 571–2.

participation in Nazi crimes was a noble stag.[2] After the war, Frevert made light of the killing of *Theodorisch* as an accident. This was not the case and was further evidence of how Frevert manipulated memories of the crimes, to warn men like Gohrbrandt to remain silent. This is an example of why the postwar stories of the hunt, during the war, are so unreliable.

At 9.30 pm on Friday 25 September 1942, Himmler arrived in Rominten, ostensibly for a long weekend of hunting. Scholars have claimed Himmler and Göring spent the weekend discussing the *Rote Kapelle* spy ring. Meetings between Himmler and Göring always led to diabolical outcomes. Earlier that week Himmler had met with Hitler and during an eight-hour meeting had discussed the full range of SS-Police responsibilities including the Jews, *Bandenbekämpfung*, and resettlement. After a week of extensive travelling, inspecting and assessing the progress of his responsibilities he arrived in Rominten. The presence of Gohrbrandt and the medical experiments, the onset of the industrialised killing phase in the Holocaust, and events in *Urwald Bialowies* suggest the two leaders had more ominous issues to discuss. Himmler's arrival also coincided with the SS decision, on 26 September, to deposit stolen valuables from Jews sent to the gas chambers with the Reichsbank. To continue their discussions and planning, on 27 September Himmler and Göring travelled together by train to Berlin. The *Matador* ceremony marked a crucial point in Göring's involvement in the Holocaust.

In October 1942, Ulrich Scherping published an article, 'To Be a Hunter'. The theme of the article: the skills of the hunter skills granted the German soldier a tactical advantage over the Russian. Scherping alleged that an article in a German Army periodical had inspired him. The author, an army captain, had asserted: 'the German soldier in the east doesn't face an enemy on the same cultural level as himself.' The captain believed, 'the greatest advantage of the Bolshevist is his highly developed animalistic instincts and his insensitivity to the weather and terrain.' The solution to overcoming the Russians was to 'feel at home in swamp or forest'; 'orient

---

2   Gohrbrandt was famous in the 1920s for conducting the first gender reassignment surgery. The patient is now recalled in the film The Danish Girl (2016).

oneself to the night and fog'; and, 'to educate soldiers in the fight against Bolshevism they have to be sent out into the marshy forest in day and night, through summer and winter.'³ Scherping was particularly taken by one of the recommendations: 'One has to be able to stalk and creep up like a hunter, and be capable of building quarters in the forest.'⁴ Having praised the captain's article, Scherping referred to letters he had received from hunters serving on the eastern front. They had convinced him that basic hunting skills learned in boyhood granted the Germans an advantage in the fight against Bolshevism. He identified five skills that enhanced soldiering: orientation in difficult terrain; the instinct to predict the moment when the enemy was about to strike; rapid appreciation of a situation (also coping with the terrain and the ability to pass an enemy strongpoint unnoticed); a talent for scouting, reporting information and leading patrols; and finally, the hunter's physical strength and lack of sensitivity to extreme weather.

Scherping recalled his time as a cavalry officer serving on the eastern front during the Great War. Several of his men were hunters in civilian life. In his squadron, they were proud to volunteer for every patrol because of their superior skills. These troopers were born and bred in the countryside and were natural hunters. They were also expert marksmen and exceptional in close combat fighting. During a patrol, one of these troopers observed a Russian in a tree over 200 metres away. His comrade on the patrol, a tram driver by profession, couldn't see the Russian even when pointed out. Scherping was scathing and ridiculed the tram driver as the 'master of technology' but 'next to useless in the field.' He recalled two master shots rang out; the first killed a Russian at 300 metres, and another killed the horse of a second Russian that tried to flee. The marksman had aimed at the horse's neck for a one-shot-kill. Scherping then compared the two wars in the east claiming there were similarities. The dense terrain and difficult landscape had remained unchanged, and he was convinced hunters were best equipped to overcome these conditions. He went on to ponder:

---

3   Hauptmann Schott, 'Kampferfahrungen eines Offiziers', *Militärwochenblatt*, Nr. 9, 28 August 1942.
4   Ulrich Scherping, 'Jäger sein', *Wild und Hund*, Nr. 27/28, 4 October 1942.

> What makes a hunter? This was someone in their youth who stalked rats and sparrows, who valued the crow as game as much as professional hunters value the wild turkey, and who spent hours on his tummy to shoot his first Roe. This person will appreciate the signs of nature that will help them creep up on the enemy in a life and death situation.

In his opinion, it was unnecessary to train young hunters with stags because even the smallest animals with their wild senses were a challenge. He confessed that stags were craved as the most important game because the hunting fraternity was 'crazy' over trophies. The crane and pigeon, however, were more 'challenging in war games'. He opined: 'The hunt is the bride of war'. The hunt made an important contribution to the campaign in the east by training future combat leaders. He asserted there was no war in German history when hunters had not played an important role, and the *Jäger* (light infantry) battalions had always been the elite. He concluded: 'we shall take care that the youth become real hunters and not just hunt followers. The Fatherland can rely for all time on its hunters in the event of war. This fight is for Germany.'[5]

One cold bright moonlit winter night in November 1942, district forester Seeger sat in his hide four metres above ground in *Urwald Bialowies*. The pale light illuminated the carcasses of his *Luderplatz*. A Luderplatz is a patch of ground covered with bait to attract animals for the hunter to shoot. Seeger had spread the carcasses of a horse, cows, and two lambs. He was hunting for predators, boars, wolves or foxes. The shooting distance to the bait avoided the need for a telescopic sight. He was keen to bag a wolf, having observed several pairs of wolves less than a hundred metres from his house. It was a very cold night with deep snow, and although he heard wolves howling, they stayed away. Seeger took a large nip of Vodka against the cold. After a long time without moving, he began to imagine all kinds of game. He had tracked a wild bear a few months before, or the lynx he had observed in December 1941 or just wolves. As the severe cold began to creep into his mind he began to long for his bed. Then a fox arrived and began sniffing the bait. The chill was rendering Seeger indecisive, and he couldn't

---

5   Scherping, 'Jäger Sein', p. 2.

make up his mind whether to kill the fox and then go home. The fox reached inside the horse's torso when Seeger shot it with his 4 mm (.22) rifle. He moved about, after sitting for several hours. He then took a drag from a cigarette, another large swig of Vodka, and began his *Bruch* for the fox. His thoughts passed over the beauty of the forest in the pale moonlight and his past hunting exploits.

He heard the approach of a *Panzerschwein*, a large female wild boar. The moonlight shone over its body and created a beautiful picture that caused Seeger to almost shake with emotion. His hunting passion roused, Seeger took aim with another rifle, squeezed the trigger, and the boar bolted. Seeger knew the sow was shot, despite the cold, he shrugged off his fur coat, and took another cigarette. He followed the blood trail that got thicker over fifty metres, whereupon he found the dead boar. Seeger placed both carcasses in his hide, before going home on his skis. The moon disappeared, the darkness closed in, and the hunt was over.[6] Like most hunting tales they only reach fellow hunters. Dull or not this is the only known public story of the hunt in Białowieża during the Nazi occupation and when the Luftwaffe was the primary security force. At the time of publication, Seeger was recovering in the *Lw. Reservelazarett* (reserve military hospital) in Bialystok. Seeger adopted a famous German poem by the romantic Joseph von Eichendorff (1788–1857) as his inspiration. *Mondnacht* (moonlit night) was popular, it's spiritual about nature and inner reflection.

This romanticised tale could be a metaphor for *Bandenbekämpfung* in *Urwald Bialowies*. The Germans hiding away in their strongpoints waiting for the partisans to come within safe shooting distance. *Bandenbekämpfung*, however, went further than hunting and was about the politics of violence. It was not about anti-partisan warfare, counterinsurgency, asymmetric warfare, counter-guerrilla warfare or any other form of German security warfare that existed before 1942. The sole purpose of Bandenbekämpfung was to exploit the territorial expansion from a military victory, consolidate occupation and implement either colonisation or *Lebensraum* whichever

---

6   Revierförster Seeger, 'Eine Mondnacht im Urwald von Bialowies', *Wild und Hunt*, November 1942.

was deemed appropriate. *Urwald Bialowies* was about Göring's fantasy; but while the men of the Green were quenching their passions with an imaginary hunt, the men of the blue were dismantling the Luftwaffe's moral code by killing Jews and civilians. The Nazi leadership was not interested in fanciful techniques or brilliant small-unit tactics, the ethos was about the application of brute force for wanton destruction and mass extermination. In this context, Bandenbekämpfung was an essential adjunct in the Holocaust. Once the doctrine was formalised in a Hitler directive, in August 1942, the Wehrmacht, the German Army and the other armed forces acceded to the dogma. There was no ethical resistance, on the contrary, the Wehrmacht and the SS adopted Bandenbekämpfung 'iron fist in glove'. The armed forces incorporated the doctrine *carte blanche*. Consequently, no German generals or soldiers could claim that they had not participated in Bandenbekämpfung. All had been exposed to serious allegations of perpetrating heinous crimes.

I. Post-Stalingrad politics

Berlin: 11.00 am on 30 January 1943. The air raid sirens whined, drilling the masses to the shelters. Berliners had dubbed the sirens Meier's Waldhorn (forest horns) because Hermann Göring, Hitler's deputy, had once boasted that if ever a bomb landed on German soil, he should be called Meier.[7] Göring's Nazi dogma of flying and hunting, represented in his roles as chief of forestry, hunting and the Luftwaffe, had worn thin and receiving public ridicule. The first daylight air raid on Berlin coincided with the tenth anniversary of the Nazis' takeover of power and within days of the capitulation at Stalingrad. The RAF was determined to add salt to Germany's wounds. Göring, as Germany's highest-ranking officer and Hitler's top political soldier, had the onerous task of informing the nation, and the Wehrmacht, of the impending catastrophe at Stalingrad. The sombre

---

[7] Michael Balfour, *Propaganda in War: Organisations, Policies and Publics in Britain and Germany*, (London, 2010), p. 433; see also Marlis G. Steinert, *Hitlers Krieg und die Deutschen: Stimmung und Haltung der deutschen Bevölkerung im Zweiten Weltkrieg*, (Düsseldorf, 1970), p. 367.

ceremony of defeat contrasted with victory parades of 1940 and the Luftwaffe's prominence in Hitler's victories. Göring was about to deliver his speech as the Nazi broadcaster announced, 'a dignified ceremony of a military character is taking place in the Hall of Honour', when Berlin Radio went off the air and Göring was forced to seek shelter. Three aircraft, led by Squadron Leader Reynolds and his navigator Ted Sismore from RAF No.105 Squadron, arrived with perfect timing.[8] Mosquitos: a high performance all-purpose twin-engine aircraft. They carried out the raid unmolested by the Luftwaffe. Later that day, three more Mosquitos raided Rostock just before Josef Goebbels' delivered his celebratory speech.[9] Göring's calamity was not just the inadequate defence of Berlin or failing to save Stalingrad through air supply or that his ambition for forestry science had not achieved a comparable result to the Mosquito, but that all these failures were displayed before the public on that sacred day.

The calamities did not end with the raid. The Nazis placed a lot of credence on public engagement through the media and propaganda, but the speech was pitiful. Forced to wait for an hour, Göring opened his speech with an 'appeal to the Wehrmacht at a low point in German history'.[10] He eulogized the end in Stalingrad and articulated the continuation of the war as a European crusade. In the struggle of race and ideology, the people were sermonised to stand against Plutocracy and Bolshevism, as they had done in 1933. After reflecting on ten years of Nazi struggle, turgid fantasies about the inner threat of Jewish Bolshevism, he declared the transformation of the *Reichswehr* (inter-war army) into a *Volksheer* (People's Army). The consequence, in his opinion, was that the Wehrmacht could no longer remain detached from politics. Historically, Prussia had stood against Russian hegemony in Europe; Hitler had shouldered the burden in the struggle against Bolshevism. This was Europe's eternal battle that would decide the fate of the west. Although cast as a European crusade it was Germany's armies that would shatter Russia

---

8   Obituary, 'Air Commodore Ted Sismore', The Times, 5 April 2012.
9   Edward Bishop, *Mosquito: Wooden Wonder*, (London, 1971), p. 70–4.
10 *Völkischer Beobachter*, 'Der Appell des Reichsmarschalls: Europe der Felsen, an dem sich die bolschewitsche Welle brechen wird', 2 Februar 1943, Nr. 33, p. 3.

and exterminate Bolshevism. Reacting to the impending defeat of Sixth Army he declared: 'rising above the gigantic battle like a mighty monument is Stalingrad. One day it will be recognized as the greatest battle in our history.' The soldiers' obstinate resistance was likened to the Battle of Thermopylae (480 BC) and the spirit of the 300 Spartans. Their sacrifice was for both Germany and Europe; a sacrifice akin to the heroic *völkisch* struggle of the *Nibelungen*. The blame as usual was attributed to treachery and vastly superior numbers. To the shattered rabble that was once the proud Sixth Army, this rambling eulogy painted Göring as a humiliating sycophant.[11]

Hitler's proclamation for 30 January, the anniversary of the Nazis coming to power, was delivered by Josef Goebbels. He was followed by Göring and other Nazi leaders across Germany. The British translated the speeches within a matter of days.[12] A British summary cut through the rambling and focused on the racist Nazi dogma that was being peddled to fit the Nazi scheme for European hegemony. There were some familiar slogans: 'The fiendish thoughts of destruction were embedded in the brains of the enemy, led by the Jews.' They also noted Göring's public confession and his burning desire for revenge: 'He, Commander-in-Chief of the *Luftwaffe*, suffered exceptionally when he heard of the results of the bombings, but although they did their best to prevent it from happening it must be recognized as unavoidable, and must not influence their will for resistance. At the moment the bulk of the *Luftwaffe* was fighting in the South, in the East, and in the North. It was his most sacred conviction that the struggle in the east would someday end with the last power of resistance of Bolshevism broken, and then they could retaliate.' For 1943, Göring pledged more offensives for 1943 in the east and revenge for Stalingrad. In regard to Hitler's

---

11 Ibid., p. 100. Joachim Wieder & Heinrich Graf von Einsiedel (ed), trans. Helmut Bogler, *Stalingrad: Memories and Reassessments*, (London, 1983), pp. 177–178. *Stalingrad und die Verantwortung des Soldaten*, (Munich, 1962). Jürgen Forster, 'The Shock of Stalingrad and the Crisis of Military-Ideological Leadership', MGFA, Ralf Blank et al (ed), trans. Derry Cook-Radmore et al, *Germany and the Second World War: German Wartime Society 1939-1945: Politicization, Disintegration, and the Struggle for Survival*, vol. IX/I, (Oxford, 2008), pp. 584–613.
12 RIIA, *Bulletin of International News*, Vol.20, No 3 (Feb. 6. 1943), pp. 100–104.

speech (delivered by Goebbels) the British noted it typically opened with references to the Treaty of Versailles and Weimar Germany's path toward self-destruction; the often-demonised journey from Democratic-Marxism to 'Jewish Bolshevism'. Goebbels announced Germany's role as the defender of Europe against 'Asiatic Bolshevism'. The invasion of Soviet Russia, Operation Barbarossa (22 June 1941) was recast as the protective shield for Europe. Goebbels referred to a speech in June 1942, when he had claimed 'only strong men could take the blows of fate.' He extolled everyone to make further sacrifices, like the men of Stalingrad and concluded the war was forced upon Germany just as it had been in 1914.[13] Alfred Rosenberg, the Nazi idealist, also gilded the Thermopylae theme in his article about the 'heroes of Sixth Army', and endorsed the rhetoric of the European crusade. The speeches confirmed a sea change in the Nazi leadership's strategic thinking post-Stalingrad.[14] In response to the speeches, Anglo-American secret services and special forces increased the incursions, acts of sabotage and support for resistance movements across Nazi-occupied Europe.[15]

After the surrender of the Sixth Army, Stalin and the Soviet Union took a more cautious stance after almost two years of setbacks. Evan Mawdsley referred to Stalin's cautious claim in February 1943 to have taken the initiative in November 1942 and that he intended to keep it.[16] Stalin's subsequent May Day speech was euphoric about the strategic situation. He pointed to the victories, the liberation of cities and towns, and the destruction of two German armies at Stalingrad. Stalin described how the Red Army had blunted the Wehrmacht operational doctrine of mass encirclement, but he chose not to explain the application of the double encirclement, exploiting Soviet advantages in warfare. Stalin projected a more realistic grasp of the strategic situation than the Nazi leadership, and he had good reason to believe German morale had

---

13 Ibid., p. 100.
14 *Völkischer Beobachter*, 'Die Helden der 6. Armee', 4 February 1943, front page.
15 M.R.D. Foot, *Resistance: European Resistance to Nazism 1940–45*, (London, 1976).
16 Evan Mawdsley, *Thunder in the East: The Nazi-Soviet War 1941–1945*, (London, 2016).

suffered a serious blow from Stalingrad. His speech highlighted the Soviet partisans and their extended operations in the German rear areas. Chris Bellamy estimated 250,000 Soviet partisans by 1943 and served in crucial functions in Soviet strategy.[17]

Stalingrad nearly broke the Hitler-Göring partnership. At best they were an odd couple, a strange political partnership that was stretched to breaking during the war. In Richard Overy's opinion, Göring was bound by loyalty to Hitler from back to 1922 as his 'first paladin'.[18] Strangely, this was their unbreakable bond. On 12 January 1943, in a moment of pathos typical of their relationship, Hitler sent Göring a letter of goodwill for his fiftieth birthday. Yet by the end of January 1943, Göring was in the proverbial 'dog-house' and by March the partnership was on rocky ground. The tensions were heightened by the allied bombing, but erupted over his increasingly questionable leadership, as Albert Speer said, 'We have not only a "leadership crisis", but strictly speaking a "Leader crisis"!'[19] Hitler was particularly angry with those among Göring's cronies who filled his head with illusions and fantasies. The extent of Hitler's displeasure can be gauged by an entry in Goebbels' diary on 9 March 1943. Hitler's mood was so sour that Goebbels decided it was not the best time to raise Göring's restoration. Hitler was also angered by the Nazi elites, the *Reichsleiter* and *Gauleiter*, for their privileges but blamed Göring for depending on his Great War comrades and friends.'[20] Hitler's aloofness caused Göring considerable stress and anxiety. In a meeting with Goebbels, in April 1943 Erhard Milch, Göring's deputy, was highly critical of his boss. Goebbels listened but concluded Göring deserved support.'[21] This fundamental faith in Göring, in the shadow of Stalingrad, partly explains why he was able to maintain his position until the final days of the regime. Politically, Goebbels efforts finally paid off on 9 November

---

17 Chris Bellamy, *Absolute War: Soviet Russia in the Second World War*, (London, 2007), pp. 573–575.
18 Richard Overy, *Goering*, (London, 1984), pp. 7–10.
19 Ian Kershaw, *Hitler: 1936–1945 Nemesis*, (London 2000), p. 559.
20 *The Goebbels Diaries*, trans. Louis P. Lochner, (London, 1948), pp. 212–214. Goebbels advocated the introduction of the one-course meal.
21 Ibid., pp. 246–247.

1943 when Göring delivered a speech to the party faithful. Although the speech was not perfect it still revitalized his standing in the Nazi fold. Goebbels wrote, 'personally he is an exceptionally lovable character.'[22] Reading Goebbels diary one might assume Göring had done penance and was a reformed character. However the month before, Göring ordered his elite *Hermann Göring* Lw.Panzer Division to evacuate art treasures from Italy. Teams of soldiers packed treasures into crates and brought them back to the division's barracks at Reineckersdorf in Berlin.[23] Göring had weathered the storm and was back to plundering occupied Europe.

Image 18: Reichsjägermeister Göring and his prize — *Matador* — the ceremony for the dead stag — 22 September1942

Bundesarchiv, Bild 146-1979-183-22 / CC-BY-SA 3.0

---

22 Ibid., p. 411.
23 Lyn H. Nicholas, *The Rape of Europa: The Fate of Europe's Treasures in the Third Reich and the Second World War*, (New York, 1995) p. 240, pp. 35–37, 380–381.

Göring's predicament in 1943, introduces the reader to a strange political relationship with Hitler and his command position in shaping the future of the Third Reich. In simplistic terms, he was not just the chief of various institutions but a significant partner in a nation-building scheme. Nation-building is a modern context to explain Göring's ambition to re-engineer Germany's eastern frontier. He was responsible for realising the Nazi dream of the Greater German Reich and in this capacity, a plan was devised to redraw the eastern frontier. The plan called for an extension of territory eastwards, protected by a natural barrier of extensive forest wilderness. This was a fantastic objective to recreate ancient *Germania* in Eastern Poland and Belarus; but it was also drawn to suit the interest of his political cronies like Erich Koch, the Gauleiter of East Prussia, who was one of his staunchest supporters. However, this was only one major project of many. Göring was heavily burdened with responsibilities to Hitler including—finding the 'final solution' of the Jews in 1941–42; maintaining the power of the Luftwaffe and air superiority; leading the strategic initiative in conferences; and maintaining Nazi authority within the Reich. The calamity of 1942 bled into 1943 at a time when *Lebensraum* and the Holocaust were on the same parallel as the conduct of the war. In the critical post-Stalingrad period, Hitler opted for his ideology over strategic realism. The war against the Jews and the pacification of occupied lands were intensified, while the *Wehrmacht* was ordered to hold ground at all costs. In this maelstrom of extermination and genocide, Göring's tentacles were driven deeper into the body politic of the Third Reich. Hitler could ill-afford to break with Göring. This partly explains why it was not until the final days of the regime when their relationship broke.

The third and final phase of Nazi occupation was from March 1943 to August 1944. This period saw the full realisation of the merger of the Blue and the Green as a special military force. It was part of fulfilment of Göring's plan to build a Luftwaffe-forestry-hunting Nazi military elite. Ground forces expanded in what Edward Westermann has mistakenly assumed to have been the Nazis' *Levée en Masse*.[24] The expansion of the Luftwaffe ground forces was the continuation of a process of militarization that begun in 1935.

II. Dissolution

On 1 March 1943, the LWSB recorded its last company level patrols (GIS Map 14) before its tour of duty was terminated. The final muster roll and deployment were included in Herbst's last report of 5 March (see table 14). The muster roll identified the numbers of men assigned to either *Jagdkommando* duties or strongpoint duties. The *Jagdkommando* had employed a third of the officers, about twenty per cent of the NCOs, and forty-five per cent of the ORs. The NCOs commanded all the *Jagdkommando* of fifth and sixth companies. The final deployment shows the completion of the Sixth and the Fourth company's missions. Their outposts had been recalled and were holding position in their primary strongpoints. The destruction of both ghettoes in the south removed any need to continue long-range patrols in search of fugitives.

The process of dissolution of the LWSB took some twists and turns, which revealed more details about the inner workings of the *Luftwaffe*. The end was inadvertently triggered on 4 January 1943 when Herbst made some bold recommendations for the future in a report to *Luftgau I*. This led to an investigation of the general situation in Białowieża by a team of inspectors from *Luftgau I*. A copy of Herbst's original proposals no longer exists but in his thirteenth report of 7 January, he re-itemised them for Brauchitsch. He requested two additional administrative clerks for the war diary and to handle the general increase in paperwork. To further justify his requests, he argued that his forces were equivalent to two battalions (a regiment) and that it was necessary to form a larger staff. He also proposed the adoption of supply carts with teams of four horses. This would increase supply performance partly due to the forest's poor transport network and partly because the rifle companies were dispersed

---

24 Edward B. Westermann, *Flak: German Anti-aircraft Defenses 1914–1945*, (Kansas, 1998), p. 125.

across the full extent of *Urwald Bialowies*, in areas not served by the forest railway. He also requested the supply of thirty bicycles to increase the mobility of the *Jagdkommandos*. Herbst also proposed raising a headquarters company, a guard platoon, and an escort staff. In effect: a sergeant major, four NCOs and twenty-five ORs.

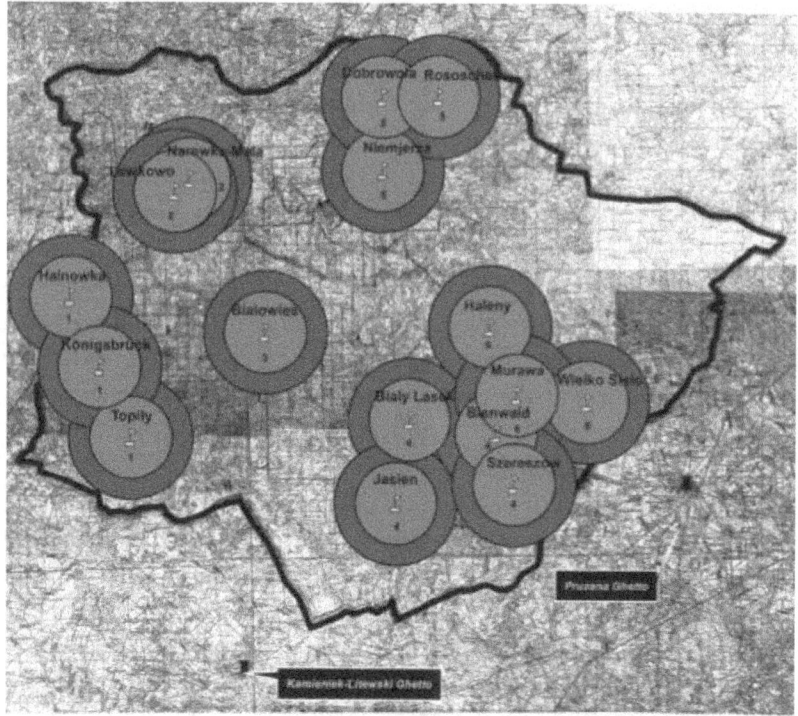

GIS Map 14: The Final Deployment — 5 March 1943
The layers for this map displayed the normal battalion configuration for the companies after deployment. The outlying smaller outposts were closed and reallocated to the platoons.

The extracts make it difficult to fully comprehend what Herbst was saying or trying to achieve. For example, to compound the sense of personal empire-building he rationalised his request for a guard platoon by comparing it in size with a fire control staff of an anti-aircraft artillery battalion. Then rather confusingly, added that his mission differed substantially from that of a fire control staff. In another thread, he wrote that in his experience it was necessary to integrate NCOs and ORs within the staff company and concluded, 'the momentous mission of the battalion was considered while setting up the table of organisation.' He added, 'the manpower savings could be implemented for other missions with even greater savings.' Herbst's reporting to Brauchitsch implied *Luftgau I* had all but approved his proposals confirmed by Lw.order number Ib (Fl) Nr. 2177/42 (no copy).[25] The fragmentary evidence shows, however, that Herbst received a two-day inspection tour (8–10 February 1943) from no less than the general commanding Luftgau I. The general inspected the battalion's strongpoints in Gnilicza, Popielewo, Niemerza, Lancino, Swinoroje and the companies in Strongpoint Białowieża and Strongpoint Narewka Mala.[26]

On 14 February 1943, Göring, Scherping and Frevert held a meeting in *der Rominterner Heide* (Göring's palatial hunting lodge) to discuss the future of *Urwald Bialowies*.[27] There is no record of what was discussed but it is possible to isolate the issues. The conference had the benefit of several reports including the inspection report from *Luftgau 1*; Major Herbst's situation reports; the *Oberforstamt* forestry reports and, Frevert's recent knowledge of the forest. Göring's fieldcraft from hunting and basic infantry skills probably enabled him to grasp the tactical situation. In the Great War, Scherping was a staff officer and had in-depth knowledge of the forest. Based on the best evidence, they planned the next phase of the occupation with the priorities of maintaining the initiative against the partisans, killing Jews, and imposing Nazi rule. The central problem was how to satisfactorily end the LWSB's service and Herbst and replace them with a viable alternative. The official decision to disband the LWSB was announced on 20 February 1943. A letter from Brauchitsch (*Adjutanturkanzlei des Reichsmarschall*, Tgb.Nr. 335/45 geh – no known copy) confirmed the decision. Brauchitsch conveyed Göring's thanks and good wishes to

---

25   BArch, RL 31/3, document 86, report 13 period 6–7 January 1943, Major Herbst, 7 January 1942.
26   BArch, RL 31/3, document 93, report 15, period 2–12.2.1943), Major Herbst, 12 February 1943.
27   Gautschi, *Der Reichsjägermeister*, p. 220.

Herbst.[28] In his final report to Göring, Herbst wrote: 'the LWSB was redundant because there was no longer any need to deploy a battalion of 650 men.'

Table 13:   Final deployment of the LWSB on 5 March 1943[29]

	Officers	NCO	Men		Officers	NCO	Men
Strongpoints				Jagdkommando			
1 Company:	2	15	52				
Hainowka	1	13	34	'Elch' (Elk)	1	2	18
Topiło							
Königsbrück				'Keiler' (Boar)	1	2	18
2 Company:	3	17	82				
Narewka	1	12	37	'Fuchs' (Fox)	1	2	18
Lewkowo				'Kranich' (Rabbit)		2	13
3 Company	2	15	63				
Under Bialowies				'Falke' (Hawk)		2	13
4 Company	1	19	91				
Czereszow	1	5	4	'Sperber' (Sparrowhawk)		3	13
Bienwald		1	7	'Geier' (Vulture)	1	2	13
				'Wildkatze' (Wildcat)	1	2	18
5 Company							
Rosochek		8	1	'Jaguar'		3	18
Dobro				'Luchs' (Lynx)		2	18
Niemerca		1	9	'Panther'		2	18
6 Company:	1	20	89				
Murawa	1	11	19	'Buzzard'		3	18
Haleny		1	9	'Reiher' (Heron)		2	16
Wielko-Siolo		1	9	'Burger'		1	16

The construction of a viable profile for Lw.Major of Reserve Emil Albert Paul Herbst is challenging. For a reserve officer, commanding the LWSB was a high-profile job with many opportunities to ingratiate himself within Göring's inner circle, and advance his career. Major Herbst was a soldier-perpetrator of Nazi crimes and any

---

28   Gautschi, *Der Reichsjägermeister*, p. 220.
29   BArch, RL 31/5, Einsatz, Sonderkommando d.Lw. Bialowies, 6 March 1943. Topiło remained on the roster even though it had not been allocated troops. These kinds of small discrepancies fill the files and one has to make a judgement to keep them in or ignore them.

assessment of him requires a different set of values than just ideological commitment. Herbst was born in Cuxhaven on 5 May 1894, and his chosen profession was *Prokurist,* possibly an attorney, a notary, or senior company executive; the particular context is unknown. There are no details of any Great War experience but his medals in a faded picture point to possible war service; we have no indication of his political affiliations or even his education record. He was a major of reserve, reasonably well educated, and his promotion was activated in early 1942. His known postings before Białowieża was with Kdr.K.Gr.z.b.V 105, a *Junkers 52* squadron that had taken part in the parachute assault on Crete and later supplying the troops in the Demyansk pocket. From the same photograph we know he was a tall man and, from a faded picture he may well have been awarded the Luftwaffe pilot's badge. There is a reference that Herbst served in Bosnia before commanding the LWSB.

Did Herbst play the system? The departure of the LWSB from Białowieża provides further clues as to why Herbst was willing to perpetrate crimes and alter figures. Before joining the battalion, Herbst met Göring in Berlin, but they didn't discuss specific operational plans. The meeting was possibly determined by the protocol for *Aktion Reinhard.* Herbst eventually learned of the operational side of his mission when he attended *Luftgau 1* on 29 July. At that time, he was not responsible for the civilian deportations, which were the responsibility of *Oberforster* Wagner of the *Oberforstamt.* Thus, it's more than likely Herbst was ideologically prepared for his meeting with Generalmajor Müller (27 August 1942) when he was informed, again verbally, that the LWSB was assigned to support SS operations. Herbst's report to Göring of the meeting was written confirmation of the system of verbalised orders. If Herbst played the system, it was not just bearing secrets and implementing genocide — there had to be a reward.

Herbst's reward for compliance was to become commander of a guard battalion, securing the *Luftwaffe's* high command staff train. This was a highly exclusive posting in March 1943. The process of transferring and forming the guard battalion was in stark contrast with the arrival of the LWSB in July 1942. If Frevert's 'influence' over Herbst's final report happened on the 22 February and coincided with Göring's order to change the LWSB into a guard battalion (dispatched from *Asien*, the headquarters' train). Herbst immediately ordered the LWSB to make ready to become a guard battalion, with preparations to depart set for the next day. On 27 February Frevert arrived at the former Tsarist hunting lodge to take command of the replacing unit. On 6 March, 60 NCOs and 329 ORs were assigned as a cadre to Frevert. The next day *Lw.Oberleutnant* Barkowsky issued an order from *Luftgau 1*: the LWSB had to concentrate at railheads and be ready for transportation out from 8 March onwards. On 8 March 1943, *Lw.Oberst* Gerlich called Herbst to form the guard battalion at Insterburg airbase and confirmed General Büttge[sic][30] had agreed to the assembly in Insterburg. The conclusion: Herbst had not only played the system but had traded with Göring into receiving a plumb posting.

The first movement orders arrived on 9 March 1943 — a telegram about transportation was received from *Lw.Oberst* Merkel requiring a list of the remaining LWSB troops and equipment. On the same day, the fifth company congregated in Białowieża town. The second company formed in Hajnówka and then the sixth company in Białowieża town on 10 March. Herbst sent a dispatch messenger to Insterburg to confirm the troops were ready for transportation. The following day the loading order for troops stationed in Białowieża town arrived — they were to be loaded on trains between 7.00 am and noon with departure set for 1.00 pm on 12 March. On the same day troops in Hajnówka were to be loaded between 7-11.00 am with a departure time of 11.20am. Meanwhile, the fourth company began assembling in Białowieża but at 12.20 pm (11 March) Herbst sent a request to the transport quartermaster of *Luftgau 1* to prolong their stay for further delousing. After several requests, discussions began to loop, as *Luftgau 1* explained to Herbst that extra delousing would cause a delay of 24 hours in Bialystok. Then at 7.00 pm Herbst was informed an empty train was set to depart from Kaschau (today: Košice in Slovakia) at 8.00 pm

---

30 The name was miss-transposed for Lw.Generalmajor Boettge, chief of Luftwaffe recruitment at recruit depot 31.

but would not arrive on time. On 12 March the train was delayed and the loading of the battalion staff, with the fourth, fifth, and sixth companies didn't begin until 1.00 pm. The train arrived in Bialystok before midnight on 13 March and delousing began at 12.30 am. The train from Hajnówka arrived at 6.00 am for delousing. The Białowieża train departed from Bialystok and arrived at Insterburg Fliegerhorst at 3.00pm the next day, followed by the arrival of the Hajnówka train at 1.30 am. On 15 March the remnants of the LWSB were assigned their new quarters. They were assembled and told they had become *Wachbataillon der Luftwaffe Robinson Ort 2*. They filled sixty per cent of the company jobs and continued forming for the next two days to complete the task. Finally, the LWSB was dissolved on 18 March 1943; and Herbst was able to begin his new job without any remorse over his behaviour or altering figures for his commander-in-chief.

III. Body count politics

Examining the calculations of the final body count revealed a wholly unexpected twist—Göring had ordered Frevert and Herbst to cover up the numbers of Jews killed. From the beginning in July 1942, Herbst had not spared any details of the killings in his reports to Göring. He was precise, almost to a pedantic degree. In his final report on 5 March 1943, however, his figures were re-hashed to portray an altogether different set of results. The working ratios of 'new' figures have been tabulated to give an alternative impression of the LWSB's mission since July 1942 (see table 14). The number of Jews killed was reduced to 6, all described as 'shot while running away'. In contrast, the number of partisans killed was raised to 86. This re-numbering gave the impression the LWSB's primary mission was Bandenbekämpfung and its performance moderately successful.

Table 14: Herbst's amended body count[31]

	Deaths	Wounded	Camps & Bunkers	
Germans:				
In action	7	7	Winter	66
Accident	1	13	Summer	55
Hospital	2		Observation bunker	1
Disease	1			
Enemies			**Booty**	
Partisans	86		Heavy Machine Guns	2
Jews	6		Light Machine Guns	4
Court sentence	98		Small arms and rifles	31
Under death sentence	6			
Hostages shot	174		**Resettlement**	
SS-SD Executed	90		Deportations	10,000
SS-SD Arrested	34		Misc. items to the value	5,600RMs

An analysis of the LWSB's results from the prior reports set a different benchmark. The total number of partisans killed was 48: 18 from July to the end of October; 30 from November; and, 10 in February 1943. Between July and October, the partisans were killed in 'ones' and 'twos', there were no operations involving large body counts. The LWSB's reported casualty count was: 9 dead and 6 wounded. However, these figures only relate to the period after 12 August 1942 and returns posted with the Wehrmacht's personnel office. There were 3 killed between 28 July and 6 August including one by accidental gunfire (so-called blue-on-blue).[32] The reported total number of Jews killed by the LWSB was 116 between September 1942 and February 1943. The numbers included all sexes and ages. There were two identifiable phases: the first coincided with the arrival of fifth and sixth companies when 48 Jews were killed in the forest; the second phase from 2 February 1943, when 68 Jews were killed. There were no reported casualties during these incidents indicating the Jews were unarmed or defenceless. There is a

---

31 BArch, RL 31/3, documents 96, 97, 98, 99, report 16 (13.2-5.3.1943), Major Herbst, 5 March 1943.
32 DDSt, Namentliche Verlustmeldung Nr. 1-Nr. 2, Luftgau 1 Der Chef des Generalstabes, 25 June 1943.

sensitivity to the figures of approximately plus or minus 5 per cent because of the vague statements in Herbst's reports about Jews killed 'inside' or 'outside' the forest. The total number of locals killed by the LWSB was 445. Herbst's vague references in his first reports might render this number overstated by 25 persons. The most significant reprisal was in response to the death of Ciré and his corporals that led to 252 killings. The other phase of intense killing was in August–September 1942 when Herbst reported 159 suspected Soviet agents and *agent provocateur* condemned to death by the summary courts-martial or killed in firefights. The figures show the LWSB killed twice as many Jews as partisans but killed four times more locals than Jews. In effect, the LWSB was a battalion of cold-blooded killers of civilians.

Why did Herbst alter the body count figures? In seeking an answer to this question, it should be noted that the existence of two sets of figures and the rigid bureaucratic rules, which placed any battalion commander in an awkward position. Whichever format selected, he could be charged with falsifying records or misrepresenting the LWSB's performance or misleading his commanding officer. A poignant comment in Herbst's report was a reference to discussions with Lw. Captain Walter Frevert, mentioned just before the summarised tabulation in the text. The 'presence' of Frevert in Herbst's final report looks odd. Frevert arrived at the LWSB's headquarters on 22 February, in advance of his Luftwaffe command set to begin on 7 March 1943. It has to be assumed Frevert's presence was influential in Herbst arriving at his final tally. Given the heightened level of security surrounding *Aktion Reinhard*, it's probable that Göring, like Hitler, wanted all evidence of culpability removed from the documentation. The recast figures didn't entirely absolve the LWSB from litigation in a German court, but critically reduced the killings to within the bounds of military necessity. More importantly, this difficulty with the tally points to Herbst's recognition that the LWSB's actions were illegal. This was the red thread in his paper trail. He had strenuously drafted reports to minimise the impact of responsibility by adopting institutional anonymity. His reports identified the company, the patrol, the *Jagdkommando*, but never the names of soldiers. The anonymity cloaked the existence of any written or verbal killing orders. We can conclude that decisions to kill, carried out in the field, were often made by NCOs. This implies the NCOs, as much as the officers, had a pivotal role in the killings.[33]

---

33 MIS No.15, The German Rifle Company.

10. Göring's Hunter Killers

Hitler hated hunting. His first experience of the hunt was serving as a beater for his regimental commander during the Great War; he found it a disagreeable experience.[1] If we accept less well-documented accounts, Hitler was apt to lampoon and deride hunters among his headquarters staff. On 20 August 1942, Hitler had entertained his guests from the Reich Chancellery and Justice Ministry with a rant, '... a poacher kills a hare and goes to prison for three months! I myself should have taken the fellow and put him into one of the guerrilla companies of the SS. I am no admirer of the poacher, particularly as I am a vegetarian; but in him, I see the sole element of romance in the so-called sport of shooting ...'[2] He expressed his loathing of hunting during a luncheon, on 30 October 1941, with SS-Gruppenführer Karl Wolff, his SS liaison officer, and Colonel-General Alfred Jodl the OKW's chief of operations. Wolff had returned from a rabbit hunt and Hitler had ridiculed him, 'I expect you used explosive bullets ...'[3] The diabolical outcome from Hitler's outburst was announced by Himmler in one of his rambling speeches:

> In 1941 I organised a "poacher's regiment" under Dirlewanger ... a good Swabian fellow, wounded ten times, a real character — a bit of an oddity ... I obtained permission from the Führer to collect from every prison in Germany all the poachers who had used firearms and not, of course, traps, in their poaching days — about 2,000 in all.[4]

The *SS-Sonderkommando Dirlewanger* was a masterstroke that granted the SS skilled manpower languishing in German prisons. Many poachers were marksmen and capable in fieldcraft, and initially, the unit adopted the *Jäger* or light infantry configuration.

---

1 Thomas Weber, *Hitler's First War: Adolf Hitler, The Men Of The List Regiment And The First World War*, (Oxford, 2010), p. 204.
2 Martin Bormann, *Hitler's Table Talk 1941–1944*, H.R. Trevor-Roper (Intro.), Trans. Norman Cameron & R. H. Stevens, (London, 2000), p. 99.
3 Ibid., p. 640.
4 French MacLean, *The Cruel Hunters: SS-Sonderkommando Dirlewanger Hitler's most notorious anti-partisan*, (Atglen, 1998), p. 15.

This was a bold move by Himmler, grabbing skilled manpower from under Göring's radar, and as an established hunter prepared to show he could break the code in the national interest. In 1943, amid Göring's rising unpopularity, the *SS-Sonderkommando* became a rival to be copied by a hunting-Luftwaffe alternative. The pact between 'The Blue' and 'The Green' was sealed in the *Jäger-Sonderkommando Bialowies der Luftwaffe zbV*. (referred to hereafter as the JSKB). The Göring and the Luftwaffe received regular reports from *SS-Sonderkommando Dirlewanger* throughout 1942 and the 'successes' rankled with Göring, not because of the cruel crimes but the breach of his social order. A meeting between Göring-Scherping-Frevert, in February 1943, set about breaking Göring's predicament. While Göring was retreating publicly, with later claims to have fallen into a spiral of fantasy, he indulged his hunters not only with the JSKB but also support troops unavailable to Herbst. The *Sonderkommando* or 'special commando' was a feature of German military organisation prominent throughout the war. They were typically an *ad hoc* unit, raised for a particular problem by utilising expertise or special capabilities. The Luftwaffe, like the SS, raised several *Sonderkommando,* and a similar formation to the JSKB was formed in Vienna, but its mission remains unknown. The JSKB represented a wholly different approach to Herbst's conduct of *Bandenbekämpfung*. Herbst's methodology of military efficiency and unit integrity was exchanged for aggressive and mobile hunting. This was to be the hunter's solution to Bandenbekämpfung, working towards an entirely different direction to Herbst's traditionalism or Dirlewanger's murderous poachers. The JSKB worked through two phases. The first phase: March 1943 to October 1943 covered the period while Göring was a political outcast. The second phase, from October 1943 to August 1944, when Göring was restored, and the Luftwaffe returned to traditional methods.

I. The chosen man

From March 1943, *Urwald Bialowies* became Frevert's hunting reservation, where the game was human beings: partisans, Jews, and locals. The story of the JSKB was shaped by its officers because

Frevert expected them to lead hunts or patrols and be examples to the rank and file. *Auftragstaktik* was assumed, but military efficiency was to be enhanced by risk-taking, skills adapted to the terrain and aggressively taking the fight to the partisans in the forests — 24 hours per day. This was relentless, pitiless violence against 'soft' targets and hard fighting against the partisans. Frevert's idealism appealed to notions of Germanic racial superiority and unleashing the power of the individual by removing all rules and moral restraint. This was reflected in the *Sonderkommando's* profile, no longer companies, but groups enforcing a primary group style of the ethos of small storm-troop units. This was high-risk because it relied on cohesion among those troops remaining behind after Herbst departed, then integrating the replacements, and shuffling the visiting troops assigned for forest combat training. The risk multiplier lay in the partisan initiative, which in the wake of Stalingrad, meant they emerged from the winter rejuvenated, resupplied and resolved to wage a bitter conflict.

Frevert was an opportunist but his methods were not entirely based on Nazi violence. Technically, he had a strong military record, which started in June 1915, when he volunteered for the army at seventeen years old. His first posting was to a reserve artillery battalion (11th Artillery Regiment). In April 1916, he was promoted to NCO, and later in November to reserve second lieutenant. He was a courageous soldier, receiving the Iron Cross first class for serving in the battles of Verdun and Cambrai. The short notes of his war record sprinkled throughout his personnel papers identified Frevert as an accomplished young officer with hard-earned frontline combat experience. He retained his reserve army officer status, was reactivated in 1936, and mobilised to serve with 29th Artillery Regiment in Korbach (Hesse).[5] His second war started in Poland, where he received the Iron Cross Second Class on 25 September 1939 and remained in the campaign until 27 September. Later served with the 1st Cavalry Division during the opening phases of Operation *Barbarossa*. In the autumn of 1941, while serving in the

---

5   Gautschi, *Der Reichsjägermeister*, p. 76.

Białowieża, Frevert was admitted to a Berlin hospital for surgery. He suffered a cranial nerve injury. On 23 March 1942, during convalescence, Scherping wrote to General Bodewin Keitel, chief of army officer personnel, and requested Frevert's release from 'the horse-drawn artillery regiment to serve in the state hunting reserve in Rominten'[6] On 20 April his transfer was confirmed, assigned to a replacement battalion in Suwalki (Suwałki: Poland). During his convalescence, in 1942 Frevert began a new edition of Raesfeld's 1914 hunting book but also transferred from the army to the *Luftwaffe*.[7] He was awarded the *Kriegsverdienstkreuz mit Schwertern* (War Merit Cross with Swords) second class, in September 1942[8], for non-military war service in Rominten and *Urwald Bialowies*.[9]

Frevert was officially posted to Białowieża on 27 February 1943, but his service times and status remain unclear. According to the Luftwaffe, he was assigned to *Urwald Bialowies* on 4 March 1943, with the rank of reserve captain and commanding the JSKB. In May, Frevert's preliminary assessment for promotion to the rank of major was processed by *Lw.Fliegerhorstkommandantur Bialystok*. The assessment note Frevert's, 'special mission of the pacification and evacuation of the Białowieża forests on behalf of the *Reichsmarschall*.'[10] The commanding officer made several observations of Frevert:

> Very confident, clear headed and an active person with open character. He stands solidly within the National Socialist state's teachings.

---

6   BArch, Lw. Personalakte Walter Frevert: letter from Der Reichsjägermeister Stabsleiter Scherping to General of Artillery Keitel, 23 March 1942. It's unclear whether Scherping was writing to General of Infantry Bodewin Keitel, chief of army personnel department.

7   Ferdinand von Raesfeld, *Das Deutsche Weidwerk: Ein Lehr- und Handbuch der Jagd*, (Berlin, 1914).

8   BArch, Lw.Personalakte: Walter Frevert: file note UK-Stellung von Hauptmann (d.R.) Walter Frevert, 20 April 1942.

9   BArch, Lw.Personalakte: Walter Frevert, Vorschlag zur Beförderung eines Offiziers (d.B.) zum nächsthöheren Dienstgrad, 1 June 1943, Fliegerhorstkommandantur Bialystok, 3 May 1943, 'Befürwortet' Kommandierende General und Befehlshaber im Luftgau 1 Generalleutnant Putzier, 26 May 1943.

10   BArch, Lw.Personalakte: Walter Frevert: Sonderauftrag des Reichsmarschall zwecks Befriedung und Evakuierung des Urwaldes Bialowies, June 1943.

> He has an extraordinary physique and capability, as well as being very good mentally, and always with a fresh reserve of energy.[11]
> He has artillery experience. His experiences through occupation and the practice of *Bandenbekämpfung* have increased his skills.[12]

The assessment noted that he had 'no special infantry experiences', but his qualities were his independence, activity, and clear thought. A generous assessment of Frevert might argue he was learning by doing. His *Auftragstaktik* ability was taken for granted, embellished by his hunting skills, but was not accepted as adequate for advancement. A weak review could not hold up Frevert's advancement. On 1 July 1943, he was promoted Lw. Major (Reserve) and received the distinction of being a 'very good' candidate by the promotion board.[13] According to his personnel file, his promotion was due to his positive character traits: 'initiative', 'improvisation' and 'his National Socialism was beyond reproach'. On 9 March 1944, Frevert received his *Kriegsbeurteilung* (war confidential assessment) confirming his promotion was officially dated to 1 April 1944. The confirmation adopted the same words.[14]

Frevert continued operational training, which was evident during the early period of his command.[15] He introduced a full training schedule with close-combat drills and the use of the

---

11 BArch, Lw.Personalakte Walter Frevert: Kriegs-Beurteilung, 1 June 1943, Fliegerhorstkommandantur Bialystok 3 May 1943; Generalleutnant Putzier 14 May 1943.
12 BArch, Lw.Personalakte Walter Frevert: Vorschlag fur Beförderung eines Offiziers (d.B.) zum nächsthöheren Dienstgrad, 3 May 1943. Einverstanden Nichts hinzufügen, Kommandant Kommando Flughafenbereich Insterburg, 3 May 1943. 'Einverstanden', Fliegerhorstkommandantur Bialystok, 7 May 1943, Luftgau I, Generalleutnant Putzier 14 May 1943.
13 BArch, Lw.Personalakte Walter Frevert: Lw.P(III), Beförderung Hauptleute d.R. am 1 Juli 1943, Walter Frevert, Sehr Gut, 2 Juli 1943.
14 BArch, Lw.Personalakte Walter Frevert: Kriegs-Beurteilung, 1 April 1944; Generalleutnant Bieneck 13 April 1944. Frevert's personnel file disclosed a change in commanding officer at Luftgau I and a reorganisation of the Luftwaffe hierarchy in Bezirk Bialystok. Lw.Lieutenant General Richard Putzier had been general officer commanding Luftgau I but on 5 August 1943 was replaced by Lw. General of Flyers Hellmuth Bieneck (1887–1972) who remained in position until the end of August 1944. The nature of their relationship cannot be determined, but in 1948 Bieneck provided Frevert with a 'clean' testimonial to the allied authorities that enabled him to once again undertake civil service post.
15 Frevert, *Mein Jagdleben*.

compass, a necessary skill for navigating through deep forest in the midnight hours. On 15 March, a permanent three-day field course was introduced as '*Bandenbekämpfung* and the fight in the *Urwald*' intended for NCOs and ORs. In April, the training schedule was intensified. On 2 April, an advanced course for combat training with emphasis of 'firing on the move', and 'in the fieldcraft'.[16] Three days later there was more 'combat in the forest' training. On 13 April, there was a 'shooting at moving targets' exercise, which was repeated four days later. Two days later there was a light-machine gun training course. On 23 April, there was fieldcraft training and the conduct of combat in the forest. On the same day, the troops were tested for their shooting skills and weapons handling abilities. The next day, possibly as a consequence of the results, there was intense rifle training and handling skills. On 25 April, there was a course on using the compass on the march, and the signals troops carried out a work-up exercise. On 28 April, all the strongpoint detachments ran local training for combat in the forest. On 22 May, there was more shooting training and two days later there was an advanced combat firing exercise in Białowieża. There were competitive shooting exercises on 1 June, and 26 July, marking the end of the first training phases.

Training resumed in October 1943 with the large intake of reinforcements. Three days were set aside for training and target shooting exercises from 23 October. The overall prize winner was Corporal Schulze. Sergeant-major König won the solo prize in the carbine class, and Grenadier Böhnert was most proficient with the machine pistol. On 25 October, there was an advanced combat firing exercise, which involved shooting moving targets and firing while on the move. On 16 November, there was an exercise devised and managed by the training unit, a detachment not previously mentioned in the diary of the order of battle. The next day the training exercises included street fighting, conducted in Brody, which continued until 18 November. The last references to training were on 31 January 1944, when Second Lieutenant Lopsien's platoon was recalled to Białowieża town for training. Then on 14 April, a

---

16   BArch, RL31/4, JSKB, Kriegstagebuch, 1–2 April 1943.

Ukrainian platoon was assigned training under the JSKB. The ammunition expenditures and fuel consumption (see table 15) of the *Sonderkommando* reflected the intensified training programme. These expenditures do not relate to periods of intense firefights. The fuel consumption reached a peak when the signals vehicles were in almost constant usage. These consumption figures were costly and to criticism of Frevert's methods.

Table 15: JSKB expenditures—fuel and ammunition

Date	Ammo	Expend	Resupply	Date	Diesel	Used	Resupply
5.3.43	389,218	nil		5.3.43	2,745	-	-
21.3.43	386,388	2,830		21.3.43	2,425	2,820	2,500
11.6.43	348,313	11,685		11.6.43	1,975	3,710	5,000
21.8.43	296,933	14,835		21.8.43	2,653	3,010	-
1.10.43	299,248	5,670	18,340	1.10.43	6,128	4,236	3,000
1.12.43	240,939	18,764		1.12.43	6,557	5,210	
21.1.44	219,449	14,730		21.1.44	3,612	3,575	
1.3.44	193,679	15,179		1.3.44	8,901	1,520	-

Frevert's extended periods of training did not reflect a higher performance rate in comparison with Herbst. His results will be discussed in detail later, but it's important to note at this stage that the elevated hunting skills did not raise the soldiers' performance. Fieldcraft raised the readiness to 24-hour round-the-clock operations, but was Frevert running his troops into the ground? Errors of judgement and serious mistakes, even by experienced senior NCOs, pointed to high-risk methodology in danger of running out of control and breaking the integrity of the *Sonderkommando*. The later operational problems originated with the training.

II. Command and control

In contrast to the LWSB, the officers of the JSKB were forced into a bold and conspicuous posture. The officers under Frevert represent an interesting group and the war diaries identified 23 line officers.[17]

---

17 BArch, RL 31/1, Kriegstagebuch Nr 1, Sicherungsbatl. d.Lw. The references suggest they were called up relatively late, two in 1940, ten in 1941 and the rest in 1942.

Most were reservist line officers and remained with JSKB until the retreat in 1944. There were transfers, five officers from the *Hermann Göring* Lw. Panzer Division exchanged with five from the JSKB. Four officers came from Luftwaffe security battalions. Several personnel files, all particularly important to the JSKB, have survived in the *Bundesarchiv*. The adjutant was Erich Weinreis, prominent since the German invasion of Białowieźa in 1939, and probably the most experienced officer of the *Sonderkommando*. He was born on 24 November 1896, a catholic married with two children. He became a career forester employed in the forestry district of Gumbinnen (Gusev: Kaliningrad Oblast) in East Prussia. During the Great War, he served in the 7th *Jäger* Battalion from September 1914 until February 1919. In May 1935, he joined the reserve as a sergeant major in the 117th Border Regiment. As a reservist, he attended and completed: five service weekends, four field instructions days and forty-five training days. He was promoted to second lieutenant in the *Landwehr*; the army reserve for men aged over thirty-nine but below forty-five. The 6th *Jäger* Regiment, through *Wehrbezirkskommando Gumbinnen*, handled his officer candidate application, which was part of *Wehrkreis I*. He was posted to the 413th Infantry Regiment.[18] From 26 August 1939, his regiment was assigned to the invasion of Poland. His regiment breached the German-Polish border on 4 September. Seven days later the regiment crossed the Narew River and occupied Hajnówka (12–21 September). Afterwards, the 413th Infantry Regiment then took up position along the Narew River in the town of Ostralenka (today in Poland: Ostołęka).

Weinreis had a successful Polish campaign and on 5 November 1939, it was recorded in his personnel file. As a senior NCO, he had stepped in to take control of the first battalion's preparations at a critical moment. Without explanation, the file noted the battalion's senior sergeant major had 'failed'. His high level performance continued through the campaign proving his courage, consideration for the men, and overall reliability. Through several combats, he remained clear-headed under fire, and since the end of the

---

18   BArch, Lw. Personalakte Erich Weinreis: Vorschlagsliste, Wehrkreiskommando I, 10 Juli 1935.

campaign, his bearing was exemplary. His commanding officer acclaimed him as a company commander in-waiting, with a good tactical ability and excellent knowledge of weaponry. Unusually, his regimental commanding officer went further and recommended Weinreis receive a backdated promotion to 1937. Weinreis had successfully completed a lieutenant promotion course, in November 1937, but there were no available officer slots. Having missed out, his comrades had already been promoted to captain.[19] The recommendation worked because his promotion was accepted on 1 January 1940 and confirmed from February.[20] Between 4 December 1939 and 26 February 1943 Weinreis changed from the army to the RFA and then to the Luftwaffe. He became the RFA's district forester of Podlany in Białowieża. On 27 February 1943, he transferred to the LWSB prior to its dissolution, but then joined Frevert's first officer cadre. In June 1943 *Lw.Fliegerhorstkommandantur Bialystok* confirmed his candidature as a *Luftwaffe* captain.[21]

Lw.Lieutenant Fritz Lopsien was the deputy adjutant and was responsible for headquarters security. His duties included 'control over the use of ammunition, supply of ammunition, equipment and rations, bringing up transport echelons.' Lopsien commanded the battalion reserve based in Strongpoint Białowieża and led many search actions. Little is known of Lopsien, but participated in a wolf hunt, 11 October 1943, identifying another hunter. The war diary noted that Lopsien was called to duty after the hunt. Lopsien was one of the few mentioned in Frevert's postwar writing, explaining he was a Rominten forester and suffered harshly under Soviet captivity.[22]

---

19 BArch, Lw. Personalakte Erich Weinreis: Vorschlag, Inf. Regt 413. Ostralenka, 5 November 1939.
20 BArch, Lw. Personalakte Erich Weinreis: Beförderung zum nächsthöheren Dienstgrad, Chef des Heerespersonalamts, 1 February 1940.
21 BArch, Lw. Personalakte Erich Weinreis: Luftwaffenpersonalamt, 22 February 1943. After the war Weinreis testified on behalf of Frevert during a preliminary war crimes investigations; he remembered him as an excellent commanding officer.
22 Frevert, *Mein Jägerleben*, pp. 132–201.

Waldemar Nowarre was a career policeman and was the first commander of the *Überfallkommando* (rapid reaction force). He was born in Breslau on 24 August 1908, a protestant and married with two children. He attended forestry training school (*Volksschule Forstbildungsschule*) and then police training school (*Polizeiberufsschule*) followed. On 1 April 1930, he began training in the Police School at Sensburg, and was promoted to *Polizeiwachtmeister* (police NCO) and assigned to the *1 Polizei-Bereitschaft* (police department) in Breslau on 1 April 1931. He remained in that post until May 1935, when he transferred to a *Luftwaffe* flying school in Cottbus for one month. During this period, he was promoted to *Polizeistabswachtmeister* (police staff officer), in October 1934, and *Oberwachtmeister* (senior police warrant grade NCO) in April 1935. Following his brief period at flying school, he attended *Flugzeugschule* (flying school) at Ludwigslust and then from 1938, assigned to the *Ludwigslust Fliegerhorstkommandateur* (Air Station security). During this time he was successfully promoted from sergeant to sergeant major and then to *Offiziersanwärter* (officer-candidate) with the *Luftwaffe*. On 12 December 1940 Waldemar's police area commander wrote the following assessment:

> He has completed 11 years of service. He has conducted himself well during his whole term of service and he deals with figurative tasks, especially during manoeuvres, the solving of which gives him great contentment. He promises to be conscientious and an honest character; to the good officer judges, he will become a member of the officer class as well as an outstanding officer candidate.[23]

In July 1941 he transferred to the *Luftwaffe* ground forces officer candidate school in Prag-Rusin and on 26 January 1942 was commissioned. By October 1942 he had been assigned to the 3rd Security Battalion of the *Luftwaffe* (probably in Austria) and then on 13 March 1943 was posted to the JSKB as a Lieutenant.

The most important officer after Frevert was Gustav Rühm. He was born in Munich on 15 September 1904, a catholic and the son of a senior veterinarian practitioner. He completed the full

---

23 BArch, Lw. Personalakte Waldemar Nowarre.

educational process to *Beamten* (civil service) status starting from *Gymnasium* (grammar school) and taking his *Abitur* (entrance exams); then University and the *Staatsexamen* (civil service exam). His chosen branch of service was forestry and his career was successful as a *Regierungsforstrat* (district forester) when called up in March 1938 for basic training with 5th Lw.Flak Regiment. In May 1938, he entered NCO training and in May 1939 was promoted *Wachtmeister* (sergeant of mobile troops). In April 1939, he was an officer candidate serving with the 502nd Lw.Reserve Flak Detachment. In May 1940, Rühm passed his officer board and in August was promoted to second lieutenant. Rühm's first command was under the 502nd Lw-Reserve Flak Detachment as a platoon commander. His personnel assessment noted he held a good sense of duty; suitable for service at the front; and a potential instructor. Rühm's leadership skills and character were: 'mature, quiet and secure, confident, active, purposeful, considerate, and careful.' In his comrades' opinion, Rühm was caring, helpful, and popular. He had the necessary abilities to carry out his work and his attitudes were 'correct'. In September 1940 his papers showed his unit's participation in the occupation of Czechoslovakia. Afterwards, he was awarded the Sudetenland Commemorative Medal (*Die Medaille zur Erinnerung an den 1 Oktober 1938*), but there was no citation for the award among his papers.[24]

In 1941 his personnel assessment noted that he spoke French and English and had a reputation for commitment. His qualities included: 'correct', 'cunning' (positive context), and 'capable'. He maintained a distance from subordinates and was a well-educated instructor. The review concluded that he was a young officer (37 years old) with strong potential. The following year his review described him as slim and of average height, his commander believed he enjoyed life and mixed well during social gatherings. Rühm was also known for being a convinced National Socialist who communicated these convictions to his men. Rühm mastered all the requirements for being a second lieutenant and was recommended for promotion. He was on temporary assignment to the JSKB from 768th

---

24 BArch, Lw. Personalakte Gustav Rühm.

Lw.Light Flak Detachment, but this became a permanent posting on 4 September 1943. He was then described as mature, active and energetic. In addition, he was without character flaws; he understood Nazi doctrine with a strong national perceptiveness. His fitness and agility were again appreciated alongside his ability to improvise. His strongest leadership traits included being a 'good organiser' and 'instructor'. Rühm's only negative point was his lack of combat experience in the infantry, which was addressed by his posting to the JSKB.

The JSKB was assigned a signals detachment from the 1st Lw.Signals Regiment. The commander was Werner Beyrich, born in Leipzig on 3 March 1919. Beyrich completed his schooling and passed his finals on 21 March 1937. He became a schoolteacher and had served in the RAD between April and October 1937. He was called-up on 2 November 1937, as a private; and by 1940 a reserve sergeant and on 1 June 1940, he was promoted to second lieutenant. He joined the 1st Luftwaffe Signals Regiment and became a radio team leader. On 16 November, he was promoted to First Lieutenant of a signals company and posted to Insterburg airfield. The personnel assessment by his commanding officer at Insterburg noted:

> Beyrich has a decent open character and possesses a youthful fresh nature; throughout a reliable personality with a receptive mental disposition and tall slim appearance ... He must appropriate himself with more experience with his men ...[25]

His career trajectory indicated he was a high achiever destined for senior command, and perhaps this was the reason he was given control of this vast array of equipment. He received praise from by both Herbst and Frevert:

> Since his promotion and his arrival, he has taken an extensive involvement in tasks. His employment of National Socialism is positive his philosophy optimistic. His behaviour amongst senior officers is always correct. His subordinates understand and respect his seniority. Amongst his circle of comrades, he is well liked. His ability to improvise and use his initiative is sufficient at this time.[26]

---

25 BArch, Lw. Personalakte Werner Beyrich: Beureilungsnotiz, Oberstleutnant Wenig16 November 1942.
26 BArch, Lw. Personalakte Werner Beyrich: Beureilungsnotiz, Major Herbst, 26 February 1943.

Beyrich was killed in combat April 1943. He was replaced by Lw.Second Lieutenant Meinicke, responsible for combat training and the *Soldatenheim* (recreation).

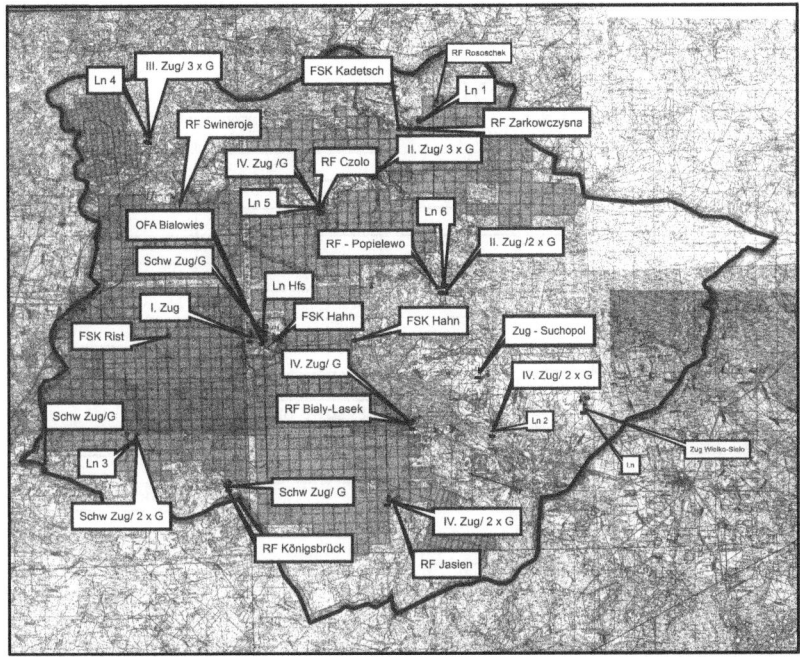

GIS Map 15: JSKB deployment – 6 March 1943
This map illustrates the JSKB deployment during the period March–October 1943, with platoons (Züge) and special sections (Ln = signals, Schw. Zug = heavy platoons). The map highlights the integration of the Oberforstamt Bialowies, RFA (RF) offices, and the FSK platoons also into the system. The Überfallkommando Bialowies (rapid reaction force) was to respond to sightings of partisan bands or to intervene in firefights. The strict regime of training raised the individual troop's abilities, thereby increasing the overall performance of the Sonderkommando. In theory, this plan offered the JSKB greater mobility, a heightened offensive posture, that would impose a constant state of movement, forcing the partisans into exhausting their supplies by abandoning their shelters.

In regard to Bandenbekämpfung, the officer cadre's collective relevant expertise was in hunting, security and policing. State foresters, police and signals lacked infantry skills. The signals capability was not exploited to its fullest potential, highlighting how inept the *Sonderkommando* was in technology. The JSKB hosted 'visits' from frontline divisions, ostensibly for training but increasing the overall firepower. Göring could freely indulge the JSKB with detachments from his bodyguard division, without triggering criticism from his political rivals. Thus, the JSKB was a training formation with a special mission to conduct Bandenbekämpfung.

Table 16:   JSKB roster, 6 March 1943[27]

Unit	Commanding officer	Strongpoints	Jagdkommando
1 Zug (platoon)	Oberleutnant Weinreis	Bialowies	Überfallkommando
2 Zug	Leutnant Schröter		
3 Gruppen (sections)		Niemerza	No codename
2 Gruppen		Popielewo	
3 Zug	Oberfeldwebel Lüttge		No codename
3 Gruppen		Levkowo-Stare	
1 Gruppe		Czelo	
4 Zug	Feldwebel Ewert		No codename
2 Gruppen		Biewald	
1 Gruppe		Bialy-Lasek	
1 Gruppe		Jasien	
Schwerer (heavy) Zug	Oberleutnant Nowarre	Bialowies	
1 verstärkten (reinforced) Gruppe			
1 Zug			Jagdkommando
1 verstärkten Gruppe		Topiło	
1 verstärkten Gruppe		Königsbrück	
Ln. (Signals) Zug	Oberleutnant Beyrich	Hauptfunkstelle Bialowies	
Nebenfunkstellen in:		Zarkewezysana	
		Bienwald	
		Topiło	
		Levkowe-Stare	
		Czelo	
		Popielewo	
		Niemerza	

---

27   BArch, RL 31/5, Einsatz, Sonderkommando d.Lw. Bialowies, 6 March 1943. The reduced order of battle included references to the eight forest districts and three FSK platoons.

On 6 March, Frevert announced the JSKB's activation roster (see table 16). The most significant difference compared with the LWSB was the absence of companies. This JSKB was designated a light Sonderkommando. The first cadre included troops from the LWSB: 5 officers, 62 NCOs and 329 OR's. The JSKB's primary mission was to 'guarantee the security of the Oberforstamt Bialowies so that it can conduct its business.' Frevert's idea envisaged eleven strongpoints to house his Jagdkommando but this was not a 'static' deployment. From the outset the 'spirit' of the JSKB was offensive, taking the fight to the partisans. The JSKB's combat instructions and mission were closely linked with the 461st Reserve Division, which was still garrisoned in Bialystok. The addition of two infantry battalions and seven companies of Landesschützen riflemen had in theory increased the division's fighting power. This enabled the JSKB to operate independently with heavy support close at hand.

Table 17 outlines the manpower structure of the JSKB between March and October 1943. Until August 1943, Frevert had to depend upon his troops and limited resources. Until at least May the JSKB was not receiving replacements for losses. Table 16 also highlights the JSKB remained constant in size until October 1943. The local militia fluctuated but eventually disappeared from reports. There was another indication of Göring's underhand support for Frevert because from 24 August 1943 he received regular short-term postings of armoured infantry platoons from the Hermann Göring Lw.panzer division. These platoons boosted the fighting power of the JSKB but were kept to platoon size to avoid attracting unwanted attention from Göring's rivals. The first platoon arrived with 14 reservists, but on 18 September an officer and 26 ORs were welcomed to the JSKB by Lw.Lieutenant Nowarre. On 11 December, another detachment arrived with an officer, 5 NCOs and 54 ORs. The irregular postings continued into the first part of 1944: February (1 officer, 5 NCOs and 49 ORs) and in May (1 officer, 5 NCOs and 57 ORs); three further platoons arrived in late May; and in July, at the time of the retreat, there were two platoons in the forest.[28] These figures indicate Frevert was to mind his casualty ratio and preserve his formation.

Table 17:   JSKB muster March–October 1943[29]

Date	Officers	Men & NCOs	Horses	Pilot	Vehicles	Mg's 38/40 MG15	Rifles 98k	militia
5.3.43	4	346	27	1	27	65	354	
21.3.43	4	329	27	1	27	65	354	
1.5.43	4	293	26	1	27	65	354	96
21.8.43	5	367	27	1	34	97	454	133
11.10.43	8	525	28	1	34	97	446	

Frevert was able to draw on three FSK formations. The overall standing and order of the JSKB and are included in GIS map 15. They were administered and controlled by the RFA but by 1942–43, the FSK had established an independent command garrisoning forests in occupied territories. The increasing numbers of partisan incursions into Poland had forced a policy change from lightly arming the FSK to issuing them with rifles, light machine-guns, and began training in Bandenbekämpfung. There is a claim that a hybrid force from the *Hermann Göring* Lw. Panzer Division and the FSK formed an FSK II. They based their opinion on the recollections of H. Ströh who alleged his FSK II detachment was raised from escort troops from the division based in Schörfheide and Rominten. Ströh was part of a group of young men that formed an escort troop for dignitaries but was despatched to serve with FSK II, armed with MP40 machine pistols and issued with anti-mosquito nets, especially for working in the swamps. Ströh recalled a shooting range near Stoczek for weapons training, and the field services and combats in the forest. Ströh's recollections are not confirmed by the war

---

28   Ripperger et al, p. 303.
29   BArch, RL 31/4, Kriegstagebuch, front pages. The actual numbers of Self-Defence men began on 1 April 1943 with 96 and concluded on 1 July 1943 with 133. On 22 May new replacements for casualties arrived (27 NCOs, 14 ORs).

diaries. They do not confirm the existence of an FSK II, but there is no evidence to confirm this account.

A financial statement for the *Forstschutzkommando-Abteilung Bialowies* (FSKAB) has survived among the RFA financial papers covering the period 1 April 1943 to 31 March 1944.[30] In regard to the RFA budget process, the FSKAB accounted for one *Forstmeister* and two *Revierforstmeister*, both serving as its field officers. The FSKAB drew a budget for 135 men including 5 *Beamte* (officials), 3 senior sergeant majors, 13 junior NCO's, 32 corporals, and 83 privates. Their combined salaries were 346,500 *Reichsmarks* based upon a daily rate of 7.30 marks per day (no adjustments were included for ranks); with an additional allowance for 'foreign' service of 182,900 *Reichsmarks*. Within this allowance, the privates were allocated 75,800 *Reichsmarks* and for the *Beamte* (civil servants) 12,000 *Reichsmarks*. The 1943 budget was a significant increase from the 1942 budget when salaries were 475,500 Reichsmarks with a 'foreign' service allowance of 259,900 *Reichsmarks*. The budget also included ten cleaning ladies and cooks with a combined salary of 13,000 *Reichsmarks*. The budget schedule also itemised five cars, five motorcycles, four trucks, and twelve horses.[31]

III. Technology and security

Göring's game-changer was the signals detachment. This was a strategic level unit usually assigned to army level formations within theatre level operations. This signals capacity was expected to fulfil several roles. First, to increase the wireless coverage from *Urwald Bialowies* to connect to the German homeland network. Second, it added to the border signals alarm system for national security. Third, to add a relay booster function to the military network. Fourth, JSKB could tap into this system and raise its communications in operations. Finally, this improved signals communications,

---

30 BArch, R 2/4699, RFA, Forstwesen, Urwaldgebiet Bialowies, Reichsfinanzministerium, abt.1, May 1944.
31 BArch, R 2/4699, RFA, Ausserordentlicher (Kriegs) Haushalt XVIIa Teil XXI Unterteil I; Haushalt für das Forstschutzkommando Abteilung Bialowies für das Rechnungsjahr 1943, (1.4.1943–31.3.1944).

between Göring-Brauchitsch-Frevert and thereby reducing the necessity for a large headquarters staff with clerks. The implication was a reduced reporting record. This was hoped to be a masterstroke on Göring's part because the detachment received motorised assets of a regimental level.[32] The signals capability enabled patrols to remain in regular contact with Frevert's command post. This heightened the flow of intelligence and enabled Frevert to respond faster to situations. This scale of communications was direct and kept Göring in the loop without complicated network protocols.

The major technological advancement arising from the Second World War was in signals. Vocal communications equipment like telephones, radios or 'walkie-talkie' extended command authority in the field. Specialist signals troops were experts in the use of their equipment and treated as highly valuable resources at high command levels. A battalion signals section usually contained about sixteen men, a commanding NCO, with a telephone section and a wireless section. The signals NCO provided the commander with all the details required to manage signals effectively. They also maintained constant supervision of communications; keeping radio transmission discipline; and running cyphers outwards and deciphering inward traffic. The NCO set the battalion signals net and coordinated links with higher offices through to the chain of command. They were required to warn their commanders immediately of any breaks in the lines or network.[33] A postwar report confirmed the use of signals communication:

> The wild, uncultivated forests of European Russia present unusual obstacles to the construction and maintenance of telephone lines. Radio, therefore, is the proper means of communication not only for higher echelons but particularly for front-line units. Blinker communications are suitable in the more open marshes but not in dense forests.[34]

---

32 This section has greatly benefitted from the guidance of signals specialist Ben Nock of the Military Wireless Museum, Worcestershire, UK.
33 TNA, WO 208/3777, Distribution of duties in the HQ of an Infantry Battalion, 1 March 1945.
34 TNA, WO 208/3230, US Army Pamphlet 20-231, 'Combat in Russian Forests and Swamps', Department of the Army, July 1951, pp. 8–9, p. 34.

There are few references in the war diary to the signals detachment. The detachment reported directly to its parent unit, the 1st *Luftwaffe* Signals Regiment garrisoned in East Prussia. This was following the usual protocol for the garrisons within the Home Forces Area. GIS Map 16 illustrates the signals network and the extent of coverage across the forest. The areas of coverage fluctuated and changed shape during operations when the mobile units were in the field. The diagram also shows how the signals network was integrated into the RFA's forest telephone system. The German armed forces had very effective methods of tactical communications that included field telephones, radios, visual signals, pyrotechnics (flare and smoke), candles, smoke grenades, flags, marker panels, signal lights, arm or hand signals, and messengers. One study has explained that the range of most radios was limited, and the field telephones were the most common and most reliable. The field telephones were connected to a switchboard by landlines, laid by a wiring party of a few men. There was a weakness in the system in that enemies could tap or break the line. Switchboards could connect to other units to relay messages. The networks were labour intensive, and wire units of a few men worked constantly to maintain and repair broken lines. The radio systems came in three forms: the voice transmission through AM (amplitude modulated); the CW (continuous wave) which used key tapping Morse code; and, the FM (frequency modulated) radio usually referred to as 'walkie-talkie'.[35]

---

35 Gordon L.Rottman, *World War II Battlefield Communications*, (Oxford, 2010).

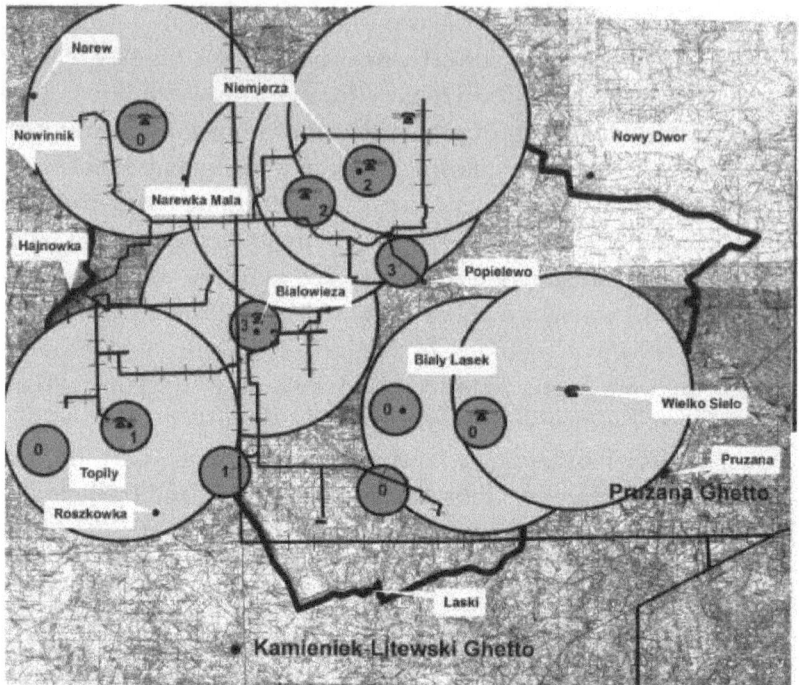

GIS Map 16: Luftwaffe signals network and the German frontier 1943–1944
This map identifies the communications network arranged by the 1st Luftwaffe Signals Regiment completing the incorporation of Białowieźa into the national homeland net. The large grey roundels identify the signals stations set up through the forest. The legend: 0–3 = Lw. Signals Regiment outposts, telephones represent signal masts, and there were several towers including the large tower at Wielko Sielo.

The chronological changes in the signals detachment are tracked in table 18. It shows the quota of signals equipment. Examined in stages: the first level of equipment was the nine '5-Watt senders', probably the Fu 9 transmitter, and was normally issued to larger formations such as divisions or brigades. Their range of radio transmission was about 10 miles AM and 36 miles in CW.[36] According to Ben Nock, a military signals specialist, this was a general-purpose medium frequency, low-power transmitter contained in a case of a light metallic alloy. It was used in divisional and regimental signals nets of the German army and could be deployed in a vehicle or on

---

36   US War Department, 'Handbook on German Military Forces', p. 438.

the ground. It was used with portable receivers and could be operated while on the move. For mobile communications, there were four tactical radios called the *Tornister Funkgerät d2* (known as *Dora 2*). They could be operated on the move and were carried in two sections by two men: one carrying the transceiver and the other the battery pack. They took ten minutes to assemble. The detachment was also assigned radio vehicles and it is likely these mobile communications extended the network beyond the forest. Their transmission range was over 15 kilometres. *Fernsprechtornister* (radio-backpacks) were carried on the backs of men from to the *Fernsprechanschlusstrupp* (telephone connection troop) — an NCO and three men. There were 51 ground-return telephones, weighing in at twelve pounds each. The *Feldfernsprecher 33* was a small telephone box containing a handset and a handle to power up calls through cables to the switchboard. The central switchboard was a large thirty-two lines box installed in Frevert's CP.

Table 18: LW Signals Regiment 1 schedule[37]

Date	Officers	NCO/Men	5 watt Sender	Electrical Sender	Radar	Switch Board 52	Middle phone	Radio Phones	Radio Backpacks	Bicycle	Grenade	Mgs 38/40	Rifles 98k	Instruments	Vehicles
5.3.43	1	65	9	1		1	2	51		1	-	10	62	9	16
21.3.43	1	64	9	1		1	2	51		1		10	62	9	16
1.5.43	1	64	9	1		1	2	51		1	-	10	62	9	16
21.8.43	1	63	9	1	4	1	2	51		1	-	10	62	9	13
11.10.43	1	62	9	1	4	1	2	51		1	-	10	62	9	13
10.11.43	1	64	9	1	4	1	2	51		1	-	10	65	9	12
21.12.43	1	57	9	1	4	1	2	68	10	1	-	10	64	9	7
1.1.44	1	65	9	1	4	1	2	68	10	1	65	10	64	9	7
1.2.44	1	65	9	1	4	1	2	68	10	1	65	10	64	9	7
1.3.44	1	62	9	1	4	1	2	68	10	1	65	10	64	9	7
10.6.44	1	61	9	1	4	1	2	68	10	1	65	10	64	9	7

37 BArch, RL 31/4, Luftwaffe signals troop, pp. 146–8.

Image 19: The signals was regarded as the advanced branch of the Luftwaffe. Recruits received a full training schedule equivalent to apprenticeships in industry.
Source: NARA, Hoffmann Collection.

IV. Stalin's partisans

In his final report to Göring, Major Herbst advised of changes in the partisans' behaviour. He noticed their activities had increased outside the forest area. The general withdrawal of the LWSB's presence beyond the forest, with strong points being abandoned, had encouraged the partisans to return to the forest during the handover to the JSKB. The partisans had plundered villages and killed local officials. German army counter-intelligence forces confirmed that Moscow had issued orders to raise bands in the southern area of the forest. Soviet agents had received radio signals from Moscow for them to join the partisans. Moscow had announced an air-bridge with regular overflights by the Red Air Force.[38] Stalin was fanatical about denying the Nazis' any possibility of imposing their culture on Russia. Throughout the occupation (June 1941 to July 1944) the Białowieża partisans continually resisted the Nazis. This determination to frustrate Göring's ambitions in the forest differed from all other Soviet

---

38 BArch, RL 31/3, documents 96, 97, 98, 99, report 16 (13.2–5.3.1943), Major Herbst, 5 March 1943.

partisan campaigns — Białowieża turned into an ideological battleground between the dogma of Scherping's middle-class hunt and the workers of Stalin's advance guard.[39] The Soviets gradually militarised the partisan bands through trained agents, with detailed knowledge of the forest and the populace, and provided expert training and leadership. After the Soviet victory at Stalingrad, the partisan campaign intensified. In supporting the campaign, the Soviets distributed propaganda leaflets to draw local support. These leaflets were either dropped by the Red Air Force during night flights or distributed by forest bands from their printing presses.

On 12 May 1943, the *Luftwaffe* collected leaflets dropped by the Red Air Force. They were translated as: 'Death to the German occupants!' and included Stalin's May Day speech of 1943. In the wake of Stalingrad, this was Stalin's survey of the new strategic situation:

> The Red army has inflicted serious defeats on Hitler's troops during the 1942–43 winter campaign. ... It encircled and destroyed two German armies in Stalingrad. It captured or killed more than 300,000 soldiers and officers of the enemy and liberated hundreds of Soviet cities and thousands of villages. ... The attempt of Hitler's command staff to seek revenge for Stalingrad failed.

Stalin described how the Red Army had not only blunted *Wehrmacht* operational doctrine of mass encirclement but had destroyed German invincibility in the process. He projected a firm grasp of the strategic situation and was determined to explain why Germany was finished:

> The Nazis aim to overcome the crisis with total mobilisation ... the fascists are in a serious crisis. This crisis is obvious because they have been forced to abandon Blitzkrieg. It is no longer fashionable to speak of Blitzkrieg among the enemy. Talk about Blitzkrieg has turned into sad conversations about a long war. In the past, the German command praised Blitzkrieg but now it is abandoned. The German fascists no longer praise themselves for Blitzkrieg. Instead, they praise themselves for cunningly escaping encirclement by English troops in North Africa and from encirclement by Soviet troops in the Demjansk pocket. The fascist's newspapers are full of reports about German troops retreating from the frontline and thereby preventing a new Stalingrad. It seems Hitler's strategists have nothing left to boast about.

---

39   CMH Pub 104-19, *The Soviet Partisan Movement 1941–1944*, (Washington DC, 1956), pp. 3–6.

Stalin emphasised how the illusions of victory from Blitzkrieg had whipped the Germans into a state of euphoria between 1939 and 1941. Since Stalingrad, he could now sense the decline in Germany's declining morale and war-making ability. He then referred to the role of the partisans:

> The partisans shall strike severe blows against the rear services of the enemy, against his transport network, military camps, against the staffs and his operatives. They shall destroy his telephone lines. The mass population of the Soviet Union shall be integrated into the aggressive struggle for liberation. The struggle for liberation shall rescue the citizen of the Soviet Union from being abducted into German slavery and from being destroyed by Hitler's animals. They shall take revenge without mercy for the blood and the tears of our women and children, mothers and fathers, brothers and sisters. They shall support the Red Army with all might in its fight against Hitler's mean oppressors.[40]

A German soldier reading these claims could not fail to comprehend the great reversal of fortunes since Stalingrad. For the German troops in Białowieża, the threat of an aggressive Soviet partisan campaign was a very serious prospect.

During the summer of 1942, *The Partisan Guide* was all the rage in Moscow according to Alexander Werth.[41] He wrote, 'The superficial impression the book made on the uninitiated reader was that the Russian partisan was a sort of glorified boy scout and that although it must be "difficult to live in the snow" and not very satisfactory to eat moss and bark in emergencies, the partisan's life was a wonderful life all the same.' The partisans in the Polish/Belorussia borderlands were praised for their heroic stand. Gradually the partisans began to form into regions (*partizanskie kraia*). Each region built airstrips maintaining communications with Moscow, kept them fully supplied, and ferried out wounded. The regions were able to build supply dumps that kept the partisans in continuous operation. From July 1943 the partisans were ordered to conduct the all-out 'Rail War'.[42]

---

40 Although difficult to ascertain its format, the translation indicated that it was a newspaper format: 'News from the Soviet Union, 1 May 1943, Order of the high commander 1 May 1943, Nr. 195, Moscow.'
41 TNA, HS 7/205, Soviet Partisan's Companion. A copy of the guidebook was translated for British intelligence. The propaganda section is almost replicated in the partisan propaganda in chapter ten.
42 Sebastian Stopper, '"Die Strasse ist deutsch". Der sowjetische Partisanenkrieg und seine militärische Effizienz', *Vierteljahreshefte für Zeitgeschichte*, 29(3), 2011, pp. 385–411.

According to Werth, Soviet scholars claimed the partisans had killed 500,000 Germans. They also acknowledged the partisans were on a 'constant lookout for traitors and the physical and psychological need to kill them'. They were concerned about the attitude of the peasantry who supplied them with food. This Soviet literature included accounts of German deportations and killings as constantly recurring reasons why there was widespread support for the partisans. Werth thought, 'The atrocities committed against both captured partisans and allegedly pro-partisan peasants and their families must rank among the worst atrocities committed by the Germans ...'[43]

The Soviet press was committed to portraying the partisans favourably in the western media. Hutchinson Press, a London-based publisher, carried a collection of Soviet-inspired literature, which included works on or by the partisans. Most of these works were highly propagandised.[44] International opinion was not always swayed by the Robin Hood image, and controversy often surrounded irregulars, guerrillas or partisans. During the Cold War, the Soviet partisan became a symbol of the ideological enemy within, a fifth column. The partisan attracted considerable scholarly attention among the US armed services that raised the paranoia of America's ideological campaign against the Soviet Union.[45] In a BBC documentary about the Nazi-Soviet war, civilians from the region were interviewed about living under Nazi occupiers and contact with the partisans. Ivan Treskovski from Usyazha, a village in Belorussia, explained what it was like when the partisans arrived: 'If you didn't let them in they would break the door down or get in through the window. They would always get in.' The partisans arrived in winter and smashed a window with a rifle, 'Give us some bacon fat or we'll kill you' they demanded. His father climbed to the loft to get food from their store. There was a glimpse of the dystopia: 'Who knew if they were partisans or bandits? Anyone with a gun was a master.'[46]

---

43 Alexander, Werth, *Russia at War, 1941–1945*, (London, 1964), pp. 641–653.
44 S. A. Kovpak, *Our Partisan Course*, trans. Ernst & Mira Lesser, (London, 1947).
45 John A. Armstrong, *Soviet Partisans In World War II*, (Madison, 1964).
46 BBC, 'Spiral of Terror', War of the Century, part two. 1999, interview with Ivan Treskovski from the village of Usyazha in Belorussia.

11. *Bandenjagd*

While Frevert was preparing the formation of the *Sonderkommando*, the partisans prepared for the forthcoming campaign in March 1943. They printed and distributed propaganda leaflets to warn Białowieża's locals of what to expect. These were ominous signs that the fighting between the partisans and Germans was about to intensify in violence and viciousness. The partisan 'commander of the forest' addressed the local youth and intelligentsia: 'Don't think of the partisans as bandits, as they are called by that dog Hitler and his Swabian followers'. 'What wrongs have the partisans done to you? What good have the Germans done to you?' Adding, 'the partisans conduct a war against your enemies. The Germans shoot and hang while your fathers, mothers, brothers, sisters and children are abducted for heavy toil in Germany. Half-starving, they are worked for the German war effort, which inevitably leads to your destruction.' He threatened the populace with dire consequences for siding with the Germans or denouncing the partisans:

> Betraying the partisans or giving away their positions is a severe crime against your own people ... Anyone, who betrays his people, who gives away positions or identifies the 'partisan-helper' among a village population, will be shot on the spot under Soviet law. They will be shot and their property will be confiscated in favour of partisan groups.

The 'commander of the forest' explained how the partisans had treated people with mercy the previous year. For the coming year, he promised changes, and the partisans' warfare would be extreme. He announced the right to burn down villages where a partisan was killed. Such villages would be treated as disloyal to the nation, and its fighting heroes. Having warned the locals, he then addressed the local youth:

> Lads, be careful when talking to traitors. Don't think that partisans are not present. They are there, they are alive and they will be alive. They have carried the battle and will do so in future. There are not just a few partisans, but thousands.

> Those persons, who fight for a good future, are neither scared of the night nor the snow or obstacles and not even death. They have conducted and will conduct the battle until the total destruction of the enemy.[1]

The Soltys of Dubiese (Bielsk district) acquired copies of the leaflets and handed them over to the *Sonderkommando* on 29 March 1943. They were translated into German on 20 April 1943, Hitler's fifty-fourth birthday. Frevert ordered his troops to read the translation adding, "the leaflet is hand-written with ink and is addressed to the natives; it requests the local population to support the bandits ... and is signed by the *commander of the primaeval forest*. This was ideological training — giving the hunters a scent of the enemy.

The first incident was at 11.30 am on 9 April 1943, a band of partisans fired at Revierförster Andres and four of his men. The group were beside the forest railway nearby Draisine. There were no casualties, but the alarm had been raised. An hour later a JSKB reconnaissance troop searched a panjewagen in Zirkzil (northeast Hajnówka) near Jagen 181. They unaccountably triggered a firefight, and the "commander of the primaeval forest" was shot dead in the melee. How the Germans identified him was not explained in the diary.[2] The ongoing claims of the 'commander of the forest' were never clarified in any Luftwaffe files. For more than eighteen months a 'commander' had been the subject of several different reports, and several times confirmed as killed. The inconsistencies in the reporting indicate Frevert was less interested in understanding the partisans or comprehend their strategic mission. He planned to strike and respond to every incursion, which led to a confusing pattern of outcomes — this was wild hunting.

I. Stalking partisans

The exploitation of individual initiative, or, as we now call it, *Auftragstaktik* was the leitmotiv running through all the after-action

---

1　BArch, RL 31/5, document 18, Übersetzung aus dem Russischen Aufruf! Undated or classified.
2　BArch, RL 31/5, document 17, Kommandeur der Sicherheitspolizei und des SD für den Bezirk Bialystok, to Jagdkommando d.Le. Herren Hauptmann Frevert, Bialowies, 10 April 1943.

reports. On 31 March 1943, *Oberjäger* Rudolf Trabus compiled a short-handwritten report about actions in Topiło area. This was a squad leader report for a twenty-four-hour period. Twenty partisan raiders seized the hamlet of Zwirki. A villager raised the alarm at 6.00am and Strongpoint Topiło sent a *Jagdkommando* under *Oberjäger* Rudolf Trabus in two RFA trucks. They arrived at 7.00 am. District forester Klarmann informed Trabus that the partisans had burned down the Gabrze hamlet. Trabus identified tracks, but they proved a false lead. He then led his *Jagdkommando* to Bobinka where they were given three forest vehicles to drive to Topiło via Starzyna. The *Jagdkommando* rode to within *Jagen* 725 in the deep forest where they dismounted, and then Trabus led the troops to *Jagen* 726. From a distance, they observed two waggons, and a hundred metres further a woman wielding a carbine. Trabus followed procedure and ordered his troops to surround the encampment. Trabus led a sixty metres dash as six more partisans appeared. The Germans shot the woman and two men in the dash but were forced to seek cover. For five minutes the partisans countered with a hail of withering machine-gun fire. A serious firefight developed and six more partisans were killed (including another female) and four others wounded, but they managed to escape. The Germans suffered one slightly wounded *Luftwaffe* aircraftsman. The *Jagdkommado* secured a light machine gun, a semi-automatic rifle, two bolt-action rifles and two pistols. One of the dead partisans was a soldier from the Red Army's 36th Cavalry Division. On 2 April, one of the four wounded partisans from this firefight surrendered, there is no record of what happened to him.[3]

On 10 July, there were several skirmishes. Nearby the settlement of Zach Josefin, partisans initiated a short but vicious firefight. Two partisans were wounded without any German losses. Clothing and fifty-nine German carbine cartridge cases were collected later. There was a similar incident at the Narewka River crossing, a kilometre north of Kolami. A partisan was wounded, a light machine gun and a bag of bullets were secured. At the time, entries in the war diary did not

---

3   BArch, RL 31/5, document 8 (second page missing), Meldung, Stützpunkt Topiło, Uffz. Trabus, 31 March 1943.

elaborate details about these actions. However, on 31 July Frevert filed a recommendation to Brauchitsch, that the men involved in those incidents should receive the Luftwaffe ground combat badge.[4] This was the only case when either Herbst or Frevert had requested awards band he wrote an account of why they were deserved:

> On 10 July 1943, sixty bandits had attacked the village Rudnia on the river Narew at 11.45 pm. The Strongpoint Niermerza attacked the village immediately with two groups from the northern and southern directions.
> One group managed to approach the partisan positions to within hand grenade range. The bandits opened fire with two machine guns, two machine pistols and twelve carbines, but were thrown out their positions after a fight lasting a half an hour. They fled to the east and to the northeast.
> The second group encircled the village and successfully stopped all attempts by the bandits from breaking out. This group became involved in close combats. The partisans left behind their stolen food and articles of clothing. At least five bandits were severely wounded, according to statements of the inhabitants of the village. Four of the five wounded bandits died, as were discovered later. There were several slightly wounded men and there were many blood trails. We suffered no losses in combat.
> The conditions for the award of the ground combat badge are fulfilled according to strict regulations. I ask you, therefore, to recognise to award the Luftwaffe ground combat medal to following soldiers: Lieutenant Schröter; Technical Sergeant Müller; *Objägers'* Jentjens, Lemke; Corporals Nehls, Lübbers, Kemper, Hiemenz, Kogge. Müller, Karl, Schmalle, Moos, Stroms, Weiss, Holländer, and Struck.[5]

There is no record of any awards or medals being granted.[6] The award application included a 'Skizzie', a rough hand-drawn map

---

4   Erdkampfabzeichen Der Luftwaffe (ground combat badge of the air force), initiated by Göring on 31 March 1942 and designed by Professor von Weech of Berlin. Awarded for three separate ground actions for hand-to-hand, assault or support combat. Airmen killed in action were awarded the badge automatically. The making of badges and awards for the Wehrmacht gave work to 130 companies, with central mints in Berlin and Vienna and regulated by the Leistungsgemeinschaft deutschen Ordenshersteller (LDO).
5   BArch, RL 31/5, documents 25, Frevert to Brauchitsch, Antrag auf Anerkennung einer Kampfhandlung für die Verleihung des Erdkampfabzeichens d.Lw., 31 July 1943.
6   It is probable, but not certain, the medals were denied because the Bandenkampfabzeichen (see *Hitler's Bandit Hunters*, p. 310) had become the official award for participation in counter-partisan operations. However, because of Göring's morbid fear of snakes the award was not granted to any members of the Luftwaffe serving in the forest.

of the action. The Skizzie used German military symbols for terrain, tactical units, and movements. They were the normal means of conveying an impression of the action without fully detailed maps.

On 20 July, an FSK detachment was caught in a firefight with forty partisans. Lieutenant Rühm led the *Überfallkommando* to their rescue. He compiled an after-action report two days later. Rühm explained that the FSK's Strongpoint at Zarkowszczyzna had raised the alarm before midnight because one of its *Jagdkommando* had suffered serious losses against partisans and was dispersed. The *Überfallkommando* set out at 2.00 am on 21 July with two trucks, a radio car and an ambulance. The total complement included Rühm, six NCOs and thirty-one ORs and along the route, they collected an NCO and eight troopers from Strongpoint Czolo. The *Überfallkommando* finally arrived in Zarkowszczyzna at 4.30 am. A lone FSK rifleman had returned to the strongpoint to report the situation to Rühm. Since 19 July the FSK had maintained an OP at a junction of *Jagen* crossing points (127-128-141-142) in deep forest. The OP was on rotation, with an NCO and sixteen ORs armed with two light machine guns placed in enfilading positions. They were arranged into three sections: a light machine gun behind a fallen tree trunk covered the crossing point of the *Jagen*; another light machine gun fifty metres to the west was placed among a clump of birch trees, and then another section dug in fifteen metres north of the crossing point. A chaotic picture emerged:

> One section was relieved on 20 July at 5.30 pm. The bandits had probably observed the change over. At about 7.00 pm, an FSK rifleman stood and was immediately shot at from a distance of 15 metres. A firefight developed between the FSK and the bandits—a band allegedly 40 strong. Both sides lobbed hand grenades and fired machine guns at each other. Then both sides withdrew from their positions as the firing subsided.
> The FSK suffered one man severely wounded and another slightly wounded. Bullets had hit four or five bandits and an eyewitness recalled how they had fallen. Two FSK riflemen, one of them slightly wounded, ran to Zarkowszczyzna to report the incident. The rest of the FSK then departed, together with the severely wounded trooper carried on a horse cart, first to Bojary and then on to Zarkowszczyzna. Four bandit caps were found on the field. Among their clothing was a German fighter pilot's flying helmet and a strange hat with a Soviet star. They also found a discarded empty Soviet machine-gun magazine drum and fifteen cartridge cases.

The *Überfallkommando* travelled to the scene of the incident but found no bodies or blood trails. The heavy rain overnight prevented tracking. Rühm thought the caps probably belonged to dead and wounded partisans. The partisans were wearing Polish army uniforms, their commands had been given in Polish, but one partisan was seen wearing a German forester's uniform. The *Überfallkommando* searched the entire area then received a radio message that the FSK had returned safely to its base. Rühm returned to Białowieża at noon.[7] There was a sense that Rühm and the troops were not impressed by the FSK performance. Reading between the lines of a subsequent war diary note, there was a dismissive tone about an FSK trooper seriously injured whilst cleaning his machine pistol and died the following day. There was no expression of sympathy.[8]

GIS map 18 was generated to analyse the JSKB patrols in this period and identified several clusters in the southeast and the continuation of *Judenjagd* initiated by Herbst. The cluster of patrols and operations in the Jasien-Suchopol-Wielko-Solo triangle was an extension of those conducted by the fourth and sixth companies of the LWSB. The Pruzhany ghetto was officially liquidated in January 1943, but Jews were still fleeing to the forest. The Wielko-Solo strongpoint was situated to extend patrols to the marshes, swamps and moors. The patrols in the swamplands were particularly hazardous because the partisans formed ambushes in the small clumps of solid terrain. The reinforcements on temporary assignment were being filtered into the patrols. On 24 August, fourteen reservists from the *Hermann Göring* panzer regiment arrived in Białowieża.[9] Another platoon arrived from the *Hermann*

---

7   BArch, RL 31/5, document 40, Bericht über den Einsatz des Überfallkommandos am 21 July 1943, Oberleutnant Rühm, Bialowies, 22 July 1943.
8   Ibid.
9   See Franz Kurowski, *The History of the Fallschirmpanzerkorps Hermann Göring: Soldiers of the Reichsmarschall*, trans. David Johnston, (Manitoba, 1995), and, Roger James Bender and George A Petersen, *"Hermann Göring": From Regiment to Fallschirmpanzerkorps*, (Atglen, 1993). This deployment was the first of a series of attachments from its parent division. The recollections of an FSKII mentioned in chapter 10 were likely connected to the arrival of HG-Division troops. Given

Göring on 29 August without explanation for its purpose or deployment. The diary noted on 30 August that Strongpoint Topiło had arrested five partisan supporters and they suspected the presence of sixty-five partisans in the locality. GIS Map 18 highlighted how Frevert extended across the forest arena with his mobile forces and exploiting the wireless.

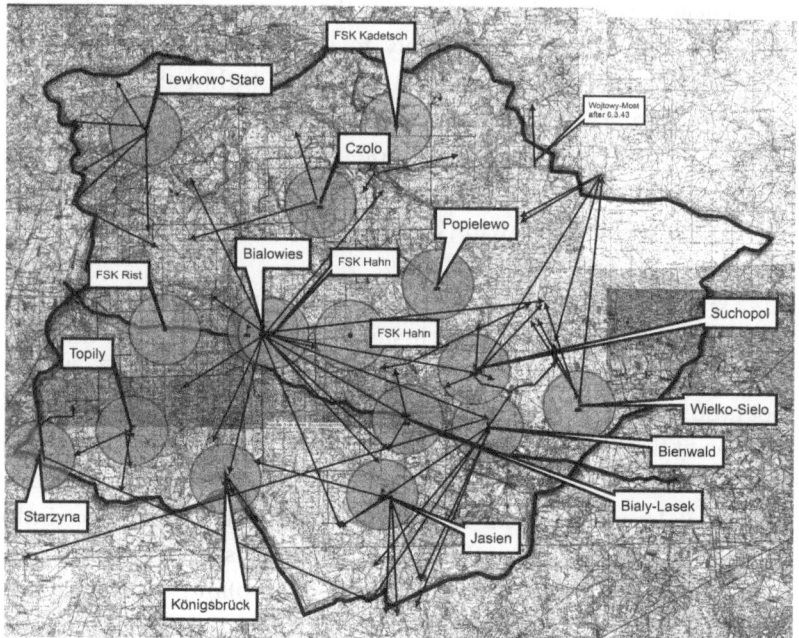

GIS Map 17: JSKB hunting patrols — March to October 1943
This map highlights how a much smaller force could cover the forest. By supporting and coordinating a thinly dispersed deployment with powerful field communications, Frevert could almost dominate the forest. The circles represent an area of 3.5 km, the usual sphere of front per SP. The names are the sites of strongpoints, FSK strong points and command posts. The lines represent the full extent of Jagdkommando patrols.

---

the reputation the division generated with perpetrating war crimes during and after the war; it's little wonder Herr Ströh cloaked his posting.

II. Dubious beaters

An incident on 3 April, stirred the old inter-service rivalry that had plagued Herbst's early days. The war diary noted two partisans had entered the hamlet of Panasiuki (typically spelt as Ponasinki by the German clerks) at 4.00 am. The local strongpoint received an alarm call at 5.30 am and dispatched a *Jagdkommando* in two panjewagen. Arriving at the village outskirts the troops received information, presumably by radio, that the two partisans had moved on to Zwirki (Czwirki in the original report). Approaching within five hundred metres of the village, the troops were warned by a local that the partisans were in a house. The troops observed from a hundred meters away as the partisans moved from house to house. A trooper fired a shot and a partisan fell dead, the other was arrested sheltering in a house. The captive partisan claimed they were trusties from a local gendarmerie company. The war diary conveyed Frevert's frustration that he had not been informed of their presence. The trusties had behaved like partisans and were treated accordingly.

The situation called for reports from the squad leader and Frevert, who presented his 'authority' in a letter to the *Wehrmacht* commander in Bielsk. Frevert confirmed the JSKB had received an alarm that 'two bandits had entered Panasiuki at about 4.00 am.' The inhabitants of Zwirki had revealed the whereabouts of the 'bandits'. At about a hundred metres from Zwirki, people came running to report 'that both bandits were in the village.' *Oberjäger* Trabus observed the 'bandit's movements and one drew a pistol when he saw the Germans. Trabus 'shot the bandit immediately.' The other fled into a house, was pursued, and 'dragged out of the house with his hands up.' The men were searched and both carried guns, but no identity papers. The captive claimed they were trusties from the *Landesschützenbataillon 238*, the same battalion that tangled with Herbst.

'My comment on this incident', Frevert wrote angrily, 'is that it is incredible that the *Landesschützenbataillon 238* sends trusties on such missions in my area, in Zwirki in the heart of the primaeval forest, without informing me.' He continued:

> This is particularly so in such a delicate matter. I suppose the trusties should provoke the population by pretending to be bandits to find out if they assist the bandits. Such methods are very risky, but it is completely inappropriate if the responsible command posts—in this case, the JSKB and the Strongpoints Topili [sic] and Starczyna [sic] are not informed.

Frevert added it was 'inappropriate' to give trusties weapons, but not official identity papers. 'The members of my *Sonderkommando*', he continued, 'have orders to shoot every civilian with a gun or without German documents. I cannot change this order now; otherwise, we would not discriminate between real bandits and trusties.' Frevert confirmed that he had 'interrogated the Soltis [sic] of Panasiuki intensively.' The Soltys had told Frevert that the trusty had held the pistol to his throat, harangued him with German expletives, and threatened to burn down the entire village because it was 'Germanophile' (meaning collaborators). The two men had also tried to prevent the population from bringing their horses for examination in Białowieża as ordered by the German authority. Frevert continued, 'they had threatened to kill everybody and anybody, who brought horses to the Germans. We can believe the Soltis' [sic] statements, especially since he recognised the pistol the bandit had used to threaten him.' Frevert judged this 'method of employing intermediaries absurd. I ask you to inform me in future about your employment of trusties ...'[10] The importance of this incident is that it reveals Frevert's shoot-to-kill order, without formal documentation in the war diary—a verbal order to all men serving in the *Sonderkommando*.

The diary noted on 13 May 1943 that, 'forty-one locals from several villages were brought to the school in Bialy-Lasek to train as *Selbstschutzleute* (self-defence militia) and for employment in *Bandenbekämpfung*.' Partisans assassinated eleven family members of the militia on 19 June in a cruel act of reprisal. Two days later

---

10 BArch, RL 31/5, JSKB, Betr. Erschiessung eines V-Mannes am 3 April 1943 in Zwirki, zu Wehrmachtbereichstandortältaesten Bielsk, 5 April 1943.

several strongpoints began preparing to protect the remaining family members of the militia. It's not clear if they were brought to the strongpoints or guarded in their villages. On 2 August 1943, seventy-four inhabitants were conscripted into the civic guard. This was the final reference to the Polish militia in the war diary. There were several references to *Ostarbeiter* (eastern labourers) conscripted for work in Germany. On 6 July 1943, Strongpoint Topiło arrested two *Ostarbeiter*, both had escaped from Germany. They were handed over to the local gendarmerie. A week later, on 14 July a fugitive *Ostarbeiter* was arrested and handed to the gendarmerie. On 4 August, a fugitive *Ostarbeiter* and a bandit-helper were arrested and taken to the security police. These short diary entries help indicate how population policy had shifted from mass deportations to conscript labour and local militia duties.

At 11.30 pm on 12 August 1943, thirty-seven trusties parachuted into the southern area of *Urwald Bialowies*. Their task was to identify a partisan band and monitor their behaviour. A local strongpoint received orders not to conduct patrols until the trusties had completed their mission. The trusties reached Chilowszczy at about 4.00 am the next day. They observed a partisan at the entrance to the village. The trusties' leader held a brief conversation with the partisan and learned that forty partisans were in the village, asleep in houses. The trusty then shot the partisan while the others surrounded a house occupied by five sleeping partisans, two of them women. The rest of the band fled south across the Lesna River. On 25 August two trusties parachuted into the area south of Jasien. The following day, at 4.15 am they located a band of fifteen partisans three kilometres from Stoily. There were no reports of the outcomes. There were a number of entries in the diaries about trusties, with little comment. If the trusties were expected to flush out the partisans, they were dubious beaters at best. Their activities certainly raised the levels of confusion, fear and violence across the forest arena.

III. Death in the forest

The heightened level of aggression implemented by Frevert had direct consequences. On 12 March, the alarm was raised following a partisan attack on a post office vehicle north of Königsbrück. At 8.10 am, *Überfallkommando Bialowies* set out and arrived on the scene at 8.40 am. A field investigation revealed the attack took place a hundred metres north of *Jagen* 740/773. The vehicle had received bullet strikes, caught fire, struck a ditch, and overturned. The driver, a soldier, and two women were burned to death inside the vehicle. Two soldiers and a Polish woman lay dead in front of the vehicle, but it was not clear if they were passengers or partisans. A bloodhound was released, one of Frevert's hunting dogs. The dog picked up the partisan's scent, but their tracks led into the swamp area and the trail was lost. The pursuit ended at 6.00pm. This was the first hint that Frevert was using hunting dogs for tracking partisans.

On 2 April a wounded partisan surrendered to troops and after recovering he was interrogated six days later. He revealed a camp with more than a hundred partisans, about 2.5 kilometres northeast of the village of Laski. He alleged the villagers aided the partisans. The war diary recorded that a large-scale operation was being prepared to exterminate the band. The operation was planned for 12 April, but the war diary stated it was 'a blowout because two platoons stirred the partisans who quickly vacated the camp.' Large quantities of food were secured, and the camp's bunkers destroyed.[11] The war dairy recorded, at 1.30 pm on 13 April Lieutenant Beyrich (signals platoon) received orders to drive the captive partisan with two signallers to the site of the camp to search the area. It seems likely they expected to use the captive to find clues as to where the partisans had gone. Then at 6.00 pm Strongpoint Königsbrück reported to Frevert that partisans had intercepted Beyrich's party. He was seriously wounded and Corporal Heinz Steinberg, a 26-year-old radio operator, was dead. The diary noted that Beyrich was carried to his vehicle by his men and driven to Czernaki where he lay hurt. At 6.40 pm a *Jagdkommando* was

---

11   BArch, RL 31/5, JSKB war diary, 2 April 1943.

ordered to collect Steinberg's body and deliver Beyrich to the field hospital in Bialystok. They set out at 7.05 pm from Białowieża and arrived at 8.45 pm. Beyrich was taken by ambulance to Bialystok, probably a three-hour trip. By that stage, he had suffered ten hours with field medical aid. The *Jagdkommando* formed a skirmish line to search the area. After an hour they were forced to give up due to poor light. They spent the night in Czernaki and began again at 5.00 am and finally recovered Steinberg's body. He had been stripped down to his underwear and shirt. The body was taken to Białowieża.

In his report to 461st Replacement Division, in Bialystok, Frevert gave a slightly different version of events. He explained that Beyrich had led a reconnaissance mission to the area of Dziadowka-Mala. He was ambushed by a strong band in an area described as a rough field on the southern edge of the forest. A fierce firefight erupted and at a distance of fifty metres. Steinberg was killed by a 'sheet of fire', while Beyrich received a graze on his thigh and a bullet to the stomach. Beyrich was transported as quickly as possible to the general hospital in Bialystok and received surgery that evening. His condition was described as serious according to the doctor in attendance. The losses of the enemy could not be determined because Beyrich's men had been forced to disengage due to the superior firepower of the partisans.[12] In his report to the Wehrmacht records office, Frevert confirmed that Lieutenant Werner Beyrich was seriously wounded in the forest four kilometres from Czermanov on 13 April and died of wounds in the 2nd Reserve-Hospital in Bialystok.[13] Lieutenant Nowarre added a note to the war diary that Beyrich succumbed to his wounds at 1.30 am on 15 April. His body was returned to the JSKB for burial the next day, with full military honours in the Białowieża's *Heldenfriedhof* alongside Steinberg.[14] The death of Beyrich and Steinberg was an awkward outcome for Frevert. The marginally different accounts of the incident and the

---

12 BArch, RL 31/5, letter from Frevert to the 461st Reserve Infantry Division, 14 April 1943.
13 DDSt, casualty report to the RLM on the 13 April 1943.
14 BArch, RL 31/5, JSLB, Kriegstagebuch, 16 April 1943.

failure to eradicate a large partisan band pointed to incompetence. Frevert responded with violence.

On 4 May, Frevert announced the village of Laski had been selected for a *Vergeltungsmassnahme* (revenge operation). The death of Beyrich and Steinberg were not blamed for triggering the action, but it is difficult not to see the connection. The instructions for the operation included a breakdown of forces: a battalion from SS-Police Rifle Regiment 34; an SD-SIPO detachment; the Gendarmerie; representatives from the SS-HSSPF; the Order Police (Königsberg); chief of civilian administration (Bialystok); 461st Replacement Division; and the district commissar of Bielsk. Frevert planned the operation in detail and explained the necessity for the action:

> Intense bandit activity over the last month in the southern border of the *Reichsjagdgebiet* is mainly due to the support and assistance of local inhabitants. Statements of arrested bandits and investigations have clearly confirmed that the inhabitants of Laski, 14 kilometres northeast of Kaminiec-Lit.[sic], in the district of Bielsk had been supporting the bandits and had been in permanent contact with them since winter 1942/43.
> The bandits have erected bunkers, 2.5 kilometres northwest of the Laski settlement. The village supplied the gang for months, upwards of 80 to 90 men, with bread and other food. The village women had constantly washed and cleaned the clothes of bandits. It can also be confirmed that the people of Laski had delivered building materials for bandit bunkers.
> Furthermore, the people have kept the bandits fully informed, especially about the movement of the German army and police forces. Consequently, many operations in this area have been without success. These facts prove without any doubt that the bandits receive support and cooperation from the inhabitants of Laski.
> The people of Laski are partly responsible for the numerous attacks of the band at the southern border of the *Reichsjagdgebiet* because their behaviour created the preconditions for the activities of the bandits. Therefore, the entire population of Laski will be shot in an action of revenge and as a warning to the populations of the border areas of the primaeval forest. The village will be burned down after the execution and the *Amtskommissar* has secured the harvest and material goods. There are about forty houses in the village with about 220 inhabitants. The execution will be conducted on 4 May 1943.

The command-and-control function was handled by the battalion of SS-Police Rifle Regiment 34. The JSKB's role was to encircle the village. The SS-Police troops were ordered to carry out the executions as per Frevert's plan. The encirclement of the village was set for 4.20 am on 4 May. The SS-Police battalion was to arrive punctually at 4.20 am at the road junction Wisznia-Czemery-Wola-Laski (two kilometres north of Wola). They were ordered to arrive exactly on time but warned not to be too early as they might disturb the populace in the village. The SS-Police troops were to then advance on Laski, the JSKB's troops were ordered to shoot on sight anybody trying to escape. A detachment from Bialystok SD led by *Kriminalkommissar* (chief inspector) Erdbrügger was to screen all persons not included in the killing. The encirclement was to remain in place until the end of the operation and the village burnt down.[15]

SSPF-Bialystok sanctioned Frevert's plan for the destruction of the village. The war diary noted at 0.30 am on 4 May the troops assigned to the task were awoken. They had been resting in Białowieża and fell in at 1.30 am in the battalion's training room and were issued with rations for a full day. Frevert announced to his men that the inhabitants of Laski were to be killed and the village destroyed. The diary noted why: 'the village had been washing the bandit's clothes and baking bread for a gang 110 strong. The bandits often went into the village with musical instruments and celebrated with the villagers.' It was believed the partisans spent the winter in bunkers near Laski and had been there since October 1941. The killings were to be conducted in three phases because the village was divided into three sections. The operation worked to the plan: the JSKB arrived at 4.00am and by 4.30am the blockade was complete. By 12.30 pm the village was burned down, and 207 people killed. The diary confirmed the troops had returned to Białowieża at 3.30 pm. There were no references to which troops carried out the killings.

On 8 May 1943, four days after the destruction of Laski, partisans ambushed and destroyed a *Jagdkommando* patrol. This incident was not recorded in the diary but was the subject of an after-action report by Lieutenant Nowarre. The report was quite detailed and opened with the incoming call to *Hauptfunkstelle Bialowies* (the main radio control station) from Strongpoint Wielko Solo at 6.30 pm

---

15 BArch, RL 31/5, document 19, 20, 21, Vergeltungsmassnahmen, SS- und Polizeiführer für den Bezirk Bialystok, Ia-30-70 Nr. 101/43 (g), Bialystok, 2 Mai 1943.

warning that partisans had attacked a *Jagdkommando*. The *Jagdkommando* commander Sergeant Major Marteck was dead; *Oberjäger* Trabus and several others were reported wounded. The general alarm was raised and the *Überfallkommando* led by Lieutenant Nowarre was dispatched at 6.55 pm and arrived in the Wielko-Solo area at 8.05 pm. Nowarre met a self-defence militiaman wounded by a shot in the thigh. He spoke with two other self-defence men from the 'destroyed' *Jagdkommando*. They gave statements, which Nowarre incorporated into his report.[16] This was one of the few reports that detailed the function of the signals.

The annihilation of Marteck's command led to series of local investigation under Frevert's oversight. Piecing together the evidence it was noted that at 8.30am locals in Wielko-Solo reported partisans observed north of Bakuny, moving in a northerly direction toward Radeck. Strongpoint commander Sergeant Marteck took control and led his *Jagdkommando* of five Germans, three trusties, and eleven locals from the self-defence militia to intercept the partisans. They identified tracks in the forest north of Bakuny and followed them. The tracks led deep into the moor, a swampland with a number of wooded islands including Wielki Hrud. At 3.30 pm the *Jagdkommando* arrived at the edge of a six-hundred-metre-wide moor. The Narew River was up to four metres wide running through the middle of the area. Wielki Hrud was situated at the far end of the area to the north. The partisan's tracks led towards the island. The *Jagdkommando* moved across the moor and approached the Narew River and began searching for a crossing point. After several hundred metres they found two strong planks, which were used as a makeshift bridge to cross the river. The *Jagdkommando* formed a squad column and moved towards the islands. After a few metres, they received incoming fire from machine guns and machine pistols. Sergeant-Major Marteck was the first killed in a hail of bullets. *Oberjäger* Trabus and three other soldiers were wounded. Trabus and a militiaman managed to crawl to the riverbank using mutual firing to support their moves. Then Trabus

---

16 BArch, RL 31/5, document 35, Bericht des Überfallkdos. über den Einsatz am 8. Mai 1943, Lieutenant Nowarre, 10 May 1943.

collapsed into the river, but the militiaman dragged him out leaving him lying on the riverbank. The militiaman made good his escape together with two others, nothing was known about the fate of the others. At the time the militiamen thought their comrades had remained behind with the wounded and were awaiting assistance. The strength of the partisans was estimated at fifty men. The three survivors of *Jagdkommando Marteck* knew nothing of any partisan losses because of the intense firing from at least six machine guns and machine pistols.

Marteck's designated deputy sent out a relief troop of five Germans and nine men from the militia with a panjewagen at about 6.15pm. They took one of the survivors with them and arrived at a point about a kilometre away from the scene of the attack. Then the *Überfallkommando* under Lieutenant Nowarre arrived. The relief troop informed Nowarre that they could not locate Marteck's path. The *Überfallkommando* took the relief troop with them but sent the militiamen back to their strongpoint on lorries. By then it was 9.30 pm and very dark. They dismounted from the motor vehicles and leaving behind a guard the rest advanced in squad column formation. The point men, an NCO and five men led the way twenty metres ahead. After five hundred metres Nowarre issued the order to halt because visibility had reduced to a radius of fewer than ten metres. He believed the point of the attack was about five hundred metres ahead but decided, 'If our soldiers are still there, they should react to signals from us.' He gave the order to fire two green signal flares (the signal for friendly forces). Nowarre allowed ten minutes to pass but there was no sign of men or movement. He accepted it was pointless in the dark, they returned to their motor vehicles and waited in the area.

At 10.00 pm Nowarre sent a radio message to Frevert, in Białowieża, that they would spend the night in the forest and take up the search at dawn. In the darkness, the *Überfallkommando* had not realised they had taken up positions on an embankment. At 10.50pm Nowarre received a signal informing him that the police had occupied the nearby Nowy Dwor–Radeck road, in the swamp area south of Starzyna (east) and west of Zamos. Then at 0.21 am another signal advised the police had blocked the road at point 165 five kilometres south of Starzyna (east). Then a warning call came in: 'Be careful!' Clearly, the partisans were still in the proximity and posed an extreme threat. At 4.00 am Nowarre was told to expect a vehicle with rations. The ration vehicle arrived at 4.40 am and the troops quickly devoured their field rations. Ten minutes later Nowarre restarted the search for Marteck. Two machine guns were set up to provide fire protection on the edge of the marshes. Two men advanced to scout for a crossing point over the Narew River. The main body of the *Überfallkommando* then followed across the river.

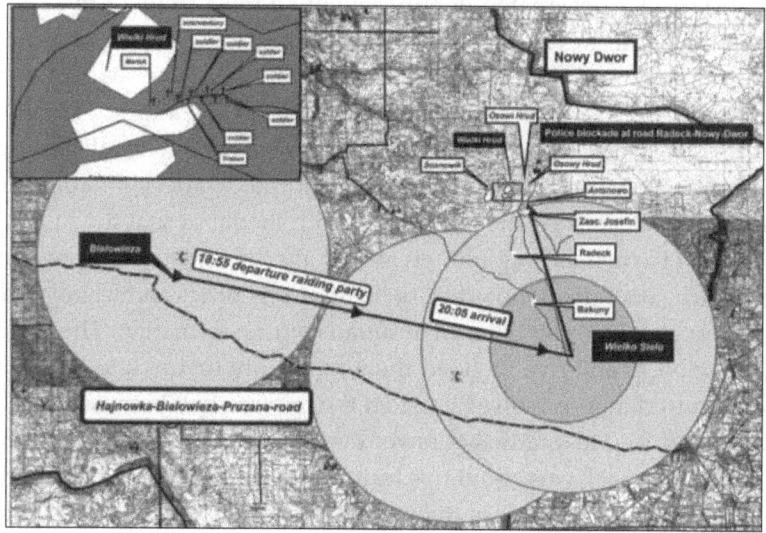

GIS Map 18: destruction of Jagdkommando Marteck
The partisans had the high ground. This map identifies the route taken by Marteck's Jagdkommando set against the potential blind spots in the signals network. The inset illustrates the position of the bodies as they were located by the search parties. The men were killed in a line or possibly while in a column. Along the main Hajnówka road, the communications were very good but once the Jagdkommando moved into the forest and swamp its communications began to breakdown.

The Germans began an intense search of the area and eventually came across the bodies of Marteck's men. The first soldier was found dead a hundred metres along the riverbank. They located all sixteen men. Four troopers lay to one side of the riverbank and four on the other, and the rest scattered. Marteck was dead beside his trusty 150 metres ahead of his men. All the corpses had been stripped and mutilated. A subsequent medical post-mortem confirmed mutilations to several bodies. It was believed the mutilations were both pre- and-post mortem. Most had crushed skulls from an axe handle or heavy club. The medical report stated: Lw.Sergeant Major Rudolf Marteck (born 29 June 1907 in Berggiesshubel, Saxony) of the second company, was killed from nine bullet wounds. *Oberjäger* Rudolf Trabus (born 27 April 1920, in Charlottenburg Berlin) of the first company had suffered a shattered shoulder and his skull cleaved in. Twenty-year-old private Eric Lunge from Kiel, first company, was hacked to death. Gustav Töpfer, the second company, a twenty-one-year-old from Stykow, died from a single blade—a wound which sliced his torso in half (from shoulder to waist) and had received two non-fatal stabbings to the upper chest and left eye. Nineteen-year-old Karl-Heinz Evers from Lemkenhafen, the second company, had suffered damage to his right hand and right shoulder, and his skull had been smashed in. Only three JSKB troopers and a forester, all wounded, returned to the battalion headquarters in Białowieża.[17] The resort to companies seems to have been a clerical decision by the military hospital clerks had jotted down companies instead of platoons.

A field investigation identified a perfectly positioned machine gun position at the southwest corner of an island, with a small elevation. The island was about six hundred metres wide and up to two kilometres long, surrounded by watery marshes. The island top was completely dry with broad pathways leading to the centre area. It was assumed the partisans had probably been living there for several months. An excavated grave of a partisan was found three hundred metres into the island. This partisan was recently buried and was assumed wounded eight days before during an attack at Strongpoint Wielko-Solo. The ground search ended with an order to 'collect the wounded and the bodies of the dead men.' After collecting all the German corpses, they departed the area at 10.15 am. Ten corpses of

---

17 DDSt, Jägersonderkommando d. Lw. Bialowies, Feldpostnummer L53 046 Lgpa. Konigsberg Flg. Ers.Btl. I Powunden Nr 2. 13 April 1943, Lw. Befh. Mitte and R.L.M., Fliegerhorstkommandant Bialystok 16 May 1943. Ripperger et al, Der Traum Vom Urwald, pp. 298–301, published the document revealing the names of the men killed to the public domain. There seems little point in trying to maintain their anonymity. The men still carried their LWSB company designation.

militiamen and the trusty were left behind. Five Germans, a trusty and the wounded militiaman were transported to Białowieża. The *Überfallkommando* arrived in Białowieża town at 12.55 pm.[18] A final entry in the diary stated: 'At 3.00 pm on the 11 May, the comrades killed in combat are buried in a dignified manner in the graveyard of heroes. Their death shall be an obligation on us to continue the fight against the bandits until their complete destruction.' Today, Marteck and Trabus lie in the *Deutsche Kriegsgräberfürsorge e.V.*, in Bartosze, Poland.

The deaths of Beyrich and Marteck marked the fundamental problem of Frevert's leadership in mingling hunt dogma and military orthodoxy. In advocating *Auftragstaktik* and *Jagdliches Brauchtum* he had unwisely encouraged his troops to take risks and stray beyond the signals network into desolate areas. Beyrich was a serious loss because of his job in the national strategic signals network. The incident exposed the naivety of an officer being caught at the scene of an incident without proper security. An official investigation report was drafted but was 'missing' from the records. The *Jagdkommando Marteck* incident was a calamity and exposed Frevert's inability to safeguard the integrity of his command. Depending on the count, it resulted in a five per cent loss ratio. The positions of the dead, suggest Marteck was not followed, there was no primary group bonding having being found so far ahead of his dead troopers. Marteck formed a column and charged machine guns, both ill-advised manoeuvres in Bandenbekämpfung. Without fire support and flanking manoeuvres, it was an ill-judged death charge. The loss of an entire *Jagdkommando* had a psychological impact on German invincibility. In the realm of incompetence, Frevert was a tactical failure but his field skills had ended in a total calamity. The logic of military efficiency, as practised by Herbst had succeeded, whereas Frevert's display of arrogance had culminated in deaths.

In one respect Frevert's methods claimed a high standard of *Judenjagd*. At 8.30am on 29 May 1943 *Oberjäger* Nönning led a three-man patrol from his strongpoint towards Bialy Lasak. GIS Map 20 was the most straightforward mapping exercise because of the reliability of the coordinates in relation to the after-action report. A

---

18   BArch, RL 31/5, documents 22-23-24, Bericht des Überfallkdos. über den Einsatz am 8 May 1943, LW-Lieutenant Nowarre 10 May 1943.

kilometre north of Okulniki, he turned just as five 'Jews' broke cover from the forest at *Jagen* 791 and began moving across a field towards the forest on the opposite side. Nönning un-slung his rifle fired several times. He killed two Jews, both from about five hundred metres away. After examining the bodies, Nönning reported to headquarters. The three remaining Jews escaped, possibly wounded, into the forest. The patrol could not pursue because of the onset of darkness. Having received word of the incident, at 3.15 am on 30 May Frevert immediately ordered Second Lieutenant Spies (signals) to drive with twenty-five men to Bialy Lasek. They were to continue the pursuit of the Jews, tracking them to locate the bunker. The troopers systematically searched *Jagen* 791 and followed tracks believed to be from the first sighting. They located fresh tracks leading from *Jagen* 790 into *Jagen* 789 and on to *Jagen* 788. They came across a well-trodden path. Spies ordered his men to spread out to five paces between men, moving forward in a sweep of the area. Spies later wrote:

> We discovered on the way several tracks, which indicated a human dwelling nearby. Suddenly we noticed a woman, but she had seen us first and escaped into the undergrowth. We discovered a bunker in the course of the pursuit, which we immediately surrounded. We opened the bunker from the top and threw several hand grenades inside. Then we examined the bunker's interior. We found a seventeen-year-old, slightly wounded Jew and a dead man. We also collected three bags of flour, a roll of cloth, a small quantity of leather and a variety of different utilitarian objects.
> The Jew was interrogated and gave us information that the bunker was inhabited by ten persons. There was one married couple with their sons aged between 15 and 25; and, some close relatives. Five men had left the bunker on the previous evening to bring supplies. They were fired on by *Oberjäger* Nönnig. The three Jews, who escaped, had not yet returned. The Jew was later shot.
> Two Jews had escaped together with the woman. I left a squad of nine men under the command of *Oberjäger* Findenig at the bunker because I assumed the three wounded Jews, as well as the woman together with the two other Jews, would return to the bunker.
> The two Jews, who had escaped together with the woman, returned at dawn. They tried to flee when they realised the bunker was still occupied. They were caught up after a brief chase and shot. During the chase, one soldier walked into an outside area and straight into the fire of three partisans. The partisans disappeared into the undergrowth, as they heard the approach of our trucks, which had just arrived in pick-up the squad.[19]

---

19 BArch, RL 31/5, document 35, Meldung, LW-Leutnant Spies, Nachrichten Zuges, 1 June 1943.

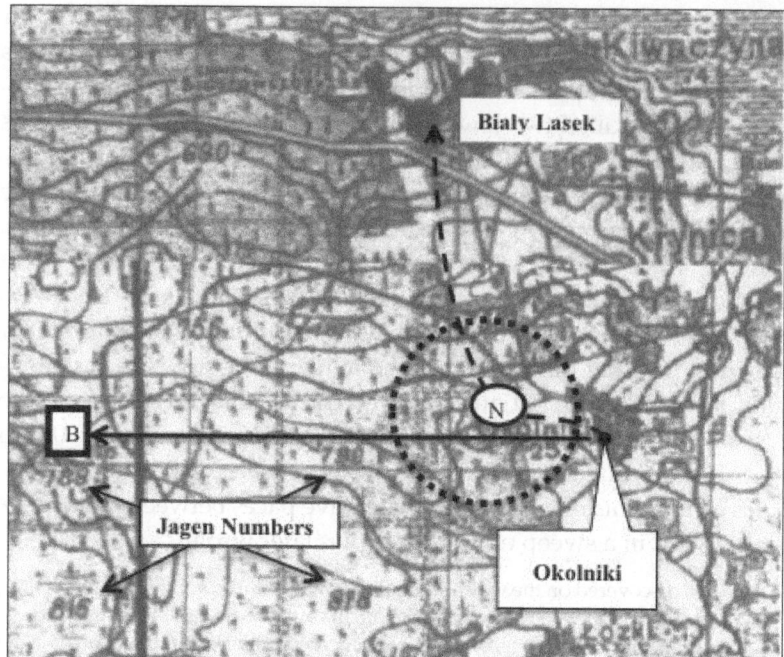

GIS Map 19: the Nönning Judenjagd
A patrol under Oberjäger Nönning set out from Okolniki for Bialy Lasek SP at dusk on 30 May 1943. They reached point 'N' when a small group of Jews fled across open ground. Nönning fired on five Jews killing several but the rest made their escape. Their bunker was in position 'B'.

The war diary recorded several incidents involving Jews. On 16 June, it was a quiet day except for killing a 'Jew' and no explanation. On 27 October, in the vicinity of Königsbrück, 'a 'Jew was shot while attempting to flee'. That same day the diary mentioned that Corporal Malinka was killed in action – neither incident received an explanation. The following day a detachment under Sergeant Trönneke was engaged in a brief skirmish with eight partisans. Three partisans were shot, two of whom were recorded as Jews. According to the diary, the last Jews to be killed was on 12 December, a couple, a man and a woman shot after they were found hiding in a bunker.[20] The aggressive hunting of Jews was probably more

---

20   BArch, RL 31/4, Kriegstagebuch Jägersonderbatillon Bialowies.

intense than these cases show, The Nönning incident report was exceptional but reveals the intensity of the search to locate the bunker and killing the other Jews. The absence of alcohol and other inducements was more than telling. No other incident, from among the Luftwaffe records, revealed such an explicit bloodthirsty drive, by all ranks, to find those people and kill them.

IV. The politics of large operations

Frevert, as Göring's huntsman and chief gamekeeper of Rominten, was experienced in hobnobbing with Nazi leaders and officials. He was schooled in the ways of the German military and the establishment. In this regard, planning and preparing an operation, like a large-scale *Druckjagd* (driving hunt) with beaters and many hunters, was part of his everyday work. Redirecting that experience to organising large-scale partisan hunts with the SS-Police and the army was not a challenge. June 1943 was a busy month for the JSKB with only twelve incident-free days and was perhaps a reason for Frevert's decision to commit to a large-scale operation. *Unternehmen Vatertag* (Father's Day), illustrated in GIS Map 21, details a planned operation. The purpose of the exercise was to destroy a strong band in the Wielki Hrud and Sosnowik (Jagen 1183) areas, nearby where Marteck was killed. The action was planned for Thursday 3 June with a significant show of force committed: SS-Police Rifle Regiment 34; several JSKB *Jagdkommando*, reinforced by two hundred combat troops from *Fliegerhorst Bialystok* (airbase troops — all recruits in final training); an infantry gun, four antitank guns, two machine guns teams supplied by 461st Replacement Division; an FSK rifle detachment from the *Oberforstamt* in Białowieża; and, two fighter bombers (Messerschmitt ME110 aeroplanes) assigned to close air support.

The SS-police were set to take positions around Starzyna (east), to control the forest's border. Close by a JSKB detachment, under Second Lieutenant Schröter was to take up positions on the forest border west of Ur-Izbisko and an embankment toward the eastern border with Jagen 207, 216b. The right-wing held the northern bank of the Narew River. Frevert assigned eighty troops from the JSKB and eighty troopers of the airfield company to travel by forest railway set to arrive 4.45 am in Jagen 177, approximately three kilometres west of Borki. They were armed with fifteen machine guns and had the support of a tactical radio squad. JSKB Staff Sergeant Ewert leading eighty-five airbase troopers set off in trucks at 4.30 am for Popielewo to collect the bulk of the garrison of Strongpoint Popielewo. They were to dismount north of Krasnik Wielkin, and after leading a reconnaissance of the area were to take up positions along the southern bank of the Narew River nearby Siewiec. Frevert warned Ewert in writing, to be in position no later than 7.45 am at the latest. Ewert's force was issued with fifteen machine guns.

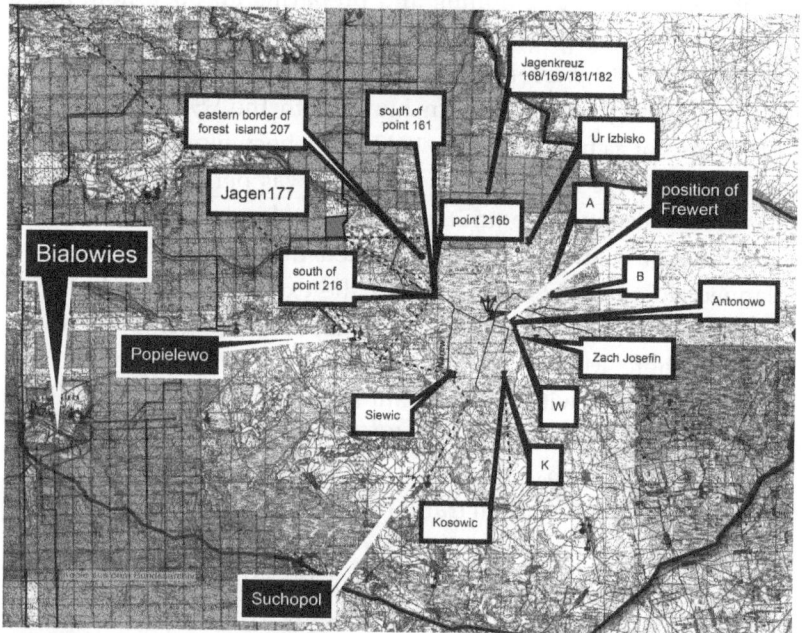

GIS Map 20: Unternehmen Vatertag – 3 June 1943
Mapping the 'major' operations was always difficult due to the constant changes in planning or unit performances. This map provides an indication of the scale of operation with the Jagen boxes on the map representing a little over a square kilometre. The letters represent: A = Frevert's position, B = Borki, K = is the 'K' Kozowik, and W = the 'w' in Antonow.

Lieutenant Nowarre, leading 105 men was designated command of the assault group pressing from Antonowo to Wielki Hrud to drive the partisans. He was to conduct a 'search and destroy' march through Wielki Hrud and then turn west to carry on through Sasnowik. He was to halt after pushing through the forest islands and swamps to the north. It was noted that Nowarre was assigned a detachment of engineers, three troopers and three *Selbstschutzmänner* (best described as carriers); four light mortars handled by twelve garrison soldiers with eight munitions carriers; a signals troop (field radios); and a forward artillery observer. The FSK troops from *Oberforstamt Bialowies* were ordered to occupy a line in an easterly direction from Siewiec up to the forest border. Frevert, leaving nothing to chance explained that they were to take up a position 'at the end of the letter 'K' in Kozowik on their 1:25000 map.' They were also ordered, in writing, to be in position no later than 7.45 am. *Abteilung Rumpeltin* a mixed detachment of twenty-five JSKB men and fifteen airbase troops was ordered to take up positions 'from the end of the letter 'K' of Kzowik (GIS Map 21) on the forest's border moving in a northerly direction up to five hundred metres south of the letter 'W' of Antonowo on their 1:25000 map.' They received four machine guns for fire support.

Frevert applied his artillery skills to position the heavy weapons and support units in positions northwest of Antonowa. They were primed to fire in the direction of the southern edge of Wielki Hrud. He added, 'it is not possible to conduct a reconnaissance of the fire position in advance.' District forester Kadersch, with twenty-five men and three machine guns, was expected to cover the crossing points at Jagen 168/169 from 6.00 am onwards (we can presume Kadersch knew the direction he was to face). The reserve detachment under Staff Sergeant Stefan** consisted of thirty JSKB troopers and was to make contact with the left-wing of the SS-Police battalion. An operational signals hub and collection point for the casualties were placed on the road north of Zasch Jozefin. The parole (passwords) for the operation was: *bumble-bee-bumble-bee*. The

JSKB was ordered to wear camouflage jackets with mosquito nets over their 1943 style caps.[21]

The final instructions for the operation were mostly to do with command, communication and control. Frevert advised that his command position would be near Antonowa. He instructed all blocking units to remain in positions until he ordered them to stand down. Reports of successes, losses, and observations from messengers were to be passed to Frevert's CP via the signals network. Lieutenant Schröter was to report successes through the signals post south of Borki. Ewert was assigned to use the regular telephone line from Popielewo to Białowieża; which would then be relayed to Frevert's command post. Sundry instructions included the note that the army's heavy weapons battery and the 200 men of the airfield company were to arrive in Białowieża by 4.00 am on Wednesday 2 June at the latest. The attack was to begin immediately after a bombing run by the two *Messerschmitt* Me110 aeroplanes, at about 8.15 am. On 3 June, the war diary noted that the large operation, conducted in the northeast area of the forest was unsuccessful. The partisans refused to fight and departed from the area a short while before the operation started. The only casualty was Lw.private Schakeit wounded after driving his vehicle over a mine.[22] This was an echo of Herbst's plans being 'betrayed', but Frevert did not conduct an internal investigation.

The next large-scale operation was in August following a number of incidents. The momentum for the hunt started on the evening of 2 August when fighting erupted with a partisan attack in the Strongpoint Rubeck area. Two partisans were shot without German casualties. There was more night-fighting the next evening involving two *Jagdkommando* west of Bzradowka Mala. By 4 August the construction of the new strongpoint at Woytowy Most, in the southeast area, not far from the swamplands, was almost complete. This position was to lead to a shift in the axis of Frevert decided to cleanse the marshlands of partisans. At 5.35 am partisans attacked the soldiers working on the strongpoint and a firefight lasted

---

21 BArch, RL 31/5, document 36, Unternehmen Vatertag, Frevert, 3 June 1943.
22 BArch, RL 31/5, document 36, Unternehmen Vatertag, Frevert, 1–3 June 1943.

twenty minutes without any casualties. Strongpoint Woytowy Most was involved in another firefight without losses. Strongpoint Woytowy Most sent a radio message to Frevert that according to local police '300 partisans' were forming in the area of *Jagen* 157/158 — deep forest.

Frevert planned a large-scale hunt for 14 August to counter the '300'. Three assault groups, each with an officer and thirty-five ORs were set to rally at the junction of *Jagen* 168/169/181/182. They were to advance together in a west to east march plan. The plan envisaged the inclusion of an encirclement around *Jagen* 157/158, which was completed by 1.00 pm. A group led by Lieutenant Schröter arrived at the start point at 10.45 am and on the march, they observed two partisans. Three partisans were shot in a firefight and several more believed wounded. The troops secured a German MG34 machine gun, two rifles and a pistol from the partisans. Lieutenant Nowarre's group with an FSK group became entangled in a brisk firefight. A partisan was captured; the FSK suffered one dead, two slightly wounded and a slightly wounded local militiaman. A detailed after-action report was originally filed in the collection of papers as "Anlage 19" but is missing from the *Bundesarchiv* files. The next day a local man from Bojary reported the presence of a wounded partisan to Strongpoint Wotowy Most and he was captured. On 20 August two *Jagdkommando* from Wielko Sielo and Suchopol initiated a five-day patrol. They stumbled across two deserted camps in *Jagen* 182, and 190/191 and secured two Soviet rifles, a machine pistol-drum and 150 rifle bullets. Later that day, five partisans were reported a kilometre south of Nowy at 10.30 am. The Germans went in hot pursuit but after two kilometres were forced to stop due to the loss of tracks. The next day Strongpoint Woytowy Most announced it was fully operational for patrols.

On 14 October 1943, the JSKB initiated *Unternehmen Charki* a joint operation involving encirclement and a 'search and destroy' mission aimed a covering a large area. Postwar changes to the frontier make a reconstruction of these operations quite difficult. A partisan camp had been detected in the area of Koziszcze (present-day Poland), Charki (Belarus), Banjoturowski (Belarus), and Zosimy

(Belarus). This reflected the present-day border zone. The operation set an intensive search from the south to north because of the partisans' proximity to the strategic Brest-Litovsk-Baranovichi railway line. The JSKB contributed 200 hundred men for the left wing of the attacking group. They were joined by troops from the Slobottka field training school. A further 130 JSKB riflemen including a reserve platoon from the HG-division, and thirty-five *Hiwis*. The Hilfswilliger were foreign volunteers in the Wehrmacht.[23]

An assault group was led by Lieutenant Nowarre and supported with the JSKB's heavy machine guns. Frevert insisted the men were clothed in camouflage jackets, coveralls, and caps but without their anti-mosquito veils. The men were to wear their coats during the drive to the collection point but then leave them behind in the trucks for the duration of the action. The marching route was from Białowieża to Königsbrück, collecting troops from several strongpoints along the way, and then on to Kaminiec-Litewski. They were then to follow a road southeast via Pruska Wielowiejska, through Dymniki, then Zawersze, and finally arriving in Zauzowie. The vehicles were to halt by the eastern exit of Zauzowie, dismount the troops, and then drive off to Czerniczno. The JSKB with the *Hiwis* were to congregate nearby the eastern edge of the forest at Czerniczno. The left-wing of the assault group formed on the southern bank of the Horodeczna River and the right-wing at the southwest end of the forest. They were then to march eastwards. The reserve platoon, commanded by Captain Theis was to divide into two groups: one occupied a rugged position about a kilometre northeast of Czerniczno, on the edge of the forest, with two emplaced machine guns. From that position, the rest were to fan out in skirmish order moving toward the northeast, east and southeast directions. A second group designated the shock group was to occupy the eastern exits of Czerniczno, and close in on the partisans. A third group was to occupy Stasinki guarding its exits. The fourth group was to take up positions at the northwest exit of Koziszcze and was expected to cover the north and northeast direction of the operations.

---

23 Hiwi or Hilfswilliger was the name given to foreign volunteers in the Wehrmacht. In the east, they were usually former Polish or Soviet Russian PoWs.

Frevert explained to his officers that once he gave the order, the shock group was to advance easterly direction without stopping. They were to 'search and destroy' the forest area thoroughly and reassemble at a position north of point 147. The shock group was to then cross the Horodeczna river and a detachment of sixty men to break off and 'search and destroy' the narrow section of forest to the north. The second detachment of a hundred men was to 'search and destroy' through the forest area of Sosnowo in a northerly direction toward the marshland. After that was completed, the troops were to collect in Koziszcze where their motor transport would await them. Frevert planned a field radio net with a *Doragerät* (Dora-radio set) placed in his CP. This led to the issue of a portable radio to the strike group, a radio was set up in Lieutenant Grote's CP in Stryje. Another radio setup was issued to the HG-division's platoon. Frevert placed himself northwest of Koziszcze, designated the collection point for casualties. During the fighting, Frevert expected to transfer to the crossing point across the Horodeczna River. All the men were issued with 24-hour rations.[24] There was no after-action report on file but on 14 October a diary entry was jubilant about the encirclement but critical of the overall 'search and destroy' performance.

V. More body counts

October 1943 concluded Frevert's first phase. The evidence shows his *Jagdliches Brauchtum* had failed and his *Auftragstaktik* was below average. Partway through May 1943, he was recalled to Rominten for a meeting with Göring to present a report for the period 5 March–5 May. There is no record of their meeting. On 2 July, Frevert was once again called to Göring to report on the second phase, there are no details. Regardless of the quality of the reports the overall tally for the campaign was: 51 partisans killed in fighting or after capture; 207 civilians were killed solely on the grounds of 'suspicion', and another 10 Jews were murdered in the field by patrols.

---

24 BArch, RL 31/5, document 44, Unternehmen Charki, Major Frevert, 13 October 1943.

There were 10 civilian arrests of persons under suspicion of being bandit-helpers and another 10 released because their names were listed for assassination by the partisans. There were also more than 10 cases when the alarm was raised by local communities including from Bojary, Nowy Dwor, Suchopol, Rudnia, and Königsbrück. Frevert was not the usual Nazi perpetrator, crossed the path from ideologue to practitioner. It is perhaps fortunate that his incompetence prevented a higher body count.

12. 1944: Retreat

There was a bitter end to Göring's fantasies for Białowieża Forest. This final phase saw the continuation of Bandenbekämpfung from mid-October 1943 until 9 July 1944, when the JSKB faced the onslaught of the Red Army offensive. The story of this end phase touches on a much larger historical canvas than the fate of a Luftwaffe battalion. The most significant being the wholesale destruction of Göring's eastern national frontier strategy. The fantasy of the Germanic *Urwald* as a bulwark against the Bolshevik hordes was utterly destroyed, but in its destruction, it indirectly impeded the Wehrmacht's defence measures. In 1945 a German geographer under interrogation claimed that Lw.Lieutenant Schultz-Kampfhenkel was responsible for mapping the entire eastern front. His foremost mission was to map the eastern frontier incorporating natural obstacles such as forests, marshes and rivers to shape the Wehrmacht's defensive strategy. The geographers conducted fieldwork across the entire eastern front. Their maps, mass produced, were meant to be easily readable and contribute to decision-making, through accurate terrain information. The British interrogator observed, 'a good' map, in this context, being an instrument, which adequately conveyed topographical information and intelligence to the fighting troops.[1] In other words, Schulz-Kampfhenkel's maps were intended to convey spatiality and terrain advantages to field commanders, highlighting impassable areas for their own troops to avoid, but to force the Soviets through to stall their advance. These German army maps of forests were a spectacular failure, not least because the Soviets were better at fighting in the forests than the Germans.

The third manifestation of the Luftwaffe organisation was the transformation of the JSKB with increased manpower and resources for a battalion. On 11 October 1943, the battalion muster was: 8 officers and 525 ORs, with a monthly average of 614, all

---

1   TNA, WO 208/3619, Interrogation Reports, CSDIC(UK), SIR 1706–1718, interrogation number 1709, 19 July 1945.

ranks, prior to July 1944. The diary tracked changing muster levels as summarised in table 18. The battalion acquired an increase in horses and handlers and, two light artillery field guns for local fire support. A 'pilot' was assigned but without an aircraft aeroplane signifying he was the air-ground liaison officer. Prominent in this 'new' formation was the place of Hiwis (Hilfswilliger), those captured soldiers in German service. There are few detailed studies about Hiwis and hardly any about Polish detachments.[2] Whether they were Hiwis in the usual sense or retitled local Polish militia is uncertain. There were two platoons of Hiwis under training in Bialy-Lasek and Białowieża town. They were broken up and the men distributed to other strongpoints: nine were sent to Strongpoint Czolo to serve under private first class Hellner. Strongpoint Popielewo shuffled five Hiwis to Strongpoint Wielko-Sielo, but in return received ten Hiwis. Strongpoint Topiło released five Germans and five Hiwis to Strongpoint Suchopol but received nine Hiwis in exchange. Strongpoint Königsbrück passed three Hiwis to Strongpoint Jasien and received nine Hiwis from the reserve. Strongpoint Bialy-Lasek and Strongpoint Roubek each received three Hiwis, while the remaining Hiwis joined the reserve. The fluctuations from 1 February 1944 were not explained.

Table 19:   JSKB muster October 1943 to August 1944[3]

Date	Officers	Men & NCOs	Horses	Pilot	Vehicles	MG's 38/40 MG15	Rifles 98k	Hiwis
10.11.43	14	621	69	1	33	97	446	
21.12.43	8	603	68	1	33	97	462	
1.1.44	9	594	68	1	33	97	462	
1.2.44	6	599	68	1	33	97	462	215
1.3.44	6	602	68	1	33	97	462	206
10.6.44	7	615	69	1	36			204

2   Mazower, *Hitler's Empire*, p. 461. A more detailed study of the subject can be found in Bundesarchiv (Hrsg.): *Europa unterm Hakenkreuz, Achtbändige Dokumentenedition, Ergänzungsband 1, Okkupation und Kollaboration (1938–1945). Beiträge zu Konzepten und Praxis der Kollaboration in der deutschen Okkupationspolitik*, (Berlin, 1994).
3   BArch, RL 31/4, Kriegstagebuch, front pages. The actual numbers of Self-Defence men began on 1 April 1943 with ninety-six and concluded on 1 July 1943 with 133. The MG15 machine gun was derivative of the Great War model 08/15.

There were changes to the officer cadre the most significant was the rise of Gustav Rühm to nominal second-in-command and eventually field command replacement for Frevert. On 25 October the JSKB was redeployed. The arrival of reinforcements encouraged Frevert to change the platoon/strongpoint deployment structure originally introduced in March. The battalion was sectored into a north-south divide across the entire *Urwald Bialowies* area. The Hajnówka-Białowieża-Pruzhany road was a partial demarcation line between both sectors. Each sector was assigned an officer, while the battalion CP and support troops remained unchanged in the former Tsarist palace in Białowieża. Under the new deployment (see GIS map 22), Lieutenant Gustav Rühm was commanding officer northern sector, based in Białowieża town. His assigned strongpoints included: Lewkowo (Lieutenant Lüttge); Niemerza and Popielewo, (Lieutenant Schröter); Czolo (Lieutenant Mulack); Witowy-Most (Lieutenant Theiss); Wielko-Siolo (Lieutenant Langer); Murawa (Sergeant Lemke); Suchopol (private first-class Wegner); and Roubeck (private first class Wunderlich). The northern sector incorporated the FSK's strongpoints at Chwoinik, Frevertshof, Zarkwszysna, Rosoczek and the bison compound. Lieutenant Meinicke was assigned to command the southern sector also based in Białowieża. The southern sector strongpoints were: Starzyna (*Oberjäger* Schild); Topiło (Sergeant major König); Königsbrück (Lieutenant Lange); Bienwald and Jasien (Lieutenant Frömke); and Bialy-Lasek and Kryniza (*Oberjäger* Nönning). Map 22 highlights the configuration of this deployment and the cluster of activity around Bienwald. This deployment appeared to make the marshland to the southeast of Wojtowy Most a void. However, detailed scrutiny shows this strongpoint received mortars and was reinforced with heavily armed panzer grenadiers from HG-Division on a temporary assignment.

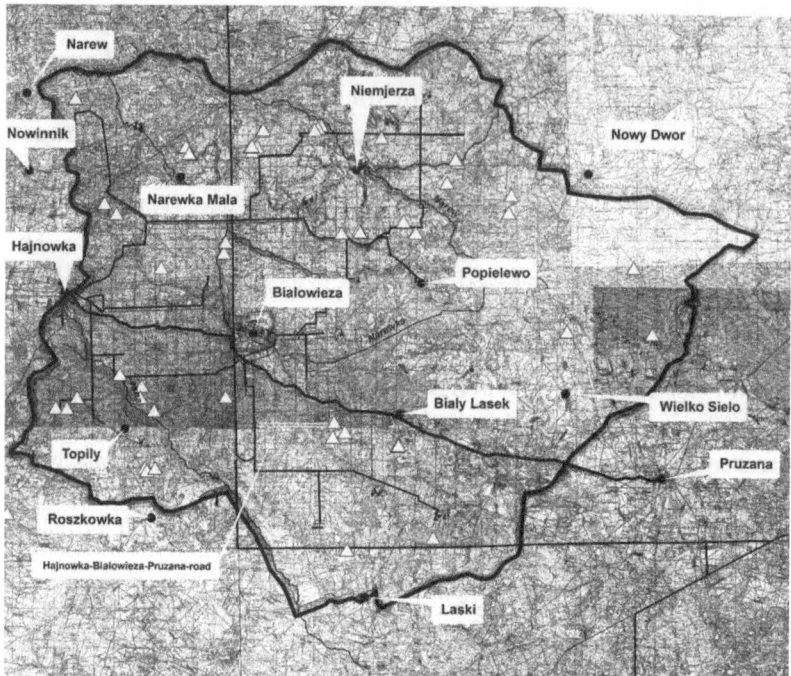

GIS Map 21: JSKB second phase north/south final deployment
The final phase of Nazi occupation began with Frevert's reorganisation of the JSKB's deployment into a north-south configuration. The expansion of the Sonderkommando led to a greater area of deployment but the partisans' incursions increased exponentially.

Frevert pushed his officers hard, demanding improved performance and aggressiveness with the locals bearing the brunt of these methods. There was a level of detail to what was expected from the sector commanders' performance. The officer's primary task was to impose rigid control over their strongpoints. They were expected to achieve this through regular visits and inspections, spending several days with the troops, and leading the *Jagdkommando*. The purpose was to raise the intensity of patrolling and impose an aggressive posture. Platoon commanders were ordered to project 'German power' at all times. Strongpoint commanders were to pass on all tactical reports to their immediate superiors as soon as possible without lingering. Frevert was succinct as to what was required of his senior subordinates: 'the activities of the platoon commander shall under no circumstances be reduced to office work.'[4] The tone of orders and instructions were different with officers ordered to participate in patrols. There are indications that the battalion was being returned to the 'military efficiency' ethos and Frevert's hunting methodology waned.

I. The final phase

Göring's political troubles had calmed down. On 26 October, Erich Koch made a final official visit to *Urwald Bialowies*. Frevert organised an honour guard, set roadblocks, and cordons of security. The security measures were necessary as the overall average of monthly partisan incursions increased, and their effectiveness was entirely related to the support proximity of the Red Army. The partisans particularly targeted the forest railway with mines and improvised explosive devices (IED). On 27 October, a patrol led by Sergeant Käbisch was entangled in a serious firefight with ten partisans. They captured a partisan, after interrogation they were able to identify him as an explosive expert serving with the 'Kirow band'. This was typical of the incomplete entries in the war diary during the end phase. However, the significance of the entry became the identification of the culprit behind the explosions, rather than the damage caused. The forest remained a sanctuary for all kinds of fugitives and a formation known as *Group Tillmann* was mentioned in the diary as conducting civilian manhunts. Again, the absence of clarification was typical of the shortened entries in the war diary. Meanwhile, Frevert ordered Rühm and his northern sector troops to prepare two field exercises. Rühm's report mentioned no contact with insurgents but following the exercise, the troops intercepted five partisans and two were captured.

On 5 November 1943, Frevert issued detailed orders for Rühm to lead an exercise in the area neighbouring *Jagen* 188a. The absence of an after-action pointed to a workup training exercise in the deep-forest for the new deployment. At 6.00 am the next day three

---

4   BArch, RL 31/5, documents 45–46, JSKB reorganised for tactical reasons from 25 October 1943 Commando order Nr. 20/43, 18 October 1943.

sections commanded by Corporal Laube were set to occupy the northern edges of *Jagen* 196//197. Frevert also sent troops from Strongpoint Popielewo reinforced by a platoon from Suchopol. Strongpoint Niemerza was reinforced by a section from Czolo and prepared as the cordon detachment to the eastern border of *Jagen* 187, divided into three groups commanded by Second Lieutenant Schröter. Second lieutenant Lopsien led a line of skirmishers from the Białowieża command reserve, reinforced with a section from Königsbrück. They were to take up positions on the embankment in *Jagen* 178 with their front-facing southwards. The right flank was to make contact with troops in *Jagen* 177//178 and the left-wing was to be the main point of effort. At 6.00 am troops from Strongpoint Wojtowy Most were ordered 'stand to' on the embankment in *Jagen* 178, forming a skirmish line facing towards the south. The right-wing was to have contact with Lopsien's force. Another subgroup from Wojtowy Most, under Captain Theis, was to cordon *Jagen* 178//188a on the eastern edge facing south. The designated attack formations of Theis and Lopsien set off at 7.00 am searching through *Jagen* 178//188a in a southerly direction. Rühm, the exercise commander was ordered to march beside Theis. Support weapons included mortars from the Wojtowy Most. A white signal flare was to signify: 'Stop the mortar fire', we can assume the orders to open fire were transmitted by radio. The troops were issued with 24 hours field rations. The operation was to be concluded when four green signal flares were fired in a sequence one after another by Rühm; the troops were to then march back on their own to their strong points.[5] This exercise signified Rühm was being groomed for promotion and command.

On 11 November, the gendarmerie in Duntrowiece arrested and delivered a Soviet parachutist. Then next day *Jagdkommando Birke* captured a 'bandit' deserter.[6] Under interrogation, both men identified four Soviet partisan liaison agents in Dubrowola

---

5   BArch, RL 31/5, documents 47, JSKB Kommando Befehl, Frevert 5 November 1943.
6   Some *Jagdkommandos* were given names like those under the LWSB but no schedule of names exists in the files.

pretending to be trusties. They were listed as operating as double agents and were arrested. The next day there was an unsuccessful search for a partisan camp through *Jagens* 53, 64, and 82 in the deep forest. On 20 November, the four agents were hanged in public in Dubrowola. Further searches came to an abrupt halt due to the deterioration of the weather. There was little activity until February. On 24 December, Frevert's headquarters held a Christmas party in Białowieża with smaller parties being held in the strongpoints. On 6 January, the Red Air Force dropped propaganda leaflets in the area of Charki and Czarnesew (sic). A large IED exploded along the Hajnówka-Białowieża road announcing the return of partisan activity from February 1944. Frevert reported to *Luftwaffe* command, on 24 February, a *Flugmeldeplatz* (air observation post) had been formed for monitoring the increasing number of Red Air Force intruder flights. Throughout the month there were many partisan attacks against the forest railway mostly directed against bridges, locomotives, and the sabotage of railway lines.

Partisan incursions increased. On 1 March 1944, the forest railway line was severed at *Jagen* 205 in an explosion but with few casualties. There were increasing signs that the partisans were carrying the fight to the Germans. On 25 March, seven partisans were cornered near Debrowo at 3.00 pm and they opted to fight it out. The fighting spilt over into *Jagen* 901 and the partisans lost their supplies. Two partisans were killed but the others escaped leaving behind a machine gun and an automatic rifle. A firefight near Nowy-Dworce led to ten partisans being killed, two wounded, and one captured. A nearby gendarmerie detachment had a small success in Zalesie. The police arrested ten partisans, securing five machine pistols and three rifles without losses. The band splintered to evade capture but was ambushed in what the diary described as 'a well-performed German-style counter move'. In Babinka on 12 March, three partisans were observed and pursued by a patrol from Strongpoint Staczyna. A running gun battle ensued; two partisans were killed, and two others wounded. The *Jagdkommando* suffered two deaths, Corporal Tony and *Hiwi* Cebük. Corporal Awe was seriously wounded, and Lance corporal Schleifer only slightly wounded. There was a military ceremony for the burial of Corporal Tony on 15 March, but no details were provided for Cebük's funeral. There was no reference to arrangements for Cebük.

The JSKB's medical records identified two Polish *Hiwis* wounded on the evening of 19–20 March 1944.[7] There was a sizeable action that day, but the after-action report has been lost. They were Paul Soldatow born on 20 July 1924 in Siemienowka near Bielsk and Stefan Bielecki born on 5 July 1924 from Hajnówka. The casualty report was marked with blue crayon and inscribed with *auch Hiwi!!* (*also a Hiwi*). The war diary referred to *Hiwis* on 16 October 1943, when seventy-one 'swore an oath in a very dignified manner.' There was a curious diary entry on 6 February 1944, when an unnamed *Oberjäger* shot a Hiwi without explanation. March 1944 was a period of sustained casualties. The Hiwi losses were not being lodged with the official *Wehrmacht* records. The *Hiwis* were mentioned again on 10–13 April when an unknown number swore oaths in Białowieża and Szersyno. On 17 April, five *Hiwis* were kidnapped from their homes during a partisan raid; they had been granted Easter leave to go home. Two of the *Hiwis* were eighteen, and a *Jagdkommando* was sent out in pursuit but returned without success. Two days later fifty-four locals in the 1926 age group were drafted as *Hiwis* (thirty-two from Bialystok and twenty-four from Dubrowola). On 3 May, a *Hiwi* escaped from the partisans and returned, but there were no further details on record. In June, a *Hiwi* vanished following a firefight, and in another incident, two *Hiwis* were targeted by partisans and bombed out of their quarters. The evidence points to all the *Hiwi* being local Poles from Białowieża.

In April, a *Jagdkommando* searching for stragglers surprised six partisans and killed all of them. Elsewhere, partisan raids in villages across the forest kept the Germans chasing shadows. A train on the forest railway ran across mines in Jagen 146, they were placed within 500 meters from each other to increase their effectiveness. The train suffered only minor damage. Irrespective of the JSKB manpower increases, it was gradually being overstretched,

---

7   DDSt, JSKB casualty report 13, 20 March 1944.

and could no longer respond to every alarm. In May the situation in the forest deteriorated still further as partisan raids began gnawing away at all available German reserves. On 3 May, a patrol car of the RFA ran over a mine on the Bialy-Lasek road. Troops responded by searching several villages for twenty-four hours but without success. On 11 May, an ambush and pursuit were planned without success in the Czerlanka area, almost within earshot of Frevert's headquarters. That same day a firefight broke out with six partisans cornered in a barn. All six were shot and in the process the barn caught fire. The fire spread and destroyed an unnamed neighbouring hamlet. The troops found two automatic rifles. A motorcar from the battalion motor pool drove over a mine along the Białowieża-Pruzhany road. The vehicle sustained slight damage, and its three passengers received minor injuries including the JSKB adjutant Lieutenant Weinreis who suffered perforated eardrums.

On 29 May, the Luftwaffe made its last attempt at power projection in *Unternehmen Paul*. The mission was directed toward the destruction of a camp of 200 partisans. Rühm set the battle plans and jump-off positions. The camp had been confirmed by aerial and ground reconnaissance, about 1,700 metres due south of Porochwnia. A report claimed the partisans had: maintained constant attacks against Strongpoint Nowy-Dwor; interrupted traffic between Lyslow to Nowy-Dwor; and had inflicted serious casualties to the police. The operation was assigned mixed troops including the fifth company from SS-Police Rifle Regiment 34; two army companies designated 'Cäsar/Ewald'; and a fighting detachment and an *Absperrkommando* (a blockade commando) from the JSKB. Their jump-off (see GIS Map 23) placed the police in the forest and swamp area in the eastern corner, at a point a kilometre south of Kornedz on the road to Porochownia. The army companies Cäsar/Ewald were placed in Porochownia in reserve. The JSKB were formed up in Nowy Dwor to search for a suspected partisan camp two kilometres south of Porochownia. The blocking force was to cordon the swamplands preventing fleeing partisans from escaping through the swamps. The call signs for the operation were 'Eichfeldt' (applicable from noon 28 May until noon 29 May) and

Heidelberg (noon 29 May until noon 30 May).[8] Lieutenant Lopsien commanded the assault group from the JSKB, reinforced by a platoon of panzer-grenadiers from HG-Division. This HG-Division was led by Second Lieutenant Würdig with six NCOs, thirty ORs, and four machine guns. Second Lieutenant Pallas commanded the second platoon of panzer-grenadiers from HG-Division (three NCO's, fifty-three OR's) with five machine gun teams. This level of machine gun power was far greater than the entire JSKB. Sergeant Blocksdorf led a third platoon made up of troops from Strongpoint Niemerza (one NCO, fifteen ranks and two machine-guns); a group from Strongpoint Czolo (one NCO, eight ranks and a machine gun); and a group from Strongpoint Popielewo (an NCO, ten OR's and a machine-gun). Sergeant major König commanded the reserve platoon including a signals section, and the heavy weapons (five NCOs, forty-nine ORs and four machine-guns).[9]

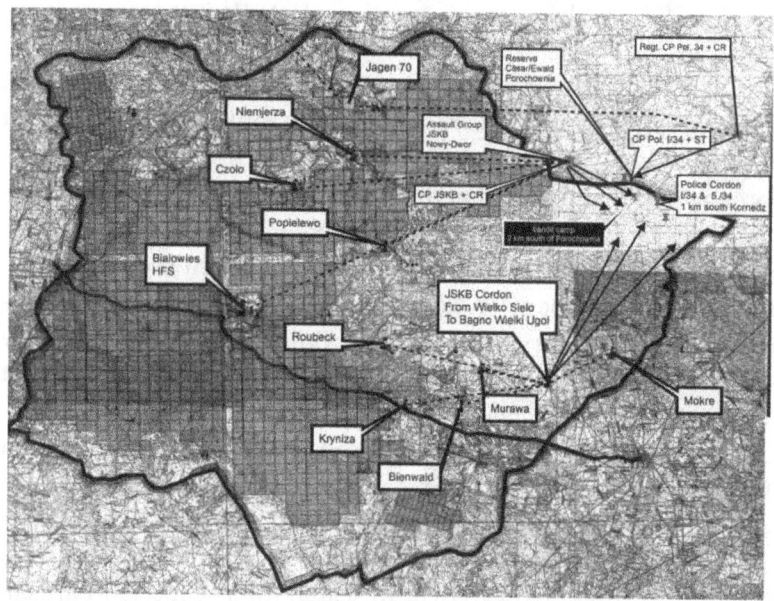

GIS Map 22: Plan for Unternehmen Paul, 28–29 May 1944

---

8   BArch, RL 31/5, document 57, Unternehmen Paul, possibly an SS-Police working paper or an operational plan by the JSKB.
9   BArch, RL 31/5, document 66, Einsatzbefehl für das Unternehmen 'Paul', Oberleutnant Gustav Rühm, 27 Many 1944.

The only after-action reference to *Unternehmen Paul* was a handwritten diary entry for 29 May. The diary mentioned a clash with a band thirty strong and sporadic fighting with small groups of partisans (each of about six). There were no known losses of either partisans or Germans, but some items of clothing and three horses were secured. On 30 May there was a firefight with partisans in *Jagen* 536 near Topiło but without losses. A camp was discovered, and equipment secured. The next day there was even more serious fighting around Porochownia. Nine partisans were shot and a *Bandenhelfer* arrested without German losses. A machine gun, a rifle, ammunition, and documents were secured later. By 1 June, the battalion was alone in securing *Urwald Bialowies* and the border areas. The area Lesna-Lena River and Lesna-Drawa River districts, up to the point where both rivers formed a natural demarcation line for the limits of operations. There were several firefights every day, reduced to one-line entries in the war diary. On 5 June, four partisans entered *Jagen* 15, and they were confronted by troops, and in the ensuing firefight, a partisan was wounded. The troops searched Siemnowka and sixty-three locals were arrested and taken by the police to Bialystok possibly for aiding the partisan escape. In Dubny two partisans and a female bandit-helper were arrested in Narewka. From 6–8 June thirty-five bunkers were blown up in the area of Siemnowka and Obkowka, and one was purpose-built in concrete. On 16 June, three *Bandenhelfer* were shot dead in a village high street by troops. The Red Air Force dropped eight bombs and an incendiary on Niemerca without damage or injury. The troops disarmed several IEDs on several railway tracks. Sixteen hostages were arrested, it was alleged their family members of the saboteurs. Siemienowka area was identified as the focal point of partisan activity.

The first days of July exposed the JSKB's powerlessness. Low flying Soviet combat aircraft carried out strafing sorties unhindered. A bomb was dropped nearby Rudnia without casualties. Taking advantage of the aerial diversion, partisans torched the turpentine factory in *Jagen* 828 in the early hours and successfully evaded pursuit. This was the last entry in the diary about the

Białowieża's partisans. The culmination of the process of collapse occurred at 3.00 am on 6 July. Three *Hiwis* armed with pistols 're-belled' within Strongpoint Ogrodniki and shot six Germans. They killed a corporal, severely wounded a sergeant major and three ORs, and a trooper was slightly wounded. Two *Hiwis* escaped but a third was wounded and arrested. Under interrogation, the wounded *Hiwi* said it was an act of revenge because of the severe punishment they had received from the Germans. The Germans dubbed them the 'traitors of Ogrodniki' and on 10 July their family members were arrested. The next day the fathers and mothers of the rebels, alongside four *Bandenhelfer* were executed in public. On 12 July, two *Hiwis* were arrested for theft and handed to the security police for execution.[10]

II. Vikings, Bears and Panthers

The Wehrmacht's retreat from the east was a chaotic rout. On 22 June 1944, the Red Army unleashed *Operation Bagration* on the anniversary of Hitler's *Operation Barbarossa*. The offensive lasted until 19 August 1944 and concentrated on Western Belorussia (today: Western Belarus).[11] Five Soviet fronts (army groups) were directed against four German armies of Army Group Centre. In preparation for the offensive, the Soviet partisans were ordered to cause maximum chaos behind German lines and in particular disrupt the transport network. German intelligence discovered the concentration of Soviet forces in early June. The Wehrmacht could only wait for the sucker punch.[12] The offensive swept away the defenders. By mid-July the Red Army had wiped out several German corps, many frontline divisions, destroyed the last reserves and was bearing down on Białowieża virtually unopposed. The Red Army's *Operation Bagration* shattered all belief in the power of Hitler's warfare.

---

10   BArch, RL 31/5, report of the period 25 July 1944.
11   Militärgeschichtliches Forschungsamt, Karl-Heinz Frieser et al (ed), *Das Deitsche Reich und der Zweite Weltkrieg: Die Ostfront 1943/44*, Band 8, (München, 2007).
12   David M. Glantz & Harold S. Orenstein, *Belorussia 1944: The Soviet General Staff Study*, (London, 2001).

The German high command was powerless, and the army staggered. The German leadership believed Białowieża was a natural obstacle but ignored Clausewitz' maxim: 'One must above all distinguish between dense, impenetrable, overgrown forests, and extensive, cultivated woods that may have numerous clearings and be traversed by a large number of paths.'[13]

In July 1944, the *Luftwaffe Jäger Sonderbataillon Bialowies* was reassigned to Second Army, commanded by General Walter Weiss and his chief of staff Major General Henning von Tresckow.[14] The Second Army looked reasonably powerful, on paper, with five corps, three panzer divisions, and several frontline infantry divisions. However, there were weaknesses especially among the formations of the Royal Hungarian Army, which were already displaying disturbing signs of collapse and disintegration. They were not the only troops in a poor condition. After almost continuous uninterrupted combat the 20th, *Korps Harteneck*, and 23rd Corps were reduced to shattered remnants. Retreat after retreat and the constant struggle to close-up gaps opened by Red Army probes, feints and main assaults had sapped the army's fighting power. As the three corps fell back on *Urwald Bialowies* more German divisions were trashed by the Soviets. The Germans were powerless to break the Red Army's momentum and limited to localised counterattacks for the troops to escape encirclement.[15] Although the Soviet onslaught was expected, the JSKB was not prepared.

The Germans in the Białowieża area faced the Red Army's First Belorussian Front, commanded by Army General Konstantin

---

13   Carl von Clausewitz, Michael Howard and Peter Paret ed. & trans., *On War*, (London: 1993), p. 545
14   Christian Gerlach, 'Men of 20 July and the War in the Soviet Union', in Heer & Naumann, *War of Extermination*, p. 139. Gerlach examined Tresckow's papers and found on 28 June 1944 he had signed the Heu-Aktion (Hay Action) to round up Polish children. By disclosing this, Gerlach was proving the underlying hypocrisy that surrounded members of the resistance. There is no evidence that this policy was adopted in the forest and this represents another example of how Bezirk Bialystok was treated differently. See also Bodo Scheurig, *Henning von Tresckow, Ein Preusse gegen Hitler*, (Berlin, 1987).
15   Rolf Hinze, *Das Ostfront-Drama 1944: Rückzugskampfe Heeresgruppe Mitte*, (München, 1988), p. 312.

Rokossovsky. To maintain the momentum of his advance, the Soviet general had planned the deployment of three cavalry corps to infiltrate the forests and swamps. The Soviet high command designated 65th Army, commanded by Lieutenant General P.I. Batov, with two rifle corps, a mechanised corps and the I Guards Tank Corps to strike through and take the forest.[16] At noon on 12 July 1944, the diary recognised the JSKB's transfer from *Luftgau I* to *Flughafenbereich 10/XI* (Bialystok). Henceforth, the battalion was downgraded from an independent unit under Göring's direct command to a battalion under *Fliegerhorstkommandanturen E* (air-station network). By 1944, the *Luftgau* structure was rationalised and no longer commanding formations in the Home Forces Area.[17] Lieutenant Weinlich entered the transfer of command in the war diary, signing the document in Frevert's name: 'The JSKB is temporarily under the command of *Generalleutnant* Stephan in all operations.'[18] The JSKB structure was reorganised as 1 *Jägersonderkommando* (under Lieutenant Rühm and Second Lieutenant Romanischky); and, 2 *Jägersonderkommando* (Second Lieutenant Schröter); and, 3 *Jägersonderkommando* (under Second Lieutenant Meinecke); two platoons from the HG-division (commanded by Second Lieutenants Würdig and Pallas); a supply and support train (Corporal Meier); and, Frevert's headquarters company. In addition, a *Jägerkommando* from *Stab Stephan* (Staff Stephan) transferred to Białowieża. The strongpoints of Mokre, Wielko-Sielo, Starzyna and Topiło were placed on alert. Strongpoint Woitowy-Most was abandoned, destroyed, and the troops marched to Białowieża town. The main fighting line was concentrated centred upon Białowieża town running along the Narewka River, north and along the road to Königsbrück to the south.

---

16 David Porter, *Order of Battle: The Red Army in WWII*, (London, 2009), pp. 142-143.
17 I would like to thank Dr Bernd Lemke of the ZMSBw for his advices on the Luftwaffe command structure after 1942.
18 BArch, RL 31/5, Anruf. Flughafenbereich 10/XI, Oberstleutnant Stephan, Fliegerhorstkommandantur E (v) 264/III, Aktennotiz, Oberstleutnant Weinlich, 15 July 1944.

On 13 July the strongpoints Wielko-Sielo, Mokre, Roubeck, and Kymica were abandoned, destroyed, and their troops collected in Bialy-Lasek. The Pruzhany road was prepared for the defensive and the JSKB readied itself for an emergency situation. Göring then intervened and personally ordered Frevert to pack up and leave for Rominten. He was to bring along: five officers, twenty-two NCOs and 161 ORs, and the entire signals detachment to Rominten. Lieutenant Rühm became the commanding officer. That same day Colonel Schmidt, commander of *Flughafenbereich 10/XI* in Bialystok, confirmed Göring's order that Rühm was to take command. Rühm was advised that if the enemy pressure was too strong his reporting line could be transferred to another Luftwaffe airbase at Bielsk. In effect, he had the indirect authority to retreat.[19] On 14 July a Red Army breach came shattered the 129th Infantry Division and dispersed remnants through Nowy Dwor. This allowed the Soviets to cut through the forest and drive through the demarcation line between *Korps Harteneck* and 23rd Corps. The Soviets forced a 25–30-kilometre gap in the German lines. The 23rd Corps struggled against being sucked into the forest. The fears over the impassable forest influenced command decisions. In the area of Pruzhany there was a confusing struggle as the corps, supported by the 4th Panzer Division, attempted to stall the Russians, but the Soviet 65th Army continued to press on towards Hajnówka.[20] At 3.00 am Frevert's evacuation detachment, destined for Rominten, departed with all haste. For 'security reasons' Strongpoints Bienwald and Jasien were abandoned, and their troops transferred to Bialy-Lasek. The garrisons of Königsbrück and Lewkowo were also withdrawn, and their quarters given to an army motorised combat engineer (*Pioniere*) battalion. Their job was to fell trees blocking the road, laying mines, and setting booby traps. At 2.00 am the strongpoints of Popielewo and Czolo received their orders pack-up and leave for to Białowieża town, collecting soldiers without specific orders or duties.

---

19 BArch, RL 31/5, document 49, Verlagung des JSKB, Flughafenbereich 10/XI, Oberst Schmidt, 13 July 1944.
20 Hinze, *Das Ostfront-Drama 1944*, p. 312.

The Soviets continued to press forward on 15 July. The German 20th and 23rd Corps formed up either side of the forest, struggling to hold fronts and flanks. Massive gaps began tearing the German frontline into islands of shattered units. The 7th Infantry Division joined the line with 23rd Corps, while the 20th Corps took the full brunt of the offensive drive towards Bialystok.[21] The JSKB was subordinated to *Stab Stephan* (part of 23rd Corps) as it took over local command and fixed defences around Białowieża town.[22] Once the engineer's roadblocks were complete along the Pruzhany-Czolo road, all German traffic ceased from 4.00 am. Security and guard posts were placed alongside the roads into Białowieża, and patrols were stepped up, equipped with radios or telephones. At 2.00 pm Strongpoint Niemerca received orders to destroy everything and retreat along the road to the junction with Popielewo. The troops were warned to be mindful of security and prepare to counter any Red Army reconnaissance probes coming from an easterly direction. The army engineers began laying mines and felling trees to blockade the roads in the northern area of the forest. At 5.00 pm a radio message from Niemerza indicated that Rudnia was receiving Soviet artillery fire directed at the edge of the village. The JSKB's CP moved to Hajnówka and was set up in a school headmaster's office. At 11.00 pm the forest front was placed under the direct command of the army engineer battalion. A note was attached to the war diary that stated there were no signals messages or orders for the period 14–19 July 1944, because the command came under *Stab Stephan* and *Stab Merker*.[23] The growing level of confusion and lack of detail means it's almost impossible to know whether orders were carried by messengers or relayed by signals.

On 16 July, the 20th Corps began to retreat again. The corps was breaking up as it tried to desperately avoid being sucked into the forest, incorrectly assuming Białowieża was impassable. At 1.55

---

21 Ibid., p. 313.
22 W. Victor Madeja, *The Russo-German War: Summer 1944*, (Allentown, 1987), p. 50. Stab Stephan has remained a mystery throughout the research. This was the only reference to its existence, in an order of battle chart for 15 July 1944.
23 BArch, RL 31/5, document 51, Anmerkung für Anlage zum Kriegstagebuch, undated.

pm, Red Army tanks with infantry were observed approaching Białowieża town from the northeast. Five minutes later, another report was received that troops in the Czolo area had observed a strong Soviet formation approaching in *Kettenfahrzeugen* (tracked vehicles) with an advance guard of thirty or forty men. Since 10.00 am a temporary command post under a corporal (possibly part of *Company Meinecke*) took a position nearby the bison reserve and observed Russians approaching Białowieża town. At 6.00 pm Company Meinecke was in Zastawa, south-east of Białowieża town. The CP at the bison reserve was ordered to secure a rapid withdrawal, they moved into the mayor's offices in Hajnówka. By 11.00pm, the frontline units along all sectors were placed under the command of *Pionier-Bataillon 80*.

The fighting continued throughout the night and at 1.00 am on 17 July JSKB received new orders:

> Hold positions for as long as possible. If the enemy pressure is too strong, *Pionier-Bataillon 80* will withdraw to Hajnówka. The JSKB will secure the withdrawal along either side of the road. JSKB is placed under the command of *Pionier-Bataillon 654*.[24]

Later in the day, the 4th Panzer Division entered the command chaos by issuing orders about recognising German night fighters.[25] *Luftflotte 6* was supposed to be carrying out night operations and remarkably the divisional order warned of recognising the sound of their aircraft guns. In addition, a green flare signal would be fired just before they arrived. The instructions were intended to prevent friendly fire incidents.[26] There was no sign of any aerial support from the Luftwaffe during this period. At 5.30 am the Red Army

---

24 Pionier-Bataillon 654, had a staff, three companies and transport column, was assigned to Ninth Army in 1944 at the time of Bagration. The Pionier-Bataillon 80, an Austrian formation, had served with the 44th Infantry Division Hoch- und Deutschmeister in 1943. This engineer battalion included a bridging column.
25 Robert Michulec, *4. Panzer-Division on the Eastern Front (2) 1944*, (Hong Kong, 2000). There are very few studies of this division although it played an important part in stabilising the German line after Bagration.
26 BArch, RL 31/5, document 55, Kernzeichen eigener Nachtjäger, Unknown Oberleutnant, 17 July 1944.

launched an attack toward Białowieża town. The diary recorded the presence of a Hungarian formation nearby and complained they had prematurely abandoned their positions undermining the defence. There was no explanation about the Hungarians, but they were probably elements of a cavalry regiment. After serious fighting, the Red Army occupied the Tsar's former palace. The Russians then attempted to cross the bridge over the Narewka River south of the town, under the protection of mortars positioned on the palace terrace. Suddenly at 6.30 am two Panther tanks of the *Waffen-SS* drove into Białowieża town, briefly halted, and then began rolling up the Red Army's penetration. For a brief time, the JSKB had support from tanks and used the moment to capture Soviet anti-tank guns and remove them. The tanks then moved off southwards, covering the left flank of the *5th SS-Panzer Regiment*.

The 5th SS Panzer Division *Wiking* was reforming and refitting, in Poland, after a winter of hard fighting.[27] On 14 July the division was assigned to the Second Army under Army Group Centre reserve and was ordered to take up positions concentrated in the Kamieniec-Litewski area. Nearly six hundred vehicles passed through Bielsk on their way toward Bialystok. The lead elements of the 5th SS-Panzer Regiment formed CPs in the Białowieża Forest area while the combat formations concentrated around Hajnówka. Their initial mission was briefly interrupted to blunt Red Army penetrations inside the forest. Then on 16 July seven divisional trains arrived and unloaded in Hajnówka. Second Army had ordered the division to form OPs in the Hajnówka area and despatch only armoured reconnaissance detachment towards Kamieniec-Litewski. The SS division's commanding officer disagreed. He formed his forces into *Kampfgruppen* (combat groups), and disobeying the orders, set out on a drive for Kamieniec-Litewski. The two *Panthers* that briefly stemmed the spearheads of the Red Army's 65th Army were part of the move south. They descended on Białowieża town providing local support, but their actual mission

---

27 Peter Strassner, trans. David Johnston, *European Volunteers*, (Winnipeg, 1988), pp. 165–171.

was probably securing the division's flank as it moved south.²⁸ By the end of the day, in the southern area of the forest, *SS-Wiking's* tanks were still concentrating along the Kamieniec-Litewski line and Topiło.²⁹ It remains unclear what this divisional commander was trying to achieve, but indicates panzer divisions could act independently in the field.

At 9.00 am on 17 July, an urgent order was received from *Stab Stephan*: 'All troops retreat to Hajnówka. Roads and bridges will be blown-up or closed down.' The JSKB's line of retreat through the forest was to be protected by Lieutenant Schröter's and Second Lieutenant Meinecke's platoons. The JSKB was fractured into small groups as sporadic firefights broke out with Red Army tanks and infantry. Severe fighting continued into the afternoon. The situation rapidly deteriorated although from 5.00 pm stragglers began to find their way to Hajnówka. Some men continued to pass through Soviet lines along the forest's western borders during that evening. The diary scribe was down beat as he wrote of casualties who could not be identified and that the better part of the battalion was missing. An official record identified five casualties; two killed and two missing but appeared later.³⁰ That evening, the Hajnówka command was dismantled, and the staff turned into platoon replacements. Then *Stab Stephan* disappeared. The remnants of JSKB under Rühm were reassigned to *Grenadier-Regiment 1071*.³¹ They were tasked with securing the Hajnówka railway junction for maximum readiness. Before they could settle into their positions a heavy Soviet artillery bombardment saturated Hajnówka railway station and surrounding marshalling yards.

---

28 Ewald Klapdor, *Viking Panzers: The German 5th SS Tank Regiment in the East in World War II*, (Mechanicsburg, 2011), pp. 297–321.
29 Hinze, *Das Ostfront-Drama 1944*, p. 322.
30 DDst, JSKB, Namentliche Verlustmeldung, Lw.Ers.Btl. I, Powunden, Nr. 1 28 June 1943//Nr. 18, 25 August 1944. The two dead corporals were both shot in the head: one was a 34-year-old and the other 24 years old.
31 Grenadier-Regiment 1071, formed on 1 July 1944 in the General-Government through 154th Reserve-Division. It was disbanded 5 August 1944, the remnants absorbed into 4th Panzer-Division.

At 4.15 am on 18 July, another heavy Red Army artillery bombardment, believed to be *Stalin-organ* (rockets) straddled the JSKB's positions.³² The Soviets had surrounded Hajnówka. The Germans could not hold the junction as counterattacks failed under the shelling. *Grenadier-Regiment 1071* ordered a general breakout and the JSKB to withdraw along the road to Bielsk. The scattered elements of the JSKB searched to break out of encirclement or to retreat. By this stage, the *Luftwaffe* troopers had stubbornly refused to be overwhelmed by the Soviets. Tanks, from 4th Panzer Division, offered support as the troopers made good an escape with few losses. At about 8.30 am the fighting lost its intensity as the tanks relieved the pressure and forced the Soviets back into Hajnówka. The JSKB raised a CP a kilometre north of Dolna. The radio station guard from Bialy-Lasek reported having fought their way through to join them. The diary explained, 'after four days and several fights we managed to arrive in Bielsk.' Elsewhere the tanks of *SS-Wiking* became involved in serious fighting in the Topiło area on 18 July. Those JSKB troops in the southern area of the forest around Topiło or Kamieniec-Litewski were caught up in the heavy fighting and disappeared from the record. The German command had again misread the situation assuming their troops had rallied, and the Soviets were spent. Another illusion just as Bialystok was captured.³³

On 19 July the Red Army shifted their attacks towards the 35th and 7th Infantry divisions, and both divisions were in danger of being rolled up or dispersed. The *SS-Wiking's Sturmgeschütz* (assault gun) battalion repulsed an attack, but the German's fighting power was waning.³⁴ The JSKB diary noted that on 19 July, the regimental train was in Zoncz but had moved to Syty to avoid heavy enemy artillery fire. Rühm's CP arrived in Zoncz at 9.00 pm but heavy artillery fire forced them to move on seeking protection from tanks. The retreat westwards continued until they reached the

---

32 DDst, JSKB, Namentliche Verlustmeldung, Lw.Ers.Btl. I, Powunden, Nr. 1 28 June 1943//Nr. 18, 25 August 1944. Two men were killed: Corporal Karl D** was 24 years old and from Berlin and Jäger Theo S** a 26-year-old from Stettin.
33 Noble, *The Darkest Hour*, p. 75.
34 Hinze, *Das Ostfront-Drama 1944*, p. 323.

Orlanka River (a tributary of the Narew River) at 10.00 pm. The battalion tried to form a fighting line, but its front was five kilometres wide and there were insufficient troops to hold the line. The JSKB's scribe noted sombrely that the remnants were no longer sufficiently equipped to fight as infantry. Fortunately, there was no further enemy pressure during that night. A combat report by Lw.Sergeant Major König explained that at 10.00 pm the fighting remnants under Rühm were ordered by *Grenadier-Regiment 1071* to take up positions along the Orlanka River. The diary scribes tried to compare the positions near a bridge and alongside a riverbank being like the former strongpoints in *Urwald Bialowies* that often extended across a 3.5-kilometre front.[35] The comparison had some bearing but has been lost in time, however, it was a reflection of men were under extreme pressure.

History remembers 20 July 1944 for the bomb plot against Hitler. Henning von Tresckow, chief of staff of Second Army, was one of the central conspirators. His day began with hope but for the rest of the troops in his army, it was beset by disaster. At 4.00 am the JSKB secured a bridge across the Orlanka River on the Hajnówka-Bielsk road and moved into positions inside an unnamed village. A temporary combined 35th Panzer Regiment/JSKB CP was established. The situation was dire, a medical orderly could only provide first aid, and the signals section led by an NCO and eleven ORs, had only three serviceable radios.[36] The Colonel commanding 35th Panzer Regiment 'press-ganged' the signals section and confiscated their equipment. This rendered the JSKB without signals communications. Lw.Sergeant major König gave a more detailed report of what happened on 20 July. In the morning the command took over an area of 1,800 meters of *Hauptkampflinie* (main fighting line), running along the southern edge of a village, and parallel with the banks of the Orlanka River. The men dug shallow trenches, but it

---

35   BArch, RL 31/5, document 60, Fhj.-Ofw König.
36   BArch, RL 31/5, document 53, Grenadier Regiment 1071, 20 July 1944. This was a confused memo from Grenadier Regiment 1071 which seemed out of sequence with events recording the positions of medical aid stations. It also stated that artillery observations were cautioned to correct their ranges as many sightings were inaccurate. It had no bearing on actual events.

was slow progress because there were few entrenching tools. A CP was set up at the southern exit of the village. Messengers on horseback maintained contact with neighbouring units. König noted the day was slow, with no Red Army attacks.

The diary entries were short on detail on 21 July. The entire support train had moved to Dorniewce. It claimed the effectiveness of the troops was much reduced because the train had divided into three parts. In effect, the troops had supplies of weapons, ammunition or clothing. König once again filled the gaps. Hostile Red Army movements were detected in the early morning hours (mostly cavalry and motor vehicles). They were Soviet scouts and probes targeting the JSKB for artillery interdiction. The JSKB hastily improved its trenches, which was prescient because just after lunch, their positions were straddled with indirect heavy artillery fire, direct anti-tank fire, tanks, and mortars, machine guns and even snipers. After receiving all that firepower, the troops suffered only one casualty (unnamed). The Red Army lobbed smoke shells from mortars on their positions and exploited by a river assault. The Soviets stormed into the rye field before the German positions but received concentrated machine-gun and rifle fire. The Red Army swept into the German line at several points during the night. There was vicious hand-to-hand fighting as the Germans struggled to fend off successive assaults. The Russians were repulsed having failed to break the main fighting line, but the JSKB suffered three more casualties. By this Henning von Tresckow's Second Army headquarters, in Krolowy Most, fifty miles away from the JSKB. The hopes of the conspirators also ended in failure that day. Tresckow drove to the forest in Krolowy Most, primed a grenade, and committed suicide. He had intended to cloak his death as just another combat casualty to prevent his family from facing *Sippenhaft* (family liability punishment).[37] The calamity of Göring's fantasies of the forest bulwark had contributed to a 175-kilometre breach of the German defences in just eight days.

---

37 Robert Loeffel. *Family Punishment in Nazi Germany: Sippenhaft, Terror and Myth*, (Basingstoke, 2012), see also Joachim Fest, *Plotting Hitler's Death: The German Resistance to Hitler, 1933–1945*, (London, 1997), pp. 289–290.

On 22 July, the diary was again short on details. It recorded the day began quietly in the morning, but a sudden firefight erupted and Rühm was killed by grenade shrapnel. König took over command as the Red Army pressed once again. Concentrated Soviet heavy weapons' fire continued to rain down on the JSKB's positions and its CP. There were many breakthroughs and even messengers were forced to fight in hand-to-hand combat. The JSKB machine-guns gradually stopped firing. Four received direct hits and were destroyed, and two others were jammed by sand that clogged the firing mechanism. König explained, 'the 08/15 machine-guns are too sensitive and not suitable for trench warfare. It is very difficult to feed the drum with munitions.' Russian soldiers persisted in their attempts to enter the rye field but were kept at bay by sustained German machine-gun and rifle fire. Red Army tanks took up positions in a small copse in front of the German positions and fired directly at their machine-gun positions and the village. The Russian anti-tank guns, captured at the Tsar's palace, continued to help hold off the Red Army's tanks until the ammunition was exhausted, at which point the JSKB was forced to withdraw. According to König, during the melee Russian tanks killed Rühm and a machine-gun team.[38] The left-wing of his command was severely weakened by heavy losses and König requested reinforcements from Second Army. He was only told to hold his position to the last man. Seven tanks attacked the JSKB's positions at 7.00 am, three were destroyed, and the others withdrew. König rounded up some stragglers and led them back to the trench lines. He conducted the classic German counterattack: leading his men out of their trenches prior to a Russian attack, counterattacked and returned to the trenches. This forced the Russians to redirect their attack toward the village and against the CP. They were thrown back in close-quarter fighting and by machine gun fire. König's command was

---

38   DDST, JSKB, Namentliche Verlustmeldung, Lw.Ers.Btl. I, Powunden, Nr. 1 28 June 1943//Nr. 18, 25 August 1944. The records show for 22 July: Rühm was killed by a shell splinter; Corporal Paul W** a 25-year-old from Flechum in Lower Saxony, was shot in the head, and Corporal Karl H** a 21-year-old from Alsfeld in Hesse, was killed without details. They were killed along the Ogrodnika road.

reduced to twenty-nine men (with two 08/15 machine guns) and ordered to hold their position until relieved by a reserve company (army) under Lieutenant Asche. The army company arrived and König offered advice before handing over his positions and retreating towards Rominten.

The war diary finally recorded good news on 23 July: 'Our soldiers were relieved, directed towards the regimental CP and placed in reserve.' At 1.00 pm, the 4th Panzer Division ordered the JSKB to pull out of the line and immediately march towards Rominten, leaving behind their signallers and radios. A motorised convoy awaited them in Schötterburg and a horse-drawn column in Ostrow. At 4.00 pm, *Column Stephan* (altered in the original without explanation) set off and travelled until 10.00 pm when they rested for the night. The next day the column set out at 7.00am arriving three kilometres west of Wisokie without incidents. On 25 July, the march resumed to Lomscha where five trucks from Rominten awaited the enlisted personnel and their equipment. Second Lieutenant Schröter took command of the vehicles and the convoys. They arrived in Rominten at 9.00 pm but there were no orders awaiting them. The detachment ordered from Białowieża to Rominten under Frevert was already employed in personal escort duties for Göring, and they welcomed the column. Meanwhile, the horse-drawn convoy continued its march collecting more stragglers along the way and arrived in Rominten the next day. On 29 July, the troops set about repairing their weapons, equipment and clothing. Traditional German military efficiency had helped save the remnants of the JSKB, and the ORs, under strong leadership, had resorted to hard soldiering.

III. *Rückkampf*: memories of a retreat

Rudolf Hinze claimed Białowieża was not blockaded, with few defensive preparations. In his opinion, if the Germans had taken the fight into the forest, their defensive actions would have slowed the Russians. He believed the Germans would have been denied mobility but at the advantage of the barrier of impassable swamps and dense forestry. The illusion that the forest was impassable has remained constant since 1945.[39] Within days of arriving in Rominten, the scribes began compiling a record of the retreat to close the diary. The after-action reports and the quickfire diary entries were padded with officer reports. Recollections of the retreat by the supply trains were written up almost as soon as the JSKB's officers reached the sanctuary of Rominten. Reading the day-to-day combat reports and the diary highlights the confusion of the battle but also the soldiers' collective recollections. The reports are a window on the German soldiers' determination to escape the Soviets, as well as focusing upon their expertise. The significance of the retreat might be lost in battle details, but became the start point of modern Germany's memory of the war. This was a traumatic period, and these accounts reinforced a perception of the Germans as victims.

On 3 August, Second Lieutenant Meinecke compiled a *Gefechtsbericht* (after-action combat report). He detailed how *Company Meinecke* had started with an overall fighting strength of seventy men. Together with two reconnaissance groups from Białowieża, they had marched into the Chwoinik area on 15 July. Their mission was to report on Red Army spearheads believed to be driving towards Białowieża town. Initially, they came into contact with a Hungarian cavalry reconnaissance squad, but there was no sign of the Russians. Meinecke received orders via his radio to retreat to the bison compound by way of Białowieża, then being secured by Hungarian troops and German engineers. They were forced to traverse minefields and abates (trees felled as obstacles) and reached the bison compound at noon. At 5.00 pm they received another radio message that the Hungarian soldiers had abandoned their positions due to enemy pressure and had withdrawn to a second trench line. The lead units of the Red Army were just entering the northeast sector of Białowieża town. *Company Meinecke* set out toward prepared positions to the western side of the town. Meinecke recalled hearing machine-gun and rifle fire during that night.

---

39 Hinze, *Das Ostfront-Drama 1944*, p. 314.

Meinecke blamed the Hungarians for abandoning 'good' positions and undermining the defence. On 17 July at 5.30 am, after a brief firefight with the Red Army, the Hungarians once again abandoned Białowieża without a fight. Meinecke could not prevent them from fleeing and claimed he let them go and was prepared to take on the Red Army alone. Then the Hungarians then rallied and formed a line behind Meinecke's company. Several German patrols cautiously pushed their way forward towards Białowieża-Zastawa to see whether the Russians were following the Hungarians. They weren't but suddenly the Germans came under heavy anti-tank and mortar fire. By chance three *Panther* tanks, not two mentioned in the diary, from SS-*Wiking*, arrived and began driving toward Kaminiec-Litewski via the Białowieża-Pruzhany road. Captain Dr Wanser (JSKB medical officer) and Meinecke rode with the tanks to the bridge over the Narewka River in the town. Supported by mortars the tanks attacked the enemy positions. The tanks continued on towards Königsbrück. *Company Meinecke* took possession of a number of discarded Soviet anti-tank guns in the palace grounds and press-ganged an unknown Hungarian anti-tank gun unit. The company then inched forward to positions enabling them to open fire on the advancing Russians. A fierce firefight erupted with machine-gun and rifle fire. The Tsar's palace was still intact, but the fighting led to artillery rounds landing within the vicinity. There is no evidence that the Germans torched the palace as was later alleged.

An engineer platoon arrived with orders to block the Białowieża-Hajnówka road with mines and cut down trees. The Hungarians and Meinecke's company covered the engineers as they worked. Once the task was completed, all troops withdrew towards Hajnówka. The fighting steadily increased as Red Army cavalry and infantry closed in on the bison compound. Company Schröter had joined the fighting by the Narewka River (it is not known where they came from). The Hungarians were again blamed for causing confusion, this time it was their khaki tunics clashing with the Red Army's uniforms. The Hungarians ran, triggering false alarms, and cases of friendly fire. The Germans in the bison compound took lunch, but a serious firefight broke out as Red Army snipers in the trees and hedges preceded the arrival of Soviet cavalry. The Russians continued to press towards Hajnówka. The Soviet anti-tank artillery joined in, which finally routed the Hungarians. The 'Meinecke' and 'Schröter' companies were forced to adopt a fighting withdrawal retaining cohesion while covering both sides of the road toward Hajnówka.

Seven Soviet tanks suddenly burst onto the scene firing all their 'tubes' (main guns) and inflicted heavy losses on the routed Hungarians. Armoured infantry guns accompanied the assaulting tanks and together they advanced in a southerly direction forcing the German companies to divide. Meinecke led fifty men and Lieutenant Schröter across the road to the south taking cover while six Soviet tanks passed by. As the tanks rolled onwards in a southerly direction, a seventh Russian tank appeared with accompanying infantry threatening to outflank them. Meinecke again ordered a fighting retreat through the forest. Sergeant Armann with twenty men became separated from Meinicke and Schröter. He was quickly reduced to a section of fewer than ten men but led their escape in a westerly direction through Topiło.

Schröter and Meinecke led twenty-six men in a southwest direction through the marshes avoiding all contact with the Russians. The heavy rainfalls rendered the marsh area impassable to tanks, which perhaps enabled their escape. They eventually fled from the forest in the area between Loszice and Oreskowo under the cover of darkness. They arrived in Witstock at 1.00 am on 18 July after crossing the Hajnówka-Ceremcha railway embankment, which had been mined. The civilian population had fled. Meinecke recalled they were all completely soaked with wet sore feet. All was quiet as they set out from Witstock at 4.00 am. By that time the men were completely exhausted, and the majority no longer had serviceable boots. They reached the Hajnówka-Bielsk road at noon when they joined *Kampfgruppe Rühm*.[40] Meinecke concluded, 'The radio station was blown up because we could not transport it.'[41]

---

40 This was the first mention of Kampfgruppe Rühm, which was not officially endorsed.

41 BArch, RL 31/5, document 61, Gefechtsbericht, Leutnant Meinicke, 3 August 1944.

On 3 August, *Oberzahlmeister* (paymaster) Meier submitted his after-action report. He recalled the events of the JSKB baggage train in its retreat from Białowieża to Rominten. At 4.00 am on 15 July, a movement order had been received for the horse-drawn baggage train, the *Luftwaffe* signals platoon and the motor vehicle squadron, to travel to the *Luftwaffe* airbase at Bielsk. Sergeant Wiskandt commanded the motor squadron and Staff Sergeant Andrejak commanded the baggage train. The movement plan called for the convoy to arrive in Bielsk by 4.00 pm on 16 July 'following a long lunch break'. The strength of the convoys included the motor squadron with fifteen vehicles and thirty-five ORs. The *Luftwaffe* Signals platoon and the horse-drawn trucks had about forty-five motor vehicles with fifty-five NCOs and ORs. The baggage train had two NCOs and eighteen staff ORs under Meier. Connections between the different parts of the train were maintained through radio transmissions under the codename 'Mosel'. Even though it was summer, the weather was blizzards and strong rainfall.

On 16 July the baggage trains rested in Bielsk. At noon Meier borrowed a motorbike and rode to the bison compound. He took command of a baggage train with another forty motor vehicles, two NCOs and thirty-eight ORs. The JSKB CP then moved to Hajnówka. Meier set off from the bison compound at 7.00 pm toward Nowo-Berisowo. Enemy tanks managed to destroy two cars, killing six civilian drivers, and two *Hiwis*. The train finally arrived in Nowo-Berisowo at 3.00 am. Another BMW motorbike joined the train ridden by Corporal Struck but broke down along the route. On 17 July all telephone connections with the JSKB's CP abruptly stopped. The motorbike was repaired, and Meier rode back to Hajnówka. He received an order to transport the entire stock of ammunition and rations with the motor vehicles to Hajnówka at 3.00 pm and to send the rest of the train from Nowo-Beresowo to Bielsk. The vehicles with the ammunition and ration sacks moved out from the larger convoy and at 5.00pm set off for Hajnówka. Meier observed strong artillery explosions landing in and around Hajnówka. He also observed the troops fleeing from the town. He decided to halt, and this led the convoy across a field road about three kilometres north of the artificial Hajnówka-Bielsk road via Ogroniki (sic) to Bielsk. They briefly considered using the motorised vehicles to transport ammunition and rations to the retreating command but decided against it. They arrived in Bielsk at 9.30 pm (still dragging the useless motorbike behind a horse cart). The base commander explained that Wiskandt and Andrejak had already departed toward Ostrow-Maz. At 10.00 pm Meier was ordered to leave because the airbase was about to be destroyed. His convoy arrived in Grabowiec at 2.00 am and still had no contact with General Stephan's staff or JSKB's CP.

In the early hours of 18 July, Corporal Korsch the guard commander woke Meier and reported that passing troops had told him the Soviets had broken through as far west as Bielsk (apparently this was treated as enemy propaganda). The convoy set off again at 6.00 am toward Bransk. They arrived in Rudka at 11.00 am and took a long break until 4.00 pm before setting out again. Once in Bransk Meier met up with Andrejak's train and all vehicles were reorganised into a single convoy. Meier then drove with Wiskandt in a field car to Bielsk (after ordering the entire train to wait until he returned) in order to scout the general situation and locate the JSKB CP. Meier located General Stephan and General Merker, but neither could provide information about the whereabouts of the JSKB. Meier called Major Harder, the commander of *Flughafenbereich 10/XI* (Bialystok) and received orders to march his train to Ostrow-Maz. Once there he was to report to Major Harder again and await further orders. Meier caught up with his column and in Bransk were joined by Sergeant Schild, Sergeant Armann and many other stragglers. By that stage, the train had grown to 140 vehicles including fifteen motor vehicles, with 170 NCOs/ORs. Meier then led the train to Ciechanowiec and gave Staff Sergeant Wiskandt the order to drive the motor vehicles, (without the communication vehicle) to Ostrow-Maz and to await fresh orders.

On 19 July Meier's column departed towards Ciechanowiec at 6.00 am via Nur-Malkinia and Kaikowo where they spent the night. On 21 July Meier's column joined with 'troop Fichtel' and more stragglers including Meinicke and Schröter. However, they lost fifteen vehicles, twenty horses, thirty *Hiwis* and twelve civilian horse cart drivers. Stragglers and refugees replaced the drivers of the horse carts. Damaged vehicles were cannibalised and discarded. The missing horses had either been stolen in the night or pushed into other columns on the road by civilian drivers and *Hiwis* who were keen to flee Meier's column. With Fichtel, Meinicke and Schröter the train was 150 vehicles, with 170 NCOs/ORs. The column rested for two days in Podberce giving time to replace the horseshoes, repair vehicles, and await orders. Meinecke departed for Rominten and Meier drove with a vehicle from *Luftwaffe Signals Regiment 563* to Warsaw to make contact with Staff Sergeant Wiskandt and purchase rations. On 25 July the convoy set out for Boguscyce.

Meier's caravan convoy moved towards Lomscha at 7.00 am on 26 July and it arrived at 11.30 am. After lunch, they transferred ammunition and weapons to motor vehicles from Rominten and then spent the night in Lomscha. The next day they rode to Szczyczyn and the day after drove to Obrittki, between Grajewo and Postken. On 29 July Meier's convoy finally crossed into East Prussia and bizarrely went through the process of customs regulations with border officials. The columns defensive machine guns were dismounted under the army regulations of not openly bearing arms in the homeland. After a final customs check, the train moved on toward Seefrieden, in the district Lyck. On 31 July the convoy departed at 7.00 am towards Wiedmannsdorf in the district of Goldap. Finally, on 1 August, they arrived in Hardteck where Meier delivered 127 vehicles, 185 horses (with two foals) and a unit muster roll of 2 officers, 14 NCOs, 92 ORs and 48 *Hiwis*.

Oberzahlmeister Meier's report appear strange in comparison with the fighting reports. On first impression, they do not appear related. However, Meier and Meinicke were the two sides of the same coin of traditional military efficiency. In Meier's case it was in his function as *Oberzahlmeister* or paymaster. He did not just end his report with their safe arrival. His general observations explained how the march was conducted. The convoy was confined to night movements because of Soviet pressure. The convoy averaged thirty-five kilometres per day. There had only been quarters in Ciechaniwiec and they had slept in tents in forests or under vehicles. The troops received rations up to the time they reached Lomscha, cooking their food on open fires. After Lomscha the field kitchens supplied the men. They had found it particularly hard to plunder potatoes at that time of the year, so rations were thin. Bookkeeping was particularly challenging to maintain because it was difficult to identify soldiers, horses and vehicles. The continuing arrival of stragglers compounded his bookkeeping problems. There were no light vehicles available to enable him to impose proper control over the convoy. The behaviour of the troops on the march was very poor. The NCOs were too weak in bringing order to the columns. The exhausted soldiers kept sleeping and could only be woken up 'violently'. The troops failed to attend to the horses properly; although the soldiers did maintain their respect towards Polish and German populations, and nothing was stolen or plundered. Meier congratulated five NCOs Mundt, Petritzki, Haselroither, Hellmich and Wolters for keeping their troops together and attending to their horses.[42] The JSKB began to reform. At 6.30am on 1 August, they occupied fifteen emplacements in Rominten each with one NCO and two privates. The next day a *Jägerzug* (light infantry platoon) was raised to take over the cavalry section for the escort regiment *Hermann Göring*. Lieutenant Meinecke commanded the *Jägerzug* with a fighting strength of an officer, twenty NCOs and 110 ORs. The JSKB finally returned sixty-nine horses, fifty-three carts, and sixty-six *Hiwis* passed to OKW authorities for duties elsewhere. At 2.00 pm on 1 August, the horse-drawn convoys and Otto Schröter's unit finally arrived in Rominten and took up quarters near Schelrow.

---

[42] BArch, RL 31/5, documents 62–65, Bericht über den Verlauf der Ereignisse beim Trose des Jägersonderkommando d.Lw. Bialowies für die Zeit vom 15.7.–1.8.44, Oberzahlmeister Meier, 3 August 1944.

July marked the end of German control of the forest. Frevert's total results was 114 partisans killed, twenty *Bandenhelfer* and 153 others arrested, and 227 civilians killed, a hundred arrests, and ten Jews killed. Total German casualties of 42 dead and 16 wounded. This closed the record of the JSKB's operations in *Urwald Bialowies* but left many questions unanswered. For example, Meinecke's report claimed to have started with 70 men. Schröter's 'company' also joined the group but during their final retreat, they were down to 26 men and another 10 with Sergeant Armann. Meinecke was lax in his accounting, whereas Meier provided a detailed account. One convoy arrived with 2 officers, 14 NCOs and 92 ORs. The *Jägerzug* was raised with 20 NCOs and 110 ORs suggests, but the numbers of fighting men remained vague. The final order of battle had accounted: 7 officers and 615 NCOs/ORs and 204 *Hiwis*. Frevert was ordered out with 7 officers, 22 NCOs and 161 ORs. While losing 140 *Hiwis* was plausible through desertion, death and missing, the unaccountable loss of upwards 300-400 men seems more than careless.

Image 20: Sites of memory — Soviet military cemetery located within Hajnówka town. Engraving reads: Hero of the Soviet Union, Guards Junior Lieutenant Aleksii Vasilevich Florenko. Born 6 February 1922. He died in the fight to liberate Hajnówka region 25 July 1944.

Source: Author, 2009, translation Dr. Nicholas Terry 2021.

Conclusion:
Memories of a Never Happened History

On 30 July 1962, Walter Frevert was killed in a hunting accident. At the time he was the state forest superintendent of Kaltenbronn in Gernsbach, Baden-Württemberg (West Germany). He was three months shy of his sixtieth birthday. Frevert's passing went largely unnoticed in the rest of the world, but in Germany, the story was headline news. He was found in a forest lying on his back with his hunting bitch *Blanka* still guarding his body. The entry point of the bullet wound was unusual. The bullet's upward trajectory entered through his left thigh passing through his torso causing traumatic internal injuries and almost certainly his immediate death. His dog's leash was wrapped around his right hand and his rifle lay to the left. The criminal police were brought in to investigate but a post-mortem ruled that it was an accident. Almost immediately rumours circulated within forestry and hunting circles about his death. There had been speculation over his wellbeing before the incident, and doubts were cast about his capacity to carry on his duties. Rumours circulated that dark memories of his Nazi past were haunting him. Given the strange manner of his death, some civil servants pondered whether he'd committed suicide.[1] Suicide had been a phenomenon among the Nazis in 1945 when the regime finally collapsed, but in 1962 there was little evidence of that old fervour.[2]

'Nazism did not die in the ruins of Berlin in 1945 nor on the gallows of Nuremberg in 1946, it merely buried its uniform, slipped into mufti, and sauntered into the postwar world', as Jonathan Meades jovially announced in the opening of a television documentary. He might well have been describing Frevert.[3] The immediate postwar environment was difficult for former prominent Nazis like Frevert to pursue their civil service careers. After his release from a

---

1 Gautschi, *Frevert*, p. 152.
2 Christian Goeschal, *Suicide in Nazi Germany*, (Oxford, 2009).
3 Jonathan Meades, 'Jerry Building', BBC, 1994.

Canadian PoW camp in July 1945, he struggled for two years. In October 1947 he became director of Murgtal forestry district in the Black Forest. Former Lw.General Hellmuth Bieneck, at one time commanding officer of *Luftgau 1*, granted Frevert a favourable reference or less reverently called a *Persilschein* (clean status) that washed away his Nazi past. In 1948 Frevert was 'betrayed' and forced to face the denazification process. He was declared a *Mitläufer* (lowest level of Nazi follower), the penalties included travel restrictions, loss of employment, and fines. Unemployed, he again turned to write books about the hunt. Relying upon his hunting expertise and reputation to provide an income from writing. From 1949, West German governments allowed amnesty for former Nazis and war criminals. Norbert Frei has called this Adenauer's 'policy for the past'.[4] Under this policy, Frevert's status as a *Mitläufer* was waived, and he became forest superintendent of Kaltenbronn in 1953.

In the early years of 'policy for the past', many former Nazis mistook amnesty as a general release, and some faced criminal investigation. Several prominent Nazis were indicted in extensive prosecutions that carried on throughout the 1960s. In desperation to mitigate against the prospect of long prison sentences, many turned evidence against former comrades. To those trying to avoid the judicial spotlight, the appearance of turncoats made life uncomfortable. In Frevert's case, Göring was dead but there were still witnesses at large who knew of his crimes in Białowieża. These men include: Fritz Wagner, former chief of *Oberforstamt Bialowies*; Erich von dem Bach-Zelewski, the *SS-Gruppenführer* and chief of SS-Police, responsible for the killing actions in 1941; and, ex-*Gauleiter* of East Prussia and Bezirk Bialystok Erich Koch, a major beneficiary of *Urwald Bialowies*. The Soviets sentenced Wagner to twenty-five years of hard labour in January 1947 for his crimes in Białowieża. Bach-Zelewski was a turncoat at Nuremberg and granted immunity from prosecution by the US Army in 1947. His life in West Germany was dull and he began making provocative remarks about

---

4   Norbert Frei, *Adenauer's Germany and the Nazi Past: The Politics of Amnesty and Integration*, (Cambridge, 2004), p. 1.

giving an SS poison ampule to Göring before his suicide. He was prosecuted and sentenced to a term of imprisonment in 1958. Koch was arrested by the British authorities in 1949 and extradited to Poland. A Polish court sentenced him to life imprisonment. Thus by 1957, it seemed all the men who could cause Frevert problems were no longer a threat.

Irrespective of the prosecutions, former prominent Nazis still hankered for their lost lifestyle, and Frevert was no exception. But like a common criminal, he began delving into his sordid past. He was holding a 'smoking gun' and made careless mistakes. The first was to publish *Rominten* in 1957 drawing unwanted attention with its anecdotes from his Nazi past.[5] Heincke Frevert, his second wife, claimed writing *Rominten* opened old wounds that festered into his final days. She recalled he was racked by memories from that period and removed pictures from old photograph albums.[6] Hard to determine which was the aberrant behaviour, leading to killing actions during the war or his memories in the 1950s. His catalogue of ghastliness included: mass deportations, the killings, , the Jew hunts, driving his wife to suicide and the destruction of Laski. Frevert then followed up his *Rominten* error with a bizarre lapse in political judgement. After strenuously avoiding public associations with prominent Nazis for so long, he granted hunting rights for Franz von Papen, the former vice-chancellor (1933–1934), to hunt in Kaltenbronn in December 1958. The story caused a major political storm, which was compounded by Frevert's absence. He went on a hunting safari in Africa. In his absence, the newspapers accused him of being Göring's *Leibjägermeister* (personal master hunter), which he late strenuously denied. In his final few years, it's believed Simon Wiesenthal, the famous Nazi hunter, visited Frevert in Kaltenbronn, which fuelled speculation, but their discussion was not on public record. Perhaps *Rominten* had backfired but his subsequent behaviour never suggested he was remorseful.

Two years after Frevert's death evidence of his criminal past began to surface. An SS-Police war diary was discovered in Prague

---

5   Frevert, *Rominten*, 1957.
6   Gautschi, *Frevert*, p. 154.

that covered the period June–August 1941, including the destruction of Narewka Mala. In 1971 a Darmstadt prosecutor decided to investigate Frevert and twenty-three others; they were not aware of his death in 1962. From the 1970s the story turned from memory to history as the last survivors passed. Bach-Zelwski died in prison in 1972 while serving a sentence of life imprisonment; and, former Lw.Major Emil Herbst died on 21 December 1974, after successfully avoiding war crimes justice. In 1977 Frevert's publishers invited Heinke Frevert to write a foreword for the twentieth anniversary of *Rominten*. She hoped to preserve her husband's memory, labelling 1977 as a year of anniversaries. Thirty years before Frevert had been released from a Canadian PoW camp. When Erich Koch died in a Polish prison in 1986, he was the last of the prominent Nazis involved in *Urwald Bialowies*.

I. Memories of Rominten

In 1938, a professor of forestry reflected on the hunt: 'No people has received so many decisive cultural impulses from the chase, in both good and bad directions, as has the German people.'[7] The observation was prophetic, within three years senior representatives of the German hunt perpetrated the first wave of Nazi genocide in Białowieża. Between 1848 and 1914, the hunt became an invented pastime of the German middle class. During the Great War, the hunt was radicalised, but under the Nazis, the radicalisation meant re-invention through the lens of the *Volksgemeinschaft*. The old hunt quest for individual professionalism as a signifier of middle-class status was transformed into a social order bound by cult ritualism and sacrificial death. The culmination of the death ritual, the sacrifice of the pedigree stags to Hitler's war and Holocaust was the *Matador* ceremony in September 1943. Those behind that ceremony also devised the Nazi hunt code and were the same men who organised the post-war hunt in West Germany—Ulrich Scherping and Walter Frevert. They did not go quietly into hiding after the war, instead, they pressed with their Nazi inventions but without the physical

---

7   Franz Heske, *German forestry*, (New Haven, 1938), p. 182.

symbolism. Thus, to date the German hunt has not faced *Vergangenheitsbewältigung* the process of coming to terms with its Nazi past.

This is visible from the hunting literature of the postwar decades. Frevert's publications were not politically neutral as at first appeared. Few realised at the time, or subsequently, how Frevert was using bland recollections of 'The Green' as means to preserve past memories. He published *Rominten* (1957), in a style that imitated Nineteenth-Century hunt literature. The overbearing sentimentality was underpinned by the banner of the 'lost lands in the east'. A blatant nostalgia for the *völkisch* lifestyle. In the last weeks of 1944, the Rominten estate remained open to hunters with the lodge hosting up to 8–10 hunting guests daily. The frontlines were closing in on the estate with the sounds of guns booming and shells exploding. There was a surreal atmosphere heightened by Göring's opulent presence as Frevert set out on his last hunt in October 1944. Göring had planned to shoot *Leutnant,* a magnificent royal stag, but was unsuccessful and passed the honour to Frevert. On 9 October, Frevert set out to stalk *Leutnant* with his hound. In 1957, Frevert choreographed the death of *Leutnant* as a Wagnerian tragedy. The narrative was flush with the undisguised *völkisch* ramblings of a Nazi perpetrator. The description of the ceremony redefined his 1936 invention in a 1957 setting. The hunting horns sounded to the cacophony of Red Army shelling and howling bombs. Afterwards, Göring ordered his HG-division to pack his valuables and ship them to Bavaria. Ten years later, the West German hunt hosted an exhibition in Düsseldorf. Presently, the horns of *Leutnant* and *Matador* are on public display in a Munich hunting museum.

Frevert recounted meeting Göring for the first time during the rutting season of 1936. Keudell, the RFA chief, introduced him to Göring as a bloodhound expert and experienced in red deer game management. Göring boasted he didn't need a bloodhound because he never missed his target. Frevert claimed he was warned never to lie to the 'iron man' (as the inner circle referred to Göring), adding the only people who had trouble with Göring were the 'slimy' types who lied or were evasive. He compared working in Rominten as like regal court service, in which Göring's lifestyle was like that of a 'demigod'. Göring was addicted to Rominten and the stags, and it was not always easy to control his bloodlust. During a boar hunt, in the winter of 1936–37, Göring failed to bag a boar because he had ignored Frevert's request to hold his position. In his impatience, he moved which allowed the boar to escape. Disappointed, Göring forced Frevert to walk the ground to show him how he had set up the boar to be killed, and why it was his fault that the boar escaped. The hunting lodges were destroyed on 20 October 1944. Frevert made his way to Holland where he was eventually captured by allied forces.[8] In May 1945 Göring's jailers completed his prison induction card. It was a small red index card that itemised his basic personal details such as assets and home address. Göring listed *Jagdhaus Romintener Heide* as one of his prime residences. Göring's plans for Białowieża had been hatched and dispatched in Rominten but in May 1945 his jailers were blissfully unaware of this and were only interested in charging him as a 'swindler'.[9] These anecdotes of Frevert's relationship with Göring also disguised a darker side of Rominten.

Frevert was married twice. His first wife, Gertrud Habich was the daughter of a pastor. The couple discovered early in the marriage she could not bear children, and Frevert took this badly. In January 1940 Gertrud made a *faux pas* during a hunt and while she was bending over, in front of witnesses, Frevert slapped her posterior three times.[10] Several hunters sniggered while others remained stony-faced, this was an indication of his bullying behaviour. Later he began an affair with Heinke Barckhausen, the widow of Dr Paul Richard Barckhausen, Frevert's friend killed in action near Warsaw on 19 September 1939.[11] Frevert spent his birthday in 1940 with Heinke but the next day learned Gertrud had committed suicide. Her final letter explained she was making way for the lovers.[12] On 6 December 1942 one of Frevert's children was baptised under the

---

8   Frevert, *Rominten*, p. 25.
9   TNA, WO208-3785, Goering, Hermann four arrest cards.
10 Max Egremont, *Forgotten Land: Journeys Among the Ghosts of East Prussia*, (London, 2011), p. 689.
11 Gautschi, *Frevert*, p. 66.
12 Egremont, *Forgotten Land*, pp. 346–7.

CONCLUSION: MEMORIES OF A NEVER HAPPENED HISTORY

antlers of a stag, which angered the pastor of Rominten because of its obvious pagan associations.[13]

Frevert bound *Rominten* to the popular *Heimat* genre that emerged in the 1950s, making a profound political statement about heritage and nation. After 1945, the indigenous German population of East Prussia (including Rominten) was expelled. Later, as refugees in the west, they established an agenda of protest as victims of both Hitler and Stalin, and the war. In the reconstruction of their lives, they encased their memories in the *Heimat*, a word with a greater spiritual meaning than just homeland. The word has a powerful resonance to the unique relationship between people, birthplace, dialect, community, and an affinity with the landscape.[14] In many respects, this conformed to the old *völkisch* notions of Germany. Although a spiritual homeland for the *Heimat* movement, East Prussia also retained a prominent place in German history and culture. Königsberg was immortalised for its cultural achievements and as home to the philosopher Immanuel Kant. The refugees began to rebuild their lives forming communities that founded newspapers, established museums, and raised memorials. A memorial stone to this movement can be found in an abandoned graveyard in Aachen, a granite boulder with the simple inscription *Die Heimat 1945–1947*. The *Heimat* genre had positive connotations, but not all memories were cherished. The genre downplayed the Nazi legacy, which was continually sanitised, and that legacy has remained an indelible stain.

Frevert borrowed heavily from the *Heimat* genre as a platform for his book, but his real purpose was to hail the German hunt under Göring's mastery. It was a confusing autobiographical memorial of fiction and memories. To embellish the Nazi hunt, Frevert invited Scherping to write the foreword. Scherping was by then the director of the West German hunting association, and his reputation as the father of the hunt was untarnished by his Nazi past.

---

13   Gautschi, *Frevert*, p. 65.
14   See Alon Confino, *The Nation as a Local Metaphor: Württemberg, Imperial Germany, and National Memory, 1871–1918*, (Chapel Hill, 1997); also by the same author, *Germany as a Culture of Remembrance: Promises and Limits of Writing History*, (Chapel Hill, 2006).

Scherping described *Rominten* a 'magnificent opus' and a major contribution to the memory of the *Heimat* and its cultural work. He recalled Rominten after the Great War, in need of restoration following the devastating invasion by a Tsarist Army in 1915. He claimed hunters from across the world would recognise Rominten's lost reputation, for red deer and its expertise in-game management. He lamented that Germans were no longer granted access to restore Rominten to its rightful owners. In his opinion, *Rominten* was destined to give an impression of its greatness and its painful loss for Germany. Frevert blamed Britain for the war. He pointed to British intransigence over the Danzig question, the British foreign minister's refusal to accept four royal stags as a bargaining gift and to settle the Polish crisis in Germany's favour. Frevert thought it had been a 'good war' and echoed the old post-1918 nationalist aspirations. The Soviets and Poles accused of harbouring political ambitions over East Prussia, in a rehash of Nazi rhetoric about 'Bolshevik' criminality. *Rominten* was a record of a German nationalist's compromise to Nazism, it wasn't an apology it was a justification.

Frevert's *Rominten* has attracted many writers. In 1970 Michel Tournier explored a vision of Rominten without ever having visited the forest. *Rominten* introduced Tournier to Nazi heraldry and the powerful *völkisch* symbolism that underpinned Nazism. In his celebrated work of fiction, *Le Roi des Aulnes*, Tournier adopted hunting as a metaphor for Nazism.[15] The leading character in *Le Roi des Aulnes* is Abel Tiffauges, a young Frenchman, who follows a twisted path to eventually turn into an ogre. The narrative follows Tiffauges' conscription into the French army in 1939, his capture by the Germans, and eventual arrival in Rominten. Tiffauges senses the spiritual power of the game and its cultural symbolism. He feeds a blind elk, which leads to a meeting with an unnamed *Oberforstmeister* in his sixties, almost certainly Frevert in a 1950s guise. Tiffauges' meeting with Göring informs us of Frevert's relationship with Göring the demigod. *Oberforstmeister* hails Göring as the 'master of animal droppings'. In a scene where Göring was bent over a

---

15 Michel Tournier, trans. Hellmut Waller, *Der Erlkönig*, (Frankfurt a.M., 1989), pp. 201–243; see the original Le Roi des Aulnes, Paris, 1970.

set of discarded antlers, Tiffauges pictured a phallic symbol and came to see hunting as a phallic sacrifice. Familiarity with the archival evidence and the region breaks the impact of Tournier's satire. When Tournier visited the former site of the Rominten estate, in 1975, there was no correlation to the impressions drawn from *Rominten*. Saul Friedländer has criticised Tournier for 'aestheticizing the horror of fascism and inducing pleasure in readers and spectators, awaken nostalgia for the fascist period and invite complicity with fascistic tendencies in contemporary society.'[16] While Friedländer raises an important argument, the findings from the research for this book raise a different warning. This was a 'lesson of history' moment: investing in the Nazi past without first making a verification of the content, can have serious consequences.

By far the strangest case of misusing Frevert's content was Max Egremont's *Forgotten Land* (2011).[17] This account followed the tales of Rominten and Białowieża through a 2008 edition of Frevert's *Rominten*, Gautsch's *Walter Frevert* (2005) and David Irving's *Göring* (1989). Egremont argued that Frevert was a product of 1918 and that *Rominten* was a physical portrait of Frevert's demigod Göring. Egremont tried to explain the impact of the Nazi order on Rominten by writing, 'The revival of order and confidence, the surge in prosperity and the power handed Frevert at Rominten made him reluctant to seek out distant truths.' In the case of *Urwald Bialowies*, he noted Frevert's part in the clearing of villages and the 1941 killings. He claimed that up to summer 1942 over 900 people were killed. In discussing the Nazi terror, he added, 'Wehrmacht commanders warned that such tactics would encourage support for partisans who were fighting the Germans.' This statement runs against the archival evidence and the records of the senior German commanders that endorsed the brutal treatment of partisans and civilians. Frevert's behaviour, his perpetration of killing actions from 1941 to 1944, the destruction of Laski, and his endorsement of the Nönning *Judenjagd* were not the actions of a man radicalised by

---

16 Saul Friedländer, trans. Thomas Weyr, *Reflections on Nazism: An Essay on Kitsch and Death*, (Indiana, 1984).
17 Egremont, *Forgotten Land*.

1918. He was a hardened Nazi who did his masters' bidding. Egremont's narrative incorporated many of Frevert's toxic memories. However, his greater failing was to not verify his sources or at least make a superficial attempt to search the archives or scholarly literature.

Scholarship about Białowieża evolved slowly. Konrad Kwiet contributed a chapter about the Narewka Mala and Białowieża killings in 1941 in an edited work about Nazism.[18] He examined the SS-Police war diary of PB322 and was surprised at its contents. It was located in Prague's Military Archives and contained directives, orders and reports. More importantly, it named perpetrators. Kwiet's approach was to scrutinise the killing procedures, the psychosomatic symptoms displayed by the perpetrators, their obedience to orders, and their relaxation after the killings. He noted that after the war under West German investigations most of the men claimed to have seen nothing or marksmen confessed to having killed only partisans and not Jews. The men excused the killings as acts carried out on behalf of the Greater German Reich, while others enjoyed their time in the forest especially hunting game. Simon Schama's cultural history, *Landscape and Memory*, is his search for the 'ruins of myth and memory'. He perceptibly argued that the Holocaust was increasingly turning into history without a landscape, without features, and was a grey zone of death. Schama has a family legacy to the Lithuanian Jews who worked in the forest.

II. A Białowieża fantasy

After the war, Walter Frevert wrote of a hunt along the Narewka River. This tributary of the Narew River flows through Belarus and eastern Poland via Białowieża. The story opened with Frevert trekking along the riverbank, sinking up to his knees in mud and water. The river meanders through the town and both banks are covered with extensive reed beds. The swamp and marshlands, fed by the

---

18 Konrad Kwiet, 'From the Diary of a Killing Unit', John Milful, *Why Germany? National Socialist Anti-Semitism and the European Context*, (Oxford, 1993), pp. 75–90.

rivers and springs, create large islands. In places, the forest touches close to the riverbank, but there are also open meadows. Frevert always described Białowieźa as an *Urwald* of thick spruce stands and mixed areas of beech, oak, and hornbeam. The abundance of predators, the wolves and lynx, had forced the game to graze on cultivated fields or the open spaces *along* the riverbanks. He observed a roebuck at 500 metres on the opposite riverbank. It was grand, so stunning it took his breath away. This 'old buck' took up a secure position ensuring it would be warned if predators approached. Although plagued by the armies of mosquitoes, endemic to the area, the buck was constantly vigilant. As the daylight faded Frevert attempted to close in on the buck and crossed the river but only to 400 metres, realising any closer would scare the buck away. At that moment, Frevert decided to hunt the buck and would use the river to make his kill. As in so many hunting tales, he pondered whether kill or not kill the buck, but then typically dismissed his thoughts as stupid sentiment. He then quickly sketched a skizzie map to plan the hunt.

The preparations for the hunt began with building a flat raft from six tree trunks. A *Gajowi*, a local Polish gamekeeper,[19] assisted him. The raft included a small trellis fence, camouflaged with reeds, and a three-metre-long ladder, which he intended to use as a shooting highstand. The *Gajowi* would propel the raft with a long pole punting through the reed banks. Stormy weather delayed the adventure for a few days, but eventually, they set out at 4.00 pm on the day of the hunt. Along the way, Frevert climbed the ladder to orientate himself. The weak trellis collapsed and Frevert was pitched into the river. He held onto his rifle, but the muzzle was full of mud, and the breech filled with water. They were a kilometre away from the planned position, and the *Gajowi* turned the raft around so the broken trellis was at the rear, and they carried on. The raft reached a point 120 metres from the last position when he

---

19 Ašarūnas Liekis, 1939: *The Year That Changed Everything in Lithuania's History*, (Amsterdam, 2010), pp. 82–83; see also Norman Davies, *Europe: A History*, (London, 1996), p. 904. The German-Polish relationship was conflicted between Nazi race dogma and the practicalities of occupation. Whether this person was a 'collaborator' is impossible to verify.

observed the buck. They rested, had a cigarette, and Frevert recalled a similar hunt in East Prussia—spending two hours lying in wait in a stream for the game while covered in mud.

Frevert again climbed the ladder to observe the buck, which was visible only by its antlers and ears above the reeds. He crouched on his ladder. The buck and its smaller companion moved into an open space. As Frevert unslung his rifle, he was concerned his bullets might be wet. He rested the rifle on the ladder, took aim, fired, and the bullet struck the buck in the left front leg. The *Gajowi* began gesticulating and rocked the raft. Frevert swore because he was without his dog and did not want to lose his kill. Frevert pointed in a direction and the *Gajowi* pushed off. They followed a blood trail and drag marks, the sign of a broken leg; then located the dead buck 80 metres further on. An examination of the carcass found the meat weighed 24 kilos, the teeth of an 8–10-year-old, and the antlers weighed more than half a kilo. Frevert didn't mention *Totenwacht* (guard the dead) ceremony but claimed the Russians had captured the antlers in Rominten in 1944.[20] The importance of this hunt illustrates Frevert's expertise, determination and thought process. The date of Frevert's hunt remains to be determined except for a vague reference to early June, which would have been 1943. It is difficult to comprehend why this tale was recalled as important. Frevert's entire life as a forester, hunter and war criminal, is encapsulated in that torrid tale.[21]

III. The lost Jewish Past

In Białowieża today, there is a memorial stone with a tourist information placard with an English translation; it reads:

> The erratic block [glacial boulder] in front of the Orthodox Church commemorates historic events. In the beginning of the 20th Century a monument to Aleksander II was funded [sic] in that place. In the interwar period, the

---

20 Frevert, *Meine Jagd Leben*, (2013).
21 Walter Frevert, *Jagdliches Brauchtum*, (Berlin, 1936). Scherping wrote the foreword in his opaque style, 'The German people are grateful to the Führer for restoring and awakening old and beautiful customs.' Hitler was a vegetarian who despised the hunt.

CONCLUSION: MEMORIES OF A NEVER HAPPENED HISTORY

> monument was replaced with a granite rock and a plaque with an effigy of Marshal J. Pilsudski. The plaque was destroyed during the Russian occupation in the Second World War. The next plaque with an inscription honours local inhabitants that had been murdered in this place. In 1942–1943, during the German occupation over 90 people were hanged in mass executions on the trees in front of the Orthodox Church. The erratic block is also an inanimate natural feature of historic importance about 150,000 years old [sic].[22]

Attached to the 'erratic block' is a metal commemorative plaque that states: 'Heroes Fighting for Freedom and Socialism'. This old memorial, like so many across Eastern Europe, retains the Soviet subtext that has survived the Cold War. On either side of the 'erratic block' are two smaller concrete blocks each with a metal plaque bearing the lists of victims of Nazism. Over time the metal from both plaques has bled bluish trails into cracks exposing the weathering and lack of maintenance. Look closer: one plaque records the town's victims during two incidents in 1942 (12 August and 9 September), a list of 18 locals; the other plaque is for 1,011 victims from the neighbouring villages. The first indication of different interpretations: the figures don't match to the German records, and there is no reference to Jewish victims. To add to the confusion, the tourist information guidepost mentions 90 persons; who were the other 72 people?

A short walk from the 'erratic block' is the former *Heldenfriedhof*, the German military cemetery during world wars; today the site of three memorials. The first is a small stone pillar with the names of 'twenty-one souls' executed on 14 August 1942. The memorial is regularly tended with flowers and candles. Beside that is a more ornate memorial raised in 1964 with the inscription: 'This place is sacred by the blood of 222 people of Białowieża, and surroundings murdered by Nazis on 14 August and 24 December 1942. May the memory of them live on! Białowieża, 22 July 1964'. A third memorial is a twin set of Catholic and Orthodox crosses standing in an area gradually becoming overgrown by shrubbery. The inscription in Polish and Russian announces: 'Here rest innocent people brutally murdered by German fascists on 24 December 1942.

---

22 Tourist Information post, 'Orthodox Church in Białowieża', Białowieża Neighbourhood Programme, 2004–6.

Lord hear their cries, give them peace in heaven.'[23] Again, these numbers do not match German records, while the remains of German soldiers had disappeared.

Image 21: Sites of memory—located in the centre of Białowieża town, the memorial stands on the site where public executions were conducted during the Nazi occupation.
Source: Author, 2009.

Deep inside the national park's protected reservation, about a mile away, there are more memorials. Near the front gate are stone carvings of prominent Polish administrators of the forest, killed by Germans and Russians. Deeper, inside the protected reservation there is another memorial with the inscription 'Here rests the remains of the resistance movement murdered by Nazis in the years 1941–44. Honour their memory.' Under the darkness of the primaeval forest canopy, hidden away from the general public's gaze, this memorial is not tended and appears to be rotting away. Perhaps the resistance movement was not all that popular. Beyond the record of death, the

---

23 Thank you to Dr Tomasz Samojlik of the Mammal Research Institute Polish Academy of Sciences Białowieża for the Polish and Russian translations.

irreconcilable numbers, and the uncertain interpretations; what remains are pitiful scars. On 24 February 2020, a Polish news blog announced, 'a march in memory of the cursed soldiers.' The march, organized by nationalists, was set through Hajnówka to commemorate the Polish partisan movement that resisted Soviet communism. The partisans had also been responsible for crimes against ethnic minorities.[24] There is still so much that remains unknown.

In the Narewka Mala area, there are more memorials and public information signs, but the accuracy of their story is also questionable. There is a plinth over the grave pits where the Jews were killed by the SS-Police, but it's incorrectly dated 5 August 1941. In over fourteen years of research, it has been impossible to identify any survivors. A few documentary and literature sources offer a glimpse into the story of a lost community. There are indications the Jewish community was already in decline before 1939, as many families emigrated to the USA and Israel. The families that escaped the Holocaust have tried to preserve the memories of their lost community. Leib Lejzon (1929–2013) was born in Narewka Mala but in 1937 his family moved to Kraków. He never again saw his extended family, all killed in 1941. During the war, he became the youngest member of Schindler's List. After the war, he moved to the USA and changed his name to Leon Leyson. Locals living in Białowieża believe a handful of Jews returned after the war but then emigrated during the Soviet-backed anti-Semitic pogroms of 1968. Today, all that remains of the Jewish community are a few buildings along Ogrodowa Street. The old Jewish cemetery with its *mazevas* survived but is gradually being absorbed by the forest. The only detailed historical narrative for the Jews of Narewka Mala murdered during the summer of 1941 remains the entries in the German police diary. The destruction was too quick, too efficient, and too complete leaving little trace of the Jews' existence.[25]

---

24 https://notesfrompoland.com/2020/02/24/an-unwanted-march-polish-natio nalists-honour-anti-communist-partisans-accused-of-war-crimes/

25 Ernst Klee, Willi Dressen and Volke Riess (ed), *'The Good Old Days': The Holocaust Through the Eyes of the Perpetrators and Bystanders*, (London, 1991), pp. 4–5.

Bartov advised Holocaust historians to engage with local testimony and records, but many times it is a futile task.[26] After the war, Dr Szymon Datner wrote about Jews escaping Bialystok and reaching the forests only to be slaughtered by rural police patrols.[27] Unfortunately, none of Datner's work could be corroborated with the German wartime records in my possession. In 1918 Simon Dubnow wrote a history of the Jews of Imperial Russia that included the Bialystok and Białowieża region. Dubnow was born in Belarus in 1860 inside the area designated the Pale of Settlement (the territory within Imperial Russia where Jews were allowed to settle). Dubnow was imprisoned by the Nazis in the Riga ghetto and was a victim of the Rumbula massacre on 8 December 1941.[28] Thirty-six years before he wrote:

> In the manufacturing city of Bialystok, the centre of the Jewish labour movement, the Cossacks assaulted Jewish passersby on the streets, invaded the synagogues and Jewish homes, cruelly maltreating their inmates and frequently searching them and taking away their money (April 9–10) ... A regular butchery was engineered by the soldiery in Bialystok (June 30). During the entire day, the city resounded with the rifle shots of maddened soldiers who were firing into peaceful Jewish crowds. Fifty dead and a still larger number of wounded were the results of these military exploits.[29]

The pieces of evidence from Dubnow's work and the few surviving documents barely constitute a full local history. From known prewar sources between 1880 and 1935 Narawka Mala was a small town with a population of up to 1,000 inhabitants of which the Jewish community fluctuated around 758–778, but the community had already experienced extensive emigration.[30] Before arriving in Narewka

---

26 Omer Bartov, 'Eastern Europe as a Site of Genocide,' *The Journal of Modern History*, Vol.80, No.3 (September 2008), pp. 557–593.
27 Szymon Datner, 'Eksterminacja ludności zydowskiej w Okręgu Białostockim', *Bulletin of the Jewish Historical Institute*, Warsaw, October–December 1966, no.6: pp. 3–29.
28 The Rumbla massacre was a two-day killing spree conducted by Einsatzgruppe A and the Arajs Kommando (collaborators) that accounted for 25,000 Jews.
29 Simon M. Dubnow, trans. Israel Friedlander, *History of the Jews in Russia and Poland: From the Earliest Times to the Present Day*, three volumes, (Philadelphia, 1918), pp. 473–4.
30 Stanislaw Lenartowicz, *Przewodnik Po Polsce: Polska Północno-Wschodnia, Tom I, Warszawa: Wszystkie Prawa Zastrzeżone*, p. 163, and Filip Sulimierski et al., *Słownik geograficzny Królestwa Polskiego i innych krajów słowiańskich*, (Warszwaa, 1902).

Mala in 1941 the Germans killed 89 Jews mostly in Białowieża town. On 15 August there were 703 Jews in Narewka Mala; this compared with the known average of 778 Jews. We can assume: the extermination of 792 Jews represented the entire Jewish community inside Białowieża in June 1941. These findings highlight the continual battle historians face at chipping away the Nazi legacy.

Image 22: Sites of memory—located within the Narewka town limits, the Jewish cemetery survived the Nazi occupation.
Source: Author, 2009.

The old Jewish cemetery of Narewka Mala lies on the edge of town. The rain had curtailed my scheduled visit the previous day. A signpost in English and Hebrew marked the entrance: 'Narevka's Jewish cemetery renovated by students of "Mekif Het" High school, Beer Sheva, Israel 2006–2007 (sic)'. There is a path leading up through the trees to the graves. This is the only human connection with Białowieźa's old Jewish heritage—on the side of a hill, under a copse, and in some places overrun by thick undergrowth. Later a short drive, perhaps two kilometres through the town, led to a remote spot by a railway line where the Jewish men had been killed and buried. They had marched through the town by the Order police in 1941. The remoteness of the site, shrouded by trees, and close-by the railway was deliberately chosen by the Nazis to cloak the extermination.

There are other jumbled traces of the past. A wooden synagogue on Szkolna Street was turned into a grain store during the Soviet occupation in 1939. This so offended the community they destroyed it.[31] The last known serving rabbi of Narewka Mala was Ajzyk Grajewski (1895–1941); his entire family were murdered in the Holocaust. Another victim was Rabbi Shlomo Barelkowski, 67 years old and born in Jashinowka; he retired to Narewka Mala. Moshe Birenbaum born in 1918 joined the Red Army on 6 June 1941 and avoided the Nazi occupation. He returned to the town in 1957, met with many locals and heard accounts of the occupation, who then emigrated to Israel. Several men from the town served in the Polish army but died in German captivity, they included: Mieczyslaw Geller (born 1915) a sapper; Szepsel Polojko (born May 1910) a baker and an NCO and, Szolem Fajngold (born 1889), died of malnutrition in July 1942 in the Lodz ghetto.[32] Gradually my searches drew to a close as the sources dried up. Then in 2016, a Polish backed initiative founded a virtual museum to restore the memory of the Jewish community in Białowieźa. Visits by émigrés to America and Israel returned the community to open the museum.[33]

---

31 Wisniewski, Jewish Bialystok, pp. 93–95.
32 http://kehilalinks.jewishgen.org/narewka/
33 http://www.jewish-bialowieza.pl/about-the-museum/description-of-the-project/

Image 23: Sites of memory—located nearby Białowieża town. They are memorials to the mass killings and destroyed villages in 1942. They stand in the grounds of the former German military cemetery, first constructed during the Imperial German Army occupation in 1915–18.

Souce: Author, 2009.

The story of Białowieża under Nazi rule is complete. The leading perpetrators are dead. The senior hunters, foresters and officers had passed away by 1970. The troopers, the young men, began to retire in the late 1960s and have now passed on. The wartime German dead have been re-interned in a prefabricated cemetery. The Jewish community was never restored, the old cemetery an overgrown memory of what was once a vibrant community. The Red Army dead from 1944 lie in a well maintained Hajnówka cemetery. The partisans, civilians, local foresters and lost villages have been memorialized. In the Cold War years, the forest was divided between Poland and Belarus within the Soviet empire. In the Polish area, reconstruction restored the forest's game stocks. Tourism, forestry and hunting have again flourished as the main sectors of the local economy. In 1976 UNESCO designated the Polish section a biosphere. In 1993 the Belarus segment was declared a biosphere. Today, the combined biosphere is 141,885 ha, reduced from the 1939 claimed area of 166,000ha. Regardless of memorialization and reconstruction, the spectre of the Nazis' Grossdeutschland lingers, besides other attempts to harness nature to politics. The forest's geopolitics extends into 2020, as Białowieża is once again on a frontier between the European Union and Belarus. Meanwhile across Europe, the rise of popular nationalism has witnessed an upsurge in racism and anti-Semitism.

IV. Myth of the clean Luftwaffe

If the memory of the Nazi hunt became a satirical travesty, in the post-war years, then 'Hitler's clean Luftwaffe' must rank as one of the great charades of military history. This narrative of the Luftwaffe was set in place long before any German literature was published. In 1948 the Air Ministry in Britain published an operational history of the Luftwaffe.[34] Basil Liddell Hart interviewed senior Luftwaffe officers and broadened the narrative to include ground war.[35] The British were followed by Adolf Galland *The First and the*

---

34 Air Ministry, *The Rise and Fall of the German Air Force (1933 to 1945)*, London 1948.
35 Basil Liddell Hart, *The Other Side of the Hill*, (London, 1948).

Last (1950), and Hans-Ulrich Rudel *Stuka Pilot* (1949). In the 1950s, popular histories followed a peculiarly German nostalgic dimension. Udo Walter's story of fighter ace Hans-Joachim Marseille, killed during the war, was turned into the film *Der Stern von Afrika* (1957). Cajus Bekker's book from 1964 was translated three years later as *The Luftwaffe War Diaries*. The West German *Heimat* film genre also shaped the narrative about the Luftwaffe with *Des Teufels General* (1955). British writers continued to build on the narrative with Alfred Price a prolific author. Galland contributed to one book with a foreword entitled, 'Goliath brought down'.[36] In another of the series, Galland's foreword was: 'Quarter century of greatness'.[37] In 1973, Rudel's memoir was republished with a foreword by Douglas Bader, the former RAF fighter ace. Bader wrote: 'The book is not broad in its scope because it is confined to the activities of one man — and a brave one — waging a war in a very single-minded fashion. It does however shed an interesting light on Rudel's opposite numbers on the Eastern front, the Russian Air Force pilots.'[38] However prolific this narrative, it only related to the air war, and was largely based on anecdote. Bader had conjured an honourable adversary who he imagined the RAF had duelled in the skies above Kent and thus inflated the status of 'the few' as saviours of Britain in 1940.

The story of the clean Luftwaffe was universally accepted by the 1970s.[39] There were contradictions between anecdote and evidence. While Galland was an advisor to Guy Hamilton, the film director *Battle of Britain* (1969), he walked off the set when an actor playing senior Luftwaffe officer made the Nazi salute.[40] Hamilton later explained that Galland believed the battle was fought by knights of the clouds, the last ethical warriors of the modern age.[41]

---

36 Alfred Price, *Luftwaffe: Birth, Life and Death of an Air Force*, (London, 1969).
37 Martin Caidin, *ME109: Willy Messerschmitt's peerless fighter*, (London, 1968).
38 Rudel, *Stuka Pilot*, passim.
39 James S. Corum, 'Building A New Luftwaffe: The United States Air Force and Bundeswehr Planning for Rearmament, 1950-60,' *Journal of Strategic Studies*, 27:1, 89–113.
40 S.P. Mackenzie, *The Battle of Britain on Screen*, (Edinburgh, 2007), p. 88.
41 Special edition DVD, The Battle of Britain, (MGM, 2004), additional supporting digital programmes.

Galland's participation in the *World at War* television documentary series referred to his flying with *Jagdgruppe 26* during the Battle of Britain. He told an interviewer the daylight battle became more disorganized and eventually ended. 'The night raids of our bombers were sometimes very successful, as in Coventry.'[42] The inconvenient memory of the Luftwaffe's involvement in the Spanish civil War, in the Nazis eternal battle against 'Bolshevism', was wiped from the memory.[43] In 1968, Raymond Toliver and Trevor Constable published a book of anecdotes from the top Luftwaffe's fighter aces. Superficially, it extolled the virtues of the *Experten* (experts), but the book stirred some old and long forgotten dogma:

> The patron saint of the German fighter pilots was St. Horridus, who had his origin in mess parties rather than the pantheon. During combat, the Luftwaffe fighter pilots would call Horrido on the radio when they had scored a kill against enemy aircraft. The distinctive cry alerted other pilots airborne to watch for a crash or a flamer, and also alerted ground stations. This practice helped confirm many victories.[44]

The marriage of hunting and aviation was proclaimed and glorified, but the meaning of the airborne hunter had deep ideological implications. The *Jagdflieger*, the fighter pilots, combined combat and hunting. According to two German scholars, the hunt enabled German flyers to better comprehend their missions and combat.[45] A British writer identified the hunting traits in German tactics. The 'spirit' of the Luftwaffe, according to Bungay lay in its language. He noted the flying *Schwarm* manoeuvre came from the image of a swarm of bees and the *Rotte* was a pack of hunting hounds. The Luftwaffe wanted its fighter pilots to behave with 'the flexible but purposeful aggressiveness of a band of hunting animals.'[46] In this sense, the leader's

---

42 Richard Holmes, *World at War*, (London, 2007), p. 226, 228, 234.
43 Werner Beumelburg, *Kampf um Spanien: Die Geschichte Der Legion Condor*, (Berlin, 1939). Roger James Bender, *Uniforms, Organisation and History of the Legion Condor*, (Santa Cruz, 1992). The campaign medals were engraved: 'In the fight against Bolshevism' (Im Kampfe Gegen Den Bolschewismus).
44 Raymond F. Toliver and Trevor J. Constable, *Horrido!* (New York, 1968), p. xiv.
45 Neitzel & Welzer, *Soldaten. Protokolle vom Kämpfen*, pp. 132–135, also *Soldaten* (London, 2012), pp. 56, 65–69, 161.
46 Ibid., p. 494.

only job was to identify prey for the pack. The purpose behind this tactic was to increase the opportunities for the kill in what was known as the *freie Jagd* (free hunt).[47] Comparing British and German aerial tactics, Bungay thought the Luftwaffe copied from James Fennimore Cooper's descriptions of Indian attacks on British Redcoats — he was perhaps closer to the truth than he realized.[48]

There was a further dimension to the clean Luftwaffe, which stemmed from Galland's influence as the General of Fighters. In 1944, he granted permission for the release of a combat shooting handbook for fighter pilots that was entitled *Horrido!*[49] This *Schiessfibel* (shooting primer) was a cartoon styled training manual with most of the sketches drawn by Johannes Trautloft (1912–1995), a fighter ace who served on Galland's staff. The manual was meant to train with humorous advice to young pilots on how to shoot down American *Flying Fortresses*. The content was modernistic in the sense that it adopted comic sketches, sexist jokes and silly quips; to reinforce the key lessons learned from aerial warfare for the purpose of transforming rookies into fighter pilots in the shortest time possible. The booklet concluded with a sketch of the successful fighter pilot having shot down a *Flying Fortress* with the caption: 'the hunter unlike any other has the concentrated feelings about the fight and victory. This makes us happy and proud, so to all hunters — *Horrido!*'[50] The manual incorporated a subliminal racial tone. To strengthen the trainees' motivation as to what the war was about, there was a sketch on page twenty-one to remind them. A cartoon illustrated the fighter using deflection shooting at a *Flying* Fortress. At that time victories achieved through deflection shooting were called the 'the money shot.' In the lower right-hand corner, drawn inside a small cloud, was a Nazi stereotype of a Jew holding a bag of money. There was no caption only the subliminal message — the war was being waged in the air against enemy aeroplanes funded by the Jews. In 1944, Galland endorsed the handbook including the Jewish cartoon. When Galland hunted in the

---

47 Ibid., p. 495.
48 The Luftwaffe call sign for enemies was 'Indianer' while the RAF used 'bandits'.
49 Toliver et al, Horrido.
50 Deutsche Luftwaffe 5001, *Horrido! – des Jägers Schiessfibel*, Juni, 1944.

forest of Dünaberg in, during the German army's march on Moscow he was in the same killing ground for 10,000 Jews during October–November 1941. Decades later Gitta Sereny recalled interviewing Galland and he confessed:

> The first indication which made one think seriously of genocide was while flying over Russia, around March 1942 with Himmler and Speer, the minister of armaments. … Himmler pointed down where we could see a lot of people moving about, and he said, 'last year we had decided to kill them all – this year we need them for the [arms industry]. That remark jolted me. I thought what does it mean "kill them all"?'[51]

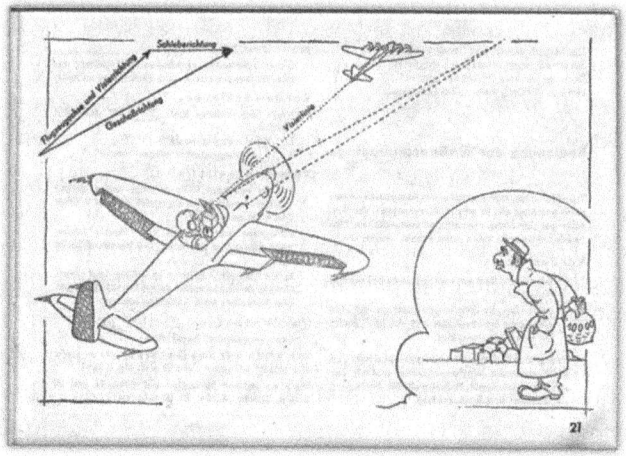

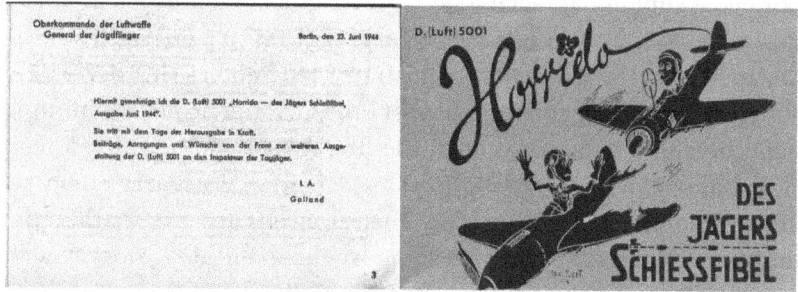

Image 24: In his position as General of Fighters, Adolf Galland approved and endorsed this anti-Semitic trope in comic form. The connections between hunting, the Luftwaffe and training had reached complete integration.
Source: Adolf Galland Horrido, Des Jägers Schiessfibel Ausgabe Juni 1944. Internet Archive | Opensource.

---

51   Gitta Sereny, *Albert Speer His Battle with the truth,* London: 1997, p. 354.

CONCLUSION: MEMORIES OF A NEVER HAPPENED HISTORY

The Luftwaffe was the third arm of the Wehrmacht (OKW), alongside the Navy and Army. The OKW issued instructions, orders and guidelines that were specific to the Luftwaffe. For example, on 5 September 1942 the OKW war diary recorded that the Luftwaffe had assigned 10,0000 men under training for combating partisans in the rear areas of the eastern front.[52] Twelve days later, Göring announced merit awards for participating in ground combat.[53] On 18 September 1943, Göring issued a general warning from the operations on *Robinson* (headquarters train), about Soviets using German PoWs as agents and saboteurs in the *Operations- und Heimatkriegsgebiet*.[54] For the remainder of the month, (September 1943) Göring issued notices for volunteers for all Luftwaffe ground forces. On 20 November 1942, Goring announced the formation of two *Lw.-Feldbataillons zbV*.[55] The list goes on but their overall importance was their standing as OKW official communiques. By 1942-3, the strategy in the east was no longer just about Göring's ambitions or Frevert's fantasies. The search for rapid training methods not only effected the flying branch, but the ground forces were also in dire need of trained men. The Luftwaffe was set a very important part in the defence of the Home Forces Area and the rear areas. This was also about re-calibrating training for a wider purpose than solely preparing troops for conventional combat.

In 2006 Hew Strachan was perplexed by an historical dilemma: 'Germany lost the two world wars, and yet its army continued fighting until the very end of both.'[56] He also observed, 'its performance in 1944–45 is truly astonishing given the fact that the probable outcome of the Second World War, unlike that of the first, was clear at least twelve months before it ended.' Strachan believed the British had a comparable record but the solution to understanding why involved morale. In this regard he noted three possible

---

52   Rudolf Absolon, *Die Wehrmacht im Dritten Reich*, Band IV, 19 Dezember 1941 bis 9 Mai 1945, (Boppard am Rhein, 1995), p. 664.
53   Ibid., p. 666.
54   Ibid., p. 761.
55   Ibid., p. 680.
56   Hew Strachan, 'Training, Morale and Modern War', *Journal of Contemporary History*, Vol 4(2), 211–227, 2006 Sage, New Delhi.

reasons: the primary group ethos, ideological indoctrination, or discipline; he concluded they were inadequate to explain why the Germans kept fighting and decided the answer lay with training. In Strachan's opinion, 'the value of training was psychological: it is an enabling process, a form of empowerment, which creates self-confidence.' The critical point, vis-à-vis this book, was his observation that 'training teaches men to kill.' Training reduced combat preparation to 'the last 200 yards' and the importance of the bayonet as a psychological tool rather than as an actual weapon. He redirected from killing to discuss SLA Marshall and the debate about shooting averages. This was the closest Strachan came to 'blooding' and the 'first kill' in war. He veered off into weapons, military history, training grounds and other issued. Strachan claimed the Wehrmacht consolidated its training methods after the fall of Poland. The gaps between short campaigns were used to digest experience and apply it to training. In 1941 the army introduced a psychological dimension in training 'leaders and men for ruthless aggression ...' Strachan drew on an unreliable anecdotal statement about 1942 to argue the training was getting harder. Having 'dodged the bullet' about blooding, Strachan could not explain why the Germans kept fighting in 1944–45, because the answer lay outside the field of military history.

Military history alone cannot explain German military culture. This requires an engagement, with Nazi politics of violence, genocide, and the Holocaust. Researching Luftwaffe troops, in Bandenbekämpfung, involves re-evaluating the impact of *Auftragstaktik*, military efficiency and fighting power within *Sicherheitskrieg* or security warfare. *Auftragstakitik* enabled German soldiers to apply their initiative to any given situation. In theory, well-trained and gifted with freedom of action, the German soldier was highly effective at conducting warfare. The mechanistic socialisation of German soldiers into *Auftragstaktik*, beside conventional training was inexpensive, consistent across political epochs and adaptable to the changing conditions of war. Unrestrained *Auftragstaktik*, as applied by the Nazis', however, pushes the story beyond the bounds of military history and into the realm of politics of violence. The introduction of a 'shoot-to-kill' order, against 'soft racial targets', shifted the balance of civil-military relations away from the military, and into the political realm of ethnic-killing and genocide. In effect, the division of labour in the perpetration of Nazi crimes and killings was shared by the SS-Police and small units of the Wehrmacht. The absence of scholarly research of small units within battalions — the squads, platoons, companies — is particularly problematical for German military history. This partly explains why it has taken the demise of the last *Landsers* before research of the rank and file could be undertaken. While doctrine, strategy, and tactics are moderately straightforward topics, they do not explain the nature of Nazi military culture. Any question of rank-and-file guilt must obviously lie with the middle-class officer corps, regardless of the 'trigger pullers', because they issued the orders in the field. German soldiers, irrespective of branch or arm, were taught to conform to a particular style of fighting. The Wehrmacht produced effective soldiers because they trained recruits to kill soft targets. This led to their heightened military efficiency, reduced their training time and reinforced their fighting power to the end of the war. The Prusso-German way of combat had developed over decades and was a cultural totem of Germanic society. The hunter, the warrior, the warlord; to be master of the battlefield, whether infantryman or general, was the perpetual quest of the mechanistic military culture. Winning was not regulated by ethical methods or monitored by moralistic scruples — war was fought aggressively to win.

Vernichtungskrieg or extermination warfare was not only a doctrine or a political slogan, but a way of combat instilled in the recruits and perpetuated by the military system. This system barely changed between 1870 until 1942. Then Bandenbekämpfung was introduced, and training doctrine was lifted by the act of blooding against 'soft' targets. The rationality of the system remained in direct correlation to the demands of military efficiency and building unit cohesion — killing did not undermine morale, it supercharged it. The outcome of this kind of training was the increase in fighting power, which had other consequences such as an overtly aggressive mentality and risk-taking with higher casualties. The universality of this kind of fighting power, however, was its applicability to the politics of violence. From combating banditry in the forests of East Prussia or the Franc-Tireur in the Nineteenth Century, to fighting the Herero warriors in Namibia, to coercing civilians through violence in Belgium in 1914 to the hunting of Jews in the Second World War, this was the red thread of military culture with tragic consequences.

The flexibility inherent to the German military culture was evident in the changeover expressed by the men of the JSKB in 1944. They smoothly adjusted to conventional combat, during the retreat from Białowieża, after an extended period of conducting Bandenbekämpfung. The command remained conditioned to maintaining unit integrity, retaining cohesion, utilising military efficiency, and sustaining their fighting power. Under repeated attacks from tanks, artillery barrages and infantry assaults, the JSKB defended the retreat. In the face of differential odds, the enforced change of commander, and loss of support weapons, the soldiers continued to perform and hold ground. That final chapter in this story opened a window on the common characteristics of German military culture. Without postwar anecdotal evidence, these records are the purest illustration of emerging fighting power, which also explains why the troops perpetrated killings over the previous two years. To kill Jews, civilians and partisans was institutionalised blooding, what came after was the motivational boost of crossing a social barrier. Thus, we observe a rabble turn into a fighting combat group; explained by the correlation of killing Jews through *Auftragstaktik*.

The overall hypothesis of *Birds of Prey* was, however, concerned with the employment of *Bandenbekämpfung* by the *Luftwaffe*, its implications in the Holocaust and its wider participation in Nazi crimes. This microhistory has disclosed why it was an inexpensive methodology and relatively easy to practise. Nicholas Stargardt has written that the Second World War was a German war like no other.[57] This was true, but it was also a continuation of previous

---

57   Nicholas Stargardt, *The German War: A Nation Under Arms, 1938–1945*, (New York, 2015), p. 28.

wars. *Sicherheitskrieg* was an institutional dogma that empowered the German armed forces, from 1870 to 1945, to exploit its fighting power within the realm of politics of violence. Any serious study of Hitler's *Bandenbekämpfung* involves engaging with a period of modern history's darkness. We are revolted by Nazism and its threat to civilised values. *Bandenbekämpfung* was an ideological weapon for genocide, and a large swathe of Germany's civil-military infrastructure engaged in its implementation. *Bandenbekämpfung* was borne out of strategic confusion, political intrigue, and institutional rivalry. Regardless, *Bandenbekämpfung* was incorporated into the military code, without complaint, by leading generals of the *Wehrmacht*, men hailed after the war as the moral standard bearers of German soldierly honour. The *Wehrmacht*, without oversight or prodding, prosecuted *Bandenbekämpfung* as vigorously and violently as the SS-Police. By the end of the war, the hardened military purveyors of *Bandenbekämpfung* could no longer recognise the difference between conventional enemy soldiers and insurgents.

Epilogue

JSKB war diary 5 June 1943: 'A *Jagdkommando* from *Bialowies* encountered bandits at about 6.00 am in *Jagen* 578 on the Topiło road. One bandit was shot and a camp with food and clothing secured. A rifle and two pistols were secured. *Oberjäger* Adams was killed in the action.'[1] Adams joined the other 700,000 German soldiers killed during 1943, a figure roughly equivalent to total UK/USA killed in action during the whole of the Second World War. German deaths in 1944/1945 were much greater, but the 1943 losses were the final hiatus of the Wehrmacht that went to war in 1939. Although seemingly insignificant, Adams' death in Bandenbekämpfung represented the purest phase of ideological conflict between Hitlerism and Stalinism. This was a death struggle between rival political, cultural, and socially engineered societies dominated by charismatic dictatorships. Each side fought without any laws or codes of war, it was barbaric and unrestrained. Lost in that maelstrom, Adams' story emerged by chance in the search for documents. His records were the most complete and throughout the research for this book became an important source in structuring the story of the common German soldier. In *Hitler's Wehrmacht*, Rolf-Dieter Müller discussed the importance of the NCO and observed, 'their story had not yet been written.'[2] In examining Adams' and the other rank and file, we can break down their existence into several parts: the person and their civilian life, military experience, and death in war (or postwar life).

Siegfried Edgar Gunter Ferdinand Adams was born in the Elberfeld part of Wuppertal in 1916. Rudolf, his father, was a city official and a protestant. Siegfried, the name underlined on all his military papers, was middle-class in upbringing, schooling and in his civil life. In 1937 Siegfried was legally declared an orphan when his father died. His mother had passed away in 1923 when he was seven years of age leaving no other traces of family. The family home, in 1937, was 27 Obergrünerwalder Strasse and was still his

---

1   BArch, RL 31/4, JSKB Kriegstagebuch, 5 June 1943.
2   Rolf-Dieter Müller. *Hitler's Wehrmacht, 1935–1945*, (Lexington, 2016), p. 206

place of residence at the time of his death. Today, the site of a modern building, with a car park, all the original buildings were probably destroyed in the bombing. At twenty years he was 1.70 metres (five foot six inches) tall, which was about average for rank-and-file German soldiers in the Second World War. There are no photographs of Siegfried, but his appearance was described as a slim build weighing 54 kilos (8 St. 7lbs), with an oval-shaped face, brown eyes, black hair, blood group A, and wore spectacles. His military medical found he suffered a slight problem in the left eye (6/18) and severe myopia in the right (6/24). He struggled with short-sightedness without corrective spectacles. He passed his military medical and during his period of service was regularly inoculated against smallpox, typhus, dysentery, and cholera; there was no adverse reaction to his cocktail of immunisations. Adams was forced to seek work after school but were assisted by the level of his *Abitur* or final school examination.

From civil society, we know he was 17 when the Nazis came to power. Wuppertal had a population of 408,000 in 1933 in the Bergisches Dreieck area of present-day North-Rhine-Westphalia. Wuppertal was home for Erich Koch, the Nazi Gauleiter of East Prussia. On a sunny day in May 2014, I visited Wuppertal. The city oozes middle-class gentility like all modern industrial German cities in Germany on a Sunday. It was formed from the amalgamation of seven towns, the largest of which being Barmen and Elberfeld. After a referendum in 1930, the city was named Wuppertal. There is a particularly interesting urbanity since Barmen and Elberfeld grew lengthwise along the river valley. Wuppertal gives the appearance of being a very long but relatively narrow city. This is even more pronounced by the electric railway known, the *Schwebebahn*. In 1894 the city fathers agreed to the construction of an elevated electric railway designed by Eugen Langen. The railway follows the river, supported on huge steel stanchions placed at regular intervals along the riverbank. The railway binds with a swift, efficient, and low-priced transport system opened in 1903. In the 1890s Wuppertal, like so many other industrial cities, was at the forefront of German modernity. At around the same time the *Schwedebahn* was being built,

Aspirin was being synthesised by Bayer AG. in Wuppertal. Imperial Germany was not only a major industrial power, but its scientific advances were also collecting Nobel prizes, the legal code was highly respected, and the education system was the envy of the world. To an outsider, the city has quiet middle-class areas and lively working-class communities. There are parts of the old city from before 1939, but there is no impression of the Nazi past. Wuppertal first experienced heavy bombing was on the Barmen district during the night 29–30 May 1943. There is evidence to indicate Siegfried was in Elberfeld during the raid. Although more than sixty years later, the contrast between Wuppertal and Białowieża was profound.

On 7 April 1933, the Nazis enacted the law for the reconstitution of the civil service, which essentially meant Aryanisation.[3] This was the first Nazi legal instrument to impact Siegfried's chosen career. The second was the Nuremberg Race laws (September 1935) and the third came from his call up to the Luftwaffe. On 20 December 1936, he completed the conscription paper trail including a 'Declaration of Aryan Descent' issued to all recruits. The signed document confirmed no Jewish heritage. This document does not confirm Siegfried was an anti-Semite, but it does highlight how many racial profiles a soldier might pass before attending basic training. We do not know if he had a particular political upbringing but given his choice of career, he was possibly a conservative. The grade of his Abitur allowed him to enter public service with a junior rank in the Düsseldorf higher court. He was an apprentice *Justizinspektor*, an entrance level justice official, still residing in the family home. The military system began to process Siegfried after he was 20. There is an indication that he was content with his public service status and referred to it in his official correspondence with the Luftwaffe. Early into the military process, Siegfried expressed a reluctance for military service. He made a vain attempted to defer or even avoid serving because his new public service career would be terminated. We might conclude his civilian life as a young middle-class man, physically lightweight, perhaps even bookish, but

---

3   Richard Bessel, *Nazism and War*, (London, 2004) p. 66.

had a strong sense of duty, career, and ambition. Interestingly, his uncle was declared his elder guardian for processing purposes.

Siegfried's protest was in vain. He was called up before *Wehrmeldeamt Wuppertal* and on 8 January 1940, was sent to *Luftwaffenbaukompanie 45/XI* (basic training company). His training was completed on 10 April, having been taught with weapons: the *Mauser* 98k carbine, the machine gun MG15, and the *Luger* .08 pistol. As a *Flieger* (aircraftsman) he was sent to *Flieger Ausbildung-Regiment 52* for three months of operational training and became *Gefreiter* (corporal). He joined the command services staff in July 1940 and was assigned to the judge advocates branch and the Luftwaffe courts-martial in *Luftgau 1* in Elbing. His commanding officer assessed him as 'vibrant, with an open character, a positive work ethic and service attitude. He is also gifted and his professional knowledge above average. He enjoys his profession as well as his duties as a soldier.' Siegfried's personnel file included a *Lebenslauf*, between a Curriculum Vitae and a state of ambition, which was usual for NCO/officer candidates but not the common soldier. His ambition was to become an officer in the legal branch of the Luftwaffe. He tried to establish a permanent position within the first assignment, but his reports marked him for advancement through the promotion system. In the summer of 1942, he was sent to NCO candidate school in Luftgau I. He was promoted to *Obergefreiter* (senior corporal) on 1 April 1942. Somewhere along that journey, between April 1940 to May 1943 he was married to Marie and they resided in Neue Friedrich Strasse 13, in Elberfeld.[4]

On 13 July 1942, he was joined an *Unteroffiziere Lehrkommando*, (NCO operational training course) until 19 September 1942. As was the norm, he was issued with a five-day travel warrant and sent to Wuppertal to receive his instructions from his local recruitment office. This happened seven times during his service in the Luftwaffe. Upon completion of his course, the training officers made important and detailed assessments of Siegfried. He was observed as mid-size, with a weak physique, not physical but reasonably proficient in

---

4　BArch, Lw. Personalakte, Wehrstammbuch Oberjäger Siegfried Adams, Wehrnummer Wuppertal 16/1/3/.

sports. His general knowledge was excellent and had a 'sprightly intellect'. He held a 'positive opinion of himself' and was 'self-assured'. His character was described as 'cool'. His command speak was loud and assertive. The negative points were the tendency to question or object. He was regarded as somewhat aloof, clean but had unexplained 'little habits'. In the field, Siegfried was above average, but better in theory where he excelled, than in practice where he was average. His best quality was his ability to train others. He could bring his imagination to bear and had excellent verbal skills. The course commander rated him, 'with an above-average performance and the potential to become a leader.' However, although a good NCO he was registered as under schooling for front service. The military bureaucracy required frontline experience. Siegfried was received by *Flieger Ersatz Bataillon 1*, in Powunden, as a replacement ready for an operational posting. His service in the *Heimatkriegsgebiet* was completed as 16 August 1941 to 30 September 1942.

Siegfried was transferred to operational duty through a posting to *Feldausbildung Bataillon der Luftwaffe 1*, Gütersloh, and then *Fliegerhorstkommandantur Neukuhren* where he was assigned to a field company (sixth) on 14 October 1942. He was posted to the LWSB as an *Oberjäger* or 'Corporal of Rifles' with the rest of the sixth company. He was assigned to *Kampf gegen Banden* (combating banditry) until 15 March 1943. On 1 March 1943, he officially transferred to the JSKB and was assigned to service in *Einsatz im Kampf gegen sowjet russ. Banden* (combat operations against Soviet bandits). There was no explanation for the second tour in Białowieża or with the JSKB. On 24 January 1943, he was given an X-ray at the Bialystok reserve field hospital. On 19 April 1943, he was diagnosed with *Gelbsucht* (Jaundice) and was hospitalised in Bialystok until 18 May, under the (*Kriegsverwaltungsinspektor*) war administration inspector. He was awarded home leave by an *Oberfeldarzt* (senior military doctor) and issued with a five-day travel pass with a return date of 3 June. There is a question over his length of convalescence that might have undermined his awareness and led to errors in the field.[5]

---

5   BArch, Lw. Personalakte, Soldbuch-Luftwaffe, Nr. 245, Oberjäger Siegfried Adams, Wehrnummer Wuppertal 16/1/3.

Image 25: Sites of memory—German dead relocated from Białowieża cemetery. The search for Siegfried Adams burial place marked by my index finger.
Source: Author, 2009.

Siegfried's death in the forest was not Wagnerian. According to the JSKB diary, a meeting engagement took place in *Jagen* 578 near Topily. A short note in the medical report explained he was shot in the throat by rifle or machine pistol fire. His *Soldbuch* (soldiers' pay book) included an entry the JSKB, 'Killed in action 5 June 1943, *Urwald Bialowies*, *Jagen* 522, 3 kilometres nearby Czerlanka, shot in the throat.' The processing of his death through *Luftgau 1* was completed on 26 June 1943. The area where the incident occurred is not scenic and constantly changes with the seasons. The forest has an undulating floor, with deep hollows and high hanging crests caused by severe soil erosion and poor drainage due to rainfall or flooding. Siegfried probably crested one of the gentle slopes, exposing his head and shoulders and was shot in the throat. He was buried in *Heldenfriedhof* (military cemetery), in Białowieża, but there was no specific reference to a military funeral in the diary. Today, Siegfried is buried in the modern prefabricated German cemetery in Bartosze, in eastern Poland, with the rest of his comrades killed in Białowieża. On 26 June 1943, Lw.Captain Weinreis, JSKB adjutant, compiled a final personnel report. He was identified as a *Gruppenführer* (group leader) within the JSKB. Siegfried was described as reliable, dutiful and a popular person. His performances were always well above average, a very good leader and with a high intellectual capacity. This confirmed his merit award from Frevert, which ensured his widow would receive extra compensation and acknowledge his bravery in local announcements.

Siegfried represented an enigma. For example, how was he informed and socialised into the killing mission of the sixth company? Somewhere along attending the *Unteroffiziere-Lehrkommandos*, in September 1942, posting to *Fliegerhorstkommandantur Neukuhren* in October 1942, and his arrival at the LWSB (October–November 1942), Siegfried's company was advised of the mission. Within two weeks of its arrival, the men of the sixth company had killed Jews without coercion or compunction. The airbase at Neukuhren was a central sorting base for recruits and replacements to operational service. This was the same base that received and placed Erich Hartmann, the German fighter ace, for frontline training. Hartmann had studied in a *Napola* (Nazi school), taught gliding in the Hitler Youth, and began his military training in 1940, the same year as Siegfried. If Siegfried's mission was explained in the airbase, then the Home Forces Area was implicated in the preparation process of the Holocaust. The Luftwaffe air bases were critical to the military socialisation process but how far they instructed in Nazi dogma remains open to speculation.

Epilogue

As a long-term candidate for legal service, Siegfried was assigned to the sixth company with the tasks of killing and deporting civilians and Jews. To the men of the sixth company, he was very different on many levels. He was a twenty-six-year-old NCO in a rifle company with an average age of nineteen-year-olds. In comparison, he was well educated, had already established a civilian career and was married. They were mostly working-class men or farm labourers with minimal education and destined to become farm or factory hands. Their military service was determined by training in flak artillery, infantry, signals, and aircraft maintenance. Siegfried was middle class, a public servant and trained in the administration of military law. He was almost certainly conversant in the basic regulations of the military code. The soldiers' pay-book contained the "ten commandments" of sacred rules of military life. Article 7 of the Luftwaffe and Wehrmacht's code of conduct stated: "The civil population is untouchable. The soldier is not allowed to plunder or to destroy them on purpose."[6] There is a tantalising thought that his reputation for questioning carried over into the duties of the sixth company or whether he approved, we will never know definitively. Siegfried came to represent an important personal microhistory of Hitler's war and the German people. This book has explained how ordinary soldiers, like Siegfried Adams, perpetrated Nazi crimes.

---

6 BArch, Lw. Personalakte Luftwaffe airmen's pay-book. "Die Zivilbevölkerung ist unverletzlich. Der Soldat darf nicht plündern oder mutwillig zerstören."

Appendix 1: German Ranks

Ranks/Force	Luftwaffe	SS	Jäger/Jagdamt[1]
Göring	Reichsmarschall		Reichsjägermeister
Generals ranks	Generalfeldmarschall	Reichsführer-SS	
	Generaloberst	Oberstgruppenführer	Oberstjägermeister
	General der Flieger	Obergruppenführer	Landesjägermeister
	Generalleutnant	Gruppenführer	Stabsjägermeister
	Generalmajor	Brigadeführer	Gaujägermeister
			Kreisjägermeister
Field Officers	Oberst	Standartenführer	Hegeringsleiter
	Oberstleutnant	Oberführer	Oberforstmeister
	Major	Sturmbannführer	Forstmeister
Captains	Hauptmann	Hauptsturmführer	Forstassessor
			Forstamtmann
Lieutenants	Oberleutnant	Obersturmführer	Oberförster
	Leutnant	Untersturmführer	
Senior NCOs	Stabsfeldwebel	Sturmscharführer	Revierförster
	Oberfeldwebel	Hauptscharführer	
	Feldwebel	Oberscharführer	
Junior NCOs	Unterfeldwebel	Scharführer	Förster
	Unteroffizier	Unterscharführer	Unterförster
Men/corporal	Stabsgefreiter	Stabsrottenführer	
	Obergefreiter	Rottenführer	
	Gefreiter	Sturmann	Hilfsförster
	OberJäger	SS-Oberschütze	
	Flieger	SS-Schütze	Forstaufseher

---

1 Many rank and file hunting and forestry field ranks overlapped.

Appendix 2: Luftwaffe Soldiers

There is a dark archaeology to studying dead German soldiers of the Second World War. This became apparent after reading an account from the American Civil War.[1] The American dead, both victor and vanquished, have been preserved in records, letters, graveyards, monuments and memorials. There is a familiarity of names even down to the common soldier. The same cannot be found for German soldiers killed in action, or POWs, or in old age. Although there is a wealth of German historical literature, many of those that lived into the postwar period passed into old age and death virtually unnoticed. The cases of discovered mass graves of dead German soldiers, in the east, continues daily. Those re-inturned in prefabricated politically neutral cemeteries are without unit identification, the branch of service or place of death. Only their name with dates of birth and death marking their brief existence. Younger generations of Germans barely notice the mass incarceration when they are posted as a news item on their iPhones. The bodies are inconvenient, long forgotten by both nation and family—there is no courtesy granted to the dead. The common German soldiers were cannon-fodder of the Nazi cause, but in order to complete this book, they had to be treated as individuals and their identities restored. This appendix surveys the surviving records of the young men of the Sixth Company, the small collection of personnel files readily identifiable from archival searches.

Driving through Eastern Poland means passing Soviet war memorials and cemeteries. Most, if not all, have fallen into decay or have been vandalised. To the Polish people, they don't represent liberation but mark a long and painful Soviet occupation. The Red Army cemetery on the outskirts of Giżycko, formerly Lötzen, was constructed in 1951 and contains the remains of 1,715 dead—all killed in the area during 1944-1945. The graves are without names; it is a cemetery entirely for unknown soldiers. The red stars etched into the concrete grave sections are fading. Unlike British, American, and German war

---

[1] Drew Gilpin Faust, *This Republic of Suffering: Death and the American Civil War*, (New York, 2008).

cemeteries, Soviet atheism rendered this cemetery bereft of all religious symbolism. The Russian dead are buried with uniformity common to all military cemeteries. The individual graves retain a military posture in a quiet setting, with a memorial of the Red Army as the centrepiece rendering the overall effect of a 'lost' regiment. Just after leaving behind the Red Army cemetery, there was a signpost for the *Volksbund Deutsche Kriegsgräberfürsorge e.V.* the German burial service cemetery in Bartosze. This is a cemetery where Germans bury Germans in Poland. Boulders and rocks at the entrance with a stairway that leads to communal grave-pits, facing a large East Prussian cross of Golgotha. Three smaller crosses of Calvary and several standing stones by each communal grave to complete the bureaucratised process of mass internment. There was no sign of visitors, with one wreath among the 13,000 dead.

I. Sixth company officers

Two officers were assigned to the sixth company. The company commander was Lieutenant Konrad F** born in Offenhausen in September 1909. He passed through ground forces training school but there is no personnel file and no other references to him other than his listing in the war diary aged thirty-three years. Rudolf N**, the second officer's records, have survived. He was born on 24 April 1907 in Syrin near Ratibor (Racibórz: Poland). He was Catholic and his father a deputy rector. He followed the usual path of schooling for an engineer, attending Gymnasium, and then an engineering academy. His career in uniformed Nazi organisations begun with the RAD as an *Oberstfeldmeister* (the equivalent of a captain). He married in March 1935 and according to his records had no children during his military service. His entry date into the *Luftwaffe* was March 1938 when he was assigned to tenth Company, 13th Flak-Regiment. Rudolf rose rapidly through the ranks from sergeant to sergeant-major, and in May 1941, was promoted to second lieutenant. His personal assessment stated:

> N** is a conscientious soldier with stable character and good general education. He is energetic and purposeful, as well as independent in the structuring and handling of tasks. His seniors regard N** as sure and reliable. As a

Appendix

> comrade his seniors respect him. His soldierly bearing is good and his physical education is sufficient. He has a good appearance. His flak-artillery skills and expertise are in general good. His position on National Socialism is positive he understands and accepts the ways of National Socialism. N** promotion to war reserve-officer is both suitable and unrestricted.[2]

Rudolf's field service began with the Polish campaign. He was the commander of a 37mm flak battery in the east. After the campaign, he was granted leave and travelled to Lemberg (Lviv: western Ukraine) but arrived earlier than expected. The local railway inspector convinced him that he could add the time to his holiday allocation. He also received advice that he could fly back making the return trip sooner. Both were wrong and Rudolf arrived back at his depot nine days late. During the preliminary investigation, he compounded his problems by lying (details unknown) to his commanding officer. On 1 February 1942, a preliminary court-martial hearing was convened, and he was advised:

> The judgement of 19 November 1941 is revoked. N** had led the 37mm gun section in the winter battles under the severest conditions with ability. But N** has dishonoured himself by the considerable delay in returning from leave, without reason. He is allowed to return to his battery on 29 January 1942. Any further discipline has been handed over to the unit in question.[3]

On 24 June 1942, Rudolf was sentenced to four months imprisonment and a reduction in rank. Six days later there was a reprieve:

> The acting unit commander has made the following decision: N** is to serve his term of imprisonment for the purpose of probation in a Field-Regiment. In 6 months a further detailed judgment is to be submitted.

The punishment was a posting to the sixth company, where he was listed as the twenty-eighth officer within an entire battalion compliment of thirty-one officers. Little is known about his performance except a personal assessment delivered by his company commander Konrad F** on 25 February 1943:

---

2   BArch, Lw. Personalakte, Lieutenant Rudolf N**: 24 May 1941. Accepting the ways of National Socialism, for career purposes, was not the same as being a Nazi.

3   BArch, Lw. Personalakte Lieutenant Rudolf N**: court-martial judgement, 1 February 1942.

> Mentally alert, circumspect and lively in a practical way. Solid, resolved character, slim build, deft physique, however, in the field, he gives the impression of tiring due to a stomach illness. His physical potential is thereby hindered. N** is Flak-officer and has in a short time become skilled in the techniques of the infantry. His appearance at the front is positive and decisive. His seniors and subordinates bring him into the circle of comradeship, and he pays attention to his subordinate's welfare. He uses his own initiative and talent for improvisation. He stands by the National Socialist way and gives great thought to it.

It's difficult to gauge what Konrad's reference to 'stomach illness' meant, was it a psychosomatic or a physical condition? Until his leave transgression, Rudolf had a good track record. Was his 'stomach illness' a reaction to the physical conditions of serving in *Urwald Bialowies* or was it his discomfort about the mission? One could speculate but on 15 March 1943, Rudolf was transferred to *Fliegerkorps XIII* whereupon his records ended abruptly. The *Bundesarchiv* officials believe he was one of the many who simply disappeared from the record system at the end of the war, and his part in Białowieźa remains a mystery.

The difficulty of completing an accurate company command profile was complicated by the incompleteness of records. The shortfall of primary sources reduced the social profile for the sixth company. Different muster rolls allowed age profiles. Diagram 1 charts the age range of officers and NCOs of the sixth company. A breakdown of the ages of officers and NCOs revealed some important points: the officers were significantly older than the NCOs but there was some overlap between the ages of NCO's and the enlisted men. The oldest NCO was not the most senior. The combined results present the impression of a very youthful company led by middle-aged officers. The over twenty fives group were a distinct minority. We can safely assume that age and experience, as well as rank, determining authority and hierarchy. A large study of a German Army infantry division formulated a social profile from an extensive database, but this proved inconclusive as a benchmark to measure the sixth company.[4] It is impossible to assess whether this was truly representative of the entire battalion.

---

4   Christoph Rass, '"Menschmaterial". Sozialprofil, Machtstrukturen und Handlungsmuster einer Infanteriedivision der Wehrmacht im Zweiten Weltkrieg',

APPENDIX

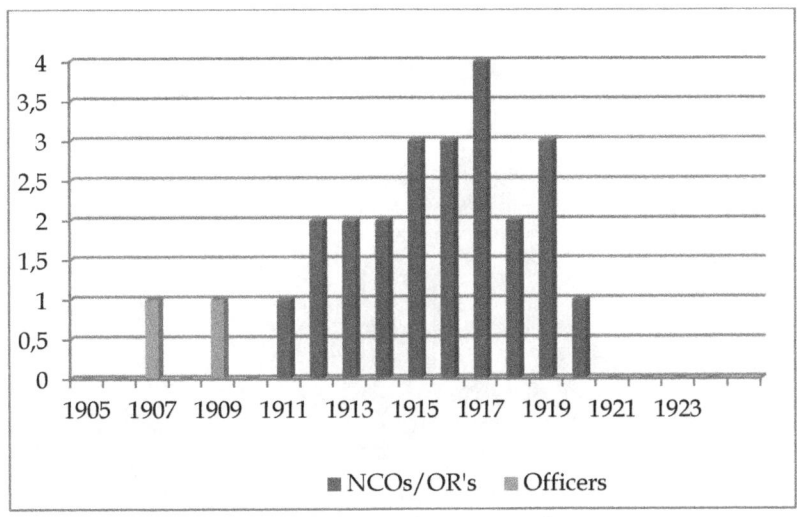

Diagram 3: age range of sixth company officers and NCOs[5]

Richard Holmes thought the German leadership culture in the field was quite unique. He noted how platoons were often commanded, 'by those senior non-commissioned personnel of which it had a bewildering variety. Tasks which might have been entrusted to a subaltern in the British army were carried out by a *Feldwebel*, *Fähnrich* or *Offizierstellvertreter* in the German.'[6] Unfortunately, from the mass of leadership studies, there has been less examination of the specific role of the German battalion commander. They served a unique purpose in Nazi Germany's civil-military relations. In the killing actions, we must assume Herbst was issuing verbal orders to kill or arrest. This was more than an ideological go-between, the battalion commanders had to organise, deploy, and manage their troops to ensure the maximum efficiency in the killings. Herbst's orders were conveyed to the two officers of the sixth company, but we can only assume the killing orders were verbal.

    PhD thesis, Rheinisch-Westfälischen Technischen Hochschule, (Aachen, 2001), pp. 221–227.
5   Ibid.
6   Holmes, *Firing Line*, p. 345.

Image 26: Heimatkriegsgebiet - Luftwaffe troops in training building small unit cohesion.
Source: Author's collection.

Image 27: Dress uniforms and other duties.
Source: Author's collection.

II. Company men

Herbst distilled his leadership through the hierarchy authority, strict discipline and firm training. This was manifested in exacting unit cohesion through overall battalion efficiency. The reports reflected functionality in the sense of doing a job rather than conducting a typical military campaign. The forest arena forced Herbst to rely on the troops utilising their initiative, but not die or suffer unit destruction. In effect, the troops were expected to develop a strong sense of teamwork but had only a short time to build the bonds of comradeship. The common soldiers were aircraftsmen, ground troops, serving as infantrymen. An 'airman', according to the Collins English Dictionary, is either an aviator or a man who serves in his nation's air force. According to the 1936 *Militär-Wörterbuch*, a

German-English military dictionary published by the German Army translated airman to *Flieger*. The *Wörterbuch* defined *Flieger* as an aviator but also referred to *Gemeiner der Luftwaffe* a private soldier or aircraftsman in the *Luftwaffe*. The popular name for the German soldier was the *Landser*, the equivalent of the British 'Tommy', or the American 'GI', defined by the *Wörterbuch* as a 'comrade'. The official terms for the ordinary soldier included: *aktiver Soldat* (regular), *Gefreiter* (private first class), and *Rekrut* (recruit or conscript).[7] The *Landser* of the sixth company served as infantrymen, but their range of skill sets was many and varied.

Image 28: The Luftwaffe troops assigned to the LWSB/JSKB were generally young and often reassigned from non-combat branches.
Source: Author's collection.

The surviving personnel records of the LWSB's men included the *Wehrstammbuch* (military service record book) with the *Wehrpass* (soldier's copy) and the soldier's *Soldbuch* (paybook). The research process

---

7   Eitzen, *Deutsch-Englishes Militär-Wörterbuch*. The Landser was defined as a Kamerad (comrade) and a regular.

APPENDIX

located several personnel files that contained two official forms. The first was the *Erklärung arischer Abstammung* (Declaration of Aryan Descent) introduced on 7 November 1935, which was signed by all the *Luftwaffe* troopers at the point of recruitment that confirmed: 'My parents, grandparents are not Jewish or members of the Jewish religion or related to Jews or convict.'[8] The second was the record of soldier's postings from basic training and all subsequent transfers during the war. The troopers examined experienced an average of seven transfers. The transfer document contained: name, place and date of birth, religious affiliation, schooling, occupation, height, weight, eyesight and distinguishing marks. They also recorded war service, general performance, and remarks from the commanding officer. The remaining paperwork in the soldier's records depended upon their war service, general administration, or death in service. Some troopers placed their *Wehrpass* and *Soldbuch* in protective wallets. There were cases when these items were returned covered in congealed blood, due to wounds sustained in combat. Curiously for a military culture bewitched by bureaucracy, there were a large number of misfiled documents.

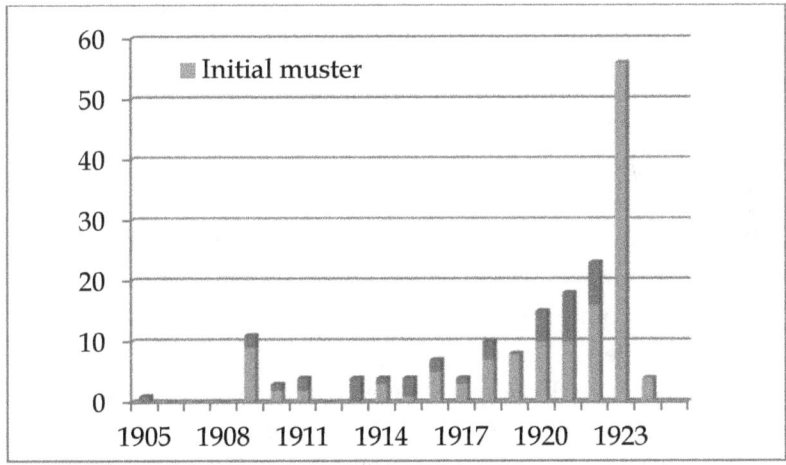

Diagram 4: age profile of sixth company[9]

---

8   One trooper requested permission to marry. Both he and his future wife filed a completed Aryanisation form (marked 1933) and she was made to declare her Aryan status prior to their marriage in 1942. The problem it seems stemmed from his Italian great grandmother. The Luftwaffe wanted to ensure he was free of Jewish blood.
9   DDSt, sixth company, age profile of LWSB, as of January 1943.

The personnel files of the *Landser* showed most had received pre-military training in paramilitary organisations and Nazi institutions. From 1 December 1936, the *Hitlerjugend* (Hitler Youth—HJ) became a nationwide institution. All males aged ten to fourteen were required to join the *Deutsches Jungvolk* (DJ), and males aged fourteen to eighteen joined the HJ. The curriculums of these organisations included sports, fieldcraft, and political indoctrination. The HJ incorporated very basic military training, discipline, and imposed notions of uniformity. Training also included target practice with small-calibre weapons, throwing dummy grenades, marches over twenty kilometres, map reading and ground orientation, camouflage and concealment, and the communication of messages. The ideological spirit of the HJ espoused individual sacrifice for the nation and to Hitler. A British post-war study of HJ training concluded, 'The war training in the Hitler Youth was a good preparation for routine duty in the Armed Forces, especially when work with special units was concerned.' The report added that boys, 'developed a resistant and hardened physique.'[10] The men of the sixth company's personnel records included cases of service in the *Reichsarbeitsdienst* or Reich Labour Service (RAD). The RAD incorporated a para-military training but harboured institutional ambitions of being a militarised organisation. The RAD institutionalised pre-military training to parade ground drill, field craft and physical exercise. The organisation was driven to building confidence in its officers while imbuing a sense of responsibility toward the community and creating a strong work ethic among the rank and file.

Some of the sixth company's men had prior service in different branches of service in the *Luftwaffe*. There was no indication that all the troopers were posted to the LWSB direct from basic training. The overall distribution of the branches of service is illustrated in diagram 6. The largest compliment came from the flak branch and

---

10   TNA, WO 208/3979, A Study of German Military Training, Combined Services, May 1946.

mostly based in the Rhineland and Ruhr. The ground combat troops came from security battalions from units serving in Russia or southeast Europe. The 'other' category included clerks and non-specific administrative duties. In other words, they were not all young men under training.

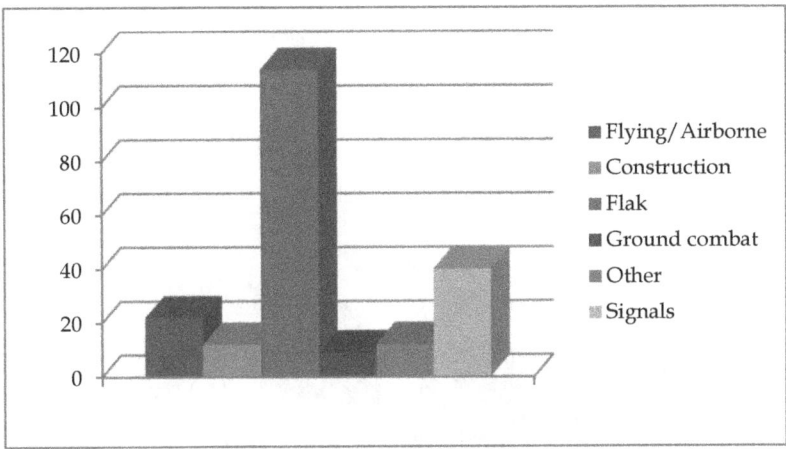

Diagram 5: Original branch of Service with transfers

In the *Luftwaffe*, the signals and flying branches were normally assigned the most capable manpower, graded with an above-average intelligence or technocrats. These specialist branches would not normally release unless they were designated redundant or were incompetent. The 'other' category included a multitude of positions including pay clerks, legal assistants, filing clerks, bookkeepers, medical assistants, switchboard operators etc. Examining the flak contingent identified particular units illustrated in diagram 6. The diagram identified a common group from the homeland flak regiments and being replaced by Hitler Youth and *Luftwaffe* female auxiliaries were serving in flak batteries enabling men to be released to the front.

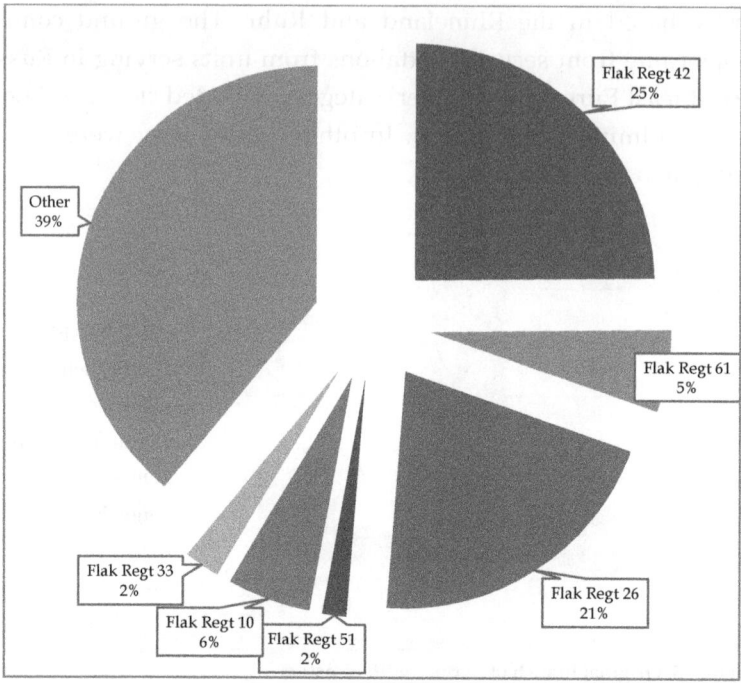

Diagram 6: Personnel assigned from Flak regiments

The personnel papers that have been preserved include junior NCOs and men aged from nineteen to twenty-seven. Two were volunteers and the rest conscripted. The junior and lowest level NCOs are included in this section. All the records found in the archives were men mustered in the Rhineland-Ruhr-Westphalia area, the *Wehrmacht's Wehrkreis VI*. The men were equally divided between Catholic and Protestant faiths, reflecting the balance of the catchment area. The range of their previous occupations included: a baker, boys straight from school, a young farmer, a silk weaver, a druggist, a sheet metal worker, a farmhand, a laboratory assistant, a locksmith, a hospital clerk, and a justice official. Three men were married, and one had children. Under medical examination, prior to basic training, the men showed an array of different physiques. These medical opinions were not consistent throughout a soldier's service. One trooper was reported to have short legs and a propensity to put on weight, but a subsequent report stated that he was very fit and agile. Another trooper received all the required vaccinations for serving on the eastern front including pox, dysentery, cholera and typhus whereas the other didn't. There were indications that the *Luftwaffe* medical officials were very concerned with TB and would call for X-rays at the slightest indication of symptoms. During basic training, the silk weaver was treated as physically challenged due to his work because he could no longer stand straight, and his torso was slightly twisted. A second opinion declared he was physically overworked and incapable. Neither opinion stopped him from being posted to a field company.

The absence of consistency continued with personal assessments periodically given to each man, usually by the next commanding officer. There were enough positive and negative assessments to form a picture of how they were structured. They came in two formats: individual qualities and job performance. Positive personal traits included: 'good intellect', 'good oral skills', 'socially aware' 'outgoing', 'clean', 'friendly', and 'cool attitude'. The positive job traits were: 'strict disciplinarian', 'reliable', 'good at administration', 'good training' and the ubiquitous 'potential leader'. Leadership (*Führung*) and the potential for leadership were strong indicators of performance that not only graded candidates but also reflected back on the trainers and commanding officers. The negative personal assessments received typically adverse comments. The common character faults were: 'slow', 'naughty', 'sloppy', 'big mouth', 'backward' and physically weak. Those aircraftsmen labelled with: 'poor technical ability', 'a poor shot' and 'requires permanent supervision' were never likely to be favourites with their commanding officers. It was noticeable that those cases experienced a disproportionate number of transfers and postings.

In one example of inconsistency, the personal assessments actually undermined the morale of an aircraftsman. Heinrich Alosius U** was born on 7 October 1919 in Duisburg. His father was a waiter, he had a brother and two sisters. He was raised as a catholic and attended *Volksschule*. His 1934 school report remarked that he was a busy, well-behaved boy who was quite good at maths. He did well in all subjects and took up an apprenticeship as a locksmith. Heinrich was happily employed by a Saarland company between 24 April 1934 and 13 November 1937. They gave him an excellent reference: 'he has accepted his life as a locksmith and his overall performance is good.' While under apprenticeship he attended the *Berufsschule Oberhausen* (apprentice school) where he passed his entrance test on 15 March 1937. He also had ambitions to fly and volunteered for the *Luftwaffe* in Oberhausen (Ruhr). He was required to get his father's permission to serve. On 20 September 1937, he signed papers that declared he was not Jewish, and that none of his family members were Jews. During basic training he was taught to use the pistol, a light machine gun and the 98k carbine. More importantly, he received a positive personal assessment: 'good physique', 'well-disposed intellectually', 'average shot', 'a little awkward in sports', 'decent character', and 'had the makings of becoming a good soldier'. In 1939 he was transferred to the Lw. reconnaissance forces in Münster. Between 25 November 1939 and 14 December 1940, he served with a motorised reconnaissance squadron based in Radom, Poland, and was assigned to security duties within the General-Government of Poland.

Having completed his basic training, and service in the field, Heinrich volunteered for flying duty as a radio operator in 1940. On 20 June, he was passed medically fit but his examination revealed *Phimosis*. This is a medical condition in men that prevents the retraction of the penis foreskin. The *Luftwaffe* doctors were not prepared to perform a circumcision even on sound medical grounds that contributed to Heinrich's decline. On 28 June his commanding officer appraised him as: 'intellectually above average', 'open and calm man', 'good performances', 'good leadership qualities', 'full of excellent qualities' and 'should be promoted'. Then on 19 October, he received a negative NCO assessment. He was described as 'simple', inattentive, 'not interested', 'lacks affection', and 'incapable of becoming a flyer or a paratrooper.' However, as confusing as his record was, from 17 November to 13 December 1941, he attended an NCO course and succeeded. On 28 January 1942, he requested a transfer on the grounds that he only volunteered for the Luftwaffe to fly. On 28 February 1942, he was again assessed and found to be 'mentally average', 'lacked interest in things', 'quiet', 'not tough', 'sensitive', 'needs a good leader but accepts authority' but a 'good mechanic'. In compensation for having been a volunteer, but failed the grade, his commanding officer offered him a choice of transfer. He selected to become an aircraft mechanic. By the time Heinrich was posted to the sixth company on 13 October 1942, he had served in three Nazi occupations and had participated in the invasion of Soviet Russia.

Even a junior NCO promotion was treated very seriously in the *Luftwaffe* administration and was a highly bureaucratic process with courses extended over long periods of time. A typical example was Heinrich H** born in Bielefeld, 22 August 1918. He attended Lenzinghausen Protestant *Volksschule* and became a linen-weaver. He was single, 171 cm tall and served with the RAD between 2 February 1938 and May 1939. During this time, he signed the papers confirming there were no Jews in his family on 22 April 1938. As previously mentioned, his medical tests were far from satisfactory. His first posting was to the second company, 10th Flying Training Regiment, in Neukuhren. His training included the 98K carbine, the machine-gun MG15 and the Luger pistol. He volunteered to become a *Fallschirmjäger* (paratrooper) but failed. From the 26 August 1940 to 26 October 1940, he attended the *Unteroffizier-Anwärter-Lehrgang* (NCO candidate school) 8/40 in Heiligenbeil. The course commander wrote of his performance:

> Honest, modest, very obliging, average build, slim, mentally ponderous and tough. Speaks and shouts quite well, loud and clear. He began badly but in all areas he has improved. Educationally inadequate but acceptable for that required of an NCO candidate. Suitability as an NCO: approved.

There were cases of ill-discipline in several personnel files. One trooper was arrested for three days because he arrived back to base late from home leave. Another recruit was placed under arrest for three days because he was late for the start of his induction into the *Luftwaffe*. The strangest case was Helmut F**, born on 12 September 1920 near Düsseldorf. Helmut joined the HJ (1935–1939) but this experience had not instilled in him any military bearing. After school, he became a sheet metal presser, until October 1939 when he was conscripted. His first posting for basic training was to second battalion *Fliegerausbildung Regiment 72* in Detmold. From the beginning, he was typecast as 'hopeless'. In 1940 he tried to become an air mechanic and was declared *mangelhaft* (poor and inadequate). While serving with an airfield reserve technical battalion he was arrested on 19 November 1940. His charge sheet stated:

> Standing to attention before an NCO he moved without permission. When the NCO shouted at him he shouted back 'don't scream at me'. He was then taken before the *Hauptfeldwebel* (senior battalion NCO) and lied under questioning about his reasons for moving without permission. He was sentenced to ten days arrest.

On 4 August 1941, he received six days arrest for returning five hours and forty-five minutes late from home leave. In 1942 he unsuccessfully attempted to become a cook but failed the exam. His poor discipline continued and in one assessment there was a note of irony, 'behaviour quite good after his recent punishment.' Helmut F** was transferred fifteen times during the war, between March and November 1943, to five different battalions of the same field regiment. There was a case of disorderliness within the sixth company in a report of a misdemeanour from 24 January 1943. Richard D** was arrested for drunkenness and insulting a sixth company sergeant. Richard was the company medical orderly and was arrested for three days by the battalion *Oberarzt* (medical officer). Although a minor infraction it does show that the LWSB had access to alcohol and there were some tensions between the men. Richard D** eventually became a senior medical NCO and completed nine postings during the war.

Nearly all the men of the sixth company arrived in the forest during the period 10–14 October 1942. About half the men had served in Poland, France and Russia either as signallers, mechanics, flak gunners or guards. Three had received the *Ostmedaille* 1942. This was given to all soldiers that had served on the eastern front during the winter of 1941 and derided by the soldiery as 'the order of the frozen meat'. On 15 November 1940 aircraftsmen received the *Kriegsverdienstkreuz II Klasse*, the war merit cross, which was instituted on 18 October 1939. This was usually only given to civilians for their war work; there was no citation on file. Many of those men transferred out of the sixth company in 1943 were eventually sent to Norway where they were categorised as serving in 'the air war against England'. Five troopers were re-assigned to *Robinson Ost 2*, Göring's *Luftwaffe* guard. As well as serving in flak, and signals detachments based at Zossen (south of Berlin) the *Wehrmacht* central headquarters during the war and at Göring's headquarters at Rominten Heide. The distribution of transfers when the battalion was dissolved indicates Herbst was monitoring and tracking the performance of the troops.

All the men were trained in the use of infantry small arms especially the 98K carbine, the Luger .08 pistol, the MG15 or MG13 light machine guns and the MP38/40 machine pistol. Most officers and NCOs received the Luger .08 pistol, firing a 9mm calibre bullet. This pistol was prone to clogging from dirt and was carried in a leather holster attached to the waist belt. The 7.92mm Karabiner 98K bolt-action was the standard Wehrmacht carbine during the Second World War. It entered production in 1934 and was initially produced with a milled and laminated beech wooden stock, later changed for a nut tree wood stock. This carbine had iron sights for up to 2000 metres, but its effective range was 800 metres. Its fixed magazine was fed manually by clips of five bullets. The bolt action was then closed in a turned down 'locked and loaded' mechanism. Each carbine came with a twelve-inch cleaning rod, a rubber muzzle cap, a cleaning kit with extra patches, cardboard boxes of fifteen rounds and stripper clips to hold the bullets when loading. The LWSB's troops did not receive attachments such as telescopic sights for sniping or grenade launchers. The officers and NCOs were issued with MP38/40 machine pistols, which fired a 9mm bullet from a thirty-two-round magazine.

Several of the personnel records include the *Schiessbuch* (shooting book), a record of the ability in shooting and marksmanship. A complete shooting record was in Heinrich, the silk weaver's file. Firing the 98k, the recruit was expected to hit a five-centimetre target from one hundred metres. Heinrich scored fourteen hits of the outer circle and eight of the inner circles. He consistently shot well on five different exercises. He was asked to do the same with a light machine gun and again scored high marks. Yet during his time at NCO school, a year later was recorded as a poor shot but allowed to progress as an NCO. He served as a junior NCO rifleman in the sixth company. The battalion's machine guns were all 7.92mm *Machinengewehr 08/15*, the light version of the heavier standard model from the First World War. They used fabric belts of bullets each of 250 rounds or more usually with a drum magazine. The battalion was also issued with the 7.92mm *Maschinengewehr 15* that had originally been fitted to aircraft but was adapted for the ground forces. These re-engineered machine guns were prone to jam and were only used outside the strongpoints during an operation when mounted on tripods.

German soldiers were regularly kitted out with new or renovated clothing. Their uniforms were the least satisfactory of all the belligerents during the war. The earliest uniforms of the *Reichswehr* and *Wehrmacht* were made of high-grade wool. After 1936 the production of dress tunics stopped in favour of a utility uniform. The 1936 model uniform was composed of wool with a small proportion of synthetic rayon. A lining was added to prevent chaffing. By 1940 uniforms were still mostly wool but with increasing levels of rayon or flox increased. To add protection to the wearer an extra button was fastened to keep the front fully closed. The extra buttons were made of wood or compressed pulp. By 1942 the wool content was further reduced. In 1943 a field blouse, without lining, replaced earlier uniforms but most significantly the wool content was reduced to less than fifty per cent of the finished product. By 1944 a hundred per cent synthetic uniform of canvas gabardine twill was issued in the style of British battledress. The troops arrived with the standard blue-grey uniform in July 1942.

Their underwear was natural coloured cotton tricot fabric and artificial yarn. They had a twill waistband and held up by running the braces through loops sewn into the pants. Uniform dyes were inconsistent in quality and subject to fading. It was common practice to change uniforms so as to recycle parts and remnants. The uniform branch of service coloured thread, known as *Waffenfarbe*, buttons and badges were usually made of synthetic fibres and wood. Insignia was made in cloth, velvet cuts, cardboard, aluminium, zinc, rayon, artificial yarn, aluminium twill or gold cord for generals. Military undershirts were made from *Baumwolle* (wood wool). In 1938, the *Luftwaffe* introduced a *Trikothemd* (tricot shirt) made from a mix of cotton and *Zellwolle* (artificial yarn). They reputedly lost their shape after washing. Even the famous 'Jackboots', made of leather, were subject to rationing from 1943 when ankle boots with canvas garters became commonplace. The soldier's *Mantel* (overcoat) was the only part of the uniform to remain in general service, throughout peace and war. It was also the only really warm item the common soldier could rely on.[11] There is no indication that the LWSB was issued with camouflage clothing during its deployment.

Since 1900 Germany had made considerable strides in the development of synthetics many of which were derived from wood. Research into synthetic fibres included rayon, viscose rayon, and a stable fibre, all produced from plant cellulose. Synthetic factories were established across Germany and Göring placed great hope on the substitute industry. There appears to have been no proper testing of these materials under the rigours of wartime conditions — a decision that German soldiers would pay for with their lives.[12] Helmut Pabst, a German army signals NCO, kept a diary of his first days in *Barbarossa*. He described the conditions of life in the nearby forests, during the summer of 1941: 'We marched towards Grodno ... Swamps left and right of us ... mosquitoes — there is enough of those, and dust ... We were sweating horribly. The thunderstorm was a roaring barrag ...'[13] The weather and forest conditions took a toll on the soldiers' uniforms. In April 1942 the British government's Joint Intelligence Committee noted:

> Textiles. — This is a serious German deficiency. Synthetic fibre is not an adequate substitute for wool or cotton. The quality of German uniforms has already deteriorated and is likely to deteriorate further. The substitution of synthetic fibre for wool means less resistance to cold and wet. The clothing

---

11 John R. Angolia & Adolf Schlicht, *Uniforms and Traditions of the Luftwaffe*, (San Jose, 1996), p. 342.
12 Adam Tooze, *The Wages of Destruction: The Making and Breaking of the Nazi Economy*, (London, 2006), pp. 112, 115-6, 130-2.
13 Helmut Pabst, *The Outermost Frontier: A German soldier in the Russian Campaign*, (London, 1986), pp. 13-16.

of the German armies this winter on the Russian Front was inadequate, and if they have fought there next winter their condition will be considerably worse. Should Germany be fighting in Russia next autumn a further drastic cut in the already reduced civilian clothing ration is likely.[14]

The Luftwaffe uniform had a distinct style and cut from the army and navy. The basic uniform colour was blue-grey with the national emblem, worn over the right breast pocket was the Luftwaffe eagle, in flight, symbolising the Swastika being carried into battle. Until 1943 the Luftwaffe troops were issued the *Schiffchen* cap similar to the British 'chip bag' style. From 1943 the standard army issue mountain ski cap replaced them. The caps were the same for NCO's and ORs. All troops received the German steel helmet in rust-resistant paint coloured blue-grey. From September 1942 a helmet camouflage net was issued which could hold dry leaves, blades of grass, twigs or reeds in place over the helmet. The soldiers received badges for awards, technical abilities or lanyards for marksmanship. Only one trooper had a complete clothing allowance in his *Soldbuch*. He received new clothing every three months during the period 1939 to 1943. Some items were duplicated such as underwear with three sets but only one tunic was issued. Behind the image of the impressive uniform, the *Landser* had to cope with wearing uncomfortable items like badges, medals, rough stitching, and unreliable quality. Given the conditions in Białowieża and the lack of warmth or comfort from uniforms, this provides another perspective on the *Landser* in the forest. It's likely the men of the sixth were not entirely comfortable in the winter of 1942–43. The soldier's papers did not list camouflage uniforms.

From the literature available to the troops, we know they contained subliminal messages reinforcing authority. The nature of superior orders was handled through humour in German soldiers' literature. In 1941 the Wehrmacht issued a comedic publication that explained various situations of military culture an enlisted soldier might face during his service. One particular segment referred to *Befehl ist Befehl* (orders are orders). The situation depicted Christopher,

---

14 TNA, FO 371/30895/C3953, War Cabinet papers, JIC (42) 113, Axis Strength and Policy 1942, p. 31.

a young farmhand, newly enlisted and on parade in his uniform. The enlisted soldiers were brought before a *Hauptmann* (captain), who welcomed them. The *Hauptmann* stood before Christopher who snapped to attention. He asked how he liked the surroundings and Christopher bellowed: 'Herr Feldwebel, all is good.' The *Hauptmann* explained he was not a *Feldwebel* and Chistopher blushed. Recognising an 'order is an order', Chistopher bellowed: '*Jawohl, Lieber Herr Hauptmann!*'[15] Serving subliminal messages through comics and unsophisticated pulp literature was a cheap, but highly effective means of integrating lowly educated working-class enlisted soldiers into the military culture. These messages re-established authority and hierarchy, as well as reinforcing the power of discipline and the sanctity of higher orders. In contrast, there were no subliminal messages to explain the circumstances when an enlisted should disobey orders. In other words, they were control literature to instruct soldiers to carry out orders regardless of their criminality.

A few men claimed their military pensions after the war. Richard D**'s wife claimed his pension on 24 January 1973. He died on 6 February 1973 and she only had the minimum of details of his war service. The authorities took three months to reply but confirmed his call up year as 1940 but offered no further war service details. They confirmed he was an NCO medical orderly serving in the flak and had been captured. After a period of French and American PoW captivity, he was released in 1945. The ill-disciplined Helmut F** claimed his military pension on 1 February 1980. The state authorities accepted he was sixty per cent handicapped but did not explain whether this was due to his war service. On 14 May 1980, he received confirmation that his service record ran from 1939 to March 1944. They denied his claim to include 1945 because there were no other reports on his file, but requested he supply them with details if he wished to take the matter further. Heinrich T* requested his pension on 31 March 1980 and received a response on 12 September. The authorities could not prove his claims when he was discharged but noted he had served in the field police.

---

15 Hans Riebau, Hans Reimann, Manfred Schmidt, *Lachendes Feldgrau*, (Bremen, 1941), pp. 111-2. (literally Yes sir, dear Mr. Captain!)

Hermann H** was a twelve-year volunteer and would have been eligible for release from the *Luftwaffe* on 31 March 1949. He claimed his pension on 9 November 1976 and received a response on 25 November proving the Federal authorities could expedite matters if they desired it. He probably received preferential treatment because he was a public servant. In 1982 he requested something the details of which are unknown. He received a brusque reply that he was registered as an NCO with the field police on 25 October 1944. There was no follow-up. Interestingly all the pensioners could recall significant details of their military records, but none made any reference to their service within *Urwald Bialowies*.

III. A summary of casualties, 1942–1944

Assessing the LWSB/JSKB's casualty records is an exercise in balancing incomplete records, an art form usually associated with accountants. There are two sets of numbers: those held in unit war diaries; and, the former official *Wehrmacht* record. Today the *Deutsche Dienststelle* (WASt) in Berlin holds the Wehrmacht's casualty records. The *Wehrmachtsauskunftstelle für Kriegsverluste und Kriegsgefangene* (WASt) kept a complete record of combatants, casualties and POWs for all land and air forces, and marines. Its record combines the LWSB/JSKB into a series of brief reports of individual cases running consecutively throughout the period August 1942 to January 1945 (there is no explanation for the extended period). Diagram 8 graphically shows the peaks and troughs in the casualty records for the entire period.

In the first phase of JSKB's operations the war diary and official record identified 10 dead and 3 wounded. During the second phase, the JSKB suffered 30 killed and 13 wounded. Compared with the losses of the LWSB, the JSKB's losses reflected Frevert's heightened aggressive stance.[16] The ratio of killed was eight per cent and the overall casualty ratio was eleven per cent. On an individual basis, a cross-section of casualties highlights the absence of indis-

---

16   DDSt, JSKB, Namentliche Verlustmeldung, Lw.Ers.Btl. I, Powunden, Nr. 1 28 June 1943//Nr. 18, 25 August 1944.

crimination in war. Private Walter B** (third company, LWSB) was the first fatality listed in the Wehrmacht record; shot in the head on 12 August 1942 while standing by the Lesna Bridge. Walter was just twenty-five years of age born in Tilsit in 1917. Two of his comrades were also severely wounded during that incident—one in the shoulder and the other in the pelvis; they were twenty-three and eighteen respectively. The youngest was Grenadier Hugo B** (JSKB) who was born on 30 March 1926; he was eighteen, killed by a bullet to the head on 21 June 1944, and was buried in Białowieża. The oldest killed in action was Lw. Lieutenant (Reserve) Theodor Lüttge (JSKB) born in Hamburg in February 1897. He had led trusties on special operations and was serving in the Rudziski area on 4 March 1944 when he was shot three times (twice in the lung and once in the heart) from a partisan's machine pistol.[17] The Wehrmacht files recorded an average age of twenty for those killed in action.

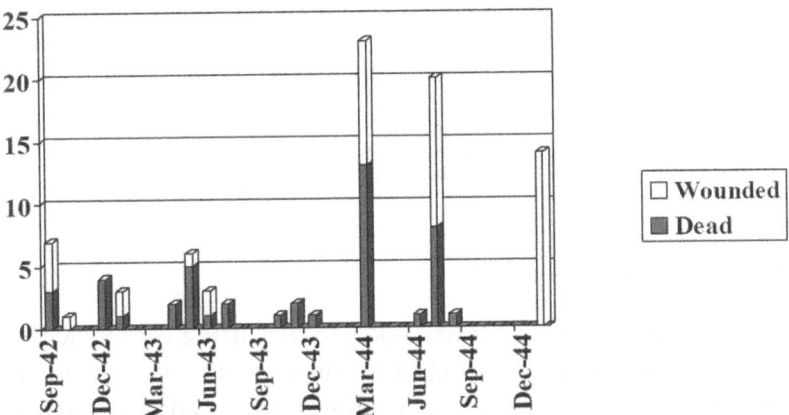

Diagram 7: LWSB/JSKB casualties

Diagram 9 provides an analysis of the weapons and causes of death. This diagram illustrates the range of wounds. There were several cases of *Durchschuss Gesäss* (shot in the arse). Limbs, legs and arms were prone to serious injuries and the most severe cases led to

---

17   DDSt, Namentliche Verlustmeldung Nr. 9, 4–11 April 1944.

death. One trooper suffered an eye injury and lost his sight. A serious thigh wound turned gangrenous and the trooper died of blood poisoning. Private Alfred N** a twenty-three-year-old from Berlin was shot in the liver. Doctors could not remove the bullet and he eventually died of peritonitis. There was one case of TB, LWSB trooper Leonhard W** from Freising Upper Bavaria was twenty-two and he died in the field hospital in Bialystok. On 11 August 1943 Corporal Weiss (JSKB) died after a short but severe illness not explained in the war diary; he was buried in Białowieża three days later. The diary noted, 'the *Jägersonderkommando* loses with him a determined and exemplary soldier.'

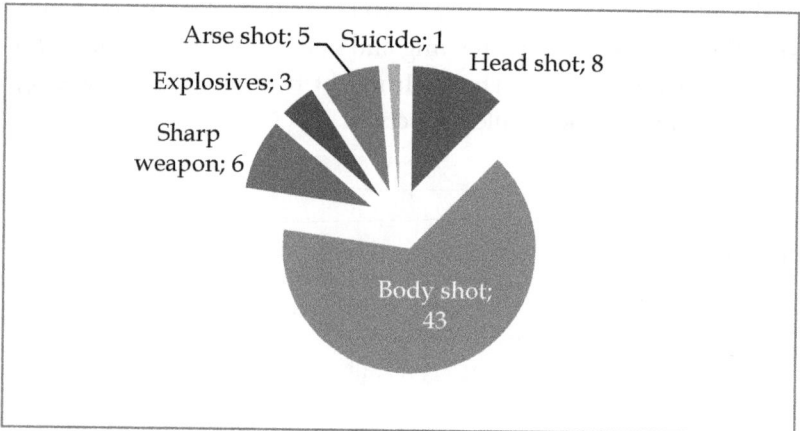

Diagram 8: cause of fatal wounds

There was an account of a wounded soldier being treated with a Marfantil Prontalbin dressing, a Sulphonamide solution. Blood transfusions from the preserved form were not used by the armed forces. The normal method was direct from donor to recipient. Blood substitutes were also used, Tutofusin and simple saline. Treatment also included the use of circulatory stimulants such as Sympatol or Cardiazol. The greatest weakness in the treatment process was Germany's lack of penicillin. Many base hospitals had been deliberately placed in Poland out of the range of allied bombing. The seriously wounded in Białowieża faced a long ride to base hospitals in Bialystok. Some men were wounded in the remotest parts of the forest, difficult for ambulances to access. The seriously wounded were transferred to one of the two reserve Luftwaffe military hospitals in Bialystok. The dead were buried in one of the military graveyards in Bielsk, Bialystok, and Białowieża. The total number of wounded was forty, the vast majority being serious cases requiring intensive medical treatment. It is possible that lightly wounded casualties were treated at Frevert's CP and not included in the official record.

Once a soldier was in an ambulance the journey to Bielsk or Bialystok could be more than two or three hours along poor roads and in badly sprung vehicles. Once the wounded arrived they entered facilities with 500 and 1,500 beds. Once the patient was fit enough to travel they were sent home via a local hospital for recuperation. According to one source until 1942 troops wounded in the field were then placed on an ambulance train but only those destined for the soldier's original Wehrkreis (military district), later this practise was abandoned and wounded were placed on any free bed on the first available train irrespective of destination. Severe cases, in need of long-term treatment, were transported to a hospital nearby their home when a bed was available. Soldiers declared unfit for service were discharged in a process that took about six weeks.[18]

Remarkably, after so much effort to remove the German presence from Polish Prussia, Poland has allowed the proper burial of German soldiers. The remains of the men killed in action while serving with the LWSB/JSKB now lie in the Deutscher Soldatenfriedhof Bartossen (German military cemetery Bartosze) in Poland. Many comrades from the LWSB/JSKB lie side-by-side in communal graves but the whereabouts of Beyrich's remains are unknown. His body seems to have disappeared after those men buried in the Heldenfriedhof were reburied in a new German cemetery and his name is not listed with the rest of the men from both formations. The cemetery is maintained by the Volksbund Deutsche Kriegsgräberfürsorge e.V., (German war grave commission). The

---

18 TNA, WO 208/3615, interrogation of Assistant Dr Dammann, Sanitätskompanie 1190, 6 March 1945.

Volksbund was founded in 1919 and has remained in existence ever since. After 1946 the Bund once again began constructing cemeteries and had built 400 in Germany. From 1954 the Federal authorities commissioned the bund to tend graves in overseas countries. According to the Bund's official statement: 'since 1991 the Bund has taken care, repaired and constructed 330 cemeteries of World War II and 188 graveyards of World War I in Eastern, Central and South Europe. 759,110 war dead have been interned in 82 war graves.' There are other German cemeteries in Poland including Modlin (near Warsaw), Danzig (Gdansk), Joachimov-Mogily (near Warsaw), Krakau (Krakow), Posen (Poznan), Neumark (Stare Czarnowo), Laurahütte (Siemianowice), Mlawka, Gross Nädlitz (Nadolicr Wielkie), Przemysl and Pulawy. The Bund is a not-for-profit organisation; it depends on donations and volunteers and promotes the principle Gedenken und Frieden (remembrance and peace).

Bartossen (Bartosze: Poland) is not far from Lyck (Elk: Poland), an area that lies in the Masurian Lakes district of northeast Poland about 171 miles northwest of Białowieża. Before 1945 Bartossen was in East Prussia and not far from where the LWSB was originally mustered. At the entrance of the cemetery, there is a huge boulder signpost and visitors climb the long stairs to the graves. Work began on building the cemetery in 2001, covering five hectares of ground and was opened in the autumn of 2003. In 2002 the total was 7,000 dead German soldiers interned in the cemetery from the former East Prussia and Bialystok burial sites. Today the site contains 13,824 war dead but is planning for an increase to 20,000; in regards to the management of the dead, the Second World War remains open.

Bibliography

Archival sources

German Archives:

Arolsen Archives (AA)

1.2.7.6., 9038100, Incarceration Documents, Notices and reports o Pol. Batl.322 Operation against Jews in Bialowieza, Bialystok, Narewka Mala.

1.2.7.7., 905880, Incarceration Documents, I. Train Car numbers from the German railroad, railroad administration Königsberg, 29.22.1942–18.8.1943.

I, 9028000, Incarceration Documents, Reports about the organisation of the deportation of the Jews in the district of Bialystok, Easz Prussia.

Bundesarchiv (BArch)

R 2/ 4699, RFA, Forstwesen, Urwaldgebiet Bialowies, Reichsfinanzministerium, abt.1, May 1944; Ausserordentlicher (Kriegs) Haushalt XVIIa Teil XXI Unterteil I; Haushalt für das Oberforstamt Urwald Bialowies, Staatsjagdrevier in Bialowies für das Rechnungsjahr 1943.

R 20/45b Kriegstagebuch von dem Bach.

R 37001-2231, RFA, Organisation 20 August 1941.

RH 27-1/98, 1st Panzer Division, 18 August–10 September 1942. Zusammenstellung von Jgdkos zur Bandenbekämpfung, (31 August 1942).

RL 31/1 – Partisanenkrieg in Bialowies.

RL 31/2 – LW Sicherungsbataillon z.b.V., Anlage 1 zum Kriegstagebuch des Sicherungsbataillon. d. LW.z.b.v. (27 July–3 August 1942).

RL 31/3 – Anlage 2, zum Kriegstagebuch des Sicherungsbataillon. d. Lw. z.b.V report (August 1942–March 1943).

RL 31/4 – Jägersonderkommando d. Lw. Kriegstagebuch 1(5 March 1943–20 September 1944).

RL 31/5 – Jägersonderkommando der Luftwaffe (6 March 1943–3 August 1944) Einsatzbericht fur den 12 Marz 1943.

Formerly Zentralnachweisstelle, Aachen-Kornelimünster (BA ZNS)

Various personnel files of officers and ordinary ranks including: Walter Frevert; Erich Weinreis; Werner Beyrich, Gustav Rühm, and others.

Deutsche Dienststelle (DDst), Berlin

LWSB/JSKB: Sicherungsbataillon d. Lw. z.b.V. Feldpostnummer L49 006, Luftgaupostamt Konigsberg/ PR:

Namentliche Verlustmeldung – Nr. 1, 1–31 August 1942 (27.7–29.8.42).

Namentliche Verlustmeldung Nr. 10, 19–24 March 1944.

Namentliche Verlustmeldung Nr. 9, 4–11 April 1944.

United Kingdom

Imperial War Museum (IWM)

Nazi Conspiracy and Aggression Volumes I-VIII, (Washington 1946–48):

Document L-221: Memorandum For the Record, 8/17/1941 [translation].

Document, NO-1667, Der Reichsführer-SS, Kommando Abt Ia Tgb Nr. Ia 490/42 g.Kdos, Unterdrückund der Bandentätigkeit in Regierungsbezirk Bialystok, 7.8.42. 'Wisent' – Prützmann, SS-Brigadeführer und Generalmajor der Polizei Müller.

Document 032-PS, Secret letter from Rosenberg to Himmler, 2 April 1943, pp. 92–94.

Document 032-PS, Chefgruppe Forst und Holz, Beeunträchtigung forstlicher Belange im RKU: Waldgebiet Zuman, Oberforstrat Lerp, 30 March 1943, pp. 95–96.

IMT, Trial of The Major Criminals Before the International Military Tribunal, Nuremberg 14 November 1945–1 October 1946, Vol. XXV, Nuremberg, 1947, Document 032-PS, Secret letter from Rosenberg to Himmler, 2 April 1943, pp. 92–94.

National Archives, formerly the Public Records Office (TNA)

FO 371/30895, case C3953, War Cabinet papers, JIC(42) 113, Axis Strength and Policy 1942, p. 31.

HS 7/205, Soviet Partisan's Companion.

HW 16/6, British decrypts of German police signals covering period 15–31 August 1941, MSGP 27, 21 August 1941

HW 16/6 British decrypts of German police signals covering period 15–31 August 1941, General situation assessment.

HW 16/6, British decrypts of German police signals, MSGP 13, 11 September 1940.

HW 16/6, British decrypts of German police signals, MSGP 28, 12 September 1941

WO 208/3000, 'The German Squad In Combat, Military', Intelligence Service, US War Department, Washington DC, 25 January 1943.

WO 208/3009, Germany Basic Handbook, Part III: Nazi-Occupied Europe, October 1944. A colour map plate from an allied occupation handbook (1944).

WO 208/3230, US Army Pamphlet 20-231, 'Combat in Russian Forests and Swamps', Department of the Army, July 1951.

WO 208/3608 CSDIC SIR 1329, Establishment of a Jgdko by Secret order of the Befehlshaber Südost, interrogation of UFF'S Kotschy and Boscmeinen, 13 December 1944.

WO 208/3615, interrogation of Assistant Dr. Dammann, Sanitätskompanie 1190, 6 March 1945.

WO 208/3619, Interrogation Reports, CSDIC (UK), SIR 1706–1718, interrogation number 1709, German Army Warrant Officer Dr. Bartz 19 July 1945.

WO 208/3777, Vorschlag zur Gliederung und Aufgaben-Verteilung des Bataillons-Stabes im Gefecht und im inneren Dienst. Acquired in February 1945.

WO 208/3785, Goering, Hermann four arrest cards.

WO 208/3979, A Study of German Military Training, Combined Services, May 1946.

WO 208/4168, SRGG 1065, General Ramcke, September 1944.

WO 208/4170–C.S.D.I.C. (UK), S.R.G.G. 1228(C), Generalleutnant Galland (JV44), Captured Tegernsee 5 May 1944, interrogation on the 16 May 1945.

United States of America

National Archives (NARA) of Washington D.C.: College Park, Maryland.

T 77/100 100/145/301 (OKW Wi Ru Amt) mobilisation of the Reichsforstministerium.

T 77/145 (OKW Wi Ru Amt) Reichsforstmeister 1935–42, mobilisation plans.

T 77/301 (OKW Wi Ru Amt) Reichsforstmeister.

T 77/1421 OKW-Wehrmachtführungsstab, Poland and Bialystok.

T 77/780/5506284-5506484 (OKW Wi Ru Amt) Wehrmacht Ersatzplan 1945, section 62, Reichsforstamt.

T 78/880, Kriegsgräber fürsorge, II band 1943–1944, various WGO papers.

T 175/13/ 2515813-2515890, Die Völker der Erde.

T 175/13/2515813-2515890, Richtlinien für die kolonialtaktische Ausbildung an den Kolonialpolizei-Schulen (n.d.).

T 175/42/1, Lieutenant-General Ramcke, farmstead in the east.

T 175/140/2668141-355, Weisung Nr. 46: Richtlinien für die verstärkte Bekämpfung des Bandenunwesens im Osten, Der Führer, OKW/WFSt/Op. Nr. 002821/42g.K., Führerhauptquartier, 18 August 1942

T 314/404-408, IX German Army Corps 1941.

T 580/216/0473. Ansprache des Chefs der Ordnungspolizei anläßlich der Tagung der Inspekteure der Ordunungspolizei am 21. Januar 1941, 24.

T 580/222, Bekämpfung des Wildererunwesens im Warthegau, 8 March 1940.

T 580/222, letter from Chief of Order Police Kurt Daluege to Scherping, 8 April 1940.

FMS, D-257, Heinz Krampf, 'Anti-Partisan protection of the railways'.

RG 319, IRR, Winiza (sic) massacres, September–October 1952, 66 Counter Intelligence Corps Detachment, 17 October 1952.

Yad Vasham Archive, Jerusalem

0-53/127, Police Bicycle Battalion 322 war diary, Tagesmeldung am Pol. Btl.322, 30 July 1941.

0-53/127, Police Bicycle Battalion 322 war diary, Stichwortartiger Bericht über Einsatz des Batl.

I. Official codes, reports, handbooks, manuals, dictionaries

Absolon, Rudolf, *Die Wehrmacht im Dritten Reich, Band IV, 19 Dezember 1941 bis 9 Mai 1945*, (Boppard am Rhein, 1995).

Air Ministry, *The Rise and Fall of the German Air Force (1933 to 1945)*, (London 1948).

Blasé, Richard, *Die Jägerprüfung*, (Melsungen, 1970).

Bundesarchiv (Hrsg.), *Europa unterm Hakenkreuz, Achtbändige Dokumentenedition, Ergänzungsband 1, Okkupation und Kollaboration (1938–1945)*. Beiträge zu Konzepten und Praxis der Kollaboration in der deutschen Okkupationspolitik, (Berlin, 1994).

BIBLIOGRAPHY

Cologne District Court Judgement 30-11/67, The People vs Kurt Wiese and Henry Errelis, Federal Republic of Germany, (27 June 1968).

CMH Pub 104-19, *The Soviet Partisan Movement 1941–1944*, (Washington DC, 1956).

Der Reichsführer-SS und Chef der Deutschen Polizei, *Bandenbekämpfung*, I Ausgabe, (München, 1942).

Eitzen, Kurt Hilmar, *Militär-Wörterbuch*, (Berlin, 1936).

Generalkommando des XIII. Armeekorps, *An Der Mittleren Ostfront: Ein Deutsches Korps im Kampf gegen die Sowjets*, (Nürnberg, 1942).

Glówna KomisjaBadanaia Zbrodni Hitlerowskich w Polsce Rada Ochrony Pomników Walki I Męchzenstwa, *Obozy hitlerowskie na ziemiach polskich 1939–1945: Informator encykloedyczny*, (Warszawa, 1979).

Hubatsch, Walter, *Hitlers Weisungen für die Kriegführung 1939–1945: Dokumente des Oberkommandos der Wehrmacht*, (Osnabrück, 1999).

Laura, Craigo, and Alexander Kruglov, 'Kamieniec Litewski', United States Holocaust Memorial Museum Encyclopedia of Camps and Ghettos_, ed. Geoffrey P. Megargee, Vol. 2, *Ghettos in German-occupied Eastern Europe*, ed. Martin Dean, (Indianapolis, 2012).

Keilig, Wolf, *Das Deutsche Heer 1939–1945, Gliederung, Einsatz, Stellenbesetzung*, (Bad Nauheim, 1956).

Mantel, Kurt, *Reichsjagdgesetz*, (München, 1934).

Militärgeschichtliches Forschungsamt, Boog, Horst et al. (ed), trans. Dean S. McMurray et al, *Germany and the Second World War: The Attack on the Soviet Union*, vol. IV, (Oxford, 1998).

Militärgeschichtliches Forschungsamt, Karl-Heinz Frieser et al. (ed), *Das Deitsche Reich und der Zweite Weltkrieg: Die Ostfront 1943/44*, Band 8, (München, 2007).

Militärgeschichtliches Forschungsamt, Ralf Blank et al. (ed), trans. Derry Cook-Radmore et al, *Germany and the Second World War: German Wartime Society 1939–1945: Politicization, Disintegration, and the Struggle for Survival*, vol. IX/I, (Oxford, 2008).

Military Intelligence Service, *German Military Abbreviations*, (Washington, 12 April 1943).

_____, No.15, *The German Rifle Company*, (Washington DC, 1942), 1942, partial translation of Ludwig Queckbörner, *Die Schützen-Kompanie: Ein handbuch für den Dienstunterricht*, (Berlin, 1939).

Müller Rolf-Dieter, and Gerd R. Ueberschar, *Hitler's War in the East 1941–1945: A Critical Assessment*, (Oxford, 1997).

Noakes, J., & G. Pridham (ed), *Nazism 1919–1945, A Documentary Reader: 3. Foreign Policy, War and Racial Extermination*, (Exeter, 1995).

Tessin, Georg, *Verbände und Truppen der Deutschen Wehrmacht und Waffen-SS im Zweiten Weltkrieg*, Erster Band: Die Waffengattungen-Gesamt-übersicht, (Osnabrück, 1977).

_____, *Verbände und Truppen, der deutschen Wehrmacht und Waffen-SS im Zweiten Weltkrieg 1939–1945*, Achter Band, Die Landstreitkräfte 201–280, (Osnabrück 1975).

_____, *Verbände und Truppen, der deutschen Wehrmacht und Waffen-SS im Zweiten Weltkrieg 1939–1945*, Zehnter Band, Die Landstreitkräfte 371–500, (Osnabrück 1975).

_____, *Verbände und Truppen, der deutschen Wehrmacht und Waffen-SS im Zweiten Weltkrieg 1939–1945*, Sechzehnter Band, Verzeichnis der Friedensgarnisonen 1932–1939 und Stationierungen im Kriege 1939–1945, (Osnabrück 1996).

The Goebbels Diaries, trans. Louis P. Lochner, (London, 1948).

Ultrichter, Major General Friedrich, *Der Reserveoffizier: Ein Handbuch für den Offizier und Offizieranwäter des Beurlaubtenstandes aller Waffen*, (Berlin, 1941).

U.S. Army CMH Pub 104-19, *The Soviet Partisan Movement 1941–1944*, (Washington, D.C., 1956).

Reichelt, Katrin, Laura Craigo, and Martin Dean, 'Prużany', United States Holocaust Memorial Museum Encyclopedia of Camps and Ghettos, ed. Geoffrey P. Megargee, Vol. 2, *Ghettos in German-occupied Eastern Europe*, ed. Martin Dean, (indianapolis, 2012).

US War Department, 'Handbook on German Miliatary Forces', War Department Technical Manual, TM-E 30-451, (Washington DC, 15 March 1945).

Witte, Peter, et al (eds), *Der Dienstkalender Heinrich Himmlers 1941/42*, Forschungsstelle für Zeitgeschichte in (Hamburg, 1999).

V. Oral sources: interviews, newspapers, television and radio.

Documentary, 'Alltag im Fliegerhorst', Gescher, Polar Films, 2004.

Siegień, Paulina and Wojciech, 'An unwanted march: Polish nationalists honour anti-communist partisans accused of war crimes.' *Notes from Poland*, February 24, 2020. https://notesfrompoland.com/2020/02/

24/an-unwanted-march-polish-nationalists-honour-anti-communist-partisans-accused-of-war-crimes/.

Special edition DVD, *The Battle of Britain*, (MGM, 2004).

Television: Jonathan Meades, 'Jerry Building', BBC, 1994.

Television: 'Nazis — A Lesson From History', programme 6, BBC 1995.

Television, 'Spiral of Terror', *War of the Century*, part two, BBC 1999, interview with Ivan Treskovski.

The Times, *Air Commodore Ted Sismore*, Obituary, 5 April 2012.

Tourist Information post, 'Orthodox Church in Białowieża', Białowieża Neighbourhood Programme, 2004–6.

VI. Doctoral theses and open access sources.

Blood, Philip W., 'Bandenbekämpfung, Nazi occupation security in Eastern Europe and Soviet Russia, 1942–45,' PhD diss. (unpublished), Cranfield University, 2001.

_____, https://www.academia.edu/43096984/Weidmanns_Heil_a_history_of_Social_Hunting_and_the_German_Middle_Class_1848_1914_ 27 April 2020.

Michael Imort, '"Forestopia": the use of the forest landscape in naturalizing National Socialist policies of Volk, race and Lebensraum 1918–1945', PhD Thesis, Queen's University, 2000.

Pipping, Knut, 'Infantry company as a society', PhD diss. published, Helsinki: National Defence University, 2008.

Christoph Rass, '"Menschmaterial". Sozialprofil, Machtstrukturen und Handlungsmuster einer Infanteriedivision der Wehrmacht im Zweiten Weltkrieg', PhD thesis, Rheinisch-Westfälischen Technischen Hochschule, (Aachen, 2001).

VII. Books and articles

Articles and books before 1945

Beumelburg, Werner, *Kampf um Spanien: Die Geschichte Der Legion Condor*, (Berlin, 1939).

Dubnow, Simon M. *History of the Jews in Russia and Poland: From the Earliest Times to the Present Day*, three volumes, trans. Israel Friedlander, (Philadelphia, 1918).

Frevert, Walter, *Jagdliches Brauchtum*, (Berlin, 1936).

_____, 'Zehn Jahre Jagdherr in Rominten', *Wild und Hund*, (1943).

Galland, Adolf, 'Oberst Galland', *Wild und Hund*, No. 47, 1941–42, pp. 357–358.

Gritzbach, Erich, *Hermann Göring, Werk und Mensch*, (München, 1938).

Heck, Lutz, *Auf Tiersuche in Weiter Welt*, (Berlin, 1943).

———, 'Hermann Göring, der Schützer des deutschen Urwildes', *Wild und Hund*, 1943, No. 39–40, pp. 154–157.

Henderson, Sir Nevile, *Failure of A Mission: Berlin 1937–9*. (New York, 1940).

Heske, Franz, *German forestry*, (New Haven, 1938).

Jentsch, Fr. 'Das Preussische Reitende Feldjägerkorps', *Tharandter Forstliches Jahrbuch*, Band 90, Heft ¾, 1940.

Kobylinski, Manfred von, *Bunte Strecke, Aus dem Leben eines ostpreussischen Jägers*, (Berlin, 1935).

Leopold, Aldo, 'Deer and Dauerwald in Germany. I. History', *Journal of Forestry* 34, No.4 and 5 (1936).

Lenartowicz, Stanislaw, *Przewodnik Po Polsce: Polska Północno-Wschodnia*, (Warszawa, 1935).

Raesfeld, Ferdinand von, *Das Deutsche Weidwerk: Ein Lehr- und Handbuch der Jagd*, (Berlin, 1914).

Richthofen, Manfred Freiherr von, *Der Rote Kampfflieger*, (Berlin, 1933).

Röhrig, Fritz, *Wald und Weidwerk: In Geschichte und Gegenwart*, (Potsdam, 1933/38).

Scherping, Ulrich, 'Bialowies wieder in Deutscher Verwaltung', in *Wild und Hund*, 19 December 1941.

———, 'Jäger Sein', *Wild und Hund*, Nr. 27/28, 4 October 1942.

Schott, Hauptmann, 'Kampferfahrungen eines Offiziers', *Militärwochenblatt*, Nr. 9, 28 August 1942.

Seeger, 'Eine Mondnacht im Urwald von Bialowies', *Wild und Hund*, November 1942.

Books and articles since 1945

Allen, William Sheridan, *The Nazi Seizure of Power: The Experience of a Single German Town 1922–1945*, (London, 1984).

Aly, Götz, *Final Solution: Nazi Population Policy and the Murder of the European Jews*, (Oxford, 1999).

Angolia John R., & Adolf Schlicht, *Uniforms and Traditions of the Luftwaffe*, (San Jose, 1996).

Bibliography

Angrick, Andrej, Martina Voigt, Silke Ammerschubert und Peter Klein, '"Da hätte man schon ein Tagebuch führen müssens": Das Polizeibatailon 322 und die Judenmorde im Bereich der Heeresgruppe Mitte während des Sommers und Herbstes 1941', Grabitz, Helge, Klaus Bästlein, Johannes Tuchel, Peter Klein und Martina Voigt, *Die Normalität des Verbrechens*, (Berlin, 1994).

Arad, Yitzhak, Shmuel Krakowski & Shmuel Spector, *The Einsatzgruppen Reports*, (New York, 1989).

Armstrong, John A., *Soviet Partisans In World War II*, (Madison, 1964).

Autorenkollektiv, *Bilanz des Zweiten Weltkrieges – Erkenntnisse und Verpflichtungen für die Zukunft*, (Oldenburg, 1953).

Balfour, Michael, *Propaganda in War: Organisations, Policies and Publics in Britain and Germany*, (London, 2010).

Bartov, Omer, 'Eastern Europe as the Site of Genocide', in *The Journal of Modern History*, 80 (September 2008).

_____, *Erased: Vanishing Traces of Jewish Galicia in Present Day Ukraine*. Princeton: Princeton University Press, 2007

_____, *Hitler's Army: Soldiers, Nazis and War in the Third Reich*, (New York, 1992).

_____, *The Eastern Front, 1941–1945: German troops and the Barbarisation of Warfare*, (New York, 1986).

Bellamy, Chris, *Absolute War: Soviet Russia in the Second World War*, (London, 2007)).

Bender, Roger James and George A. Petersen, *'Hermann Göring': from Regiment to Fallschirmpanzerkorps*, (Atglen, 1993).

Beorn, Waitman Wade, *Marching Into Darkness: The Wehrmacht and the Holocaust in Belarus*, (Harvard, 2014).

Bessel, Richard, *Nazism and War*, (London, 2004).

Bishop, Edward, *Mosquito: Wooden Wonder*, (London, 1971).

Blood, Philip W., 'Securing Hitler's Lebensraum: the Luftwaffe and the forest of Białowieża 1942-4', *Holocaust and Genocide Studies*, (2010).

_____, *Hitler's Bandit Hunters: The SS and the Nazi Occupation of Europe*, (Virginia, 2006).

_____, 'Kurt Daluege and the Militarisation of the Ordnungspolizei', in Gerard Oram, *Conflict and Legality: Policing Mid-Twentieth Century Europe*, (London, 2003), pp. 95–120.

Borcher, W., 'Der Todeswald von Bialowieza', *Der Landser*, (1961).

Bourke, Joanna, *An Intimate History of Killing: Face-To-Face Killing in Twentieth Century Warfare*, (London, 1999).

Breitman, Richard, *Official Secrets: What the Nazis Planned, What the British and American Knew*, (New York, 1998).

Browning, Christopher, *Nazi Policy, Jewish Workers, German Killers*, (Cambridge, 2000).

_____, *Ordinary Men: Reserve Police Battalion 101 and the Final Solution in Poland*, (New York, 1998).

_____, *The Path to Genocide: Essays on launching the Final Solution*, (Cambridge, 1992).

_____, *The Origins of the Final Solution: The Evolution of Nazi Jewish Policy 1939–1942*, (London, 2004).

_____, 'A reply to Martin Broszat Regarding the Origins of the Final Solution, in Michael Marrus (ed), *The Nazi Holocaust: Historical Articles on the Destruction of the European Jews*, vol.3, (Meckler, 1989), pp. 168–87; see also the original "Zur Genesis der Endlösung.' Eine Antwort an Martin Broszat." *Vierteljahrshefte für Zeitgeschichte*, 25(4), 1984, pp. 739–775.

Bullock, Alan, *Hitler: A Study in Tyranny*, (London, 1952).

Bungay, Stephan, *The Most Dangerous Enemy: A History of the Battle of Britain*, (London, 2010).

Burrin, Philippe, *Hitler and the Jews: The Genesis of the Holocaust*, (London, 1994).

Bussenius, Ingeburg Charlotte, *Die preussische Verwaltung im Süd- und Neuostpreussen*, (Hamburg, 1960).

Caidin, Martin, *ME109: Willy Messerschmitt's peerless fighter*, (London, 1968).

Charlesworth, Andrew, 'The Topography of Genocide', in Dan Stone (ed), *The Historiography of the Holocaust*, (Londond, 2004).

Citino, Robert M, *The German Way of War: From Thirty Years' War to the Third Reich*, (Kansas, 2005)

Clausewitz, Carl von, Michael Howard and Peter Paret ed. & trans., *On War*, (London: 1993).

Clayton, Anthony, *Warfare in Woods and Forests*, (Bloomington, 2012).

Condell, Bruce and David T. Zabecki ed, *On the German Art of War: German Army Manual for Unit Command in World War II*, (Mechanicsburg, 2001).

Confino, Alon, *Germany as a Culture of Remembrance: Promises and Limits of Writing History*, (Chapel Hill, 2006).

_____, *The Nation as a Local Metaphor: Württemberg, Imperial Germany, and National Memory, 1871–1918*, (Chapel Hill, 1997).

Corum, James. S, 'Building A New Luftwaffe: The United States Air Force and Bundeswehr Planning for Rearmament, 1950–60,' *Journal of Strategic Studies*, 27:1, 89–113, (2004)

_____ 'Die Luftwaffe, ihre Führung und Doktrin und die Frage der Kriegsverbrechen' in Wolfram Wette & Gerd R. Ueberschär (Hrsg.) *Kriegsverbrechen im 20. Jahrhundert*, (Darmstadt, 2001).

_____, *The Luftwaffe: Creating the Operational Air War, 1918–1940*, (Lawrence, 1997).

Cox, Dan G. and Thomas Bruscino (ed), *Population-Centric Counterinsurgency: A False Idol?* SAMS Monograph Series, CSIP, US Army CAC, (Kansas, 2011).

Craig, Gordon, *The Politics of the Prussian Army, 1640–1945*, (Oxford, 1978).

Creveld, Martin van, *Fighting Power and US Army Performance 1939–1945*, (London, 1983).

Curilla, Wolfgang, *Die deutsche Ordnungspolizei und der Holocaust im Baltikum und in Weissrussland 1941–1944*, (Paderborn, 2006).

Dalby, David, *Lexicon of The Mediaeval German Hunt: A Lexicon of Middle High German Terms (1050–1500) associated with the Chase, Hunting with Bows, Falconry, Trapping and Fowling*, (Berlin, 1965).

Dallin, Alexander, *German Rule in Russia, 1941–1945: A Study of Occupation Policies*, (New York, 1957).

Datner, Szymon, 'Eksterminacja ludności żydowskiej w Okręgu Białostockim', *Bulletin of the Jewish Historical Institute*, (Warsaw, 1966).

Davies, Norman, *Europe: A History*, (London, 1996).

Desbois, Father Patrick, *The Holocaust by Bullets: A Priest's Journey to Uncover the Truth Behind the Murder of 1.5 Million Jews*, (Basingstoke, 2008).

Dixon, Aubrey and Heilbrunn, Otto, *Communist Guerrilla Warfare*, (London, 1954).

Duffy, Christopher, *Red Storm on the Reich: The Soviet March on Germany, 1945*, (London, 1991).

Egremont, Max, *Forgotten Land: Journeys Among the Ghosts of East Prussia*, (London, 2011).

Ellis, John, *The Sharp End of War: The Fighting Man in World War II*, (London,1980).

Fest, Joachim C., *Plotting Hitler's Death: The German Resistance to Hitler, 1933–1945*, (London, 1997).

Flachowsky, Sören, und Holger Stoecker (Hg), *Vom Amazona an die Ostfront. Der Expeditionsreisende und Geograph Otto Schulz-Kampfhenkel (1910–1989)*, (Köln, 2011).

Foley, Robert T., *Alfred von Schlieffen's Military Writings*, (London, 2003).

Foot, M.R.D., *Resistance: European Resistance to Nazism 1940–45*, (London, 1976).

Forster, Jürgen, 'The Shock of Stalingrad and the Crisis of Military-Ideological Leadership', MGFA, Ralf Blank et al (ed), trans. Derry Cook-Radmore et al., *Germany and the Second World War: German Wartime Society 1939–1945: Politicization, Disintegration, and the Struggle for Survival*, vol. IX/I, (Oxford, 2008), pp. 584–613.

_____, 'The Wehrmacht and the War of Extermination 1941', *Yad Vashem Studies* 14, (1981).

Frevert, Walter, *Rominten*, (München, 1957).

_____, *Das Jagdliche Brauchtum: Jägersprache, Bruchzeichen, Jagdsignale und sonstige praktische Jagdgebräuche*, (Berlin, 1981).

_____, *Meine Jägerleben*, (Berlin, 2013).

Foucault, Michel, *The Birth of the Clinic: An Archaeology of Medical Perception*, trans. A.M.Sheridan Smith, (New York, 1994).

_____, *Discipline and Punish: The Birth of the Clinic*, (London, 1991).

_____, *The Order of Things*, (London, 1989).

Frazer, Sir James, *The Golden Bough: A Study in Magic and Religion*, (London, 1993).

Gilpin Faust, Drew, *This Republic of Suffering: Death and the American Civil War*, (New York, 2008).

Frei, Norbert, *Adenauer's Germany and the Nazi Past: The Politics of Amnesty and Integration*, (Cambridge, 2004).

Friedländer, Saul, *The Years of Extermination: Nazi Germany and the Jews, 1939–1945*, (London, 2007).

_____, *Reflections on Nazism: An Essay on Kitsch and Death*, trans. Thomas Weyr, (Indiana, 1984).

BIBLIOGRAPHY

Frydel, Tomasz, 'Judenjagd: Reassessing the role of Ordinary Poles as Perpetrators in the Holocaust', in Timothy Williams and Susanne Buckley-Zistel, *Perpetrators and Perpetration of Mass Violence*, (London, 2018), pp. 187–203.

Galland, Adolf, *The First and the Last: The German Fighter Force in the World War II*, (London, 1970).

Gautschi, Andreas, *Walter Frevert: Eines Waidmanns Wechsel und Wege.* (Melsungen, 2005).

_____, *Der Reichsjägermeister: Fakten und Legenden um Hermann Göring*, (Suderburg, 1999).

Gellately, Robert, *The Nuremberg Interviews: Conversations with the Defendants and Witnesses Conducted by Leon Goldensohn*, (London, 2006).

Gerlach, Christian, 'Men of 20 July and the War in the Soviet Union', in Hannes Heer & Klaus Nauman, *War of Extermination: The German Military in World War II 1941–1944*, (Oxford, 2000).

_____, *Kalkulierte Morde: Die deutsche Wirtschafts- und Vernichtungspolitik in Weissrussland 1941 bis 1944*, (Hamburg, 1999).

Geyer, Herrmann, *Das IX Korps im Ostfeldzug*, (Vowinckel, 1969).

Glantz, David M., *Barbarossa Derailed: The Battle for Smolensk, the Encirclement Battle, and the First and Second Soviet Counteroffensives, 10 July–10 September 1941*, (Solihull, 2010).

Glantz, David M., & Harold S. Orenstein, *Belorussia 1944: The Soviet General Staff Study*, (London, 2001).

Goeschal, Christian, *Suicide in Nazi Germany*, (Oxford, 2009).

Goldhagen, Daniel Jonah, *Hitler's Willing Executioners: Ordinary Germans and the Holocaust*, (London, 1996).

Grabitz, Helge, Klaus Bästlein, Johannes Tuchel, *Die Normalität des Verbrechens: Bilanz und Perspectiven der Forschung zu den nationalsozialistischen Gewaltverbrechen*, (Berlin, 1994).

Grabowski, Jan, *Hunt for the Jews: Betrayal and Murder in German-Occupied Poland*, (Indiana, 2013).

Gregory, Ian N.& Paul S. Ell, *Historical GIS: Technologies, Methodologies and Scholarship*, (Cambridge, 2007).

Gross, Jan Tomasz, *Revolution from Abroad: The Soviet Conquest of Poland's Western Ukraine and Western Belorussia*, (Princeton, 2002).

Gryc, Alls, (ed) *Alla, Hajnówka W Starej Fotografii*, (Hajnówka, 2007).

Guderian, Heinz, *Panzer Leader*, trans. Constantine Fitzgibbon, (Aylesbury, 1974).

Hale, Christopher, *Hitler's Foreign Executioners: Europe's Dirty Secret* (Stroud, 2011).

Hamburger Institut für Sozialforschung (Hg.), *Verbrechen Der Wehrmacht: Dimensionen Des Vernichtungskrieges 1941–1944*, (Hamburg, 2002).

_____, *Vernichtungskrieg. Verbrechen der Wehrmacht 1941 bis 1944*, (Hamburg, 1995).

Hart, Basil Liddell, *The Other Side of the Hill*, (London, 1948).

Häusler, 'Hermann, Forschungsstaffel z.b.V. Eine Sondereinheit zur militärgeografischen Beurteilung des Geländes im 2. Weltkrieg.' *Schriftenreihe, MILGEO Institut für Militärisches Geowesen*, Heft 21/2007.

Heer, Hannes, 'Killing Fields: The Wehrmacht and the Holocaust in Belorussia, 1941–1942', in *Holocaust and Genocide Studies*, Spring 1997.

Heer, Hannes & Klaus Nauman, *War of Extermination: The German Military in World War II 1941–1944*, (Oxford, 2000).

Heiber, Helmut, David M. Glantz (ed), *Hitler and his Generals: Military Conferences 1942–1945*, (New York, 2002).

Hilberg, Raul, *Sources of Holocaust Research: An Analysis*, (Chicago, 2001).

_____, *The Destruction of the European Jews*, (New York, 1985).

Hinze, Rolf, *Das Ostfront-Drama 1944: Rückzugskampfe Heeresgruppe Mitte*, (München, 1988).

Holmes, Richard, *World at War*, (London, 2007)

_____, *Riding The Retreat: Mons to the Marne – 1914 Revisited*, (London, 2007).

_____, 'Battle: The Experience of Modern Combat', in Charles Townshend ed, *The Oxford History of Modern War*, (Oxford, 2000).

_____, *Firing Line*, (London, 1985).

Hobsbawm, Eric, *On History*, (London, 1997).

Hobsbawm, Eric, & Terence Ranger, *The Invention of Tradition*, (Cambridge, 1983).

Jones, Nigel H., *Hitler's Heralds: The Story of the Freikorps 1918–1923*, (London, 1987).

Kershaw, Ian, *Hitler: 1936–1945 Nemesis*, (London 2000).

Keneally, Thomas, *Schindler's Ark*, (London, 1982).

Klapdor, Ewald, *Viking Panzers: The German 5th SS Tank Regiment in the East in World War II*, (Mechanicsburg, 2011).

Klee, Ernst, Willi Dressen, and Volker Riess (ed), *The Good Old Days: The Holocaust as seen by its Perpetrators and Bystanders*, (New York, 1991).

Klemann, Hein, & Sergei Kudryashov, *Occupied Economies: An Economic History of Nazi Occupied Europe, 1939-1945*, (London, 2012).

Klemperer, Victor, *The Language of the Third Reich*, (London, 2000).

Knopf, Volker and Martens, Stefan, *Görings Reich: Selbstinszenierungen in Carinhall*, (Berlin, 1999).

Knowles, Anne Kelly, Tim Cole, Alberto Giordano (ed), *Geographies of the Holocaust*, (Bloomington, 2014).

Knowles, Anne Kelly, (ed), *Past Time, Past Place: GIS for History*, (California, 2002).

Koehl, Robert Lewis, *RKFDV: German Resettlement and Population Policy 1933-1945*, (Cambridge Mass., 1957).

Kossak, Simona, *The Białowieża Saga*, (Warsaw, 2001.

Kovpak, S.A., *Our Partisan Course*, (London, 1947).

Krakowski, Shmuel, trans. Orah Blaustein, *The War of the Doomed: Jewish Armed Resistance in Poland 1942-1944*, (New York, 1984).

Kreidler, Eugen, *Die Eisenbahnen im Zweiten Weltkrieg*, (Hamburg, 2001).

Kühne, Thomas, *Belonging and Genocide. Hitler's Continuity 1918-1945*, (New Haven, 2010).

_____, 'Kameradschaft – "das Beste im Leben des Mannes", Die deutschen Soldaten des Zweiten Weltkrieges in erfahrungs- und geschlechtergeschichtlicher Perspektive,' *Geschichte und Gesellschaft* 22 (1996).

_____, *Kameradschaft: Die Soldaten des nationalsozialistischen Krieges und das 20. Jahrhundert*, (Göttingen, 2006).

Kurowski, Franz, trans. David Johnston, *The History of the Fallschirmpanzerkorps Hermann Göring: Soldiers of the Reichsmarschal*, (Winnipeg, 1995).

Kwiet, Konrad, 'From the Diary of a Killing Unit', John Milful, *Why Germany? National Socialist Anti-Semitism and the European Context*, (Oxford, 1993).

Leopold, Aldo, *A Sand County Almamanac: And Sketches Here and There*, (New York, 1949).

Liekis, Ašarūnas, *1939: The Year That Changed Everything in Lithuania's History*, (Amsterdam, 2010).

Longerich, Peter, trans. Jeremy Noakes and Lesley Sharpe, *Heinrich Himmler*, (Oxford, 2012).

_____, *Holocaust: The Nazi Persecution and Murder of the Jews*, (Oxford, 2010).

Lower, Wendy, *Nazi Empire-Building and the Holocaust in Ukraine*, (Chapel Hill, 2007).

Mackay, Richard W., *The Zabern Affair 1913–1914*, (Lanhan, 1991).

Mackenzie, S.P. *The Battle of Britain on Screen*, (Edinburgh, 2007).

MacLean, French, *The Cruel Hunters: SS-Sonderkommando Dirlewanger Hitler's most notorious anti-partisan*, (Atglen, 1998).

Madeja, W. Victor, *The Russo-German War: Summer 1944*, (Allentown, 1987).

_____, *Hitler's Dying Ground: Description and Destruction of the German Army*, (Allentown, 1985).

_____, *German Army Order of Battle: The Replacement Army, 1939–45*, (Allentown, 1984).

Madajczyk, Czeskaw, *Die Okkupationspolitik Nazideutschlands in Polen 1939–1945*, (Stottgary, 1987).

Magnusson, Sigurdur Gylfi, and István M. Szijártó, *What is Microhistory? Theory and Practice*, (London, 2013).

Mann, Michael, *The Dark Side of Democracy: Explaining Ethnic Cleansing*, (Cambridge, 2005).

Marshall, S.L.A., *Men Against Fire*, (Alexandria, 1947).

Mawdsley, Evan, *Thunder in the East: The Nazi Soviet War 1941–1945*, (London, 2016).

Mazower, Mark, *Hitler's Empire: Nazi Rule in Occupied Europe*, (London, 2008).

Meindl, Ralf, *Ostpreussens Gauleiter: Erich Koch – eine politische Biographie*, (Osnabrück, 2007).

Merker, Ludwig, *Die 78. Infanterie- und Sturm-Division 1938–1945*.(Berlin, 1981).

Merridale, Catherine, Ivan's War: *The Red Army 1939–1945*, (London, 2010).

Meyer-Detring, Wilhelm, *Die 137. Infanterie-Division im Mittelabschnitt der Ostfront*, (Eggolsheim, 2006).

Michulec, Robert, *4. Panzer-Division on the Eastern Front (2) 1944*, (Hong Kong, 2000).

Monkiewicz, Waldemar, *Białowieża w cieniu swastyki*, (Bialystok, 1984).

Mosse, George L. *The Crisis of German Ideology: Intellectual Origins of the Third Reich*, (New York, 1998).

Murray, Williamson, *The Luftwaffe 1933–45: Strategy for Defeat*, (Maxwell Air Force Base, 1983).

Musial, Bogdan, *Sowjetische Partisanen 1941–1944: Mythos und Wirklichkeit*, (Paderborn, 2009).

Neitzel, Sönke (ed), *Tapping Hitler's Generals: Transcripts of Secret Conversations, 1942–45*, trans. Geoffrey Brooks, (Barnsley, 2007).

Neitzel, Sönke & Michael Walzer, *Soldaten: On Fighting, Killing and Dying*, (London, 2012).

_____, *Soldaten. Protokolle vom Kämpfen, Töten und Sterben*, (Hamburg, 2011).

Nicholas, Lyn H., *The Rape of Europa: The Fate of Europe's Treasures in the Third Reich and the Second World War*, (New York, 1995).

Noble, Alastair, *Nazi Rule and the Soviet Offensive in Eastern Germany, 1944–1945, The Darkest Hour*, (Brighton, 2009).

Pabst, Helmut, *The Outermost Frontier: A German soldier in the Russian Campaign*, (London, 1986).

Paul, Wolfgang, trans. Helmut Bögler, *Hermann Göring: Hitler Paladin or Puppet?* (London, 1998).

Porter, David, *Order of Battle: The Red Army in WWII*, (London, 2009).

Price, Alfred, *Luftwaffe: Birth, Life and Death of an Air Force*, (London, 1969).

Overy, Richard, *Interrogations: Inside the Minds oft he Nazi Elite*, (London, 2001).

_____, *Goering: The 'Iron Man'*, (London, 1984).

Raper, Jonathan, *Multidimensional Geographic Information Science*, (London, 2000).

Rass, Christoph, 'The Social Profile of the German Army's Combat Units 1939-1945', in Ralf Blank et al., *Germany and the Second World War, Volume IX/I, German Wartime Society 1939–1945: Politicization, Disintegration, and the Struggle for Survival*, (Oxford, 2008).

Reitlinger, Gerald, *The House Built on Sand: The Conflicts of German Policy in Russia 1939–1945*, (London, 1960).

Riebau, Hans, Hans Reimann, Manfred Schmidt, *Lachendes Feldgrau*, (Bremen, 1941).

Ripperger, Waleri, & Wjatscheslaw Semakow, *Der Traum vom Urwald: Streifzüge durch die Bialowieser Heide*, (Tessin, 2008).

Rose, Edward P.F., Dierk Willig, 'German Military Geologists and Geographers in World War II', in *Studies in Military Geography and Geology*, 2004.

Roseman, Mark, *The Villa, The Lake, The Meeting: Wannsee and the Final Solution*, (London, 2002).

Rottman, Gordon L., *World War II Battlefield Communications*, (Oxford, 2010).

Rubner, Heinrich, *Deutsche Forstgeschichte 1933–1945. Forstwirtschaft, Jagd und Umwelt im NS-Staat*, (St. Katharinen, 1997).

Rudel, Hans-Ulrich, *Stuka Pilot*, trans. Lynton Hudson, (Exeter, 1952).

Russell of Liverpool, *The Scourge of the Swastika*, (London, 1954).

Rutherford, Jeff & Adrian E. Wettstein, *The German Army on the Eastern Front*, (Barnsley, 2018).

Samojlik, Tomasz, *Conservation and Hunting: Białowieża Forest in the Time of Kings*, (Białowieża, 2005).

Saris, Wilhelm P.B.R., and Mathieu de Wolf 'Das Forstschutzkommando des Reichsforstmeisters', in *Internationales Militaria-Magazin*, Mai-Juni, (2008).

Schafft, Gretchen E., *From Racism to Genocide: Anthropology in the Third Reich*, (Illinois, 2004).

Schama, Simon, *Landscape and Memory*, (New York, 1995).

Shepherd, Ben, *Hitler's Soldiers: The German Army in the Third Reich*, (London, 2016).

_____, *Terror in the Balkans: German Armies and Partisan Warfare*, (Harvard, 2012).

_____, *War In The Wild East: The German Army and Soviet Partisans*, (Cambridge Mass., 2004).

Shils, Edward A. Morris Jannowitz, 'Cohesion and Disintegration in the the Wehrmacht in World War II,' *The Public Opinion Quarterly*, Vol.12, No.2 (Summer 1948), p. 280–315.

Stargardt, Nicholas, *The German War: A Nation Under Arms, 1938–1945*, (New York, 2015).

Steinweis, Alan E., *Kristallnacht 1938*, (Cambridge Mass., 2009).

Strassner, Peter, trans. David Johnston, *European Volunteers*, (Winnipeg, 1988).

Steinert, Marlis G. *Hitlers Krieg und die Deutschen: Stimmung und Haltung der deutschen Bevölkerung im Zweiten Weltkrieg*, (Düsseldorf, 1970).

Stopper, Sebastian, '"Die Strasse ist deutsch". Der sowjetische Partisanenkrieg und seine militärische Effizienz', *Vierteljahrshefte für Zeitgeschichte*, 29(3), 2011.

Strachan, Hew, 'Training, Morale and Modern War', *Journal of Contemporary History*, Vol 4(2), 211–227, 2006 Sage, New Delhi.

Streit, Christian, *Keine Kameraden: Die Wehrmacht und die sowjetischen Kriegsgefangenen 1941–1945*, (Stuttgart, 1978).

Sunseri, Thaddeus, 'Exploiting the Urward: German Post-Colonial Forestry in Poland and Central Africa, 1900–1960', *Past & Present*, Vol 214, Issue 1, February 2012, pp. 305–342.

Taylor, A.J.P., *The Course of German History: A Survey of the Development of German History Since 1815*, (London, 1961).

Tooze, Adam, *The Wages of Destruction: The Making and Breaking of the Nazi Economy*, (London, 2006).

Trouillot, Michel Rolph, *Silencing the Past: The Power and Production of History*, (Boston, 1997).

Tournier, Michel, *Der Erlkönig*, trans. Hellmut Waller, (Frankfurt a.M., 1989).

_____, *Le Roi des Aulnes*, (Paris, 1970).

Uekoetter, Frank, *The Green and the Brown: A History of Conservation in Nazi Germany*, (Cambridge, 2006).

Vale, Michael, *The Princely Court: Medieval Courts and Culture in North-West Europe, 1270–1380*, (Oxford, 2002).

Vetter, Fritz, *Die 78. Infanterie und Sturm-Division 1938–1945: Eine Dokumentation in Bildern*, (Bad Nauheim, 1981).

Weber, Thomas, *Hitler's First War: Adolf Hitler, The Men Of The List Regiment And The First World War*, (Oxford, 2010).

Wegner, Bernd, *Waffen-SS: Organization, Ideology and Function*, trans. Ronald Webster, (Oxford, 1990).

Werth, Alexander, *Russia at War, 1941–1945*, (London, 1964).

Westermann, Edward B., *Flak: German Anti-aircraft Defenses 1914–1945*, (Kansas, 1998).

Wieder Joachim & Heinrich Graf von Einsiedel (ed), trans. Helmut Bogler, *Stalingrad: Memories and Reassessment's*, (London, 1983).

_____, *Stalingrad und die Verandwortung des Soldaten*, (Munich, 1962).

Winder, Simon, *Germania: A Personal History of Germans Ancient and Modern*, (London, 2010).

Yerger, Mark C., *Allgemeine-SS: The Commands, Units and Leaders of the General SS*, (Atglen, 1997).

Zalc, Claire and Tal Buttmann (ed), *Microhistories of the Holocaust*, (New York, 2017).

Zantop, Susanne, *Colonial Fantasies: Conquest, Family, and Nation in Precolonial Germany 1770–1870*, (Durham, 1997).

Index

A

Adams, Siegfried, Lw.Oberjäger 55, 422, 424, 425, 426, 427, 428, 429
Army Division z.b.V., Bialystok 150, 152, 155, 157, 158
Auftragstaktik 26, 235, 259, 260, 271, 283, 309, 311, 333, 350, 359, 418, 420

B

Bach-Zelewski, Erich von dem, SS-Obergruppenführer 106, 107, 110, 113, 114, 118, 126, 134, 394
Bader, Douglas (RAF pilot) 413
Bandenbekämpfung 19, 23, 24, 26, 27, 30, 32, 55, 58, 136, 138, 146, 152, 156, 157, 166, 169, 181, 195, 199, 239, 241, 255, 261, 276, 283, 286, 289, 303, 308, 311, 312, 319, 322, 340, 350, 361, 418, 419, 420, 422
Bandenhelfer (bandit-helper) 181, 189, 197, 371, 372, 392
Bartosze, Poland (former Bartossen) 350, 428, 432, 455, 456
Bartov, Omer (historian) 32, 40, 274, 408
Bekker, Cajus 413
Belarus (Byelorussia) 41, 56, 93, 109, 116, 137, 152, 175, 261, 296, 357, 372, 402, 408, 412
Beyrich, Werner, Lw.Signals 318, 319, 320, 342, 343, 344, 350, 455

Bezirk Bialystok 33, 46, 115, 121, 122, 123, 125, 126, 127, 128, 136, 139, 147, 151, 152, 155, 175, 201, 202, 204, 205, 221, 239, 242, 247, 249, 394
Białowieża arena (Nazi security area) 44, 128, 149, 202, 235, 239, 242
Białowieża forest 25, 33, 45, 106, 140, 235, 310
Białowieża town 110, 141, 268, 302, 312, 350, 362, 363, 374, 375, 376, 377, 378, 385, 409
Bialystok 25, 33, 46, 92, 93, 94, 96, 97, 98, 104, 106, 107, 108, 114, 117, 121, 122, 123, 124, 125, 126, 127, 129, 130, 133, 137, 139, 140, 149, 150, 151, 152, 154, 155, 157, 158, 161, 162, 175, 182, 183, 189, 191, 199, 201, 202, 207, 209, 211, 212, 213, 214, 215, 216, 217, 220, 221, 223, 224, 227, 234, 242, 246, 249, 269, 289, 302, 310, 315, 321, 343, 344, 345, 353, 368, 371, 374, 375, 376, 378, 380, 389, 408, 426, 454, 455, 456
Brauchitsch, Bernd von, Göring's ADC 79, 80, 91, 144, 146, 149, 154, 156, 168, 170, 204, 215, 223, 285, 297, 299, 324, 335
Brix, Friedrich (Nazi commissioner) 124, 215, 221
Browning, Christopher (historian) 32, 34, 42, 113, 116, 237

C

Casualties/killed/wounded/missing 17, 21, 29, 33, 55, 59,

60, 68, 70, 72, 85, 87, 89, 91,
92, 95, 96, 102, 115, 119, 133,
135, 137, 145, 146, 148, 149,
171, 172, 176, 183, 184, 187,
189, 191, 195, 196, 197, 198,
200, 210, 227, 229, 231, 232,
233, 240, 243, 245, 246, 250,
251, 254, 257, 258, 261, 264,
265, 270, 274, 278, 282, 287,
303, 304, 307, 319, 322, 328,
329, 330, 332, 333, 334, 335,
336, 337, 342, 343, 345, 346,
348, 349, 350, 351, 352, 353,
355, 356, 357, 359, 367, 368,
369, 371, 379, 382, 383, 390,
392, 393, 398, 401, 402, 406,
407, 408, 409, 410, 413, 419,
422, 427, 428, 431, 452, 453,
454, 455

Ciré, Walter, Lw.Oberleutnant
176, 231, 305

Colonial, Nazi colonialism,
Lebensraum 27, 44, 46, 118,
138, 201, 220, 259, 289, 296

D

Daluege, Kurt (chief of order
police) 118, 131

Datner, Szymon 247, 408

Deutsche Kriegsgräberfürsorge
(German war graves
commission). 350, 432, 455

E

East Prussia 27, 33, 42, 45, 46,
52, 69, 77, 102, 107, 118, 121,
122, 123, 124, 126, 128, 139,
154, 166, 239, 296, 314, 325,
390, 394, 399, 400, 404, 420,
423, 432, 456

F

Fighting power 255, 321, 373,
380, 418, 419, 420, 421

Forschungsgruppe-Schultz-
Kampfhenkel 48

Frevert, Walter 43, 71, 72, 75,
85, 86, 87, 91, 98, 102, 103,
115, 129, 130, 169, 239, 285,
286, 299, 301, 303, 305, 308,
309, 310, 311, 313, 315, 316,
318, 321, 322, 324, 327, 332,
333, 335, 338, 339, 340, 342,
343, 344, 345, 346, 347, 350,
353, 354, 355, 356, 357, 358,
359, 363, 364, 365, 367, 369,
374, 375, 384, 392, 393, 394,
395, 396, 397, 398, 399, 400,
401, 402, 403, 404, 417, 428,
452, 455

Friedländer, Saul (historian)
113, 401

Fromm, Werner (SS-PF
Bialystok) 126, 137, 149, 150,
154, 160, 177, 184, 187, 198,
199, 200

FSK 130, 131, 132, 133, 142, 153,
172, 203, 253, 319, 322, 336,
337, 338, 353, 355, 357, 363

G

Galland, Adolf 17, 76, 77, 79,
80, 83, 87, 412, 413, 415

German Army including
Divisionskommando.z.b.V
17, 25, 31, 33, 39, 92, 107, 124,
129, 138, 146, 161, 178, 193,
195, 196, 219, 241, 255, 256,
257, 275, 280, 286, 290, 326,
328, 344, 361, 416, 434, 438,
449

Geyer, Hermann, Army General
94, 95, 96, 97, 98

Index

Goebbels, Josef 61, 291, 292, 294
Gold, Schaja and Jakob 247, 248
Göring, Hermann 20, 23, 25, 26, 33, 36, 41, 44, 45, 47, 48, 56, 59, 60, 61, 62, 63, 66, 67, 68, 69, 70, 71, 75, 76, 77, 78, 79, 80, 81, 83, 84, 85, 86, 87, 89, 90, 91, 92, 99, 102, 103, 106, 112, 113, 116, 117, 121, 123, 128, 130, 134, 136, 139, 144, 147, 149, 151, 154,161, 168, 169, 170, 171, 178, 199, 204, 212, 215, 221, 223, 239, 247, 259, 276, 285, 286, 290, 291, 292, 294, 296, 299, 300, 301, 302, 303, 305, 307, 308, 314, 320, 321, 322, 323, 328, 337, 353, 359, 361, 365, 374, 375, 382, 384, 391, 394, 395, 397, 399, 400, 401, 417, 430, 447, 449
Grossdeutschland (Greater German Reich) 25, 46, 52, 61, 89, 103, 121, 122, 128, 136, 296, 402, 412
Guderian, Heinz 97

H

Hajnówka 41, 92, 93, 96, 104, 107, 114, 126, 127, 129, 133, 140, 145, 154, 156, 157, 158, 165, 173, 174, 197, 202, 206, 252, 253, 254, 265, 302, 314, 333, 348, 363, 367, 368, 375, 376, 377, 378, 379, 380, 381, 386, 387, 388, 407, 412
Hart, Basil-Liddell (military historian) 412
Heck, Lutz 70, 71, 134
Heimatkriegsgebiet (Home Forces Area) 124, 136, 140, 146, 234, 239, 255, 325, 374, 417, 426, 428

Hemmerich, Gerlach-Hans (Army General) 47
Henderson, Nevile, British diplomat 90, 91, 117
Herbst, Emil, Lw.Major 144, 146, 147, 148, 149, 150, 151, 152, 153, 154, 155, 156, 157, 158, 159, 160, 161, 162, 164, 166, 168, 169, 170, 171, 172, 173, 174, 175, 177, 178, 179, 181, 183, 184, 185, 186, 187, 188, 189, 195, 197, 198, 199, 200, 204, 207, 208, 209, 210, 211, 212,213, 214, 219, 220, 221, 223, 225, 227, 228, 232, 234, 235, 239, 242, 243, 246, 247, 249, 251, 252, 258, 259, 261, 262, 264, 265, 266, 268, 269, 270, 276, 297, 298, 299, 300, 301, 302, 303, 304, 305, 308, 309, 313, 318, 328, 335, 337, 339, 350, 356, 396, 435, 437, 447
Heydrich, Reinhard 112, 113, 123
Hermann Göring Division 82, 83, 358, 359, 363, 370, 374, 397
Himmler, Heinrich 19, 26, 61, 68, 71, 108, 112, 113, 126, 135, 136, 139, 143, 151, 201, 234, 263, 269, 286, 307, 308, 416
Historical GIS 34, 35, 45, 51, 53, 55, 56, 57
Hitler, Adolf 18, 19, 24, 25, 26, 27, 31, 32, 33, 34, 38, 40, 44, 46, 61, 63, 66, 67, 71, 75, 78, 83, 89, 94, 119, 121, 136, 138, 140, 146, 169, 181, 193, 201, 234, 241, 246, 257, 270, 273, 274, 276, 285, 286, 290, 291, 292, 294, 296, 305, 307, 329, 330, 332, 333, 372, 381, 396, 399, 412, 421, 422, 428, 429, 440, 441

Hiwis (Hilfswilliger) 358, 362, 368, 372, 388, 390, 391, 392
Holocaust/genocide 24, 26, 27, 32, 33, 34, 35, 36, 51, 54, 55, 60, 76, 112, 113, 117, 119, 121, 129, 181, 201, 235, 238, 259, 260, 271, 285, 286, 290, 296, 301, 396, 402, 407, 408, 410, 416, 418, 420, 428

J

Jagdamt (hunting bureau) 63, 64, 67, 91, 134, 143, 430
Jagdkommando 19, 54, 149, 153, 162, 163, 164, 167, 187, 197, 198, 225, 226, 229, 241, 243, 244, 245, 246, 250, 253, 261, 262, 263, 264, 266, 271, 278, 297, 300, 305, 320, 321, 334, 336, 338, 339, 342, 345, 346, 348, 350, 353, 356, 357, 364, 366, 367, 368, 422
Jagdliches Brauchtum (1936) 71, 72, 75, 84, 86, 285, 350, 359
Jagen (1 kilometre square forest sector) 57, 143, 144, 145, 149, 153, 172, 173, 188, 192, 195, 196, 197, 198, 208, 226, 229, 231, 243, 244, 245, 247, 253, 266, 267, 268, 270, 333, 334, 336, 342, 351, 353, 354, 355, 357, 365, 367, 368, 371, 422, 427
Jägermeister/Göring's Schnapps 85
Jews 24, 25, 26, 31, 32, 33, 34, 42, 44, 56, 68, 70, 89, 92, 105, 106, 108, 109, 113, 114, 115, 116, 117, 118, 119, 132, 133, 152, 162, 166, 168, 171, 177, 193, 201, 223, 224, 234, 236, 237, 238, 239, 240, 242, 243, 246, 247, 249, 250, 251, 252, 253, 254, 259, 275, 276, 278, 282, 285, 286, 290, 292, 296, 299, 303, 304, 308, 337, 351, 352, 359, 392, 402, 407, 408, 409, 415, 420, 428, 429, 439, 444, 445
JSKB, Luftwaffe Jäger Sonderbataillon Bialowies zbV. (March 1943-August 1944) 163, 308, 310, 313, 316, 317, 318, 319, 320, 321, 322, 323, 328, 333, 337, 338, 339, 340, 343, 344, 345, 349, 353, 355, 357, 358, 361, 362, 363, 364, 368, 369, 371, 373, 374, 375, 376, 377, 378, 379, 380, 381, 382, 383, 384, 385, 386, 388, 389, 391, 392, 420, 422, 426, 427, 452, 453, 454, 455
Judenjagd 55, 58, 234, 237, 239, 283, 337, 350, 352, 401

K

Kamieniec-Litewski (ghetto) 42, 165, 166, 241, 242, 247, 378, 380
Kobylinski, Manfred von 126, 140, 142, 143, 147, 148, 149, 150, 153, 154, 155, 157, 161
Koch, Erich (Nazi Gauleiter) 33, 46, 121, 122, 123, 126, 128, 136, 201, 228, 296, 365, 394, 396, 423
König, Lw.Sergeant Major 312, 363, 370, 381, 382, 383

L

Laski (destroyed village) 111, 173, 342, 344, 345, 395, 401
Lithuania 45
Luftgau I 139, 145, 149, 152, 154, 155, 159, 166, 178, 181, 221, 297, 299, 374, 425

Luftwaffe 17, 19, 20, 23, 24, 26, 27, 28, 29, 30, 31, 33, 34, 36, 37, 38, 40, 42, 44, 50, 53, 54, 56, 59, 62, 63, 76, 77, 78, 79, 81, 83, 84, 85, 88, 89, 92, 101, 106, 124, 130, 132, 136, 137, 138, 139, 144, 147, 148, 153, 166, 169, 170, 172, 179, 186, 199, 201, 202, 204, 234, 235, 255, 257, 258, 273, 274, 282, 285, 289, 290, 292, 296, 297, 301, 303, 305, 308, 310, 314, 315, 316, 318, 325, 326, 329, 333, 334, 335, 353, 361, 367, 369, 373, 375, 377, 380, 388, 390, 412, 413, 414, 415, 417, 418, 420, 424, 425, 426, 428, 429, 430, 431, 432, 438, 439, 440, 441, 443, 444, 445, 447, 449, 450, 452, 455

Luftwaffen Kommando Ost 20

Lüttge, Theodor (Lw. Lieutenant) 195, 320, 363, 453

LWSB, Luftwaffe Sonderbataillon Bialowies zbV. (July 1942-March 1943) 139, 140, 142, 145, 147, 148, 150, 151, 152, 153, 154, 155, 156, 157, 161, 162, 163, 165, 167, 172, 173, 176, 184, 186, 187, 188, 189, 190, 193, 194, 196, 207, 209, 215, 217, 225, 228, 229, 231, 232, 235, 237, 239, 240, 242, 246, 247, 250, 251, 252, 253, 254, 255, 259, 261, 265, 268, 269, 270, 273, 278, 279, 281, 283, 297, 299, 300, 301, 302, 303, 304, 305, 313, 315, 321, 328, 337, 426, 428, 438, 440, 446, 447, 449, 452, 453, 454, 455, 456

M

Marteck, Rudolf 346, 347, 348, 350, 353

Meinecke, Lw.Lieutenant 374, 377, 379, 385, 386, 387, 390, 391, 392

Military efficiency 257, 258, 278, 283, 308, 309, 350, 365, 384, 390, 418, 419, 420

Müller, Rudolf (Police general) 127, 137, 151, 152, 189, 211, 212, 269, 301

N

Narewka Mala 42, 105, 107, 109, 111, 116, 127, 129, 153, 156, 158, 160, 195, 233, 242, 267, 285, 299, 396, 402, 407, 409, 410

Nolte, Ernst (Army General) 124, 149, 150, 154, 155, 158

Non Commissioned Officers, NCOs 39, 47, 97, 144, 145, 241, 251, 271, 272, 273, 276, 280, 282, 300, 309, 314, 316, 317, 323, 324, 327, 336, 347, 370, 381, 391, 410, 422, 425, 429, 434, 444, 445, 446, 448, 449, 450, 451

Nowarre, Waldemar, Lw.Lieutenant 316, 320, 321, 343, 345, 347, 355, 357, 358

O

Oberforstamt Bialowies 129, 134, 158, 162, 202, 203, 205, 207, 319, 321, 355, 394

Operation Bagration 372

Order Police Battalions (Ordnungspolizei) 115, 118, 126, 131, 137, 154, 189, 234, 236, 344

P

Pipping, Knut (sociologist) 281, 283
Poland/General-Government 131, 146, 152, 444
Police Battalions 34, 108, 109, 110, 111, 113, 114, 115, 117, 118, 126, 133, 153, 154, 268
Population/resettlement 107, 126, 181, 209, 211, 212, 213, 214, 215, 217, 218, 219, 223, 224, 228, 234, 249, 280, 286
Prisoner(s) of War (PoW) 38, 102, 109, 156, 177, 178, 185, 191, 200, 275, 394, 396, 451
Pruzhany (Ukraine) and ghetto 41, 52, 98, 107, 108, 116, 133, 165, 190, 202, 241, 242, 245, 248, 250, 251, 254, 269, 337, 363, 369, 375, 376, 386

R

Raesfeld, Ferdinand von (hunter) 65, 72, 310
Ramcke, Hermann-Bernhard 79, 122
Red Army/Russian soldiers 17, 18, 20, 30, 92, 94, 95, 97, 99, 101, 105, 106, 109, 133, 177, 178, 190, 191, 193, 195, 229, 236, 238, 266, 275, 293, 329, 330, 334, 361, 365, 372, 373, 375, 376, 377, 378, 379, 380, 382, 383, 385, 386, 397, 410, 412, 431
Reichsforstamt (RFA) 63, 64, 67, 69, 71, 77, 81, 89, 91, 103, 119, 127, 128, 130, 131, 134, 136, 141, 145, 147, 149, 153, 155, 158, 169, 172, 181, 185, 202, 203, 204, 205, 207, 220, 221, 315, 319, 322, 323, 325, 334, 369, 397
Reprisals, revenge actions 23, 128, 133, 171, 176, 184, 225, 231, 232, 292, 305, 329, 330, 340, 344, 372
Richthofen, Baron Manfred von 60, 78, 83
Röhrig, Fritz 65, 66
Rokossovsky, Konstantin, Red Army General 374
Rominten 45, 47, 59, 69, 84, 86, 88, 90, 103, 117, 130, 134, 136, 139, 285, 286, 310, 315, 322, 353, 359, 375, 384, 385, 388, 390, 391, 395, 396, 397, 399, 400, 401, 404, 447
Rudel, Hans-Ulrich 30, 83, 413
Rühm, Gustav 316, 317, 336, 337, 363, 365, 369, 374, 375, 379, 380, 383, 387

S

Scherping, Ulrich 67, 68, 71, 76, 89, 91, 102, 103, 104, 105, 110, 113, 115, 117, 121, 123, 129, 130, 131, 134, 136, 153, 169, 202, 206, 207, 212, 221, 239, 285, 286, 287, 299, 308, 310, 329, 396, 399
Schulz-Kampfhenkel, Otto, (geographer) 48, 361
Second Army 373, 378, 381, 382, 383
Soltys (Lithuanian, village leader) 168, 186, 187, 198, 199, 205, 208, 210, 216, 217, 227, 246, 252, 333, 340
Soviet partisans 26, 29, 177, 196, 204, 294, 372
SS Wiking Panzer Division 378, 380, 386

SS-Postschutz/Reichspost case 127, 159, 160
Stab Stephan 374, 376, 379
Stalingrad 18, 26, 175, 199, 201, 249, 290, 291, 292, 293, 294, 296, 309, 329, 330

T

Tournier, Michel (French writer) 400
Trabus, Rudolf 334, 339, 346, 349, 350
Training, Basic and Operational 77, 125, 235, 255, 256, 259, 272, 279, 311, 317, 424, 425, 439, 440, 442, 444, 445
Tresckow, Henning von 373, 381, 382
Trusty/collaborator 30, 181, 187, 190, 270, 340, 341, 348, 350

U

Udet, Ernst (aviator) 77, 86, 87
Uiberall, Peter (Nuremburg interpreter) 62

V

Violence, politics of 177, 235, 289, 418, 420, 421

W

Waffen-SS (militarised Schutzstaffeln) 82, 126, 189, 269, 270, 378
Wagner, Fritz, Chief of Oberforstamt Bialowies 129, 169, 189, 212, 221, 301, 394
Weinreis, Erich 130, 221, 314, 320, 369, 428
Werth, Alexander 330
Wuppertal (Barmen/Elberfeld) 422, 423, 425

About the Author

Philip W. Blood is an independent historian and writer. BA (Hons) at Lancaster University (Politics, Strategic Studies, and Civil-Military Relations). MBA from Aston University Business School. PhD at the Royal Military College of Science, Shrivenham, Cranfield University. Lecturer at the Working Men's Education Association, at Surrey University, and at the RWTH Aachen (Germany). Blood served as Chief Administrator and Senior Fellow with the American Academy in Berlin, under Henry Kissinger and Richard Holbrooke, setting austerity budgets against the effects of the global financial crash. He also worked as historical advisor to the Association of the US Army for seven years before becoming an independent writer.

For further information readers can engage with the author through various social media platforms and webpages:

Twitter — author page: @BloodPhilip
Twitter — book page: @Birdsof79875803

Academia: https://cranfield.academia.edu/PhilipBlood

Webpage/blog: https://www.philipwblood.com/

Facebook: https://www.facebook.com/philip.w.blood

Instagram: philip.w.blood

ibidem.eu